THE PERENNIAL S

THIRD EDITION

THE PERENNIAL STRUGGLE

Race, Ethnicity, and Minority Group Relations in the United States

Michael C. LeMay

California State University–San Bernardino

PEARSON

Prentice
Hall

UPPER SADDLE RIVER, NEW JERSEY 07458

Library of Congress Cataloging-in-Publication Data

LeMay, Michael C.
  The perennial struggle : race, ethnicity, and minority group relations in
the United States / Michael C. LeMay.—3rd ed.
    p. cm.
  Includes bibliographical references and index.
  ISBN-13: 978-0-13-208021-7
  ISBN-10: 0-13-208021-4
  1. Minorities—United States—Political activity. 2. Minorities—United
States—Political activity—Case studies. 3. Political
participation—United States. 4. Political participation—United
States—Case studies. I. Title.
  E184.A1L435 2009
  323'.0420973—dc22

                                        2007052962

Executive Editor: Dickson Musslewhite
Associate Editor: Rob DeGeorge
Editorial Assistant: Synamin Ballatt
Marketing Manager: Laura Lee Manley
Marketing Assistant: Jennifer Lang
Production Manager: Mary Carnis
Production Liaison: Marianne Peters-Riordan
Operations Specialist: Maura Zaldivar
Cover Art Director: Jayne Conte
Cover Design: Bruce Kenselaar
Cover Photo: Bob Gomel/Time Life Pictures/Getty Images
Image Permission Coordinator: Annette Linder
Full-Service Project Management/Composition: Michael Krapovicky, Pine Tree Composition, Inc.
Printer/Binder: R.R. Donnelley & Sons

Credits and acknowledgments borrowed from other sources and reproduced, with permission, in this
textbook appear on appropriate page within text.

Pearson Education LTD.
Pearson Education Singapore, Pte. Ltd
Pearson Education, Canada, Ltd
Pearson Education—Japan
Pearson Education Australia PTY, Limited

Pearson Education North Asia Ltd
Pearson Educación de Mexico, S.A. de C.V.
Pearson Education Malaysia, Pte. Ltd
Pearson Education, Upper Saddle River, New Jersey

10 9 8 7 6 5 4 3 2 1
ISBN-13: 978-0-13-208021-7
ISBN-10:   0-13-208021-4

To my wife, Lynda,
who makes it all worthwhile

CONTENTS

CHAPTER 4

THE STRATEGY OF ACCOMMODATION: THE TACTIC OF POLITICAL ACCOMMODATION   122

PREFACE

The struggle among racial and ethnic groups is a highly persistent and nearly world-wide phenomenon. Its resurgence in recent decades to the forefront of world concerns is evidenced by such dramatic events as the tragedy of ethnic cleansing in Darfur and Somalia, and in Bosnia and Kosovo; the civil war in Rwanda, resulting in the genocidal slaughter of thousands of innocent Tutsi civilians and the mass exodus of millions of refugees; the cease-fire by the Irish Republican Army after three decades of bloody terrorism on both sides of the conflict; and the rapid breakup of the former Soviet Union into various republics, often driven by a sense of ethnic pride and a yearning for national identity and autonomy, as in Chechnya. Turkey has struggled for years with its Kurdish separatist movement, and India with Kashmir rebels seeking independence; Liberia has suffered a decade of civil war with deep ethnic overtones. Since the U.S. invasion of Iraq, there has been an outbreak of civil war between the Shiia and Sunni Muslims and between Muslims and Kurds, and it seems beyond the ability of the U.S. occupying forces to keep the lid on the religious-based strife. All these ethnic conflicts have resulted in a cumulative death toll of many millions. One can truly characterize the conflictual relationships between ethnic minority groups and a majority society as a "perennial struggle." Racial and ethnic tensions are always just below the surface, ready to break out into violent confrontation.

In the United States, one sees both the persistence and the renewed strength of minority group politics. Continual examples of hate crimes demonstrate that racism is far from over. Yet the Hispanic and Black Congressional Caucuses have increased in size and have played key roles in molding a critical compromise in several areas of public policy, such as in immigration policy changes during the Clinton and the Bush administrations, in compromises made in welfare reform, and in legislation concerning racial profiling, to cite but a few examples of their efforts.

The Perennial Struggle is about race, ethnic, and minority group relations and how they interact in group politics in the United States. Understanding these relationships is critical to understanding American society in general and American politics in particular.

Understanding these relationships is key to a grasp of American society because of the rich diversity of our racial and ethnic composition. The United States is a *nation of nations*; it receives more immigrants to its shores by far than does any other nation of the world.

Some decades ago historian Oscar Handlin (1951) wrote a Pulitzer Prize winning book, *The Uprooted*. In it Handlin related that he had started out to write a history of the immigrants to America, but soon discovered that the immigrants *were* American history! To paraphrase his observation, the perennial struggle of minority groups in America is enduring; it displays a richness of styles, methods, and techniques. Ethnic politics can no longer be understood as just the old-style urban political machine. Political incorporation and segmented assimilation are social science concepts that have largely replaced the concept of inevitable and uni-directional assimilation.

In the past several decades much has appeared in books, periodicals, newspapers, and the mass media about ethnic groups and their problems. The respective civil rights movements of blacks, Hispanics, Native Americans, the elderly, women, and gay Americans have impressed upon American society an acute awareness of the presence of many minority groups—of their discontent with their status and of their struggle to cope with and overcome, or at least mitigate, the effects of that status.

Early works by social scientists raised expectations of more or less complete assimilation as the processes of industrialization and urbanization reduced the salience of ethnicity. The explosive decades of the 1960s and 1970s laid to rest the myth of the "melting pot" nature of American society. Recent scholarly examinations of ethnic relations have largely rejected such expectations. New studies have demonstrated the richness and complexity of racial and ethnic relations with majority society and have underscored the persistence of those relations and their relevance for political, social, and economic behavior. In place of an inevitable and linear progression to full assimilation, scholars posit a segmented and pluralistic picture of varying degrees of incorporation. Groups vary in the degree to which they remain distinctive culture subgroups. American society varies in the degree to which groups are incorporated—culturally, economically, politically, socially, and so on.

As various minority groups developed into interest groups struggling to get "their fair share of the pie," it has become increasingly evident that the perspectives of all the social science disciplines are needed to effectively study racial and ethnic relations. The perspectives of the anthropologist, the historian, the political scientist, the sociologist, the social psychologist, and the economist all add to our theoretical knowledge of ethnicity and ethnic relations. Integration of these perspectives is essential to understanding the rich complexity of race and ethnic relations—how public policy effects may limit minority group conflict and how better to promote a healthy pluralism in our society. Such broader and deeper understanding may help limit minority group conflict, both among minority groups and between them and the majority society.

Many colleges and universities are themselves struggling with issues of diversity. They have integrated the various perspectives of the social science disciplines into courses such as Race and Racism, Roots of American Racism, and Minority Group Politics in the United States. If American society is to avoid the woes of a Darfur, Bosnia, Kosovo, Northern Ireland, or Rwanda, or even to prevent the development of separatist movements as in French-speaking Canada, we need to better understand the perennial struggle of ethnic relations and its impact on politics and policy. We need to understand the history, contribution, and special problems of particular and often exemplary minority groups in American society. In short, we need to understand the how and the why of their perennial struggle.

This book, then, has several goals. It uses many historical examples to illustrate how the United States came to its rich mixture of minority subcultures, how race and ethnicity interact with class status to form persistent patterns. It applies the insights of the various social sciences to an analysis of racial and ethnic relations to clarify their similarities and differences. It examines social mobility in the United States, developing a systems framework of race and ethnic relations to better view the wide variety of factors that influence the rate, degree, and type of social interactions of various minority groups struggling within our society. It also examines why some groups reject assimilation or are largely excluded from such assimilation by the majority. Using the examples of a rich array of group experiences, it develops a typology of the strategies employed by minority groups to cope with their status—accommodation, separatism, and radicalism. It distinguishes two tactical approaches to each of these coping strategies employed by minority groups. It examines various public policy arenas, describing how policy is used by the majority in a top-down approach to social interactions to channel the access and routes of social interaction of various minority groups. It shows how various minority groups, in a bottom-up approach to social interaction, use those same policy arenas to cope with and mitigate the policy effects of their status. The book describes how public policy is used by minority groups to change their role and status in the majority culture, or at least to mitigate some of the vexing problems they face as a result of their minority status.

THE STRUCTURE OF THIS BOOK

This book is intended to serve as a core text in such courses as Race and Racism, Racial and Ethnic Relations, and Minority Group Politics. It loses none of the richness of insight the various social science perspectives offer to the study of ethnic and racial relations, while integrating those perspectives into a consistent viewpoint that a core textbook can bring to such a rich and complex area of study.

Chapter 1 concerns the language of race and ethnic relations. It discusses the basic concepts of the struggle between minority and majority groups and provides definitions for all the key terms or concepts used by both the United States government and by the social sciences in the study of racial and ethnic relations. It delves into the dimensions of self- and group identity and how these identity issues influence social interactions between the majority society and the various minority groups within it. It discusses the concepts and the use of top-down and bottom-up approaches to social interactions. Its end-of-chapter reading raises the issue of whether or not minority groups should try to assimilate or simply to incorporate in some areas of interaction.

Chapter 2 presents various theories about race relations and then develops a framework to understand race and ethnic relations. It outlines previous approaches from the social sciences that offered more or less single-variable explanations for variation in social interactions and in rates of incorporation or segmented assimilation. It discusses how policy effects can be used to explain or measure the outcomes of social interactions between the majority and various minority groups. Its end-of-chapter reading offers a bio-sketch of Senator Barack Obama and illustrates how the political incorporation of Black Americans, so personified by his candidacy for president, depends on the gains made by the civil rights movement of the 1960s and the work of the late Dr. Martin Luther King, Jr.

Chapter 3 then examines in detail the strategy and tactic of economic accommodation. It reviews the experience of many minority groups who have adopted this strategy to cope with their minority status. It looks at national-origin minority groups and subgroups of Asian Americans, European Americans, Hispanic Americans, and Arab Americans who adopted economic accommodation in one or another of its tactical approaches as the best method to survive and prosper. It ends with a reading that raises the issue of inter-minority group competition and conflict, in this case among Koreans and Blacks and Hispanics.

Chapter 4 continues the discussion of the strategy of accommodation, focusing on the tactic of political accommodation. It discusses Irish Americans, Italian Americans, Greek Americans, Polish Americans, Jewish Americans, some Asian Americans (the Vietnamese and Asian Indians), some Hispanic Americans (Puerto Ricans and Cubans) and African Americans and how they used politics to pursue their perennial struggle. It continues on to discuss how politics can lead the way to cultural and economic incorporation. It examines the use of the strategy and tactic by gays and lesbians. Its end-of-chapter reading asks the reader to consider the question of whether or not Latinos are the key to winning national elections in the future.

Chapter 5 examines the strategy of separatism, with a review of several groups practicing the tactic of physical separatism to isolate themselves from the majority culture. It examines the Mormons, Native Americans, Amish and Mennonites, and those African Americans who followed Black Nationalism, exemplified by Marcus Garvey and his "Back to Africa Movement." Its reading at the end of the chapter asks students to consider whether tribal gaming will lead to economic and political sovereignty.

Chapter 6 then looks at separatism from the perspective of the tactic of psychological separatism to achieve isolation from the majority culture. It examines the Black Muslims, Muslim Americans today, Hasidic Jews, and Jehovah Witnesses and how these groups used this tactical approach to separatism. It closes with a reading on the basics of the millennial movements and how such movements provide the power over individuals to so shape their lives as to provide that "psychological" ability to separate oneself from majority society by rejecting key aspects of the values of the majority society.

Chapter 7 examines the strategies of old-style radicalism. It covers the "isms" of socialism, communism, fascism, and Nazism and finally the rise of white radical nationalism to show how these political ideologies sought to enroll minority group members in an effort to radically reform American society, its values, and its politics. It explains how each attempted, with little success, to gain the adherence of racial and ethnic minorities to their ideological and political cause. Its end-of-chapter reading discusses how the communist party, for a time, effectively used the defense of the Scottsboro defendants to appeal to Black Americans (then referred to as Negroes).

Chapter 8 discusses the politics of new-style radicalism—the civil rights movements from W. E. B. DuBois to Dr. Martin Luther King, Jr., from Black Power to Brown and Red Power to Gay Power. It looks at protest movements and civil rights movements and how groups used nonviolent protest in an attempt to drastically alter U.S. society. The reading at the end of this chapter is perhaps the most eloquent and explicit philosophical defense for the use of civil disobedience, the famous Dr. Martin Luther King, Jr.'s "Letter from a Birmingham Jail."

Chapter 9 looks at the use of public policy to place groups into minority status, and how such groups seek to alter public policy to change their status and roles in society. It examines the major arenas of conflict between majority society and minorities: the policy effects in education, employment, immigration, housing, law enforcement, and political participation that reflect the policy effects on the outcomes of social interactions between the majority society and its multiplicity of racial and ethnic minority groups. Its end-of-chapter reading discusses the state of American diversity as the nation enters the twenty-first century.

To enhance its educational value as a core textbook for a highly complex and controversial subject area, this book uses various pedagogical devices designed to enrich the discussion, provide special or extra insight, and make the study and review of the material more "user friendly." This third edition offers—in each chapter—new photographs, tables, figures, and cartoons to illustrate various topics. Each chapter presents "boxed" material, brief readings that highlight a topic central to the chapter. The third edition presents two dozen such boxes, many of which present "Bio-Sketches" of persons who played a significant role in the struggle. To add visual interest to the text, nine pointed cartoons are used, one per chapter. A dozen varied figures use bar, line, and pie graphs to illustrate key points in visually dramatic ways. More than two dozen photographs add visual punch or "put a face" to key actors in the perennial struggle. There is a copious use of tables, more than three dozen throughout, to present specific data to demonstrate key points about the many groups covered in the book. Each chapter ends with a Summary, a glossary of the Key Terms introduced in the chapter, and a list of Review Questions to provide a special means of study, followed by an Additional Readings section, which includes useful scholarly books that students can consult for further exploration of the topics of the chapter. Finally, each chapter closes with an end-of-chapter reading—a more lengthy reading than the boxed matter that further elaborates on a major theme of the chapter. There is an extensive bibliography at the back of the book, as well as an author index and a subject index, to facilitate reader's access.

ACKNOWLEDGMENTS

I wish to thank several individuals for their assistance with this project: Prentice Hall Executive Editor Dickson Musslewhite, who originally reviewed the manuscript and decided to do the project; Rob DeGeorge, who served as the Associate Editor for this third edition of the book; Michael Krapovicky of Pine Tree Composition, who served as its project manager there; Linda Duarte, also of Pine Tree Composition, an excellent copy-editor whose careful editing of the manuscript improved my efforts; and finally, Laserwords, who did some fine art work, turning my sometimes poorly hand-drawn illustrations into usable figures.

A debt of gratitude is owed to several readers who improved the manuscript with their suggestions. The following reviewers constructively critiqued the first edition: James

Button, University of Florida; N. Hart Nibbrig, George Mason University; Robert C. Smith, San Francisco State University; and Theodore J. Davis Jr., University of Delaware. James D. Fairbanks of the University of Houston–Downtown and Pei-te Lien of the University of Utah contributed to the review of the second edition with very helpful suggestions. Useful comments for revisions to the third edition were provided by Donald G. Baker of Long Island University, C. W. Post Campus; Kenneth E. Fernandez, University of Nevada, Las Vegas; and by Melissa Michelson, California State University, East Bay. Dino Bozonelos, of the University of California, Riverside, offered many contributions to the third edition. He helped redraft figure 2.1 to present it graphically in a manner better understood by students. He contributed some original material used in boxes and end-of-chapter readings, and he read and critiqued chapter drafts for all nine chapters, offering useful suggestions to improve each. Needless to say, any faults that remain are solely those of the author.

Several colleagues at California State University–San Bernardino read the original manuscript and offered helpful suggestions. I wish to thank Professors David Decker, Cecilia Julagay, Mary Texeira, and Elsa Valdez in the department of sociology. I wish to thank the CSUSB Foundation for its support of a sabbatical leave that enabled the author to complete the original manuscript. Two students who deserve special thanks are Stephanie Fairman, who drew a couple of the cartoons, and Kevin Grisham, who researched some of the photographs via the Internet. The departmental secretary, Mrs. Debbi Fox, was helpful in many ways, as always. I wish to thank the many students in sections of my Race and Racism class with whom I classroom-tested much of this material. I wish to thank my sister-in-law, Sharon K. Nash, who refined nine of the figures used as illustrative matter throughout the textbook.

Michael C. LeMay

The Perennial Struggle

CHAPTER 1

———— •●• ————

THE LANGUAGE OF THE STRUGGLE

The Basic Concepts of Majority/Minority Relations

INTRODUCTION: WHO CONSTITUTES AMERICA?

The United States of America is arguably the most ethnically and racially diverse nation on earth. Who is an American, and perhaps more critically important for the discussions of this book, who ought to be considered an American has been and continues to be a vexing issue. Although there is widespread consensus that a person born in the United States is legally a native-born American citizen, there are many Americans who believe and who argue that children born of illegal residents ought not to be considered native-born American citizens. Such persons would deny citizenship to the children of unauthorized resident aliens. An additional and equally vexing issue is how we describe or categorize Americans. There are many tens of millions of naturalized American citizens who were born in a dizzying array of countries of origin— nearly two hundred such. How such individuals identify themselves, and how the government categorizes them has changed over time, and has important implications for politics and public policy.

The United States Bureau of the Census, which is assigned the task of counting the American population, employs a number of classifications associated with the concepts of ethnicity and race. In terms of race, the Census Bureau breaks down Americans into White, Black, Asian, American Indian and Alaska Native, Native Hawaiian and Other Pacific Islander, and Hispanic. In terms of ethnicity, the Census Bureau recognizes and counts over one-hundred categories of claimed ancestry and for the foreign-born residents, their countries of origin. To illustrate the point, Table 1.1 (on page 2) lists a selected number of claimed ancestries for the purpose of this introductory chapter. Complicating the issue of who counts as an American is the fact that people are legally free to marry across ethnic and racial lines (although that was not always the case for all such groups), and for the children arising from such mixed ethnic and racial unions, the government has the additional issue of identifying and counting mixed-race

Table 1.1   Persons by Claimed Ancestry, Selected Ancestry Groups, 2003

Ancestry Claimed	2003 Population	% of Total Population
Arab	1,258,000	.40
Austrian	790,000	.20
British	1,153,000	.40
Canadian	698,000	.20
Czech	1,416,000	.50
Danish	1,435,000	.50
Dutch	5,059,000	1.80
English	28,403,000	10.03
European	2,164,000	.76
Jamaican	825,000	.29
Lithuanian	720,000	.25
Norwegian	4,494,000	1.58
Polish	9.304,000	3.28
Portuguese	1,349,000	.47
Russian	2,975,000	1.05
Scotch-Irish	5,099,000	1.80
Scottish	5,811,000	2.05
Slovak	811,000	.28
Finish	778,000	.20
French	9,678,000	3.40
Fr. Canadian	2,188,000	.77
German	47,842,000	16.91
Greek	1,229,000	.43
Hungarian	1,495,000	.52
Irish	33,992,000	12.01
Italian	16,726,000	5.91
Haitian	666,000	.23
Subsaharan Africa	1,884,000	.66
African	1,144,000	.40
Swedish	4,254,000	.40
Swiss	984,000	.34
Ukranian	870,000	.30
Welsh	1,890,000	.66
West Indian	2,129,000	.75

Source: Table by author LeMay, from U.S. Bureau of the Census, *Statistical Abstract of the U.S., 2006,* data from Table 46, p. 47.

persons. Recognizing this fact, as of the 2000 census of population, the Census Bureau now allows respondents to identify with two new categories: Two or More Races, or Some Other Race.

Table 1.1 lists various ancestry groups in the United States as of 2003, by declared ancestry and by their percentage of the total population.

The federal government, through the Census Bureau, clearly states that their racial classifications are "socio-political constructs and should not be interpreted as being scientific or anthropological in nature." Thus, to avoid any issue of miscategorization, the bureau allows respondents to self-identify their race. However, the bureau has limited the number of major categories. These categories are determined by our politicians and tend to reflect societal definitions of race. The federal government considers race and ethnicity to be two separate and distinct concepts. So even though one is freely able to identify with their ethnic heritage, e.g., a person who claims Italian ancestry, on the census they would be coded within one of the racial categories, in this case, White. However, the Census Bureau has provided a separate ethnic category for Hispanics to reflect the country's growing diversity. Thus, those who identify themselves as "a person of Cuban, Mexican, Puerto Rican, South or Central American, or other Spanish culture or origin regardless of race," are considered Hispanic or Latino.

Yet even though Hispanics are separated on the U.S. census, they are still required to choose one of the listed racial categories. Hispanics, therefore, can be of any race. For example, the 2000 census showed that nearly half (48%) of all Hispanics reported White, while approximately 42 percent reported Some Other Race when responding to the question on race. Less than 4 percent of Latinos reported Black or African American, American Indian and Alaska Native, Asian, or Native Hawaiian and Other Pacific Islander. This explanation accounts for why one sees Non-Hispanic White in census of population reports. Non-Hispanic Whites are those respondents, then, who identify themselves as White and did not mark the Hispanic origin box on the 2000 census, questionnaire. To illustrate this distinction, in the 2000 census, with a total population of over 297 million Americans, the racial category White was used by 75 percent of respondents, or 222.75 million. However, when one subtracts the number of Hispanics who also marked off White, that figure, referred to as Non-Hispanic White, drops to 69 percent, or 197.3 million.

This issue of how the government uses race and ethnicity illustrates the importance of terms, categories, and classifications. The government is not alone in defining such key terms. Society, or common parlance, develops and over time changes definitions of terms central to this book. Likewise, the social sciences develop definitions for these key concepts and seek consensus as to those definitions over time. When beginning any field of study, therefore, it is helpful to start by defining key concepts. This can be problematic when such concepts are emotionally charged and when common vernacular uses different definitions of those key concepts than does scholarly discussion. In a diverse society such as the United States, we are all members of various groups. Our group affiliations shape attitudes we have toward the basic concepts central to this book—concepts such as political power and privilege, majority and minority group, ethnicity, prejudice, stereotyping, discrimination, racism, assimilation, incorporation, and pluralism, to name but a few. A common understanding of basic concepts and analytical distinctions about the manner in which they are used is essential to better deal with subjects as complex and rich as racial and ethnic relations and minority group politics in the United States. A clear focus is necessary to understand all aspects of American society because American behavior so often reflects biases, power and influence struggles, prejudice and discrimination within members of the majority group, and reactions of minority groups to those attitudes and to such treatment. Much of American history, then, reflects majority society's attempts to deal with the presence of so many and such varied minority groups.

DEFINITIONS OF MAJORITY/MINORITY

From the perspective of the social sciences, a **majority group** is defined as one that is superordinate (above) in a superordinate/subordinate relationship. The majority group is considered the majority because it possesses political, economic, social, and cultural power. It need not be a numerical majority, although in most societies it is. It simply must have sufficient power to determine the values and norms of society. It must be able to set public policy. In America, there are a number of subordinate cultures whose central identity is based on religion, race, ethnicity, region, or class. America's dominate identity is based on the Anglo-Protestant Culture (often referred to as White-Anglo-Saxon-Protestant, or simply WASP). Samuel Huntington characterizes it as having six central elements: common ancestry, religion, principles of government (or political values), manners and customs, and a common war experience (60). Similarly, John McElroy stipulates what he calls the central or basic beliefs of the American culture: that God created nature and human beings; that improvement is possible; that every person is responsible for his/her own well-being; that human beings will abuse power when they have it so a written constitution is essential to government; that society is a collection of individuals; and that America is a "chosen" country (by God) (223).

Political power does not exist in a vacuum. It is *structured*, woven into the very fabric of society, much like the structure of a dress determines whether it is an a-line, an empire dress, an evening gown, a simple house dress, a maxi, midi, or mini, and so on. Majority political power is manifested in the ability to *control*: to control the making of laws, the military and police apparatus of a society, the basic economic operations of a society, its social norms and customs, the distribution of goods and services—in short, who gets what, how, and why. Members of the majority occupy the positions of social and political power. They and their children are the first hired and the last fired. They attend the better schools. Their neighborhoods are better served by municipal government—trash pick up, police and fire services, street maintenance, and so on. They belong to prestigious social organizations. By definition, then, such group members are the "discriminators" rather than the subjects of discrimination. In the case of American society, they enjoy the fruits of "white privilege."

This perspective views political power through the prism of *interest group theory*. Interest groups are defined as organized bodies of individuals who share some common goals and who try to influence public policy in order to better pursue those goals (LeMay 1987, xv). The group theory of politics suggests that public policy is the struggle among groups. It sees public policy as "the equilibrium reached in this [group] struggle at any given moment, and it represents a balance which contending factions or groups constantly strive to weight in their favor" (Latham 1965, 36). As groups gain and lose power and influence, public policy is altered in favor of those gaining influence at the expense of those whose influence is waning (Anderson, 18).

"The legislature referees the group struggle, ratifies the victories of the successful coalitions, and records the terms of the surrenders, compromises, and conquests in the form of statutes. Every statute tends to represent compromise because the process of accommodating conflicts of group interests is one of deliberation and consent" (Latham, 35-36). Laws reflect who has power in a society and are designed to maintain that power.

In American society, the White/Anglo/Saxon/Protestant majority emerged out of the colonial era as the dominant group along the Atlantic seaboard. By 1800, they became the "host" or "native" group of the United States. They dispossessed the Native American Indians and they surpassed in influence all other Western European immigrant groups, becoming the predominate "Euro-Americans." English language and customs, and the ideas of people coming from the British Isles regarding commerce, law, government, and religion came to predominate in the emerging American culture. In 1790, when the new nation took its first census of population, it recorded a population of 3,227,000, mostly the descendants of seventeenth- and eighteenth-century arrivals, or recent immigrants themselves. More than 75 percent were of British origin. About 8 percent were of German origin. The rest were of Dutch, French, or Spanish origin, although approximately one-half million were black slaves and about the same number were Native American Indians residing east of the Mississippi River. The U.S. Constitution enshrined the prevailing sentiment among the citizens at the time: that their nation was a brave and noble experiment in freedom. They felt this freedom should be broadly shared by any and all who desired to be free, regardless of their former nationality. They established an "open-door" policy with respect to welcoming immigration, but expected newcomers to conform to their perception of the "good society," the "American ideal" (LeMay 1987, 7). By 1815, Anglo conformity had become dominant and unchallenged. All other groups were pressured to conform to their ideal of society.

The emergence of Anglo conformity came when intellectual credence, based on biblical and pseudo-scientific support, was increasingly given to the concept of *white supremacy*—that is, to the belief that the military and economic success of the "white race" could be attributed to the biologically inherited differences among racial groups. Anglo conformity held that the more nearly a person approximated the Anglo-American model, the more nearly "American" that person was judged to be. Immigrant groups were seen as more or less desirable according to how closely they resembled the Anglo-American pattern, how rapidly they departed from their own cultural patterns, and how successfully they became socially invisible within the newly emerging WASP-American society. Anglo-conformity is well characterized by the "melting pot" metaphor of American society. Minority group members were expected to lose their subcultural distinctiveness to become more and more like the members of the majority.

Any group that was either unwilling or unable to fit into the developing American majority pattern was viewed as a "problem" group. Race was a term then used more broadly than how it is used today. By the end of the Civil War, in common parlance, the "Anglo-native Americans" referred to others as "the Italian race," "the Greek race," "the Slavic race," and so on. Either a group's clannish refusal to accept the "superior" ways of life of the majority, or the possession of some undesirable physical trait that made it difficult or impossible to become "WASP-like," was sufficient to brand such a group in some way deficient, and the group was thereby subjected to discrimination. Huntington and others fear that the immigration process itself leads to diversity and dispersion and a constant threat of discontinuity (192–197). In subjecting any such group to discrimination, the majority group of society in essence created or defined any such "other group" (the "They") as a **minority group**.

Common usage of language emphasizes the numerical aspect of minority. Webster defines minority, for instance, as "the smaller in number of two groups constituting the whole," or "a group having less than the number of votes necessary for control." In this book, minority is a political concept referring to a *power relationship*. It is a group on the subordinate end of a superordinate/subordinate relationship. Its members are viewed as differing from others in some characteristic and subjected to differential treatment. Thus, until 1994, blacks in South Africa were the minority even though they made up roughly 80 percent of the population. Women are still a minority in the United States yet they constitute just over 52 percent of the population.

The concept of minority is a power/status concept. Group relationships (ethnic, racial, religious) between the dominant and minority groups are not determined by numbers but rather by the distribution of power. The minority's presence implies the existence of a corresponding dominant group with higher social status and greater privileges. The minority is excluded from full participation in the life of society—they are not fully incorporated. Minority groups may be described as subordinate groups in a social/political hierarchy with inferior power and less secure access to resources than has the majority (Kottak and Kozaitis 1999).

Minority status in the United States is based on many characteristics. The two primary bases for such status have been *race* and *ethnicity*. The distinction between the two is important because the differing base for minority status affects the manner in which a group copes with resulting problems. It affects the manner in which the majority accepts or rejects a group, and the way the majority society channels the options open to its members. It affects the methods and tactics used by members of a minority group to cope with their status. Race is institutionalized and structured in such a way that public policy creates patterns of racial distinction in politics and society. The institutional structure of the welfare state played a central role in transforming the racial structure of American politics and society (Lieberman 1998, 7).

Ethnic Minority Groups

Members of an ethnic group show cultural similarities and differences from other groups that foster a sense of peoplehood. Such groups may be viewed by their members and/or outsiders as religious, racial, national, linguistic, or geographic. Ethnic group members have in common their **ethnicity**, or sense of peoplehood, which represents a part of their collective experience. "In a society made up of many cultural groups, like the United States, the intensity of ethnic identity or ethnicity is apt to be determined by the attitude of the members of the 'host' society toward the 'strangers' in their midst" (Rose, Peter, 1990, 7).

German sociologist Max Weber, considered by many to be the "Father of Sociology" as a scholarly discipline, articulates how human similarities and differences (manifested as cultural or physical traits) influence social interaction and lead to a sense of "consciousness of kind." That sense of kind in turn promotes a mono-political closure in which certain individuals are invited to become part of the "we," that over time affects genetic mixing or selection, patterns of migration, and as contact with the "other" takes place, conscious stressing of difference. Within a cohesive group of individuals a commonality of language, religious belief, similarity in physical appearance, similarity of customs, and ultimately a common political community give rise to the perception of ethnicity—to *consanguinity* that is actual or perceived. This ethnicity is expressed as the sense of "peoplehood."

Ethnic minority groups develop a sense of "symbolic ethnicity." They use the symbols of their ethnic group—eating certain foods, observing certain ceremonial holidays, supporting specific political issues confronting the old country—as cultural markers that show outsiders as well as their fellow ethnics that they belong. These characteristics are often *ascribed*, that is, acquired at birth.

A group of people having a sense of peoplehood often seeks *political sovereignty*—the authoritative (accepted as legitimate) right to rule over a particular place (a society, a nation-state). A given set of people (say, the German people) may seek to govern a geographic area (which becomes the nation-state of Germany). These involve cases wherein ethnics are seeking nationhood. Historically, we can also distinguish cases in which nation-states (for example, a former colonial area that becomes independent) are struggling to engender within their population a sense of "peoplehood" (we are all Yugoslavians, rather than Serbs, Croats, or Bosnians; or we are all Iraqis, rather than Shiite, Sunni, or Turks). Ethnicity is typically an important, often the major, determinant of political sovereignty. Sovereignty is another example of a complex concept that has many dimensions. Figure 1.1 shows a kaleidoscope metaphor or image of the many dimensions that typically comprise political sovereignty.

Racial Minority Groups

In a primordial sense, **race** would refer to the differential concentrations of gene frequencies for certain traits that, so far as we know, are confined to physical manifestations such as skin color, hair texture, and facial features. However, race has become accepted in the social sciences, is a socially constructed concept. It has no intrinsic connection with cultural patterns or institutions (Gordon 1964, 27). **Racism** refers to an ideology that considers the unchangeable physical characteristics of a group to be linked in a direct, causal way, to their psychological and intellectual functioning, and on that basis, distinguishes between superior and inferior races.

When racism permeates a society, it may result in *institutionalized racism,* in which society's norms and values so reflect the racism of the majority society that *racial stratification*—the system of distributing social rewards on the basis of racial discrimination—occurs. In its extreme form, such structurally institutionalized racism may establish a racial caste system.

Figure 1.1   The Dimensions of Diversity—The Kaleidoscope Metaphor

Racial groups are a subcategory of ethnic groups in that racial identity is usually a basis for "commonly shared cultural traditions," or a sense of "peoplehood." The distinction between ethnic and racial groups is analytically useful since racial groups often experience special barriers.

> A [racial group is a] human group that defines itself and/or is defined by other groups as different from other groups by virtue of innate and immutable physical characteristics. These physical characteristics are in turn believed [by the racist society] to be intrinsically related to moral, intellectual, and other non-physical attributes or abilities. (Van den Berghe, 5)

DIMENSIONS OF PERSONAL IDENTITY

Identity is based on a number of sources from which an individual may take it or even be given it. It may be *ascriptive:* such as age, ancestry, gender, kin, ethnicity, or race. It may be *cultural:* such as clan, tribe, ethnicity, language, nationality, religion, or civilization.

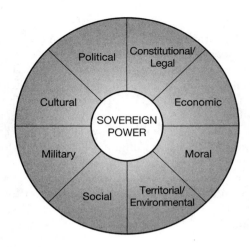

Figure 1.2   A Kaleidoscope Image of the Dimensions of Political Sovereignty

It may be largely *territorial:* the neighborhood, village, town, city, province, state, nation, continent, or hemisphere. It may be *political:* a faction, clique, leader, interest group or movement, cause, party, ideology, state. It may be *economic:* based on one's job, occupation, profession, work group, employer, industry, economic sector, labor union, or socio-economic class. It may be primarily *social:* friends, club, team, colleagues, leisure group, status (Ibid, 27). For most individuals, their identity comes from some combination of those sources.

Based on these sources, is identity then *primordial,* i.e. inherent or natural, or *constructed,* as determined by the individual or society? This is important for understanding the role of ethnicity and race in intergroup relations. If ethnicity or race is primordial, that is, existing first in time and from the very beginning, then it is something that is highly immutable, difficult, if not impossible, to change. Primordial dimensions of identity would make full assimilation and even high levels of segmented assimilation nearly impossible unless the society accepted and even encouraged bi-racial marriage. If, on the other hand, race and ethnicity are social constructions, then society can change how it defines race and ethnicity. Socially constructed dimensions of identity can more readily change over time and would more readily allow pluralism, incorporation, and segmented assimilation.

If we accept the standard social science view that race and ethnicity is socially constructed, then people can have multiple sources of identity. For instance, a useful way of thinking about multiple dimensions of identity is represented in Figure 1.2, a *kaleidoscope image* of the dimensions of diversity. The innermost circle represents an individual's self-image, or his or her own personal identity. The innermost ring depicts the primary sources of diversity. The second ring shows the secondary influences. The outermost ring represents tertiary dimensions or the types of influences that typically impact a person somewhat later in life, generally during adulthood. Imagine this kaleidoscope image as colored, like pieces of glass in a kaleidoscope, where the intensity of the color represents the degree to which that dimension influences that person's self-image, that is, his or her personal diversity.

A "hypothetical person"—someone we will call a Mrs. Sheila O'Brien (nee Sheila Murphy)—might color in her personal kaleidoscope to depict the various influences on her own identity as follows. Let us say Mrs. O'Brien is a forty-five-year-old woman married to Jack O'Brien. She and Jack are the proud parents of a boy and a girl. Sheila is a recently promoted executive, an associate vice-president for Quality Control, of an international, Fortune 500 corporation headquartered in Atlanta, Georgia. The family resides in the suburbs there. Sheila is Irish American on her father's side; Italian American on her mother's side. Her father is a retired U.S. army officer and Sheila was raised all over the world and in the United States. She might color her inner circle—her personality and personal identity—as fiery red, depicting how she sees herself as having a "fiery personality." In the innermost ring she might color in the "ethnicity" dimension as Kelly-Green and Olive-Green, representing her Irish- and Italian-American heritages. For the race dimension she selects white. She colors in the age dimension a light blue to depict her mildly blue attitude about being over forty. She depicts her sexual orientation as light pink to reflect her "femininity and heterosexuality." Her gender she depicts as "hot pink." For the religious dimension she uses a dark green to relate to her "Irish-Catholicism." She colors the physical ability dimension a light flesh color since, having no particular disability, it is not a strong factor in her personal life nor her self-perception.

For the secondary ring she might select the following colors: Appearance is represented by navy blue, her favorite color and that of her most frequent business attire. She colors her parental status a bright yellow to signify that she is warm about being the mother of two, and her marital status a cherry red to reflect her being happily married and nuts about her Jack. Geographic location is shown as a pale green in that it doesn't mean much to her as she has moved so often in her life. The income dimension is a dark green, reflecting her upper-income bracket. Her personal habits she depicts as a very light yellow, as this is not a weighty factor in how she sees herself. To depict her educational background she selects a light blue to represent her M.B.A. degree in business administration taken from Yale University. To depict her work experience, she selects a light grey to indicate that it was a hard climb up the corporate ladder.

The outer ring representing her tertiary influences might be colored in as follows: a deep purple for management status to show she is proud of having achieved upper-level status and reflecting her "organizational power." Her functional classification she shows as light purple for being in management. For her "work content or field" dimension she uses a light grey to show her take on the VP for Quality Control, her boss. Seniority she represents as a "bluish-grey" to show that while she is "up there," she has mixed feelings about age as well as implications of organizational power. She depicts the organizational culture dimension as light green to reflect her attitude that ultimately it is all about the bottom line. Work location she colors in as pale greenish-grey to signify being in the South but also that it is relatively unimportant to her personal life and identity. Union affiliation is uncolored as it is not and has never been a factor in her life.

In addition, social scientists have also accepted the role that generation can have in constructing personal identity. Joseph Fichter (1954) developed a typology for his study of members of a parish that can be usefully adapted to understanding the primordial vs. constructed dichotomy. It helps us to understand the individual's relation both to the group and its members (the "we") and to those of outgroups (the "they"). These distinctions help us grasp the dynamics of intergroup relations and why some groups vary in the degree of intensity of their members' group-relatedness. Such distinctions help us understand the rate at which members of a group shed a sense of "we-ness" and merge into a group of "theys."

Fichter categorizes four types of persons in terms of their group-relatedness: nuclear, modal, marginal, and dormant. A *nuclear member* of a group is one whose self-identity is totally involved in the group. Such an individual exhibits all the norms, values, and physical or cultural traits associated with that group. If we applied this concept to a national-origins group, say, Italian Americans, our nuclear member might be a seventy-two-year-old Italian grandmother who immigrated to the United States at age sixteen. Though widowed for many years now, she still dresses in all black every day. She attends mass daily, praying the rosary often. She speaks Italian almost exclusively, her English being very broken and with a heavy Italian accent. She lives in an Italian-American neighborhood, say in South Boston, above a little Italian delicatessen that she and her late husband operated for some thirty years. All of her friends are Italian American. Her social life revolves totally around her parish and her family. Her married children still come over virtually every Sunday for a big family meal. She eats Italian food three times a day, every day. One could pick her up and deposit her into some village in Italy and she would hardly notice except for the absence of her family and friends. She is, in short, more Italian than American.

The *modal type* is one who accepts most of the norms and values of the group and manifests nearly all of the physical or cultural traits of the group. For our hypothetical case, it might be the fifty-five-year-old son of the Italian grandmother. He speaks Italian fluently but, having been born in the United States, he also speaks English as a native language and with no accent. He married an Italian-American woman from the neighborhood, a childhood sweetheart. He owns and operates an Italian-American restaurant, where he and his wife and several of his nine children and other relatives all work. He is a practicing Catholic, attending mass on Sundays and all holy days. He eats Italian-style food at least once a day. His social life, too, revolves largely around his family and friends, except for two close non–Italian-American buddies with whom he served in the U.S. army. His clothing and physical features are such that even a total stranger seeing him would likely guess him to be an Italian American. If he migrated to Italy he would adjust well. He is, in short, very "*Italian* American." He thinks of himself in precisely those terms.

The *marginal type* manifests but few traits and internalizes only some of the norms and values of the group. Such a person might be the thirty-year-old grandson of our Italian immigrant. He has left home and the neighborhood to attend a university, majoring in business administration. He recently joined a major corporation as an assistant personnel manager and is working at a branch office located in a small midwestern town that has few Italian Americans. He married a non-Catholic and non-Italian woman (say of Norwegian-American background). He no longer practices Catholicism regularly, attending church only a few times a year (at Christmas and Easter and for weddings and funerals). He occasionally attends his wife's Lutheran church services. But when he does, he harbors guilty feelings about that fact. He speaks a little Italian with a heavy American accent. He reads the language poorly, and now that he has so little chance to use it, he is fast becoming rusty in Italian. His new wife cannot cook very well, and certainly cannot cook traditional Italian dishes. He eats

Italian food occasionally, at restaurants or when visiting his family in Boston. He dresses like all the other rising young executives of the company. A stranger meeting him might guess him to be of Italian-American heritage, judging from his features, but not necessarily so. To more readily incorporate, he legally changed his name from Antonio Marcconi to Tony Marks. He sees himself as "an American of Italian descent."

Tony's daughter, who will grow up with a non–Italian-sounding name and acquire yet another name upon marriage, and who will be raised in a non-Italian environment, exemplifies the *dormant type*. She exhibits few if any of the physical characteristics typical of the group and internalizes in a latent manner only some of the norms and values of the group. By adulthood, she will be a person who will speak about as much Italian as the typical American, that is, only a few words picked up from the popular culture. She will not practice Catholicism and will rarely attend the service of any denomination. She also will marry a non-Catholic, let us say of German-American heritage. She can not read, write, speak, or well understand Italian. She knows, of course, that her grandparents on her father's side are Italian Americans and that her paternal great-grandmother was an immigrant from Italy. She loves her grandparents dearly, even though she only met them on a few occasions for a week or so when she was younger and went on family vacations to visit her father's family back east. She has some emotional ties as a result, however, and they are strong, if largely subconscious. Given the right stimulus, they do surface. She does, for example, react strongly to any "dumb Italian" or "cowardly Italian" jokes. If asked to do so, she would describe herself as "an American of Norwegian and Italian descent." She is not likely, on the basis of such weakened ethnic heritage, to vote Democratic in most elections.

These examples employ a generational gap to illustrate the differing degrees or types of group-relatedness, but the reader should understand that such a time continuum is not essential. An immigrant stepping off the ship could be, psychologically speaking, a marginal type. The type of group-relatedness depends on a person's internalized *self-identity* with the relevant group. A third-generation Greek American might behave as a modal or a nuclear type. Religious groups provide good examples of this effect. Adult converts to a religious denomination often behave in a more modal or even nuclear way than one born and raised in a given denomination.

DIMENSIONS OF GROUP IDENTITY

Personal identity is shaped by such dimensions, and by the groups to which one belongs. Group members share in shaping group identity. Individuals within any group vary in the extent to which they identify with it. For some members, and for certain types of groups, belonging to the group becomes central to their own identity. For others, their social and patterned behavior and many of their internalized norms and values are deeply dependent upon the group. Still others may be but tangentially involved with a group, and internalize that connection only weakly.

The concept of group is not a simple one. When does a collection of individuals comprise a group? In 1963, sociologist Peter Rose first argued in his ground-breaking book on race relations entitled *They and We* that people exaggerate and intensify everything in their own folkways that is peculiar to them to set them apart from others.

This process is defined by Rose as *ethnocentrism* (the belief that one's own group is unique and right), wherein he cites Rudyard Kipling to capture the essence of ethnocentric thinking: "All good people agree, and all good people say, all nice people like us, are We; and everyone else is They." As professor Samuel Huntington notes: "The need of individuals for self-esteem leads them to believe that their group is better than other groups" (25).

One's perception of the "We" and the "They" is at the very heart of ethnic/racial relations. It forms the basis of the majority group/minority group distinction. Essential to the perspective of this book is the distinction between majority and minority and how that distinction influences power and the perennial struggle for power that characterizes American politics. As Huntington puts it, identity is an attribute of both individuals and groups. People can aspire to an identity, but not be able to achieve it unless others who have that identity welcome them to share it with them (25).

A group consists of persons of varying status whose behavior in large measure is determined by the expectations of its members. As long as all individuals follow the expected pattern of behavior, the group is at equilibrium. If individuals are forced or allowed to deviate from their accustomed pattern of behavior, ideas, norms, and ideals, then group equilibrium suffers, and if sufficient deviation occurs, the group disintegrates. When minority groups successfully assimilate into the majority group, they lose their distinctive sub-cultural group identity.

We can distinguish various types of groups. **Ethnic groups** are *primary groups,* those characterized by intimate face-to-face association and cooperation. A primary group involves a mutual identification for which "we" is the natural expression. The very essence of a primary group is the sense of "we-ness" that develops among its members. Members are, generally speaking, "born into" such groups.

Groups may be seen from an internal versus external perspective. The external tradition is more often used by sociologists. This perspective views groups as a whole and stresses the relationship to other groups in society. But we can also view groups, as does Gordon Allport (1958), from an internal perspective. Groups are assemblages of individuals. This view stresses factors of solidarity and anomie; the pressures and positive or negative rewards that induce individuals to comply with the group's wishes, to form social relationships that strengthen group solidarity. The forces of anomie are those factors that induce individuals to avoid social contract and to behave independently of one another. Groups are collections of individuals with significant interdependent relations.

TOP-DOWN APPROACH

The group identity can derive in a top-down manner. That is, the superordinate group, the majority, defines or categorizes the subordinate group and who belongs to that group. It assigns social significance to the group membership. It perceives of the members of the subordinate group being more or less readily able to assimilate into the majority. Members of the subordinate group may not initially see themselves through the prism of that group membership. Only after being treated by the majority members as one of that group may they gradually come to share that identity in a personal way. The majority culture defines the social significance of the group and whether its "defining characteristics" are viewed as admirable, desirable, positive, and so on. A Chinese, Japanese, or Korean immigrant or his or her child thinks of himself or herself as Chinese, Japanese, or Korean. The child will tend to think of him- or herself as Chinese American, Japanese American, or Korean American. But if the majority society defines them as Asian, or Asian American, and begins to treat all such persons who fit its categorization as belonging to that group, then it can define the group in a top-down manner. If society forces members sharing whatever characteristics the majority uses to define the group to live together in certain prescribed neighborhoods, by public law to attend only certain schools, by economic pressure to concentrate only in certain occupations, and so on, then over time persons sharing those societally defined characteristics may come to think of themselves, for example, as "Asian American."

The Irish immigrant fresh off the ship likely thought of himself as a "Dubliner," or from County Cork, not as an Irishman. Only after being treated as an Irishman did he come to think of himself that way. Danes, Norwegians, and Swedes became "Scandinavian" only after the majority society so categorized and defined them. A variety of characteristics may be singled out by the majority society as being "significantly different" from the dominant group's self-image to provide a basis or reason for placing a group in minority status. Those bases provide a justification for the differential treatment of all persons then so defined as belonging to that subordinate group. These bases may vary from society to society and in time and place within a society.

Important to the top-down approach is the concept of *white privilege*. This concept was popularized by Peggy McIntosh (1990). McIntosh notes that because, in American society, there are numerous interlocking hierarchies, the phenomenon of white privilege exists. She characterizes it as a sort of invisible package of unearned assets about which the majority is largely oblivious. McIntosh likens it to an invisible, weightless knapsack of special provisions, maps, passports, codebooks, visas, clothes, tools, and blank checks. This base of unacknowledged privilege underlies racial oppressiveness that is unconscious. For whites, it is like the air that they breathe and that surrounds them. They are unconscious of it unless it is somehow taken away. White persons do not see themselves as oppressors, nor as being unfairly advantaged, or as a participant in a culture that is racially biased. In America, whites are taught to think that their lives are morally neutral, normative, and average as well as "ideal." Thus, when whites work to benefit others, it is seen as work that will allow "them" to be more like "us."

In her explication of the concept, Peggy McIntosh developed a list of fifty "daily effects" of white privilege; conditions that are attached more to skin color than to class, religion, ethnic status, or geographic location, although such factors are intertwined. To illustrate the concept, we list in Box 1.1 (page 15), twenty-five of her fifty conditions of daily or frequent contact.

If the majority society is tolerant of an ethnic group, that acceptance may loosen the bonds of ethnic identity, as in the case of the Scottish and German immigrants to America. By contrast, rejection and subordination strengthen those bonds. It makes ethic minority groups stronger and more cohesive in their mutual sub-group identity.

Thus, the majority "creates" the minority group *as a group* by seeing all persons evidencing a certain characteristic as being "different" from them, attaching cultural, economic, political and social significance to those perceived differences. Such persons

Box 1.1   EXAMPLES OF THE CONCEPT OF WHITE PRIVILEGE

1. I can, if I wish, arrange to be in the company of people of my race most of the time.

2. I can avoid spending time with people whom I was trained to mistrust and who have learned to mistrust my kind and me.

3. If I should need to move, I can be pretty sure of renting or purchasing housing in an area which I can afford and in which I would want to live.

4. I can go shopping alone most of the time, pretty well assured that I will not be followed or harassed.

5. I can turn on the television or open the front page of the paper and see people of my race widely represented.

6. When I am told about our national heritage or about "civilization," I am shown that people of my color made it what it is.

7. I can be sure that my children will be given curricular materials that testify to the existence of their race.

8. Whether I use checks, credit cards, or cash, I can count on my skin color not to work against the appearance of financial reliability.

9. I do not have to educate my children to be aware of systemic racism for their own daily physical protection.

10. I can be pretty sure that my children's teachers and employers will tolerate them if they fit school and workplace norms; my chief worries about them do not concern others' attitudes toward their race.

11. I can swear, or dress in second-hand clothes, or not answer letters, without having people attribute these choices to be bad morals, the poverty, or the illiteracy of my race.

12. I can do well in a challenging situation without being called a credit to my race.

13. I am never asked to speak for all the people of my racial group.

14. I can criticize our government and talk about how much I fear its policies and behavior without being seen as a cultural outsider.

15. I can be pretty sure that if I ask to talk to the "person in charge," I will be facing a person of my race.

16. If a traffic cop pulls me over, or if the IRS audits my tax return, I can be sure I haven't been singled out because of my race.

17. I can easily buy posters, post-cards, picture books, greeting cards, dolls, toys and children's magazines featuring people of my race.

18. I can go home from most meetings of organizations I belong to feeling somewhat tied in, rather than isolated, out-of-place, outnumbered, unheard, held at a distance, or feared.

19. I can be pretty sure that if I argue for the promotion of a person of another race, or a program centering on race, it is not likely to cost me heavily within my present setting, even if my colleagues disagree with me.

20. My culture gives me little fear about ignoring the perspectives and power of people of other races.

21. I am not made acutely aware that my shape, bearing, or body odor will be taken as a reflection of my race.

22. I can worry about racism without being seen as self-interested or self-seeking.

BOX 1.1, CONTINUED

23. I can take a job with an affirmative action employer without having my co-workers on the job suspect that I got it because of my race.

24. I can think over many options, social, political, imaginative, or professional, without asking whether a person of my race would be accepted or allowed to do what I want to do.

25. I can choose public accommodations without fear that people of my race cannot get in or will be mistreated in the places that I have chosen.

Source: Box by author LeMay, adapted from McIntosh's list of 50 examples, 1990.

---

become part of the "They" and members of the "We" subject them to negative differential treatment solely on the basis of that perception. What characteristic is singled out and invested with such significant "difference" varies from society to society and even from time to time or place to place within a given society. In the United States there have been various characteristics upon which minority status is based: e.g. race, ethnicity (aka national origin), religion, political ideology, sexual orientation, gender.

Prejudice

In the vernacular, prejudice and discrimination are often treated as if they were synonymous. Such usage obscures some very important distinctions having significant impact upon public policy that help us toward a clearer understanding of general political behavior.

Gordon Allport, in his classic *The Nature of Prejudice,* defines prejudice simply as "an antipathy based upon faulty generalizations" (1958, 10). Peter Rose defines it as "a system of negative beliefs, feelings, and action-orientations regarding a group of people" (1990, 86). Such definition involves three major dimensions of all attitude systems: the cognitive (beliefs), the affective (feelings), and the connotative (predisposition to act in particular ways, or policy orientations).

Prejudice is best understood as a mind-set whereby the individual or group accepts as valid the negative social definitions that the majority society forms in reference to some minority group and is predisposed to apply those negative social definitions to all individuals who are perceived as belonging to that group simply on that basis. Prejudice is a highly emotionally charged attitude towards an outgroup (that is, majority members may be prejudiced against minority members, and vice versa). It is directed in negative and stereotypical terms based upon a social definition of the group. A person is hated, feared, shunned, and avoided merely because that person is seen, not as an individual to be judged on his or her own merits, but as a member of an outgroup.

Stereotypes differ from rational generalizations. They are oversimplistic and overexaggerated beliefs about a group, often acquired secondhand yet highly resistant to change. Today, for example, Arabs, a minority in the United States, are often subjected to negative stereotyping. Arab-American stereotypes include the belief that they are "all fabulously wealthy," "barbaric and uncultured," "sex maniacs with a penchant for white slavery," and that they "revel in acts of terrorism" (Shaheen 1984). In such over-simplification, Arab and Islamist are confounded. It is but a short step to consider all Arabs as potential "Islamic terrorists."

An individual learns such prejudicial attitudes at a preconscious or subconscious level. They have virtually no control over such attitudes which are deeply ingrained, internalized and often connected with very primary feelings or emotions. Given a stimulus, an individual will unconsciously or automatically react in a prejudicial way. The attitude may not be overtly manifested.

Prejudice can become so widely accepted that it begins to underlie the values and norms of a society. Prejudice becomes structured or *institutionalized*. Prejudicial values become structured to the detriment of some for the benefit of others. Blacks may be forbidden from joining certain labor unions, which cuts off their access to certain occupations. This may benefit the employers of blacks by holding down pay scales for the jobs they are allowed to enter and ensures the majority society of a large pool of cheap labor. It benefits whites by allowing them to hold disproportionately the more desirable occupations (white privilege). A racist society is one that has prejudicial attitudes permeating the norms and values of that society. Prejudice will be manifested in behavior, since the societal values set the norms of individual behavior.

Many early studies tried to find a simple, single-factor explanation of prejudice.[1] That focus shifted when it became increasingly clear that groups differ in the degree and direction of the prejudice they exhibit, and that the targets of prejudice may shift over time and/or place within a society. Harry Kitano (1997) stresses four categories of how prejudice develops: exploitation, ignorance, racism/ethnocentrism, and symbolism.

- *Exploitation* involves theories wherein one group dominates another sexually, economically, and socially. The "inferior" group must be kept in its place so that the "superior" group members can enjoy advantages of better employment, social status, and life styles. For instance, through subtle or even overt means, a particular group may be forced to take certain jobs to ensure employers among the dominant group of a large pool of cheap labor, or so that there will be a group of individuals who will perform necessary but socially undesirable tasks. A classic example of such an explanation is Marxian theory.

- *Ignorance* is often viewed as a simple explanation for prejudice.[2] Lack of information and knowledge leads to *stereotyping*: "an overgeneralization associated with a racial or ethnic category that goes beyond existing evidence" (Feagin and Feagin, 1996; 10). Stereotyped images, in turn, are projected through the mass media and permeate the popular culture of the society. The process of *selective perception* often works to reinforce such stereotyping by validating the attitudes. A group may be labeled "overly avaricious," always concerned with making a buck. If a member of a minority seems to fit the stereotyped image (and the society often generates pressures upon individuals of the minority inducing them to behave in ways that fit that very image), then the majority group member sees evidence to confirm the stereotype. If the minority group member's behavior does not fit the image, such behavior is explained away as an exception, which does nothing to upset the basic prejudice.

- *Ethnocentrism,* or the belief that one's own group is unique and right, is viewed as being almost universal.[3] This concept is used to explain prejudice as a weapon in intergroup conflict. Ethnocentrism serves the group in power. A racist society, for example, develops an ideology of white supremacy based upon a biblical and/or "scientific" theory that justifies the white supremacy and the institution of slavery.

- *Symbolic* explanations view prejudice as a by-product stemming from other concerns.[4] Freudian theory, for example, views all behavior as psychically determined. Prejudice is seen as a symptom reflecting a deeper, intrapsychic phenomenon. Social-psychological theory, following this perspective, emphasizes frustration and aggression as critical variables behind prejudice. Frustrated individuals feel hostility. Often they are blocked in directing that hostility toward the true source of that frustration and deal with hostility by directing it toward a convenient target—a *scapegoat*. Minority groups, because of their relative powerlessness in society, become convenient scapegoats. In czarist Russia, for example, peasants could not take out their aggression against the nobility who exploited them, so in frustration they turned their aggression against the Jews.

The sociological perspective emphasizes the link between change and prejudice.[5] The more static the society, the less its prejudice; the more diverse and changing the society, the greater its prejudice. In this view, prejudice is an attempt to *conserve the existing social order*. Anti-Semitism or antiblack prejudice would rise in the United States during periods of economic turmoil, such as severe recessions or depressions, or during periods of rapid social change brought on, for instance, by the nation's involvement in a war. This perspective views prejudice as a "social problem," and focuses on the linkage between attitude and behavior. Prejudiced attitudes do not predetermine prejudicial behavior. An individual's behavior may be determined more by the social situation at any particular time than by that person's preexisting mind-set. Both attitude and behavior are susceptible to situational change.

The sociological perspective places a new focus on how prejudice is learned. Prejudicial behavior (an act of discrimination) shapes and alters prejudice as a mind-set. The learning of prejudice is affected by social situations. The complex prejudicial practices within a community provide the family and similar traditional and peer groups with the frame of reference that perpetuates such practices and sustains or even extends prejudice. Jim Crow laws in the South were viewed as being a necessary underpinning of societal norms designed to enforce the continuation of the existing social order by which the white elite ruled. If a society wishes to change or reduce the degree of prejudice, it must begin by changing such institutional bases of prejudice, for example, by repealing its Jim Crow laws.

How a society might employ public policy in an attempt to reduce or mitigate prejudice is shaped by its perceptions of prejudice. The "cure" is designed to fit the perceived "illness." When prejudice is seen as the result of ignorance, then public policy involves various forms of education designed to alleviate that ignorance. When prejudice is seen as being caused by exploitation, a far different set of policy options is suggested: affirmative action programs or some set of quotas to end systematized occupational prejudice. When prejudice is viewed as some sort of psychological disorder, the result of flawed personality development producing people who need scapegoats or who have authoritarian personality types and are susceptible to a rigid dogmatism, then policy enacting health care programs designed to "prevent" their development would be advocated.

Discrimination

Discrimination is analytically distinct from prejudice. A person can have a prejudiced attitude without exhibiting overt discriminatory behavior. Likewise, a person, given a certain social milieu, may routinely behave in a discriminatory manner even if he or she does not possess the relevant prejudicial attitude. **Discrimination** has been defined as applied prejudice. Negative social attitudes are translated into action. Policy enforces subordination of minorities' rights.

Robert Merton (1949) describes the relationship between prejudice and discrimination in a paradigm that involves four types of persons and their typical response patterns. Merton's typology is summarized in Box 1.2.

While both majority and minority group members develop prejudice, usually only the majority group member is capable of translating prejudice into action, to discriminate, since only majority group members have the power to determine the norms of acceptable behavior. Discrimination connotes the *institutionalization* of expressions of prejudicial attitudes to socially control a minority group. Employers in a society who are of the dominant group may develop the practice of a "glass ceiling"—a barrier that blocks promotion of qualified workers in a multiracial work environment. Minority group members may be denied entry into highly skilled occupational apprenticeships. Bankers and realtors may practice "red-lining," wherein homes for sale in middle-class, all-white neighborhoods are shown to white clients seeking housing or white applicants seeking home improvement loans are accepted; and where non-white clients and applicants are only shown homes for sale in "ethnic neighborhoods" or are denied home-improvement loans as "questionable loan risks."

Discrimination is typically manifested in several ways. The majority will try to control the numbers of the minority group to better ensure their remaining powerless. It is manifested economically by barring minority members from unions or professional associations or by otherwise excluding them from certain occupations. This is accomplished by making minorities the last hired and first fired among those occupations they do manage to enter. Discrimination is shown in education, demonstrated in a reluctance to educate "inferiors," or by providing them with inferior education. Discrimination is seen in restrictions on political participation by using devices such as the white primary, the grandfather clause, the literacy test, the poll tax, or by unequal application of registration requirements or in the gerrymandering of electoral districts. Social discrimination is seen in limiting the minority's access to hotels, restaurants, public transportation, and other public facilities. Parks, pools, libraries, and even churches may be closed to them. Intermarriage is at least socially isolated and often legally proscribed. The Jim Crow laws of the South sought to segregate African Americans in all areas of life. Ghettoizing blacks and Jews and forcing Native Americans to live on reservations exemplify the use of public policy to enforce geographic segregation to isolate a minority.

A common manifestation of prejudice is the use of *defamation* or *derogation*,[6] directed at the outgroup members. Such derogation involves the use of **ethnophaulisms**, defamatory terms used by members of one ethnic group to refer to members of others (Peter Rose, 1990). Ethnic humor, based on negative stereotypes, is another such practice.

Box 1.2   MERTON'S TYPOLOGY OF PREJUDICE AND DISCRIMINATION

Unprejudiced Nondiscriminators

Merton calls them "all-weather liberals." They do not have individual prejudice, nor are they willing to behave in a discriminatory manner because of societal norms or pressure. They believe in the American creed of freedom and equality for all and practice it fully. They are vigorous champions of the underdog, take the Golden Rule quite literally, and cherish egalitarian values.

Unprejudiced Discriminators

Merton calls them "fair-weather liberals." They do not have prejudiced attitudes, but give in to social pressures and discriminate, often without thinking of it or being consciously aware of the discriminatory behavior they are manifesting. An example would be the homeowners of the urban North who deny having any personal feelings against blacks, yet steadfastly try to keep them out of their neighborhoods for fear of altering the character of those neighborhoods. More pragmatic than the "all-weather liberals," they discriminate when such behavior is socially called for, seems to be appropriate, or is in their own self-interest. Merton suggests that the "fair-weather liberals" are often victims of guilt because of the discrepancy between their personal beliefs and their actual conduct. They are especially amenable to the pressure of the liberal.

Prejudiced Nondiscriminators

Merton calls this type a "fair-weather illiberal," a sort of timid bigot. Many people of prejudice are not activists. They feel hostility toward members of an outgroup and they subscribe to conventional stereotypes of others, but they, too, react to the social situation. If the situation, by law or custom, forbids open discrimination, they comply. They would serve black customers, sit next to them on public transportation, send their children to integrated schools, and yet complain about the system that compels them to do so. The "fair-weather illiberal" does not accept the moral legitimacy of the creed. He conforms if he must, and will fail to conform when the pressure to do so is removed.

Prejudiced Discriminators

Merton calls this type the "all-weather illiberal." They are the active bigots, the "rednecks" who manifest prejudice in discriminatory behavior almost instinctively and consistently. They are the overt racists. "All-weather illiberals" neither believe in the American creed nor act in accordance with its principles. Like the "all-weather liberal," the prejudiced discriminator conforms to a set of standards, but in this case those standards proclaim the right, even the duty, to discriminate. He or she does not refrain from expressing prejudiced attitudes and is willing to defy the law, if need be, in order to protect his or her beliefs and vested self-interests. In American WASP-controlled society, that means maintaining all aspects of "white privilege."

Segregation signs such as the one shown here were used to help enforce the Jim Crow laws, which called for the separation of public facilities. (*Courtesy of the Library of Congress*)

Segregation

We may define **segregation** as the act of separating and isolating members of a racial or ethnic minority group from members of the majority society. Such isolating may be done more or less formally; that is, by custom or by law. *De facto segregation* is based on fact or social customs rather than by law (which is *de jure segregation*), resulting from more subtle processes. An example is *gerrymandering,* the drawing of electoral district lines in such a way that a social group is disadvantaged. This might be done to ensure that a school district, for example, is racially homogeneous (all white, all black, etc.). It might be done to split or dilute the votes of a racial group so they will be less able to elect one of their own to public office. Housing segregation, another example, is often maintained through such devices as redlining districts by mortgage lenders, or by real estate practices resulting in buying, selling, or renting housing in segregated patterns. Because public education is often based on the principle of the neighborhood school, de facto segregation in housing effectively segregates public schools as well.

Segregation may involve the separation of public facilities, such as drinking fountains, waiting rooms, and rest rooms, as was done by Jim Crow laws designed to isolate the majority member from contact with the despised minority group member in as many points of contact as was possible. More institutionalized segregation is

"Peaceful coexistence at last!"

exemplified in urban housing programs in which racial groups are ghettoized. Segregation may be so extensive that it involves the complete geographic separation of a racial or ethnic group, for example, the reservations for Native Americans and the use of concentration camps for Japanese Americans during World War II. Segregation is but one of the more blatant aspects of social stratification, an elaborate system that structurally institutionalizes racial and ethnic segregation.

Social Stratification

Social inequality involves the distribution of "rewards, goods and services, benefits and privileges, honor and esteem, or power and influence available to the incumbents of the different social roles and positions and associated with different roles and positions" (Matras 1975, 11–12). **Social stratification** refers to the methods and procedures used to assign individuals and groups to different roles and positions. Most societies exhibit inequalities in honor, status, or prestige; in economic influence and material rewards; and in access to military, political, and bureaucratic power. This structural ranking perpetuates unequal rewards and power in a society. Such inequalities may lead to the establishment of strata or social classes—that is, division of whole societies or communities within societies—that represent the division of a combination of such rewards. When such class divisions are organized along racial or ethnic lines, a society reflects ethnic stratification found among *all* multiethnic societies. While class lines are less rigid in the United States than in some other societies, there is ample evidence of ethnic stratification.

Sociologists who study stratification often place societies along a continuum from caste systems to class systems. A *caste system* has two or more rigidly defined and unequal groups in which membership is passed from generation to generation. Where one is born totally dictates the lifestyle and opportunities of the individual throughout his or her life. In a *class system,* inequality of status is not determined solely by birth. A class system allows for some degree of *achieved status,* where one gains in status through one's own actions. Both caste and class systems are ideal types. In the real world, most societies fall within that continuum and may change their position along it over time. Sociologist William Wilson (1987) has popularized the concept of *underclass*—the long-term poor who lack the training and skills to function well in the modern postindustrial society.

Functional sociologists see some ethnic stratification as functional.[7] They see society as needing a consensus and shared identity or "we-ness" to encourage cooperation within society among members who share certain basic values and a shared sense of identity. They see ethnocentrism as a natural tendency within society. They recognize, however, that while functionally necessary, such ethnocentrism can cause conflict and often leads to ethnic stratification.

Ethnic stratification is a problem that ought to be minimized, even if it is somewhat inevitable. Feagin and Feagin (1996) distinguish four basic types of discriminatory practices within societies evidencing ethnic stratification: isolate discrimination, small-group discrimination, direct institutionalized discrimination, and indirect institutionalized discrimination.

1. *Isolate discrimination* is harmful action taken with intent by a member of the dominant group against a member of a subordinate racial or ethnic group. Such discrimination is not socially embedded in a larger organization or community setting. A young person who goes out "gay-bashing" and intentionally beats up some person he believes to be homosexual would illustrate this type.

2. *Small-group discrimination* is harmful action taken by a small number of dominant group members acting together against members of a racial or ethnic minority group, without the support of the norms or rules of the larger society. The Aryan Nation and skin-heads terrorizing blacks and bombing black churches, for instance, illustrate this type.

3. *Direct institutionalized discrimination* refers to organizationally prescribed action that by intent has a negative differential impact on members of a racial or ethnic minority group. Discrimination by real estate agencies to create the ethnic ghetto is an example of this type.

4. *Indirect institutionalized discrimination* consists of practices having negative differential impact on members of minority groups even though they are carried out with no intent to harm members of those groups. An example of this type would be nonwhite workers suffering from seniority practices even though the seniority system was not originally set up to harm them.

BOTTOM-UP APPROACH

When members of a group develop a sense of "we-ness," of "peoplehood," then group membership is developed in a bottom-up manner. The group members themselves define what characteristics they share in common that sets them aside from others.

The group members then develop within themselves their individual identities that includes belonging to that group as a primary element. Any number of characteristics may be singled out by a minority subculture as being "significantly different" from the dominant group's traits, values, or norms, and so on and to provide, thereby, the basis for group membership. As we have seen, these bases vary from society to society and from time to time or place to place within a society.

An early theorist of ethnic relations, Richard A. Schermerhorn (1970), argues persuasively that *how* a minority becomes such is critically important to our understanding of resulting factors, such as the degree to which pressure is applied against them, the avenues opened or closed to them, and their resources to deal with their minority status. He distinguishes five inter-group sequences. First is the emergence of pariahs, such as the untouchables in India or the Eta in Japan. Then there is the emergence of indigenous isolates, exemplified by certain tribes in Africa who follow traditional lifestyles while the dominant elite, usually from another tribe, moves the rest of the nation toward modernization. A third sequence results from annexation, through military conquest or by economic means such as treaty purchase. A fourth is by migration in some manner, either forced migration such as slave transfer, the movement of forced labor, contract labor, or the displacement of persons, or by voluntary migration. A fifth sequence is that of colonization.

In the United States minority status has been based on national origin, religion, race, gender, sexual preference, age, and physical disability. It is important to remember that prejudice may be cumulative, stronger against persons exhibiting two or more characteristics upon which such status is based. The severity of prejudice and discrimination against a group greatly influences the ways in which a minority copes with its status. It has implications for political behavior by both the dominant and the subordinate groups.

Self-image is also an important distinction in understanding American minority group politics because many "groups" did not become such with a self-conscious group identity until they arrived in the United States and found themselves being treated differently. The Irish immigrant arriving in 1848 from Dublin, for example, likely thought of himself or herself as a "Dubliner." After being treated in the United States in an unequal manner, being refused jobs on the basis of signs stating "No Irish Need Apply," the immigrant began to think of himself as an "Irishman," or as "Irish-American." Group identity was a response to the discrimination they experienced.

POLITICAL IMPLICATIONS

The presence of so many and varied minority groups in American society profoundly impacts their political behavior. Ultimately, this entire book is devoted to those implications. We highlight a few here that will be discussed more fully in later chapters.

The need to absorb so many millions of persons of various subcultures and to deal with "other-group loyalties" has a significant impact on the majority culture. Elite groups in the majority have shaped public policy in ways that directly respond to the influx of minority groups. The majority is often split into factions depending on how differing viewpoints about the best policy for dealing with the "problem minority group" affects them. Some, such as the Know Nothing Party, respond with nativist reactions, advocating restrictionist immigration policy. Others, such as the Ku Klux Klan, attempt to totally isolate by violence and severe social segregation despised groups like blacks, Catholics, and Jews. Other elite factions react in just the opposite way. They may reach out to minority groups, advocating an "open-door" immigration policy and lobbying to spend public monies to recruit immigrants to the United States. This elite faction is often mixed in its pro-minority stance, actively seeking some "desired" minority group while being less than enthusiastic about certain religious or racial groups (LeMay 1987).

The latter faction of the dominant society has been among the economic elite and the more politically powerful. Their views continue to prevail in public policy. Sometimes they have pursued economic policy through nonpublic institutions of the majority society, such as railroads, steamship lines, or corporations that hired immigrant agents. They favored the large supply of cheap labor afforded by an open-door immigration policy. Others have acted through public policy, especially the leaders of several political parties. The Republican and Democratic political parties emerged as the dominant parties in the two-party system of the United States precisely because they did reach out to immigrants, building their parties as vast coalitions of various voting blocs. Today, Republicans are more divided between economic conservatives who favor easier immigration, "earned legalization," and a generous guest-worker policy, and social conservatives who see immigration, especially illegal immigration, as a threat (cultural, economic, and social) and view "earned legalization" as amnesty that rewards prior lawbreaking. They oppose any comprehensive immigration policy reform that would enact a guest-worker program.

Minority groups, too, were greatly influenced in their political behavior by their status, and continue to be so even today. Most groups exhibit at least an initial period of relatively low political participation. The length of time for an initial phase varies. In general, nationality groups become politically active to a higher degree and more quickly than do religious or racial groups. The minority's reaction, is in large measure, influenced by the majority's stance toward them. A period of relative inaction is typically followed by a stage in which they use politics very consciously to seek social and economic gains or to reduce the effects of discrimination.

Political party identification often becomes linked with ethnic loyalties, producing persistent patterns of voting behavior. Nationality groups tend to develop this linkage more quickly than do racial groups, perhaps because the former see a faction of the elite seeking their vote and rewarding their participation, which it is more reluctant to do with racial minorities. Those political parties that responded to the opportunity afforded by ethnic voting blocs that could be manipulated on the basis of ethnic loyalties thrived and became dominant. Those political parties that rejected such coalition building soon declined and disappeared (Welch et al. 1998).

Both majority and minority groups form political interest groups that seek to influence public policy. Policy questions often take on ethnic relevance. The majority develops factions seeking to pass restrictive immigration laws or to legally force certain racial groups into geographic or social isolation through such means as reservation policy, the anti-Chinese land laws, the ghettoization of blacks, Jews, and Chicanos, and the enactment of Jim Crow segregation laws. Other elite factions soon learn that stands on public policy issues of both domestic and foreign policy concerns can become convenient means to politically manipulate large blocs of voters and thereby to control the nomination and election processes to their benefit.

Minority groups respond to domestic legislative proposals designed to reduce discrimination or that otherwise socially and economically benefit them as a group. Often the mere psychological benefit accrued by simple recognition—naming a school or public park after an ethnic hero, for example—is enough to cement the loyalty of a minority group to a political party.

Minority groups have a keen interest in foreign policy when such policy can influence the government or nation to which they are loyal or hostile. The Greek, Irish, Chinese, and Jewish lobbies have been significant forces influencing U.S. foreign policy vis-à-vis Greece, Ireland and Great Britain, Cyprus, Taiwan, and Israel.

COPING STRATEGIES

Minority groups develop strategies to cope with their status. Such coping strategies determine the degree and manner of their political activity. Each strategy exhibits various tactical approaches to pursue that strategy. A given minority may develop factions and engage in more than one strategy at a given time, just as the majority may form factions over how to deal with minority groups within its culture. Edgar Litt (1970) suggests that all minorities will respond in one of three ways: *accommodation,* which we distinguish as being pursued by either an economic or political tactical approach; *separatism,* which may be either physical or psychological; and *radicalism,* which may be either old-style or new-style in its tactics. Martin Marger (2003) similarly classifies racial minorities into assimilationist, secessionist, and militant. As articulated by Booker T. Washington, black Americans advocated accommodating to racial discrimination by attempting to find an economic niche that would be nonthreatening to the middle class. Over time, he argued, they could themselves move into the middle class and be accepted. Other blacks, such as Marcus Garvey with his "Back to Africa" movement or the Black Muslims, preached separatism. Still others, from W. E. B. Du Bois to Dr. Martin Luther King Jr., have advocated a radical approach by attempting to change the basic value system of the dominant culture.

Each strategy inevitably involves the minority in the perennial struggle characterizing minority group politics in America. The dilemma about how difficult it is for racial and ethnic minorities to get along with one another is illustrated by cases of ethnic cleansing, as in Bosnia and Kosovo, and in intertribal genocide, as in Rwanda, the Sudan, Kenya and so on.

One way that minority groups cope with their status is through **acculturation**. This is the process by which a member of a minority subculture gradually absorbs the norms, values, and lifestyle of the dominant culture, or at least that portion of majority society within which he/she operates regularly. A certain degree of acculturation will take place simply as a result of the sustained contact between two cultures. It is not all one-sided. In turn, the dominant culture will absorb some aspects of the subordinate culture. The majority Anglo-American culture, for example, acquired the Christmas tree and kindergarten from German immigrants. Another example is the

Americanization of pizza, tacos, and similar ethnic foods now so broadly accepted as part of the American diet. Indeed, the American two-party system was forged and greatly shaped by the influx of over seventy million immigrants who needed to be accommodated. Much acculturation, however, is from the subordinate to the dominant culture. Minority group members gradually adopt the norms and values of Anglo-American culture. They begin to speak English, adopt the economic and political methods used here, and may even change their names or religious affiliation to be more compatible with the dominant culture.

Accommodation refers to the relations between the dominant society and its various racial/ethnic minority groups in which the minority accepts the value system of the dominant culture and wants to be accepted into it. The dominant culture recognizes the legitimacy of the minority's attempts to assimilate. The progression to assimilation is gradual, however, with some degree of conflict and competition. The friction is on both sides of the racial/ethnic lines. Depending on reactions of both sides, accommodation could result in amalgamation or pluralism.

Social passing involves a situation wherein an individual who is ascribed to one, usually racial, subgroup and experiences discrimination because of it copes with that discrimination by "passing themselves off" as belonging to the majority group. This can be done, for example, when the mixed race person who had been racially defined as being "black," or "Asian," and so on, is sufficiently "light-skinned" to pass as white. Such persons usually are too well known in their home town to be able to pass, but if he or she moves to some other typically distant location where their family origin is not known, then passing becomes a possible way to cope with the discriminatory treatment. Such "social passing," however, usually engenders a good deal of personal psychological stress as the individual "denies" an important part of their individual identity as it had developed while growing up.

Rejection is another way of coping with discriminatory treatment. The individual rejects the values, norms, or customs of the majority society. The individual may reject even "belonging" to the majority society. Rejection often engenders anger, rage, even hatred for the "outgroup." It may justify violence as appropriate reaction for the individual. Rejection may also result in self-loathing or hatred. Feelings of rejection are usually associated with the coping strategy of radicalism, and often with either forced or voluntary separatism.

Conflict is a common social interaction arising out of majority/minority relations in which there is a high degree of competition. Conflict may be more or less violent. Sometimes conflict is essentially deflected—that is, directed at another person or group perceived as being a threat to the individual or his or her group. Conflict is common between racial or ethnic minority groups and the majority society, but also, in deflected cases, between or among minority groups who see themselves in competition with each other rather than with the majority society.

SUMMARY

In many ways, this book is about the bottom-up strategies and tactics used by minority groups in coping with their minority status and in socially interacting with the majority culture. This chapter introduced the key terms and concepts that make up the "language" of the perennial struggle between majority and minority groups. It introduced the jargon of ethnic and racial relations by discussing the contributions to that field by a number of scholars of racial and ethnic relations. It focused on both individual and group identity and how identity comes to be formed and defined. It laid the groundwork for later chapters that explore the theories and strategies of racial and ethnic relations more fully, and that use the experiences of a multiplicity of such groups to illustrate key aspects of their struggle as they cope with minority status in the United States. It developed important analytical distinctions among basic terms used to study racial and ethnic relations, and presented some graphical figures to illustrate how personal and national identity factors relate to those distinctions.

The vexing issues of whether or not the United States should be a "melting pot" or a more pluralistic "salad bowl" have often been raised in the popular press over concern about America's continued high levels of legal immigration and especially concern over the estimated twelve million illegal immigrants that seem to be flooding in at a rate of nearly one million per year. Social interactions arising from the illegal immigration problem, and the policy quandary it poses is the focus of Reading 1.1, "To Assimilate or to Incorporate?" found at the end of this chapter.

KEY TERMS

accommodation   The minority group accepts the value system of the dominant culture and seeks inclusion.

acculturation   A process by which a member of a subculture gradually absorbs the norms, values, and lifestyle of the dominant culture.

discrimination   Applied prejudice where negative social definitions are translated into action and public policy by the subordination of a minority's political, social, and economic rights.

ethnic group   A self-perceived group of people who hold a common set of traditions not shared by others with whom they are in contact, including religion, language, history, and common ancestry, giving them a sense of "peoplehood."

ethnicity   A sense of "peoplehood."

ethnophaulism   A type of derogation involving the use of defamatory terms for members of one ethnic group by another.

majority group   The superordinate group in a superordinate/subordinate relationship.

minority group   The subordinate group in a superordinate/subordinate relationship; they are viewed as unique on the basis of perceived physical, cultural, economic, or behavioral characteristics and are treated negatively as a result.

prejudice   A set of attitudes that causes, supports, or justifies discrimination; a mind-set whereby individuals or groups accept negative social definitions that the majority forms in reference to some minority group as valid, predisposing them to apply those definitions to all in the group.

race   The differential concentration of gene frequencies for certain traits that are confined to physical manifestations, such as skin color, hair texture, and facial features.

racism   An ideology that considers the unchangeable physical characteristics of a group to be linked in a direct, causal way to their psychological and intellectual functioning, and thereby to distinguish superior and inferior races.

segregation   The act of separating and isolating members of a racial or ethnic group from members of the majority society. May be by law (de jure) or by custom (de facto).

social stratification   The distribution of rewards, goods, services, benefits and privileges, honor and esteem, or power and influence according to different social roles and positions; methods to assign individuals to different roles and positions.

stereotypes   Oversimplistic and exaggerated beliefs about a group, most often acquired secondhand.

REVIEW QUESTIONS

1. What are Fichter's four types of group-relatedness? Relate them to assimilation.
2. Discuss what is meant by, and the purposes of, various Jim Crow laws.
3. Discuss how discriminatory practices contribute to ethnic stratification.
4. In the United States, what have been the various bases used to assign minority status to various groups?
5. Discuss intergroup sequences used to account for how a group comes to be confined to minority status, distinguishing between acculturation, amalgamation, assimilation, and incorporation processes.
6. Can you describe the three strategies for coping with minority status?
7. What are Banton's Kitano's four categories of how prejudice develops?
8. What are Merton's types of prejudiced and discriminator persons?
9. Besides the United States, what other countries exemplify ethnic stratification?
10. Contrast the "melting pot" with the "salad bowl" image of interracial relations. What theory of race relations fits each of these images? How do the two images affect factions of the majority society in positions they take with regard to illegal immigration reform policy?

NOTES

1. For a general discussion on the causes of prejudice, including all these explanations, see Allport (1954), Berry (1958), and Williams (1947). In addition to the economic theory of Karl Marx, others argue the economic exploitation approach. See, for example, Bonacich (1976), Fox-Piven and Cloward (1975), Dahrendorf (1939), Fushfield (1973), Tabb (1970), Cox (1948), and Wilson (1987).
2. Both sociologists and social psychologists stress this view. See, for instance, Bogardus (1950), Feagin and Feagin (1996), Allport (1958), and Collins (1970). In the early twentieth century, social scientists rejected the doctrine of racial superiority, but some held the view that people *instinctively* dislike the strange and different. They saw xenophobia (the dislike of foreigners) as an inborn trait. See, for example, such sociologists as Reuter (1934) and the early work of Park and Ernest Burgess (1924).
3. For sources that emphasize ethnocentrism as an underlying factor in social/ethnic relations, see Rose (1990), Feagin and Feagin (1996), Simpson and Yinger (1965), and Levine and Campbell (1972).
4. See Freud (1950), Allport (1958), Dollard et al. (1939), and Bettleheim and Janowitz (1950).
5. See, for instance, the later work of Park (1939, 1950), Gordon (1964), Davis and Moore (1945), and Durkheim (1964).
6. Derogation refers to several types of verbal behavior that are defamatory in nature: ethnophaulisms, unintentional references to color and verbal slips that are derogatory (color-laden phrases), ethnic jokes and ethnic accents, and ethnic labeling. See Peter Rose (1990) and Palmore (1962).

7. Various social scientists represent the functional school. See such sociologists as Parsons (1953), Davis and Moore (1945), and Emile Durkheim (1964). An example of a functional economist would be Berle (1959). Functional psychologists include Hernstein (1971) and Jensen (1969). For criticism of the functional school approach, see Anderson (1974) and Matras (1975).

ADDITIONAL READINGS

Banton, Michael. *Race Relations.* London: Tavistock, 1967.

Bonilla-Silva, Eduardo. *Racism without Racists.* Lanham, MD: Rowman and Littlefield, 2003.

Brunsma, David L. and Kerry A. Rockquemore. *Beyond Black: Biracial Identity in America.* Thousand Oaks, CA: Pine Forge Press, Sage Publication, 2002.

Doane, Ashley W. and Eduardo Bonilla-Silva, eds. *White Out: The Continuing Significance of Race.* New York: Routledge, 2003.

Gallagher, Charles. 1999. *Rethinking the Color Line.* Mountain View, CA: Mayfield.

Gordon, Milton. *Assimilation in American Life.* New York: Oxford University Press, 1964.

Hero, Rodney. *Racial Diversity and Social Capital: Equality and Community in America.* New York: Cambridge University Press, 2007.

Huntington, Samuel. *Who Are We? The Challenge to American National Identity.* New York: Simon and Schuster, 2004.

Lieberson, Stanley. *A Piece of the Pie.* Berkeley: University of California Press, 1980.

McElroy, John H. *Divided We Stand.* Lanham, MD: Rowman and Littlefield, 2006.

Omi, Michael, and Howard Winant. *Racial Formation in the United States, 2nd ed.* New York: Routledge, 1994.

Portes, Alejandro and Ruben G. Rumbaut, eds. *Ethnicities: Children of Immigrants in America.* New York: New York University Press, 1997.

Rose, Peter. *They and We.* New York: McGraw-Hill, 1990.

• **Reading 1.1**

To Assimilate or to Incorporate?

The United States is one of the world's leading immigration-reception nations. It is, moreover, exceptional in the degree to which it has absorbed immigrants from other nations. As a "Nation of Nations" it has permanent residents among its population who were born in more than 170 nations of origin. The United States has welcomed, although not always warmly so, some 70 million legal immigrants, and has experienced in recent years the influx of an estimated 12 million illegal immigrants.

Immigration policy is intended to control the flow of newcomers. The unauthorized flow is a perennially vexing issue in United States politics and policymaking. In the post-9/11 era American politics struggles with heightened fears that illegal immigration overburdens governmental education, health care, prison, and welfare systems at the state and local levels. U.S. immigration policy seeks to cope with the threat that international terrorism poses through the possibility of terrorist cells infiltrating through illegal immigration (LeMay, 2006). Congress is presently engaged in consideration of a guest-worker program, the problems of human trafficking, and the dual nationality aspects of a new world order with its increasingly multiple allegiances. Policy aimed at control of unauthorized immigration illustrates how gaps in or unanticipated consequences of prior law have affected the nature and size of the illegal immigration flow. The massive size of the estimated unauthorized immigrant population (the Pew Hispanic Center puts the number at 12 million) has once again brought the issue to the forefront of the U.S. political scene, the halls of the U.S. Congress, and to the public policy agenda of a host of governments at the state and local levels.

Unauthorized immigration is comprised of two types of migration: (1) the undocumented, more popularly known as the "illegal immigrant," who enters the country without paperwork or authorization, typically crossing the southern border with Mexico, and frequently called "wetbacks;" and (2) the visa overstayer, or the migrant who enters the country with a valid but temporary visa (for example, for tourism or as a student), who then simply goes underground and stays beyond or otherwise breaks the terms and conditions of the visa and thereby becomes illegal. Such unauthorized immigrants often enter from the north, from Canada, or through the various ports of entry (airports and seaports) all over the nation. Of the unauthorized immigrants in the United States, about 60 percent are undocumented, and 40 percent are overstayers, fraudulent entrants, or persons failing to depart. Unauthorized immigrants are illegal but not criminal, as to be in the United States illegally is a civil not a criminal offense.

Many U.S. employers, certainly a part of the "majority," often desire to hire illegal immigrants as they constitute a cheap and highly controllable workforce. Since 1986, with enactment of the Immigration Reform and Control Act (IRCA), it is illegal to knowingly hire them. More immigrants—legal and unauthorized—have entered the United States between 2000 and 2005 than during any other five-year period in U.S. history. An estimated 8 million immigrants entered during this time, nearly half (3.7 million) illegally, according to Census Bureau data reviewed by the Center for Immigration Studies. The immigrant population set a national record at 35.2 million in March, 2005. Today, they make up 12.1 percent of the entire U.S. population. How the nation can absorb and effectively control this massive influx is one of the most perplexing policy issues on the national policy agenda.

Advocates of comprehensive immigration reform (both Democrats and Republicans) favor an "incorporation" perspective. They propose "earned legalization" that would allow most of the 12 million illegal immigrants to begin a path that would allow them to regularize their status and incorporate into the legal work-force. This would, proponents argue, lessen the unwanted effects of the "underground economy." They would pay fees and taxes and thus benefit the economy. They would pay into the social security system and help finance that increasingly troubled program. Being mostly young, working-age persons, who moreover have a higher natural birth rate than does the national average, they would provide, long-term, a stable workforce to offset an increasingly aging, retired group among the "native population."

Critics of the comprehensive reform approach favor stricter border control measures and oppose any legalization program. They approach the issue from an "assimilation" perspective. They fear that the very size and scope, as well as the source of origin of illegal immigrants, make efforts at "Americanization" more difficult. Illegal immigrants are highly concentrated, with the top four immigrant-receiving states accounting for a 20 percent larger share of that population than did the top four states in 1975. Critics argue that illegal immigrants are less varied than were those of the past, with more than fifty percent coming from Spanish-speaking countries. This trend, critics fear, represents a degree of ethnic concentration unprecedented in U.S. history. The very massiveness of the illegal flow, they maintain, hinders the immigrants' (both legal and illegal) economic incorporation. Finally, they argue that illegal immigrants are anti-assimilationist. They contend most illegal immigrants undergo at best a superficial assimilation. Such critics foresee the development of a visceral, emotional attachment to the United States and its history as part of a "patriotic assimilation," that they fear is unlikely to occur when the general culture is hostile to patriotism, and when communication technology enables illegal immigrants to maintain strong psychological and even physical ties to their countries of origin.

Source: Adapted from Michael LeMay, 2006. *Guarding the Gates: Immigration and National Security.* Westport, CT.: Praeger Security International, Preface; and Michael LeMay, 2007. *Illegal Immigration.* Santa Barbara, CA: ABC-CLIO, Preface and pages 1–2.

CHAPTER 2

$\bullet\ \bullet\ \bullet$

STRATEGIES OF THE STRUGGLE

Social Interaction Between Majority and Minority Groups

As legal and illegal immigration surged anew in the 1980s and 1990s, the trend renewed old fears and concerns about the ability of new immigrants to assimilate and about how willing American society should be to absorb them. As the nation struggled to cope with the renewed immigration, public opinion pressured Congress to do something about what many felt to be a lack of control of the borders. Congress passed several immigration laws designed to restrict illegal immigration and otherwise discourage immigration. It increased the border patrol, strengthened provisions aimed at document fraud and alien smuggling, tightened detention, deportation, and employee verification procedures, restricted access to a number of public benefits, and tightened asylum, parole, and short-term visa provisions.

The number of refugees during the decade of the 1990s averaged over 130,000 a year, and the number of unauthorized aliens entering the United States has been estimated at 500,000 to perhaps a million annually. The nation again faces the task of absorbing roughly a million new arrivals a year. The fact that the vast majority of the newest arrivals are either Hispanic or Asian raises additional concerns about how prepared they are to successfully "melt" and who will pay the cost for programs designed to assist them in the process of assimilation. Some Americans fear a "Hispanic separatist movement" developing in the United States, along the lines of the French-speaking separatist political movement in Quebec (see, for example, Samuel Huntington 2004).

INTERACTION BETWEEN TOP-DOWN AND BOTTOM-UP APPROACHES

Social interaction between the majority society or dominant group and the various minority groups subordinated within it is a two-way street. The majority society prefers to interact with a minority in a top-down approach and being the superordinate group, has the power to do so. How it treats the minority group, however, impacts their reaction to and interaction with the majority. Discrimination, prejudice, and the public policy effects of those attitudes such as physical or social segregation, have consequences. The minority group may reject the treatment accorded it because of the top-down approach. It may compete in those avenues open to it and attempt to acquire sufficient power to mitigate its treatment. It may acquiesce with the majority and its top-down approach, seeking to assimilate with the majority and accepting its norms and values. The minority group prefers to interact with the majority society in a bottom-up approach, but may lack sufficient cultural, economic, political, or social power to do so. How it reacts to the majority society, however, likewise has consequences. Its interactions may reinforce majority society's attitudes and images of minority group members. Majority society members may conflict or compete with minority members. Social interactions by the minority using the bottom-up approach may result in competition, conflict, and grudging acceptance. The majority society may change its attitudes, norms, and values with respect to the minority as a result of that two-way street interaction.

WHY POLICY IS CRITICAL TO RACE/ETHNIC RELATIONS

The top-down and the bottom-up approaches meet and mingle in their impact on race and ethnic relations in the arenas of public policy formation, several of the more important of which are discussed more fully in Chapter 9. As the title of this book states, race and ethnic relations involve a perennial struggle for power. The majority group, and significant factions thereof, seeks to maintain the power and privileges that result from holding power—economic, political, social, and cultural. Power is structured, and to maintain that power the majority group uses public policy to impose it on others. Influence over public policy enables them to enjoy preferential treatment.

They maintain their privileges and they impose negative status upon various minority groups, the "others," by using top-down relationships that are reflected in public policy choices they are able to decide to their benefit and to the detriment of minorities. They use public policy to ensure that they and their children attend the better schools, live in the better neighborhoods, have the more desirable jobs, are the first hired and the last fired, acquire the higher incomes, and so on.

Conversely, the minority groups seek to mitigate their detrimental treatment. They use bottom-up approaches to seek power, to attempt to influence public policy such that it will not be used to impose minority status upon them, to relegate them by law or custom to the worst schools, to force them to live in the worst neighborhoods, to deny them access to certain occupations. They try to influence public policy to end the cycle of their being the last hired and the first fired from such jobs as are open to them, to climb out of poverty and the ranks of the under- or unemployed, to avoid disproportionate incarceration, and so on. Public policy and its impacts upon society, whether intended or unintended, can be viewed as the "score-card" reflecting who is winning and who is losing in the perennial struggle among racial and ethnic groups in society.

INTERACTION HAS LED TO SEGMENTED ASSIMILATION

As stated above, the social interaction between the majority society and various minority groups within results in minorities adopting one or another of the coping strategies, or some combination of such strategies. They will either seek full or at least increased entrance into the social structures of society, seek to avoid as much as possible social interaction with the majority society, or seek to change majority society to be more compatible to their values, customs, and norms. Most minority groups adopt the strategy and tactics of accommodation, meaning they seek full or at least partial and significant degrees of assimilation.

Assimilation is the subjectively felt or psychological identification with the majority. In total assimilation, the former minority group member feels a part of the majority, and the majority accepts him or her as such. Not all minorities can or even want to assimilate. Acculturation may be viewed as a type of assimilation—cultural assimilation (Gordon 1964). In its simplest definition, assimilation means to become similar to, and the change can be in more than one direction. With respect to the process of immigration, assimilation means the creation of greater homogeneity in society through the attenuation of ethnic differences. In terms of American majority society, it entails adoption of the "American way of life"—learning English, adhering to the Anglo-Protestant culture of religious commitment, individualism and the work ethic, and identifying oneself psychologically as a patriotic American (Citrin, Lehrman, Murakami, and Pearson 2007; Huntington 2004).

Segmented assimilation refers to the gradual acceptance into the social structures of society by members of the minority. It refers to a lower degree of such assimilation that may be limited to certain areas of social interaction that the majority leaves "open" to members of the minority, and to which the minority members are willing to pursue. The minority group may assimilate only culturally, or only somewhat culturally. They may acquire access into limited areas of the economic structure—to certain jobs and to lower levels of socio-economic status. Segmented assimilation means that the minority may be "stuck" in certain areas of social interaction and levels or areas of power for long periods of time. Segmented assimilation does not presume that the interactions are uni-directional nor inevitable. Progress may be made in one area of social interaction but not in others. Progress may regress given changes in certain conditions.

Variations of Segmented Assimilation: Amalgamation and Accommodation

Within the social sciences, scholars have identified various types of segmented assimilation. For example, Milton Gordon (1964) distinguishes seven kinds of assimilation: cultural behavioral, structural, marital, identificational, attitude receptional (the absence of prejudice), behavioral receptional (the absence of discrimination), and civic (the absence of value or power conflict). He presents certain hypotheses about the relationships among these dimensions of assimilation: (1) that in majority/minority contact, cultural assimilation will take place first; (2) that acculturation may take place even if none of the other types of assimilation occurs, and that the situation of "acculturation-only" may continue indefinitely; and (3) that if structural assimilation occurs, along with or subsequent to acculturation, the other types will inevitably follow. According to Gordon, prejudice and discrimination will disappear from a society only when civic assimilation has been reached. It is possible for a good deal of cultural assimilation, and even some structural assimilation, to occur without further stages developing, or doing so only very slowly. In the United States, structural assimilation is evident with respect to Euro-American minorities, but little has yet occurred with respect to racial minorities. As various ethnic and racial minority groups are discussed in subsequent chapters, the status of their stage or degree of assimilation, whether segmented or full, will be explicitly noted and the indicators of that assessment will be illustrated.

The capacity of a specific minority to achieve the more advanced dimensions of assimilation, according to Gordon, is determined by what he labels "competitive power," the ability of individuals to compete in the reward system of a society, and by "pressure power," the ability to effect change in society in a collective fashion. Such power pressure may be manifested in one of two ways: (1) political pressure involving actions appropriate to the standard political behavioral norms of that society, for instance, actions via voting, litigation in courts, lobbying the legislature, and the like; or (2) disruptive pressures, involving acts that disrupt normal and expected routines of social intercourse, ranging from peaceful but unconventional demonstrations to violent revolution.

Scholar Michael Banton (1967) distinguishes what he calls six "orders of interracial contact." Among those, discussed more fully below, his fifth order is **amalgamation.** To exemplify amalgamation, Banton refers to interracial marriage and its variations (intimate social interaction, living together as a couple but not legally married, etc.). Amalgamation can occur without much acculturation (for example, war-bride marriages between American servicemen and Japanese, Korean, or Vietnamese during those respective wars). Such assimilation is frequently thought to be the inevitable result of integration, which is why it was so resisted in the South. Gordon maintains that once members of a minority could freely enter into social clubs, organizations, and similar institutions of majority society on an *equal* footing, then intermarriage and the remaining stages of assimilation would follow. Fear of amalgamation is found among members of the dominant group and among members of the minority racial group. In short, both groups often resent and resist amalgamation. Given segmented assimilation, such resistance to amalgamation may be more often and more clearly manifested in some areas of basic social interaction than in others.

American society is clearly witnessing a much greater degree of interracial marriage. The profusion of couples breaching once impregnable barriers of color, ethnicity, and faith is startling. Over a period of roughly two decades, the number of interracial marriages in the United States has escalated from 310,000 to more than 1.1 million; 72 percent of those polled by *Time* magazine know married couples who are of different races. The incidence of births of mixed-race babies has multiplied 26 times as fast as that of any other group. Among Jews the number marrying out of their faith has shot up from 10 to 52 percent since 1960. Among Japanese Americans, 65 percent marry people who have no Japanese heritage; Native Americans have nudged that number to 70 percent. In both groups the incidence of children parented by mixed couples exceeds the number born into uni-ethnic homes. Such amalgamation does not come without pain. The child of one such union stated, "I know that people are tolerating me, not accepting me" (*Time*). Special Issue 142, November (1993)

A common image of amalgamation, the **melting pot theory**, was especially popular during the twentieth century. It envisioned a unique American character emerging out of the intermingling of different people in this new environment. It assumed that structural assimilation would take place. While a noble one, the metaphor has never accurately depicted minority group experience in the United States, although the trend toward increasing racial intermarriage already noted may yet bring about such a society in the distant future. The melting pot theory or image is more appropriate to assimilation theory and the concept of minority group accommodation.

INTERACTION HAS LED TO INCORPORATION

Incorporation is the gradual acquisition of positions of status in society. It may be cultural, economic, political, social, or a combination of those aspects of society. While amalgamation and accommodation emphasize a gradual process that is unidirectional and by early sociologist scholars considered inevitable, incorporation is seen as multi-directional, highly varied in rate, and decidedly not uniform nor inevitable. Some groups may incorporate in some limited areas, say somewhat socially or culturally, yet lag far behind economically or politically. Some groups may essentially reject the majority culture and incorporate only minimally. Other groups may advance for some time, only to regress when attitudes or conditions change (Browning, Marshall, and Tabb, 1997). In subsequent chapters discussing various ethnic group histories, we will note the status of that group's incorporation.

Pluralism

Banton's sixth order is pluralism, in which racial differences indicate much wider variation in expected behavior than is the case with integration. **Pluralism** has been likened to separate nation states, in which groups live side by side with different languages and cultures and with a minimum of social interaction, integration, or assimilation. In place of the "melting pot" image of society, a "salad bowl" image might be more appropriate with cultural pluralism. As in a tossed salad, each ingredient remains distinct and identifiable, yet all contribute to the ultimate mix. Banton's pluralist order is more appropriate to the incorporation approach.

Cultural pluralists view the need to maintain subsocietal separation as key "to guarantee the continuance of the ethnic tradition and the existence of the group, without at the same time interfering with the carrying out of standard responsibilities to the general American civic life" (Gordon 1964, 158). For a pluralist society, wide-scale intermarriage and extensive primary-group relations across racial or ethnic lines pose a grave threat to its existence. Gordon maintained that the reality of American life is one of structural pluralism rather than cultural pluralism, although some degree of cultural pluralism still obviously remains, especially with regard to racial subcultures.

Cultural pluralism refers to the maintenance of ethnic subcultures with their traditions, values, and styles. *Structural pluralism* refers to the structural compartmentalization into analogous and duplicative but culturally alike sets of institutions. The United States, for instance, has two major racial castes, black and white, sharing the same Western culture and the same language. To be white is to belong to the upper half of the system, with its corresponding social-psychological perspectives. Members of the white power structure feel superior and responsible. They emphasize law and order and gradualism in race relations, and place a high value on rational discussion and scientific studies. They enjoy the fruits of white privilege. They feel that if the "other" would only become more like them, the ethnic stratification and boundaries would soon disappear (a top-down perspective). Those in the subordinate position, however, view the world differently. They may try to escape their minority status by changing their names or exterior appearances or by altering reality. They sometimes over-identify with the dominant group, or vent their frustrations on members of other minority groups, or even among others in their own. They often feel great impatience with the racial status quo and demand immediate action to change it.

Kitano adds yet another concept to Banton's six stages—*biculturalism,* which he describes as a variant of both acculturation and pluralism based on the observation that exposure to several cultures can be additive. A person can acquire and be comfortable with both the dominant culture and his or her own ethnic heritage, one's minority subculture. A bilingual person is one who has acquired one of the skills important to such bicultural adaptation, although language is but one such skill. An individual with a bicultural orientation would have friends in several cultures, enjoy various foods, appreciate and speak at least two languages, and be able to interact with various groups with an appropriate sensitivity to the different cultures. A bicultural perspective assumes the desirability of a variety of cultural styles. It reflects the "salad bowl" metaphor over the "melting pot" image of society. Such a response, however, is difficult in any society where one culture is thought to be superior or better than the other(s). Marger (2003) distinguishes a typology of multiethnic societies as being either colonial, corporate, pluralistic, or assimilationist. Within that typology he distinguishes various types of pluralism: egalitarian, cultural, corporate, and inegalitarian.

Integration

In Michael Banton's schema, the first order of interracial contact between groups is that of "peripheral contact" involving minimal interaction between the two cultures. If the two are of roughly equal power, such interaction tends to be formal—involving the exchange of ambassadors and consulates, and instituting formal cultural exchanges and the like. Such interaction leaves the majority of each culture autonomous and independent of one another. Institutionalized contact between *unequal* power groups Banton calls "paternalism" or "colonialism." Under paternalism, role and status are sharply defined, and social distance is maintained through etiquette, regulations, and repeated demonstrations of power by the dominant group. Paternalistic societies are rigidly stratified by racial castes. His third type of interaction is acculturation, described above. Banton's fourth type is **integration**. In this order racial distinctions are disregarded or given only minor consideration. The primary interactions among the races on most levels (in housing, schooling, employment, interest group affiliation, friendship, and social relations) are conducted on an equal basis. Rigid definitions and racially prescribed roles are discarded or greatly modified, so there is more freedom for voluntary choice and movement across racial lines. Integration may also take place on a less than equal basis. Integrated army units may be led by white officers; an integrated company may have all of its top echelon of managers be white males, even though its labor force may be fairly equally mixed. In such a case, integration may be but little evidenced in the more intimate social relationships, such as intergroup marriage.

INTERACTION HAS LED TO CONFLICT

The two-way street aspect of social interaction between the majority society and minority subcultures means that the intermingling of the top-down and bottom-up approaches, between the desires and intentions of the majority society and those of members of the minority society often result in conflict. That conflict may be manifested as **majority/minority conflict**; that is, as conflict that is more or less violent, between members of the majority and the minority group(s). Race riots, violent demonstrations and such are common occurrences as a result of the majority/minority conflict. Such violence may be perpetrated by members of the majority against members of the minority—in hate crimes, lynchings, terror tactics by the Ku Klux Klan, and so on. Such conflict may be perpetrated by the minority against the majority—by strikes, assassinations, riots, attempted coups, and so on.

The interaction may also result in **minority/minority conflict**. The majority society may induce competition between racial and ethnic groups that is evidenced in the labor market, for example. Different minority groups may blame their problems on other minority groups rather than on the majority society. Stereotyping members of another minority group, for example, may result from inter-group conflict. Violent conflict may be evidenced when minority group members attack one another in hate crimes or in riots directed at other minority groups, such as blacks against Koreans or Hispanics or Hasidic Jews, and so on.

THEORIES OF RACE/ETHNIC RELATIONS

When groups find themselves treated differentially, they have to cope with that discrimination. Minority groups develop coping strategies. Some groups reject the dominant culture. Still others seek to radically alter the norms and values of the majority society to improve their status and lives. Most groups, however, seek accommodation with the dominant culture, attempting to get their fair share of the pie and to move up the economic ladder. They attempt to assimilate. This section discusses some theories of race and ethnic relations developed in the social sciences.

Minority groups seeking to assimilate vary in the degree to which they desire to do so, and various groups historically have clearly differed in the rate at which they achieve some degree of acculturation and segmented assimilation. Some national origin groups, such as the Scandinavians, Germans, Scots, and Welsh, have moved up quickly and incorporated with little friction. As we will discuss more fully below, they have essentially reached full assimilation. Other national origin groups, such as the Irish, Italians, Greeks, and Slavs, faced stiff resistance and moved quite slowly. Religious minorities sometimes reject assimilation, and even those who accept it have tended to move more slowly than have simple national origin minority groups, and generally have been characterized as having achieved segmented assimilation. Some religious groups faced severe persecution. The Mormons, for example, were forced to give up a basic tenet of their faith before they could assimilate into the dominant culture. The presidential campaign of Mitt Romney illustrates how far Mormons have come from forced physical separation, to gradual segmented assimilation, to relative mainstream religious status and assimilation. Racial groups have experienced the greatest resistance, have been subjected to greater degrees of prejudice and discrimination, and have moved the most slowly of all (Feagin and Feagin 1996; Omi and Winant, 1994). Many reacted to discrimination by rejecting accommodation and espousing separatism.[1] Some have sought radical change to aspects of the dominant culture's value system, undergoing severe conflict before being better received. Those racial groups that have striven to assimilate have found it difficult to do so. Even among the various racial minorities in the United States, great variation is evident in the means and rates of their segmented assimilation.

What causes variations in the rate of assimilation or incorporation is by no means an easy question to answer. Several theories have been advocated by scholars of racial and ethnic relations to explain variations in rates of assimilation among different subcultures. More recently, scholars from various social sciences emphasize different variables to explain how and why subcultures incorporate into the majority culture at varying rates and why they employ different routes of access to do so. This chapter discusses some single-factor explanations of variations in those rates. The next chapter will present a multi-factor, systems framework for racial and ethnic relations that is useful for understanding segmented assimilation and incorporation.

Stanley Lieberson (1980) presents an analysis of the causes and nature of the gap between South, Central, and Eastern European groups and black Americans in their respective rates of segmented assimilation. He attempts to account for why those who migrated to the United States during and after the 1880s fared so much better than did black Americans (for briefer studies, see also Hollifield 1989, Schmidt 1989, and Stowers 1989).

Assimilation, whether segmented or full, is best viewed as a gradual process of transformation, either within an individual or within a group as more and more of its members change individually. This gradual transformation involves persons typical of a given subculture becoming more and more like individuals of the dominant culture. It is the complex process in which a person from a minority subculture gradually merges into another culture. It is manifested among members in a number of dimensions or sub-processes: cultural, structural, marital, identificational, attitude receptional, behavioral receptional, and civic (Gordon 1964, 71; Kottak and Kozaitis 1999, 48–49; for a critical discussion of the assimilation model and alternative theories, see Feagin and Feagin 1996, 30–56). Assimilation depends on both the minority members seeking it and on the majority's acceptance of their absorption. The pace depends on both sides of the relationship. It is possible to achieve structural assimilation and then to regress if hostility suddenly increases, as it did against German Americans during World War I. Milton Gordon suggests that when the rate of inter-group intermarriage increases, the pace of assimilation increases rapidly and that after extensive marital assimilation occurs (greater than 50 percent), the other stages become inevitable. In Milton Gordon's typology, complete political incorporation of members of a group is the final stage of assimilation.

As alluded in Chapter 1, Joseph Fichter's (1954) four categories of group-relatedness, the nuclear, modal, marginal, and dormant, are useful in examining the degree to which members of a group are assimilating. If a group has many marginal members, it will change or shed many of the more distinguishing characteristics, norms, values, or traits that set it apart from the majority dominant culture. The pace of acculturation to segmented and perhaps even full assimilation quickens. A dormant-member type is usually well on his or her way toward full assimilation—one who has reached the identificational stage in Gordon's typology.

Once total assimilation occurs (Gordon's stage of civic assimilation) the former minority subculture ceases to be readily identified as such. All the individuals would have become so assimilated that neither its former members nor the majority society can realistically distinguish the group as existing as a separate subcultural group. Gordon views civic assimilation as the end state of the process. It means that while a former minority group may still maintain some minor aspects of cultural identity (for example, Irish Americans celebrating St. Patrick's Day by the wearing of the green), their doing so elicits no prejudice or discrimination. Indeed, they may become so acceptable that even some members of the dominant group adopt the identity for the day and celebrate with them. Today, for example, many Anglos celebrate Cinco de Mayo. There are no barriers in politics, jobs, or intimate social contact. While members of the group occasionally manifest "subgroup relatedness," they identify with the dominant culture. They enjoy access to political power and to social/economic status commensurate with the WASP majority members. A classic example would be a woman describing herself as "an American of German-French ancestry."

The Psychological Approach to Race/Ethnic Relations

A variety of perspectives or explanations of race/ethnic relations emphasize a single variable as *the* factor that best accounts for differing rates of assimilation. Scholars stressing psychology focus on the minority group members' ability to cope with the stress of minority status. A scholar using this approach might focus on the ability or inability to change, stressing the motivation to change. An application of this perspective is the achievement-motivation studies of Bernard Rosen, who emphasizes the individual's psychological and cultural orientation toward achievement; that is, the person's need to excel, his or her desire to enter the competitive race for social status, an initial willingness or not to adopt the high valuation placed on personal material success. Rosen believes that racial and ethnic groups differ in their orientation towards achievement, as experienced in the drive for upward social mobility. He holds these differences in orientation have been singularly important contributing factors to dissimilarities in social mobility rates (Rosen and Crockett 1969). He describes what he calls the *achievement syndrome,* composed of three components. The purely psychological factor is achievement motivation, the individual's internal impetus to excel. The other two components are cultural. Value orientations, determined by the group's subculture, implement achievement-motivated behavior. Culture also influences the educational/vocations aspirations of members of that subculture according to Rosen.

A similar emphasis on the psychological dimension underlies studies that account for prejudice and discrimination among the majority society's members by focusing on personality types. The "frustration/aggression" personality studies exemplify this approach (Dollard et al 1939). Childhood patterns are viewed as contributing to the development of a pathological personality type. Early childhood restrictions and later adult limitations foster an inordinate need for power and prestige. When individuals fail to achieve their perceived needs, they may become highly frustrated. Sustained frustration levels lead to the development of an authoritarian personality type, compelling the person to aggression (conflict) and to scapegoating against a highly visible and readily accessible minority. An individual with such a personality disorder uses the minority as a means of displacing frustration. Minority members may also develop psychological disorders: social blindness, self-hatred, and identification dilemmas lead to high frustration levels. These lead some minority members into an aggressive response. Their economic, political, and social powerlessness enables the majority's power elite to exploit or control them. The minority's sense of being controlled or exploited leads to further frustration, and the cycle of conflict goes on (Kinloch 1974).

The Social-Psychological Approach to Race/Ethnic Relations

Closely related is the social-pyschological approach, which emphasizes the social milieu within which the psychological factor operates. Prejudice is seen as related to the individual's position in the social structure, that is, it is determined by a person's degree of socio-economic security. It is further influenced by racial socialization to which one is exposed and to family, peer, and regional pressures. This view sees racial prejudice as a function of the extent and quality of interracial contact to which a person has been exposed (Kinloch 1974). The social-psychological view sees several factors affecting the "speed of inclusion," whether or not people have migrated voluntarily, whether or not they desire to integrate, the racial identification of the individual or group, and the extent to which the majority is willing or not to accept the minority group members for inclusion (McLemore 1983, 6–8).

This mixture of social structural elements with psychological orientation is important in Milton Gordon's work. He discusses the variables needed to study the type and degree of assimilation (what current scholars view as segmented assimilation) and the degree of intergroup conflict. He argues that a general theory of ethnic relations must integrate all such variables. *Biosocial* variables would include a measure of the sense of self and the tendency to protect the self. These variables would recognize that a man defending the honor or welfare of his ethnic group is a man defending himself. Likewise, there are variables Gordon calls *interaction process* factors, dealing with stereotyping, frustration/aggression, felt-dissatisfaction, goal attainments, and conflict-reducing mechanisms. A measure of the level of felt-dissatisfaction is necessary for understanding the prevailing ideologies and value system of both the majority and the minority. Perceived sanctions determine how the minority assesses its chances for success. The tendency for conflict to escalate leads to the need for the majority to develop conflict-reducing mechanisms. Gordon refers to what he labels *social variables:* the absolute and relative sizes of the majority and the minority; their comparative rates of natural increases, the degree and nature of their territorial dispersion, and a value consensus or lack thereof among both the majority and minority groups. For social variables, Gordon focuses on the nature of ideologies about race, religion, and ethnic groups; on the distribution of relative power resources; and on the political nature of the majority society along a democratic to totalitarian scale (Gordon 1964; see also, Glazer and Moynihan 1975, 91–107; Lieberman 1998, 10–11).

Nathan Glazer sees social-psychological aspects of the minority as most important in affecting the rate of assimilation. He emphasizes whether or not the minority is concentrated (that is, rural versus urban settlement patterns), and whether or not the group comes from "nations struggling to become states" (such as Poles, Lithuanians, or Slovaks) or from "states struggling to become nations" (such as Italy, Turkey, and Greece) (cited in Kurokawa 1970, 74–86).

Social-pyschological studies focus on the minority's orientation toward the majority society, coupled with a structural assessment of the group's reaction to its minority status: whether the group is assimilationist or pluralist. Irwin Rinder suggests three types of pluralism: (1) *accommodated pluralism,* in which moderately deprived minorities such as the Chinese and the Jews, meet moderate barriers with a group identity that contains important centripetal strengths, such as high morale, continuity, and economic versatility; (2) *segregated pluralism,* in which severely disadvantaged minorities, stigmatized as either culturally primitive, racially different, or both, are able to sustain their members' identity by maintaining a strong traditional social order isolated from the majority society; and (3) *exotic pluralism,* in which minorities are neither severely disadvantaged nor moderately deprived, but rather, are temporarily advantaged by their distinctiveness from the dominant group—for example, immigrants from the British Isles in the twentieth century. Their differences are rewarded rather than penalized because they create no obstacles at the same time that they afford a marginal differentiation that is considered to be exotic without being unsettling (Kurokawa 1970, 43–54).

The Sociological Approach to Race/Ethnic Relations

The sociological perspective was the first approach used in analyzing race/ethnic relations because sociologists were among the first to become interested in explaining the process. Robert Park (1950) posited the idea of a race-relations cycle. He argued that when different racial/cultural groups come into sustained contact, they cannot avoid falling into competition. He proposed a race relations cycle of contact, competition, accommodation, and eventual assimilation as progressive and inevitable. Its rate may vary, but its direction cannot be reversed. Other sociologists have followed Park's lead in constructing cycles they see as sociologically determined. This view forms the basis of the entire ethnic stratification literature that emphasizes the socially structured nature of intergroup relations. Donald Noel states:

> Ethnic stratification will emerge when distinct ethnic groups are brought into sustained contact *only* if the groups are characterized by a high degree of ethnocentrism, competition, *and* differential power. Competition provides the motivation for stratification; ethnocentrism channels the competition along ethnic lines; and the power differential determines whether either group will be able to subordinate the other (1968, 157–172; Noel's italics).

The sociological perspective is implicit in Ralf Dahrendorf's (1939) discussion of class conflict in industrial societies. He emphasizes that the greater the deprivation of a group in its economic, social status, and social power resources, the more probable it is that it will resort to intense and violent conflict to achieve gains in any of those areas. As the social class position of the subordinate group rises, intergroup conflict will become less intense and less violent. Lloyd Warner and Leo Srole (1945) maintain that when similarities between the minority group and the majority group exist, the probability is greater that the relationship between the two will be relatively harmonious and that assimilation will eventually occur. The greater and the more visible the cultural differences between the groups, the greater the likelihood that conflict will occur (see also Blalock 1967).

Most sociologists studying race and ethnic relations today reject the unidirectional and inevitable nature of assimilation. They are pluralists who strongly disagree with Park's notion of an "inevitable and irreversable cycle." Pluralists recognize that minorities can maintain their distinctiveness and simultaneously interact with the larger society (Barth and Noel 1972, Kottak and Kosaitis 1999). Although arriving at far different conclusions, pluralists share Park's basic sociological perspective on how to explain differences among social groups and their rates of primarily segmented assimilation.

The Economic Approach to Race/Ethnic Relations

The economic perspective is an equally important approach to concerns about racial/ethnic relations. Marxian theory claims that economic determination explains all intergroup relations. Numerous scholars have used various forms of economic analysis to explain acculturation and assimilation. Vincent Parrillo (1985) notes that sometimes economic and technological conditions facilitate minority integration. When the economic conditions are healthy and jobs are plentiful, newcomers find it easier to work their way up the socio-economic ladder of a society. *Occupational mobility*, the ability to improve one's job position, becomes the key to rapid economic (segmented) assimilation. This view notes that downward socioeconomic mobility increases ethnic hostility among that portion of the majority society that is suffering the greatest economic decline. Numerous studies show that upward social mobility is linked to tolerance, whereas downward social mobility is to linked prejudice and discrimination (see Gallagher, 1999).

Another use of an economic perspective to explain rates of segmented assimilation is the split labor market analysis of Edna Bonacich (1976). She argues that dominant group workers realize economic gains from "keeping down" some minority group workers. The antagonism that white workers feel toward black and other minorities stems from the fact that the price of labor in the two groups differs initially, and that the capitalist class does not create, but rather is faced with, a "split labor market." Such a market is characterized by conflict among three groups: the capitalists (those doing the hiring), higher paid labor, and cheap labor. The economic interests of the two labor groups are fundamentally different. Higher paid labor is genuinely threatened by cheap labor groups, which undercut the dominant, higher paid labor group by doing the same work for lower wages. Since the business class gains by substituting cheap labor for higher paid labor, the attempt by the latter to improve their wages and working conditions by organizing and striking can be broken by the "reserve army" of cheap laborers. These economic forces often induce minority/minority conflict and are often related to a minority group's choice of new- or old-style radicalism rather than accommodation.

Implicit in these perspectives are different theories of discrimination. The psychological and social-psychological perspectives imply a cultural transmission theory of discrimination; the economic perspective reflects a group-gains theory of discrimination. The value of each perspective is its focus on a *necessary* factor to explain the complex process of assimilation. While each adds a bit of the truth in explaining rates of assimilation, no single view is adequate to account for all variations nor is equally applicable to the tactics of the various coping strategies adopted by all minority groups. A system's framework of racial and ethnic relations considers all these perspectives.

COMBINING THE APPROACHES AND SOCIAL INTERACTIONS

The concept of a **system** emerged as a major focus in the social sciences after World War II.[2] The systems concept understands that many things, from a car or a computer to an entire universe, are more than a mere collection of parts. The car is more than a bunch of steel, plastic, rubber, wires, and glass parts; its parts are assembled so that people can be moved from place to place. The computer is more than a plastic cabinet and boards or chips with programmed paths for electronic messages and storage. It is a highly sophisticated system to facilitate communication between or among individuals, including—with proper access, a World-Wide Web. One system can be viewed as being related to other, higher order systems. The car, for example, is part of a transportation system that may also be viewed as part of the ecosystem. The computer affects our government, business, education, and mass media systems. Each of these systems is markedly affected by a change from the typewriter to the word processor, and to a sophisticated technological system for data management, manipulation, computation, and storage, that impacts them all. Every system may be viewed as being a part (a subsystem) of a larger system or an encompassing one (a suprasystem).

A Systems Framework for Race and Ethnic Relations

The systems perspective (Easton 1965) focuses on the many factors that influence the rate of incorporation. One must recognize the fact that incorporation is inherently *reciprocal,* that is, simultaneously involving the actions of both the majority society and minority group(s). It reflects the interactions—the feedback effect—among the various factors, viewed here as "orders" that influence the process. Figure 2.1 illustrates a systems framework for racial and ethnic relations. The framework can graphically portray the following relationships. The rate of assimilation (segmented or full) or of incorporation varies according to the level of social interaction that a given minority group has achieved at any given point in time. Social interaction is determined by three first-order variables: (1) tolerance, the majority's willingness to accept acculturation by the members of the minority and to have close social interaction with them; (2) adaptability, the minority members' ability to acculturate; and (3) policy effects, the minority's ability to positively influence public policy. Each of these first-order variables is determined by three second-order variables, or causal effects of these first order variables.

Tolerance   The tolerance variable is determined by the second-order variable **level of majority fear**, which represents the degree to which the majority society perceives the minority subculture as a threat. The threat may be economic, value-based, cultural, and so on. In this framework, the greater the degree of fear felt within the majority society, the less willing it is to accept acculturation by the minority group members, and vice versa. The tolerance variable reflects the top-down approach to majority/minority social interaction.

Closely linked is another second-order variable determining the tolerance variable, the influence of the **perceived size of minority group**. This must be understood as a relative one; the size of the minority in relation to the majority is the key aspect of how perceived size influences the majority society's willingness or not to allow the minority to acculturate. We are dealing here with an order that refers to the majority's *perception* of the size of the minority. The visibility of the minority to the majority (highly visible physical features, geographic concentration versus dispersal, and so on) influences the majority's sense of the size of the minority. The perception of threat implicit in the minority's perceived size means that if the majority feels the *potential* size of the minority is a source of threat, it will adversely affect the majority's willingness to accept the minority's acculturation attempts (as we will see in the next chapter with the case of Chinese Americans). A religious minority that is small but growing rapidly through intense proselytism (such as the Mormons, discussed in Chapter 5) will be viewed as a larger and more threatening group than a relatively small one not aggressively seeking new converts. A minority group that may be moderately small but is experiencing massive immigration or a rapid birth rate relative to the majority society's birth rate is viewed as a larger threat (for example, Mexican Americans since the 1980s as illustrated in Chapters 3 and 4).

The systems framework depicts a third of the second-order variables determining the tolerance variable, the majority's willingness to accept the minority's acculturation as a function of the "time of entry" of the minority subculture into the majority society. The

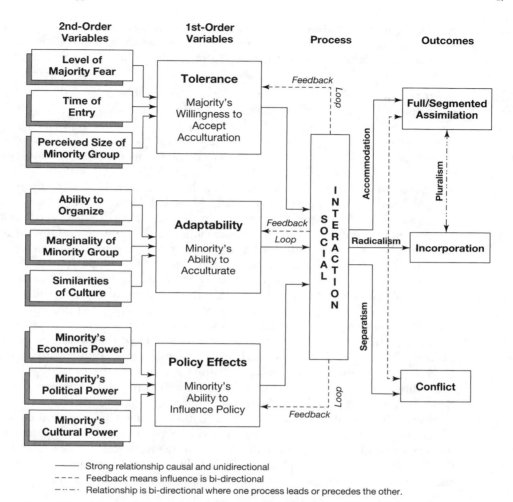

Figure 2.1   A Systems Framework for Race and Ethnic Relations

Source: Framework adapted by author LeMay and Dino Bozonelos from Michael LeMay, *The Struggle for Influence* (Lanham, MD: University Press of America, 1985), 263.

influence of this variable is dependent upon the majority's perception of the minority. A group entering during economic recession or depression, or of social upheaval and instability, will be less accepted by the majority than one coming during an economic boom. The "new" immigrant groups, who entered during the decades of the 1870s and 1880s, when the United States economy experienced depressions like the Panic of 1873, were less well received than those coming prior to the Civil War and its relative boom times as the nation's economy increasingly industrialized. "Entry" means the beginning of initial, sustained, and significant contact between the two cultures. It may be the time (often viewed as a decade) when an immigrant group arrives in substantial numbers to a new country or when an indigenous religious sect emerges. It may be the result of internal migration from one region to another within the majority's geographic area. How sustained the influx of the new group is determines the majority's perception and willingness to accept acculturation of the minority.

Adaptability   The second major or first-order variable determining the level of social interaction is the adaptability variable; that is, the ability of the minority to acculturate. This variable reflects the bottom-up approach to social interaction. With the adaptability variable, the rate of acculturation (or level and nature of social interaction) results from three second-order variables. The first is the minority's ability to organize order. Groups need to be well organized to cope with prejudice and discrimination or develop new values among their members. The more organized the group desiring to acculturate (Jews, Greeks, Chinese), the faster its rate of doing so. The less organized a group (Mexicans, Puerto Ricans), the slower its rate of acculturation.

Another second-order variable of adaptability is the minority's **marginal membership**. The greater the number of a group's marginal members, the faster its rate of acculturation and the more nuclear or modal the membership, the slower its rate of acculturation. The more rapid intermarriage rates among Japanese Americans than among Chinese Americans, for instance, illustrate this second-order variable.[3]

Finally, the minority's adaptability variable is influenced by a third second-order variable, the **similarity of cultures variable**. The closer in basic norms, customs, and values two cultures are, the easier it is for members of the minority culture to acquire the majority culture and the more likely it is that the dominant culture will adopt some aspects of the incoming subordinate culture. An incoming group using a language vastly different from English acquires the norms and values of American culture more slowly than does an English-speaking group. A foreign language linguistically closer to English enables members of the group to learn more readily. This variable also concerns such cultural aspects as urban living patterns, clothing styles, child-rearing practices, religious beliefs and practices, and so on. As seen in the historical overviews in Chapters 3 and 4, the Scotch-Irish and Welsh assimilated more rapidly and more fully than did the Greek or Slavic groups (for an excellent but critical discussion of the cultural similarities effect, see Min 1995).

The systems framework specifies that the level and nature of social interaction is *simultaneously influenced* by these three first-order variables. The framework stipulates an informational feedback process. The feedback flow (depicted by dotted lines) indicates that as a minority group acculturates, it becomes easier and more desirable for its members to do so. Likewise, the dominant culture members become more willing to accept the subordinate group members, allowing further and more positive social interaction. The majority may begin to accept into its own culture some norms and values from the minority subculture. Acculturation is a sharing process, a two-way street. Therefore, even without changing, the minority may become more like the majority, more acceptable to it. Italian, Chinese, and Mexican foods, for example, have become "Americanized." A dominant culture may drastically alter its perceptions of some aspect of the subordinate subculture. Norms and customs may suddenly become more acceptable without changing. Since World War II many Chinese norms and customs are viewed as charming, quaint, or desirably exotic. The feedback influence increases the willingness of the majority to accept the minority's acculturation, thereby reinforcing the minority's desire and capability to do so, raising the level of acculturation, and speeding up segmented assimilation or incorporation and reducing conflict.

Policy Effects   The third of the first-order variables depicted in the framework is that of policy effects. Its impact upon social interaction largely reflects a bottom-up approach, as the minority group seeks and is more or less able to influence public policy. Since power tends toward being structured, the ability of the minority to influence public policy over time impacts the level and nature of its social interaction with the majority. Majority/minority relations involve conflict or competition in the various arenas of public policy, as discussed more fully in Chapter 9.

Three second-order variables determine the policy effects variable. As the minority group increasingly achieves better economic status, it acquires greater economic power that can be employed to influence public policy. As the minority better organizes into interest groups, either by organizing ethnic-based pressure groups or by joining economic-based interest groups (for example, labor unions), it is more able to assert political power to influence public policy. As members of the minority group increasingly adapt to the majority culture, the more likely they are to be able to exert influence on policy. Some minority cultures have aspects of their culture that the majority society (or factions thereof) admires and accepts. In such cases, the minority group is capable of exerting cultural power that effects policy (for example, their religious norms and views might influence social policy regarding marriage, abortion, education, health policy, and so on).

Power to influence policy effects is reflected in the outcomes generally measured by national data. Change in the minority's relative social status can be "measured" or is indicated by data such as: median family incomes of members of the minority relative to that of the majority society (national average); national formal educational levels, national rates of (comparative) incarceration; minority under- or unemployment rates relative to the national average of unemployment; national rates of homeownership in comparison to that among members of the minority group; the number of elected officials from various minority racial or ethnic backgrounds relative to their percent of the population; registration and turnout rates of minority voters in comparison to national voter registration or turnout rates; and so on.

As the minority is better able to influence public policy, especially domestic public policy areas, the resulting social interactions tend to induce the minority to achieve outcomes of segmented assimilation or incorporation.

The systems framework of race and ethnic relations focuses on the *multiplicity* of variables and emphasizes the *dynamic* nature of the interrelationships. It is helpful to show empirical indicators for each of the first- and second-order variables that have been specified here. While the development of such indicators of the variables in the framework is beyond the scope of this chapter, some suggestions are sketched here to further clarify the framework.

The ability to develop measures is often hampered by a lack of data. Some of the groups to which we might apply the framework began their acculturation/assimilation processes long before such possible data were routinely kept or the reliability of the data is seriously questioned. Sometimes data are unavailable because we do not know how to empirically measure something or we do not have agreement among social science scholars as to whether or not some set of data accurately represents a given variable. The "similarity of cultures function," for example, depends on judgment about the compatibility, or lack thereof, concerning certain cultural norms, values, or practices. We may need to rely on surrogate measures for certain variables specified in the framework. The following, then, should be viewed as tentative suggestions regarding the nature or type of empirical data needed to make the framework more specific and/or to assess the degree to which a particular racial or ethnic minority has assimilated, achieved only segmented assimilation, has incorporated, or is still largely engaged in conflict.

Indicators of Policy Effects   Because the rate or degree of assimilation or of incorporation is the dependent variable, that is, what the framework seeks to explain, discussion of operational measures begins with those concepts. What we need to measure this element of the framework are some readily accessible data to indicate civic assimilation or political incorporation. An index comprising three or four indicators might be the most fruitful way to measure civic assimilation. To indicate incorporation achieved by a group in a civic sense, election data are likely the most obvious to use. One might construct an ordinal-level index (high, medium, low rate of civic assimilation). The degree of group bloc voting could be part of such an index. The closer the group votes, as measured by percent split in votes between the competing major parties in, for instance, presidential elections, to that of the split among the majority population, the more incorporated is the minority group; the more the group cohesively bloc votes, the less incorporated is the group. Equally important, the index would need a component that measured the turnout rate, that is, the percentage of the group actually voting from among those eligible to do so. The closer the group in question was in turnout to the general population turnout rate, the more incorporated the group, and vice versa. The index might also employ a negative indicator, such as the willingness of some group to cross ethnic lines and vote against one of its own for some other electoral reason. An illustration of this effect would be conservative black voters voting for a George Bush for President when a Jesse Jackson is on the ballot. Such **cross-group voting,** for whatever reason, indicates a degree of civic assimilation. An index might include the number of members from a minority group to have been elected to national-level office (for instance, to the U.S. House of Representatives and the Senate, or nominated or elected president). Because to get such a candidate elected to that level of office requires a high degree of acceptance of that minority member by voters of the majority, it seems logical to include such data in a civic assimilation index (Schmidt 1989, Stowers, 1989).

The "level of majority's fear variable" would need to be measured indirectly. The fear of a group is difficult to measure directly at any time and would be impossible for the distant historical past. One can no longer "opinion-poll" persons from the 1880s. Surrogate measures are possible, however, and could be used to develop an index (again ordinal-level) of the majority's fear level at a given point in the historical past. Presuming that a threat of unemployment is a major cause of fear among majority society members, the national percentage unemployed at any given time might be used. Likewise, sociological literature suggests several methods of measuring segregation (both residential and social) of a given group. A degree of segregation measure could be a possible indicator of the majority's fear of the minority. The use of **ethnophaulisms** (a racial or ethnic group's derogatory nickname for another) might also be a component of a level of fear index. A high degree of association between the amount of prejudice against an out-group and the number of ethnophaulisms for a group has been shown on a limited basis (Palmore 1962).

The number and types of racial stereotypes have been shown to correlate highly with levels of prejudice (Katz and Braley 1958). A surrogate measure might be one of ethnic violence—for times past indicated by the number of race riots or race-based lynchings. The size and strength of organized opposition groups may be useful. Estimated membership in hate groups such as the Ku Klux Klan, or percent vote for avowed nationalistic groups such as the Know Nothing Party or the American Party, or avowed racist candidates such as David Duke, might suffice. For more recent periods, an index of white flight to the suburbs might usefully be employed.

The "size of minority variable" could be measured by the relative percentage of a minority group in the total population. Since this variable concerns the majority's willingness to accept the acculturation and greater social interactions with members of the minority, however, the *perception* by the majority of the size of the minority is a key element for indicating this variable. Thus, relative birth rates among minority groups as compared to the general population might be used, because a rapidly growing minority (i.e., with high natural birth rates relative to women of childbearing age among the dominant group) would be seen as a larger threat than would be one whose birth rate was comparable to or lower than the majority society's birth rate. In the case of a religious minority group, a "conversion index" indicating growth by aggressive proselytism could be added to the natural birth rate data for the group.

The "time of entry variable" might include not only the peak decade for the relevant group's emergence within the dominant culture but also the length of the immigration or emergence period. Stanley Lieberson (1980) notes the importance of the flow of migrants in his analysis of differences between South/Central/East European groups and blacks. A continuous influx of a group over a long period of time adversely affects its occupational queuing and its ability to employ a special niche in the occupational structure of society. Sizable, continuous numbers of newcomers raise and maintain a level of ethnic and/or racial consciousness between and among members of both the majority and minority groups. The long-term migration of a group may also cause a shift in ethnic and racial group boundaries. If, for instance, the large and continuous migration of blacks to the north took place while the previously discriminated against white ethnic immigration flow basically stopped, then the negative dispositions toward those white ethnic immigrants would be muffled and modified as they came to be viewed as relatively more desirable neighbors, coworkers, political candidates, and so on, than blacks.

This effect seems relevant, for example, to account for the differences in rates of segmented assimilation between Asian Americans and African Americans. Although both are racial minorities, the rate and patterns of their segmented assimilation or of their incorporation are quite diverse. The fact that the Asian immigration influx was comparatively small (until recent years at least) and of a brief duration may be an important difference in their divergent rates of incorporation.

"It occurs to me that none of this would have happened if our forefathers had enacted stricter immigration laws."

With respect to measuring the minority's adaptability—its willingness to acculturate—each of these second-order variables would be measured by an ordinal-level index composed of several elements. The "minority's marginal membership variable" might be measured by the percentage of "outgroup" marriages. Another indicator might be the number and relative size of clearly identifiable ethnic-specific associations for a given group.

The "minority's ability to organize variable" could be tapped by several indicators. The size of the ethnic press, indicated by the number and circulation of newspapers catering to a given ethnic group, might be one such component of this index. The number and size of ethnic associations for a given group is a possible measure. The relative wealth at the time of entry are data of possible use with respect to immigration groups as are the formal educational levels and percent literacy of a group as surrogate indicators of a group's ability to organize. Job skills at the time of entry might also serve, since the immigration service has some fairly good data on occupational status at the time of entry for most groups since 1900. Lieberson suggests the use of "life expectancy" as a surrogate for the social status of a group at entry. The higher the status of a group's members, the greater is its ability to organize.

The "similarities of cultures" variable might be measured by an index of several elements. Agreement in settlement patterns might be one component. A rural-to-rural or urban-to-urban settlement pattern would be a positive indicator, whereas an urban-to-rural or rural-to-urban pattern would be a negative one. The linguistic closeness of the group's language to English could show cultural closeness. Protestant faith (measured by percentage of a group adhering to a Protestant denomination) would be a likely component of any cultural closeness index. The group's being of the Caucasian race or not would also be included. A skin-color weighting of the closeness or distance from the dominant group's white color would be suggested by an extensive body of sociological literature.

Such empirical measures, when developed, would allow using statistical measures to better articulate or understand the racial and ethnic relationships suggested by the framework. The applicability of the framework to explain past groups' incorporation could be measured. The important point here is that the very attempt to empirically measure or specify these variables illustrates the value of developing the framework. The very process of developing the framework forces one to think about segmented assimilation, about incorporation, and about racial and ethnic social conflict processes in a manner that lends itself to developing specific empirical measures of what is occurring in the very complex real world. It may suggest future collection of data not presently available that may more accurately or directly serve as indicators of the inter-relationships suggested by the framework. For example, the development of a consensus among economists about the concept of gross national product contributed significantly to economic theory. Perhaps a somewhat comparable effect can be achieved in the social sciences for development of a general theory of ethnic/race relations (although since the social sciences by necessity have to rely on ordinal data more often than interval data, it is unlikely that such a framework would ever rival econometric models).

Using a Typology to Explain Bottom-up Strategies

As stated earlier, when a group finds itself placed in minority status, it must react. Be it quickly or slowly acculturating, a group that experiences discrimination simply cannot ignore that fact. Scholars have suggested different typologies for minority group reaction to the dominant group's treatment. Harry Kitano (1997) developed a typology of reaction that includes conflict, acceptance, aggression, and avoidance. Race riots would be a form of conflict. He discusses forms of acceptance being ritualistic behavior, super-patriotism, and the internalization of stress, and he posits four kinds of aggression: direct, such as insurrection, strikes, boycotts, and race rioting; indirect, such as use of the arts, ethnic humor, or passive resistance; displaced aggression, such as scapegoating; and the change of goals, avoidance, retreatism, or withdrawal manifested by such behavior as drug or alcohol addiction, schizophrenia, or suicide.

Edgar Litt (1970) employs a schema for his analysis of American ethnic politics. He includes the politics of accommodation, separatism, and radicalism. We employ his typology as three strategies. For each of these strategies, we further distinguish two basic tactical approaches for pursuing that overall strategy. The strategy of accommodation may be pursued primarily through an economic or a political route. The strategy of separatism may rely on physical or psychological methods of isolation from the majority culture. The strategy of radicalism may be either an old-style or new-style radicalism. Each of these strategies and their associated tactical approaches is discussed briefly here, and subsequent chapters deal with each in greater detail, using the historical experiences of various ethnic and racial minorities to illustrate them.

The Strategy of Accommodation

When using the **accommodation strategy**, members of the minority group accept the value system of the dominant culture. They simply want their "fair share" of what the majority society has to offer. They want to be accepted by the dominant group, eventually to become virtually indistinguishable from it—that is, to be fully assimilated. Whether a group desiring accommodation follows an economic or political route to that end depends on several factors. Groups most likely to use an economic approach are those who voluntarily migrate to the area of the dominant culture. They want to assimilate and they accept the majority's value system, which is why they migrated to that society. If they have some desired economic skills or arrive with sufficient means to be able to use the economic approach, this tactical approach to accommodation is especially appealing (see the Asian-American groups in Chapter 3 and their ability to achieve segmented assimilation).

Timing is an important factor in the choice of economic accommodation. If an immigrant group arrives during a period of an expanding economy, it is more likely to find available points of access. During such periods, moreover, the majority's fear of the foreign (*xenophobia*) is likely to be reduced, thereby reinforcing the minority's desire to accommodate.

Groups who possess desirable job skills will not only be welcomed; they also have a means for climbing the socioeconomic ladder (economic incorporation). If they have the financial means to get to rural areas, for instance, they can more readily acquire cheap land and be more socially acceptable in the frontier regions where their labor is a more needed commodity. Some groups have sufficient capital to start their own businesses or to establish special economic niches for themselves. These often involve occupational areas viewed by the majority as noncompetitive or nonthreatening. Such groups are often called "middle-man minorities" (Schaefer 1998). The Scandinavian and German immigrant groups first used this approach. They arrived in the United States when the frontier was still open and came with enough resources to reach the interior farmland or to gain desirable jobs in urban areas during the early stages of America's industrialization process. Improved economic status was followed by improved social status, and political involvement largely followed their socioeconomic success at incorporation, and their gradual assimilation to the point of full assimilation.

Several European groups, East European Jews, Chinese, and Japanese also used this approach, particularly relying upon the **occupational niche** route. The concept is closely related to that of **occupational queuing**—the ranking of jobs by order of their desirability for a given group. Members of the majority, by definition, enjoy a favorable situation among employers. They fill as much as they can of society's more desirable jobs, leaving the less attractive ones to the minority population. If the minority population is subdivided by race or ethnic origin in terms of their "worthiness" in the eyes of the dominant group, then members of that group will open access to the remaining desirable jobs first to those ethnic groups deemed most worthy by the dominant group. One may progress downward, ranking jobs until all groups have attained their positions. If there are more potential workers than there are total jobs available, then those minorities at the bottom will experience the highest rates of unemployment or underemployment.

The dominant group tends to perpetuate its dominance. Since majority members are more likely to be employers, key co-workers, union officials, and so on, they and their offspring will be in the best position to secure the more desirable jobs. Although such a system is not entirely rigid, occupational queuing is evident in the United States.

A group at the bottom of the racial/ethnic hierarchy will tend to fill the least desirable positions in rough proportion to the group's percentage of the total population. If that minority is large, it will find some opportunities higher on the occupational hierarchy, since the majority would not be pushing as far down. If the minority is a small percentage of the total population, there will be room only at the very bottom because the majority will tend to compete successfully for the other jobs. This queuing effect makes the shift in unemployment most radical for the lowest-ranking minorities. When the economy is sluggish or in recession, the minority groups at the bottom are pushed out of jobs as the majority members are forced to "push downward." On the other hand, the minority finds new job opportunities open when the economy is booming because a labor shortage is created. In that case, the majority members cannot fill all of their traditional employment opportunities. In occupational queuing, minorities are the last hired and the first fired.

Table 2.1 illustrates such occupational queuing. It shows the percentage employed in a variety of occupations for females, blacks, and Hispanics as of 2004.

Minority group members sometimes use "special niches," concentrating in certain occupations first open to them either because of special skills and interests or because the majority considered that job undesirable or nonthreatening to its favored positions. These minority members develop a network of ethnic contacts and experience that attracts others of their group to those occupational opportunities.

When immigration by a minority rapidly accelerates, the ability of that group to exploit the special niche is reduced markedly. Such specialties can absorb only a relatively small portion of the group's work force when that group is experiencing rapid population growth. Not all Chinese men can open a restaurant or laundry in a city where they are a sizable part of the total population. Not all Jews can own their own stores or garment businesses in New York. Not all Greeks can be confectioners or restaurant owners in Baltimore. Where a given group suddenly becomes a sizable part of the total population, it is more difficult to use occupational niches.

For groups that are able to develop special niches, especially if their immigration then ceases or tapers off, they can exploit such jobs to climb the socioeconomic ladder. The job stability associated with such niches enables the group members to plan ahead and save more of their resources to enable their children to achieve greater educational levels. After a generation or two, the entire group rises up the status ladder of the society. The availability of such niches is a key factor in a group's viewing economic accommodation as desirable. The majority, in turn, views the minority as being less threatening to its favored-job-status positions. The minority sees that approach as being more likely successful and thus a more desired strategy for them to pursue.

For some groups, even if they do desire assimilation, economic opportunities are not sufficiently open to them to be the more attractive tactic. They may enter society when expanding job opportunities are not available. They may lack the necessary job skills or resources (capital to open one's own restaurant, retail store, garment business, or import/export firm) or farming skill and the capital needed to get to where free or cheap farmland is in abundance.

For some immigrant groups the economic route is blocked. When they try but are relatively unsuccessful in using that tactic, then the tactic of political action becomes an option. As with economic accommodation, political accommodation is favored by

Table 2.1   Percentage of Females, Blacks, and Hispanics Employed in Specified Occupations, 2004

Occupation	Female	Black	Hispanic
Total in work force	46.6%	11.3%	10.9%
Personnel/labor relations managers	68.2	11.4	7.3
Administrators, education and related	64.1	11.5	5.7
Managers, medicine and health	77.3	7.5	5.6
Architects	23.5	3.1	4.4
Engineers	10.4	5.5	3.5
Mathematical, computer scientists	30.1	8.6	3.6
Chemists, except biochemists	34.3	4.8	2.8
Dentists	29.3	5.6	4.6
Health assessment/treating occupations	86.1	9.6	3.8
Registered nurses	93.1	9.9	3.4
Dietitians	86.4	24.8	8.0
Speech therapists	92.1	4.3	4.2
Teachers—colleges/university	43.3	6.1	4.1
Pre-and kindergarten teachers	97.8	15.0	10.3
Elementary school teachers	82.5	10.6	5.4
Special education teachers	86.0	9.7	2.4
Lawyers and judges	29.3	5.3	3.2
Actors and directors	42.1	7.9	8.9
Public relations specialists	60.2	9.9	5.0
Dental hygienists	96.8	4.8	11.1
Licensed practical nurses	90.1	32.7	11.6
Legal assistants	83.9	9.8	5.8
Service occupations	60.4	17.9	16.3
Private household service	95.4	16.2	25.6
Child-care workers	97.0	8.1	18.8
Cleaners and servants	96.1	13.5	39.5
Food preparation/service occupations	57.0	12.4	18.1
Food counter, fountain service	67.2	14.6	14.6
Kitchen workers, food preparation	71.0	11.1	12.9
Health service occupations	89.1	29.4	11.5
Dental assistants	96.8	4.8	11.1
Personal services occupations	80.7	15.9	11.0
Barbers	25.9	23.6	18.5
Hairdressers, cosmetologists	90.4	13.1	10.5
Family child-care providers	98.7	15.3	14.6
Early childhood teacher's assistants	94.7	20.4	10.7
Precision crafts and repairers	8.7	7.8	14.7
Mechanics and repairers	4.7	7.9	11.6
Automobile mechanics	1.5	7.5	15.2

Construction trades	2.5	7.0	17.4
Operators, fabricators, laborers	23.3	15.6	17.7
Textile sewing machine operators	74.2	13.5	38.3
Pressing machine operators	74.5	29.0	36.8

Source: U.S. Bureau of the Census, *Statistical Abstract of the United States, 2006* (Washington, DC: U.S. Government Printing Office, 2006), adapted from Table 604, pp. 401–404.

a group as its overall strategy only when certain conditions pertain. Generally speaking, the political path will be all the more attractive when a group's economic path is blocked by relatively strong occupational discrimination. "No Irish Need Apply" signs preceded the development of the Irish urban political machine.

For political accommodation to work, a minority group must have the organizational skills and experience to develop a base to deliver a cohesive voting bloc. It needs such political organization to direct its political activity toward specific group goals. The group must be able to vote. Another critical ingredient is that the majority society must be politically divided into factions. One or another of the factions will desire a coalition with the minority in order to consistently win in its electoral struggle with the other dominant group faction. If the minority can demonstrate its ability to move in organized voting blocs, it becomes a desirable coalition partner. For the majority faction to acquire the sustained electoral loyalty of the minority bloc it grants some rewards to the minority coalition members, enabling them to use politics as a means to socioeconomic incorporation.

The political tactic of accommodation is the most attractive alternative to a minority group having a psychological need for the rewards that political recognition can bring. If the economy is expanding sufficiently to provide for unskilled jobs that can be dispensed by the political elite, the dominant faction can easily reward its minority coalition partners. The political strategy relies on a political organization capable of distributing these rewards for political loyalty (an urban political machine). The Irish used this tactical approach most successfully to pursue incorporation. The Slavic and Italian groups employed this approach, although less successfully than did the Irish.

Native politicians soon recognized the value of appealing to ethnic groups to attract their votes in massive and easily manipulated voting blocs (symbolic political rewards). They saw that ethnic voters were likely to vote for a co-ethnic team and responded by offering an ethnically balanced slate. Including an Irish immigrant as a council member, a Jew as city auditor, a Greek as city clerk, and so on assured the party of loyal support from those groups. Erecting a statue to Columbus in an Italian-laden ward or naming a new high school in a Polish ward after General Pulaski were easy symbolic ways to appeal to these groups for their vote.

Fred Greenstein (1970) identified five factors that propelled the development and operation of the classic urban machine. First was the explosive rate of growth of the nation's cities. Prior to the flood of immigration, only one city in the country, Philadelphia, exceeded 250,000 in population. By 1890, eleven cities had attained that size, three of which were over 1 million. In four decades the urban population had increased sixfold, while the rural population had only doubled. Chicago, in 1850, was under 10,000 in population; by 1900, it had reached 1,690,000.

The explosive growth rate of those cities meant an increase in demand for basic public services essential for survival. Large cities needed highly developed transportation systems (mostly railroads) to bring in supplies of food and other essential resources. Cities needed extensive streets, lighting, bridges, and mass transit. Massive sewer systems had to be installed and tons of garbage removed. Police and fire stations had to be built and manned. Building codes and inspection programs had to be put in place. Hospitals, health services, and school systems led to nearly overwhelming public policy demands being placed on city governments. All of those needs meant there were a substantial number of unskilled jobs.

A related factor was the disorganized municipal government structure prevalent at the time. City governments were structurally ill-prepared to meet the challenges created by an explosive rate of growth. Hundreds of officials were individually elected, sometimes annually, and thus had little incentive to work together. Power was fragmented still more by large and unwieldy city councils and a host of boards and commissions. The urban machine developed, in part, as an informal and extralegal means to unify what the formal structure so fragmented.

A third factor was the flow into the cities of millions of immigrants who formed a highly dependent population. The machine politicians soon realized the value of catering to this population through their ethnically based organizations. A fourth factor was the needs of businessmen. Businesses varied in size from the very large to the very small. All had needs to which the politician could cater through public policy effects. Some needed the government services; street maintenance, sewer and water expansion. Some needed government permits to build or expand. Some sought relief from government restrictions on plant operations, safety conditions, disposal of waste, and so on. In such cases, their prime need was to operate without government interference. Other businessmen had an opposite need. They did business with government itself; contractors, utility producers, and mass transit operators were all engaged in the profitable pursuit of serving the very process of massive and rapid urban growth. Such businesses provided the machine politicians with graft in return for favored treatment. The politicians used the graft money not only to enrich themselves but also to fund the material incentives of welfare-type services that they dispensed to needy immigrants in exchange for their loyal electoral support. This system enabled the machine to dispense private sector jobs to many loyal supporters. The *patronage system* became the oil that greased the machine's smooth operation. It figured into the political incorporation of some minorities.

The final factor was relatively unrestricted suffrage. Since even the lowliest citizen could vote, machine politicians catered to those groups who could provide bloc voting. For some time and for some localities in various states, even non-citizens were allowed to vote in local elections. The political party apparatus performed the valuable service of initiating immigrants into citizenship and teaching them the value of participating in politics. Despite the machine's raw and at times corrupt and inefficient public policy process, it accepted and welcomed immigrants and provided them with an invaluable commodity—the vote. Machine workers greeted disembarking immigrants. They were soon naturalized and registered to vote by judges controlled by the machine. Although corrupt, the urban political machine did much to reduce the hopelessness of the immigrants' conditions. These policy effects shaped social interactions. Immigrants responded with loyal and easily manipulated electoral support.

   Patronage was crucial to the machine's development because the immigrants were desperate for steady jobs. There were no government programs for employment or to pay unemployment benefits. The machine's provision of jobs was a sorely needed and much appreciated policy effect. The explosively expanding cities provided many job opportunities to be filled by loyal party workers; jobs in police, fire, sanitation, and street construction and maintenance. Private jobs in the many businesses and industries indebted to the machine politicians became part of the patronage system. The machine also provided a host of what eventually became welfare services to the immigrant. In the words of Tammany Hall Boss George Washington Plunkitt, the philosopher-king of the old-style urban machine:

> What holds your grip on your district is to go right among the poor families and help them in different ways they need help. I've got a regular system for this. If there's a fire in Ninth, Tenth, or Eleventh Avenue, for example, any hour of the day or night, I'm usually there with some of my district captains as soon as the fire engines. If the family is burned out I don't ask whether they are Republicans or Democrats, and I don't refer them to the Charity Organization Society, which would investigate their case in a month or two and decide if they are worthy of help about the time they are dead from starvation. I just get quarters for them, buy clothes for them if their clothes were burned up, and fix them up 'til they get things runnin' again. It is philanthropy, but it's politics too—mighty good politics. Who can tell how many votes one of these fires brings me? The poor are the most grateful people in the world, and, let me tell you, they have many more friends in their neighborhoods than the rich have in theirs. (cited in Greenstein 1970, 49)

   The "boss" and his party henchmen helped immigrants with all of their dealings with government. He symbolized and personified government for the newcomer who desperately needed that service. The party was friend and intermediary in dealing with the broader, majority society; with the courts, police, and local bureaucracy. Eventually the party so dominated the local government that minority group party loyalists "captured" some of those bureaucracies for themselves.

   The machine gave the immigrant group a much needed psychological boost simply by recognizing them and the value of their culture. Politicians appealed to their sense of group loyalty and bound that loyalty to a party attachment. Whether running an entire slate of officials representing a wide variety of ethnic groups living in the city or erecting a statue or naming a school, park, or other public building after some ethnic hero, or simply attending ethnic group gatherings such as weddings, funerals, dances, or similar social occasions, such symbolic rewards by the machine politician appealed to the minority group's members because such activities showed that the politician cared for the group. They *felt valued* and responded with loyal bloc-voting.

   After a generation or so, recognition politics were no longer sufficient to keep ethnic group loyalties attached to the party. Ethnic group members began pressing for more. They sought and extracted from the machine and the political system a number of collective welfare benefits. Litt refers to this as the "rule of expansion," namely, get more benefits, as in "what have you done for me lately." Where the old boss might have found a place to live for the family that was burned out, the new system demanded public housing projects, soon filled with members of the relevant minority group and in which a public housing bureaucracy was often staffed by members of the minority group.

The final phase of successfully employed political accommodation is what Litt calls *preferment politics*. In this stage the minority group has achieved sufficient access and power within the political machinery that the group is able to influence the fundamentals of the system. It is generally able to determine the allocation of political claims (policy effect) made within its framework. A group like the Irish Americans not only can succeed in getting a few divisible rewards allocated to them, they can even go beyond demanding a public housing program and bureaucracy. In this final stage, they capture the political party machinery, take over the bureaucracy, and determine the policies by which it will distribute a general welfare benefit such as public housing. As Litt notes:

> This sticky phase of ethnic political claims may be handled by party leaders in several ways. A major factor in stable accommodation is the extent to which heretofore dominant groups have secured preferments outside of their political positions. If the dominant group is secure enough to yield the social and economic benefits of party preferments to assertive ethnic claimants, accommodation is facilitated; the most difficult problems are likely to arise when relative newcomers must displace others who have not yet come to securely reap the social and economic benefits of political preferments. (p. 72)

Irish Americans used their ability to capture urban political machines as a means to get ahead. They nudged aside nativist politicians when the latter were no longer needed. Once they gained control, they used the political power to control positions to achieve broader social and economic status. An Irish immigrant eventually became mayor of Boston. The son of an immigrant went on to become governor of Massachusetts. The Ivy League schools and prestigious business enterprises, and even the more elitist social clubs, accepted a governor's son. And, in the instance of John F. Kennedy, a grandson of an immigrant went on to become President of the United States. The Boston Brahman, having a wide variety of social and economic opportunity open to them, were more willing to yield and move aside when the aspiring Irish politician applied pressure to move up the ladder.

Those same Irish politicians were less likely to step aside for the aspiring Italian- or Greek- or Polish-American politician. The Irish Americans were too new, too psychologically insecure of their place on the ladder to move aside easily. The Irish-American politician forced the later arriving ethnic politicians to seek access to upward social and economic mobility by means of economic accommodation, or through the Republican Party, as exemplified by the Republican Fiorello LaGuardia (see, for example, Levy and Kramer 1973).

The Strategy of Separatism

Sometimes the minority group rejects the value system of the dominant society. It may seek not to acculturate but simply to be left alone. It does not seek to impose its values on the majority, nor does it want the majority to do so to it. It wants the dominant groups to respect its differing values, to allow it to hold those values, and to practice its norms, values, and lifestyle without suffering discrimination. Often such groups are ones that have come into sustained contact with the majority society in some largely involuntary manner.

Forced migration, such as the importation of slaves, can bring two such cultures together. The minority rejects its status and position. Often internally developing minority groups, such as a new religious minority, come to reject the value system of the dominant society. The Mormons, as seen in greater detail in Chapter 5, provide a classic example. Sometimes the minority subculture finds itself in such status because of boundary absorption, as in the case of many early "Spanish Americans" and the various Native-American tribes. When a minority group, for whatever reason, adopts separatism, it attempts to do so in one of two ways: physical separatism or isolation; or the psychological separatism of its members from the norms, values, customs, and lifestyles of the dominant culture.

The choice of the physical route depends on the group's ability to physically isolate itself. This may be done by going to frontier or rural areas where low density enables their numerical superiority. The Amish and Mennonites, clustered in rural enclaves, exemplify this. Reducing their contacts with majority society to a bare minimum helps. Often the majority society rejects contact with the group, reinforcing the isolating effects of rural settlement. The Mormons' fleeing to ever more isolated frontier areas in response to majority society is a classic example.

Sometimes physical separatism is not really a matter of choice. It may be forced upon the group by the majority culture. Ghettos, barrios, Chinatowns, and the Mormons' flight to isolated areas to avoid persecution exemplify this effect. The military forced Native-American survivors of an earlier policy of near-annihilation to ever-decreasing areas of "reservation."

A critical ingredient for successful separatism is the group's maintaining an economic system capable of supporting its members in isolation. Generally, necessary economic interactions with the majority group hasten the decline of the group's use of separatism by bringing about subtle changes in their values that gradually signal a degree of acculturation.

The use of the psychological tactic of separatism is more often the choice of millennial movements. These are generally religious or political movements with a pervasive ideology that offers an explanation of the past, present, and future for its members that justifies or explains their situation in the world. Millennial movements construct history in a manner wherein the end gives meaning to all preceding events. Some millennial movements survive their earlier stages of apocalyptic vision to develop into stable social institutions that maintain their millennialist ideas in such fashion as to interpret them in a way that makes ordinary life possible again. The political ideology or religious theology of millennial movements is strong enough to become a means for a sort of psychological shell is built around the individual members, isolating each member from the influence of the dominant society, even though they may be living in the midst of that society. Good examples of this are the Black Muslim and Hasidic Jew. Black Muslims exhibit distinct organization and cultural norms specifically designed to compensate for the effects of discrimination by the dominant society. The group withdraws from the ongoing polity. In Litt's words, "Ethnic separatism is to a political system as third parties are to the American two-party monopoly" (p. 76).

The Strategy of Radicalism

A third and final strategy for minorities involves rejecting the value system of the majority and seeking to replace those values with their own. This radical strategy exhibits two major tactical approaches: old-style and new-style radicalism.

In *old-style* radicalism the ideology is different from the prevailing one of the majority culture, but the behavior remains standard. Groups using this route employ standard political behavior, such as electoral politics, to try to win over the majority to its new ideology and value system. It is the politics of radical third-party movements. The American Communist Party, attempting to win support among blacks, exemplifies this approach. While never very successful in winning electoral support, even among alienated blacks, its indirect impact was important.

The American Socialist Party used the old-style radical approach. A small faction of German Americans sought to win over a large immigrant following. In a few places with large German-American populations, such as Milwaukee, Socialists achieved a short-term, local electoral success. Their influence was strongest in the trade union movement, especially where Jewish influence was strong. The Socialist influence pervaded important trade unions, the Yiddish press, and Jewish social activities such as the Socialists Workingmen's Circle. From their experience with socialism, Jewish communal leaders of three decades acquired the political skills and style that influenced the American trade union movement (for instance, the International Ladies Garment Workers), the development of American intellectual life (through numerous academic and political accomplishments of "ex-radicals"), and American national politics (for instance, the role of New York's American Labor Party and the Liberal Party in electing Franklin D. Roosevelt in 1936, 1940, and 1944).

The American Alliance of Polish Socialists tried to appeal to the larger Polish immigrant group, although never as successfully as the more accommodationist Polish National Alliance. Those interested in American Socialism joined the Polish section of the American Socialist Party. A small faction of Italian Americans flirted briefly with radical politics, attracted to the American Communist Party, and another small faction supported the American Fascist Party. Neither faction achieved much size or electoral strength.

The task of the old-style radical was a difficult one. The ideologue had to convince the ethnic member that future rewards would outweigh the benefits to be gained from the present system. The radical ideologue had to convince the ethnic masses that attachments based on principle were more important in the long run than the short-term satisfactions obtained through membership in ethnic fraternal and social associations. The ideology's success depended on a degree of political awareness and sophistication among ethnic groups that in reality had low to moderate political interest, experience, or inclination. Old-style radical leaders had to forge a common bond between "blood and believer." They had to promote the ideological premises themselves.

Because of these difficulties, radical ideological politics of the old style never really caught on amongst ethnic groups. The religious beliefs and ethnic organizations of many groups provided their members with the emotional and structural support needed to cope with their strange new environment in the "New World." The ethnics' desire for social acceptance was often too strong for many to be attracted to the radical political platforms. Accommodation politics won them sufficient material gains to undercut the ideological appeal. They simply preferred the immediate gratification and emotional and psychological ties to their "own" groups to the long-term and doubtful rewards of an alien political ideology. The major political parties undercut the appeal of radical third-party movements whenever such splinter groups won some electoral strength. The major parties adopted a few aspects of the radical party's platform, bringing a few of their more popular concerns into conformity with majority society goals.

The greatest success of old-style radicalism was to focus attention on some problems, ideas, or concerns stressed by the third-party movement in its campaigns. Their political impact was indirect; inducing majority parties to adopt, albeit in some modified form, some aspects of their radical planks. Today's minority groups use *new-style radicalism,* perhaps best exemplified by the militant black civil rights movement of the late 1950s to mid-1960s. Under this approach, the minority espouses less radical ideological points but employs what is at the time considered to be radical behavior.

For such new-style radicalism to emerge, three elements must converge. The first element is a widespread feeling of anomie among minority group members. This anomie means that deprived persons, united only by common location or color, are more likely to view normal accommodation politics as ineffective and meaningless.

The second element is when a group has a weak social base. Anomie among ethnic group members becomes politically potent when it is built into enduring social relations, when the individual's frustrations are no longer screened or adequately controlled by social mechanisms. Then personal anomie is likely to produce the politics of passion. History shows that isolated social groups are the most susceptible to mass movements and extreme volatility in political behavior. Isolated factory worker groups participated in the more violent and volatile aspects of the labor movement. Ethnic groups developed the politics of radical passion. The third element leading to new-style radicalism is the broad and direct intervention of federal institutions in the core urban areas. The nationalization of ethnic politics led to tactics that encouraged passionate political activity. Radical behavior may range along the full spectrum of nonviolent, direct-action protest to full-scale revolution.

Protest politics partly explains why the civil rights movement was more successful against de jure (by law) segregation than against de facto (by social custom) segregation. It is easier to change Jim Crow laws than to change broadly accepted societal norms and customs. The successful use of this approach by the black civil rights movement inspired other groups to imitate it. Black Power inspired Red, Brown, Gray, and Gay Power movements, all of which employed variations of the direct-action protest tactic. One of the best philosophical justifications for civil disobedience is the eloquent "Letter from a Birmingham Jail," written by Dr. King (see the end-of-chapter reading in Chapter 8).

When peaceful protest tactics fail to work, groups using new-style radicalism may be driven to increasingly violent radical behavior. The need to continue to attract mass media coverage imposes a pressure toward increasingly radical rhetoric, if not violent behavior. The first time a freedom ride or sit-in is used, it is hot news. Direct-action protests soon become old hat. The national media's and the nation's attention span to any one problem is short-lived. Protest leaders are compelled to use more radical rhetoric and behavior to "keep the cameras rolling." New-style radicalism tends to encourage social interactions of conflict. Expressions like "burn, baby, burn" inspire violent reactions among some in the majority. This may instill violent reaction among minority group members. The radical approach contains a strong, though not inevitable, tendency toward more violent tactics.

The sporadic riots of the late 1960s were logical extensions of the approach. The targeted political rioting that rocked some 150 American cities during the summers of 1967 and 1968 were the emotional outbursts predicted by Dr. King. The use of gun sniping, occasional bank heists, or kidnapping by the Symbionese Liberation Army (SLA) exemplifies the more radical, violent spectrum of this approach. When less violent tactics seem to fail, or bring results many feel are too little, too late, more violent tactics may be used. The two approaches may work in tandem. The radicalness of the Black Panthers may lead city representatives to bargain with the accommodationist NAACP.

This trend toward increasingly radical behavior is neither inevitable nor irreversible. The winning of specific goals through unconventional and nonviolent protest may bring about sufficient changes in the rules of the game under which standard politics are conducted that a group previously rejecting accommodation politics as useless might change and adopt that strategy (relying on lobbying and electoral success to effect public policy to their betterment). After the civil rights movement used its nonviolent protest politics to end Jim Crow laws, blacks developed a substantial voting force in southern politics. By the late 1970s and continuing to the present, blacks used standard electoral politics to win a considerable number of elective and appointive positions via the polling booth instead of the streets. Electoral gains by some minorities helped others as well. Black political clout by the 1970s and affirmative action programs enabled other minorities to likewise achieve political gains and successes. Changes in public policy aimed at the black minority spilled over into policy effects benefiting minorities.

A given minority may pursue any one of these three basic approaches. It may employ one approach at one time, and another at some other time. Some of the larger minority groups may fragment into factions, each of which pursues a different strategy at the same time. Blacks in the 1960s, for example, showed all three approaches were possible. The Black Muslim faction advocated separatism while the Urban League followed an accommodationist approach. Dr. King and his Southern Christian Leadership Conference (SCLC) preached and used new-style radicalism. His success inspired others: the Congress of Racial Equality (CORE) and the Student Nonviolent Coordinating Committee (SNCC); even the National Association for the Advancement of Colored People (NAACP) began using similar tactics. The Black Panthers and more radical groups such as the SLA used more radical rhetoric and violent tactics in their approach to new-style radicalism. By the late 1970s, the civil rights movement changed to a predominantly accommodationist approach.

SUMMARY

This chapter presented a systems dynamic framework to better understand racial and ethnic relations or social interactions with the majority society. It discussed typical minority group responses to their status. Three major strategies were distinguished: the politics of accommodation, separatism, and radicalism. The chapter developed two main tactical approaches for each strategy: the economic or political route to accommodation, the physical or psychological route to separatism, and the old-style and new-style routes to radicalism.

Box 2.1   Strategies and Tactics of Minority Groups' Responses to Discrimination and Placement in Minority Status

Strategy	*Tactics and Groups Employing Them*	
Accommodation	*The Economic Approach*	*The Political Approach*
	Occupational queuing and use of special niches.	Machine politics and coalitions, electoral generated gains.
	Groups using:	Groups using:
	Scots, Welsh, Germans, Scandinavians, Dutch, Japanese, Chinese, Korean, blacks (Booker T. Washington followers).	Irish, Italians, Greeks, Jews, Slavs, Women (e.g., NOW).
Separatism	*Physical Separatism*	*Psychological Separatism*
	Moving to isolated areas.	Building shell around members.
	Groups using:	Groups using:
	Chinese, Amish, Mennonites, Mormons, Native Americans, blacks (Marcus Garvey followers).	Black Muslims, Hasidic Jews.
Radicalism	*Old-Style Radicalism*	*New-Style Radicalism*
	Ideological "isms."	Nonviolent to violent protest actions.
	Groups using:	Groups using:
	Socialism—Jews, Poles, Germans, Slavs, Russians	SCLC, SNCC, CORE, Black Panthers, SLA, AIM, UFW of Cesar Chavez.
	Communism—same as Socialism	
	Fascism/Nazism—Germans, Italians, White Russians, radical agrarianism, Utopian movements.	

Box 2.1 summarizes these strategies and their tactical approaches, suggesting examples of various groups that used one or more of these strategies in response to discrimination. Different groups employed different strategies over time. While the accommodationist strategy is by far the most common, new-style radicalism was a more popular approach in the 1960s to 1980s.

Some groups fragmented into factions employing the various approaches at the same time. The chapter briefly discussed which strategy is the more attractive alternative for any given group at any particular time. The characteristics of various minorities and the resources available to them are major determinants in their choice of strategy and tactical response.

Key Terms

accommodation strategy   A minority group accepts the values of the majority and seeks "entrance" and its fair proportion of societal rewards.

cross-group voting   When members of a minority group vote for someone other than a co-ethnic when they have a choice. It is a prime indicator of civic assimilation.

Amalgamation   Amalgamation is a type of assimilation best exemplified by interracial marriage and its variations.

Assimilation   Assimilation is the subjectively felt or psychological identification with the majority.

incorporation   The gradual inclusion of group members into the cultural, economic, social, and finally the political structures of the majority society.

majority's fear function   The degree to which majority society perceives the minority subculture as a threat.

marginal membership function   The number of marginal members within the minority group, which influences its rate of acculturation/assimilation.

occupational niche   Job roles or positions open to a minority because they are viewed as non-threatening by the dominant group. Minority groups show high concentrations in particular occupations.

occupational queuing   The rank-ordering of jobs by their socioeconomic desirability.

similarity of cultures function   The closeness of fit between the majority and minority subcultures.

size of minority function   The perceived relative size of the minority to the majority group.

systems theory   Theory that views relationships as being integrally related parts of a whole wherein the sum is greater than the parts. Each system may be viewed as being part (a subsystem) of another larger system or as an encompassing system (a suprasystem).

REVIEW QUESTIONS

1. What are Milton Gordon's seven stages of assimilation? Relate them to incorporation.
2. Discuss the three strategies that minorities use to cope with their status and give examples of groups using each strategy.
3. Read the reading at the end of this chapter, (pages 68–69). "Standing on the Shoulders of a King." It exemplifies that the presidential campaign of Senator Barack Obama indicates a considerable degree of political incorporation of African Americans, but states that he owes a heavy debt to the new-style radicalism of Dr. Martin Luther King Jr. and the civil rights movement of fifty years ago. Do you agree as to that "debt?" What other indicators of political incorporation are evident in American politics? With respect to other racial groups? With respect to women?
4. Discuss the process of political incorporation. How might *you* measure it?
5. Describe the characteristics typical of a millennial movement. What typical groups exemplify it? Why do such movements favor separatism?
6. Compare and contrast old-style and new-style radicalism.
7. Which political coping strategy are Arab-Americans more likely to employ? Why so?
8. Which coping strategy is more likely to be favored by Gay Americans? Why so?
9. Which coping strategy is more likely to be used by women? Why so?
10. Which minority group would you categorize today as being the least segmentallly assimilated or incorporated at this time? Why so?

NOTES

1. Elections held in Quebec, Canada, in September 1994, returned to power the Separatist Parti Quebecois by giving it a solid majority in the provincial legislature, winning 77 of 125 seats. The party leader promised a referendum within a year on the question of seceding. See Craig Turner, "Separatists Party Headed for Victory in Quebec Election," *Los Angeles Times,* September 13, 1994, pp. A1, A3.

2. See the seminal work of David Easton, *A Framework for Political Analysis* (Englewood Cliffs, NJ: Prentice Hall, 1965).

3. Rates of intergroup marriage have been shown to be important in numerous studies. See, for example, B. R. Bugelski, "Assimilation Through Intermarriage," *Social Forces* 40 (1961): 148–153; Joseph P. Fitzpatrick, "Intermarriage of Puerto Ricans in New York City," *American Journal of Sociology* 71 (1968): 395–406; C. Peach, "Which Triple Melting Pot? A Re-Examination of Ethnic Intermarriage in New Haven, 1900–1950," *Ethnic and Racial Studies* 3 (1980): 1–16; and B. B. Wessel, *An Ethnic Survey of Woonsocket, Rhode Island* (Chicago, IL: University of Chicago Press, 1931).

ADDITIONAL READINGS

Bauton, Michael, *Race Relations.* London: Tavistock, 1967.

Bauton, Michael, *Racial Theories.* New York: Cambridge University Press, 1987.

Cook, Terrence E. *Separation, Assimilation, or Accommodation: Contrasting Ethnic Minority Policies.* Westport, CT: Praeger Press, 2003.

Gerstle, Gary, and John Mollenkopf, eds. *E Pluribus Unum? Contemporary and Historical Perspectives on Immigrant Political Incorporation.* New York: Russell Sage, 2001.

Healey, Joseph F. *Race, Ethnicity, Gender, and Class: The Sociology of Group Conflict and Change*, 3rd ed. Thousand Oaks, CA: Pine Forge Press, Sage Publications, 2003.

Litt, Edgar. *Ethnic Politics in America.* Glenview, IL: Scott Foresman, 1970.

Marble, Manning, and Leith Mullings, eds. *Let Nobody Turn Us Around: Voices of Resistance, Reform, and Renewal—An African American Anthology.* Lanham, MD: Rowman and Littlefield, 2003.

Pipher, Mary. *The Middle of Everywhere: Helping Refugees Enter the American Community.* New York: Harcourt Books, 2003.

Shanks, Cheryl. *Immigration and the Politics of American Sovereignty, 1890–1990.* Ann Arbor, MI: University of Michigan Press, 2001.

Tizard, Barbara, and Ann Phoenix. *Black, White, or Mixed Race?* 2nd ed. NY: Routledge, 2002.

Wierzbicki, Susan. *Beyond the Immigrant Enclave: Network Changes and Assimilation.* New York: LFB Publishing LLC, 2003.

• *Reading 2.1*

Standing on the Shoulders of a King

The only African American serving in the U.S. Senate is the junior senator from Illinois, Senator Barack Obama. When he formally announced his candidacy for the Democratic Party nomination for the 2008 presidential election public opinion polls placed him second only to Senator Hillary Rodham Clinton of New York among the field of candidates for the party's nod. By nearly every pundit's assessment, he is the first African American with a realistic chance to win the office.

Senator Obama, however, could not be a viable candidate for president of the United States had it not been for the ground-breaking work of another African American leader, Dr. Martin Luther King, Jr. Dr. King, and the civil rights movement of the late 1950s to mid-1960s, paved the way for the current crop of African American political leaders. Dr. King received his doctor of divinity degree from Boston College and served as a minister in Montgomery, Alabama where he began his civil rights career leading the 1954 bus boycott there. Dr. King and the movement used (and best exemplify) the coping strategy of the "new-style radicalism" approach described briefly earlier and discussed more fully in Chapter Eight. After Dr. King's famous "I Have a Dream" speech in 1963, followed by his martyrdom in 1964, the civil rights direct-action protest movement culminated in Congressional enactment of the 1964 Civil Rights Act and the 1965 Voting Rights Act. More than any other single cause, these two laws enabled the shift among African Americans from the protest politics of new-style radicalism to the active engagement of political accommodation through successful use of electoral politics. Senator Obama stands on the shoulders of Dr. Martin Luther King, Jr. In his personal life and his political career, he personifies the movement from new-style radicalism in the use of civil rights and community service to the accommodation approach of standard American electoral politics.

According to the United States Senate Historical Office, Senator Obama is only the fifth African American Senator in U.S. history, and the only African American currently serving in the U.S. Senate. He began his service in the Senate on January 4, 2005 and enjoyed celebrity status from the start. He serves on the prestigious Senate Foreign Relations Committee; on the Health, Education, Labor and Pensions Committee; on the Homeland Security and Government Affairs Committee; and on the Veteran's Affairs Committee, all of which have given him a forum for his anti-Iraq War advocacy.

Senator Obama was born of mixed-race ancestry in Honolulu, Hawaii. His father was an immigrant from Kenya. His mother was born in Wichita, Kansas. They met while both were students at the East-West Center of the University of Hawaii at Manoa. They were divorced when Barack was two years old. His father went on to Harvard University to pursue Ph.D studies and eventually returned to Kenya. His mother married an Indonesian foreign student and Obama was raised and attended school in Jakarta from ages 6 to 10. His father died in a car accident in Kenya when Barack was 21 years old, and his mother died of cancer in 1995, shortly after publication of his first book, *Dreams of My Father.* In his book, Senator Obama describes his experiences growing up in his mother's white, middle-class family. As a youth, he struggled to reconcile social perceptions of his multiracial heritage.

Obama studied at Occidental College and then at Columbia University, where he majored in political science with a specialization in international relations. He took his B.A. degree from there in 1983, went on to work at Business International Corporation, then in 1985 he moved to Chicago, where emulating Dr. King to a degree, he directed a non-profit project assisting local churches to organize job training programs for residents of poor neighborhoods. In 1988 he moved to Boston to attend Harvard Law School, were he obtained his J.D. degree magna cum laude and was the first African American to be elected president of the *Harvard Law Review.*

On returning to Chicago in 1991, he directed a voter registration drive, then worked for the civil rights law firm of Miner, Barnhill and Galland, and taught constitutional law at the University of Chicago Law School from 1993 until he was elected to the U.S. Senate in 2004, winning with a landslide victory of 70 percent of the vote.

Barack Obama began his elective political career in the Illinois State Senate, representing Chicago's 13th District in the south-side area of Hyde Park. He sponsored several important bills and chaired the Senate Health and Human Services Committee. He authored the Illinois Earned Income Tax Credit law providing benefits to lower-income families, and helped pass bills to increase funding for AIDS prevention and care.

In 2000, Obama made an unsuccessful bid for the U.S. House of Representatives. After his loss, he continued in the Illinois Senate, authoring a law to require police to videotape interrogations for crimes punishable by the death penalty. He ran unopposed in 2002. He was notable in the Illinois Senate for his ability to work well with both parties and to build bipartisan coalitions. In his 2004 U.S. Senate bid he was endorsed by the Illinois Fraternal Order of Police, citing his longtime support of gun control measures and his willingness to negotiate compromises. During his U.S. Senate campaign, he came to national attention when he delivered the keynote address at the 2004 Democratic National Convention in Boston. He went on to defeat his Republican opponent, Alan Keyes, by 70 percent of the popular vote to Keyes's 27 percent.

Senator Obama announced his candidacy for the 2008 presidential election in Springfield, Illinois on February 10, 2007. He was an early opponent of the Bush Administration's policies on Iraq and in Fall, 2002, spoke at an anti-war rally in Chicago, alongside Jesse Jackson. In 2006, at a Chicago Council of Global Affairs meeting, he stated that the days of using the war on terror as a political football were over, and called for a phased withdrawal of American troops starting in 2007, and an opening of diplomatic dialogue with Syria and Iran. He speaks and writes of his religious convictions formed during his early career as a community organizer working with local churches.

Like Martin Luther King, Jr., Senator Obama is a notable author, having written two highly successful books: *Dreams of My Father,* which is a memoir of his youth and early career first published in 1995 and reissued in 2004; and in October, 2006, a book that discusses his political convictions, *The Audacity of Hope,* which has topped the New York Times Best Seller list.

Source: U.S. Senate Historical Office biography; Obama for President Campaign site; and http://en.wikipedia.org/wiki/Barack_Obama.

CHAPTER 3

• ● •

THE STRATEGY OF ACCOMMODATION
The Tactic of Economic Accommodation

Whenever an ethnic or racial group finds itself assigned to minority status by the dominant society, it must react. Historically, many such groups developed out of the immigration process. They came voluntarily to the United States seeking a better life—which for them meant more economic opportunity and greater religious and political freedom. Therefore, they desired to assimilate. Their choice of tactics to pursue a strategy of accommodation was either economic or political. This chapter discusses the economic path to accommodation, that is, first to incorporation within the economic structures of society, then for some groups followed by political and social incorporation. Since more immigrant groups came for economic opportunity than for any other reason, many pursued an economic path. Groups who immigrated during a period of an expanding economy, or who arrived with special skills or resources, were more able and willing to use this tactical approach to the overall strategy. This chapter discusses in some detail the accommodation patterns of several groups. It begins with a discussion of Asian American groups, distinguishing those who arrived pre-1965 and post-1965. Asian Americans used this tactical approach very successfully and are sometimes called "model minorities" because of that fact. The chapter then uses examples of several European groups to illustrate their use of economic accommodation, again noting the pre- and post-1965 distinction. It discusses how subgroups of Hispanic Americans pursued economic accommodation and closes with a description of Arab American employment of this strategy and tactic. Most of the people in the last two groups arrived after 1965.

ASIAN AMERICANS

Asian Americans make up one of the nation's smallest racial minorities, but are a comparatively rapidly growing minority. According to the estimated number of U.S. residents in July 2005, 14.4 million claimed to be Asian or Asian in combination with one or more other races, approximately 5 percent of the total population, up from 2.9 percent in the 1990 census. They were the fastest growing racial group between 2004 and 2005, at 3 percent annual growth. They are very well educated. As of 2004, 86.8 percent had high school degrees or more, slightly higher than the 85.2 percent rate among the total population, and 49.4 percent had four years of college or more. The corresponding rate for all adults 25 and over was 28.2 percent (*Statistical Abstract of the United States 2006*, 147). The 2005 American Community Survey found that 20 percent of single-race Asians have a graduate or professional degree (e.g., master's or doctorate), double the rate for all people 25 or older. The Census Bureau estimates that by 2050 the number of persons who identify themselves as single-race Asians will be 33.4 million, comprising 8 percent of the total population by that year. Asian/Pacific Islanders comprised 26 percent of the nation's foreign-born population in the 2000 census. Their population in 1970 totaled just 800,000. That number tripled in the 1970s, more than doubled again in the 1980s, and reached 6.9 million by 1990. Using the designation, Asian-alone population in 2000, this population increased by 3.3 million, or 48 percent between 1990 and 2000. If the Asian-alone or in combination population figure is used, an increase of 5.0 million, or 72 percent results. Thus, from 1990 to 2000, the range for the increase in the Asian population was from 48 to 72 percent. In comparison, the total population grew by 13 percent; that is, from 248.7 million in 1990 to 281.4 million in 2000. Their recent immigration rate is evidenced by the fact that 88 percent of those claiming Asian race were either foreign-born themselves, or had at least one foreign-born parent (http://www.census.gov/PressRelease/www.2002/ accessed 8/5/2003).

Table 3.1 presents the percentage of the population of Asian origin as of 2005 for the top ten sending nations.

The median household income for single-race Asians in 2005 was $61,094, the highest median income of any racial group. The median household income varied considerably by Asian groups: for Asian Indians in 2005 it was $73,575, but for Vietnamese-Americans it was $50,925 (2005 American Community Survey).

Likewise, single-race Asian poverty rate was 11.7 percent in 2005, the lowest poverty rate the Census Bureau measured for any racial group, but up from 9.8 percent in 2004. Their preference for owning their own businesses is pronounced. In 2002 Asians owned 1,100,000 businesses, up by 8 percent from 1997, and those business generated $326 billion in receipts and employed 2.2 million. Nearly half (46 percent) of all Asian-owned business were owned by Chinese or Asian-Indians. In 2002, more than three of ten Asian firms were in professional, scientific, and technical services. These businesses are geographically concentrated (as is the Asian population, as will be seen more fully later). More than six in ten of Asian-owned firms were located in California, New York, Texas, and New Jersey. The cities with the highest number of Asian-owned firms were: Los Angeles–Long Beach, California; New York; Honolulu, Hawaii;

Table 3.1   Percentage of U.S. Population of Asian Origin, 2005, and by Selected Nation of Origin (Top Ten Asian, Rank Ordered)

Population	Number (thousands)	Percent Asian	Percent U.S. Population
Total U.S.–2005	295,507	—	100
Total Asian–2005	14,400	100	4.8
Chinese–2005	4,260	29	1.44
Filipino–2005	2,800	19	.94
Asian Indian–2005	2,500	17	.80
Vietnamese–2005	1,500	10	.50
Korean–2005	1,400	9.7	.47
Japanese–2005	1,200	8.3	.40
Cambodian–2005	206	1.4	.007
Laotian–2005	198	1.3	.006
Hmong–2005	186	1.29	.0065
Thai–2005	150	1.04	.005

Source: Table by author, data from http://www.census.gov/FactsforFeatures, accessed 4/9/2007, and estimated total from *Statistical Abstract of the United States, 2006*, Table 15, p. 17.

and San Francisco, California. Table 3.2 compares Asian to Black, White, and Hispanic family income as of 2003.

Among Asian-owned businesses, 44 percent were in services; 21 percent in retail trade; 8 percent in finance, insurance, and real estate; 6 percent in wholesale trade; 3 percent each in manufacturing and transportation, communication, and utilities; and only 1 percent in agricultural services, forestry, fishing, and mining; and 10 percent were in industries not classified (http:/www.census.gov/csd/mwb/Asianp.htm, accessed 4/9/2007). Among single-race Asians 16 years or older, 47 percent worked in management, professional, and related occupations, such as financial managers, engineers, teachers, and registered nurses. Approximately 23 percent worked in sales and office occupations, 15 percent in service occupations, and 11 percent in production, transportation, and material-moving occupations (2005 American Community Survey).

About 49 percent of persons claiming Asian race lived in the western part of the United States. California alone claimed 4.9 million of those of Asian race, making it the state with the largest Asian population. Los Angeles County, in 2005, topped the nation in Asians with 1.4 million. New York, Hawaii, Texas, New Jersey, Illinois, Washington, Florida, Virginia, and Massachusetts followed in order. Those top ten states had 75 percent of the nation's Asian population as of the 2000 census. The approximate percent distribution of the Asian population by region of the country, as of the 2000 census, was: 49 percent West, 20 percent Northeast, 19 percent South, and 12 percent Midwest.

Tables 3.1 and 3.2 present statistical data that provide an overview of their numbers, origins, and economic status. Table 3.1 presents their relative percentage of the total population by selected countries of origin. Table 3.2 compares Asian-American family incomes, as of 2003, with that of blacks, whites, and Hispanics.

Table 3.2   A Comparison of All Households, Asian-American, Black, White, and Hispanic Family Income, 2003.

Income Level	All Households	Asian	Black	White	Hispanic
Under $15,000	15.9%	15.2%	27.4%	14.2%	18.9%
15,000–24,999	13.0	9.5	16.0	12.7	17.6
25,000–34,999	11.9	7.1	13.3	11.9	15.8
35,000–49,999	10.6	9.5	10.8	10.6	12.4
50,000–74,999	18.1	18.4	14.6	18.5	15.9
75,000+	26.2	36.0	13.5	27.6	15.2
Median Family Income	$43,318	$55,699	$29,645	$45,631	$32,977
Persons Below Poverty Level	12.5%	11.8%	24.4%	10.5%	22.5%
Unemployment Rate, 2004	4.4	3.8	8.1	3.9	5.7

Source: Table by author, data from U.S. Census Bureau, *Statistical Abstract of the United States, 2006.* Tables 615, 673, 674, 676, 693.

Before considering particular Asian-nation groups it is important that one understands the distinction in immigration pre- and post-1965. For Asian groups that came in the 1840s through 1920s (Chinese, Japanese, and Koreans mostly), their members were largely "laborers," what would be classified today as unskilled labor. Immigration policy changed dramatically in 1965. Box 3.1 presents a brief summary of the provisions of the Immigration Act of 1965. That law caused a significant shift in the source of immigration to the United States, away from northwestern European nations that dominated immigration under the National Origins Quota Acts (1921, 1924, and 1929), toward those from Latin America and Asia. Moreover, immigrants within the post-1965 flow were much more highly educated, often middle-class and professional in their occupations, and more likely to be somewhat older and to immigrate as families. These pattern changes in the immigration flow had profound impact upon the social interactions and their choice of strategies and tactics for coping with minority status. Also worthy of note, in 1992 for statistical reporting purposes, the Census Bureau began reporting the Asian or Pacific Islanders racial category in two categories: "Asian" and "Native Hawaiian and Other Pacific Islanders."

Chinese Americans

At nearly 23 percent of all Asian Americans, Chinese Americans are the largest Asian-American group. They were the first Asian immigrants to come to the United States in significant numbers. After the discovery of gold in California in 1848, Chinese laborers surged into the state. The largest groups came from Kwantung and Fukien provinces, in southern China. In part, they fled economic depression and resulting local rebellions, but also floods, famine, and the general social discontent in their homeland. They were also pulled by the demand for labor created by the California gold rush. Railroad and steamship companies recruited them heavily.

Box 3.1   Summary Provisions of The Immigration Act of 1965

The Immigration and Nationality Act of October 3, 1965 (79 Stat. 911) amended the Act of June 27, 1952. It ended the quota system, replacing it with seven "preference categories." The act had five goals: (1) to preserve the family unit and to reunite separated families; (2) to meet the need for highly skilled workers; (3) to help ease population problems created by emergencies, such as political upheavals, Communist aggression, and natural disasters; (4) to better the understanding of people cross-nationally through exchange programs; and (5) to bar from the United States aliens who were likely to represent adjustment problems (i.e., assimilation) due to their physical or mental health, criminal history, or dependency, or for national security reasons. It replaced the quota system with a preference system that allocated immigrant visas within each foreign state (on a basis of 20,000 per nation on a first-come, first-served approach in issuing visas) as follows:

1. First preference: unmarried sons and daughters of U.S. citizens
2. Second preference: spouses and unmarried sons and daughters of permanent resident aliens
3. Third preference: members of the professions and scientists and artists of exceptional ability
4. Fourth preference: married sons and daughters of U.S. citizens
5. Fifth preference: brothers and sisters of U.S. citizens
6. Sixth preference: skilled and unskilled workers in short supply
7. Seventh preference: refugees

In the decade after enactment, total immigration increased by nearly 60 percent. The number of immigrants from some countries increased markedly: Greek immigration rose by 162 percent; Portuguese by 382 percent; overall Asian immigration rose by 663 percent and exemplified some of the most remarkable changes: immigration from India rose by over 3,000 percent; from the Philippines by nearly 1,200 percent; from Thailand by more than 1,700 percent; and from Vietnam by over 1,900 percent. Immigration from European nations declined overall by 38 percent, including for example, those from Austria declining by more than 76 percent, those from Ireland by over 77 percent, from Norway by more than 85 percent, and from the U.K. by nearly 120 percent.

The Act's third preference category was especially important in opening up immigration from Asia. Korean and Philippine health professionals entered in exceptionally large numbers. They, in turn, could then use the family preference category to bring in their family members (second, or even later, the fifth preference categories). By the late 1970s, more than 70,000 medical doctors alone had immigrated and by 1980 there were more Filipino physicians in the United States than native-born black doctors. Nurses and other medical technicians from Asia used this provision to come in large numbers. An unanticipated consequence of the act was what came to be called "the brain drain" of highly talented persons from Asian countries to the United States.

The act also established a Select Commission on Western Hemisphere Immigration that ultimately made recommendations influencing markedly the immigration patterns from Mexico, and Central and South America.

President Lyndon Johnson signed the act into law at the foot of the Statue of Liberty on October 3, 1965.

Source: Adapted by author from: LeMay and Barkan, 1999: 257–262; and LeMay, 2004: 4–5.

Chinese laborers were welcomed for the first few years after their arrival in America. They were initially viewed as industrious, thrifty, adaptable to many types of tasks, and willing to perform labor unattractive to the majority white males. Chinese immigrants quickly became essential to the California economy. They were organized, so an employer could secure any number of workers by negotiating with a single contractor. This placed them in a comparatively advantageous position. Once employed, Chinese laborers stayed on the job, agreeing to do the most undesirable tasks. With the lack of labor generally, and especially the lack of women, they found work in the mines, building railroads, and as ranch hands, farm laborers, and domestic servants. The Central Pacific Railroad, for example, employed some 9,000 Chinese immigrants a year. By 1860, they made up about 10 percent of California's population and roughly 25 percent of its work force (Thompson 1996).

Their warm welcome was short-lived. By the mid-1850s, growing hostility was evident. In the mining regions especially, the Chinese were often robbed and beaten and occasionally murdered. By 1849, a Know Nothing judge of the California Supreme Court had ruled that the Chinese could not testify in courts against white men. Crimes against them often went unpunished.

Their problems reflected resentment against them because they were viewed as threats to white labor. The Chinese immigrants were overwhelmingly males who came to the United States as **sojourners**—intending to work here only for a few years to save money and then return to their native country to buy land. The Chinese male-female ratio from 1860 to 1900 was a few thousand to one. This problem was exacerbated when fourteen states passed *antimiscegenation laws* (forbidding marriage between the white and Asian races). Those laws, coupled with the scarcity of Chinese females, left the men with no alternative but total abstention or the use of prostitutes. Prostitution was usually associated with the opium traffic, which soon led to a severe image problem of "criminality" concerning Chinese immigrants. Difficulty in importing Chinese females contributed to the long-lasting nature of the imbalance. By 1882, Chinese labor immigration was greatly reduced. As of 1890, only 2.7 percent of Chinese were American-born. The ratio began to be redressed during the 1920s when 30 percent were native-born. But real parity was not achieved until after a 1943 law ended the total ban on Chinese labor immigration and provided a quota that allowed Chinese women to enter the country. By 1960, two-thirds of Chinese Americans were native-born, and the male-female ratio was finally nearly balanced. Outmarriage to non-Chinese was culturally discouraged.

As noted above, after enactment of the 1965 act, Chinese immigrants were more likely highly skilled or professional. They came with high educational degrees and emphasized higher educational achievement among their children, especially those born in the United States. Today, as indicated in the 2000 census data, 84.6 percent of Chinese Asians identified themselves as Chinese alone, and only 15.4 claimed themselves as Chinese and some other race or detailed Asian group.

Miscegenation laws were but one manifestation of the legal constraints imposed on the Chinese in America. By the 1850s, California expelled them from the mining work camps, forbade their entry into public schools, denied their right to testify against whites in court, and barred them from obtaining citizenship. By 1865, calls for restrictions on their immigration began. In 1867, the Democratic Party swept into California's elective offices running on an anti-Chinese platform. The Panic of 1873 brought on economic conditions that greatly increased the sense of competition from Chinese immigrant labor, and calls against the "Yellow Menace" broadened. In 1887, the Workingmen's Party, led by Dennis Kearny running on a blatantly anti-Chinese campaign, scored political success in several cities. The party called for an end to all Chinese immigration. By the 1870s, such sentiment was so strong on the West Coast that it was virtually political suicide to take the Chinese side. This anti-Chinese legal action culminated nationally in the passage of the Chinese Exclusion Act of 1882.

The policy effect of that law, first passed with a provision imposing a ten-year ban and amended in 1884 to further tighten the ban, was immediate and drastic. In 1881, 11,900 Chinese labor immigrants entered the United States and over 39,500 came in 1882. But that figure dropped to a paltry 8,031 in 1883, and by 1885 a mere 23 Chinese laborers managed to enter. In 1892, Congress renewed the Exclusion Act for another ten years, and in 1902 the law was extended indefinitely.

Laws were not the only method used to restrict Chinese life and work opportunities. Violence and social segregation were common. Anti-Chinese feelings reached a fever pitch by the mid-1870s. Many turned from law to violence. In 1871, 21 Chinese were killed in a Los Angeles riot. In 1880, Denver also experienced a severe anti-Chinese riot. A typical example of the use of violence was the Truckee Raid of June 18, 1876; whites burned two Chinese-occupied cabins and shot and wounded the residents (one of whom later died of his wound) as they attempted to flee the flames. White citizens tried for the crimes were acquitted. The Order of Caucasians advocated the elimination of the Chinese through the use of violence. They raided and burned various sections of Chinatowns. In 1885, at Rock Springs, Wyoming, a mob killed 28 Chinese and drove hundreds of others from their homes. In Tacoma, Seattle, and Oregon City, mobs expelled hundreds of Chinese from those cities. Unionized labor, particularly the Teamsters, became a major force behind the violently anti-Chinese movement. The violence subsided after the restrictions laws were passed, but strong prejudice and discrimination remained, especially in jobs and housing, well into the 1890s. Newspapers spread the stereotyped images of the Chinese with stories about prostitution, gambling, and opium dens in Chinatowns. "Chinks" and "John Chinaman" were ethnophaulisms used as racial slurs.

Job discrimination was prevalent. Violence kept many out of the mine fields, but so did legislation. In 1855, the Foreign Miners' Tax was enacted in California. It required foreign miners to pay a four-dollar-per-month tax. In addition, the tax increased each year the miner did not become a citizen. Since the Chinese were legally excluded from naturalization, they were forced to pay ever higher rates. This legislation and the violence soon forced them to seek other areas of employment.

The general lack of women in the frontier opened up the area of domestic services to the Chinese as one field in which they would not be viewed as a competitive threat to the white male labor force. Laundries, restaurants, and other domestic services required little capital or job skills. Individuals simply had to be culturally willing to accept occupations that in the dominant culture were considered unworthy of an able-bodied male. The increasing job discrimination and violence encouraged their tendency to cluster together in urban Chinatowns (i.e., self-segregation). Even there they could not escape legislative harassment. San Francisco passed ordinances between 1876 and 1880 aimed solely at the Chinese. A special tax was placed on small hand laundries, all of which were operated by the Chinese at the time. A "Cubic Air Act" was passed that jailed the occupants of overcrowded housing rather than the landlords, if each person did not have 500 square feet of living space. The city also enacted a "Queue Tax," that is, a tax on pigtails—a hairstyle worn exclusively by the Chinese. An ordinance was passed restricting the shipment of human bones, aimed at the Chinese custom of sending a deceased person's bones home for burial. Although these laws were nearly impossible to enforce very widely and were ultimately found to be unconstitutional, they contributed to the atmosphere and the institutionalization of a rigid social and geographic segregation of the Chinese in America.

When the Chinese did enter an industry, pay discrimination forced further segregation. The Chinese virtually took over the San Francisco shoe industry. The cigar industry became over 90 percent Chinese. They made up 64 percent of California's textile industry workers. In these occupations, wages fell dramatically from $25 to $9 per week (Kitano, 1997).

Chinatowns arose in Los Angeles, San Francisco, New York, Boston, Pittsburgh, and St. Louis, a pattern that continues today. Chinese Americans are overwhelmingly urban and concentrated in several large Chinatowns. As of 2005, the top ten places in the United States in terms of their Asian population are: New York, NY; Los Angeles, CA; San Jose, CA; San Francisco, CA; Honolulu, HI; San Diego, CA; Chicago, IL; Houston, TX; Seattle, WA; and Fremont, CA.

Despite the prejudicial actions and discriminatory legislation, Chinatown residents often displayed symbols of national loyalty. New York's Chinatown, as the nation neared entry into World War I, for example, was resplendent with American flags from nearly every building.

The Chinese reacted to the discriminatory pressures by forming organizations for self-protection, for social and economic benefits, and for pooling their scant economic resources. The older organizations, such as the Six Companies of San Francisco, were highly specific, limited in scope and membership, and conservative. They offered education and medical services, settled disputes among members, and gave legal aid to members involved in lawsuits with whites. During the period of heightened violence against them, they hired their own private policemen to guard property in Chinatown. They fought legal cases to overturn the anti-Chinese laws passed at local, state, and even the national level. The Six Companies helped bury their dead and cared for their graves. Before the establishment of official diplomatic and consular offices in America, the Six Companies served as the unofficial voice of the Chinese Imperial Government on behalf of Chinese residents in America (Kung 1962).

Newer Chinese organizations reflect American patterns—Chinese golf clubs, boy scout troops, and Lions Clubs. Organized religion plays a minor role. A more confrontational stance has been adopted by the Asian-American Political Alliance, a group of Chinese-American and Japanese-American youth who reject the accommodationist posture of the first generation. A middle-of-the road position was taken by the Chinese American Citizens League. Founded in 1895, the league promotes mutual interests among Americans of Chinese ancestry.

A major factor in easing the situation of the Chinese Americans was the basic attitude shift within the majority society during the 1940s, when China became a U.S. ally

Chinese Americans proudly displayed U.S. flags in New York City's Chinatown in 1913. *(Courtesy of the Library of Congress)*

against the Japanese. Suddenly the mass media began describing the Chinese people's peace-loving nature, how valiantly they fought against the "sly, tricky Jap," how different they were from their more aggressive neighbor. They were viewed as honest, hardworking, gentle, and compliant. The alliance between the United States and China against Japan led to the repeal of the Chinese Exclusion Act. A citizen's committee was formed to advocate for repeal. That law was passed on December 13, 1943 (57 Stat. 600: 8 U.S. C. 212(a)). The McCarren-Walter Act of 1952 further codified the many immigration laws into one statute, and Chinese labor quotas for immigration, though small (set at the minimum 100), were established, and restrictions against naturalization were repealed. Increased Chinese immigration was enabled by the refugee law enacted under President Kennedy in 1962. Finally, in 1965, President Johnson signed into law an act that abolished the national-origins quota system and pooled all unused nationality quotas into one group. Chinese immigration rose substantially after 1970. As noted above, the newest Chinese immigrants, many from Hong Kong, come under the third category, or a later amendment allowing for investors to immigrate.

Even in California, which previously had led the anti-Chinese immigration movement, the attitude against the Chinese changed dramatically during and after World War II. They were praised for their high ethical standards in faithfully meeting their contractual and other obligations and for their commercial abilities. The personal word of the Chinese merchant was accepted by American bankers, businessmen, lawyers, and even customs officials. They had a reputation for paying their bills, taxes, rents, and other debts.

The war period opened up other avenues for more rapid economic accommodation. Because of manpower shortages during the war, Chinese Americans entered skilled as well as unskilled positions in industry. They proved to be hardworking employees. They soon competed in many occupational fields, although today there is still evidence of more subtle discrimination in employment in that they are somewhat underrepresented in executive, managerial, academic, sales, and personnel positions and in the more highly paid crafts, such as ironworkers, operating engineers, plumbers, and electricians (Parrillo, 1996).

After 1965, the cohesive and extended family structure of Chinese-American society is seen as a contributing factor to their more rapid acculturation. Their heritage emphasizes formal education. In all-Chinese households, children are taught to speak Chinese. Indeed, an estimated 2.3 million people who are five or older speak Chinese at home, the second most (after Spanish) widely spoken non-English language (2005 American Community Survey). Third-generation Chinese Americans were able to get good educations after the post-World War II economic gains made by the first- and second-generation cohorts. With improved education, they entered the professional job market. As noted above, they have done well in formal education, now ranking among the highest educated of minority groups. The third generation of pre-WWII immigrants, and the children of post-1970 immigrants, have completely acculturated in the style of clothing, observance of American cultural holidays such as Christmas and Easter, and American national holidays such as the Fourth of July. Reflecting pluralism, however, it is still common for them to celebrate the Chinese New Year. Today, the typical Chinese American eats with a knife and fork rather than with chopsticks, and more often than not eats traditional American dishes.

Chinese laundries and restaurants are still highly popular and profitable forms of businesses. Quantitatively, the laundry business surpasses all others, but the amount of revenue is less than that of the Chinese restaurant industry. The hand laundry still predominates, but laundries that perform specific functions, such as shirt processing, are more mechanized. The Chinese restaurant has grown into an American favorite and produces good profits. Most are run either by a partnership or a single owner. Other popular Chinese-American businesses are the Chinese grocery and the import-export gift shops. The very image of Chinatown has changed. Once despised as dirty, crime-ridden dens of iniquity, today Chinatowns are viewed as bits of quaint old China set down in our streets, providing the tourist with a unique and pleasurable cross-cultural experience (i.e., exemplifying exotic pluralism).

Today's Chinese Americans are well incorporated and largely middle class. Being native-born, they speak English as their native tongue. With few exceptions they are Americanized in almost all cultural aspects. Structural assimilation has been less achieved. Segmented assimilation is indicated by individual incomes still below the national white average, although their family income exceeds that of the average white family. As a group, they still exhibit a higher than average rate of mental illness, and tuberculosis remains a nagging health problem. In housing, they remain clustered in the Chinatowns of Hawaii, San Francisco, Los Angeles, and New York. In recent decades, delinquency and gang behavior have emerged as serious social problems. Social contacts between Chinese Americans and whites still reflect a degree of racial prejudice. While the Chinese are no longer feared in the job market, there are still indicators of prejudice operating against them there. Their greatest success comes when they own and operate their own businesses. Their rate of intermarriage, another indicator of segmented assimilation, remains low. While becoming more common, intermarriage is still frowned upon on the mainland, as opposed to Hawaii, by members of both races. That is less of a problem among Japanese Americans, to whom we next turn. The heavy reliance by Chinese Americans on the use of the economic path, however, achieved sufficient success that in recent years they have become more politically involved. They have a notable tradition of effective lobbying at the national level, although such efforts were mostly directed at influencing U.S. foreign policy vis-à-vis mainland China and Taiwan or Hong Kong. Their limited use of electoral politics is exemplified by the fact that only one Chinese-American politician has held the office of a state governor. Now former Governor of the state of Washington, Gary Locke, used economic policy to make his mark in office. Box 3.2 provides a brief biographical sketch of Gary Locke.

Japanese Americans

At just over 1.2 million in population, and 8 percent of Asian Americans, Japanese Americans are now the sixth largest Asian group in the United States, according to 2005 census bureau data. Their migration to the United States began in 1868, when 148 contract workers came to Hawaii as plantation workers, but most came during the period between 1890 and 1924, and since 1965. It was not until the Meiji Restoration in 1868 that the Japanese were allowed to emigrate. Initially they were encouraged to do so and were well received in Hawaii. They first came expecting their stay to be temporary, working under a three-year contract that had been arranged by the Hawaiian government. They were viewed as a source of cheap labor and an alternative to the Chinese "coolie" labor force, and arrived as "unskilled labor," although they were quite skilled farmers which in Japan made them part of the middle-class there.

After the initial three-year period, some migrated to the mainland, concentrating on the West Coast, especially California. In 1870, there were only 56 Japanese immigrants on the mainland, but by 1890, they exceeded 24,000 and totaled just over 72,000 by the 1910 census. In 1920, they exceeded 110,000, at which level they basically stabilized because of the Immigration Law of 1924, which specifically barred them until it was rescinded in 1952. By 1941, when the Japanese attacked Pearl Harbor, there were only 127,000 Japanese aliens and Japanese Americans on the mainland, some 94,000 of whom lived in California, and among whom 63 percent were native-born citizens.

The Japanese adapted well to working conditions in the United States. The majority were young males (the ratio of male to female was about 4 to 1) from the farming class. They were highly literate; nearly 99 percent were able to read, exceeding by far the literacy of the majority population and clearly distinguishing them from their West and East European immigrant counterparts. In Hawaii, most worked in farming, usually in all-male work gangs under the supervision of an agent. Those who went to the mainland established a more diversified occupational pattern. Their most typical job was working on the western railroads, but they were also employed in canneries, in the mines, as domestic servants, cooks, and waiters, and in groceries and dry goods establishments. Troubled by their low wages, they evidenced a strong desire for upward mobility. They turned to agriculture on the mainland, particularly truck farming, and

---

BOX 3.2	*BIO-SKETCH OF GOVERNOR GARY LOCKE OF WASHINGTON*

Born to an immigrant family in 1950, Gary Locke is a third-generation Chinese American whose paternal ancestry goes back to Taishan, Guangdong Province in China. Gary Locke was born in Seattle, Washington, the second of five children. The family lived in Seattle's Yesler Terrace, a public housing project. Using part-time jobs and financial aid and scholarships, he was able to attend Yale University, earning a bachelor's degree in political science in 1972, then went on to take a law degree from Boston University School of Law in 1975. In 1994 he married Mona Lee Locke (nee Li Meng), a Seattle television reporter whose parents came from Shanghai and Hubei Provinces. Gary Locke was elected Washington's twenty-first governor in 1996, the first Chinese American governor in U.S. history. He was re-elected in 2000 and served until 2005.

Gary's political career began in service as a deputy prosecutor in King County, Washington. In 1982 he was elected to the Washington State House of Representatives, where he distinguished himself serving on the House Judiciary Committee and as chair of the prestigious Appropriations Committee. In 1993 he became the first Chinese American to be elected King County's County Executive, and in 1996 became the state's governor. After re-election in 2000 the state faced a major recession. Governor Locke's plans for dealing with the state's fiscal crisis, avoided across the board reductions. Instead he and his staff used the Public Strategies Group, Inc. to recommend selected budget cuts enabling a record-high allocation for construction projects. Essentially, they turned the budget process on its head, evolving a four-part plan of action for the budget. They established ten "result teams" to plan for specific outcomes. Even his Republican opponent for the governor's office in 2000 hailed his work as bold and impressive statecraft, praising the governor's willingness to face down the most powerful interest groups even in his own party. In January, 2004, a survey of the state's voters agreed when 64 percent endorsed the statement: "Whether or not I agree with all of the Governor's budget reduction recommendations, I respect his leadership and vision to solve the current problem and get the state's economy back on track."

He was seen as a rising star in Democratic politics and mentioned as a possible vice-presidential selection. In summer of 2003, however, Governor Locke announced he would not seek re-election, in part due to racist insults and threats. He left office in January, 2005, when he joined the Seattle office of international law firm Davis Wright Tremaine LLP, in their China and governmental-relations practice groups.

Source: Bio-sketch by author, based on the Governor's Office archives (accessed 2/27/2007; his biography in Wikipedia, accessed 2/27/2007; and Michael LeMay, *Public Administration, 2nd ed.,* Belmont, CA.: Wadsworth/Thomson Learning, 2006: 75–76.

---

they became strong economic competitors. Prior to World War I, although Japanese immigrants farmed less than 1 percent of the agricultural land in California—and that often the most marginal land—they produced 10 percent of the state's total crop.[1]

The Japanese faced immediate hostility and some violence upon coming to the mainland, when anti-Chinese sentiment was extended to them. The shoemakers' union attacked Japanese cobblers in 1890. Similar attacks by cooks' and waiters' union members followed in 1892. Fear of the Japanese "Yellow Peril" grew markedly after the success of Japan in the Russo-Japanese War of 1905. In May of that year the Japanese and Korean Exclusion League was formed. It was soon renamed the Asiatic Exclusion League. Labor and the *San Francisco Chronicle* led the protest movement in 1905.

As with the Chinese, legal action against them soon followed. In 1906, San Francisco adopted an ordinance segregating them into "Chinese" schools. In 1907, President Theodore Roosevelt issued an order, which remained in effect until 1948, that barred their entry into the United States from a bordering country or U.S. territory (that is, Canada, Mexico, or Hawaii). Opposition to their immigration rose.

In 1908, the Roosevelt administration used diplomatic and economic pressure to force the Japanese government to accept the "gentleman's agreement" to restrict emigration voluntarily. The importing of Japanese wives was excluded from that agreement, so the peak year of Japanese immigration was 1907–1908, after which it sharply declined except for the "picture-bride" marriage system that brought in brides. From 1911 to 1920, 87,000 Japanese were admitted, but 70,000 returned to Japan, for a net gain of a mere 17,000 for that decade.

Legal action continued against them. In 1913, the Webb-Henry bill, better known as the California Alien Land Act, was passed. This law restricted Japanese aliens from owning land. It limited their leasing of land to three years and forebade land already owned or leased from being bequeathed. California Attorney General Webb frankly described the law he authored as follows:

> The fundamental basis of all [restrictive] legislation . . . has been and is, race undesirability. It seeks to limit their presence by curtailing their privileges which they may enjoy here, for they will not come in large numbers and long abide with us if they may not acquire land. And it seeks to limit the numbers who will come by limiting the opportunities for their activities here when they arrive. (cited in Kitano 1976, 17)

Although most Japanese got around the law by placing ownership in the names of their native-born children, who held citizenship, or in the names of Caucasian friends, the racist nature of the law foreshadowed the troubles to come.

In 1921, the Supreme Court ruled, in *Ozawa v. the United States*, that the Japanese were not Caucasoid and therefore were subject to the Asian restrictive laws. In 1923, California attempted to plug the loopholes in its Alien Land Act by prohibiting aliens from being the guardians of a minor's property. When the United States upheld the constitutionality of that law, similar laws were quickly passed in New Mexico, Arizona, Louisiana, Montana, Idaho, and Oregon.

The Immigration Act of 1924 was the final legal restriction aimed at totally blocking Asian immigration. Restrictions on their acquiring citizenship complicated their acculturation process. The Japanese government was especially upset by this law for its blatant manifestation of racism. Not only did it feel the law was a "slap in the face" to a people whose culture made "face," or honor, all important, but they considered it a direct violation of the gentleman's agreement that specified that the United States would not adopt any discriminatory laws against the Japanese, which the 1924 Act clearly was (Kitano 1976, 28).

Table 3.3   Japanese-American Relocation Camps Rank Ordered by Their Capacities

Camp Name/Location	Dates of Operation	Numbers
Totals for All Camps		114,4900
Tule Lake, California	Jun. 1942–Mar 1946	18,800
Poston, Arizona	Jun. 1942–Nov. 1945	18,000
Gila River, Arizona	Aug. 1942–Nov. 1945	13,400
Heart Mountain, Wyoming	Sep. 1942–Nov. 1945	11,100
Manzanar, California	Jun. 1942–Nov. 1945	10,200
Mididoka, California	Sep. 1942–Oct. 1945	9,900
Jerome, Arkansas	Nov. 1942–Jun. 1944	8,600
Rohwer, Arkansas	Oct. 1942–Nov. 1945	8,500
Topaz, Utah	Oct. 1942–Oct. 1945	8,300
Granada, Colorado	Sep. 1942–Oct. 1945	7,600

*There were two camps at Tule Lake. The second was a high-security prison for the 3,500 Japanese Americans believed to pose individual threats to the U.S. war effort. None was ever charged with or convicted of spying or sabotage. Still, this small group was not released until the war was over.

**Some prisoners were released before others were interned. The total number of "evacuees" was more than 120,000.

Source: Adapted by author from data in Peter Wright and John Armor, *Manzanar,* 1989, New York: Random House.

The effect of this law was to develop an unusually pronounced generation gap among the Japanese Americans. They can be categorized by age/generation. The *Issei* were born in Japan and immigrated here. They were prevented by law from becoming citizens until 1954, and were unable to vote or to own land and were subject to miscegenation laws that banned marriage (or sexual relations legally) across racial lines. The *Nisei* were the generation born between 1910 and 1940. They are native-born citizens who could vote, own land, and the like. They have been characterized as the "quiet generation" who are now in their 70s and 80s. The *Sansei* were born after World War II and are now middle-aged. A final group, the *Kibei,* were Nisei children sent to Japan to be raised in a traditional culture, who, by the time the war broke out, were desperately trying to return to the United States (see Hosokawa 1969, Kitano 1976).

During the 1930s, as Japan extended its "co-prosperity sphere," tension between Japan and the United States increased, and anti-Japanese sentiment on the West Coast continued to rise alarmingly until culminating in racial hysteria after the Japanese attack on Pearl Harbor on December 7, 1941. That attack began a virtual nightmare for Japanese Americans living on the mainland. Nearly 120,000 Japanese Americans, some 70,000 of whom were *native-born citizens,* were sent to "relocation camps" in the interior for what was termed "military necessity." The relocation camps were a euphemism for what were, in fact, concentration camps. Their conditions were grim. Surrounded by 15-foot-high barbed-wire fences, the camps were guarded by armed troops stationed around the perimeter and on spotlight towers. Residents lived in crude barracks where stalls a mere 18 feet by 21 feet housed families of six or seven. They were partitioned off with 7-foot-high walls with 4-foot openings affording no privacy. Residents used outside latrines and camp mess halls. They were locked in by nine o'clock with a ten o'clock lights-out curfew. The camps were located in seven states, as shown in Table 3.3

A long-range view of the internment camp at Manzanar is shown here. *(Courtesy of the Library of Congress)*

on page 83, run by the War Relocation Authority and the War Relocation Work Corps. Following is a description of Poston in Arizona, whose peak population reached 17,867 by August 1942.

> The barracks were flimsily constructed. Sometimes as many as eight people lived in one room. Mattresses were made by stuffing cloth bags with straw. There was hardly any furniture. The heat was intense in the summer, and the minimum temperature during the winter occasionally fell below the freezing mark. And then there were the barbed wire and the guards. It is little wonder that some people felt betrayed at having been sent to such a place and either actively resisted or failed to cooperate fully with the administration's plans. (McLemore 1983, 179)

Table 3.3 lists the internment camps, their dates of operation, rank ordered by the numbers interned at each camp. Photograph 3.3 of the camp at Manzanar (on page 84) shows the bleakness of the internment camps. Only racial prejudice can adequately explain internment policy.[2]

The relocation program's principle author, General DeWitt, provided an openly racist rationale for its adoption as public policy and for the existence of the camps:

> In the war in which we are engaged, racial affinities are not severed by migration. The *Japanese race is an enemy race* and while second- and third-generation Japanese born on U.S. soil and possessed of U.S. citizenship have become "Americanized," *the racial strains are undiluted.* (cited in McLemore 1983, 184; italics added)

In the succinct words of one scholar, "One hundred thousand persons were sent to concentration camps on a record that couldn't support a conviction for stealing a dog (Rostow 1945, 184).[3]

Paradoxically, on Hawaii, which was in a much more vulnerable position, authorities did not attempt a mass evacuation of the 120,552 Japanese-American citizens living there. The war passed without a single proven act of espionage or sabotage by a Japanese American there or on the mainland. The army announced that "the shipping situation and the labor shortage make it a matter of military necessity to keep the people of Japanese blood on the Island." Yet the army had used the very words of "military necessity" to justify the West Coast evacuation plan (Hosokawa 1969, 457–467). The failure to evacuate Japanese Americans on Hawaii was a matter of manpower and logistics. Their skills and energies were desperately needed in Hawaii. The government did not have the ships to move 100,000 Japanese Americans, plus 20,000 military dependents, to the mainland and bring back an equal number of workers to take their place. Given an opportunity to do so, the Japanese Americans in Hawaii demonstrated that nothing needed to be done to restrict them. On the mainland they were not given that chance, although the danger of attack was more remote.

Anti-Japanese activity was particularly widespread and intense on the West Coast. Newspaper headlines, editorials, political speeches, as well as mob actions and nativist organizations, reflected the prejudice against Japanese Americans. Politicians struck out against them, exploiting the tensions of the average voter and avoiding reference to more critical issues. Even before World War II, many politicians used that prejudice to help win elections. There were strong correlations between waves of anti-Japanese agitations and election years. The Japanese-American group was small, economically and politically weak, and an ideal scapegoat. Politicians running for office could attack them without fear of reprisal. There were economic as well as political motives for such activities. Trade unions and small landowners took part in the agitation, but much of the organized opposition stemmed from the owners of huge estates. Large landowners diverted attention from their own control by attacking the Japanese farmer as the cause of everyone's problems.

The racial homogeneity of the Japanese Americans made them easy targets for stereotyping. The stereotype of the Japanese as a "buck-toothed, bespectacled, monkey-faced sneak" was easily applied to the Issei and the Nisei, whose physical characteristics made them easy to segregate. A Nisei was instantly a "Jap," no matter how removed his family, interests, and culture were from Japan. Japanese Americans were caricatured as the schoolboy, the farmer, the gardener, and the corner grocer in a Japanese military uniform. By contrast, German Americans and Italian Americans had become more or less indistinguishable. They had different heights, different shades of white skin, and hair coloring ranging from blond to brunette. Whereas the "German Nazi" and the "Italian Fascist" were verbally distinguished from German Americans and Italian Americans, the term "Jap" was applied to all of Japanese ancestry, be they long-term resident aliens, native-born citizens, friends, or enemies.

The climate of opinion created by those who saw economic and political gain in anti-Japanese agitation was an important factor in the evacuation. Those few alien Japanese who truly were a military danger were already known to the FBI and were taken into custody within a few days after the Pearl Harbor attack. That all the rest, including some 70,000 native-born citizens, should be treated as a military threat was an act of official racism. There was never a single act of convicted sabotage or related criminal activity connected to the war effort by a Japanese American. By contrast, although there were efforts of sabotage by some German Americans and Italian Americans, they were never considered for evacuation. Those public policy effects clearly exemplify the racial bias and nature of those policies.

Japanese Americans accepted the evacuation and internment surprisingly peacefully. There was one strike at Poston and a riot at Manzanar during the very early period when conditions were especially grim. But once the immediate period of hysteria passed, Japanese-American evacuees of proven loyalty were allowed to leave the camps and join the U.S. Army. Some 20,000 did so, and 6,000 served in the Pacific in the later years of the war. Most, however, were in the famed 442nd Regimental Combat Team, which became the most highly decorated unit in the European theater.

In *Hirabayashi v. the United States,* in 1943, and in *Korematsu v. the United States,* in 1944, the U.S. Supreme Court upheld the constitutionality of the evacuation order. In the latter decision, approved by a 6–3 vote, the dissenting justices rendered sharp dissents. In *Endo v. the United States* (1944), the Court revoked the West Coast Evacuation Order. Effective January 2, 1945, Japanese Americans were no longer under forcible detention. By June 1946, all the camps were closed.

Ironically, the forced geographic segregation in the internment camps ultimately contributed to more rapid acculturation of Japanese Americans and advanced their assimilation process in several ways. The wartime relocation forced them out of their "Little Tokyo enclaves." In dispersing the populations of the Little Tokyos of San Francisco and Los Angeles, it ended the nearly feudalistic control that the Issei generation, the Japanese father, held over his children. It emancipated the Japanese-American women. Power within the ethnic community shifted from the Issei to the Nisei and propelled them into the mainstream of American life. The Nisei entered new occupations, improved their economic status, and helped pull down the legalized racial barriers against them.

Educational barriers particularly began to fall. By May 1942, the National Student Relocation Council was organized. That fall, hundreds of Nisei were enrolled in interior schools. By 1942–1943, 928 students in the relocation centers were enrolled in colleges and universities, in addition to 650 Nisei students who were not evacuees. Over 280 colleges and universities in 38 states accepted them. About 20 percent were able to finance their own educations; the colleges, universities, and various church boards and foundations aided the other 80 percent. They did well. Reports from the receiving institutions were highly commendatory. The Nisei students demonstrated an encouraging desire and ability to assimilate once freed from the oppressive strictures of life on the West Coast.

A related spur to their dispersal was the increasing need for manpower. Sugar producers and processors created an insistent cry for evacuees to be released as laborers in the beet fields of the states outside the restricted military zones. Seasonal work permits were granted to approximately 1,700 evacuees, most of them young men, during the spring and summer months. They were effective workers, and during the fall harvest the demand was even greater—nearly 10,000 evacuees went out on seasonal work permits.

By the fall of 1942, work permits granting indefinite leave were given to those not found to be "security risks." As manpower needs grew desperate, employers in the Midwest began to call for Nisei help. Many Nisei urged others in the camps to move out. This completely altered the prewar employment patterns. On the coast they were farmers, produce merchants, fishermen, gardeners, and domestic helpers. In Chicago and other midwestern cities, they worked in factories and in such diverse areas as social work, teaching, chemistry, and engineering and as dental and lab technicians, draftsmen, and mechanics. Soon they were earning two to ten times as much as they had received in prewar employment. Some Nisei were supervising persons of other races, a situation unheard of on the coast. Less than 10 percent were employed domestically. Many soon had their own businesses. Nisei women were hired as stenographers, at first reluctantly, eventually enthusiastically, as their good qualities became known. They rarely had a chance at secretarial jobs in California. Many of the women found well-paying jobs in the clothing industry, operating sewing machines.

In Chicago, Japanese-American–owned stores were interspersed with others, and they had to cater to the general public, in contrast to Los Angeles where they had to look to their own for such employment and as customers. In the Midwest, instead of setting up their own churches, they attended more than 100 of Chicago's established churches and found themselves welcomed. This new atmosphere, in part due to the regional shift, in part made possible by the careful work of the Relocation Authority in soliciting the approval of responsible citizens, contributed to the success of relocating the evacuees. Usually a War Relocation Authority (WRA) officer would spend two to three weeks conferring with local government officials, union leaders, heads of civic organizations, and ministers before authorizing any resettlement.

The Japanese American Citizens League (JACL), founded in 1930, began during the war to lobby quietly but effectively against the prejudice and discrimination they faced. The JACL worked with the WRA, the American Civil Liberties Union, the Common Council for American Unity, Norman Thomas of the Post–War Council, the American Baptist Home Mission Council, the YWCA, and the Friends Service Committee to help evacuees find jobs and housing. The JACL held the Nisei together and kept them in touch with one another through its paper, *The Pacific Citizen.* It gave the Nisei a strong, clear editorial voice when most newspapers were either against or simply ignoring them. It was through its paper that the JACL expressed its goal as an organization for Japanese Americans: the emancipation of all Japanese Americans from the stigma of limited citizenship and the cloak of questioned loyalty through their full assimilation into the general culture and their complete acceptance as co-Americans by their fellow citizens.

The wartime dispersal was fairly widespread. Nearly 43,000 had resettled in nine states: Illinois, 15,000; Colorado, 6,000; Utah, 5,000; Ohio, 3,900; Idaho, 3,500; Michigan, 2,800; New York, 2,500; New Jersey, 2,200; and Minnesota, 1,700. The Nisei liked their new homes, as they had job challenges and opportunity unknown to them in California. After the war, the JACL continued its work. It led the fight for naturalization of the Issei, recognizing that only as citizens would the Issei have equal protection under the law. It fought to remove the discriminatory aspects of U.S. immigration law.

Congress moved slowly. An amendment to the Soldiers' Brides Bill was passed allowing the Japanese spouses and children of American servicemen to enter the United States without regard to the Oriental Exclusion Act. Individual congressmen sponsored more than 200 private bills benefiting the Issei and Nisei. Tenure, which had been canceled as a result of the evacuation, was restored to Nisei under the federal civil service. The JACL found strong support in Congress from Representative Francis E. Walter of Pennsylvania and Senator Pat McCarren of Nevada. The McCarren-Walter Immigration and Naturalization Act of 1952 (66 Stat. 163) provided for the repeal of the Oriental Exclusion Act of 1924, extending to Japan and other Asian countries a token immigration quota. It also eliminated race as a bar to citizenship. Truman vetoed the bill for reasons not linked to Japanese Americans, but the JACL made a determined lobbying effort to override the veto. The Nisei sought editorial support in local newspapers, and Nisei veterans got in touch with men they had known while in uniform. Congress passed the bill over the presidential veto by a vote of 278–113 in the House and 57–26 in the Senate.

The McCarren-Walter Act was a big step for the Issei. Hundreds of them enrolled in citizenship courses sponsored by local churches, JACL chapters, and other organizations. Further JACL legal successes came with passage of the Immigration Act of 1965, which ended the national-origins quota system. Since 1970, Japanese immigration has averaged about 4,000 annually. They are overwhelmingly skilled workers and professionals, and many are business investors. They arrive with high levels of formal education, strong English-language skills, and middle-class or higher status.

Since 1965, Japanese Americans, and more especially the Sansei, have achieved remarkable success. By nearly any criterion they have become the most successful of all minority groups. As one scholar wrote: "Perhaps the model choice for handling the problem of visibility has been 'psychological passing': identifying and acquiring the American culture at such a rapid rate that they have been termed as America's model minority" (Kitano 1976, 200; see also Marger 2003, 353).

The Nisei and Sansei have higher average formal education than any other group in the United States, including whites. They have been very upwardly mobile. In occupational choice, they have concentrated in the professions, particularly architecture, medicine, dentistry, engineering, teaching, and pharmacy. They have moved into highly technical fields. Their average income exceeds that of all other nonwhites and is comparable in amount and distribution to that of whites. As a group, and in contrast to Chinese Americans, they have exhibited low rates of juvenile delinquency, divorce, and mental illness. They overwhelmingly live in middle-class housing. Their out-marriage rate exceeds 50 percent. More than 15 percent of them hold professional jobs, far higher than any other minority group and on a par with whites. Over 88 percent have high school degrees and over 35 percent graduated college. At less than 3 percent below the poverty level, they exceed the national average and the rate of whites in poverty. A Japanese-American child can expect to live six to seven years longer than a white child, and ten to twelve years longer than a black child. Crime figures are even more telling. While arrest rates for white, black, Hispanic, and Native American adults have soared during the past three decades, those for Japanese-American adults, which were never high, declined sharply.

They exhibit considerable evidence of secondary and even primary cultural assimilation. Their record in business, the professions, housing, joining voluntary associations, and dating is remarkable. Their out-marriage rate is higher than for any other racial minority, changing from 11 percent in 1949 to 20 percent in 1959, to 33 percent in the 1960s. A 1973 study found 50 percent of Sansei married outside their race. It peaked at 63.1 percent in 1977. By 1989, another study found their out-marriage rate was 51.9 percent. In the 2000 census, 69.3 percent of those self-identifying as Japanese did so as "Japanese alone," but 30.7 identified themselves in combination with another racial group—the highest of any detailed Asian subgroup in the census.

Several theories have been advanced to account for their remarkably successful assimilation. The **value-compatibility theory** holds that traditional Japanese values are highly compatible with white middle-class values and stress upward social mobility. Politeness, respect for authority, attention to parental wishes, and duty to the community, plus the stress on hard work, cleanliness, neatness, and honesty coupled with an emphasis on formal education, are traditional Japanese values that mirror traditional values of Anglo Americans, and their acceptance of these values played an important part in the relationship of the two groups. The **community cohesion theory** accounts for why these values were so effectively socialized among the Nisei and Sansei generations, stressing the way their values were transmitted to the entire ethnic group (McLemore 1983).

Despite this impressive record there are gaps, so they are categorized as having a high level of segmented assimilation rather than as being fully assimilated. While third and fourth generations are rapidly entering the professions, Japanese Americans remain heavily concentrated in agriculture. Gardening is still dominated by them in California. In business they have yet to achieve the higher corporate levels except in Japanese-owned firms, and they are significantly underrepresented in the art and entertainment fields. Outside of Hawaii, where they compose about 37 percent of the population, they have comparatively little political power, and their impact on mainland politics has been minor. Congressional representatives of Japanese American descent are from Hawaii and California.

Korean Americans

At just under 10 percent of the Asian-American population, Korean Americans rank in fifth place in 2005. They exhibit a classic case of using the economic path to accommodation. They often play the role of the "middleman minority"—acting as a sort of buffer between the dominant society and other minority groups, especially blacks and Hispanics, among whom they live and work. Though small in total numbers (currently just about 1.4 million), they are Asian Americans who illustrate a pattern of accommodation typical of that wider community, even as they present some characteristics that differ from those of other Asian Americans, particularly Chinese Americans and Japanese Americans.

Korean immigration can be described in terms of three distinct phases or waves. Their early immigration was brief: 1903–1905. The second wave was between 1951 and 1965; the third, and largest, wave has occurred since 1965.

The earliest group of Korean immigrants, like the Chinese and Japanese before them, came first to the territory of Hawaii. From 1902 to 1905, just over 7,000 Koreans migrated to Hawaii to work on the islands' plantations. This migration was organized by the Hawaii Sugar Planters Association. They typically were young males between 18 and 35 years of age. The ratio of male to female was 6 to 1. About 1,000 of those original immigrants went on to the mainland, mostly California, in 1905. Unusual for Asian immigrants, a significant portion were Christian, which aided in their segmented assimilation, some acculturation and acceptance by white Americans (Kim 1977). Their involvement in Christian churches not only assured them a more sympathetic reception by whites, it gave members of the Korean community who were not in clan associations or sworn to a brotherhood group a chance to engage in social interaction outside of their work camps. Even non-Christian Korean parents saw the value of sending their children to Christian schools.

The first group of Korean immigrants was from the lower class in Korea. They were contracted to work in Hawaii as cheap labor to replace the Chinese and Japanese, and their wages were lower than that paid to the latter two groups. In the American labor force, the early Korean immigrants were concentrated in agriculture as laborers, or in urban areas as dishwashers, kitchen helpers, and janitors. They largely devoted whatever political activity they engaged in to lobbying around issues relating to their homeland.

At the time of their original migration, Korea was under the influence of both diplomatic and economic pressure from Japan. The Japanese government went so far as to induce the Korean government to appoint the Japanese consul in Hawaii, Saito Kan, as the honorary Korean consul in May 1905. The Korean community did not accept the consul, however, and continued to petition the government to appoint a Korean national as their consul. After 1905, the Korean government bowed to Japanese pressure and no longer allowed Koreans to emigrate. Some in Hawaii returned home; others moved on to the mainland. By 1910, Korea was colonized by Japan, and further immigration was limited to about 1,000 "picture brides," who came between 1910 and 1924.

The second wave of Korean immigrants came during 1951–1965. Numbering about 25,000, they were mostly wives of American servicemen, Korean War orphans adopted by Americans, and students. Instead of being located mainly in one area, they were geographically widely dispersed.

The third wave of Korean immigration, the largest and most significant influx, came after 1965, when the U.S. government repealed the national-origins quota system that was the basis of U.S. immigration policy since 1924. This latest wave averaged over 15,000 Korean immigrants per year from 1965 to 1980 and over 33,000 per year since 1980. Unlike the pre-1965 waves, they are higher educated, from middle-class backgrounds, skilled workers or professionals, or businessmen. They more often migrate in family units.

The 2000 census data has Korean-American population at just over 1,228,000, and over 56 percent of them had entered from 1980 to 1990. As with other recent Asian immigrants, Korean immigrants are decidedly middle- to upper-class with high levels of education achieved in the United States. By 1993, their median family income, at $33,909, approached the national average of $35,108. By the 2000 census their median family income exceeded the national average. In the 2000 census data, over 80 percent of Korean Americans are high school graduates (compared to the national average of 58.8 percent), and 34.4 percent have college degrees (compared to the national average of 20.4 percent). Their employment patterns reflect that higher educational background and family income status. While 13 percent of Korean Americans were employed as operators, fabricators, and laborers (as compared to the national average of 18.6 percent of the 1990 labor force), and 15 percent were employed in service jobs (compared to the national average of 18.1 percent), over 13.3 percent worked in the professions, exceeding the national average of 12.3 percent. A study of the Korean-American community in Los Angeles found that over 40 percent of the heads of households were self-employed (as compared to 8 percent of the general population), and 80 percent worked in Korean-owned firms, mostly in the service and retail trades. The Korean settlement in Los Angeles, historically the nation's largest, grew tenfold in the decade after 1965. The Korean-American community is fairly dispersed geographically.

The large influx of Korean immigrants since 1970 led to an organizational resurgence among Korean Americans. The explosive growth of the Korean-American population in the Los Angeles metropolitan area, for example, gave rise to over 50 nonprofit community organizations, 50 church groups, 4 Buddhist temples, and more than 50 high school alumni groups (Kim 1977).

Among Korean-American business enterprises, major-sized firms are concentrated in oriental foods, packing, and truck farming. Most Korean-American businesses, however, involve small firms, concentrated mostly in retail and service enterprises. Among retail businesses, they are most often found in grocery, market, and liquor stores; in hardware and electric appliance shops; in software retail stores; in gift shops; and in wholesale trading, especially wig shops and grocery wholesalers. Among service businesses, Korean Americans are concentrated in food and entertainment; in semiprofessional services such as travel, insurance, and real estate; in professional services such as accounting, income tax preparation, medicine, and dentistry; in such small-scale service enterprises as photography and art studios, printing shops, beauty shops, and shoe repair shops; and in larger-scale services such as auto repair and garages.

As mentioned earlier, in their role as small businessmen, and because of the location of their business enterprises, Korean Americans have become the "middleman minority," the buffer between the dominant white society and other racial minorities, especially blacks and Hispanics (Blalock 1967; Bonacich 1973; Bonacich and Modell 1980; Marger 2003; Turner and Bonacich 1980; Zenner 1991). That role has led them typically to being cast as scapegoats and the target of interracial violence. Among the black communities in Los Angeles and New York, where Korean Americans operate one-quarter of the small businesses, they are resented by blacks, who commonly accept the stereotypical image of Koreans getting help in starting such enterprises from the government and at the expense of the black community. In reality, the base of Korean venture capital comes from pooling family resources.

Korean-American immigrant success in business has undoubtedly contributed greatly to their achieving middle-class economic status in the United States. The degree of Korean-American segmented assimilation correlates with the following characteristics: education, length of residence, present occupation, religion, and proficiency in the English language.

Other Asian Immigrant Groups, Post-1965

A number of other Asian groups have relied heavily on the economic accommodation tactic that arrived overwhelmingly after and often as a result of the changes in immigration policy enacted in the 1965 act and its amendments. This section will be limited to a brief discussion that highlights the experience of Filipino Americans and Southeast Asians.

Filipino Americans   Filipino Americans are the second largest group that identify themselves and are categorized by the Census Bureau under Asian Americans. In 2005 they numbered just over 2,800,000 or about one percent of the U.S. population and about 22 percent of the Asian American population. They are concentrated in California, Hawaii, Washington, Guam, and in the Chicago and New York City Metropolitan areas. They are the second largest group of citizens who became naturalized since 2000.

Culturally, the Philippines is the most Westernized nation in Asia, with a lengthy legacy of Spanish and American colonial rule, and that history makes them often Catholic in religious tradition and fluent in speaking English. Filipino immigrants, therefore, experience minimal cultural shock. There the most common language is Tagalog, which is the fifth most-spoken language in the United States, with over 1,200,000 speakers.

As mentioned above, Filipinos arrived heavily after 1965, and they especially utilized the third preference category coming as nurses and other health care professionals. Filipino immigrants are, therefore, highly educated persons. Census Bureau data indicate some 60,000 professionals immigrated in the 1990s. Many come as university and post-graduate students and then become permanent resident aliens. Since 2000, Filipino immigrants are second only to Mexican immigrants, with an average 70,000 migrating annually. About 75 percent consist of family-sponsored immigrants, with the remainder being employment-oriented. Since 2003, Filipino immigrants are eligible for dual citizenship, and in 2004 some 6,000 chose to do so.

Among Asian Americans, Filipino immigrants settle in a more dispersed pattern, living in settlements across the country and in neighborhoods that are racially and ethnically diverse. Their dispersed pattern and the ease with which they have integrated and assimilated into the United States have earned them the label of "Invisible Minority." The label reflects their lack of political power and representation, but also that their fluency in English meant they assimilated rapidly. Their political involvement is largely at the municipal level. Intermarriage is common and they have the highest rate of interracial marriage among Asian immigrant groups, with nearly 22 percent of Filipino Americans identified as of mixed-race blood.

In 1965 the Delano grape strike began when members of the Agricultural Workers Organizing Committee, comprised mostly of Filipino farm workers, walked off the farms of area grape growers demanding the federal minimum wage. Filipino labor leader Philip Vera Cruz served as the second vice-president and on the managing board of the United Farm Workers. Their role is discussed in Chapter 8. Filipinos have begun to use the political accommodation strategy in recent years. In 1987, Benjamin Cayetano became the first Filipino American and second Asian American elected Lt. Governor of a state, and in 1990 David Valderrama became the first Filipino American elected to a state legislature on the mainland (Maryland). In 1992 Velma Viloria became the first Filipino American woman elected mayor of a city (Lacey City in the Seattle area). In 1994, Benjamin Cayetano became the first Filipino American governor.

Southeast Asian Americans The post-1965 immigration changed dramatically in part as a result of the post-Vietnam War refugee flow. For the United States, in the decade after 1975 more people arrived from the same region and in such a short time and under such dire conditions than at any other time in its history. From 1975–1985, some 100,000 Southeast Asians arrived annually to the United States. The Vietnam War had resulted in millions of deaths of Vietnamese, Cambodians, and Laotians.

Southeast Asian refugees generally lived in camps in Asia for six months during which time they learned some English and basic information about the United States. They were sponsored into the country by church groups and American families. Having lost so much of their property and so many family lives, generally speaking the transition of the refugees involved a more difficult adjustment than that experienced by voluntary immigrants. Many came with few transferable skills, and faced considerable language barriers, and they often lived in substandard housing in densely populated urban neighborhoods. They relied very much upon economic accommodation, working long hours as factory workers, custodians, restaurant workers and other such positions that demanded less by way of English language proficiency and job skills.

As a group, they employed a pattern of many family members working to contribute to the household income. Many soon developed small business enterprises to attain some segmented assimilation. Cambodians, Laotians, and Thai are briefly highlighted here.

Cambodians and Laotians and hill tribe refugees (the Hmong and Mien) came to the United States in two waves: one after the fall of Saigon in 1975, and the second and larger wave in the early 1980s. In the 1980 census, about 16,000 persons claimed Cambodian (Kampuchean) ancestry. Many others of the refugees, however, identified themselves as ethnic Chinese. In 2005, about 206,000 Cambodians, comprising about 1.5 percent of the Asian population here and about a half-percent of the total population, were identified. Cambodians made great strides from 1975 to 2005 in pursuing careers and in education of their young. They established mutual assistance organizations and worshiped at Buddhist temples. Resettlement programs helped their transition into the United States economy. They developed a commercial district in such California cities as Long Beach in which they ran markets, tailor shops, and jewelry stores. The largest Cambodian enclave was in Los Angeles. In 1980 the United States government established a refugee resettlement program designed to settle them in twelve cities outside California. Many later returned to the state, however, and California is currently home to the greatest number of Cambodians living in the United States. Besides relying on economics for segmented assimilation, their adjustment to life in America has been marked by extended family ties, and strong ethnic communities to cope. They often self-segregate into low-rent areas in California to be among friends and relatives.

Laotians arrived in a large wave between 1979 and 1982, settling especially on the West Coast. In the 1980 census, just over 53,000 claimed Laotian ancestry, and about another 3,000 claimed Laotian and other ethnic ancestry. This number was undercounted as nearly 111,000 refugees were admitted prior to 1984. By 1986, some 162,000 Laotian refugees had arrived. Included under the national identity of Laotians are the various hill tribes, most notably the Hmong and the Mien. They had allied themselves with the United States against the communist Pathet Lao, which took power in Laos in 1975, and began a campaign to exterminate the Hmong, killing an estimated ten percent of the population. By 2005, 186,000 claimed Hmong ancestry. The Hmong and Mien came to the United States from refugee camps, mostly in Thailand. They faced a much greater cultural transition: from slash and burn jungle agriculture to a largely urban settlement in the United States. The hill tribes formed associations based on clans and religious practices, and ran the gamut from soccer teams to self-help associations, to meal programs for the elderly. For jobs, they most often found work in low-paying jobs, such as meat packers, and clothing manufactory workers. They, too, used the extended family ties and mutual help associations. They exhibit slow occupational advancement, heavier reliance upon public welfare programs, and have remained socially isolated, with very small out-marriage rates. They sought a return to agricultural occupations, mostly as farm laborers in California's Central Valley, especially near Fresno and Merced, California. More recently, Hmong have settled in Missoula, Montana, an area similar to their Laotian homeland, and in or near Portland, Oregon, and Minneapolis-St. Paul.

Thai   In the 1980 census, just over 52,000 claimed Thai ancestry, and another 11,000 claimed Thai and some other ethnic ancestry. That number of roughly 64,000 is undercounted because 70,500 Thais immigrated to the United States between 1960 and 1984. Most Thai are ethnic Thai, but a number are ethnic Chinese who comprised about 12 percent of the country. Most came to the United States as students, temporary visitors, or spouses of U.S. military personnel rather than as refugees. In 2005, about 150,000 claimed Thai ancestry, comprising just over one percent of Asian Americans and about one-half of a percent of the total population.

Los Angeles has the largest Thai American population, with about 66 percent of all Thais in America, but other concentrations are found in Chicago, New York City, Houston Texas, and Philadelphia Pennsylvania. Many smaller Thai communities are found around U.S. military bases around the country. By 2002 some 80,000 Thais resided in the Los Angeles metropolitan area. Thais have notably started their own businesses, especially Thai restaurants, which are fast becoming ubiquitous. Thai Buddhist temples offer Thai language classes, music and culture for Thais who grew up in America, and are the centers and meeting places for Thai cultural festivals. Their children are students, many finding jobs upon graduation in the professions and in white-collar occupations. In terms of religious affiliation, Thais are Hinayana Buddhists or Muslims, although in America there are now many Thai Christians found among mainstream churches. Thais have been largely politically inactive to date, exhibiting some lobbying in foreign relations controversies involving their homeland politics. In 2006 a city councilman of La Palma became the first, and so far only, elected official of Thai descent, although two others ran but lost in city government elections, one in Houston and one in Anaheim, California. In the 2006 mid-term congressional election, a Thai American who is an Iraq war veteran ran for the United States Congress to represent Illinois' sixth district, but she was narrowly defeated. Had she won, she would have been the first Thai American in Congress.

European Immigrants

German Americans

Immigrants from Germany exceed those from any other nation. According to the 2000 census, nearly 46 and one-half million persons reported German ancestry. They rank first among all Euro-American ancestry groups. Their migration has been long and consistent, going back to colonial times and before the government started counting persons entering. Among the foreign-born persons reporting in the 2000 census, persons of German birth comprise about 2 percent. Over 10 percent of all persons legally entering the United States from 1990 to 2000 came from Germany. Total German legal immigration exceeds 7 million. Given the size of their migration, German Americans exhibit the use of several coping strategies. Most came when their job skills were desired and opportunities were abundant and they pursued economic accommodation. Their experience serves as a case study for most European immigrants to the United States. In educational attainment, over 80 percent claiming German ancestry are high school graduates, with 22 percent having a bachelor's degree, and over 7 percent having a graduate degree. Their median age is just over 33. As of 1998, over 68 percent of those over 16 years of age were employed, and only 4.5 percent were unemployed. Their median household income (1998) was $38,216. Only 5.5 percent were below the poverty level.

Three major currents of German immigration are commonly distinguished: the colonial period, when they came mostly for religious and economic reasons; from 1848 to the Civil War, when they came for political and economic reasons; and post–Civil War, when they came primarily for economic opportunity, often having been recruited by the various state governments, the railroads, several industries, and by friends or relatives already here.

German immigrants were never one nationality; their distinctive "Germanness" developed here, when they were treated alike, as German Americans. Until 1870, there was only a loose federation of many German states. Indeed, for much of modern history, the Germans have been a hybrid people of German-speaking states in Central Europe and Austria, Hungary, Luxembourg, Switzerland, Poland, Czechoslovakia, and Russia. In America, they were all considered the same, categorized for immigration purposes based on their common language. Although the WASP majority viewed them as a single people, they were a fairly diverse group splintered by regional strife and along religious lines.

During the colonial period, German-American immigration patterns were distinguished by the movement of entire communities bound together by family relations and often sharing the same religious sect, a pattern of immigration referred to as "chain migration." They sought and cultivated some of the richest farmland in colonial America, serving as the "breadbasket" for Revolutionary forces. Scattered thinly among the total population, they were united only by language and had little political clout or interest beyond their local affairs. They had high intermarriage rates with the Anglo native stock, facilitating a rapid assimilation. Geographically, they came from Europe as Palatinates, Salzburgers, Wurttenburgers, and Hanoverians. Religiously, they were Mennonites, Dunkers, Lutherans, Calvinists, and (a few) Jews.

The outbreak of the Revolutionary War changed attitudes toward Germans. Though widely scattered, they still made up the single largest nationality group after the British. They felt no special loyalty to the British crown and were unfriendly to the Tories, who favored continued union with England. At first reluctant to become involved in colonial politics, they did become converted to the cause of independence. Several German regiments were raised and fought prominently and well in the Revolution. Their service was widely recognized and helped develop a spirit of respect. Several states even passed laws that translated statutes and other government proceedings into German. Their Revolutionary wartime service was a major step toward being accepted and toward their assimilation. As their general social and economic conditions improved, they began to take a more active part in public affairs. In partisan politics, they tended to align with the Democrats, since, as small farmers, they never were at home with the eastern establishment.

During the 1830s and 1840s, Germans immigrated for different reasons. The agricultural revolution hit Central Europe, and inheritance laws requiring land to be equally divided among all children led to small subsistence farms that became too small to support them in tough times, forcing many off the land. They turned to manufacturing—clocks, tools, and the like—but even this left them overly vulnerable to economic change. When the potato famine struck, their choice was often to emigrate or starve. Fortunately, this coincided with the opening of the American Midwest. Texas, the Great Lakes region, and the Ohio River valley all became home to these new settlers. As midwestern cities exploded in population, they attracted large German migrations. Chicago, Detroit, Milwaukee, Cincinnati, and St. Louis led the way to a swath of land some 200 miles wide, stretching across the northern tier of states from New York down to Maryland and across to the Mississippi River, known as the "German belt."

Political turmoil in Germany, culminating in the 1848 Revolution, caused many German intellectuals to flee to America. The "forty-eighters," as they became known, contributed significantly to the liberal movement in states where they settled. Even though they numbered only about 10,000, this cohort of immigrants wielded influence far beyond their numerical strength. They started German-language newspapers, reading societies, theaters, and other cultural activities. Though the full extent of their influence is debated, the forty-eighters provided important leadership in the American labor movement. In the newly emerging conservation movement, the forty-eighter Carl Schurz led the drive to save virgin forestland and became the first secretary of the interior in 1877. Further, they were prominent in the antislavery movement and instrumental in the founding of the Republican Party, where they took credit—undoubtedly an inflated claim—for the election of Lincoln, who had invested in a German-language paper.

During and after the Civil War, German immigrant labor filled slots in the desperately needed northern industrial labor force caused by the war. The booming economy drew them to areas of high demand, and became a major factor in their rapid absorption into mainstream American life. The largest wave of German immigrants came after the Civil War period. The Homestead Act of 1862 offered free land to the overcrowded population of Germany. Western states advertised for German farmers, who had a reputation of being hardworking and highly productive. State governments joined the railroads in sending agents to induce German immigrants to settle and develop the abundant lands. An additional draw was America as a haven from the military conscription during the years of the German wars of unification.

German immigrants faced some opposition, most notably from the Know Nothing Party of the 1850s. German Catholics competed with the large wave of Irish Catholics, who dominated the hierarchy of the Catholic Church in America until the early 1900s when German clergy finally began to fill some leadership roles. World War I resulted in a temporary setback in their assimilation. They initially opposed the war, which resulted in a period of heightened nationalism. Once the United States formally entered the war, opposition ceased and the German-American community supported the war effort.

Another uniting issue was German-American opposition to Prohibition. The importance of beer to their cultural heritage, and the fact that America's brewing industry was nearly exclusively in their hands, accounted for their opposition. Prohibition threatened the brewers with financial disaster.

In 1916, Congress established the Council of National Defense to speed up assimilation of German and other nationality groups. Its impact was debatable but the act was extended to the states. Several midwestern state legislatures enacted comparable statutes granting the state government, and often local and county councils, sweeping powers to investigate and punish for contempt. The councils forbade the use of the German language in schools, churches, over the telephone, and in semipublic places. While forced acculturation is problematic at best, the banning of the use of German probably sped up the process of acculturation. Postwar isolationism reflected a phobia against everything foreign. Isolationist voting was strongest in those states with heavy German-American populations. Perhaps the disillusion after World War I turned them inward.

After President Franklin D. Roosevelt's election in 1936, his administration adopted a distinctly anti-German foreign policy, triggering a substantial defection of German Americans from the Democratic Party at all levels. While as a group they demonstrated their loyalty to the nation by their sons' conduct in the war effort, in the privacy of the voting booth they voted anti-Roosevelt. After his death they came back to the party in the 1948 election in significant enough numbers that they contributed to President Truman's surprise victory. After World War II, they were no longer a distinct voting bloc. Today, they are part of the Anglo-Teutonic white stock that composes the majority society and they are fully assimilated. Their pattern of assimilation was closely followed by immigrants from Scandinavia.

Scandinavian Americans

According to 2000 census data, 1,505,450 persons identify themselves as Danish, 4,524,953 as Norwegian, and 4,342,150 as Swedish. Thus, nearly 10 and one-half million Americans claim Scandinavian background.

Scandinavians were among the first European people to explore the New World. Viking explorations and tiny settlements have been traced back to the period of 800 to 1050. In the mid-1600s, several scandinavian settlements were established in what is now Delaware. A few immigrants continued to come from Norway, Sweden, and Denmark, but their numbers were not substantial until after the Civil War. From then on, motivated by such factors as religious dissension, voting disenfranchisement, crop failures, and related economic factors, Scandinavians emigrated in large numbers. Total Scandinavian immigration to the United States exceeds 2.5 million. The Swedes hit their peak in 1910 and the Norwegians in the 1920s. Although the Norwegians, Swedes, and Danes came from countries with diverse governments, traditions, and languages, their physical characteristics and a tendency to settle together in the United States led to the use of the term "Scandinavian" to refer to all three groups.

Scandinavians were a very successful group of immigrants. They were willing to work hard. They arrived in better financial shape than most groups, which enabled them to escape the poverty, slums, and resulting stereotyping and social stigma of the eastern seaboard cities with their "teeming immigrant masses." By 1880, the average Scandinavian immigrant arrived with $60 to $70. Such sums enabled them to reach the Midwest and its abundant and cheap land on which their farming skills could be put to good use. Farming was not their only trade. They went into business, commerce, manufacturing, finance, and the professions. In the frontier settlements they succeeded in setting up their own stores, shops, factories, and banks. Before the 1890s, they were concentrated in the midwestern states whose soil and climate reminded them of their homelands, and where their successful settlements attracted others. Minnesota, Wisconsin, Iowa, Illinois, and the Dakotas all saw dramatic increases in their populations due to this influx. By the 1890s, they were increasingly attracted to the industrial opportunities in the Northeast and to the lumber industry of the Pacific Northwest. By 1920, Chicago had the largest number of Swedes of any city but Stockholm and more Norwegians than any city but Oslo.

Scandinavian assimilation proved comparatively easy. They entered the majority society largely through the economic path. Their political involvement generally followed economic and social success. Several factors account for the relative ease of their assimilation. They did not have to overcome the stigma of some "undesirable" trait. They were Caucasian and escaped racial prejudice. They were strongly Protestant, avoiding anti-Catholic sentiment. They came in relatively small numbers over a long period of time, compared to the huge waves of Irish and Italians, who came by the millions in a decade. Thus, Scandinavians did not suffer the scapegoat effect. Anti-immigrant hatred was directed toward the Irish and Italians arriving at the same time who were feared as job competitors and as "papists." Coming in smaller waves and with sufficient money and job skills to reach the Midwest, they were not viewed as threats to dominant society's labor force. They also worked hard at becoming "Americans." Strongly desiring to assimilate, they soon mastered English. Schools were important in their settlements and they insisted on schools that taught English.

Being overwhelmingly Protestant, their religion gave them a common bond with the majority. They were mostly Lutherans and were considered more devout and strait-laced than German Lutherans. Their stern faith frowned on drinking, dancing, and levity, and stressed piety and the work ethic. Many were anti-Catholic and were accepted more readily by a native stock with whom they shared a common enemy. Unlike the Irish and Italian groups whose loyalty to a unified Catholic church kept ties to the old country and customs, earning them the suspicion and enmity of WASPs, Scandinavians formed numerous new churches often based on American ideas, easing their incorporation.

Financial success helped them socially. The Homestead Act of 1862 provided cheap land, so they became established without going heavily into debt. Their standard of living was soon comparable to that of the dominant society located in frontier settlements. Describing Norwegian settlers in the Dakotas in the late 1890s, one writer said: "Most of them came with just enough money to buy government land and build a shack. Now they loan money to their neighbors . . . every county has Norwegians worth $25,000 to $50,000, all made since settling in Dakota" (cited in Dinnerstein and Reimers 1988, 97–98).

By the turn of the century they understood American-style politics with its numerous points of access: elections, representation, constitutions, and fragmented political power distributed among many local governments. They were patriotic. They organized political groups to get information on laws and elections, and learned American-style politics by organizing new townships, working on town government, levying and collecting taxes, and laying out new roads. In the early stages of their political development, sometimes more than a fifth of the men participated in town affairs.

The first Scandinavian-born politician to enter state-wide politics was a Norwegian, James Reymert, who represented Racine County in the second constitutional convention of Wisconsin in 1847. After the Civil War Scandinavians became more visible in state-level politics. Norwegian-born Knute Nelson was the first state governor. He was elected, in succession, to the legislatures of Wisconsin and then Minnesota, to the U.S. Congress, and as governor of Minnesota on the Republican ticket in 1892. By the turn of the century, many Scandinavians served in the state legislatures of Wisconsin, Minnesota, and the Dakotas. They tended to be Republicans, whose stand against slavery and status as the party of "moral ideas" appealed to them. By the mid-1900s, they had ceased to be thought of as a foreign ethnic group. Third-generation Scandinavians were firmly and fully part of the WASP majority. Since the 1970s, only a few thousand have emigrated from the Scandinavian countries to the United States. Those coming today tend to be highly skilled craftsmen, professionals, or prospective business executives. They tend to assimilate quickly and easily. They are less likely than those of the past to have feelings of ethnic community.

Immigrants coming to the United States in massive numbers between 1880 and 1920 are categorized as the "new" immigrants. They came in larger waves, mostly from South, Central, and Eastern Europe. They came for various reasons, responding to several push factors. Their greater variety in immigration patterns shows a propensity to use several coping strategies. The next section of this chapter discusses groups who use both economic and political tactics to accommodate. Here we examine Russian Americans and their use of the economic route.

Russian Americans

The earliest Russian immigration to America goes back to Alaska and California in the mid-1700s. In 1792, the first Russian Orthodox Church was built in America, and by 1812 a sizable settlement was founded in Sonoma, California, which lasted for thirty years before the entire group of several hundred was recalled to Russia by the Czar. The headquarters of the Russian Orthodox Church in America moved to San Francisco in 1872, after which time the first sizable immigration wave came, mostly Mennonites who fled to the Grain Plains area and numbered about 40,000. Between 1900 and 1913, some 51,000 Russian immigrants arrived, of which about 45 percent were Jews fleeing persecution in Russia. Their peak period was between 1880 and 1914. Most came seeking better economic opportunity. In 1917, the Russian Revolution essentially ended emigration until about 1970.

The 1965 Act permitted more extensive immigration from Russia, and their pattern now is more typical of the post-1965 trend. In the 2000 census, nearly 3 million claimed Russian ancestry, up from 1990 when just over 2 million persons claimed it. In 1990, 9.2 percent were Russian-born, over 34 percent of those arrived between 1980 and 1990. Their median age is 41.6, compared to the median age of the total population of 33. Like most of the post-1965 wave of immigrants, Russian Americans are well-educated. Among persons 25 years or older, 90.8 percent are high school graduates, 49 percent hold a bachelor's degree or higher, and 24.3 percent had a graduate degree. Sixty-six percent of Russian immigrants were in the labor force, and only 4.2 percent were unemployed, compared to 6.3 percent of all persons.

Occupationally, Russian immigrants had 51.5 percent in managerial and professional ranks; another 33.7 percent were in technical, sales, or administrative jobs. Only 5.5 percent were in the service sector, and a mere .6 percent were in farming. In industry, Russian immigrants were in production, craft, and repair jobs; with only 4.1 percent in blue-collar jobs as operators, fabricators, and laborers. In terms of class of workers, over 73 percent were in the private sector with wage or salary occupations, 8 percent worked for local government, 4.2 percent for the state, and 2.6 percent with the federal government. Nearly 12 percent of Russian Americans were self-employed in 2000. In terms of workers per family household, 26.4 percent of Russian-American families were single-wage-earner families, 49.1 percent were two-wage-earner families, and 11 percent depended on three or more workers. Their household median family income was above the national average, and their poverty rate below the national average. Their family percent in the poverty level was 3.6 compared to that of 10 percent for all persons; and their percent of persons in poverty was 6.1 compared to that of 13.1 percent for all persons (http://www.census.gov/population/socdemo/ancestry/tables01-07).

Russian immigrants pre-1965 worked in coal and other mines and in the iron and steel mills of Pennsylvania and the slaughterhouses of Chicago. They were heavily employed in the clothing and cigar industries in New York City. They held unskilled jobs in construction and with the railroads. They tended to be non-unionized, except for the United Mine Workers and the Industrial Workers of the World. Their pay was typically low-scale. By 1910, they worked an average 12 hour day for just over $2. As late as 1919, Russian immigrants in Chicago earned only $12 to $30 per week.

A few Russian immigrants did establish agricultural settlements, which were small and scattered. Most Russian immigrants live in the cities, in substandard housing. Those working in construction gangs lived in three-tier bunkhouses. In the congested enclaves of Eastern European immigrants in the steel and iron mill towns, health problems were severe.

Post-1965, they have begun to become involved in American politics, focusing on lobbying about U.S. foreign-policy vis-à-vis Russia. Those who do participate in politics tend to vote Democrat. The post-1965 wave includes Jewish refugees, and today those fleeing the post-Soviet Russia for better economic opportunity. They can be described as being partially segmented assimilated, and at the beginning stages of political incorporation. To date there are no prominent elected Russian Americans in upper level positions in state or national government.

Greek Americans

Americans claiming Greek ancestry in the 2000 census numbered 1,175,591. According to a 1998 census bureau report, 77.9 percent have high school diplomas, 28 percent are college graduates, and nearly 11 percent have graduate degrees. Their median family income was $43,330, and just 5.2 percent of their families were reported in the poverty level. Among those claiming Greek heritage, nearly 68 percent of those over 16 years of age were employed, and just over 5 percent were unemployed. Twenty-one percent of those claiming Greek ancestry identified themselves as foreign-born. Their median age was 33.6

Greeks have been coming to America since colonial times. A scattering came as explorers, sailors, cotton merchants, gold miners, and as settlers of the ill-fated Smyrna colony in Florida in 1768. They arrived in significant numbers after 1880. Between 1900 and 1920, they reached their peak immigration when 350,000 arrived. Although they came from all parts of Greece, the majority were young, unskilled males from the villages in the south.

As with other South, Central, and Eastern Europeans, various push factors led to their migration. Although political persecution played a role, economic conditions in Greece was the most compelling. The rapid rise in population led to an overpopulation that the islands could simply no longer support. By 1931, even after decades of extensive emigration, there were 870 persons for every square mile of cultivated land (Thernstrom 1980). Another push factor was the ongoing state of war between Greece and Turkey. The Balkan War of 1912–1913 caused the peak period of Greek immigration to the United States, when many fled the compulsory military service in what they considered to be a Turkish tyranny. Many Greeks, like the Italians and Chinese, came as "sojourners," young men intending to earn enough money to provide a substantial dowry for the prospective brides in their families. The fact that about 95 percent of the early Greek immigrants were young males meant that many returned home for brides.

The opportunity for better jobs was the single most important factor drawing Greeks to the United States. Greek immigrants who arrived in the 1880–1920 period settled in one of three major areas: the West, to work on railroad gangs and in the mines; New England, to work in the textile and shoe factories; and New York, Chicago, and other large cities, to work in factories or as busboys, dishwashers, bootblacks, and peddlers.

Greeks used and were exploited by a padrone system. The padrone found jobs for the immigrants, assisted with language problems, and settled disputes. Often the padrone's "clients" were young boys sent directly to the padrone, who arranged for their room and board and a small wage. The wage was prearranged and agreed to by the parents. Unfortunately, they did not know the conditions under which the boys lived—squalid and crowded basement rooms in the heart of the tenement slums. They worked 18 hours a day with no time set aside for lunch. The system was highly profitable for the padrone, who made an average of $100 to $200 and in some cases as much as $500 per year per boy. The boys themselves would receive about $100 to $180 annually in wages. The padrone system has been described as a modernized version of the indentured servant system of the late seventeenth and early eighteenth centuries (Soloutos 1964).

Although the majority of Greek immigrants were young and unskilled, some educated and skilled Greeks immigrated, meeting with unforeseen problems here. Greek lawyers could only practice law after learning English, studying for one year in an American law school, and then passing the bar exam. Greek physicians had it somewhat better; they were able to take a qualifying exam in Greek. Unless they were able to master a reasonable amount of English, however, their practice was confined to serving other Greek Americans. Many college graduates caught the emigration fever, but had few opportunities to proceed in their various interests. For the educated Greeks, it was difficult to find employment equal to their educational qualifications, and they felt it was beneath their dignity to work as unskilled laborers.

A fairly sizable number started their own businesses. They concentrated on confectioneries, candy stores, and restaurants. After World War I, there were an estimated 564 Greek restaurants in San Francisco alone. After World War II, there were 350 to 450 Greek-American confectionery shops and 8 to 10 candy manufacturing concerns in Chicago alone (Moskos 1980; Parrillo 1985).

Many Greeks went back and forth several times before finally staying in the United States. This back-and-forth migration pattern undoubtedly slowed their acculturation and assimilation rate. It led to a mutual lack of understanding (with the majority society) and often severe conflict. In 1904, for instance, a strike broke out in the diesel shops of Chicago. Heated union-management conflict left the city in a bad situation. Unaware of the conditions of the strike, inexperienced Greek immigrants served as strike-breakers. Since they broke the strike, they were considered the enemy by local unions. A period of severe anti-Greek press followed. Eventually the strike ended with the regular employees returning to work. By then, a strong anti-Greek sentiment had developed. In the West, a virulent nativist reaction directed at Greek immigrants erupted. In McGill, Nevada, three Greeks were killed in a 1908 riot. In Utah, where Mormons seemed particularly anti-foreign and anti-Greek, they were characterized in the Utah press as a vicious element unfit for citizenship and as ignorant, depraved, and brutal foreigners. A 1917 riot in Salt Lake City almost led to the lynching of a Greek immigrant accused of killing Jack Dempsey's brother. In Price, Utah, local citizens rioted and attacked Greek stores, forcing the American girls who worked in them to return home. The Ku Klux Klan was very active in Utah in the early 1920s, and Greeks were singled out as special targets (Moskos 1980). In Omaha, in 1909, a sizable Greek community of seasonal workers led to a strike-breaking situation that resulted in an ugly riot that caused thousands of dollars of damage to the Greek section of the city. Even supposedly scholarly work, such as that of sociologist Henry Pratt Fairchild, reflected anti-Greek sentiment. His work stereotyped Greek and Italian immigrants as being disproportionately "criminal types" and despaired of their ever being able to assimilate (see Fairchild 1911).

Greek immigrants often settled in small colonies where they could socialize with one another and practice their religion. Since the church and state were not separate in Greece, almost every Greek immigrant was a member of the Greek Orthodox Church. An unwillingness to practice their faith with others, even with other branches of the Eastern Orthodox Church, tended to isolate Greeks from the mainstream of religious society, slowing their assimilation rate.

Greek social life tended to isolate them. In the Greek community, the community council and the coffeehouses played a major role:

> In the Greek community, the *kinotitos*, or community council, was the governing body of the people. It provided for the establishment of churches and schools, hired and fired priests and teachers, and exerted a constant influence on Greek affairs. One could always gauge the feelings of the group by the actions of the *kinotitos*. For recreation, the Greeks flocked to their *kuffenein*, or coffee houses. These served as community social centers where men smoked, drank, conversed, and played games in what became literally a place of refuge after a hard day of work or an escape from the dank and dreary living quarters. No Greek community was without its *kuffenein*, and one chronicler reported that in Chicago before World War I, "every other door on Bolivar Street was a Greek coffee house." (Dinnerstein and Reimers 1988, 54)

The Greek church, the Greek-language press (such as the *Atlantis*), and the more than 100 Greek societies all encouraged cohesiveness and slowed assimilation. The largest and most notable of the Greek societies was the American Hellenic Educational Progressive Association (AHEPA). It was founded in 1922 to preserve Greek heritage and help immigrants understand the American way of life. Greek family life was close-knit and stressed education, particularly higher education. Law and medicine were especially valued. Greek education impacted the whole family. Greek children went to two schools: the public school and the Greek-language school. Mandatory for most children, the purpose of the latter was to maintain communication between the parent, the child, and the church, and to preserve the Greek heritage in the new land. These schools were usually taught by priests to ensure the church's lifelong influence on the new generation. Children went to public school until mid-afternoon, then the Greek-language school until early evening. This process of dual education made it impossible for Greek children to participate in the after-school activities of the public schools, slowing their assimilation and that of their families. As of 1978, some 400 Greek-language schools were operating in the United States (Moskos 1980).

The beginnings of their change from sojourners to Greek Americans can be traced to the 1920s, when Congress passed restrictive immigration laws. The quota system of 1924 limited Greek immigration to 100 per year. This number contrasted sharply with the 28,000 Greeks who arrived in 1921, the last year of open immigration. In 1929, the Greek quota was changed to 307, where it stayed for the next 30 years. Non-quota immigration allowing families to reunite resulted in a yearly average of about 2,000 entering between 1924 and 1930. Closing the door had a profound impact on Greek America. Initially there was a scramble to acquire citizenship, for only naturalized citizens could bring over family members or be assured of returning if one visited Greece. Without the continued arrival of new immigrants, American-born Greeks soon became the majority within their group, and their ascendancy was inevitable. The new immigration policy set in motion forces that affected both individuals and demographic forces that shaped the entire Greek-American community.

Another important event was World War II. Italy's invasion of Greece in 1940 brought Greece into the war. The initial and heroic success of the Greek army in throwing back the Italian invasion had an exhilarating effect on the Greek-American community. Very favorable coverage of "Greek heroism" by the American mass media allowed Greek Americans to bask in unaccustomed glory. A Greek American War Relief

Association was immediately formed. It raised $5 million in five months, helping to save an estimated one-third of the Greek population. When the United States entered the war in 1941, Greek-American support of the war effort was overwhelming. With Greece and the United States joined in the struggle against the Axis powers, Greek and American interests came together as never before. AHEPA joined in the drive to sell war bonds and eventually sold a half-billion dollars worth. One AHEPA member, Michael Loris, was named the U.S. Champion War Bond Salesman in 1943 for selling 24,142 individual bonds. The Andrew Sisters, whose "support our boys" tunes made them the most popular singing group during the war years, were second-generation Greek Americans. World War II became a watershed in Greek America. The war effort became a matter of Greek pride combined with American patriotism.

That war effort, plus American involvement in the civil war in Greece that broke out after the war, deepened the tie. The 1947 Truman Doctrine capped a number of foreign policy moves that tied Greece to the American sphere and made President Truman a hero within the Greek-American community. At a White House gala in 1948, Truman became the only president to be initiated into AHEPA, and in 1963 the association erected a statue in Athens memorializing him.

The changed attitude among Greek Americans was reflected in a changed attitude within majority society toward them as well. Today, few negative comments about Greek Americans are heard. When they are singled out, it is to serve as a model of a nationality group that has been accepted, achieved economic security, and become Americanized while retaining a strong pride in their heritage. The postwar years saw increasing numbers of Greek Americans entering the middle class, with a majority of them in white-collar and professional occupations.

Table 3.4 presents data on the socioeconomic status of selected Euro-American ethnic groups as of 1990, rank ordering them by median family income and detailing the percent of college graduates among each of the selected national origin groups.

The postwar years saw renewed efforts to change their limited quotas. In the 1950s, non-quota Greeks coming to the United States numbered over 17,000, and by additional "borrowing on future quotas," some 70,000 Greeks entered between 1945 and 1965. The Immigration Act of 1965 abolished the quota system and led to a new wave, contributing to a lingering of Greek ethnic consciousness and a pluralistic adaptation to American life.

Today's Greek-American community numbers over 1,175,000. It is overwhelmingly urban, with over 94 percent of Greek Americans residing in urban areas, as compared to 73 percent of the total population. Nearly half of them live in or near eight large cities: New York, Chicago, Boston, Detroit, Los Angeles, Philadelphia, Cleveland, and Pittsburgh.

The central Greek-American institution today remains the Orthodox Church. Remarkably, the American-born generations are in many ways more Greek Orthodox than their contemporaries of the middle-class youth in urban Greece. The introduction of English into the service exemplifies the process of Americanization of the church. That acculturation is reflected to a lesser degree in new architectural design and other aesthetic aspects, in the changing role of women in the church, and in the number of non-Greeks joining the church through marriage. In the 1960s, mixed-marriage couples accounted for three out of ten church marriages. By the late 1970s, about half of all such marriages were mixed. The Greek Orthodox Church stands midway between an ethnic religion and a mainline church in its status. Its ethnicity is self-evident, but a striving for mainline status is

Table 3.4   Socioeconomic Status of Euro-American Ethnic Groups, 1990

Group	Median Family Income	Percent College Graduates
Russian	$58,826	49
Dutch	43,415	18
Greek	43,330	28
Scottish	43,293	34
Hungarian	42,778	27
Italian	42,242	21
Polish	41,700	23
English	40,875	28
Swedish	40,459	27
Slovak	40,072	22
Scotch-Irish	38,816	28
Portuguese	38,370	12
German	38,216	22
Irish	38,101	21
French	36,237	18

Source: Adapted from Martin N. Marger, *Race and Ethnic Relations, American and Global Perspectives,* 4th edition. © 1997. Reprinted with permission of Wadsworth, a division of Thomson Learning: www.thomsonrights.com. Fax 800 730-2215.

apparent in its acceptance of the legitimacy of other religions based not on sufferance or tolerance but as a tenet of its own religion in the pluralism of America (Moskos 1980).

HISPANIC AMERICANS

Mexican Americans

In the Southwest many Hispanics can trace their ancestry back to generations before Anglo Americans ever set foot in the area. They are nonetheless viewed as Mexicans and are seen as Catholics, as are virtually all Hispanics, even those who are Protestant or nonpracticing. Many are treated as racially different from Caucasians despite the fact that a majority are Caucasian. They are, in fact, quite diverse. They are many in number, so it should not be surprising that they vary in the strategies they employ to cope with their status. Chapter 4 will discuss their political route. Here, we describe their economic route to accommodation.

Since the mid-1950s, immigration to the United States has shifted dramatically from European countries to those of North America, Central America, South America, and Asia. From 1956 to 1976, while Asian immigration rose by a spectacular 369 percent and South American immigration rose by 27 percent, immigration from European countries declined by 27 percent.

In Census 2000, of the 281.4 million in total population, Hispanics were 35.3 million, or 12.5 percent. Among the total population, 7.3 percent were Mexican, 1.2

percent Puerto Rican, .4 percent Cuban, and 3.6 percent other Hispanic. An additional 3.8 million Hispanics were enumerated in the Commonwealth of Puerto Rico. From 1990 to 2000 the Hispanic population increased by 57.9 percent compared to an increase of 13.2 percent for the total U.S. population. Differing growth rates from 1990 to 2000 resulted in shifts in their proportionate distribution. In 2000, Mexicans were at 58.5 percent, down from 60.4 percent in 1990; Puerto Ricans were at 9.6 percent, down from 12.2 percent in 1990; Cubans were at 3.5 percent, down from 4.7 percent in 1990; and "other Hispanic" (mostly South and Central Americans) were at 28.4 percent, up from 22.8 percent in 1990. In 2005, the Bureau estimates the Hispanic population at 42.7 million, making people of Hispanic origin the largest racial/ethnic minority in the United States. They are also the fastest growing minority group, with continued legal and illegal immigration and natural birth rates more than double that of the national average.

Hispanics are decidedly urban, 90 percent of them living in about a dozen metropolitan areas, particularly Los Angeles, New York, Miami, Chicago, San Antonio, Houston, San Francisco, El Paso, Riverside/Ontario (California), and Anaheim (California). They are also concentrated in just a few states. In 2000, 27.1 million, or 76.8 percent, of Hispanics lived in just seven states, each of which had in excess of one million: California, Texas, New York, Florida, Illinois, Arizona, and New Jersey. Hispanics in New Mexico were 42.1 percent of the state's total population, the highest proportion of any state. The largest Mexican populations lived in Los Angeles, Chicago, Houston, San Antonio, and Phoenix. The largest Puerto Rican populations lived in New York, Chicago, and Philadelphia. The largest Cuban populations lived in Hialeah, Miami, New York, Tampa, and Los Angeles. The largest Central-American populations lived in Los Angeles, New York, Houston, Miami, and San Francisco, while the largest South-American populations are found in New York, Los Angeles, Chicago, and Miami. Mexicans now make up 64 percent of the Hispanic-origin population. The estimated Hispanic population of LA county in 2005 was a whopping 4.6 million. Hispanics are the largest minority population in nineteen states.

Table 3.5 presents data that compares Hispanic with Non-Hispanic White, Black, and Asian population as to their levels of income, employment, and education as of 2003 and 2004. It shows that Hispanics are at the lowest level of these socio-economic indicators.

They are a young population. As of 2005, the Census Bureau estimated the median age of the Hispanic population as 27.2 years, compared with 36.2 years for the population as a whole. The Hispanic population under 18 was 35.0 percent, compared to 25.7 percent for the total U.S. population. Their youth, high birth rates, and high immigration rates portend continued significant changes. The U.S. Bureau of the Census projects that by the year 2020, the Hispanic population will reach 39 million, displacing blacks as the nation's largest minority (http://www.census.gov/CensusBriefs, The Hispanic Population). By 2050, they are projected to grow to 102.6 million, which would constitute 24 percent of the nation's total population (http://www.census.gov/Press-Release/www/releases/archives/population/001720.html. Accessed 4/9/2007).

Differences in the tactical approach used by the various Hispanic groups reflect their status and opportunities. Many Cubans entered under a protected status of "refugees." They tend to be better educated, organized, and equipped to acculturate into the American job market structure. The majority society seems more willing to accept them,

Table 3.5   A Comparison of Hispanic, Non-Hispanic White, Black, and Asian Income/Employment/ Education, 2003–2004

	Median Income (2003 Dollars)	Poverty Level (2004)	Unemployed (2004)	High School Graduates (2004)	College Graduates (2004)
Non-Hispanic white	$55,768	10.5%	3.9%	85.8%	28.2%
Black	34,369	24.4	8.1	80.6	17.6
Asian	63,251	11.9	3.8	86.8	49.4
Hispanic	34,272	22.5	5.7	58.4	12.1

Source: U.S. Bureau of the Census, *Statistical Abstract of the United States, 2006* (Washington, DC: U.S. Government Printing Office, 2006), Tables 679, 214.

and they have been aided by special legislation and resettlement programs. This has eased their transition, enabled them to better employ the economic route, and assimilate more rapidly than any other Hispanic group. By contrast, Mexicans, many of whom have entered the United States illegally, remain much less organized and at the mercy of an economic system designed to exploit them. Economically, they remain at the lowest level of society, living in a social and cultural world apart from the majority society and lacking a real political voice because of their illegal status. The majority culture rejects them, seeing them as persons who, at best, will lower wages and depress working conditions and, at worst, will swell the ranks of the welfare and criminal justice systems. These differences in attitudes and receptions are reflected in the ratios at which these two Hispanic subgroups have achieved citizenship status.

Hispanics overall are making considerable economic progress. The census bureau in 2002 put the number of Hispanic-owned businesses at 1.6 million, and their rate of growth from 1997 to 2002 was 31 percent, compared to the national average of 10 percent. Those businesses generated $222 billion, up 19 percent from 1997. Mexicans owned 44 percent of all Hispanic-owned businesses in 2002. Nearly 3 in 10 Hispanic-owned firms were in construction and other services, such as personal services, repair, and maintenance. Retail and wholesale trade accounted for 36 percent of Hispanic-owned business revenue. States with the fastest rate of growth in Hispanic-owned firms were New York (57 percent), Rhode Island and Georgia (56 percent each), and Nevada and South Carolina (48 percent each). Counties with the highest number of Hispanic-owned firms were Los Angeles (188,472); Miami-Dade County (163,188), Harris County, Texas (61,934), and Bronx County, New York (38,325).

In terms of jobs, in 2005 68 percent of Hispanics age 16 and older were in the civilian labor force, among which 18 percent were in managerial, professional, and related occupations; 24 percent were in service occupations; 22 percent in sales and office jobs; 15 percent in construction, extraction, and maintenance jobs, and 19 percent in production, transportation, and material moving occupations.

Although success stories are to be found, the majority of Hispanics suffer from low status, high crime, low educational levels, ethnic discrimination, and economic exploitation. Those in rural areas (about 10 percent of the total) typically live in run-down shacks provided for migrant workers in an economic system akin to slavery. Those in urban areas are frequently limited to slum areas. In 2005, 21.8 percent of all

Hispanic families live below the poverty level, and their median income was $35,967. Gangs are rife among urban Hispanics, and gang-related violence is the major cause of death among their youth.

Hispanic poverty is linked to their low occupational backgrounds. They continue to have among the highest levels of unemployment in the United States: Hispanic poverty is also linked to their lower levels of formal educational achievement. Hispanic high school graduation rate in 2005 was 58 percent, and those with a bachelor's degree or higher was 12 percent. In 2004, an estimated 11 percent of all college students were Hispanic.

An especially important policy effect influencing the Hispanic population's post-1965 immigration pattern, particularly that from Mexico, is the **bracero program**, which legally brought in tens of thousands from Mexico annually.

Just over 4,000 workers entered under contract with the bracero program in 1942. The annual total rose steadily until its peak year of 1956, when 445,197 entered. During the period 1953 to 1960, the average annual influx was about 300,000. The programs coincided with a new wave of illegal migrants known as **wetbacks**. "Operation Wetback" in the 1960s entailed a concerted effort to deport the illegal immigrants. Over a five-year period, some 3.8 million illegals were apprehended and returned to Mexico. The program and its significance is described more fully in Box 3.3.

This wave of illegals from Mexico resurrected the restrictionist opposition. As amended, the 1965 Act imposed a regional quota system that allowed only 170,000 from the entire Western Hemisphere. The measure passed in no small measure due to the support of organized labor, which feared the impact of cheap labor from Mexico. The discrimination Mexican Americans faced was both intense and pervasive. They were referred to by a variety of derogatory slang terms: "cholo," "spik," "Mex," "beaner," "pachuco," and "greaser." They faced discrimination in jury selection, voting rights, and school enrollment. Even in 1970, Houston had a plan to "integrate" African and Mexican Americans into their schools and have whites attend their own. Next to the Native American, the Chicano ranks lower than any other group in American society in such areas as education, housing, and economic conditions. They are still highly segregated in housing, show low levels of intermarriage, and manifest highly ethnic-related friendship patterns. Their degree of incorporation more nearly resembles a "mixing bowl" than it does a "melting pot." They remain among the least 'Americanized' of all ethnic groups in the United States.

Three factors inhibited their incorporation: their continued pride in their Mexican culture, heritage, and language; their poor education; and the racial bias they face (about 40 percent are full-blooded Indians and approximately 95 percent have at least some Indian blood). Their close proximity to Mexico means their culture survives intact, more so than does that of most other minority groups. Conquest, racism, nativism, and the continued dependence of Mexico's economy on the United States have all played a part in keeping Chicanos in the role of servants. They make up a "secondary labor force"—concentrated in such unskilled jobs as laundry workers, packers, and taxi drivers or in such semiskilled crafts as masons, painters, plasterers, and bakers. Over 60 percent are unskilled or semiskilled blue-collar workers, and the Chicano male is even more underrepresented in white-collar jobs than is the female. Only recently have they improved their economic opportunities, and then rarely are these opportunities open to the first-generation immigrant.

BOX 3.3   **THE BRACERO EXPERIENCE: IMMIGRATION AND WORK**

●

From 1880 to 1940, immigration policy was increasingly restrictive. Early in World War II, a profound policy shift took place that echoes to the present day. It became clear that American military recruitment had siphoned off a large portion of available workers. In response, Congress created the bracero program in 1942. This "guest worker" program filled the need for workers by introducing aliens into the labor pool on a temporary basis. Strongly backed by the farm sector, the bracero program allowed migrant workers to enter for as long as nine months per year to work in agriculture.

The bracero program (the word refers to a pair of open arms) was implemented via a treaty between Mexico and the United States that allowed Mexican farm workers to come on a temporary basis under contract to U.S. employers. Although inspired by war-time needs, the program remained in place long after the war ended. During its twenty-two years, it involved nearly five-million workers, most often for seasonal agricultural work. As with many immigration policies, the program had its dark side. The often tragic conditions endured by the migrant workers were documented in studies showing their often severe exploitation.

The program was phased out in the mid-1960s, ending with the Immigration Act of 1965. A long-term effect of the program, however, was a largely unforeseen consequence—a massive flow of unauthorized immigration. The bracero program resulted in millions of Mexicans becoming accustomed to working in the United States. They told friends and relatives that the pay far exceeded what they could hope to earn at home. Workers forged ties and patterns of immigration that fed the unauthorized flow that accelerated rapidly when the program was ended in 1964. The Immigration Act of 1965, amended in 1976, put the annual limit on legal immigration from both Eastern and Western Hemisphere nations at 20,000 per country. But 20,000 legal immigrants from Mexico were far short of the demand for their labor, and soon hundreds of thousands entered illegally (a civil offense, not a criminal offense). These workers soon expanded from agriculture to other industries, notably: operatives, construction, personal services, restaurants, wholesale and retail sales, and domestic and hotel/motel workers. Groups of illegal immigrants often relied on human traffickers—smugglers called "coyotes"— to help them enter the United States undetected and without authorization. Tragically, hundreds die each year while attempting to illegally cross the border.

Source: Box by author, with information from: Calavita, Kitty, ***Inside the State: The Bracero Program, Immigration, and the INS.*** New York: Routledge, 1992; Conover, Ted, ***Coyotes: A Journey Through the Secret World of America's Illegal Aliens.*** New York, Vintage Books, 1987; Immigration Plus. ***Immigration and Illegal Aliens: Burden or Blessing?*** Farmington Hills, MI: Thomson/Gale, 2006; and Nevins, Joseph, ***Operation Gatekeeper: The Rise of the Illegal Aliens and the Making of the U.S.-Mexico Boundary.*** New York: Routledge, 2002.

The political movement against illegal aliens came to a climax with passage of the Immigration Reform and Control Act of 1986 (IRCA). This act made it against the law to knowingly hire illegal aliens. Its "employer sanctions" approach sought to "demagnetize" the attraction to illegal aliens of the American labor market. Apprehensions of attempted border crossings dipped in the months after its enactment, but the numbers began climbing again and by 1990 were up to pre-IRCA levels. Continued agitation to do something about illegal aliens culminated in enactment of California's Proposition 187, which eliminated such incentives as welfare, education, and health benefits to illegal aliens and their children. Although many of its provisions were declared unconstitutional, it set the stage for Congressional enactment of immigration and welfare reform acts in 1996 that enacted many of the provisions of 187.

Central Americans

South and Central Americans are yet other groups that came predominantly after 1965 and used the economic tactic of accommodation as their primary coping strategy. Space constraints do not allow discussion of all their national origin histories. This section will briefly highlight the case of central Americans whose immigration patterns are different from the Mexican foreign-born previously discussed, and because of some special U.S. foreign policy considerations that shaped the immigration policy response in their cases.

Immigrants from Central America (Nicaragua, El Salvador, Guatemala, and Honduras) arrived in large numbers almost exclusively post-1965, and mostly came for "push" reasons. That is, their immigration patterns were shaped by political events and natural disasters in their home nations that compelled large numbers to flee. In the 1980s, asylum applications from Nicaragua and El Salvador were determined by U.S. foreign policy towards their home country, and the United States drafted specific immigration policies for them in the 1990s. As of 2004, an estimated 374,000 Central Americans are living in the United States under terms of protected status.

According to the 2000 census, there are over two million Central American foreign-born in the country, roughly half are from El Salvador and Guatemala and are concentrated in five states: California, Florida, New York, Texas, and New Jersey. Central American immigrants have among the lowest high school graduation rates, partly because significant legal and illegal immigration from Central America to the United States began in the 1980s when civil wars in Nicaragua, El Salvador, and Guatemala, combined with their weak economies, spurred their exodus. Other compelling emigration streams followed severe natural disasters in the region, such as Hurricane Mitch in 1998, two earthquakes that rocked El Salvador in 2001, and Hurricane Stan in 2005.

The influence of U.S. foreign policy is evident in the fact that between 1984 and 1990, 25 percent of the 48,000 asylum seekers from Nicaragua were granted asylum compared to only 2.6 percent of the 45,000 claims from Salvadorans and 1.8 percent of the 9,500 claims from Guatemalans. U.S. anti-communist policy accounts for the difference in the late 1980s; Nicaraguans were classified as fleeing communist oppression, while the United States was supporting the Salvadoran government against a Marxist insurgency.

In 1991 the American Baptist Churches filed a class action suit alleging discrimination in the treatment of asylum cases on behalf of Guatemalans and Salvadorans. In *American Baptist Churches vs. Thornburgh* the case was settled with the result that Guatemalans and Salvadorans physically present in the United States prior to October 1, 1990 and September 1, 1990 respectively, were granted a new interview and asylum decision. In 1997, President Clinton signed the Nicaraguan Adjustment and Central American Relief Act (NACARA). Among its provisions are various forms of immigration benefits and relief from deportation for certain Nicaraguans, Salvadorans, and Guatemalans (and certain refugees from Cuba and nations of the former Soviet bloc countries and their dependents). Instead of having to prove ten-year residency and that hardship to U.S. citizens or legal permanent-resident family members would result from their deportation as stipulated under the Illegal Immigration Reform and Immigration Responsibility Act of 1996, immigrants from these countries only have to prove seven years of residency and prove hardship to themselves. NACARA granted legal permanent resident (LPR) status to Nicaraguans continuously present in the United States since 1995 who applied before March 31, 2000. Under NACARA, Salvadorans and Guatemalans present prior to October 31 and October 1, 1991 respectively are eligible for LPR status adjustment under more lenient qualifications.

The Temporary Immigration Protected Status (TIPS) program enacted after the 1998 and the 2001 natural disasters granted special status to 290,000 Salvadorans, 80,000 Hondurans, and 4,000 Nicaraguans. They were granted work authorization and protection from deportation by the Attorney General of the United States but not automatic change to LPR status. TIPS ended for Guatemalans and Salvadorans in March, 1999, and for Hondurans and Nicaraguans it was extended until July, 2007. After two earthquakes in El Salvador in 2001, TIPS was extended for them until September, 2007.

According to the U.S. Census 2000, there were over two million Central American foreign-born in the United States. Table 3.6 lists in rank order by country the numbers and their percent of the foreign-born.

In 2004, Central Americans were admitted under the following classes: 46.4 percent under cancellation of removal orders; 28.9 percent as immediate relatives of U.S. citizens; 14.3 percent under family-sponsored preference; 4.3 percent under employment-based preference; 3.2 percent under other preferences, 1.8 percent under refugee and asylee adjustment; and 0.1 percent under the Diversity preference (Department of Homeland Security, Office of Homeland Security, 2004 Yearbook, accessed 4/26/2007).

Central Americans are concentrated in low skill occupations (e.g., hotel and restaurant workers, domestic work) in large measure due to their lower formal education status. According to Census 2000 data, only 44.3 percent of Central American born people aged 25 or older had a high school diploma and only 8.3 percent a college degree or higher, and over 34 percent had less than a ninth grade formal education.

ARAB AMERICANS

Arab American is a term used to describe individuals who can trace their ancestry to the Arabic speaking regions of Africa, West Asia, and Southwest Asia. It describes the shared community of these individuals, both immigrants and U.S.-born members. Arab Americans have a variety of skin tones and hair types and live a variety of lifestyles. In formal religious affiliation, they are Christian (Eastern Orthodox, Roman Catholic, or Protestant), Muslim (Sunni, Shi'a, or Druze), or even Jewish or atheist. Occupationally, they are doctors, lawyers, politicians, professors, students, community leaders, and entrepreneurs, and they hold a wide range of political and ideological beliefs.

Table 3.6   Central American Foreign-Born in the United States, 2000 Census, Rank Ordered by Country and Percent of the Total Foreign-Born

Country	Number	Percent of Foreign-Born
El Salvador	817,336	40.3
Guatemala	480,665	23.3
Honduras	282,852	14.0
Nicaragua	220,335	10.5
Panama	105,177	5.2
Costa Rica	71,870	3.5
Other Central America	47,915	2.4

Source: Table by author LeMay, based on U.S. Census Bureau data, Census 2000.

Yet as a group, Arab Americans have had some of their basic civil liberties restricted. The events of September 11, 2001 have exacerbated the already negative attitudes that many Americans have toward Arabs, Arab Americans, Middle Easterners, and Islam. Indeed, many Americans fail to realize that Arabs are an integral part of U.S. history.

The greatest dangers to Arab Americans and their image in the United States are widespread ignorance and misunderstanding of events in the Middle East. This lack of knowledge contributes to a lower degree of tolerance and, recently, to overt forms of discrimination, hatred, and violence directed against the Arab-American community. The media's portrayal of Arab communities and the "War on Terror" have exacerbated fears about Arabs and Arab Americans.

Arabs have been a part of U.S. history for over a hundred years. They have come to the United States looking for the economic, political, or religious opportunities denied them in their respective countries of origin. Arab migration to the United States occurred in two major waves. The first wave took place during The Great Migration (1880–1924). Of the nearly 20 million immigrants who came to the United States during this period, approximately 200,000 were Arabs, with most from Greater Syria. The second major wave occurred after the easing of immigration restrictions with the 1965 Immigration Reform Act. Arab migration patterns, assimilation, acculturation, and incorporation in the United States are multi-faceted and are affected not only by the American experience, but also by events taking place in the Middle East.

The first significant wave of Arab migration to the United States began in 1875. Differing push and pull factors encouraged migration to America: rapid urbanization and industrialization, the shortage of labor, the opening of American borders to a large influx of migrants, the entry of the Ottoman Empire into the world economy, and a drive to succeed. Merchants from the Ottoman Empire, especially from the Greater Syria region of the Arab world, participated in the Philadelphia Centennial Exposition of 1876. This opened the door for Arab-American participation and economic success in the Age of Peddling when immigrants would travel from door to door selling their wares. Many of them eventually opened their own businesses, some of which still exist today. In addition to the burgeoning merchant class, a minority of Arab immigrants joined the booming industrial labor force or the agricultural industry.

Most Arab immigrants during the first phase were Christians. Before they built their own churches, many attended churches established by other immigrants, such as the Greek, Irish, Italian, and Polish. In the 1890s, the Arab-American community published the first Arabic language newspaper in the United States and the first Arab-American novel. That decade saw Arab Eastern-Orthodox, Assyrian, Maronite, and Syrian Catholic churches formed. The first Arab-American mosque was built in 1923. During this period, the U.S. Bureau of Immigration classified the new immigrants as Syrians. This designation replaced the previous classification of Arabs as "Turks from Asia." In 1924, the United States severely restricted immigration. Nativist groups in the United States helped pass the Johnson-Reed Quota Act, which effectively ended the first wave of Arab immigration.

Pre-1965 Arab immigrants faced many obstacles. Because of their different skin tones, Arabs could not be classified as black or white, and they were ostracized by both communities. Court records indicate widespread use of race-based discrimination against Arab Americans. Only in 1989 did Arabs gain protection as a designated minority group under civil rights laws. Overwhelmingly negative stereotypes of Arabs penetrated U.S. culture in songs, jokes, films, and so on. In the 1920s, eighty-seven films contained an Arab theme, starting with the famous movie starring Rudolph Valentino in *The Sheik* (1921). The stereotypical Arab was a rich, backward, camel-rearing, exotic yet deceitful strongman with numerous wives who lived in the desert. In fact, most Arab states do not have oil, and Arabs have a rich cultural and intellectual heritage in which family, honor, courage, and generosity are highly valued. Inhabitants throughout the region encourage education, and most of the region's history has been centered in urban areas.

During the late nineteenth century, many North African states had fallen to the French, and Egypt had come under the control of the British. In 1915, during World War I, a deal with the Allies stated that if the Arabs revolted against the Ottoman authorities, they would be granted status as independent states. Instead of receiving independent status, the region was colonized primarily by the British and French. As opposition to colonialism mounted in Palestine, Syria, Egypt, and elsewhere, the British promised the Zionist Movement support in establishing a Jewish homeland for them, which they were eventually granted in Arab Palestine. Rising anti-Semitism in Europe and Russia, which included pogroms and the Holocaust, influenced mass migration. The influx of European Jews into Palestine was viewed by the Arab world as another means of European colonialism and denial of Arab self-determination.

Immigration to the United States slowed down dramatically between 1925 and 1965. As quotas were set as to who and how many could enter the United States, first-wave Arab Americans sponsored family members to enter. This second-wave period was marked by the Great Depression, World War II, the Cold War, creation of the United Nations, the establishment of the state of Israel, independence movements across the globe, and the post-colonial period in the Arab world. Despite U.S. support for Israel, Congress passed the Refugee Relief Act of 1952, which recognized refugee status for displaced Palestinians, allowing 2,000 to migrate. In 1957 this law was extended to allow an additional 985 Palestinians to be admitted between 1958 and 1963. During this time, Palestinian immigration exceeded Syrian and Lebanese immigration. But even with the special allotments, strict U.S. quotas pushed Arabs from Greater Syria to migrate in larger numbers to other parts of the world, especially Latin America.

The passing of the 1965 immigration act enabled the arrival of 400,000 new Arab immigrants between 1965 and 1992. Most were Lebanese, followed by Palestinians and Egyptians. A new influx of Egyptians made them the third largest Arab community in the United States. A major difference between these post-1965 immigrants and earlier waves is religion. Nearly 60 percent are Muslim. Most are Sunni, with a limited number of Lebanese, Iraqi, and old Yemeni Shi'a. The influx of Muslims from other countries created a unique mosaic of Arab and non-Arab Muslim neighborhoods within the larger framework of the established Arab Christian communities.

The new immigrants built upon the foundations set in place by the earlier immigrants. Many new immigrants came with family members, recreating whole family systems in American neighborhoods. Others created networks of Arab communities based on shared cultural similarities, regardless of religion. Today, the largest concentrations of Arab Americans are in the Detroit metropolitan area, Southern California, and New York. Within these Arab-American communities one can find a mixture of common items of Arab culture: restaurants, markets, books, music, films, religious institutions, and delicacies of the Arab world.

The 1990 census data divides Arabs according to their nationality. This includes Egyptian, Iraqi, Jordanian, Lebanese, Moroccan, Palestinian, Syrian, and general Arab. Together they amount to just over 1.2 million. However, Arab-American groups put the total closer to 3 million. The reason for the large discrepancy lies in the way the government classifies its citizens. The government officially labels people from the Middle East as non-Hispanic white. Anybody from the Middle East, regardless of complexion, is lumped with the majority culture. Consequently, descendants of the earlier Arab Christian migrations have assimilated more easily into the American mainstream.

With the establishment of the State of Israel in 1948, 418 Palestinian villages were destroyed and roughly 800,000 Palestinians were displaced. With no sovereign state to call their own, the majority of these people and their descendants are classified as refugees by the United Nations. The plight of the Palestinians has become the cause célèbre in the Arab world, but Israel's advanced military has kept neighboring Arab countries from overtly helping the Palestinians. Lacking an official army, Palestinian militias fight asymmetrically, using bombings, night-time raids, and hijackings to promote their interests. These actions are viewed negatively in the United States and other Western countries. Many Arabs, however, view these actions as legitimate tactics in the struggle for independence. This difference of opinion has hardened over the past two decades, leading to much mistrust and fear between the United States and Arab nations.

Arabs have been a part of U.S. history for well over a hundred years. Arriving from many parts of the Middle East and North Africa, Arab immigrants have experienced

Figure 3.1   Arab Americans in the United States

Source: Figure by author. Data from U.S. Census Bureau, Census 2000 Summary File (SF4).

significant discrimination. Despite these hardships, Arab Americans have established themselves within U.S. society, and they have laid the groundwork for other ethnic groups seeking to accommodate themselves in the United States. For their part, Arab Americans view themselves as a bridge between two worlds, often at odds with one another. They can best be described as having achieved limited segmented assimilation. Their political incorporation is, at best, just in the beginning stages. They have begun lobbying, focused mostly on U.S./Mid-East foreign policy issues. A few from the older waves have achieved some electoral success: for example, Ralph Nader, consumer advocate and twice a presidential candidate; Donna Shalala, who served as Secretary of Health and Human Services in the Clinton Administration, Senator John Sununu, and Congressman Darrell Issa.

Figure 3.1 presents a map of the Arab-American population in the United States as of 2000.

Summary

This chapter explained and exemplified the use of the economic tactic to the accommodation strategy. Both racial and national-origins ethnic minorities have employed—with varying degrees of success—this path to accommodation, to incorporation within the larger society culturally, economically, politically, and socially. It began with a discussion of Asian Americans as a sort of prototype—a best-case scenario for the successful use of the economic tactic. Coming to the United States in small enough numbers and early in the period of U.S. economic development, the Chinese, Japanese, and Korean immigrant groups were able to find economic niches in the labor system and achieve middle-class status. Its use by Filipinos and Southeast Asians has, to date, been less successful.

The chapter discussed examples of the "old" immigrant groups, northwestern Europeans who successfully relied on the economic path to accommodation. German Americans served as their prototype. They came early enough to enter the frontier farmlands. They enjoyed access to skilled trades and often founded industries that provided their economic niche. Scandinavian Americans came at an opportune time. The Homestead Act provided abundant free land. They arrived with sufficient resources to escape the urban immigrant slums and ethnic enclaves and to get out to the frontier regions where their cultural similarities and economic success enabled them to quickly and, eventually, fully assimilate into the dominant culture.

Russian Americans, coming somewhat later, represent the "new" immigrant groups who came mostly from South, Central, and Eastern Europe. Many attempted the economic path with some success. They came in small enough numbers and were sufficiently dispersed to mostly avoid the trap of ethnic enclaves.

Hispanic Americans—exemplified herein by Mexican Americans—also tried the economic approach. Differences in the traits, the timing of their entrance, and the size of their immigration waves accounts for their limited success in employing the economic tactic of the accommodation strategy. The case of Central Americans, with special refugee or other foreign-policy related policy effects, illustrates even more limited success in using economic accommodation. Central Americans can, at best, be described as having some very limited economic segmented assimilation.

The chapter closed with a brief discussion of Arab Americans, emphasizing their diversity. It focused on their use of economic incorporation and some limited political involvement in lobbying and electoral politics.

KEY TERMS

bracero program   A 1942–1964 program of legally imported "temporary agricultural workers," mostly from Mexico.

community cohesion theory   A theory accounting for the rapid rate of Japanese-American assimilation, stressing the organizational features of their community.

sojourner   An immigrant who intends to stay only a short while before returning to the country of origin.

value-compatibility theory   A theory explaining the rapid rate of assimilation of an immigrant group, stressing the values of its culture in common with middle-class Anglo-American culture.

wetback   Term for illegal aliens, mostly from Mexico.

REVIEW QUESTIONS

1. Describe an "occupational niche." What factors make it more or less useful to a group in pursuing economic accommodation?
2. Discuss the immigration laws first used to restrict Asian immigration.
3. What law revised the U.S. immigration policy of national-origins quota system by first allowing token quotas for immigrants from Asian nations?
4. Describe the approach of the law that replaced the national-origins quota system with a preference system.
5. What U.S. law provided the cheap land that enabled many "old" immigrant groups to achieve economic success? Relate it to other pull factors influencing immigration.
6. Among the groups discussed in this chapter, which one has achieved the highest extent of economic incorporation? What statistical evidence can be used that substantiates your assessment of that ranking?
7. Discuss the effort to "demagnetize" the U.S. labor market as a pull factor by enactment of the Immigration Reform and Control Act in 1986. Why wasn't it successful?
8. What law most enabled Filipino immigration? How did this policy effect their use of the economic tactic of accommodation?
9. Describe the use of the bracero program and how this policy effected subsequent patterns of Mexican immigration to the United States.
10. What factors impact the very limited success in using the economic tactic of accommodation among Central Americans? Why has their success been so limited?

NOTES

1. For more on this topic, see, for example, Kitano (1976), Parrillo (1985), and McLemore (1983).
2. See, for instance, Eugene Rostow, "Our Worst Wartime Mistake," *Harpers Magazine,* September 1945, 193–201; and Ken Ringle, "What Did You Do Before the War, Dad?" *Washington Post Magazine,* December 6, 1981, 54–62. See also McLemore (1982). This assessment is also reached by other scholars: Hosokawa (1969), Simpson and Yinger (1965), and Kitano (1997).
3. See "Disguised Blessing," *Newsweek,* December 29, 1958, 23. See also others who make this point: Kitano (1997), Hosokawa (1969), Parrillo (1985), McLemore (1982), as well as "Success Story: Outwhiting the Whites," *Newsweek,* June 21, 1971, 24–25.

ADDITIONAL READINGS

Cheng, Lucie, and Edna Bonacich, eds. *Labor Immigration under Capitalism.* Berkeley, CA: University of California Press, 1984.

Degenova, Nicholas, and Ana Yolanda Ramos-Zayas. *Latino Crossings: Mexicans, Puerto Ricans, and the Politics of Race and Citizenship.* New York: Routledge, 2003.

Fawcett, James T. and Benjamin V. Carino, eds. *Pacific Bridges: The New Immigration from Asia and the Pacific Islands.* New York: Center for Migration Studies, 1987.

Isaac, Allan Punzalan. *American Tropics: Articulating Filipino America.* St. Paul: University of Minnesota Press, 2007.

Light, Ivan and Edna Bonacich. *Immigrant Entrepreneurs: Koreans in Los Angeles, 1965–1982.* Berkeley: University of California Press, 1988.

Ng, Wendy. *Japanese American Internment During World War II.* Westport, CT: Greenwood Press, 2001.

Yoo, Jin-Kyung *Korean Immigrant Entrepreneurs: Networks and Ethnic Resources.* Ames, IA: Blackwell Publishing, Garland Studies in Entrepreneurship, 1998.

• *Reading 3.1*

Inter-Minority Group Economic Competition: Koreans vs Blacks and Hispanics

As noted in Figure 2.1, an outcome of ethnic/racial relations is often conflict. Such conflict is typically between the majority society or some faction thereof and the racial or ethnic minority. Another fairly common conflict outcome, however, is between racial and ethnic minority groups. Competition between minorities is especially found in the economic arena where they compete for jobs or other public resources distributed by government through public policy programs. The split-labor market effect noted in the chapter works, in part, because majority employers can pit one minority against another and their competition for jobs helps lower wages and/or the costs of labor conditions, thus benefiting the majority with cheaper labor.

Conflict between minorities can also occur in access to housing, especially public housing; low-cost government loans; welfare benefits, and so on. On occasion, the conflict is manifested in violence, be it more individually directed (for example, hate crimes) or group directed (for example, race riots). This reading discusses the case of such conflict between Korean immigrants and blacks and Hispanics.

The conflict between these minority groups is largely a result of the increased influx of Koreans since the United States enacted the Immigration Act of 1965. The growth in the Korean population has been dramatic. In 1965 Asians comprised less than half a percent of the total population. By the mid-1980s they made up over 4 percent. By 2005, they comprised 5 percent of the population. Among them, Koreans make up nearly ten percent. Today, Koreans alone are now nearly one half a percent of the total population. As is typical of newly arriving immigrant groups coming in significant waves, they tend to settle in the poorer neighborhoods of the major metropolitan areas of the country, which puts them into direct competition with other minority groups—in this case, Koreans compete with Hispanics and blacks for low-cost housing. The metropolitan areas of Los Angeles, New York, San Francisco, Chicago, Miami, Washington, DC, and Houston are home to more than a quarter of the total U.S. population and to more than 60 percent of all foreign-born residents.

In 1992, the Rodney King verdict in Los Angeles set off riots in which Koreans were in violent confrontation with African Americans. This violence erupted in "Koreatown" where Korean merchants, playing the role of the middle-man minority discussed previously, were essentially cast as the "enemy" to Black Americans. Korean American Angela Oh, a Korean American activist who emerged from the riots in 1992 as a leader of the Korean American community there noted: ". . . you witness this persistence of segregation, the fragmentation, all these fights over resources, this finger-pointing. You would have to be blind not to see it" (cited in http://www.washingtonpost.com/longterm/meltingpot/melt0222.htm, accessed 4/29/2007).

Where some see the nation's megacities as examples of great racial and ethnic diversity, as a tremendously mixed society, the reality at the street level is often one of high racial homogeneity in ethnically segregated neighborhoods. Such deep-seated ethnic segregation extends to the American workplace, with "ethnic niches" in the labor market that are enduring and remarkably resistant to outsiders since jobs are often a matter of whom one knows. In Los Angeles, for example, Mexican immigrants are employed overwhelmingly as gardeners and domestics, in apparel and furniture manufacturing, and as cooks and food preparers. Koreans open small businesses typically retail outlets in electronics, small appliances, food and liquor convenience stores, and wig shops; while Filipinos become nurses and medical technicians, and African Americans work in government jobs, an important niche increasingly being challenged by Hispanics who want into that niche.

Public opinion polls indicate that African Americans tend to resent the portrayal of Koreans and other Asian immigrants as the "model minority" people of color, implying, thereby, that African Americans were the "problem" people of color. African Americans often held the belief that Korean shopkeepers were given special treatment in acquiring low-cost business loans from the government to set up the retail shops and businesses which were serving black or Hispanic neighborhoods. In reality, Korean enterprises were more often financed from saving partnerships called "kyes" that involved family and friends in order to stockpile sufficient finances to open a business. The Korean-owned shops that burned down in the Los Angeles riots were usually uninsured, which meant those Korean merchants whose stores were lost, lost everything.

Some of these perceptions arise simply from cross-cultural differences. Many Korean merchants, following the customs from their retail stores in Korea, put out bowls with change in them to enable their customers to easily and conveniently take any change coming to them after a transaction. They trust the customers to take only the correct amount of change as a matter of honor. African-American customers have interpreted this custom differently: that the Korean merchants want to take their currency but do not want to "hand" them back their change because they dislike touching African Americans. Such cross-cultural misperceptions easily lead to inter-racial conflict.

Another contributing factor to such cross-cultural misperceptions is the broader culture's tendency to "lump" minorities together. A Salvadoran refugee sees himself as Salvadoran, not as a Latino or Hispanic. Asian immigrants from Korea, or Cambodia, or Laos, have little in common. Korean immigrants see themselves as Koreans. But in the United States, they are often categorized and dealt with as "Asians," not as Koreans or Korean Americans or just plain Americans. They hear the public say things like, "the Asian students are so smart," or that "Asians have no interest in politics." For people who see themselves as Koreans, they have to wonder, "who are these Asians?"

After September 11, 2001, many Americans made no distinction between the terrorists who attacked and people who "looked" like them. Shootings and other violent hate crimes were perpetrated against and violated the civil rights of South Asians, Filipino Americans, Latinos, and other Asians as well as Arab Americans and Muslim Americans. The Violent Crime Control and Law Enforcement Act of 1994 (38 U.S.C. 994) defines a hate crime as a crime in which the defendant intentionally selects a victim, or in the case of a property crime, the property that is the object of the crime, because of the actual or perceived race, color, national origin, ethnicity, gender, disability, or sexual orientation of any person. For example, after 9/11 a 21-year-old college student went on a three-day shooting rampage in Illinois and Indiana, begun on July 4th, killing an African American and a Korean man, and injuring other Asians, Jews, and African Americans (Asian American Legal Defense and Education Fund website, accessed 4/29/2007). Hate crimes have been on the rise since 2001, and are considered widely under-reported as some Asian American victims of hate crimes are uncomfortable with or incapable of reporting their experiences because of a lack of bilingual law enforcement personnel, mistrust of local police, and an ignorance about hate crimes and other civil rights protections. In addition, some law enforcement personnel misidentify or fail to identify hate crimes or they either do not take them seriously or deliberately avoid a thorough investigation to prove a hate-crime motivation.

America's dual economy, that of the haves and the have-nots, pits economic competition those at the bottom rungs of the economic ladder, particularly Mexicans and Central Americans with limited education and blacks with limited education. Blacks and Latinos see themselves as locked in conflict over decreasingly available jobs at the lower end of the economy, and with joblessness comes frustration. Blacks often see Hispanic and Asian immigrants as willing to work in low-end jobs for less pay and for poorer working conditions. This drives down the wages for all un- or low-skilled labor. It reflects the policy effects of the split-labor market described by Edna Bonacich, that inevitably leads to economic competition or conflict among certain racial or ethnic minority groups.

Source: Reading by author LeMay. Data and examples were drawn from the following: Jennifer Lee, "Retail Niche Domination Among African American, Jewish, and Korean Entrepreneurs," *American Behavioral Scientist,* Vol. 42, No. 9, 1398–1416 (1999); Jin-Kyung Yoo. *Korean Immigrant Entrepreneurs: Networks and Ethnic Resources.* Ames, IA: Blackwell Publishing, Garland Studies in Entrepreneurship, 1998; Light, Ivan and Edna Bonacich, *Immigrant Entrepreneurs: Koreans in Los Angeles, 1965–1982.* Berkeley: University of California Press, 1988, Hamamoto, Darrell. "Black-Korean Conflict in Los Angeles" *Z Magazine,* July 1, 1992: 61–62.

CHAPTER 4

• ● •

THE STRATEGY OF ACCOMMODATION

The Tactic of Political Accommodation

Chapter 3 discussed an economic tactic to pursue the strategy of accommodation. For some groups, it simply is not an attractive strategy. They may enter majority society at an inopportune time, during a major recession or depression, for example, lacking expanding job opportunities. They may not have the resources in capital or job skills to enter the occupational structure of the dominant society in sufficient numbers to make headway in climbing the socioeconomic ladder. It takes capital to open one's own restaurant, retail store, garment factory, and the like. It takes farming skill and the money to get to where cheap land is available to own a farm and thereby thrive economically and socially.

When a group wants to assimilate but finds its economic path blocked, the tactic of choice becomes political action. As with the economic tactic, political accommodation is favored by a group only when certain conditions are evident. This chapter examines groups who used the political tactic. Political accommodation is primarily a bottom-up approach that requires racial or ethnic minorities to have both the organizational skills and the experience to develop and deliver a consistent bloc vote. It needs leadership capable of articulating specific goals to bargain with a faction of majority society in return for bloc vote support. The majority society must be factionalized, with some who desire to form a coalition with racial and ethnic minorities to win consistently in the electoral struggle with other majority factions. When the minority demonstrates its ability to deliver bloc votes to provide the winning margin in elections, it becomes a highly prized coalition partner. In a top-down manner, the majority faction is then willing to grant rewards. This enables the minority to use politics to climb the socioeconomic structure of society.

Political prowess is "cashed in" to gain material (largely economic) and social rewards. Irish Americans are the classic example of a white ethnic minority group successfully using the political route to accommodation. They developed the prototype that others followed. They are, by virtually any way one might choose to measure it, a group that is fully politically incorporated. They have arrived, in Milton Gordon's term, at civic assimilation. This chapter begins with the use of political accommodation by Irish Americans. It goes on to discuss subsequent use of this tactical approach by Italians, Greeks, Poles, Jews, by some post-1965 Asian Americans, and by factions of Hispanic-American groups, especially Puerto Ricans and Cubans. It closes with a discussion of how black Americans are now successfully using this tactic of accommodation, perhaps best exemplified by Barack Obama, U.S. Senator from Illinois, and candidate for the Democratic Party nomination for president.

IRISH AMERICANS

At over 33 million, residents claiming Irish-American ancestry in the 2000 census rank second only to German Americans in number and percentage of the total population. They are evenly balanced in their regional distribution throughout the country: 24 percent reside in the Northeast, 25 percent in the Midwest, 33 percent in the South, and 17 percent in the West. Among them, less than 200,000 are foreign-born, comprising but 1.2 percent of the foreign-born population. About 18 percent of Irish immigrants have come since 1980. Of those recently immigrated Irish Americans, 64 percent are naturalized. Their median age is 34.9, close to the median of 33.0. for all persons. Among those claiming Irish designation in the 2000 census, 79.6 percent were high school graduates, above the 75.2 percent for all persons; 21.2 percent were college graduates, compared to 20.3 percent for all persons; and 7.2 percent had graduate degrees—the same percent for all persons. Among the Irish, 66.2 percent were in the labor force, just above the national average of 64.4 percent; and 5.2 percent were unemployed, compared to all persons at 6.3 percent.

A 1998 census bureau analysis of their positions in the occupational structures of the economy found that 28.5 percent were in managerial/professional occupations, 33.8 percent were in technical/sales/administrative occupations, 12.1 percent were in service occupations, only 1.8 percent were in farming and farm-related occupations, 11 percent were in production, craft, and repair occupations, and 12.6 percent were operators, fabricators, and laborers, that is, blue-collar workers. Among those in the labor force, 77.7 percent were in private sector wage or salary jobs, 7.3 percent worked for local government, 4.6 percent worked for state government, 3.6 percent for the federal government, and 6.8 percent were self-employed. Their family size and members in the household who worked were close to that for all persons: 27.1 percent of Irish-American families had a single wage earner, 47.2 were two-worker families, and 13.5 percent depended on three or more workers in the family for the household income. At $38,101 in median family income, Irish Americans exceeded the national average of $35,225 median family income. Only 8.7 percent of Irish Americans were in the poverty rate level, compared to the national rate for all persons of 13.1; and only 6.5 percent of Irish-American families were in the poverty ranks, compared to 10.0 for all families. In short, by all relevant measures, they have achieved middle-class status and full assimilation. These socio-economic gains followed their successful use of political incorporation described in the section following. The election of an Irish Catholic as president (John F. Kennedy, 1960) indicates full political power (http://www.census.gov/population/socdemo/ancestry/tables01–07).

Irish immigration can be traced back to colonial times, when they settled mostly in the colonies of Pennsylvania and Maryland. By 1790, they were about 2 percent of the nation's total population of nearly 3 million. They trailed German immigrants but were a significant minority, generating strong and overt discrimination. Irish immigrants after 1830 and before the Civil War were fleeing political and religious persecution under British rule. By late 1840, Irish immigration became a flood.

The potato famine precipitated a massive migration. For many Irish the choice was emigrating or starving to death. Between 1847 and 1854, approximately 1.2 million Irish arrived in the United States. That wave peaked in 1851, when nearly a quarter-million arrived. This famine-induced immigration was important because it meant a deluge of poor Irish immigrants settled on the East Coast, which activated existing prejudice. Their sheer numbers, religion (Catholicism), and openly anti-British sentiment contributed to the antipathy toward them evident in the native stock. Perhaps equally important for understanding their failure to use the economic route and their ability to develop the political path was their poverty. It trapped them within the nation's explosively expanding Eastern seaboard cities. That concentration enhanced the effect of bloc voting.

The Irish immigrants' high rates of illiteracy and general lack of job skills forced them into unskilled work. They were of lower-class status precisely when the United States developed class consciousness.[1] They were seen as a particular threat, a great concentration of "indigent foreigners," and a lower class of people who formed the first huge pool of manual labor (O'Grady 1973). The Irish were the first ethnic group to face overt job discrimination. Job advertisements in New York, Boston, and other eastern cities included the line "No Irish Need Apply" for some time. They accepted whatever jobs were open to them—unskilled jobs such as stevedores, teamsters, ditchdiggers, dockers, and terriers. They formed construction gangs who razed or erected the buildings of the ever growing cities. They built the roads, canals, and railroads connecting the East with the Midwest and beyond. Much to their dismay, not only were the streets of America not paved with gold; they discovered the streets were unpaved and they would do much of the paving!

These jobs were seasonal, low-paying, and periodic. They were subject to constant job threat and labor competition from the Chinese or blacks. Irish immigrants became trapped in an existence that was depressingly grim. Social barriers and meager and insecure incomes forced them to live in enclaves in the slums. Many "escaped" such conditions by abusing alcohol. This contributed to the stereotypical image of the Irish as excessive drinkers.

They broke the vicious cycle and moved up the socioeconomic ladder by their involvement in the beginnings of the American labor movement and by use of politics to enter local government bureaucracies. It was the only route realistically open to them. While few Irish immigrants had experience in labor union affairs, their precarious economic position led them into labor associations. They were early leaders in the formation of unions from New York to San Francisco, which ran the gamut from skilled craftsmen to longshoremen to simply "unskilled laborers." In the 1850s, unions operated solely at the local level, but by the 1860s they appeared at the national level. In 1861, Martin Burke helped form the American Miners Association. By the late 1870s,

"Who Stole the People's Money?" (Thomas Nast, from *Harper's Weekly*, August 19, 1871; neg. #31110 from the Collection of The New-York Historical Society)

a second-generation Irish American, Terrence Powderly, gained control of the first truly effective national-level labor union, the Knights of Labor. Peter J. McGuire, the "Father of Labor Day," helped form the American Federation of Labor in 1886.

They became politically active and organized mostly after the Civil War, and it took roughly a century (1860–1960) for them to achieve full political incorporation (the election of John Fitzgerald Kennedy as president of the United States undeniably certifying their arrival at that status) using the political accommodation tactic.

Massive urbanization between 1840 and 1850 required rapidly increasing local government work forces, especially police departments. The Irish were quick to join, and some rose rapidly to levels of responsibility. By 1863, John A. Kennedy led New York City's police force. In 1870, a new detective, Michael Kerwin, became police commissioner. The police job was especially attractive to Irish immigrants. The status of the uniform and the steady employment were magnets, as was the potential power of the position. In Ireland they had been oppressed by the police—evicted, taxed, seized for questioning, imprisoned, and even killed. In America, they exercised such power. Using wide discretion, they applied the law with flexibility befitting their interests and those of the political bosses, and the political morality of the day justified that practice (Levine 1966, 123).

Since politicians controlled appointments to the police force, Irish immigrants soon realized that job security depended on the success of the growing urban machine's slate. Irish-dominated police departments became the mainstay of ward and district organizations of the Democratic political party.

Politics set the pattern of immigrant minority group/majority society relations that served as the model for most of the "new" immigrant groups. It served as the prototype for many subsequent groups, none of whom were able to employ it quite as successfully as did the Irish. Social conditions changed by the time later groups emulated the Irish model.

Huge numbers of Irish living in enclaves formed an ethnic voting bloc that provided the margin of victory. Ward leaders and precinct captains of the urban political party machine were often Irish immigrants. Using church and related ethnic organizations, they established the machine apparatus that gradually controlled the electoral machinery. By the 1870s, they gained control of the Democratic Party machine in Brooklyn. Irish Americans served as mayors in Richmond, Memphis, Baltimore, Wilmington, and Scranton. In 1871, an Irishman entered Congress as a representative from New York; in 1876 another won a seat from Pennsylvania. The highly influential Irish Catholic Benevolent Union (ICBU) sent several of its prominent members to seats on the city council of Philadelphia in the 1870s. One of them, William Harrity, served as chairman of the Philadelphia Democratic City Committee. He later served as chairman of the Democratic National Committee during President Cleveland's 1892 campaign. This set the precedent for a long tradition of Irish Democratic Committee chairmen. The ICBU also provided eight men who held judgeships during the 1870s, and by 1880 its founder, Dennis Dwyer, won a seat on New York State's Supreme Court.

This success was duplicated in various parts of the nation, but the early political clout of the Irish reached its zenith in New York City through their 50-year control of Tammany Hall, the first of the classic urban machines. As the late Senator Daniel Patrick Moynihan so aptly described it:

> "Dick" Connolly and "Brains" Sweeny had shared power and office with Tweed, as had any number of their followers, but with few exceptions the pre-1870s Irish had represented the canaille. With the dawning of the Gilded Age, however, middle-class and upper-class Irish began to appear; thus ranging across the social spectrum, the Irish appeared to dominate a good part of the city's life for half a century. They came to run the police force and the underworld; they were evident on Wall Street as on the Bowery; Irish contractors laid out the subways and Irish laborers dug them. The city entered the era of Boss Croker of Tammany Hall and Judge Goff of the Lexow Committee, which investigated him; of business leader Thomas Fortune Ryan and labor leader Peter J. McQuire; of reform mayor John Purroy Mitchel and Tammany Mayor "Red Mike" Hylan. It was a stimulating miscellany, reaching its height in the Roaring Twenties with Al Smith and Jimmy Walker. (cited in Fuchs 1990, 79–80)

Successive waves of immigrants caused the nation's cities to virtually explode upward and outward. By 1920, immigrant groups made up 44 percent of New York, 41 percent of Cleveland, 39 percent of Newark, and 24 percent of Pittsburgh, Detroit, Boston, Buffalo, and Philadelphia. The waves of immigrants coming after 1880 had low levels of skills and resources similar to those that characterized the Irish peasants. Like the Irish, they used politics to cope with their minority status. However, they used it less successfully because of changing conditions and because the Irish, who arrived before them, were more reluctant to budge from their newly acquired middle-class "rung" than were the Yankees before them.

By the 1970s, however, Irish Americans had so fully incorporated into all aspects of society—culturally, economically, politically, socially—that they no longer relied upon politics as their means to "make it in America." Having arrived, they began to split their vote and exhibit political participation and voting behavior essentially the same as that for all white Americans.

ITALIAN AMERICANS

Italian-American immigration occurred almost exclusively after 1870. At over 5.5 million immigrants, Italy is second only to Germany in the total number of immigrants coming to the United States. In the 2000 census, 15,916,396 persons claimed Italian ancestry. In a 1998 census bureau report, 11,286,815 Americans claimed Italian ancestry. Today they remain concentrated in the East where over 51 percent reside; the remaining are distributed at 17 percent, each in the Midwest and the South, and 15 percent in the West. They continue to come. Among them, over a half million people (643,203) acknowledged being born in Italy, among whom 9 percent came since 1980. Among those foreign-born, 72.6 percent were naturalized citizens and 27.4 percent were not yet citizens. Their median age was 33.8, compared to the 33.0 for all persons. These newest (post-1965) immigrants are better educated than their earlier compatriots, although they lag behind both Asian and Irish immigrants. Among all Italian Americans, 77.3 percent were high school graduates and 21.0 percent claimed college degrees; 7.4 percent among who claimed graduate degrees. Among Italian Americans, 66.9 percent were in the workforce and only 4.9 percent were unemployed. In occupations, 29.6 percent of them were in managerial/professional jobs, 35.7 percent were found in technical, sales, and administrative occupations, 12 percent were in services, 1 percent in farming, 11.1 percent worked in production, craft, and repair jobs, and 10.7 percent worked as operators, laborers, and fabricators. In terms of class of workers, 79.1 percent were in private sector wage or salary occupations, 7.7 percent worked for local government, 3.6 percent worked for state government, 2.7 percent were employed at the federal government level, and 6.6 percent were self-employed. In terms of workers in Italian-American families, 27.0 percent of them were single-wage-earner families, 45.6 percent depended on two workers, and 14.9 percent had three or more persons in the family in the labor force. Their median household income was just over $36,000 and the mean household income among them was $44,865, well above the averages for all persons of $30,056 and $35,225. Their per capita income was $17,384. Their poverty rate for families was 4.9 percent, and persons below the poverty level was 6.9, both less than the national averages of 13.1 and 10.0 percent respectively. In short, these data indicate that Italian Americans are fully incorporated (http://www.census.gov/population/socdemo/ancestry/Italian/tables 01-07).

There was some colonial and pre–Civil War immigration from Italy. As early as the 1620s, the Virginia colony had a few Italian wine growers. Pre–Revolutionary War immigrants from Italy were lightly scattered among Virginia, Georgia, the Carolinas, New York, and Florida. Repression in Europe in the 1870s forced a number of Italian intellectuals and revolutionaries to emigrate. Although small in number, those pre-1880 immigrants, mostly from the northern provinces of Italy, had a considerable impact on the areas where they settled. They founded the opera in the United States during the 1830s and 1840s. From the 1820s to the 1870s, Italian artists were brought in by the federal government to create commissioned public artwork. By 1848, two Italian immigrants had been elected to the Texas state legislature. A year later, in New York, Secchi de Casali founded *L'Eco d' Italia,* a prominent Italian-language newspaper that supported the Whig Party and later the Republicans.

By the 1850s, there was an Italian settlement in Chicago, where they served as saloon keepers, restaurateurs, fruit vendors, and confectioners, as well as common ditchdiggers and commissioned artists. They were also being lured to California by the gold rush. Instead of mining, however, most became wine growers, vegetable farmers, and merchants, giving rise to "the Italian-American folklore that 'the miners mined the mines, and the Italians mined the miners'" (Iorrizzo and Mondello 1971, 13). Early Italian Americans were often skilled craftsmen of middle to upper class background who came seeking better economic opportunity. This changed radically after the 1870s.

The Risorgimento, resulting in the unification of Italy in 1870, sparked a mass exodus of nearly 9 million Italians who crossed the Atlantic to both North and South America to seek better economic conditions denied them by the very movement they had supported at home. The trickle of northern Italians became a flood from the south. From 1881 to 1910, more than 3 million Italians came to the United States. Most settled in the cities of the industrial Northeast. By 1930, New York City's Italian-American immigrants numbered over 1 million and were 15.5 percent of its total population.[2]

This flood of immigrants was by no means a static bloc. There was considerable mobility after their arrival, as they moved back and forth between Italy and America. They lived in enclaves known as "Little Italy" in the United States. Data from 1910 to 1914 show that about half of those who arrived returned to Italy to winter there, working the remainder of the year in America (Nelli 1970).

Several push and pull factors influenced Italian immigrants to undertake the arduous and uprooting migration to the United States. Most left Italy because of economic factors, fleeing the economic shackles of poverty. During the 1890s, agricultural workers in Italy earned between 16 and 30 cents per day, and during the winter season that fell to 10 to 20 cents per day. Italian miners received from 30 to 56 cents per day. General laborers received $3.50 for a six-day workweek, compared to $9.50 for a 56-hour workweek in the United States. Carpenters in Italy earned 30 cents to $1.40 per day, or $1.80 to $8.40 for a six-day week. That same worker in the United States received an average $18 for a 50-hour workweek.[3] Floods, volcanic eruptions, and earthquakes plagued the country and contributed to its bleak agricultural outlook, especially in the south. That region was also especially hard hit by phylloxera, a disease that killed off agricultural plants on a scale similar to the potato blight of the 1840s. Southern Italy was further troubled by frequent and severe epidemics of malaria. Others fled compulsory military service.

Far more important were the pull factors. The development of the steamship lines made the journey cheaper, faster, and easier. The glowing reports of relatives and acquaintances about the wealth of opportunity drew others. Returning "Americani," some of whom made the trip back and forth, had sufficient money not only to return to Italy temporarily for brides but also to attract many others to emulate their success in America. State governments, such as those of Illinois, New York, Pennsylvania, California, and Louisiana, hired agents to contract for laborers. And the laborers came—from 1890 to 1914 they arrived in excess of 100,000 per year. Between 1900 and 1914, a total of 3 million came. So massive was the out-migration that one author told the humorous and probably apocryphal tale of a mayor who greeted the Prime Minister of Italy then touring the provinces: "I welcome you in the name of five thousand inhabitants of this town, three thousand of whom are in America and the other two thousand preparing to go. (Iorrizzo and Mondello 1971, 48)"

The southern Italian was often a "sojourner" in his mentality, associated with the cultural and social background of the peasant, as opposed to the background of the earlier immigrating northern Italians. For historical reasons, the *Mezzogiorno* (the south) was more traditional, more backward, and poorer than the north. The *contadini* (peasants) were at the bottom of a still largely feudal society. Oppressed and exploited by *signori* and *borghesi* alike, they were despised as *cafoni* (boors). Illiterate, unschooled, lacking in self-confidence, the peasantry was preindustrial in culture and mentality—not a very good preparation for life in America's teeming tenement slums!

Their motive to immigrate was not only to escape grinding poverty but to improve their family's lot by earning money to buy land in Italy. Many came intending to work, save, and return after several years with a few hundred dollars. Like the Chinese, to whom they were often compared, the Italians were sojourners: predominantly male and youthful. Of the millions who emigrated, about half did return to their villages, either in triumph or defeat. Even those who remained in America often nourished thoughts of the day they could return. That mentality was an important condition affecting their adjustment. Why learn English, why become a citizen, why Americanize, if one were going back to the old country, if not this year, then the next?

Italians settled in the teeming cities where they found a variety of jobs: common laborers on the railroads, digging canals and waterways, digging the sewer systems, and laying the pipes for the water supply. Many took up fruit vending and vegetable farming. In contrast to their experiences in Italy, truck farming in the United States was a good investment. Match and shoe factories recruited laborers and soon found that "chain" migration (depending on the personal word of mouth or letters from one relative or friend to another) was so effective they no longer needed recruiting agents.

Some settled in more rural areas and occupations. In San Francisco they dominated the fruit and vegetable truck farming business; they were so prominent in that market in California that "Del Monte" became a household word. In 1881, the Italian-Swiss colony established at Asti in Sonoma County sparked the development of the wine industry. A smaller but comparable role was played in the wine industry in upstate New York. Other important agricultural settlements included Vineland and Hammonton, New Jersey, and Geneva, Wisconsin. In 1850, Louisiana had more Italian laborers in the cotton fields than any other state, and New Orleans had a larger population of Italians than any other city. By 1920, however, New York City led the nation with its more than one-half million Italian residents.

They arrived by the hundreds of thousands precisely when the United States was experiencing an economic downturn. The turbulent socioeconomic unrest following the Panic of 1873 and the subsequent crippling depression led to rising anti-Semitism, the emerging Jim Crow movement, and growing antipathy toward European immigrants, especially those coming from South, Central, and Eastern Europe. The latter were viewed as radicals and criminals who filled the ever-growing slums, fueled class conflicts, and contributed to the developing urban machine and its blatant political corruption.

They did seem to be filling the cities. According to the 1910 census, Italian immigrants accounted for 77 percent of Chicago's foreign-born population, 78 percent of New York's, and 74 percent of Boston's, Cleveland's, and Detroit's. In the late 1880s and 1890s, depression-induced violence swept the country and was frequently directed at the Italians and the intense discrimination against them affected their living conditions. Nearly 90 percent lived in "Little Italy" enclaves of the major cities where conditions were grim. Jacob Riis describes the slums in and around "The Bend," "Bandit's Roost," and "Bottle Alley." They characterized the Mulberry Street—Mulberry Bend area composing New York City's first Little Italy section. He says about the area:

> Half a dozen blocks on Mulberry Street there is a rag-pickers settlement, a sort of overflow from "the Bend," that exists today in all its pristine nastiness. Something like forty families are packed into old two-story and attic houses that were built to hold five, and out in the yards additional crowds are, or were until very recently, accommodated in shacks built of all sorts of old boards and used as drying racks by the Italian stock. (Riis 1971, 49)

Conditions like those described by Riis were all too common. Other studies documented similar conditions. One survey found that 1,231 Italians were living in 120 rooms in New York. Another report stated they could not find a single bathtub in a three-block area of tenements. In Chicago, a two-room apartment often housed an Italian family of parents, grandparents, several children, cousins, and boarders. A 1910 survey in Philadelphia noted that Italian families had to live, cook, eat, and sleep in the same room, and many tenants shared outhouses and a water hydrant—the only plumbing facilities available—with four or five other families. In addition, many kept chickens in their bedrooms and goats in their cellars (Dinnerstein and Reimers 1988, 48).

Concentration in enclaves helped them to cope. One way was the **padroni** system. Although probably exaggerated as to its exploitive nature and extensiveness, this "boss" system was nonetheless an important mechanism for the immigrant. The padroni, the bosses, knew individual employers, spoke English, and understood American labor practices. They were invaluable to American business in need of gangs of laborers. The newcomers depended on them for jobs and other services—collecting wages, writing letters, acting as a banker, supplying room and board, and handling dealings between workers and employers.

Although the Foran Act of 1885 forbade contract labor, the golden era of these padroni was from 1890 to 1900. Conditions of poverty drove many families to work long and hard and forced their young to forgo school and to work at very early ages. In 1897, an estimated two-thirds of the Italian workers in New York City were controlled by padroni. Though exploitive, the padroni system, nonetheless, helped them find jobs and eased the acculturation process. After 1900, it declined rapidly when others provided social services previously given out by the padroni. Railroad and construction officials investigated and became aware of the worst abuses. They found laborers without the padroni. Finally, the sheer massive numbers of immigrants pouring into the settlements exceeded what the padroni could handle. Later immigrants were less dependent on bosses for housing, jobs, and persons to assist them with English or with contacts with government or labor officials.

Unlike the Irish, the Italians found the church less useful in their assimilation process. Their anti-Irish attitudes spilled over into their relations with the church, whose hierarchy was usually Irish-dominated. Gradually, however, Italian-American priests were ordained who better met their needs, and inroads into the upper levels of the hierarchy were achieved by the 1930s. After that, the church did prove useful as a means of their assimilation.

Also aiding them to adjust to life in America was a wide variety of mutual aid or benevolent societies. These self-help associations began early in the Italian-American experience. San Francisco, for instance, had an Italian Mutual Aid Society in 1858. The Italian Union and Fraternity was started in New York in 1857. By 1912, there were 212 such societies in New York City alone; by 1919, Chicago had 80 societies. They often began as burial societies or as groups to help their members find jobs and housing. They soon developed into organizations providing insurance, a host of social services, and the basis of the social life of many immigrants.

Mafia and crime-related organizations emerged in similar fashion. The mob violence and discrimination directed against Italian immigrants contributed to the rise of criminal activities, in part as self-protective associations. Careers in crime became "a curious ladder of social mobility" (Vecoli and Lintelman 1984, 205). When the urban machines and crime organizations linked in the 1910–1930 period, crime organizations provided leaders to political clubs and party activity, especially in Chicago, where Colosimo, Torrio, and Al Capone emerged. Crime became a source of the derogatory stereotyping of all Italians as criminals. That image, plus the 1913 depression, undoubtedly played a part in the revival of anti-Italian immigrant fervor by such groups as the Ku Klux Klan in the early 1900s and to a resurgence in the use of pejorative terms like "wop" and "dago."

War influenced Italian-American incorporation as well. Although to a lesser degree than the Irish, Italian Americans saw a benefit to their image and acceptability to Anglo America by their service in the Civil War. New York City sent a regiment, the Garibaldi Guard, to fight with the Union forces. Their war record was substantial. In addition to the Guard, 100 Italians from New York served with Union forces, and three reached the rank of general. The effects of World War I, in which some 300,000 Italian Americans served, were also profound.

In politics, the Italians used the Irish model, but arriving in substantial numbers three to four decades after the Irish, they did so less successfully. They moved into the political arena more slowly and often came into conflict with the Irish politicians who had arrived before them and were reluctant to share power or to move over to make room for the newcomers. Such Irish-Italian conflict was common, often severe, and occasionally violent.

Initially, Italian-American politicians emerged from the various clubs and societies. They ran as Democrats, Republicans, Socialists, Independents, and Progressives. The Progressive and Republican parties, however, were the most popular among them.

Before the 1920s, most of their political activity was at the local level. They typically supported machine candidates. In New York, their political activity included the creation of the Italian Federation of Democratic Clubs. In 1925, they established the Fascist League of America. Political leadership emerged out of the padroni system. In upstate New York, these included several notable leaders with connections to the Republican Party: Marnel, D'Angelo, Lapetino, Gualtieri, and later LaGuardia in New York City. In Chicago, a varied pattern was evident. The first state-level Italian-American politician in Illinois was a Democrat, Charles Cois, who was elected to the State House in 1918. At the same time, on the Republican ticket, Camile Volini was elected county commissioner, and Bernard Barasa a municipal judge. Nationally, they at times supported and worked with Democratic machines, but often as not they clashed with the Irish leadership of the party. In Chicago, for example, they had running battles with ward boss John Powers (Gianni Pauli) (Nelli, 99).

In 1919, anti-Wilson views swung many of them away from the Democrats. In New York, Republican Fiorello LaGuardia emerged as their political leader. He was elected to the U.S. House of Representatives in 1915 and, after a distinguished war service, again in 1918. In 1920, he won the seat vacated by Al Smith, the Irish American who was the Democratic Party nominee for president. In 1933, LaGuardia was elected the "reform" mayor of New York City. During the 1920s, Italian Americans split their votes, with a slight edge going to Republicans, but with their usual "wet" vote over "dry" vote on Prohibition, no matter what the candidate's party affiliation. In 1932, they returned solidly to the Democratic fold, where they have been ever since, with a 60 percent vote for Roosevelt.

During the 1930s, increasingly prominent Italian-American politicians were working themselves up to state-wide and even national-level offices. By 1937, for example, three Italian-American judges served on New York's Supreme Court. Angelo Rossi, LaGuardia, and Robert S. Maestri were, respectively, the mayors of San Francisco, New York, and New Orleans. Three U.S. congressmen from New York were prominent Italian Americans of the day: Vito Marcantonio, James Lanzetta, and Alfred Santangelo. Through judicious "behind the scenes" politics and his own business acumen, another Italian American stood at the pinnacle of success in American business: Amadeo Peter Giannini, chairman of the board of the Bank of America. By 1945, his bank had surpassed the Chase National Bank of New York as the largest commercial bank in the world.

During the interwar years, a faction of Italian Americans flirted with fascism, although both pro- and anti-Fascist groups emerged within the Italian-American communities. In part, Il Duce (Benito Mussolini) became a source of ethnic pride, reflecting a sort of communal hero-worship. An anti-fascist Italian American girl, for example, despite her opposition to Mussolini, said, "You've got to admit one thing: he has enabled four million Italians in America to hold up their heads, and that is something. If you had been branded undesirable by a quota law, you would understand how much that means" (Nelli, 241).

After World War II, Italian Americans remained aligned with the Democratic Party when measured by national, and especially presidential, voting behavior. Despite the occasional notable Republican politician of Italian heritage, such as John A. Volpe in Massachusetts, Italians are overwhelmingly Democratic. They will cross party lines to vote for one of their own. While 85 percent of the Italian-American voters in Massachusetts supported John Kennedy for president in 1960, 50 percent crossed over to vote Republican for Volpe in his gubernatorial bid.

Republicans have made some very concerted efforts to woo the Italian-American voter—most notably in the two Richard Nixon presidential campaigns. Their efforts have been far from successful since two-thirds of Italian Americans identify themselves with the Democratic Party, significantly above the rate of the general public. One of the more prominent Italian-American politicians was former governor of New York, Mario Cuomo. Another current example of a prominent Italian-American politician elected to state-wide office is Janet Napolitano, the governor of the state of Arizona. She was first elected in 2002 and re-elected in 2006 by a nearly 2–1 margin. She is the state's third female governor, the first female ever to win re-election, and the first of Italian heritage. In 2005, *Time* magazine named her one of the five best governors in the United States, and she has been mentioned as one of eight female politicians who could run for president. By most means of measuring political incorporation, Italian Americans were fully incorporated by the 1980s, taking about one hundred years to achieve that status, as did the Irish a few decades earlier. An indication of having achieved that status of "civic incorporation" was the nomination of Italian American Geraldine Ferraro (D-NY) for the vice-presidency on the Democratic Party ticket in 1984, and more recently, the selection of Representative Nancy Pelosi as Speaker of the House. The notable political office of the speakership makes her second in line after the Vice-President to assume the presidency. Her political career is highlighted in Box 4.1.

GREEK AMERICANS

Although Greek Americans tried to use the tactic of economic accommodation they were not so successful at that tactic that they ignored reliance on political action, increasingly using that strategy after achieving a modicum of economic success. In the 2000 census, 1,175,591 persons claimed Greek ancestry. The 1998 census bureau report found 79.0 percent native-born and 21.0 percent foreign-born, among whom 12.9 percent entered from 1980 to 1990, indicating over 87 percent had entered before 1980. Among them, 70.9 percent were naturalized citizens, and 29.1 percent were not yet citizens. Among Greek Americans, 77.9 percent had high school degrees, 28 percent graduated college, and 10.7 percent had achieved graduate degrees. Their median age was 33.6, just slightly above the national average of 33.0. Among them, 67.6 percent were in the labor force, above the national average for all persons of 64.4 percent; and only 5.2 percent were unemployed, compared to the 6.3 percent for all persons. In income they also ranked above the national average. Greek-American median household income was $37,212 compared to $30,056 for all persons. Their median family income was $43,440, well above that of $35,225 for all persons. Their poverty level was well below that for all persons: 7.3 percent compared to 13.1 percent for all persons; and 5.2 percent of Greek families were below the poverty level compared to 10.0 percent for all families. In terms of the number of workers in the Greek families who were actively in the labor force, 28.3 percent of their families were single-wage-earner families, 47 percent were two-wage-earner families, and 15.3 percent had three or more wage earners in

BOX 4.1   SPEAKER OF THE HOUSE, CONGRESSWOMAN NANCY PELOSI

Since 1987, Nancy Pelosi has represented what is now California's Eighth District (for her first three terms it had been numbered the Fifth), which includes most of the City of San Francisco with many diverse neighborhoods. Born in 1940, Nancy Patricia D'Alesandro Pelosi was selected as Speaker of the House in January, 2007. She is the first woman, first Californian, and first Italian American in U.S. history to be Speaker of the House. She ranks second in the line of presidential selection, following Vice-President Dick Cheney, and as such is the highest ranking woman in the history of the U.S. government.

Pelosi was the House Minority Leader from 2002 to 2007, then being the first woman in American history to lead a major party in the U.S. Congress. Prior to that, she served as the House Democratic Whip for 2001–2002, and was responsible for the party's legislative strategy in the House. She was the senior member of the House Appropriations Committee, and a member of the House Permanent Select Committee on Intelligence for ten years, the longest continuous service in that committee's history, including two years as its Ranking Democrat. Post-9/11, Pelosi led congressional reviews of the U.S. intelligence and security agencies, authored legislation to create the national commission to assess U.S. intelligence before, during, and after the attacks, and threats to international security posed by the proliferation of technologies used by global terrorism and associated with weapons of mass destruction.

Pelosi follows a strong family tradition of public service. Her father was mayor of Baltimore, Maryland for twelve years after representing the city for five terms in the Congress, and her brother was also Mayor of Baltimore. She graduated from Trinity College in 1962. She met her husband there and the couple moved to his home town of San Francisco. She was a housewife and mother until her youngest child graduated from high school, at which time Pelosi began her involvement in politics, soon serving as the Democratic party chairwoman for Northern California. She first took office in the U.S. Congress in June, 1987, in a special election. She went on to be re-elected since by margins typically in the mid-80 percent range.

Source: Box by author LeMay with information from the house website (www.house.gov/pelosi/biography/bio.html), accessed 2/27/2007; and wikipedia.org, accessed 2/27/2007.

the family. In class of workers, 77.8 percent of them had private sector wage or salary jobs, 6.2 percent worked for local government, 3.5 percent for state government, 2.6 percent were employed with the federal government, and 9.4 percent were self-employed. In occupations, 34.7 percent were managerial or professional, 32.2 percent worked in technical, sales, or administrative jobs; 13.6 percent were in service, 0.8 percent in farming, 9.8 percent in production, craft, and repair occupations, and 8.9 percent were employed as operators, fabricators, or laborers (http://www.census.gov/population/socdemo/ancestry/tables01-07).

BOX 4.2   *BIO-SKETCH OF MICHAEL DUKAKIS*

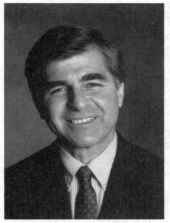

Michael Dukakis was born in 1933. His father was a Greek immigrant who settled in Lowell, Massachusetts and graduated from Harvard Medical School. His mother, Euterpe, was from Larissa, Greece and her family immigrated in 1913. She graduated Bates College. Michael Dukakis graduated from Swarthmore College in 1955, served in the U.S. Army, and then received his law degree from Harvard Law School in 1960.

He served as governor of Massachusetts from 1975–1979 (as its sixty-fifth governor), and from 1983–1991 (as its sixty-seventh governor), the longest serving governor in the state's history. His re-election in 1986 was with more than 60 percent of the vote. The National Governor's Association voted him as the most effective governor in 1986, and he was known as the only governor who rode the subway to the state capitol every day.

Using the campaign theme of the "Massachusetts Miracle" to promote his campaign, Dukakis won the Democratic Party nomination for President of the United States in 1988. Touching on his immigrant roots, he used Neil Diamond's ode to immigrants, *"America,"* as his campaign's theme song. He lost to Vice-President George H.W. Bush, the Republican nominee. His reserved and stoic character led to his being called "Zorba the Clerk." Following his loss (he received 45.65 percent of the popular vote), he served out his term as governor. Had he won the office, he would have been only the second U.S. President (after Andrew Jackson) born of immigrant parents.

After leaving the governorship, he became a professor of political science at Northeastern University in Massachusetts and a visiting professor Loyola Marymount University and the University of California Los Angeles.

Source: Box by author LeMay, based on information in: wikipedia.org, accessed 2/27/2007.

Their political involvement closely parallels that of other "new" immigrant groups, especially Italian Americans. Like them, by the 1940s most Greek Americans voted for the Democratic Party. First the New Deal, then Roosevelt's and Truman's foreign policies during and immediately after World War II solidified Greek-American loyalty to the Democratic Party.

Some inroads were made by Republicans during the 1960s reflecting the weakened hold of the Democratic urban organizations, the movement of the Greek-American middle class into the suburbs, and the appearance of Spiro Agnew as vice-presidential candidate in 1968 and 1972. Yet second- and third-generation Greek Americans still vote Democratic at a greater rate than one would expect, based solely on economic indicators of class status. Greek Americans self-identify their political party affiliation as 48 percent Democratic, 24 percent Republican, and 29 percent Independent, almost exactly the party identification of the population nationally.

Greek-American impact on American politics comes from the visibility of second-generation Greek Americans in relatively high electoral office. Although the mainstream Greek-American group is socially conservative, some prominent politicians have emerged from the liberal wing of the Democratic Party. Maryland, for example, elected Paul Sarbanes to the U.S. Senate in 1976, and he was comfortably re-elected in 1982, 1988, 1994, and 2000. He retired from the Senate in 2006. Senator Sarbanes, the son of a Greek immigrant café owner, is a graduate of Princeton University, holds a law degree from Harvard Law School, and was a Rhodes scholar. In 1978, he was joined in the Senate by Paul Tsongas, a Massachusetts Democrat, who was the son of a Greek tailor. Senator Tsongas graduated from Dartmouth and received his law degree from Yale University. He briefly challenged Bill Clinton for the Democratic presidential nomination in 1992. The most prominent Greek American still serving in the U.S. Senate is Olympia Snowe, Republican, Maine. Born in 1947, she served in the Maine legislature (House and Senate) from 1973 until her election to Congress in 1978, the youngest Republican woman and the first Greek American woman elected to Congress. She was first elected to the U.S. Senate in 1994, and was comfortably re-elected in 2000 and in 2006.

The Ninety-sixth Congress had five Greek Americans holding seats in the House of Representatives: John Brademas (D-Ind.), the then majority whip who was also a Rhodes scholar; Gus Yatron (D-Pa.); Nicholas Mavroules (D-Mass.), the son of Greek immigrants who worked in the mills, who was later elected mayor of Peabody; L. A. Bafalis, a conservative Republican from Florida; and Olympia Snowe (R-Maine). Other Greek Americans who held seats in the House in the 1970s were Peter Kyros (D-Maine) and Nick Galifianakis (D-N.C.), who ran unsuccessfully for the Senate.

The most notable Greek-American politician, and a clear indicator that as a group they have "arrived" politically speaking, is former Massachusetts Governor Michael Dukakis, who ran for president on the Democratic ticket in 1988. He lost to George Bush. His success in capturing the party's nomination for the highest elected office in the land indicates the strength and status of Greek Americans in politics. Box 4.2 presents his Bio-Sketch. Other Greek Americans who served as governors in their respective states during the 1970s include Republican Nicholas Strike of Utah in 1972; Democrat Harry Spanos of New Hampshire in 1976; and Democrat Michael Bakalis of Illinois in 1978. Many Greek Americans have served in various state legislatures and on state judicial benches. Several dozen have been elected mayors of their cities, including George Christopher of San Francisco; Lee Alexander of Syracuse, New York; George Athanson of Hartford, Connecticut; Helen Boosalis of Lincoln, Nebraska; and John Roussakis of Savannah, Georgia. Scores more have been elected mayors in the small mill towns of New England.

This electoral record is all the more impressive since, with few exceptions, none of these cities has a truly sizable Greek ethnic voting bloc on which to build a base for electoral success. All the candidates had to pitch their campaigns to the general electorate. They received substantial contributions, however, from the Greek-American community. Senator Sarbanes, in his successful bids to the U.S. Senate, raised one-fourth of his total campaign budget from Greek-American contributors from across the nation.

Perhaps the lack of a sizable ethnic bloc allowed them to remain unconstrained by a parochial ethnic base and to run with no special appeal to an ethnic loyalty. Such was the case of former Vice President Spiro Agnew. Emerging rapidly from a school board chairmanship to become governor of Maryland on the Republican ticket, the relatively unknown Agnew burst upon the national scene at the 1968 Republican National Convention. His vice-presidential election in 1968 and re-election in 1972 made him a leading contender for the 1976 presidential nomination until his resignation in disgrace in 1973 ended his political career.

Nonetheless, Agnew exemplifies the case of an assimilated ethnic. Greek American on his father's side, his name was anglicized from Agagnostopoulos. Spiro Agnew spoke no Greek and was Episcopalian rather than Greek Orthodox, but his father had been the owner of a small lunchroom, an active member of the American Hellenic Educational Progressive Association (AHEPA), and a pillar of Baltimore's Greek-American community. Not only could he be called a Greek American, Agnew articulated how most of them felt about law and order, family integrity, and upward social mobility based on one's own efforts. His was an "up-by-your-own-bootstraps" mentality. He personified the 1968 and 1972 Republican Party strategy of appealing to the white ethnic vote.

Agnew's resignation after pleading no contest to charges of income tax evasion shocked the Greek-American community. But a survey of that community shortly after revealed an ambiguity of opinion typical of ethnic minority groups when confronted with examples of corruption among their own. Some retreated to the rationale that he was never really a Greek anyway. Others responded with: "He may be an S.O.B., but at least he's our S.O.B." Most, however, reacted with dismay at his betrayal of his middle-class constituency. Agnew quickly became a nonperson within the Greek-American community (Moskos 1980).

Any inroads the Republicans may have made into the Greek-American community during the Nixon years were reversed during the Ford Administration, due to the Cyprus crisis. In July 1974, a Greek-led coup overthrew President Mihail Makarios of Cyprus. Turkey responded by invading Cyprus. By August, after numerous cease-fire agreements had failed, Turkey gained control of about 40 percent of the land area, displacing about a third of the nearly 180,000 Greeks on the island. Greek Americans organized a huge relief effort. Angered by the Ford/Kissinger tilt toward Turkey and by the Turkish invasion of Cyprus, the Greek-American community was politically mobilized as never before. Led by the Greek Orthodox Archdiocese and by AHEPA, they exerted great influence on Congress. The press began covering them as one of the most effective lobbies in Washington. Congress responded by imposing an embargo on arms to Turkey in February 1975, although restrictions were later modified.

The incident led to the emergence of the American Hellenic Institute—Public Affairs Committee (AHI-PAC). An association to promote trade between Greece and the United States, the PAC operated as the lobby arm on the Cyprus question and sought to activate the Greek-American community to become even more politically involved. Also active were the United Hellenic American Congress, headquartered in Chicago and linked to the Archdiocese, which served as its umbrella organization to coordinate Greek-American efforts, and the Hellenic Council of America, a New York—based organization that enlisted professional and academic Greek Americans to the cause.

The Cypress issue united the Greek Americans to a degree unprecedented since the Greek War Relief of World War II. These efforts reflected the political maturation of Greek Americans and demonstrated the value of working within the American political system. The political mobilization, by then staunchly "anti-Ford/Kissinger," led them back to the Democratic Party. Greek-American newspapers endorsed Carter. An estimated 87 percent of the Greek-American vote went to the ticket.

It shows the importance of the "other nation" loyalty for racial/ethnic minority groups in activating them politically to seek to influence U.S. foreign policy on behalf of their homeland's politics. Other "new" immigrant groups, such as the Slavic immigrant groups and the American-Jewish community, exhibit similar patterns and concerns in their use of the political route to accommodation. Not only is it a means to rise socially and economically in American society, it is a primary way to influence foreign policy on behalf of one's ethnic heritage.

SLAVIC AMERICANS

Immigrating overwhelmingly in the late nineteenth and early twentieth centuries, East European groups, traditionally discussed as the Slavic peoples, were treated alike and experienced many similarities in their emigration, acculturation, and segmented assimilation patterns. Like the Irish, Italian, and Greek Americans, they used politics as their main path to accommodation, but coming later and generally poorer in conditions, they are among the white ethnics who have incorporated more slowly.

They can be grouped into three regions: the Eastern Slavs, the Western Slavs, and the Southern Slavs. The Eastern Slavs include the Russians, White Ruthenians, and Ukrainians. The Western Slavs include the Poles, Czechs, Slovaks, and Lusatin Serbs. The Southern Slavs, located in southwestern Europe, primarily in the Balkan Peninsula, are Hungarians, Slovenians, Croatians, Montenegrins, Serbs, Macedonians, and Bulgarians.

Their migration is almost completely a phenomenon of the post-1870s. Increasingly large numbers arrived from 1890 until 1921, when the Immigration Act sharply curtailed them. During colonial times a few Slavic settlers reached the New Amsterdam and New Sweden colonies, and some Moravians joined the Quaker colony in Pennsylvania. The earliest Russian colonists date back to 1747, when a group settled in Alaska's Kodiak Island. Some colonial-period Ukrainian immigrants were missionaries in California. Polish Americans proudly stress the role of Generals Pulaski and Kosciusko as heroes of the American Revolutionary War.

Slavic immigrants who came after 1880 tended to settle in the industrial centers of the Northeast, some 80 percent of whom were in an area roughly bounded by Washington, DC in the southeast, St. Louis in the southwest, and the Mississippi River, Canada, and the Atlantic Ocean. Two-thirds of them can be found in New York, New England, Pennsylvania, and New Jersey, with sizable numbers also in Illinois and Ohio. The major cities in which they settled are New York, Chicago, Detroit, Cleveland, Boston, Philadelphia, Milwaukee, Buffalo, Baltimore, Pittsburgh, Providence, San Francisco, and Los Angeles.

Slavic immigrants tended to replace German and Irish immigrants in the mines and factories of Pennsylvania and the Midwest and in the slaughterhouses of Chicago.

Like the Italians and Greeks, Slavic immigrants were often sojourners, making up the majority of more than 2 million aliens who returned to Europe between 1908 and 1914. They experienced severe segregation, frequently manifested in ghettoization, and considerable economic hardship. The fact that their young boys began work at an early age, typically for a six-day, 10-hour-per-day workweek, meant that they climbed the socioeconomic ladder slowly. Their peasant backgrounds, longer periods of economic deprivation, which led to child labor and, therefore, lesser formal educational achievements among the second generation, are all factors that contributed to their slower segmented assimilation rates. This section will discuss the Poles as exemplary of Slavic groups using the political tactic to achieve incorporation. One of the more prominent politicians of Slavic heritage (Hungarian ancestry) is former governor of New York, George Pataki.

Polish Americans

In the 2000 census, 9,029,440 persons claimed to be of Polish ancestry. Estimates as to the number of Polish immigrants vary widely since official records were not always counted separately and the area itself changed, at times being part of Germany, Austria-Hungary, or Russia. Thomas and Znaniecki estimate their number at over 875,000, while others place their number at over one million.[4] In a 1998 census report, 6,542,844 persons claimed Polish ancestry, among whom 408,604 (6.2 percent) were foreign-born. Their continued high influx is evident in that among them, about 30 percent arrived since 1980, whereas 70.5 percent arrived before 1980. Of those, 62 percent are naturalized citizens, and 38 percent are not yet citizens. Among those identifying themselves as Polish Americans, nearly 66 percent were in the labor force and only 4.8 percent were unemployed. In occupational background, 30 percent were managerial/professionals, 34 percent were in technical, sales, or administrative jobs, 11 percent were employed in the service sector, about 1 percent earned their livings in farming occupations, 11 percent in production, craft, and repair jobs, and 12 percent were operators, fabricators, or laborers. Fully 80 percent of Polish Americans were in private sector wage or salary occupations, while about 7 percent worked for local government, 3 percent for state governments, 3 percent for the federal government, and 6 percent were self-employed. In terms of workers per family, among Polish-American families 26 percent were single-wage earners, 46 were two wage-earner families, and 14 percent relied on three or more workers.

In educational status, just over 78 percent of Polish Americans were high school graduates, 23 percent were college graduates, and 9 percent had graduate degrees. Their median family income was above the national average ($41,700 compared to $35,525). Among Polish-American families, 6.6 percent were below the poverty level, compared to all families at 13.1 percent. Persons below the poverty level rates were 4.3 percent among Polish Americans compared to 10 percent for all persons (http://www.census .gov/population/socdemo/ancestry/tables01-07).

Historically, about three-fourths of Polish immigrants were farm laborers, unskilled workers, and domestic servants. Less than 12 percent were classified as skilled. A fourth of them were illiterate, and virtually all came with less than $50 in their possession. Polish immigrants tended to be young male sojourners. Their attachment to the homeland was perhaps enhanced by the fact that the ills of life in Poland could be blamed on foreign occupations. Resentment of the Polish upper class seemed less than was typical among other Slavic groups.

Some Polish immigrants got into farming in the Northeast and Midwest, concentrating in truck farming in Long Island and the Connecticut Valley, and in corn and wheat farming in the north-central Midwest and in the Panna Maria settlement in Texas, which was founded in 1854 entirely of Polish immigrant families. Most concentrated in Buffalo, Chicago, Milwaukee, Pittsburgh, Detroit, and New York. Chicago ranks after Warsaw and Lodz as the third largest Polish center in the world.

Men and boys shared common labor jobs, such as working in the coal mines for ten hours per day, six days per week, for less than $15 per week. It was common for children to complete only two years of high school before working full time. That pattern perhaps explains why first- and second-generation Polish Americans were slower in upward mobility than so many other immigrant groups. It was not until they reached the third and fourth generations that Polish Americans started closing the gap. They are heavily blue-collar workers, 40 percent of whom are unionized.

The most influential institutional mechanism in the Polish-American community is the church. Numerous scholars have noted it as the unrivaled instrument for the organization and unification of the Polish-American community.[5] As with Italians and the other Slavic groups, Polish immigrants had difficulty adjusting to the Irish-dominated Catholic church. Protests against that power structure took several forms: parish mutual aid societies joining with the Polish Roman Catholic Union (PRCU), which was organized in 1873; the Polish National Alliance, founded in 1880; and the Polish National Catholic Church (PNCC), begun in 1897 and re-formed in 1904. Today there are fifty independent Polish parishes unified into the PNCC, plus an unknown number of isolated parishes that have split from Rome but have not yet joined the PNCC. The majority of Polish Americans, however, remain faithful to the Catholic church, and since 1970 inroads into the hierarchy have been made with a number of bishops and archbishops of Polish descent. And, of course, a Pole was the late Roman Pontiff.

Polonia—the term used to designate the total Polish-American population—still maintains an estimated 800 Polish-American Catholic parishes. Closely linked to the church are the parochial schools. In the late 1950s, an estimated 250,000 elementary school students were being taught by Polish-American Catholic nuns, and over 100,000 more students were in catechism classes. In the 1980s, there were still more than 600 Polish parochial schools.

During and after World War II, the link between Polonia and Poland weakened. While Polish Americans continued to send money and humanitarian aid, they sent few men. Polonia did push hard to get the Displaced Persons Act passed, which granted exceptions to the quota laws and allowed an estimated 162,400 Poles to enter the United States between 1945 and 1969. They also pressured the government against the Yalta agreement and tried to influence foreign policy to help rid Poland of its communist government and to aid the new government once that came about.

Polish Americans banded together to cope with political and social prejudice, especially against their stereotypical image of being illiterate and mentally deficient, as in the "dumb Polack" jokes. Initial reaction in Polonia was to ignore American culture and turn attention to Poland. This was followed by mixed feelings of anger, withdrawal, and inferiority. Since World War II, however, Polonia has reacted by developing an ideology of America as a pluralistic society rather than as a melting pot. They have attempted to counter prejudice by stressing Polish-American national heroes and contributions to American culture, such as Revolutionary War heroes Pulaski and Kosciusko, and by spotlighting outstanding sports figures and film stars, successful businessmen, artists, and scientists of Polish-American descent. They also formed a Committee for the Defense of the Polish Name (Anti-Defamation Committee) to counter Polish jokes.

Their political activity developed slowly. In the 1920s in Chicago, for instance, only about 25 percent of Polish Americans turned out to vote. Their political impact was weakened further by splitting their vote rather than voting in a cohesive bloc. Since World War II, however, they have been consistently and highly Democratic, reflecting their blue-collar and unionized status. Today, among all white ethnic voters, they are the most likely to vote Democratic. Over 75 percent self-identify as Democrats nationally, and 80 percent do so in the Midwest. From 1958 to 1964, in a study of 57 elections for such offices as U.S. senator, governor, or president, the Democratic percentage of their vote was 65 percent or higher in 54 of those 57 elections, and in one third (19 elections) of those, it exceeded 80 percent. At any level of office, the typical Democratic candidate can expect to receive about two-thirds of the Polish vote. In 1960, John Kennedy received 80 to 85 percent of the Slavic vote, and that dropped off by only 2 percent for Johnson in 1964. President Nixon succeeded in wooing away about 7 percent more in his 1968 and 1972 elections, but the Slavic and Polish-American vote is still about two-thirds loyal to the Democratic Party. A few Polish-American politicians have achieved prominence on the national scene, most notably former Senator Edmund Muskie (D-ME), who sought the Democratic presidential nomination, the late Clement Zablocki (D-WI), former Congressman Dan Rostenkowski (D-IL), and former Senator Barbara Mikulski (D-MD).

The most successful Republican candidates with Polish-American voters are those who are moderate to liberal, such as the former Senators Case, Percy, and Mathias. The first, and so far, only Republican to win a clear majority of the Slavic vote in a statewide race was William Cahill of New Jersey, who in his successful bid for governor in 1969 received an estimated 60 percent of their vote.

Current examples of notable politicians who are Polish Americans include Democrat Ted Kulogoski, Governor of Oregon and Republican Lisa Murkowski who serves in the United States Senate as the junior Senator from Alaska. Kulogoski served for thirty years in public service before being elected governor in 2003. He served in the state's House of Representatives; it's Senate; as Oregon's Insurance Commissioner; as Attorney General; and as an Associate Justice of the state's Supreme Court. Murkowski was appointed by her father, then the sitting Senator, to serve out his term when he became Governor of Alaska in 2002. Lisa had been previously elected to the Alaska House of Representatives in which she was elected as the House Majority Leader, but resigned that position to accept her appointment to the U.S. Senate. She was elected to a full six-year term in 2004. She is considered a moderate Republican, being one of ten Republican Senators who opposed Senate Majority Bill Frist's "nuclear option" to end judicial filibusters, and has a mixed voting record on abortion, being among the few Republican Senators who are pro-choice. Her support of oil exploration in the Arctic

National Wildlife Refuge places her among the "Main Street" Republicans in the Senate. She serves on the Senate Committee on Energy and Natural Resources, on the Foreign Relations Committee, the Committee for Health, Labor, and Pensions, and Indian Affairs. She belongs to the Republican Main Street Partnership Coalition, the Republican Majority for Choice, and Wish List, a group of pro-choice female Republicans comprised of members of both houses of Congress.

By most measures of incorporation, then, Polish Americans are now nearly fully incorporated, but exhibit a pattern of slower assimilation than many other "white ethnic" groups.

JEWISH AMERICANS

Data regarding immigration of Eastern European Jews to the United States are sketchy. About 40 to 45 percent of all South, Central, and East Europeans entering the United States from 1870 to 1930 were Jewish. They immigrated for many of the same push and pull factors motivating the other Slavic groups, but in their case they had the added push of religious/political oppression that ultimately became the most compelling cause of their emigration.

By the 1860s, the serfs, or peasant class, were attaining a degree of freedom and slowly began to develop a small middle class. By 1860, about 5 percent of Russia's labor force was Jewish. Of that segment, 11 percent were employed in industry and 36 percent in commerce. By law, Jews were forbidden to own land, so they became merchants, tailors, administrators, and other commerce-oriented businessmen. Consequently many European Jews were urbanites. This greatly facilitated their segmented assimilation in the highly urbanized areas of the United States.

The czarist government used Jews as scapegoats for long-festering social, economic, and political grievances. The government openly encouraged ethnic minorities, particularly Jews, to emigrate. Jewish immigration to the United States can be directly correlated with historical events in Russia, particularly the pogroms that swept Russia during the 1880s up to World War II. In the Pale of the Settlement area of Russia—the land between the Baltic and the Black seas—those **pogroms** were especially violent, involving looting, pillaging, riots, murders, and, in some cases, total destruction of Jewish ghettos. Government troops would sit idly by or even join in these ventings of frustrations upon the hapless Jews. Such pogroms were often followed by educational restrictions and eventually by expulsion. The photograph on page 143 shows the results of one such pogrom— a mass grave containing an estimated 10,000 victims of a 1941 pogrom.

Since the Jews fled both religious and political persecution, leaving Eastern Europe and especially Russia was not as traumatic an experience for them as for other Russian immigrants. Indeed, to remain in the homeland was to risk life and limb, to remain confined within legal limitations on education and occupational opportunities, and to suffer conscription of their youth at the age of twelve for thirty-one years of compulsory military service. Jewish immigrants were not sojourners as were many other Slavic groups.

Their main ports of entry were New York, Philadelphia, and Baltimore, where they often settled in large numbers in the low-rent areas adjacent to the city's business district. These areas quickly developed into ghetto areas.

Approximately 10,000 Jews who were killed in a 1941 pogrom are buried in this mass grave above the city of Lasi. (*Courtesy of the Library of Congress*)

Jewish immigrants differed from the other South, Central, and East European groups in several respects. They tended to immigrate in whole family units with every intention of remaining. They also came with better and more suitable job skills and a more urban background, which eased their acculturation, especially into American economic life. Sixty-seven percent of Jewish males entering the United States were classified as skilled workers, as compared to the average of 20 percent for all other groups.

They were quickly active in unionization, especially in the garment industry. The Amalgamated Clothing Workers and International Ladies Garment Workers Union (ILGWU) were predominantly Jewish. By World War II, over 60 percent of the ILGWU was Jewish, and the Dressmakers Local 22 of New York City was 75 percent Jewish. About half of the city's Jewish labor force worked in the trade. Other occupations included cigar manufacturing, bookbinding, distilling, printing, and skilled carpentry. In unskilled work, they tended toward being pushcart peddlers and salesmen. A 1900 census study by the Immigration Service found the proportion of Jewish immigrants in the professions the highest among non-English-speaking immigrants.

They experienced considerable and growing prejudice here, but nothing like the pogroms of Europe. In colonial America they were often disenfranchised, such restrictions lasting until 1877 in New Hampshire, the last state to end such restrictions. Anti-Semitic attitudes were prevalent, and stereotyping was common. Jews were often portrayed as scoundrels on the American stage. While their numbers were small, anti-Semitism was easily dealt with by the German Jews who were often middle class. They were at first fearful of the large-scale immigration of East European Jews and rejected the newcomers as a potential source of more virulent outbreaks of anti-Semitism. They were correct in their assessment of the results of such large-scale immigration. When anti-Semitism did escalate, however, they closed ranks and helped the newcomers adjust.

In the 1870s, largely latent anti-Semitism broke out into the open. In 1877, Jews were blackballed from the New York Bar Association, and in 1878, New York college fraternities followed suit. The Saratoga Springs resort began barring them, and soon a host of clubs, resorts, and private schools were doing likewise. The Ku Klux Klan, revived in the late nineteenth century, became the leading nativist group that was especially anti-Semitic.

Pogroms, which broke out again in Russia in 1903 and 1906, led to Jewish efforts to help their brethren. The American Jewish Committee, made up primarily of Americanized German Jews, actively helped the East European Jews raise money for those still suffering in Europe. By 1909, there were over 2,000 Jewish charities operating in the United States, and over $10 million was spent in that year alone. In 1913, the B'nai B'rith's Anti-Defamation League (ADL) was formed. By the 1970s, annual Jewish philanthropy exceeded a billion dollars. These charities organized orphanages, educational institutions, and homes for unwed mothers and delinquent children. They established hospitals and a wide variety of recreational facilities. They supported the Jewish Theological Seminary (which trained rabbis) and Yiddish-language newspapers. Between 1883 and 1915, they started 150 such papers, including the highly influential *Jewish Daily Forward*.

In both their religious institutions and their strongly cohesive family life, Jewish immigrants stressed formal education. Advanced learning was particularly emphasized for males. Professional jobs were held up as the ideal, highly valued for their secure incomes and their social prestige, not only within the Jewish community but in the broader culture as well. By 1915 they made up 85 percent of the student body of New York's City College, a fifth of those attending New York University, and one sixth at Columbia. Education became *the* route to middle-class status and *the* means of acculturation and assimilation.

Today, Jewish immigrants arrive in substantial numbers from Israel. The 1998 census report noted 69,018 persons claiming Israeli ancestry, among whom 43 percent were native-born and 56 percent were foreign-born. Of those foreign-born, 56 percent entered since 1980, while 44 percent had arrived before 1980. Among Israeli immigrants, 45 percent are naturalized citizens and 55 percent are not yet citizens. Israeli-Jewish Americans are a very well-educated lot: over 87 percent are high school graduates, 42 percent hold college degrees, and 21 percent have graduate degrees—all well above national averages. Among them, 69 percent were in the labor force and only 4.6 percent were unemployed. Occupationally, 45 percent held professional or managerial jobs; 34 percent were in technical, sales, or administrative positions; 6 percent were in the service sector; only 0.4 percent were in farming; just over 9 percent were producers, craftsmen, and repairmen; and 6 percent were employed as operators, fabricators, and laborers. Their employment in the private wage/salary sector was 78 percent, while 3 percent worked for local government, 4 percent worked for the state, 2 percent were employed with the federal government, and 12 percent were self-employed. As for families, 35 percent of Israeli-American families relied on a single wage-earner, 48 percent had two wage-earners, and 10 percent relied on three or more workers. Their median household income was well above the national average at a median household income of $40,242 and a mean of $57,055. The median Israeli-American family earned $47,162 and their mean family income was $66,069. Their per capita income was well above the national average at $19,195. The poverty rate among Israeli Americans was 8 percent among families, and 12 percent persons below the poverty level, compared to 10 and 13 percent respectively for all persons at the time.

Politics followed gains in economics. Jews were slow to enter the classic urban machine, although some Jewish immigrants played prominent roles in city politics. Their slowness in political involvement reflected a lack of political experience in their homelands. Jews were often uncomfortable with the big-city machine politicians with their strange skills, codes, vulgarities, and corruption. But politics was the key to power, and power was needed to protect their economic gains and to influence U.S. foreign policy.

Three American politicians of Jewish American background who illustrate their political success story are Senator Charles Schumer of New York, Governor Eliot Spitzer of New York, and Senator Joe Lieberman of Connecticut.

Charles Schumer is the senior U.S. Senator from New York, elected in 2004 to his second term as U.S. Senator after a previous 20 year career in Congress. Senator Schumer serves on the Democratic Leadership team and is a prominent member of the powerful Senate Finance Committee, the Committee on Banking, Housing, and Urban Affairs, and the Administrative Oversight Committee. Senator Schumer had served for three terms in the New York State Assembly before election to the House of Representatives and then the Senate. He was a leading sponsor of the Brady Bill, and is a long-time leading voice on immigration policy. After the 9/11 attacks, he was a lead sponsor of the federal effort to fund rebuilding in New York, and he brokered a key compromise on the anti-terrorism bill.

Eliot Spitzer serves as the current governor of New York, succeeding George Pataki in January 2007 in an election which he won with 69 percent of the vote. He is the former New York State Attorney General and had a national reputation as a leading state's attorney general, first being elected to the office in 1998. He went on to become one of New York's most recognizable Democratic politicians. He used his authority in civil actions against corporations and criminal prosecutions of their officers and led states' attorney general efforts involving federal court cases on pollution, entertainment, technology, occupational safety, and health in which New York plays a central role in setting and maintaining national standards. He was arguably the most noted state Attorney General in the United States.

The classic example of an American Jewish politician who illustrates full civic incorporation is Senator Joseph Lieberman of Connecticut, who is highlighted in Box 4.3. His selection as the Democratic Party's Vice-Presidential nominee in 2000, in which he and Gore lost the election in the electoral college and by a 5/4 decision of the Supreme Court despite having won the popular vote, illustrates the pinnacle of electoral power reached by any U.S. Jewish politician.

The broader story of Jewish American involvement in American politics, a success story to be sure, and their use of politics to influence public policy both to ensure their security here and to aid Israel through foreign policy, set an example followed by such post-1965 Asian American groups as the Vietnamese and Asian Indians. Jewish use of politics shows similarities to another group that used both the economic and political paths to accommodation, Hispanic Americans, to whom we next turn our attention.

HISPANIC AMERICANS

Rapidly increasing numbers of Hispanic Americans has led to greater political electoral strength, although their political incorporation still shows more promise than

Box 4.3   Bio-Sketch of Senator Joseph Lieberman of Connecticut

In 2007, Senator Joseph Lieberman began his fourth term of representing Connecticut in the U.S. Senate. He enjoys a national reputation as a thoughtful and effective legislator. He is best known as the Democratic Party candidate for vice-president in 2000, but he won re-election to the Senate in 2006 as an Independent. His reputation is based on a long and distinguished Senate career and he is widely regarded as one of Congress' most influential voices on national security issues, following his Senate leadership in promoting the law establishing the Department of Homeland Security. Senator Lieberman was a leading advocate for campaign finance reform and is noted for his ability to form bi-partisan legislative efforts.

Senator Lieberman was born in 1942, in Stamford, Connecticut. He took his bachelor's degree from Yale College in 1964, and his law degree from Yale Law School in 1967. He served in the Connecticut State Senate from 1970 to 1980, the last six of those years as its majority Leader. In 1980 he returned to private legal practice for two years, then served as Connecticut's Attorney General. He was first elected to the U.S. Senate in 1988, by the slimmest of margins, but was re-elected in 1996 by over 67 percent of the vote. He won a third term in 2000. In 2006, due largely to an anti-Iraq war vote in the Democratic primary, he lost that primary bid for re-election to the Senate, but went on to run and win office as an Independent. Senator Lieberman is Chairman of the Homeland Security and Governmental Affairs Committee, and a member of the Environment and Public Works Committee, and the Senate Armed Services Committee. He is a former Chairman of the Democratic Leadership Council.

His wife, Hadassah, is the child of Holocaust survivors who fled Hitler's regime to start a new life in the United States. She grew up in Gardiner, Massachusetts, the daughter of a community rabbi.

Source: Bio-sketch by author, based on information on Senator Lieberman's website, http://lieberman.senate.gov/about/. Accessed 2/27/2007.

---

performance. Their potential political clout is significant if yet but partially exercised. A number of Latino politicians became mayors of their respective large cities, an office to which they could achieve election only with the help of non-Hispanic voters. Miami elected Maurice Ferre. Henry Cisneros, mayor of San Antonio, was considered for a while as a possible vice-presidential candidate in 1984, and served in the Clinton administration as secretary of Housing and Urban Development. Denver elected Frederico Peña, who also served in President Clinton's cabinet. Robert Martines was elected mayor of Tampa, Louis Montano served as mayor of Santa Fe, and Judith Valles was the first Latina mayor of a major American city, San Bernardino, California. The largest city with a Hispanic mayor is Los Angeles, which in 2006 elected Antonio Villagrossa.

Annual Immigration (in 000s)

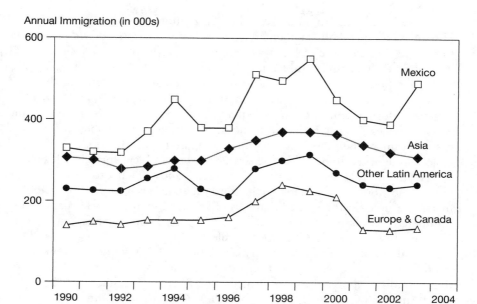

Figure 4.1   Country Groups Show Similar Trends: Rise, Peak, and Decline
Source: Figure by author. Adapted from figure presented by Roberto Suro, Pew Hispanic Center, at the Regional Conference on Illegal Immigration (NCLS, Denver, CO, December 12, 2005).

Figure 4.1 compares Mexican immigration trends with those from Asia, other Latin Americans, and those from Europe and Canada, indicating their potential political clout as their share of the population rises so dramatically.

The Hispanic Congressional Caucus, made up of the various Hispanic members serving in the House, has had a fair degree of influence over some issue areas, such as immigration policy. It has declined in numbers and influence during the Republican-controlled Congress. The most prominent Hispanic elected official today is New Mexico's governor, Bill Richardson, candidate for the Democratic party nomination for president in 2008.

Hispanic political success is a recent phenomenon. Traditionally, the Hispanic vote has been weak. Splintered and with low turnout, it was not a bloc of voters to be vigorously courted by the major parties. Some of their potential for political strength was diluted because of the large number of illegal aliens within the community. Their lack of political efficacy seems related to a high proportion of working-class members and a common sojourner attitude, a prominent feeling of political apathy and ineffectiveness, a pattern of discrimination, a violation of their civil rights, an often dispersed population, internal quarrels, and a general distrust of government. Until recently, few Spanish-speaking people achieved, nor even sought, positions of political leadership. Their relative lack of political power reflected a low level of voter turnout, which, while improving markedly in the past couple of decades, still lags behind all voters. When they do vote, they are so overwhelmingly Democratic in their voting affiliation that they constitute a virtual "captive voting bloc." Assorted surveys among Latinos from the 1960s through the mid-1990s, for example, found Mexican Americans voting Democratic 64 to 92 percent; and among all Latinos, 53 to 82 percent (Table 2.1, p. 31, in DeSipio 1996).

They have begun to mobilize and organize more effectively since the late 1970s. Hispanics are still highly fragmented in terms of both nationality and philosophic view toward dealing with the majority society. Although the majority society sees Hispanics as alike, the Cuban, Puerto Rican, Mexican, and Central-American groups see themselves as different. They conflict with one another, and unity among them is largely illusory, despite "La Raza Unida." These Hispanic subgroups vary considerably in degrees of formal education achieved, a critical background attainment to increased voter awareness, registration, and turnout. Nevertheless, their potential political clout is significant in the nine states in which they are concentrated (Arizona, California, Colorado, Florida, Illinois, New Jersey, New Mexico, New York, and Texas).

Assimilation is stronger among young Chicanos. Their **exogamy** rate (marrying outside the group) has been rising, the third generation is the most exogamous. Among married couples in the United States as of 2004, Hispanic/non-Hispanic households numbered 2,076,000 (compared to 5,611,000 Hispanic/Hispanic households) (*Statistical Abstract of the U.S., 2006,* Table 54: 51).

Another indicator of segmented assimilation is the growing involvement of Latino youth. Politically active Chicano organizations include the older and more conservative or traditional organizations formed after World War I, like the League of United Latin American Citizens (LULAC) formed in 1929; the Community Service Organization (CSO), begun in Los Angeles after World War II, in 1947; and the American GI Forum, started in Texas in 1948. More recent and more militant organizations include the Mexican-American Political Association (MAPA), founded in California in 1958; the Political Association of Spanish-Speaking Organizations (PASSO), begun in Texas in 1959; the American Coordinating Council of Political Education (ACCPE), begun in Arizona in 1959; and Cesar Chavez's union, the United Farm Workers Association that arose in Delano, California in 1965.

The latter group launched Chavez to national prominence as a leading force in the Hispanic civil rights movement. Another major Chicano leader was Reies Lopez Tijerina, known as El Tigre, who started the Alianza Federal de Mercedes (Federal Alliance of Land Grants) in 1963. Using radical tactics inspired by the success of the black civil rights movement, the Alianza led several demonstrations and takeovers. In 1968, Tijerina ran for governor of New Mexico on the Independent People's Constitution Party ticket. In 1969, the group briefly seized the Tierra Amarilla courthouse. San Antonio was the site where the Mexican American Nationalist Organization (MANO) began at about the same time.

In 1965, a "barrio youth" leader emerged on the national scene—Rodolfo "Corky" Gonzales. He started the Crusade for Justice in 1967, based in Denver, Colorado. He was also instrumental in establishing the La Raza Unida Party in 1970. He ran for several state and local offices.

A fourth major Chicano leader to emerge during this period was Jose Angel Guitierrez. He was another youth leader instrumental in the founding of La Raza Unida. He led the Mexican American Youth Organization (MAYO), also begun in 1967. Other Chicano groups with political action agendas included United Mexican American Students (UMAS), Mexican American Student Association (MAESA), Movemento Estudiantial Chicano de Aztlain (MECHA), National Organization of Mexican American Students (NOMAS), and the Association of Mexican American Educators (AMAE).

The 1970s saw the development of La Raza Unida and a voter registration drive (the Southwest Voter Education Project). In 1971, President Nixon made a concerted

BOX 4.4   *BIO-SKETCH OF BILL RICHARDSON, GOVERNOR OF NEW MEXICO*

In 2006, Bill Richardson was re-elected to a second term as Governor of New Mexico with 69 percent of the vote, the largest margin of victory for any governor in the state's history. He also completed a second straight year as Chairman of the Democratic Governor's Association, and he previously served as Chairman of the Western Governor's Association, Chairman of the Border Governor's Conference, and Chairman of the 2004 Democratic National Convention. He is often mentioned as a vice-presidential prospect.

Prior to his first term as Governor, Bill Richardson established a career in public service, academia, and the private sector. He taught courses at New Mexico State University, at the University of New Mexico, at Harvard University's Kennedy School of Government, and at the United World College in Montezuma, NM. In his diplomatic career he negotiated the release of prisoners from Saddam Hussein, and has been nominated several times for the Nobel Peace Prize. He served as Secretary of the Department of Energy.

Richardson served for fifteen years representing the Third Congressional District of New Mexico, one of the most ethnically diverse in the nation. He consistently won re-election with over 60 percent of the vote. While a congressman, he served as special envoy on many sensitive international missions, winning the aforementioned release of U.S. hostages, American servicemen, and prisoners in North Korea, Iraq, and Cuba, and the release of an Albuquerque resident held hostage in Sudan. In 1997 he was nominated U.S. Ambassador to the United Nations where he worked to increase security against international terrorism, and promoted cooperation on such issues as global warming and public health. He was confirmed as Secretary of Energy in 1998.

In 2001, Richardson assumed chairmanship of Freedom House, a private, non-partisan organization promoting democracy worldwide, and served on several boards including the Natural Resource Defense Council and United Way International, serving until his election as New Mexico's governor in 2002.

Source: Bio-sketch by author, based on information on the governor's website: http://www.governor.state.nm.us/governor.php. Accessed 2/27/2007.

effort to woo the Chicano vote through such appointments as Romana Banuelos as secretary of the Treasury, and Phillip Sanchez as head of the Office of Economic Opportunity and then as director of the Immigration and Naturalization Service. In 1980, President Reagan appealed to the Chicano vote, capturing about 30 percent in 1980 and just over that in 1984. Still, the Chicano vote is more potential than actual, with a typical turnout in the low 40 percent of their registered voters. The 1980s saw them win mayoral positions, and Anthony Ayaya elected governor of New Mexico. The best example of a major Hispanic American politician on the current national scene is unquestionably Bill Richardson, Governor of New Mexico. His career is highlighted in Box 4.4.

Puerto Rican Americans

Puerto Rican political activity is a limited and recent development. Their youth, low status, and tradition contribute to low registration and turnout patterns. Several groups make up the major community development forces among them on the mainland. The Puerto Rican Forum started in the mid-1950s. Another important group is the Puerto Rican Family Institute. Of all the grass-roots organizations, Aspira has been the most effective. The ASPIRA Association, Inc., founded in 1961, is the only national nonprofit organization devoted solely to the education and leadership development of Puerto Rican and other Latino youth. ASPIRA takes its name from the Spanish verb "aspirer," aspire. One of the most articulate spokespersons among Puerto Ricans was the director of the Commonwealth of Puerto Rico office in New York, Joseph Monserrat. Other groups include the Puerto Rican Educators Association, the Puerto Rican

Table 4.1   Hispanic versus White Electoral Percentages, 1972–2004

| | Presidential Election Years | | | | | |
| | Reporting Registration | | | Reporting Voting | | |
Year	Hispanic	White	Total	Hispanic	White	Total
1972	44.4%	73.4%	72.3%	37.4%	64.5%	63.0%
1976	37.8	68.3	66.7	31.8	60.9	59.2
1980	36.3	68.4	66.9	29.9	60.9	59.2
1984	40.1	69.6	68.3	32.6	61.4	59.9
1988	35.5	67.9	66.6	28.8	59.1	57.4
1992	35.0	70.1	68.2	28.9	63.6	61.3
1996	35.7	67.7	65.9	26.7	56.0	54.2
2000	57.3	70.4	69.5	45.1	60.5	59.5
2004	34.3	67.9	65.9	28.0	60.3	58.3

| | Congressional Election Years | | | | | |
| | Reporting Registration | | | Reporting Voting | | |
Year	Hispanic	White	Total	Hispanic	White	Total
1974	34.9%	63.5%	62.6%	22.9%	46.3%	44.7%
1978	32.9	63.8	62.6	23.5	47.3	45.9
1982	35.3	65.6	64.1	25.3	47.3	48.5
1986	35.9	65.3	64.3	24.2	47.0	46.0
1990	32.3	63.8	62.2	21.0	46.7	45.0
1994	31.3	64.6	62.5	20.2	47.3	45.0
1998	33.7	63.9	62.1	20.0	43.3	41.9
2002	32.6	63.1	60.9	18.9	44.1	42.3

Source: Table by author, adapted from Horner, *Hispanic Americans: A Statistical Sourcebook,* Table 6.02, pp. 94–95, and *Statistical Abstract of the U.S., 2006,* Table 405: 263.

Legal Defense and Education Fund, the Puerto Rican Institute for Democratic Education, and the National Association for Puerto Rican Civil Rights.

Table 4.1 presents data on the Hispanic vote versus white electoral percentage turnout for the years 1972 to 2004. It shows the percentages reporting registration and those reporting actual voting for both presidential election years (1972–2004), and for congressional election years (1974–2002).

Puerto Ricans have voted overwhelmingly Democratic, usually in the low 90 percentile range. They have voted so solidly Democratic that in 1968, Hulan Jack, a black Democrat, received 88 percent of their vote against the 14 percent cast for a Puerto Rican running on the Republican ticket.

Since the 1970s they have joined other Hispanics in La Raza Unida, and have organized for more standard electoral action and success. They, too, stress voter registration drives. These drives resulted in the election of some prominent Puerto Rican politicians: Baltasar Corrado, the Puerto Rican commissioner; Judge John Carro, the first mainland Puerto Rican to become a federal judge; Teodoro Moscoso, head of the Alliance for Progress under President Kennedy; and Robert Garcia, a Democrat from New York, member of the Hispanic Caucus, and the first New York–born Puerto Rican to serve in the U.S. Congress.

By 2000, the Hispanic voting age population (that is, 18 years and older) was 21,598,000, or 10.6 percent of the total voting-age population in 2000. This compared with 168,733,000 (83.3 percent) among the white, non-Hispanic population. Among registered voters in 2000, Hispanic voters 18 years or older were 34.9 percent, compared to 65.6 percent white; and among those 18 years and older who claimed to have actually voted in 2000, the Hispanic rate was 27.5 percent compared to 47.4 percent of white voters. (Horner 2002, *Hispanic Americans: Statistical Sourcebook,* pp. 99–103). By 2004, 34.3 percent of registered Hispanic voters actually voted, compared to 67.9 percent for whites.

The gradually increasing Hispanic political activity and growing influence is shown in Table 4.1 (on page 150), which details the Hispanic versus white electoral activity from 1972 to 2000. It shows the percent registering and voting in presidential years and in congressional election years from 1972 to 2000. Hispanic activity continuously trails by half that of white voters.

Increased Hispanic political activity has led to growing political clout and electoral results, indicated by Hispanics being elected to public office at all levels. Hispanic elected officials grew from just over 3,000 in 1985 to more than 5,200 in 2000. In 2004, there were 4,651 Hispanic elected officials at the state and local levels, 231 in state executive or legislative offices, 2,059 in city and county elected office, 638 in judicial and law enforcement elected positions, and 1,723 in elected educational offices/school boards (*Statistical Abstract of the U.S., 2006,* Table 403: 262).

As Hispanic political activity and clout grows, it does so at times in a direct clash with black Americans. While Hispanics follow the lead of the black civil rights movement and often work closely with the black Congressional Caucus on bills of mutual interest—for example, on immigration policy—they also come into conflict with one another on efforts to control local politics. It is to black American political activity we next turn our attention.

BLACK AMERICANS

Only black Americans experienced the status of slavery, an experience that shaped their incorporation rates and patterns. Most black Africans who migrated to the United States prior to 1808, when the slave trade was officially ended, were forced to come as slaves. In recent years, voluntary migration has averaged about 65,000 annually. Two hundred plus years of slavery not only slowed their acculturation and assimilation but also shaped the majority society's norms and attitudes in ways relevant today.

According to 2000 census data, black or African Americans (alone) numbered 34,658,190, or 12.3 percent of the total population. This puts them slightly behind Hispanics or Latinos, who at 35,305,818 comprised 12.5 percent of the total population. If, however, one counts persons identifying themselves as black or African American in combination with one or more other race, then their number rises to 36,419,434, or 12.9 percent of the total population. In part, this reflects the growing number of married couples of mixed race and origin. In 2000, 363,000 couples identified themselves as black/white couples; among them were 268,000 couples with a black husband and white wife, and 95,000 with a white husband and black wife. Another 50,000 couples identified themselves as married couples of black with another race mixture.

In education, in 2000, over 79 percent of African Americans aged 25 or over had graduated high school, a record high; and 17 percent had earned at least a bachelor's degree. In 2000, over one million African Americans had earned an advanced degree (master's, Ph.D., M.D., or J.D.).

The poverty rate for African Americans, at 23.6 percent, was the lowest ever measured by the census bureau, and their median income was the highest ever recorded. Just under half (48 percent) lived in married couple households. Their family size is larger than that of non-Hispanic white families (e.g., 21 percent of African-American households had five or more members compared with 12 percent for non-Hispanic white households).

The African-American population is young, with a median age of 30.4 years compared to the 35.3 median age for the U.S. population as a whole. In 2000, 54 percent of blacks lived in the South, 19 percent in the Northeast, 19 percent in the Midwest, and 8 percent in the West. Over 53 percent of African Americans resided in central-city metropolitan areas. The five states with the largest African-American populations were New York (3.2 million), California (2.5 million), Texas (2.5 million), Florida (2.3 million), and Georgia (2.2 million). The District of Columbia (Washington, DC) led all states or state equivalent with the largest percentage (61 percent) of African Americans in its total population. Cook County, Illinois (Chicago), at 1.4 million, had more African Americans than any other county. It was followed by Los Angeles, California, at just over 1 million.

In jobs, 25 percent of employed African-American women, and 18 percent of the men, worked in managerial and professional specialties (e.g., over 96,000 engineers, 47,000 physicians, 47,000 lawyers, and so on). In 2000, however, where the unemployment rate among whites was 3.5 percent, it was 7.6 percent among blacks. In 2001, the unemployment rates among whites rose to 4.2 percent, and to 8.7 percent among blacks (http://www.census.gov/PressRelease/www/2001/cb01/ff02.html).

Their historical experience with slavery shaped their educational and occupational patterns for generations, determining for all time their incorporation into the majority society. In the South the existence of slavery led to an elaborate caste system with clear and strongly delineated norms for interaction. Repression, prejudice, and discrimination against blacks were exceptionally strong. Even the free blacks of the South, of whom there were nearly one-quarter million prior to the Civil War, faced rigid discrimination because of the caste system. They lived at the margins of society, virtual slaves without masters, and had few legal rights. With few exceptions they could not vote; they were banned from schools, the militia, public places, and many types of occupations. While they could make contracts and be married, sue, and hold property, they could not testify against whites in courts or sit on juries. They faced harsh penalties if convicted of crimes.

For the millions of slaves living in the South by 1860, conditions were far worse. The interstate trade was among slavery's most inhumane aspects. Prior to the Civil War there were an estimated 4 million slaves in the United States. This practice not only degraded the individual in particular, it had profound and lasting impact on the African-American population in general by greatly influencing their acculturation. It destroyed existing links to their native culture and groupings, often destroyed family units, and dispersed their population throughout the South. The harshness of slave life was an important ingredient in subsequent African-American development, as slaves were highly limited in their occupational training and education. Slave status contributed to the development of a sense of racial superiority among whites. The antebellum slave codes were very repressive, designed to cause fear of the white man among the slaves.

Slaves were both legally and culturally considered as property—chattel—and thus, by legal definition, were subhuman. They could be bought, sold, given away, or killed at the will of their master. Slave women could be sexually used by their masters or for breeding purposes. Discipline was strict, as slaves were taught to be submissive yet productive. Slaves were fearful of and dependent upon whites. This was done to ensure their submission and loyalty. Family life was unstable to nonexistent. Morbidity and mortality rates among slaves were very high. Illness, filth, and disorder were common aspects of the slaves' everyday life. Since they were owned and maintained solely for their labor, equal social interaction with whites was unknown. Such status depressed the need for achievement. It developed a *matrifocal* (mother-centered) family life tradition that not only led to higher rates of female-headed households among blacks but also a weakening of the male role.

The effects of the slave system were not limited to the black population. Whites were also, if differentially, affected. Southern whites were obliged to defend slavery against outsiders whom they felt were incapable of understanding their peculiar problem. They also felt an ever-present need to defend themselves against slave revolt. This fear conditioned otherwise compassionate men to accept and overlook excessive brutality against blacks. It encouraged a sense of a common bond among all white men that became the basis for a unified South of one-party politics and a common perspective on national politics that had its roots deeply planted in the slave period (Dye 1971).

The Civil War and the end of slavery brought a promise of peace and equality in the reconstruction period, but reconstruction was short-lived, lasting but a decade. The radical Republicans gained control of Congress in 1867. The southern states, under military rule, adopted new constitutions that assured blacks the vote and other civil liberties. Blacks were elected to the Congress and to various state legislatures. A prominent black politician was governor of Louisiana for 40 days. The Reconstruction Congress passed the Thirteenth, Fourteenth, and Fifteenth Amendments.

Between the end of the Civil War and the late 1870s, blacks enjoyed considerable success. They voted throughout the South, and many were elected to federal and state-level offices. They were treated nearly equally in theaters, restaurants, hotels, and public transportation facilities as guaranteed by the Civil Rights Act of 1875. By 1877, though, these gains began to abate and recede.

The Compromise of 1877 ended the military occupation of the South. More importantly, a series of U.S. Supreme Court decisions spelled the collapse of reconstruction. The *Slaughterhouse* cases of 1873 nullified the privileges and immunities clause of the Fourteenth Amendment. The *Civil Rights* cases of 1883 declared the Civil Rights Act of 1875 unconstitutional. In 1884, the *Hurtado v. California* ruling severely restricted the due process clause of the Fourteenth Amendment. Finally, in *Plessy v. Ferguson,* in 1896, the Court approved the segregation of society through application of the "separate-but-equal doctrine" that essentially nullified the equal protection clause of the Fourteenth Amendment.

Even during reconstruction, southern whites used campaigns of violence and intimidation. The Ku Klux Klan led the movement to suppress the emergence into society of the new black citizens. Major riots occurred in Memphis, Tennessee, where 46 blacks were killed and 75 wounded, and in Colfax and Coushatta, Louisiana, where more than 100 blacks and white Republicans were massacred.

Segregation in its full-blown Jim Crow form took shape gradually, aligned with the rise of populism in the South. Southern blacks voted well into the 1880s. They held office, served on juries, on local government councils, and in the U.S. Congress. Blacks and whites rode the railroads in the same cars, ate in the same restaurants, and sat in the same theaters and waiting rooms. As southern whites regained control over government, a program of relegating blacks to a subordinate place in society accelerated. Beginning in Virginia as early as 1869 and spreading throughout the South, the use of Jim Crow laws and Klan intimidation characterized the "new South's" approach to the end of reconstruction.

Disenfranchisement was the initial step taken. Blacks who defied Klan pressure and tried to vote were met with an array of deceptions and obstacles. Polling places were changed at the last minute without notice to blacks. Severe time limits to complete long and complex ballots were imposed on blacks. Votes cast incorrectly in a maze of ballots were nullified. State constitutions were rewritten to disenfranchise blacks who could not read, understand, or "correctly interpret" complex and obscure sections of the constitution. Yet state constitutions permitted those who failed the test to vote "if their ancestors had been eligible to vote on January 1, 1860, when no Negro could vote anywhere in the South." In 1896, black registered voters in Louisiana totaled 130,344. In 1900, after the state rewrote its suffrage laws, only 5,320 blacks remained on the registration books. In 1883, the Supreme Court declared the 1875 Civil Rights Act void. In 1896 *Plessy v. Ferguson* promulgated the "separate-but-equal doctrine." Legal segregation reinforced social custom. Soon, blacks and whites were segregated by law on public transit and in all places of public accommodation, even hospitals and churches. Blacks and whites swore their oaths on separate Bibles in courthouses. They were even buried in separate cemeteries. Segregation meant discrimination, since the facilities, school conditions, and salaries were invariably worse for blacks. They were always separate but never equal.

Conditions in the North were not much better. Blacks were crowded by local ordinances into one section of a city where housing and public services were invariably substandard. Discrimination in employment was rampant. Blacks were limited to menial jobs. Labor unions excluded them from membership, or granted them membership only in separate and mostly powerless Jim Crow locals. Yet if blacks took jobs during strikes, they were castigated as "scabs" for undermining the principles of trade unionism.

Northern whites also resorted to violence. Anti-black riots took place in New York in 1900; in Springfield, Ohio, in 1904; in Greensburg, Indiana, in 1906; and in Springfield, Illinois, in 1908. The latter riot, a three-day rampage initiated by a white woman's charge of being raped by a black man, left six persons dead and extensive property damage. Many blacks fled the city permanently, most migrating to Chicago. Throughout the nation about 100 lynchings occurred every year in the 1880s and 1890s. One hundred sixty-one blacks were lynched in 1892 alone. "A virtual reign of terror began in the 1890s and extended to the beginning of World War I. A pioneering study by the NAACP, appropriately entitled 'Thirty Years of Lynchings in the United States, 1889–1918,' lists the names of 3,224 lynch victims" (Dye 1971, 18–19).

Those blacks who fled from Springfield to Chicago found they had left the frying pan for the fire. In 1919, the nation was embroiled in the "Red Summer" race riots, the worst of which shook Chicago, which had experienced an immigration of 60,000 blacks from the South from 1910 to 1919. The riot began when an 18-year-old black drifted across the imaginary line segregating black and white swimmers. White rock throwers caused him to drown. Soon after, blacks mobbed a policeman who refused to arrest the whites responsible. Then a crowd of Italian Americans killed the first black they saw, starting a riot that left 38 dead, 1,000 homeless, and 537 injured (Levy and Kramer 1973).

As more blacks migrated north, race riots became almost commonplace. Northern whites increasingly accepted the South's views on race relations. Social customs followed public policy in the North. Soon little signs reading "white only" or "colored" were everywhere (see photo 1.1). Although these lacked the sanction of law, black children were taught in their segregated schools to obey those signs. Segregation replaced slavery as society's method of keeping blacks "in their place." The vast majority of blacks remained mired at the bottom of the social and economic system. Segregation was supported by state law, by social practices, and by most institutions. Blacks were segregated throughout their lives, from birth in a segregated hospital, to attendance at segregated schools, to living in segregated neighborhoods, to employment in a segregated and limited job, to burial in a segregated cemetery. While some gains were made during Reconstruction, those were largely overturned in the Jim Crow era. Most political gains by African Americans have been a post-1970 development.

African Americans, as of the 2000 census, numbered 34,658,190 when counted black alone, and 36,419,434 when counted in combination with another race. Their median age was 30.2, nearly five years below that of the total population. In 2000

Table 4.2   Median Household Income Constant (2003) Dollars, 1990–2003

Year	All Households	White	Black	Asian/Pacific Islanders	Hispanic
1990	$40,865	$42,622	$25,488	$59,559	$35,429
1991	39,679	41,586	24,771	48,007	29,887
1992	39,364	41,385	24,098	48,570	29,035
1993	39,165	41,320	24,487	48,073	28,690
1994	39,613	41,779	25,816	49,703	28,756
1995	40,845	43,379	26,842	48,682	27,401
1996	41,431	43,379	27,411	50,517	29,073
1997	42,294	45,542	28,630	51,716	30,434
1998	43,825	46,110	28,572	52,562	31,929
1999	44,922	45,720	30,808	56,251	33,938
2000	44,853	46,910	31,690	59,559	35,420
2001	43,822	46,261	30,625	55,736	34,880
2002	43,381	$46,119	26,691	53,832	33,861
2003	43,318	45,631	29,645	55,699	32,977

Source: U.S. Census Bureau, *Statistical Abstract of the United States, 2006,* adapted from Table 674, p. 460.

black Americans registered some record numbers and impressive gains in several indicators of economic, social, and political incorporation, although they still lag behind other racial minorities in most categories.

In 2004, 81 percent of Black Americans had graduated high school or more; 19 percent of blacks had some college but no degree, 8 percent had earned an AA degree, 18 percent had their BA degree; and 5 percent had an advanced degree (*U.S. Statistical Abstract, 2006,* Table 216: 148). Their participation rate in the labor force approached that of the total population: 66 percent of blacks were in the labor force compared to 67 percent for the total population. African-American families tend to be larger than those of whites. Nationwide, 53 percent of African Americans resided in central cities within metropolitan areas. In 2000, African-American homeownership reached 47 percent, again the highest ever.

Economic gains were made between 1990 and 2000 but, as can be seen in Table 4.2, the median income of black Americans consistently lagged behind those of all other racial groups.

African Americans were the only race or ethnic group to show an increase in voter participation in congressional elections, increasing their turnout at the polls from 37 percent in 1994 to 40 percent in 1998, while nationwide the overall turnout by the voting-age population was down from 45 percent in 1994 to 42 percent in 1998. During those same years, black Americans increased their voter registration rates from 59 percent to 61 percent.

One of the earliest leaders using the political strategy was the brilliant W. E. B. Du Bois, a historian and sociologist at Atlanta University. In 1905, he and a small group of black intellectuals met in Niagara Falls, Canada. The Niagara movement rejected the

W. E. B. DuBois, co-founder of the NAACP (*Courtesy of the Library of Congress*)

moderation and compromise advocated by Booker T. Washington and called for radical change ending black inferior status, the loss of voting and civil rights, and the Jim Crow laws, segregated schools, inhumane conditions in southern prisons, denial of equal job opportunities, and segregation in the armed forces (Brooks 1996, 128–131). Out of this came the establishment, on February 12, 1909, on the 100-year anniversary of Lincoln's birthday, of the National Association for the Advancement of Colored People (NAACP). Over the years, the NAACP led the campaign for black civil rights through legal action. In 1915, it achieved its first major victory in one of hundreds of cases pursued at all levels of government. The U.S. Supreme Court declared unconstitutional the grandfather clause of the Oklahoma constitution. In 1954, the NAACP won an even greater victory in *Brown v. Board of Education of Topeka, Kansas,* which finally overturned the "separate-but-equal" doctrine established in *Plessy v. Ferguson* (1896). The *Brown* decision gave a constitutional blessing to the movement to desegregate the United States, effectively beginning the end to de jure segregation (segregation by law).

From World War II through the mid-1960s, a period of new-style radicalism involving the use of direct-action protest predominated, a tactic discussed more fully in Chapter 8. The successes of the civil rights movement in the 1960s paved the way for some substantial gains being made using standard electoral politics. The culminating actions of the movement were passage of the Civil Rights Act of 1964 and the Voting Rights Act of 1965. The impact of these two laws can be seen in the closing of the voting gap between whites and blacks. These two laws, strongly supported by a Democratic administration and a Democratic-controlled Congress, resulted in continued strong electoral support for the Democrats by black voters throughout the 1970s and 1980s, even as that party's white coalitions weakened and fell. Voting loyalty was often significant. Presidents Carter and Clinton owed their electoral success to the margins they received from African-American voters. The percentage of black voter turnout rose dramatically after 1965. Electoral success followed, with thousands of blacks in public office at all levels and in all regions.

For example, in 1947, there were only two black representatives in the Eightieth Congress. Their number remained under a half dozen through 1963. It reached double digits (12) in 1968, rose to 20 in 1980, to 39 in 1992, and 40 in 1998. The Black Congressional Caucus now has 80 white associate members. Since 1880, only three blacks have been elected to the U.S. Senate, Edward Brooke (R-MA) in the 1970s, Carol Moseley-Braun (D-IL) from 1992 to 1998, and Barack Obama (D-IL) in 2004.

Blacks achieved symbolically important firsts in 1983. Although these events may not rank with the 1964–1965 acts, they validated the opening of doors previously closed to blacks. Guion Bluford became the first black astronaut in space, and Miss New York, Vanessa Williams, became the first black Miss America. Important strides were made in politics as the civil rights movement shifted from protest politics to elective office. In part, this change in strategy reflected a change in black leadership. Some 1960s black leaders were assassinated: Dr. Martin Luther King Jr., Medgar Evers, and Malcolm X. Others were imprisoned: Stokely Carmichael, Huey Newton, and Bobby Seale. Still others went into exile (Eldridge Cleaver). The newer leadership (Andrew Young, Jesse Jackson) had new political resources. By 1980, the total number of black elected officials had risen to 4,890. Three hundred served in the various state legislatures and the U.S. Congress. Over 2,800 held city and county offices. Gains were made in the nation's largest cities. In 1966, no large American city had a black mayor. By 1984, two dozen cities in excess of 100,000 in population had one, and there were 245 black mayors in cities of all sizes.

The 1984 presidential election showed evidence of changing attitudes toward black politicians. Public opinion polls by Gallup, Harris, and Washington Post/ABC News showed 77 percent of the public said they would vote for a well-qualified black candidate for president, a higher percentage than those who, in 1960, said they would vote for a Catholic. Jesse Jackson won 18.3 percent of the primary votes cast in 1984, earning a total of 384 delegates and playing a role at the Democratic National Convention. In 1988, he ran again, his percentage growing to 29 and his delegate count to 1,218.

The Jackson candidacy augmented an impressive voter registration drive. The Voter Education Project, based in Atlanta, led a drive netting over 1 million new black voters across the nation. In the 1980 election, black turnout increased by 18 percent, and in some districts it, for the first time, exceeded that of white voters. In 1982, black turnout rose by 5.8 percent over the previous off-year election, which was more than double the increase in white voter turnout. In 1984, the gap between white and black registration was only 3.3 percent, and turnout was only 6.9 percent. The turnout gap in 1996 was only 5.4 percent, the lowest of any national election in history. Black voting remains consistently Democratic. By 2004, 64.4 percent of blacks reported they were registered to vote, where registered whites were at 67.9 percent. The number of black elected officials has steadily increased. As of 2001, there were a total of 9,061 blacks holding elective office: 633 in U.S. or state legislative offices, 5,456 in city or county elected office, 1,044 elected law enforcement officials, and 1,928 elected education officials (*Statistical Abstract of the U.S., 2006*, Table 403: 262).

These data demonstrate African-American weakness and minority status in the use of political power. The very failure of the Jackson campaign to create a powerful "rainbow coalition" capable of electing a black to the highest office, or even to dramatically impact national policy, demonstrates the need for alternative strategies and tactics for some racial minority groups. In 2003, running for the Democratic Party nomination for the 2004 presidential election was former U.S. senator from Illinois and former ambassador, Carol Mosely-Braun. The most serious African American presidential contender is Illinois Senator Barack Obama, whose career was described in the reading at the end of Chapter 1.

Another leading African American politician who exemplifies black use of the political accommodation approach is one of the founders of the Black Congressional Caucus, Representative Charles Rangel of New York. In the U.S. Congress, the Congressional Black Caucus is the organization of African American members that seeks to influence the course of events relevant to African Americans and others of similar experience and situation by achieving greater equality for persons of African descent in the content of domestic and international programs and services. In the 110th Congress the caucus is chaired by Representative Carolyn Cheeks Kilpatrick of Michigan (D-MI, 13th). (See Table 8.1 for a list the members of the Black Congressional Caucus as of the 110th Congress, identifying their party and district.)

Black Americans have employed all three strategies and all six tactics. Chapters 5 and 6 illustrate the use of physical and psychological separatism, each of which was pursued by significant factions of black Americans.

GAY/LESBIAN POLITICAL MOVEMENT

Like Black American and Hispanic American use of the political strategy of accommodation, gay/lesbian politics as a movement arose relatively recently—since the 1970s. Gay/lesbian political power has high potential but has been limited in its successful use to date. A relative lack of cohesion and targeted participation remains a factor in their potential for political power being somewhat "untapped."

A significant aspect of their movement's power status is that a large portion of their population remains "in the closet." This hampers their ability to organize and to direct their political action in a highly focused manner. Estimates for the size of the homosexual-preference population place it at about 8 percent of the total population (estimated at ten percent of males and six percent of females) (Fisher 1975, 193, 254; LeMay 1985: 340; Siminoski 1984, 6). Although not an accurate count of gay households, nonetheless, an indication of the increasing openness and of the size of the gay population can be gleaned from the 2006 *Statistical Abstract of the United States*, which numbers, as of 2002, the total number of households in the United States (108,419,5006), and then the number of unmarried-partner households by sex of partner. The total unmarried households in 2002 numbered 5,571,436. Of these, the male/male partner households were 363,072; and the total female/female partner households were 338,661 (Table 57: 52). To the extent that the estimated 8 percent of the population being gay is accurate, then the gay population as of 2004 would be about 2,773,400.

As Blasius notes: "Nevertheless, the birth, since the Stonewall Riots of 1969, of a lesbian and gay 'counterculture' within the stifling larger culture is somewhat of an illusion. Gay men and lesbians are therefore in a situation of constituting themselves as a political community that is dispersed throughout society fighting homophobia wherever it occurs" (1992, 647).

To be effective as a political movement, gays and lesbians need to use "identity deployment," as the lesbian and gay movement is the quintessential identity movement (Bernstein 1997, 532). The tension between political and cultural goals will always be an issue for social movements, not just for the lesbian and gay movement (Ibid: 560). The movement confronts an inherent dilemma, how best to put forward a set of unsettling demands for unconventional people in ways that will not make enemies of potential allies (Tarrow 1994, 10). Identity deployment, then, is a form of strategic use of collective action, and movement leaders within political campaigns decide whether to celebrate or suppress differences based on the structure of the social movement organizations, their access to polity, and the type of opposition they face (Bernstein 1997, 532).

When the social movement (or a portion of it) morphs into a political movement, it uses politics in a strategic way. "Politics involves a 'problematization' or a calling into question of power relations in society *by* a social movement, *through* transformation techniques that are used to govern people—exercising and submitting to power relations, and a production of knowledge (writing, reflection, scientific or other statements that make claim to truth) about the meaning of this phenomenon *as* political" (Blasius 1992, 642, his italics).

Indeed, "gay and lesbian existence should be conceived as an ethos rather than as a sexual preference or orientation, as a life-style, or *primarily* in collectivist terms, as a subculture or even as a community . . . The key to understanding ethos is through the lesbian and gay conceptualization of 'coming out,' understood as a process of *becoming* in which the individual enters into a field of relationships that constitute the gay and lesbian community" (Blasius 1992, 642–43, his italics).

Unless they "come out" and become part of the community, it means that lesbians and gay men suffer from discrimination like any other minority—in laws, housing, employment, public accommodations, police harassment, negative stereotyping, and so on—but grow up without the protective benefits of a distinct subculture. Homosexuals are not raised as homosexuals, in the sense that Jews, Catholics, Poles, Blacks, Asians and such are all raised by their families and groups to be members of that subculture. Homosexuals most often have no community while growing up in which they share their minority status and learn a tradition, a lifestyle, that shapes their values, goals, and styles of behavior and ways of relating to one another and to the world at large. They often lack role models while growing up. The homosexual is aware of his/her own sexual orientation before they are aware of the idea that others exist and share those values and that lifestyle on which to pattern themselves. They feel sexual feelings that nobody else seems to share, and they quickly learn that it is dangerous to openly acknowledge those feelings (Fisher 1995, 70–71). As Blasius puts it: "Rather than being an end-state in which one exists as an 'out' person, coming out is a process of becoming, a lifelong learning of how to become and of inventing the meaning of being a lesbian or a gay man in this historical moment" (1992–655). To survive, lesbians and gay men must either stay hidden in the closet, or come out and work together in alliance. For the latter, "political action, made possible by the creation of a lesbian and gay public sphere, effects state policies but is not itself only statist in orientation; such political action is directed at power *relations*—power as it is exercised in everyday life through procedures of subjection and the forms of domination that support them" (666). The substance of politics is defining the question, "how shall we live"?

Haider-Markel and Meier (1996) note that moral disputes over values have a long political history in the United States, and have a highly symbolic edge in part because they are more rarely enforced. Morality politics puts the government's stamp of approval on one set of values rather than another. Morality policy is similar to redistributive policy, except in this case the redistributed good is not money or governmental services and programs but values (333). A morality model of politics sees the distribution of citizen values as the determining variable in explaining public policy, rather than interest groups' influence (Ibid, 334). When studying seven policy issues directly linked to state-wide initiatives on gay civil rights issues in two states (Oregon and Colorado), however, Haider-Markel and Meier found that gay and lesbian politics resembles interest group rather than morality politics (Ibid, 343–46). Morality politics involves open conflict between advocacy coalitions with different concepts of values and morality. Because religious groups have explicit moral codes, they are frequent players in morality politics (Ibid, 337). Partisanship is also linked to morality politics. Emphasis on traditional family values results in the Republican Party as viewed as antigay while the liberal Democratic Party is seen as more supportive of gay civil rights policy.

Discrimination in jobs, housing, public accommodation and services, and mass media stereotyping drove the lesbian and gay social movement to political activism—to come out of the closet and join a "gay liberation" political movement. The Mattachine Foundation, begun in Los Angeles in 1950, can be considered the first real homosexual political movement. New York's Mattachine organization spun off an action committee whose members formed the nucleus of the New Gay Liberation Front, begun in July, 1969, after the "Stonewall Rebellion" (Fischer 1975, 186; LeMay 1985, 346). The Gay Liberation Front spread quickly in the 1970s, stressing gay consciousness raising. A more militant gay movement emerged about the same time, the Gay Activist Alliance. Alliance members emphasized confrontation and political visibility in order to promote change. The Alliance, comprised of numerous local groups and chapters, promoted a wide range of policy goals: repeal of sodomy laws, laws against solicitation, and laws used to justify the policy of entrapment and enticement procedures by law enforcement. It sought to end overt gay discrimination in jobs, housing, and public accommodation. It consciously attempted to manipulate the media to reduce the negative stereotyping, to recruit new activists, and to use the media to further its political goals and agenda. By the late 1980s and 1990s, gays were openly backing local politicians in cities such as San Francisco, Washington, DC, New York, Boston, and so on. Massuchusetts became important for showing that gay support was not necessarily a political liability. Openly gay and pro-gay legislators were elected and re-elected, as exemplified by Congressman Barney Frank, whose career is briefly highlighted in Box 4.5.

The lesbian and gay political movement illustrates well the multifaceted use of identity. The creation of community and movement solidarity necessitates mobilization. Mary Bernstein identifies three analytical dimensions of identity: 1) identity for empowerment, where activists draw on existing identity or construct a new collective identity

Box 4.5   *Bio-sketch of Representative Barney Frank, Massachusetts*

Barney Frank has represented the 4th Congressional District of Massachusetts since 1981. He was born in New Jersey and educated at Harvard College, taking his degree in 1962. He taught undergraduates at Harvard while pursuing a Ph.D. degree, but left to become Chief Assistant to Mayor Kevin White of Boston, then served a year as Administrative Assistant to Congressman Michael J. Harrington. In 1972 he was elected to the Massachusetts Legislature, where he served for eight years, during which time he entered Harvard Law School and graduated in 1977. He taught part-time at the University of Massachusetts, Boston, at the John F. Kennedy School of Government, and at Boston University.

Frank passed the Massachusetts Bar in 1979, and ran for and was elected to Congress in 1980. He soon emerged as a leading figure in the liberal wing of the Democratic Party and an outspoken critic of human rights issues, particularly gay and lesbian rights, coming out as gay in public in 1987. In 1998 he founded the National Stonewall Democrats, the national gay, lesbian, bisexual, and transgender Democratic organization. In 2004 and 2006 Capital Hill staffers named him the "brainiest" member of congress, and in the same survey he was called the "funniest" and the "most eloquent" member of the House. He has also been noted for his blunt stance on outing certain gay Republicans, called the "Frank rule," in which he stated it is acceptable to out a closeted gay person if that person uses their power or notoriety to hurt gay people.

Source: Bio-sketch by author LeMay, from information in his official Congressional website, http:www.house/gov/frank, accessed 3/2/2007; and in wikipedia.org/Barney_Frank, accessed 3/2/2007.

to create and mobilize a constituency; 2) identity as goal, where activists challenge stigmatized identities, seek recognition of new identities, or deconstruct restrictive social categories; and 3) identity as strategy, where activists deploy identity strategically as a form of collective action (Bernstein 1997, 536–37).

SUMMARY

This chapter explained and illustrated the strategy of accommodation and how various groups used the political tactic of that strategy. It discussed the Irish Americans as the prototype example of political accommodation and how they helped create the urban political machine and then used machine politics to climb the socioeconomic ladder of society. The chapter discussed other groups who employed that tactic, albeit less successfully than did the Irish: Italian Americans, Greek Americans, and some Slavic American groups, as well as East European Jews. The chapter then discussed its use by factions of Hispanic Americans, focusing especially on the Chicano and Puerto Rican groups. The chapter discussed how a faction of black Americans, particularly as illustrated by the leadership of Jesse Jackson, the Black Congressional Caucus, and currently Senator Barack Obama, showed success in employing the political approach to accommodation. The chapter closed with a brief discussion of the lesbian and gay political movement and their increasing use of the strategy and its electoral political tactics.

Key Terms

exogamy   Marrying outside of one's ethnic group.

padroni   Italian "boss" system.

pogrom   Violent outbreaks of looting, pillaging, riots, and murders in Eastern Europe directed at Jews with the government's tacit approval.

polonia   Term referring to the total Polish-American population.

Review Questions

1. Which groups discussed in this chapter would you characterize as having achieved a high level of civic incorporation, which a moderate level, and which a low level of civic incorporation? What statistical data presented in this chapter would you cite as evidence to substantiate your rankings of the groups into a high, medium, or low level of civic incorporation?

2. What was the first, and the classic, example of the urban machine? What factors have contributed to the decline of machine politics since the 1930s?

3. What groups make up Slavic Americans? Where in the United States do they tend to concentrate?

4. Compare and contrast how the "new" immigrants relied heavily on their churches and mutual-aid societies for their assimilation process.

5. Why were East European Jewish immigrants *not* sojourners?

6. Specify any three prominent Hispanic political leaders, and discuss the organizations they founded. Characterize the style of politics of each such leader/organization.

7. What are some advantages and disadvantages for a minority group of being closely allied with a particular political party organization?

8. Which black American leader has been the foremost advocate of standard political electoral behavior as a means to develop black political clout? What are some advantages and disadvantages to blacks voting according to their race?

9. Write a brief bio-sketch of any two black Americans who serve(d) on the U.S. Supreme Court.

10. What barriers to electoral success do lesbian and gay minority groups have to overcome?

Notes

1. See, for example, Parrillo (1985). Dinnerstein and Reimers (1988) cite the fact that by 1860 some two-thirds of the domestics in Boston were Irish.

2. Federal Writer's Project, *The Italians of New York.* New York: Arno Press, 1969: viii.

3. Luciano Iorizzo and Salvatore Mondello, *The Italian Americans*. New York: Twayne, 1971: 48.

4. Other sources estimate their number at over 1 million (Dinnerstein and Reimers 1988; Parrillo 1985; Dinnerstein and Jaher 1977). Lopata puts the maximum at 1,670,000 for the number who emigrated and remained here from 1885 to 1972; estimates for the total Polish-American group (Polonia) range from 6 million to 15 million (Levy and Kramer 1973).

5. See, for instance, Thomas and Znanieki (1977), Parrillo (1985), Lopata (1976), and Dinnerstein and Reimers (1988). As with the Italians and other Slavic groups, the Polish immigrants had difficulty in adjusting to the Irish-dominated Catholic church.

ADDITIONAL READINGS

DeSipio, Louis. *Counting on the Latino Vote: Latinos as a New Electorate*. Charlottsville, VA: University of Virginia Press, 1996.

Guglielme, Jennifer, and Salvatore Salerno, eds. *Are Italians White? How Race Is Made in America*. New York: Routledge, 2003.

Haider-Markel, Donald P., and Kenneth J. Meier. "The Politics of Gay and Lesbian Rights: Expanding the Scope of the Conflict," *The Journal of Politics,* 58 (2, May, 1996): 332–49.

Horne, Gerald, and Mary Young, eds. *W. E. B. Du Bois: An Encyclopedia*. Westport, CT: Greenwood Press, 2001.

Hornor, Louise L., ed. *Hispanic Americans: A Statistical Sourcebook*. Palo Alto, CA: Information Publications, 2002.

Litt, Edgar. *Ethnic Politics in America*. Glenview, IL: Scott, Foresman, 1970.

Moskos, Charles. *Greek Americans*. Englewood Cliffs, NJ: Prentice Hall, 1980.

Reeves, Keith. *Voting Hopes or Fears? White Voters, Black Candidates, and Racial Politics in America*. New York: Oxford University Press, 1997.

Segura, Gary M. and Shaun Bowler, eds. *Diversity in Democracy: Minority Representation in the United States*. Charlottesville, VA: University of Virginia Press, 2005.

Torrow, Sidney. *Power in Movement: Social Movements, Collective Action, and Politics*. New York: Cambridge University Press, 1994.

Woodward, C. Vann. *The Strange Career of Jim Crow*. New York: Oxford University Press, 2001 (Commemorative Edition).

• *Reading 4.1*

Are Latinos Key to Winning National Elections?

Latino refers to all persons originally from Spanish-speaking regions of Latin America and the Caribbean, *not* to a specific race of people. It is inclusive of indigenous, white, black, Asian, and mixed-race people from those regions. It is a highly heterogeneous population. *Hispanic* is the term used by the United States government (especially the U.S. census bureau) and by some who self-identify, to include anyone from a Spanish-speaking region, including Spain (Geron 2005, 3)

Despite a great diversity among Latinos, they share a common political legacy based on their collective experiences with the dominant U.S. political system. That system has racialized (that is, the construction of racially unequal social hierarchies characterized by dominant and subordinate social relations between groups) Spanish-speaking peoples into broad categories such as Latino, Hispanic, and Hispanic American (Geron 2005, 5).

As Latinos reach the status of being the nation's largest minority group and are nearing a plurality in some regions, they have stirred considerable debate about their growing political power. The presidential candidacy of New Mexico's governor Bill Richardson has many asking, "are Latinos emerging as the key to winning national elections?"

Both political parties are reaching out to attract the Latino vote. As noted in this chapter, the Democratic Party has traditionally received about 70 percent of the Latino vote. Latino activists, however, charge that the Democratic Party is taking Latinos for granted and that the party loyalty of Latinos may be up for grabs. Since 2000, the Republican Party has been more aggressively marketing itself to Latino voters by using symbols of sensitivity to Latino culture, and by using Spanish-speaking ads that show family celebrations. George W. Bush received an estimated 33 percent of the Latino vote. His highly visible close ties to Mexico, and his administration's proposed comprehensive immigration reform bill that includes a generous guest worker program and an "earned legalization" provision which many in his own party view as amnesty, are clearly efforts to reach out to Latino voters. They probably played a significant role in his garnering the estimated 33 percent of the Latino vote in 2004.

Latinos now represent about 14 percent of the U.S. population and continue to be the fastest growing minority. They have the *potential* to play the key role in winning national elections. The question is, Can they be sufficiently motivated to do so? On that, the jury is still out. Consider the following:

- On the one hand, an estimated million people marched across the United States in 2006 to voice their concerns about immigration reform. In 2007, the protests were perhaps half that turnout, but those demonstrations show a growing interest among young people, especially Latinos, to take political action (Wagner 2006, 1).

- On the other hand, the great diversity of Latino groups make it exceptionally difficult to achieve a unified agenda for the "Latino community." Their political needs are so varied that it is arguable that there is a "Latino community" in any political action sense. Although pan-ethnic organizations are developing, there is, as yet, no political agenda adhered to by all Latinos (Geron 2005, 4).

- On the one hand, increased voting by Latinos is evident. From 2000 to 2004, Latino votes jumped by 23 percent in the November election, more than double the growth rate for Anglo voters (i.e., non-Hispanic whites). All the trend lines point to continued growth in the Latino population in the future (Suro 2005, 1).

- On the other hand, Latino registration and voting rates still lag far behind Anglo and total voting. In the 2000 presidential election, for example, Hispanic registration was just over 53 percent compared to an Anglo rate of 70 percent, and total reported registration at 69.5 percent. In terms of reported voting, in 2000 Hispanics were at 45 percent compared to an Anglo rate of 60.5 and a total rate of 59.5 percent. In the 2004 presidential vote, Hispanics overall reported registration rates of just over 34 percent compared to an Anglo rate of 67.9 percent and a total rate of 65.9 percent. Reported voting in 2004 shows an even greater gap: Hispanics reported 28 percent compared to an Anglo rate of just over 60 percent and a total reported voting rate of just over 58 percent (*Statistical Abstract of the United States, 2006*: table 405: 263).

    The gap between Hispanic and Anglo in total registration and voting for the 1998 and 2002 Congressional races was similarly about half. In 1998, for example, Hispanic registration was at 33.7 percent and in 2002 it dropped to 32.6 percent. Comparable Anglo registration in 1998 was 63.9 percent and it too dropped in 2002 to 63.1 percent. Voting rates in 1998 and 2002 show a similar drop but the Anglo rate is basically double that of Hispanics: 63.9 percent in 1998 and 63.1 percent in 2002. Overall (total) rates in 1998 were 62.1 percent and in 2002, 60.9 percent. Actual reported voting shows an even wider gap. In 1998, reported Hispanic voting for Congressional races was 20 percent compared to 43.3 percent for Anglos and 41.9 percent total. In the 2002 Congressional races, reported Hispanic voting dropped to 18.9 percent, while the Anglo reported voting increased to 44.1 percent. Total voting likewise went up from 41.9 percent in 1998 to 42.3 percent in 2002 (Ibid).

- Although Latino organizational activity is growing and is growingly diverse, Latino membership in community-based organization still lags far behind that of Anglos. Whereas Latino membership by 1999 was a bare majority, Anglo membership in community organizations that year was found to be at 75 percent (DeSipio 2002, 3).

    These gaps, of course, reflect the fact that greater political participation among Latinos is hampered by the failure of many immigrants to complete the naturalization process. Group consciousness has been shown to increase

Latino participation, but the strength of the effect varies considerably among Latino subgroups (Stokes 2003, 361). Moreover, although it has been shown that organizational activity spurs civic engagement, and that the skills, networks, and information provided by the group focused community activity vests Latinos with the resources needed for effective politics, that group influence of organizational activity does not shape attitudes (DeSipio, 2002: 2).

- On the one hand, mid-census (i.e., 2005) reports showed that Hispanics accounted for *half* of all the population growth in the United States since the 2000 census.

- On the other hand, that same report showed that Hispanics accounted for only *one-tenth* of the increase in all votes cast in 2004 compared with the 2000 election. Only about one in four Latinos added to the population was an added voter. In part, this reflects the fact that among the most recent increase in the Latino population (2000 to 2004), an estimated two-thirds of the new arrivals have come illegally (Suro 2005, 1).

- On the one hand, as seen, the number of Latino elected officials (LEOs) is growing. In 2004 there were 4,853 Latino/Latina elected officials.

- On the other hand, those 4,853 LEOs comprised less than one percent of the nation's total elected officials, while the Latino population is at least 14 percent of total population. Moreover, Latino elected officials remain concentrated at the state and local levels. In 2004, two Latino candidates (Mel Martinez from Florida and Ken Salazar from Colorado) were the first Latinos elected to the United States Senate in thirty years (Geron 2005, 8). The number of Hispanic members in the House edged up to 27 (about 6 percent of House seats compared to their estimated 14 percent of the population) (Suro 2005, 2).

- On the one hand, Latino population growth is dramatic and the fastest among minority groups.

- On the other hand, they are young. The vast majority are under 18. The biggest source of the population increases for Latinos come from new births. The vast majority of these new native-born U.S. citizens will not be old enough to vote for some time. Approximately 80 percent of them will still be too young to vote in 2008.

While in 2004, Hispanics outnumbered blacks by nearly 5 million in the population count, blacks had nearly 7.5 million more eligible voters. Black eligible voters were 64 percent of the black population, whereas Hispanic eligible voters comprised only 39 percent of the Hispanic population. And among those eligible voters, in 2004 only 58 percent of Latinos were registered compared to 75 percent among Anglos and 69 percent among blacks (Suro 2005, 2). If Latinos had registered and voted in 2004 at the same rate as did Anglo voters of the same age, Latinos would have cast an additional 2.7 million ballots, increasing their tally of voters by 36 percent.

In summary, while Latino political power is growing, it still lags far behind their potential power based on population numbers. Latino *potential* power is concentrated. In 2004, 96 percent of Latino elected officials were from nine states (Arizona, California,

Florida, Colorado, New York, Texas, New Mexico, Illinois, and New Jersey). These nine states had 82 percent of the total Latino population, and in fact, had 75 percent of LEOs. That concentration may be seen as a limitation of their political clout. But in terms of *future presidential elections*, that concentration could be described as a plus. Those nine states make up 207 votes of the 270 electoral college votes needed to win the office. Latino elected officials bring symbolic and material benefits to the Latino community and serve as much needed role models.

Latino political incorporation is not limited to national electoral politics. Four distinct pathways to their political incorporation have been noted: (1) demand/protest (i.e., sit-ins, demonstrations, boycotts, etc.); (2) non-confrontational political evolution; (3) legal challenges to structural barriers; and (4) coalition politics (Geron 2005, 13).

Source: Created by author, based on examples and discussion in Geron, 2005; Suro, 2005; Stokes, 2003; Wagner, 2006; Mena, 2003; and DeSipio, 2002.

CHAPTER 5

— •●• —

THE STRATEGY OF SEPARATISM

Physical Separatism

Ethnic or racial minorities sometimes reject the value system of the majority society. They desire to be left alone rather than to assimilate. They do not seek to impose their values and views on the majority society but want the majority society to respect their differing values and allow them to hold their values, norms, and customs without suffering discrimination. Often such groups come into sustained contact with the majority culture in some largely involuntary manner. The minority group rejects major aspects of the new and dominant culture. It also rejects its minority status and position in the new society. Internally developed minority subcultures, such as a new religious minority, may come to reject the value system of the dominant culture. The Mormons provide a classic example of this type. Sometimes a subculture finds itself in minority status through military suppression, as in the case of Native Americans. Forced migration can bring two such cultures into contact, as in the case of black slaves forcibly brought to America.

Many groups physically separate themselves from the majority culture to the extent that is possible as a matter of their choice. Examples of groups using this tactical approach that are discussed herein are the Mormons, the Amish and Mennonites, and Black Nationalism. Their cases illustrate the bottom-up approach to using this tactical approach to a separatist strategy. At other times, such physical segregation from the majority society is a matter of force, as in the case of Native American Indian tribes. It illustrates the top-down approach to social interaction within the context of the tactic of physical separatism as a coping mechanism.

The social withdrawal of the Mormons, the Amish, and the Mennonites from the secular majority society requirements led these groups to live in rural communities as far and as separated from the majority as was possible. The emergence of Zionism, the separatist views of the Hasidic Jews, and the development of Black Nationalism are cases where an ethnic group turns inward, creating its own institutions to replenish social, psychological, and cultural values that cannot be fulfilled in the dominant society. In doing so, they develop a strategy of separatist politics, developing distinct organizations and cultural practices to compensate for disenchantment with the ongoing political and social order. When a subculture, for whatever reason, wants to pursue a strategy of separatism, it may attempt to do so in one of two ways: physical separatism (isolation) or the psychological separation of its members from the norms, customs, and values of the rejected majority society.

This chapter discusses and illustrates physical separatism. The choice of this tactical approach depends on the group being able to isolate itself physically from the majority culture. This may be done by seeking out frontier or rural areas with low enough density of settlement that the minority group members settle the area as the numerically superior group. The initial fleeing of the Mormons to ever more isolated frontier regions in response to persecution is a classic example of this tactic. A small faction of black Americans, following the separatist philosophy of Marcus Garvey's Back to Africa movement, represents another attempt at using this approach. The Amish and Mennonites, clustering in rural enclaves, are yet another example of groups using this tactic. They reduce their contact with members of the majority culture to a minimum, rejecting the media, reinforcing the isolating effect of their rural settlement.

Sometimes physical separatism is not a matter of choice by the minority racial or ethnic group. Sometimes it is, to varying degrees, forced on a group when the majority treats them in a manner that physically isolates them. The Chicanos in the Southwest are often forced into barrios, much as the Chinese were relegated to Chinatowns. The military forced survivors of Native-American tribes of an earlier policy of annihilation to ever-decreasing areas of reservations. The use of physical separatism is typically restricted to minority groups small enough to make isolation a realistic tactic. They also have to be able to maintain an economic base of support for their subculture in their physically isolated area. Such groups typically employ economic niches. Necessary economic interactions with members of the majority culture, however, tend to result in the gradual emergence of the accommodation approach being utilized by the minority group. True and effective separatism is a difficult strategy to pursue over long periods of time.

THE MORMONS

Among religious minority groups, the Church of Jesus Christ of Latter-Day Saints, commonly known as the Mormons, undoubtedly experienced the most repressive discrimination, if measured by use of violence against them, legal restrictions imposed upon them, and their ultimately being forced to change or at least suppress an important tenet of their faith because of majority society pressure. The case of the Mormons is a clear example of religious discrimination since it initially was a native-born minority faith and therefore experienced no "antiforeign" prejudice. As a noted scholar of the Mormons observed:

> The appearance of such a new religious or social movement, like an invasive organism, presents a challenge to the normative order of the surrounding host society. This challenge will be the more serious, of course, the more militant and deviant the movement

is; and survival itself might of necessity preoccupy the new movement. That so many new movements of all kinds fail to survive even one generation testifies clearly enough to their usual fragility. . . . If survival is the first task of the movement, the natural and inevitable response of the host society is either to domesticate [it] or to destroy it. In seeking to domesticate or assimilate it, the society will apply various kinds of social control pressures selectively in an effort to force the movement to abandon at least its most unique and threatening features. To the extent that the society succeeds . . . the result will be eventual assimilation of the movement. Failing to achieve sufficient domestication, the host society will eventually resort to the only alternative: persecution and repression. Movements which, like Mormonism, survive and prosper are those that succeed in maintaining indefinitely an optimum tension . . . between the two opposing strains: the strain toward greater assimilation and respectability, on the one hand, and that toward greater separateness, peculiarity, and militance on the other. (Mauss 1994, 4–5)

It is somewhat surprising to many today to learn of that past experience, since the Mormon Church today is clearly mainstream. The census 2000, based on a 1997 report, listed Mormon membership at 4,923,000 in the United States, attending nearly 11,000 churches. (*Statistical Abstract of the United States, 2000.* Population, p. 61, Table 74, *Religious Bodies, Selected Data*). Table 5.1 provides a profile of Mormon members compared to national averages.

Another scholar describes the Mormon Church as a new world religion. Projecting membership data for the main world religions to 2080, he extrapolates the following figures: Christianity—2,060,000,000, Islam—1,200,000,000, Hinduism—860,000,000, Buddhism—360,000,000, Mormonism—265,000,000 (Davies 2000, 243). Mainstream status, however, has most decidedly not always been the case.

Mormon Fundamentalism is generally used to describe splinter movements (sects) of Mormonism whose adherents cling to what they consider fundamental aspects of the faith and they break from Mormonism as practiced by the LDS headquartered in Salt Lake City, Utah. They feel the mainline wrongly abandoned such LDS tenets and practices as the Law of Consecration, the Adam-God theory, the Patriarchal Priesthood, elements of the Mormon Endowment ritual, and the exclusion of blacks from the priesthood. These sects are established in small, cohesive, and isolated communities in areas of the Western United States, as well as in Canada and Mexico. Polygamous Mormon sects continue the practice officially abandoned by the 1890 Manifesto of then Mormon president Wilford Woodruff. There are an estimated 37,000 Fundamentalist Mormons, with about half of them living in polygamous households. Some of them accept the practice of older men marrying underage girls (13–15 year olds), which is also illegal in most states. Most of them use polygamy, although a few accept polyandry (one wife, with several husbands). The most significant of these splits began in the 1920s, following a dissenter named Lorin C. Woolley who claimed a separate line of authority from the mainstream hierarchy.

The more notable of the Mormon Fundamentalist Sects include the following: (1) The Apostolic United Brethren of about 5,000 to 9,000 adherents in Utah, Montana, Arizona, Wyoming, Missouri, and Mexico; (2) The Fundamentalist Church of Jesus Christ of Latter-Day Saints of about 6,000 to 8,000 followers led by Warren Jeffs and concentrated in Colorado City, Arizona, and Hildale, Utah; (3) the Kingston clan of

Table 5.1   Profile of Mormons Compared to National Averages

	Mormon	*National Average*
Mormons as a percentage of the nation as a whole	1.8%	—
Female	58%	52%
Hispanic	4	5
Union Member	7	11
Black	4	10
Resident		
Northeast	6	21
Midwest	9	25
South	13	34
West	72	21
High School Diploma	37	35
College Graduate	17	21
Republican	45	29
Lean Republican	18	15
Independent	9	9
Lean Democrat	9	14
Democrat	19	32
Resident in Large City	14	20
Suburban	25	22
Small City/Town	44	36
Rural	15	21
Family Income		
<$20,000	21	25
$20,000–$30,000	24	19
$30,000–$50,000	33	27
>$50,000	18	21
Age		
18–19	20	22
30–44	34	33
45–64	24	27
65 and older	21	17

Source: Table by author; adapted from Kohut et al., *The Diminishing Divide, 2000*. Table A-12, pp. 152–153.

the Latter-Day Church of Christ, which has an estimated 1,200 members, and notably allows polygamous marriages of underage girls; (4) the Righteous Branch of the Church of Jesus Christ of Latter-Day Saints, which is a very small group of perhaps 200 people who live in Modena, Utah, and followed Gerald Peterson Sr. and who are led by his son, Gerald Peterson Jr.; (5) the True and Living Church of Jesus Christ of Saints of the Last Days, a group of about 300–500 members who split off in 1994 and stress the "restoration" of the "very last days" before the second coming of Jesus Christ;

(6) the Centennial Park group of about 1,500 members located in Centennial Park, Arizona, who denounce all violence and abuse, do not allow marriage to underage girls, and disavow the more extreme practices of the Colorado City/FLDS group; and (7) the Neilson/Naylor group of about 200 who trace their authority through Alma Del Timpson and Frank Naylor and are based in the Salt Lake Valley (http://www .mormonfundamentalism.com/accessed 5/14/2007)

Mormon History

Joseph Smith, the founder of Mormonism, was born in Vermont in 1805. His family moved to Palmyra, New York, in 1816, and it was near there that, as a fourteen-year-old, Smith says he first received his revelations from God. He claimed his first visit from an angel, Moroni, happened in 1823. In 1827, Smith claimed he "discovered the tablets" known as *The Book of Mormon*, which he published in 1829. On April 6, 1830, Smith and six of his followers formally established the Church of Jesus Christ of the Latter-Day Saints. Almost immediately they experienced intense discrimination.

Moving from New York to Ohio and then on to Missouri because of severe persecution, Smith was killed by a mob storming the jail in which he was being held in Carthage, Missouri, on June 28, 1844. In the words of one historian of the Mormons: "It is not surprising that the first, and until the assassination of Malcolm X in 1965 the only, American religious leader to be murdered was a Mormon, for the Saints have always inflamed passions" (Hirshon 1969, 50).

Discrimination against the Mormons developed early and involved the reactions of expulsion through the use of violence, as well as applying the force of law to pressure them to change their tenets to be more acceptable to the views of the majority society. Part of that persecution was a reaction to their dogmatism and to the "theocracy" community these established.

The tenet of faith that caused the Mormons so much trouble was polygamy, or the plural marriage principle. This tenet of faith has been officially dropped, as will be discussed later. Another tenet of their faith is that of **celestial marriage**, defined in Mormon Doctrine as "marriages performed in the temples for time and eternity," and remains a central doctrine (McConkie 1966, 117). Early Mormons stressed "speaking in tongues" and faith healing. The aspect of dogmatism aroused animosity, although that characteristic of the faith also attracted many of its early converts who came from the lower classes and were probably attracted because its dogmatism provided a sense of security in the pre–Civil War period so wracked with disorder. The Mormons revere a "priesthood." Every adult male loyally adhering to the faith was considered a priest. Mormons quickly developed a group of Melchizedek priests, the Council of Seventies, every bit as militant as the Roman Catholic Jesuits. Mormonism was a society, a total way of life. As Hirshon puts it:

"As much as a church, moreover, the Saints created a society. In specifically designated communities they gathered and became in every sense a people. Often migrating in groups, they proved a new society following some model could even be moved physically from one part of the world to another" (Hirshon 1969, 18–19). Table 5.1 compares Mormons to the national average of the population among a number of characteristics to provide a profile of Mormons today.

Because the plural marriage tenet was initially a well-kept secret, practiced only by a few leading priesthood members in 1841, and not introduced to the body of the LDS church until 1852 when they had already moved to Salt Lake, it was probably those other aspects that caused the initial hostile reactions to the Mormon sect in New York, Missouri, and Illinois. The first public announcement Joseph Smith made of his belief in the plurality of wives was at Nauvoo in 1840 (Young 1972, 67), but in New York, in their earlier history, skeptics frequently broke up Mormon meetings with jeering and by throwing stones at the faithful.

It was in New York, in 1832, that Brigham Young was converted. The church, and Young, moved to Kirtland, Ohio, where many Mormons assembled in 1832–1833. The plural marriage principle, supposedly revealed to Smith in 1831, was being secretly practiced among the elite of the church between 1841 and 1852.

The Mormons built their first temple in Kirtland in 1833, but abandoned it almost upon completion. Along with the rest of the nation, they were hit by the Panic of 1837. They fled Ohio because of financial difficulties, a rather shaky financial venture, some degree of persecution, and a desire to aid the Mormon community in Missouri (Hardy 1992).

It was in Missouri, during the years 1831–1833, that outright conflict broke out between the Mormons and the majority society, called gentiles by the Mormons. November 4, 1833 was "bloody day" when the conflict between Mormons and Missourians forced their exodus. Smith had announced the church's intention to start a New Zion in the Carthage/Panock/Nauvoo triangle of Mormon settlements in Missouri and Illinois. In 1833, Nauvoo was a malaria-ridden dot of a town of 240 settlers. By 1842, it had 7,000 people, larger than was Chicago at the time. The initial conflict broke out in Jackson County, Missouri. The area around Independence witnessed a virtual state of war between Mormons and gentiles. Some 1,200 Mormons were engaged in pitched battles. Gentiles burned down Mormon homes, destroyed a Mormon paper, and tarred and feathered several Saints. In the Far West, between 1836 and 1838, tensions resulted in a virtual state of war that started on election day, August 6, 1838. On October 25, 1838, the Battle of Crooked River took place; it became known as the Mormon Rebellion. The next day, Missouri Governor Boggs issued an extermination order. Governor Boggs was shot in the head and severely wounded in 1842, an act suspected to have been done at the instigation of Joseph Smith, for which the feeling against him grew stronger than ever (Young 1972, 60). Several battles, such as the Haun's Mill massacre on October 30, 1838, began the "Siege of the Far West" that lasted until November 6, 1838, and ended with the killing of Mormon women and children. On December 16, 1838, the Charter of Nauvoo was signed, and a militia, the Nauvoo Legion was established with Smith at its head. The Nauvoo charter had Smith as mayor, and its merging of the religious with the military and the secular political structure into a virtual theocracy troubled outsiders. In 1840 Smith ran for President, another shocking political development at the time.

In 1840, Brigham Young was sent with several others to serve as missionaries in England. Their first year resulted in nearly 9,000 converts, many of whom migrated to New Zion when Young returned there in July 1841.

In October, 1845, citizens in Quincey, Illinois, and Lee County, Illinois, asked Mormons to leave because civil war seemed imminent. In January, 1845, the Nauvoo

Brigham Young, second Mormon president
(*Courtesy of the Library of Congress*)

Charter was revoked. Increasing conflict led to Smith's arrest and on June 27, 1844, Joseph and Hiram Smith were martyred. His martyrdom led to the last great migration of the Mormons, to Utah, begun in February, 1846, after the Nauvoo Charter was revoked.

During 1845 some 150 Mormons were burned to death in Missouri. The conflict, however, was not totally one-sided. Mormons committed violent acts against their neighbors as well. As one historian put it: "If the Mormons had behaved like other people, they would never have been driven from Illinois and Missouri; but they stole, robbed, and plundered from all their neighbors and all the time" (Hirshon 1969, 63). General H. G. Parks, the commanding officer of the Missouri militia in Davies County, however, stated he found the Mormons an industrious and thriving people, willing to abide by the law of the land and deeply regretting that they could not live in peace with their non-Mormon neighbors. General Parks was under the command of General Atchison, head of the state troops, whom Governor Boggs fired when he would not support the treatment of the Mormons and execute the Governor's extermination order (The Church of Jesus Christ of Latter-Day Saints, 201).

By 1846, Nauvoo was a virtual city-state and construction of the Mormon temple in Nauvoo was completed. Brigham Young married thirty-five women in Nauvoo, after Smith's death. Young ultimately had seventy wives and fathered fifty-six children. This practice, more than any other, made him a symbol of evil to the majority society, even in death.

In February 1846, Young left Nauvoo with about 4,000 people to establish winter quarters near what is now Omaha, Nebraska. In April 1847, he led a party of 148

Brigham Young's "Empty Pillow" (in memoriam) (Used by permission of the Utah State Historical Society. All rights reserved.)

Mormons in 73 wagons to what was then the far frontier. On July 21, 1847, they saw Salt Lake Valley, stopping on July 23 at the site that became Salt Lake City. A second group of nearly 500 joined them soon after. John Nelson, a gentile frontiersman who guided the first of the Mormon parties to Salt Lake City and who joined the church for a while, described them as follows:

> The class of people who made up these Mormon caravans were generally very poor and ignorant. Some, however, amongst them belonged to a better class, and I always fancied these had joined to save their necks from the gallows of the district from which they migrated. . . . The secret of polygamy amongst the Mormons was this. They thought that if each man had ten wives, and each wife had from three to five children, in twenty years time they would be strong enough to protect themselves from the gentiles. (Nelson 1963, 118)

The death of founder Joseph Smith led to a crisis in the movement's leadership and ultimately to the first of several church schisms. This development was not surprising, since the movement arose in a crisis of authority. The Mormon movement was a divisive and ringing dissent from the existing churches and theologies of the time, and its early attempts to develop a communal utopia under theocratic control in the 1830s and 1840s led to dissenters within. Smith's death created the major split in the summer of 1844, the main line following Brigham Young west and a minor line remaining in the Midwest. The differences concerned doctrine as well as leadership. The Midwest line, The Reorganized Church of Jesus Christ of Latter-Day Saints, for example, rejected the plural marriage tenet and practice completely (Abanes, 2002; Launius and Thatcher 1994, 3–16; Tanner, 1976).

Several groups developed out of early Mormonism: the Strangites, the Cutlerites, and the Reorganized Church of Jesus Christ of Latter-Day Saints of Josephites. The Strangites remained in Wisconsin and Michigan. Sidney Rigdon led the Church of Christ, which lasted from its inception in 1845 until after his death in 1876, and was found mostly in Pennsylvania and Iowa. The Reorganized Church of Jesus Christ of Latter-Day Saints was headquartered in Independence, Missouri. It was headed for some forty years by Joseph Smith III, the son of the founder of the Mormon faith.

Life on the frontier was harsh for the early Mormon settlers. Certainly their polygamous lifestyle, which Young gradually extended from the elite to the rank-and-file members of the faith after 1852 (although LDS scholars estimate less than 7 percent of the members actually practiced polygamy), seemed strange and threatening to the majority society. Although only the leaders had many wives, non-LDS scholars estimate that up to 20 percent of the Saints were polygamists. The practice of plural marriage acquired added momentum among the migrants during their passage west. The practice, though, was not formally made public by the church until 1852, and was not actually printed in the Mormon *Doctrine and Covenants* until 1876. It was officially ended in 1890 (after it was legally banned by the United States) in a church manifesto that can be viewed as marking the end of Mormon separatism and the beginning of an uneasy compromise with non-Mormons (Hardy 1992; O'Dea 1957; Schaefer 1998). The territory of Utah was admitted as a state in 1896. They gradually became more and more accommodationist in the twentieth century.

The pressure of public law against the Mormons was upheld in two U.S. Supreme Court cases. The first, in 1879, upheld the validity of an act by Congress proscribing the advocating of polygamy against the Mormon claim of freedom of religious practice. Chief Justice Waite, writing for the unanimous Court, first expounded the "wall of separation" doctrine with regard to church and state relations. The case ruled that religious *beliefs* did not justify polygamy as a *practice*. The final case, rendered in 1890, upheld the validity of an 1887 congressional act that annulled the charter of the Mormons and declared all church property forfeit save for a small portion used exclusively for worship. This case was necessitated by the fact that the Mormons ignored the earlier ruling and continued to practice polygamy despite the law.

The manifesto did lead to some schisms and splinter groups which broke away from the main body of Mormonism to continue the practice of plural marriage. Even in the main body, polygamous marriages continued after the manifesto of 1890 with the consent of general authorities (Abanes 2002). Within the main body, however, the practice increasingly withered under the pressures of the dominant society.

The Mormon settlement in Utah grew rapidly. In 1848, there were only 5,000 Mormons in the territory, virtually all in Salt Lake City. By 1850, there were over 11,000, and by 1852, they numbered 32,000. By 1855, there were some 60,000 Mormons in the territory, over 15,000 of whom resided in Salt Lake City alone.

Box 5.1 presents a bio-sketch of one of Brigham Young's wives, later an apostate from the faith. It illustrates the pressures the tenet of polygamy raised within the faith and the resulting pressure toward accommodation rather than separatism.

BOX 5.1   *BIO-SKETCH: ANN ELIZA YOUNG (1844–?)*

•

Ann Eliza Young describes herself in her autobiography, published in 1875, as wife number 19 of Brigham Young, and as his "apostate wife" whose life was "a life in bondage." Other scholars list her as his twenty-seventh wife.

Ann Eliza Young (nee Webb) was born in Nauvoo, Illinois on September 13, 1844. She was the youngest child and only surviving daughter of a family of five children. Her mother and father were both devout Mormons, among the earliest of Joseph Smith's converts. Her father, Chauncey G. Webb, was born in 1812 in Hanover, New York, and was converted in 1833. Her mother was Eliza Churchill, born in Union Springs, New York in 1817. Her father eventually took five wives.

Her family moved with the great migration of Mormons out to Utah. Ann Eliza was seventeen when Brigham Young first asked her to marry him. She refused, however, and at age eighteen married Mr. James L. Dee, a young Englishman and Mormon convert, on April 4, 1863. It was not a happy marriage, although they had two children. He physically abused her and she divorced him in 1865. She married Brigham Young on April 7, 1869. She had considerable difficulty with his other wives, especially Eliza Burgess Young and Harriet Amelia Folsum Young. Early in their marriage, she lived with her mother. Brigham Young, however, forced her to expel her mother from their house. She took on boarders to cope financially.

On July 15, 1873, at age twenty-nine, she left Brigham Young and the Mormon faith, fled their house, and became an "apostate." She spoke and lectured on the evils of polygamy beginning in December 1873 in Denver. In July of 1874 she began divorce proceedings and in August of 1874 Brigham Young denied that he was married to her to avoid any financial obligations. Ann Eliza Young began a national campaign that culminated in passage of the "Poland Law" against polygamy, enacted by the Congress in 1874. Brigham Young's twenty-seventh wife had accomplished her mission at last.

In 1875 she was converted to Christianity—as a Methodist Episcopal, in Boston. She published her autobiography in 1875. It was republished in 1908, when she was sixty-four. The date and place of her death is unknown although it was rumored that she died in the early 1920s. That date is disputed, however, in that a grandson, Ernest Jane, claimed to have briefly seen and met her in Rochester, New York, around 1928 or 1930. If so, she would have been 86 years old.

Sources: Bio-sketch by author LeMay, based on information from Irving Wallace, *The Twenty-Seventh Wife* (New York: Simon & Schuster, 1961); Ann Eliza Young, *Wife No. 19, The Story of a Life in Bondage* (Hartford, CT: Dustin, Gilmann and Company, 1875); Kimball Young, *Isn't One Wife Enough?* (New York: Henry Holt and Company, 1954).

Flight to the frontier did not end Mormon conflict with the majority society. In December 1848, the Council of Elders of the church created a territorial government with Young at its head. He began colonizing beyond Salt Lake City, and that colonization process led to conflict with gentile settlers in the territory. Critics of the Mormons depicted him as akin to the czar of Russia; that Young ruled with near absolute power. While he was both secular and religious leader of the Mormon people, his power was not absolute. Mormon settlements in Utah, however, were more like a theocracy than like the majority society's image of a democracy.

The development and expansion of the Mormon domain was not without conflict, occasionally even violence. In the presidential election of 1856, the National Republican Party platform, reflecting the sentiment of most easterners and midwesterners, declared opposition to the "twin relics of barbarism"—slavery and polygamy. Tensions rose during the 1856–1858 period of "reformation," and violence erupted. The church leadership had petitioned for statehood as the State of Deseret in 1849, but anti-Mormon sentiment in Washington, DC, as well as fear and concern over Young's theocratic power, resulted in it being given territorial status under the name of Utah, as part of the Compromise of 1850 (while the nation was split among free state and slave state positions). When gold was discovered in California in 1848 and more and more gentile settlers traversed the Mormon-dominated territory, conflict arose between gentile settlers and Mormons. The territorial government was split, with the judiciary being held by non-Mormons. Tensions mounted.

In September 1857, a party of 120 gentiles was massacred by Mormons disguised as Indians. The Mountain Meadows massacre became enough of a national issue that President Buchanan sent a force of soldiers into Utah to suppress a "rebellion." More tension and atrocities followed.[1] John Nelson, who had earlier joined the church and led the Mormons to Salt Lake City, and is considered an apostate as he later served as a guide for the Union expedition, described the events leading up to the use of military force against the church, as follows: "Brigham Young and his Saints had outgrown their discretion, and suddenly took to murdering immigrants who did not belong to their denomination, to robbing trains, and to killing people who were bound for California" (Nelson 1963, 117). The massacre and its aftermath was enough to precipitate the use of the United States armed forces against the Mormons.

As the Union forces advanced upon them, the Mormons abandoned and burned down many of their settlements, fleeing to the stronghold of the Wasatch at Provo. The Union force and the Mormon military reached a virtual standoff without blood being shed. After weeks of tension, a compromise was reached by which the garrison of troops was stationed at Salt Lake City, showing the federal presence in the Mormon region. President Buchanan, in June 1858, granted Young and the Mormon leadership "free and full" pardon, and Young returned to Salt Lake City in July 1859. John D. Lee, a leading Mormon in its military force, was ultimately tried, convicted, and executed by firing squad at the very site of the Mountain Meadow massacre.

One of the California settlements was Fort San Bernardino, erected in 1851. It became the site of the city of San Bernardino, one of 250 Mormon settlements (colonies) in the West. In 1857, just as it was being firmly established, Brigham Young suddenly summoned the settlers back to Salt Lake City. The withdrawal of a majority of its leading citizens was orderly and demonstrated their dedication to the Mormon cause. Fully two-thirds of the population returned to Utah. Some remained and embraced the Reorganized Church of Jesus Christ of Latter-Day Saints, the Missouri-based church without allegiance to Brigham Young or to plural marriage. The persecution of the Mormons certainly tested their dedication and undoubtedly contributed to their sense of "peoplehood."[2]

During the 1858–1860 period of occupation, the soldiers interfered little with Mormon life and tensions eased. The Mormons reaped a sizable economic benefit from the occupying army (Arrington and Bitton 1992, 169). When Young died in 1877, the extensive practice of polygamy began to die with him. After the 1890 manifesto, the

Mormon and American value systems gradually grew increasingly congruent, especially between 1900 and 1920, so that by the time of the Great Depression, Utah politics had become thoroughly Americanized. The Mormons' People's Party was disbanded, with the church rank and file and the leadership becoming Republicans and Democrats in their party affiliation and voting patterns.

Mormons used politics almost from their inception. Members of the church, being native-born, could and did participate in politics without restrictions. They were so active in Ohio politics that their activities led to their being forced to flee. Smith was able to deliver the votes of his members as a bloc. Though small, they were a sizable minority in local politics and aroused much fear in Ohio, especially during the Panic of 1837. When they fled to Illinois and Missouri, Smith again entered politics, with his flock voting en mass for the Democrats. After the move to the far west, the church split into factions. By 1870 there were three main factions, whose phenomenal growth made them a force to be reckoned with. In 1850, Mormons had over 10,000 members in 16 branches. By 1870, they had 171 branches and over 87,800 members. The leader of each of the factions could and did deliver his members' votes as blocs. The largest faction, led by Young, established the State of Deseret in January 1862. It set up its own government and for eight years petitioned Congress for admission. The Congress ignored them. Young became obsessed with establishing the "Kingdom of God" with its principles of unquestioned "perfect" obedience and a holy war against the gentiles. Once statehood was achieved, the Mormons dominated Utah politics.

Currently, no overwhelming party linkage is evident, although they more often favor Republicans. There is some difference among the leadership and the rank-and-file Mormon membership in party identification. By 1960, while the general members identified themselves as 40.8 percent Republican and 38.3 percent Democrat (and 20.9 percent "other"), bishops of the church were 55.6 percent Republican and 22.2 percent Democrat (and 22.2 percent "other"), and "stake presidents" were 89.3 percent Republican and only 10.7 percent Democrat (none identified as "other"). By the ninety-seventh Congress there were two Democrats and five Republicans who were Mormons in the House of Representatives, and in the Senate, one Republican and three Democrats were Mormons.

During their early days, the Mormons' public policy focus was defensive, attempting to achieve statehood without relinquishing their tenet of polygamy. That practice was the one over which most conflict evolved. Their clinging to the tenet was more than theological. A practical reason Mormon leaders urged men to marry often was that a practicing polygamist rarely apostatized. It was also a logical means to massively and rapidly increase the size of the church membership.

While Young was governor of the territory, he used public policy to accumulate personal wealth and to build up the power of the Mormon church. He used his appointive power to rid himself of unwanted rivals. Young and the church leadership often fought with presidential appointees who were gentiles assigned to the territorial judiciary. They also tried to develop the region agriculturally, industrially, and through control of railroad development. These developments reflected a tension between the "angel and the beehive." A statue of the angel Moroni, atop the famous Temple in Salt Lake City, was the symbol of the otherworldly heritage of Mormonism. The beehive, found on many

Mormon enterprise buildings, symbolizes the worldly enterprises throughout the Mormon heartland (Mauss 1994).

In part as a result of the Panic of 1873, Young initiated the Second United Order. Between 1873–1874 he created over 100 United Orders in communities throughout the intermountain west. The community operated several cooperative enterprises, shared proceeds and dividends, and allowed the Mormon people a greater degree of self-sufficiency. This period marked the gradual change in the Mormon movement from a utopian sect into a more mainline church.

Anti-Semitic and anti-black attitudes among many Mormons led them to very conservative positions on civil rights and welfare policy. Their view of women made them active opponents of the ERA. Today, their conservatism reflects the defensive posture of a minority faith. They support policy that they feel will benefit them as a group and oppose any policy that they believe threatens them as a group. (Mauss 1994; Abanes 2002.)

The tendency toward schism has continued within the Mormon movement. A Levite Sect, known as the Aaronic Order, emerged during the 1930s and was formally organized in 1940. It was considered a "revitalization" movement by its followers. They established several communal settlements: one in Alton, Utah, near Bryce Canyon National Park; the Alpha Colony and sawmill business near Springville, Utah; Partoun, the first in western Utah as a desert community; and Eskdale, their largest and most successful Levite desert community, established in 1955 and still surviving today. The Aaronic Order has a high priesthood and maintains the integrity of polygamist marriages. They have virtually complete endogamy, allowing only a few "out marriages" to other Mormons. They are similar to Amish and Mennonites in that they wear distinctive garb or "uniforms," even to using a woman's cap modeled after the Mennonite cap.[3]

Since that split, the main Mormon church has become increasingly assimilated. A 1980s study of various religious denominations in the United States found that on matters pertaining to racial justice and civil liberties the Mormons, contrary to their racist and conservative image of the 1960s, were closer to liberal mainline denominations, such as Episcopalians, Presbyterians, and even the very liberal Unitarians, than they were to conservative fundamentalist denominations such as Baptists, Methodists, and the various Evangelicals/Fundamentalists. On lifestyle matters (abortion, extramarital and premarital sex, divorce, women's rights, etc.), however, the Mormons joined the Baptists, Assemblies of God, and other fundamentalist denominations on the conservative side.

Perhaps the best example of their now accommodationist stance, and to their arrival at mainline status, is provided by the presidential aspirations of former Massachusetts governor Mitt Romney, seeking the Republican Party nomination. Box 5.2 provides his bio-sketch. His securing the nomination and winning the election would demonstrate that the Mormons had achieved full political incorporation, but opinion polls early in the race (April, 2007) indicated that as many as 43 percent of the public reported they would not vote for him because he is a Mormon. That poll indicated that 78 percent of Republican voters and 55 percent of Democratic voters stated that a candidate's faith is an important consideration to them when voting.

BOX 5.2   BIO-SKETCH OF GOVERNOR MITT ROMNEY

Widely recognized as a leader in private enterprise and as a public servant, Mitt Romney was elected Governor of Massachusetts in 2002. The state experienced substantial economic expansion during his tenure. The good economic times enabled the governor to balance the budget each year of his administration without raising taxes or increasing state debt, even closing a $3 billion dollar budget gap from 2001–2002 and the previous administration. During his administration, the state's unemployment rate declined as many new companies moved to the state and deficits were transformed into surpluses. Governor Romney was elected to the Chairmanship of the Republican Governors Association for the 2006 election cycle, and the Association raised a record $27 million for State House candidates running that year.

Romney was born in 1947 in Detroit, Michigan. He is a great-great grandson of Latter-Day Saint leader and apostle, Parley P. Pratt, and the son of George W. Romney, the former Michigan Governor and Housing and Urban Development Secretary, and American Motors Chairman, who was an unsuccessful candidate for the Republican presidential nomination, and of Lenore Romney, a 1970 candidate for the U.S. Senate. He attended Stanford University, and served for 30 months as a Mormon missionary in France. He graduated from Brigham Young University as valedictorian, earning his B.A. summa cum laude in 1971. In 1975 he took a joint JD/MBA degree from Harvard Law School and Harvard Business School, graduating cum laude from the law school and in the top 5 percent of the business school class.

He worked for the Boston Consulting Group, went on to be vice-president of Bain and Company, a Boston-based management consulting firm, and in 1984 co-founded Bain Capital, a highly successful private equity investment firm. Romney rose to national recognition when serving as the CEO of the 2002 Olympic Winter Games held in Salt Lake City. He revamped the organization's leadership and policies, reduced budget deficits and boosted fundraising, and coordinated, in the post-9/11 period, a $300 million security budget to ensure the safety of the games, which cleared a profit of $100 million. He personally contributed $1 million to the Olympics and donated his $825,000 salary as CEO of the games to charity. He wrote a book about his experience, *Turnaround: Crisis, Leadership and the Olympic Games*.

In 1994 Romney won the Massachusetts Republican Party's nomination for the U.S. Senate, but lost to Senator Ted Kennedy in the general election. In 2002, he ran for governor on a reform platform, and on promises to reform the state's budget. Hailed for his business record and the success of the 2002 Winter Olympics, he contributed $6.3 million to his own campaign during the election, at the time a state record. He was elected Governor in 2002 with 50 percent of the vote. He served one term as governor. He announced in December, 2005 that he would not seek re-election, fueling speculation that he would run for the White House in 2008. On February 13, 2007 he formally announced his candidacy for the Republican Party nomination, and he won the Conservative Political Action Conference Straw Poll on March 3, 2007, by 21 percent of the vote over his chief rivals, former NYC. Mayor Rudy Giuliani, who received 17 percent, and U.S. Senator John McCain, who polled 12 percent of the vote.

Source: Bio-sketch by author LeMay, based on information from his presidential campaign website, http://www.mittromney .com/ accessed 3/14/2007; and http://en.wikipedia.org/wiki/Mitt_Romney, accessed 3/14/2007.

NATIVE AMERICANS

The 2000 census reported that nearly 2.5 million individuals identified themselves as Native Americans, among which about 40 percent live off reservations in the nation's cities. This reflected a 26 percent increase from 1990. Native Americans comprised 0.9 percent of the total population of the United States. At 37 percent of them reporting mixed-race status, they far exceed that of any other group in the population of over 281 million (http://census.gov/prod/2001pubs). Despite some $3 billion a year in federal aid, and despite some substantial financial success by tribes with established Indian Gaming Casinos, the majority of Native-American Indians have the lowest income and education levels and the worst housing and health conditions of any minority group in the nation. They are truly the poorest of the poor. They have the dubious distinction of leading the nation in unemployment. Native-American children are the most poorly prepared students in America, exhibit the highest dropout rates, the lowest test scores, and the worst alcoholism and suicide rates of any student group.

Like black Americans, they represent a racial case that has unique aspects. Despite their being the only truly native population in the nation, they were not legally declared citizens with the right to vote until 1924. They are the only minority group legally segregated into reservations. They are the only minority that suffered from an avowed policy of annihilation. No other minority in the country's history has the unfortunate distinction of having experienced actual genocide. And as a result of a long, and often sad, history of treaty relations, they are the only minority that has a recognized and legal claim to "limited or domestic dependent nations—quasi-sovereigns" (Wilkins 2002, 48). (See the reading at the end of this chapter for a discussion of the import of that status.)

National policy toward the Native American has taken many approaches over the years. Those policy shifts have ranged from avowed friendship, recognizing their independence, to expulsion and to genocide, forced geographic segregation, and forced acculturation through termination, to attempts to allow for cultural pluralism. In the process of these policy shifts, hundreds of treaties were made and broken. Indian affairs have been shifted and parceled out among various agencies housed within several departments of the federal government. Their history perhaps more clearly demonstrates the effects of public policy on social interactions than is the case of any other minority group.

The decimation of the Indian population because of contact with European whites, whether intentional or not, is well established. At the time of the first European settlement of the North American continent, the number of Indians residing in that territory has been estimated at 2 to 10 million. Those residing in what is now the United States numbered about 1.5 million. By 1800, their population had fallen to around 600,000. By 1850, the ravages of malnutrition and disease, coupled with the policies of expulsion and genocide, had reduced the Native-American population to around 250,000. Their population has climbed upward from that low point of 1850, reaching just over 2,386,000 today.

Native Americans were initially treated as sovereign nations, and despite some violent clashes between white colonists and the tribes, official government policy was peaceful. Native-American tribes had treaty relations with Spain, France, and England.

British policy was to protect them. When the American Revolution commenced, both sides attempted to win over and use friendship and alliance with the tribes through treaties.

After the war, the new American government followed the British tradition and continued an avowed policy of "friendship" based on treaties with independent nations. But just as the British could not stop the colonies from developing their own relations with the Indians, the new federal government could not stop the states from making their own treaties with the tribes, despite the fact that the federal government was supposed to have sole jurisdiction over trade and treaty relations with Native-American tribes. In any event, although supposedly friendly, most of the treaties resulted in the taking of Indian lands by white settlers. From 1778, when the first treaty was signed, until 1871, when the United States officially stopped recognizing Native-American tribes as independent nations, 389 treaties were ratified. In a sense, all were broken. The Northwest Ordinance, passed in 1787, promised the Indians that their lands could not be taken without consent, except in the case of war declared by Congress. Since no war was ever really declared, the numerous conflicts with Indians that resulted in whites seizing their lands were illegal.

Henry Knox, Washington's secretary of war, was the first government official to speak of assimilating the Native Americans. Knox felt the best way to do this was to introduce them to the concept and custom of private property. President Washington spoke to a delegation of Indians about learning the white man's ways of farming and raising stock. Even when the official policy considered the tribes as independent nations, the idea of assimilation and acculturation, whether benign or forced, was begun. This friendly policy, however, did not last long.

> The tribesmen presented the federal government with a cruel dilemma. On the one hand, responsible officials wanted to maintain peace; on the other hand, they wanted to satisfy the host of westward-moving land seekers. Unfortunately, any policy likely to satisfy the Indians outraged the pioneers. As a result the government seemed to follow conflicting and contradictory practices; but in reality the policy changed little. (Dinnerstein, and Nichols, (Reimers), 1990, 36)

By the early 1800s, problems with Native-American tribes had become acute, especially in the South. While technically the Indians could choose either to take a portion of land and farm as did the whites or move west, in reality few were given any choice, as greedy miners, lumbermen, and farmers pushed them aside. Federal officials soon began to demand that they migrate.

Policy seemed to vacillate for a time. Under Presidents Jefferson and Madison, a policy of removal was begun. In 1804, a provision was included in the Louisiana Territory Act for the exchange of lands; Indians were to be moved west of the Mississippi River. In 1809, 100 million acres were "appropriated" through some fifteen treaties by which William Harris, then governor of the Indiana Territory, received lands purchased from the Indians at one cent per acre. The Indians agreed to these treaties under the threat of force.

In 1815, Congress established the Indian Civilization Fund to educate Native Americans. Between 1783 and 1815, some tribes learned English, and Euro-style farming and business. The Cherokee tribe of North Carolina became bicultural. They were literate, articulate, and fully bilingual. By the mid-1820s, they owned 22,000 cattle,

1,300 slaves, 31 grist mills, 10 saw mills, and 8 cotton gins. They ran 18 schools and published the *Cherokee Phoenix,* a bilingual newspaper. Most Native Americans, however, retained their allegiance to tradition and refused to acculturate.

After the War of 1812, relations began to deteriorate. As the threat of British intervention faded, the federal government felt less need to conciliate Indian tribes. White settlers kept pushing westward and desired Indian lands. The government was forced to oblige them. A removal policy was formally adopted, although between 1816 and 1848 the pretense of "Independent Nations" continued. An Indian removal policy was first officially adopted by President James Monroe in 1825. Federal officials envisioned Indian territories and states in the far west. Apparently no one at the time anticipated the spectacular speed with which white settlers pushed beyond the Mississippi. The rapidly advancing frontier prevented any chance of the removal policy actually succeeding. President Andrew Jackson wholeheartedly approved of the policy of removal, although he felt it "absurd" to continue to deal with the Indians as independent nations. In 1830, Jackson pushed passage of the Indian Removal Act, which provided $300,000 for "an exchange of lands, compensation for improvements, and aid in the removal and initial adjustment to their new homes." (4 U.S. Statute 411, May 28, 1830) Most often, however, force was used and the majority society really did not accept their assimilation. Given the treatment they received by the government and the string of broken treaties with whites, Native Americans did not want to assimilate either.

Even those who went "voluntarily" suffered greatly in the migration. White officials oversaw the transportation and resettlement of the Indians in their new lands west of the Mississippi. Exploitation was common. Contractors supplying transportation and food bought condemned meat and spoiled flour to feed their charges. For transportation, they rented cheap and untrustworthy boats to get the Indians across major rivers, sometimes with fatal results. One steamboat crossing the Mississippi River sank, drowning 311 Indians. Nearly 4,000 of the 15,000 Cherokee who started west at gunpoint died on what the Indians called the Trail of Tears or during the first few months in what is now Oklahoma.

The Cherokee, being the most acculturated of the tribes, sought legal redress. They appealed to the U.S. Supreme Court. In *Cherokee Nation v. Georgia* (1831) and *Worcester v. Georgia* (1832), the Court ruled in favor of the Indians. President Jackson simply ignored the ruling, allegedly remarking, "John Marshall has made his decision. Now let him enforce it." In the *Worcester* case, the Court referred to the Indians as "Wards of Washington," which later became the basis for the approach of the Bureau of Indian Affairs. The refusal by Jackson to comply with the Court's ruling dashed hopes for a peaceful and legal resolution to the conflict.

Sometimes geographic separatism is forced upon a racial minority. Such is the case of the Native American on reservations. For American society, they constitute the best example of internal colonialism. In the words of General William Sherman, the typical reservation was "a parcel of land set aside for Indians, surrounded by thieves."[4]

The Bureau of Indian Affairs was established by the U.S. Congress in 1824, charged with administering all relations with Native Americans. The first reservation was created in 1830 in the Oklahoma territory. Between then and 1880, numerous others were established, mostly in Oklahoma, Arizona, and New Mexico. In all cases they were removed "from the path of progress," that is, out of the way of white settlers. They were closely supervised and controlled by the federal government. Lands set aside for reservations were routinely selected as sites judged to have no value or economic potential in the future. They were on barren land, well off the main routes of travel west, and useless for settlement or agricultural purposes, worthless for farming, and even marginal for ranching. Most had no visible natural resources.

The reservation program was designed to strip Native Americans of their dignity, of any means of supporting themselves, and of their traditional way of life and culture. They were kept powerless and totally dependent on the government for their sustenance. During the administration of President Grant, Congress created a Board of Indian Commissioners under the secretary of the interior. Relations with the tribes shifted legally from "treaties" to "agreements," symbolically reducing the status of Native Americans. Reservation programs accelerated in numbers, yet reduced their lands considerably. In the late 1860s and throughout the 1870s tribes across the nation, from the Dakotas to New Mexico, up to Puget Sound, resisted in a series of wars. Cynical soldiers referred to this policy as "feed 'em in the winter, and fight 'em in the summer."

The reservation system formed the basis of the relationship between Native Americans and the federal government from the 1830s to the present day. In many ways, the reservation program is an ironic misnomer. Far from "reserving" land, it directly led to their losing land, in millions of acres. In 1879 a policy of **forced assimilation** began. Then Secretary of Interior Carl Schurz outlined his goals in relation to Native Americans: To help them become self-supporting and break them of their "savage ways," he would turn them into farmers. Forced education would introduce the next generation to "civilized" ideas and aspirations. Individuals would get title to their farms, fostering pride of ownership rather than tribal dependence. Once individual allotments had been made, the remaining tribal lands would be sold, the proceeds of which would be set aside to meet future Indian needs, thereby reducing the federal government's obligation to support them. When all this was done, Native Americans would, he concluded, be treated like everyone else. In short, they were to be forcibly assimilated.

From 1887, with the enactment of the General Allotment Act (aka the Dawes Act), to 1934, when Congress enacted the Indian Reorganization Act (aka the Wheeler-Howard Act), native lands decreased from 138 million acres to 90 million acres. Between 1871 and 1983, Native-American tribal lands declined from over 120 million acres to just over 52 million acres, a reduction of more than 60 percent. Today, tribal lands are located within 35 states and total just over 56 million acres (see Table 5.2).

Forced assimilation involved more than turning them into farmers. Native-American religions came under attack as well. Using "Bibles, not bullets," native religious practices were undermined by Christian missionary groups. Specific reservations were assigned to the various denominations so they would not have to compete; they also gained access to a captive audience teeming with potential converts—so much for the separation of church and state and establishment clause, the constitutional prohibition against the government establishing religion. Indian reservation schools were established, at which native languages and cultures were forbidden. The founder of the

Table 5.2 Tribal Lands under Jurisdiction of the Bureau of Indian Affairs, 1996

Acreage Recapitulation by State	Tribal	Individually Owned	Total Trust	Government Owned	Total
Alabama	2,933.75	0.00	2,933.75	0.00	2,933.75
Alaska	83,879.83	1,056,530.13	1,140,409.96	0.00	1,140,409.96
Arizona	20,370,974.73	256,765.64	20,627,740.37	90,466.48	20,718,196.00
California	520,327.86	71,555.66	591,883.52	152.74	592,036.26
Colorado	797,594.51	2,699.68	800,294.19	12.24	800,306.43
Connecticut	5,028.10	0.00	5,028.10	980.00	6,008.10
Florida	165,267.39	0.00	165,267.39	189,333.30	354,600.69
Idaho	450,269.87	270,841.57	721,111.44	32,631.88	753,743.32
Iowa	7,270.99	0.00	7,270.99	5.00	7,275.99
Kansas	10,840.72	23,335.02	34,175.74	36.00	34,211.74
Louisiana	2,527.77	0.00	2,527.77	0.00	2,527.77
Maine	265,234.00	0.00	265,234.00	0.00	265,234.00
Massachusetts	467.30	0.00	467.30	0.00	467.30
Michigan	15,898.24	9,268.55	25,166.79	0.00	25,166.79
Minnesota	975,714.76	50,217.61	1,025,932.37	88.05	1,026,020.30
Mississippi	22,772.07	0.00	22,772.07	82.50	22,854.57
Missouri	0.00	374.37	374.37	0.00	374.37
Montana	2,534,379.10	2,850,445.40	5,384,824.50	94,535.96	5,479,360.40
Nebraska	23,174.00	43,288.37	66,462.37	6.79	66,469.16
Nevada	1,149,492.08	78,528.56	1,228,020.50	4,978.71	1,232,999.20
New Mexico	7,500,567.57	668,839.71	8,169,407.20	179,739.96	8,349,147.10
New York	53,188.40	0.00	53,188.40	35,341.00	88,529.40
North Carolina	51,166.11	0.00	51,166.11	112.16	51,278.27
North Dakota	245,629.60	619,337.66	864,967.26	1,927.71	866,894.97
Oklahoma	104,290.72	957,204.51	1,061,495.20	849.88	1,062,345.00
Oregon	666,106.28	130,465.87	796,572.15	16.24	796,588.39
Rhode Island	2,335.25	0.00	2,335.25	0.00	2,335.25
South Carolina	720.00	0.00	720.00	0.00	720.00
South Dakota	2,617,894.54	2,381,515.92	4,999,410.40	2,645.45	5,002,055.80
Tennessee	168.04	0.00	168.04	0.00	168.04
Texas	5,250.33	0.00	5,250.33	0.00	5,250.33
Utah	2,297,770.10	33,236.69	2,331,006.70	87.45	2,331,094.10
Washington	2,170,345.68	431,748.36	2,602,093.90	160.08	2,602,253.90
Wisconsin	352,515.39	82,969.23	435,484.62	335.65	435,820.27
Wyoming	1,794,589.22	93,646.98	1,888,236.10	1,296.15	1,889,532.20
Total	45,266,584.28	10,112,815.49	55,379,399.00	635,821.38	56,015,220.00

Source: U.S. Department of the Interior (http://www.doi.gov/bia/realty/state.html).

Carlisle Indian Industrial School in Pennsylvania observed that the school "has always planted treason to the tribe and loyalty to the nation at large." Its philosophy was to "kill the Indian to save the man."

As part of forced assimilation, native languages and cultures were forbidden at Indian reservation schools such as the Carlisle Indian Industrial School in Pennsylvania, shown here. (*Courtesy of the Library of Congress*)

Strict regulations, the use of school uniforms, and marching in formation were intended to move the youth from the desolation of the reservation to assimilation with the national culture. By separating them from their native roots, transporting them hundreds, even thousands, of miles away to distant schools in the East, many children of even grade-school ages were forced to assimilate. Reservation Indians were wards of the government in all aspects of life, controlled by the government. Today, some half-million Native Americans live on 314 reservations, where massive and persistent unemployment keeps the population in a state of dependency. Unemployment figures for reservations run three times the national average, from 23 to 90 percent.

An unanticipated consequence of the residential schools was the intermingling of children of diverse tribes who then developed a camaraderie from being thrown together into such a scary, alien environment. When they became adults, their friendships sometimes blossomed into marriages, intertribal visits, and political alliances. Ironically, "The phenomenon later called **Pan-Indianism**, a sense of shared identity that transcended tribal boundaries, arose at least partly from these schools—the very institutions designed to erase the idea of 'Indianness' from modern American life" (Marger 2003, 344).

The reservations evolved as well. Beginning as little more than outdoor prisons or holding pens that were administered by heavy-handed agents controlling barren and isolated acreage to which unwilling groups of people had been banished, they were gradually developed into tribal lands with self-governing bodies. The numbers of Native Americans also began to rebound. In 1890, their population in the United States was

The Indian Reorganization Act of 1934 forced Native Americans to live on "Trust Lands," or reservations. Shown here is a group of Native-American chiefs and U.S. officials. (*Courtesy of the Library of Congress*)

just over 270,000. By the 1990 census it had exceeded 2 million (just under 1 percent of the total population). Between 1980 and 1990, Native Americans became the fastest growing sector of the U.S. population, registering an increase of 72.4 percent.

The Indian Reorganization Act of 1934 required that persons living on the Native-American **trust lands** (i.e., reservations) have at least one-half Native-American bloodline. As of 1997, their growth rate has been more than double that of the white rate, at 15.4 per 1,000 versus 6.3 per 1,000. Their median age is much younger than the national average (26 years versus 33 years for the population generally), so a higher birth rate is likely to continue for the foreseeable future.

Currently at over 56 million acres and representing about 2.5 percent of the total U.S. land base, the reservations are home to about 42 percent of the total Native-American population. Within the 48 contiguous states there are 325 tribal nations with trust lands, and Alaska has more than 200 Native-American communities; over 100 others are seeking official recognition. They speak about 100 recognized tribal languages. Conditions on the reservation are still well below the standards for the nation as a whole. As of 1997, over 27 percent of Native-American families living on reservations were below the poverty level. Nationally, 23 percent of reservation housing, which was three times the national level, lacked complete plumbing facilities, and 49 percent of those on the Navajo reservation, one of the nation's largest, lacked plumbing

Box 5.3   THE UNBREAKABLE CODE

The U.S. Marine Corps had a secret weapon against Japan in World War II: the 420 Navajo code talkers who fought all the way from Guadalcanal to Okinawa. Using a blend of everyday Navajo speech and some 400 specially devised code words, they transmitted messages that completely baffled the enemy. Bombers were *jaysho* ("buzzards"); bombs, *ayeshi* ("eggs"); battleship was *lotso* ("whale"); destroyer, *calo* ("shark"); submarine, *beshlo* ("iron fish"). In a coded alphabet the Navajo word for "ant" was the letter *A,* the word for "bear" was *B,* and so on; thus, a place such as Bloody Ridge was spelled out with the Navajo words for Bear, Lamb, Onion, Dog, Yucca, Rabbit, Ice, Dog, Goat, and Elk. In keeping with a language that was rarely written, there was no code book. Until trained, even new Navajo recruits could not break encrypted messages.

Initially skeptical about the unconventional code, Marine officers finally had to acknowledge its effectiveness. "Without the Navajos," said one, "the Marines would never have taken Iwo Jima." In addition to the Navajo, there were Hopi, Lakota, Sauk and Fox, Oneida, Chippewa, and Comanche code talkers in Europe and the Pacific.

Source: Box by author, based on information adapted from *Through Indian Eyes* (Pleasantville, NY: Reader's Digest, 1995) 358.

facilities. Native-American family income levels hover at 35 to 40 percent below that of the general population. In 1990, Native-American median family income was $21,619, compared to the national average for the total population of $39,066. Their formal education is far below average: In 1997, the percentage of Native Americans who had completed high school was 65.6 percent, compared to 77.6 percent for the total population; and the percentage with college degrees was 9.4 versus the 24.6 percent of the white population.

Native-American assimilation and a greater acceptance and tolerance of them were influenced by war. When the United States entered World War I in 1917, Congress passed the Selective Service Act. Many American Indians joined the armed services despite the fact that as noncitizens they were deferred from the draft. By war's end, some 17,000 had enlisted, close to 30 percent of adult Indian males and double the national average. Congress gave citizenship to honorably discharged Indian veterans in 1919 and, finally, universal Indian citizenship in 1924. In World War II, likewise, their rate of service exceeded the national average. As citizens they were eligible for the draft. By 1945, over 25,000 Native-American men and 1,000 women had served, with some tribes sending as many as 70 percent of their men between the ages of 18 and 50 (Thompson 1996). Box 5.3 highlights their special contribution as **code-talkers**, Native Americans who served as communication specialists during WWII. Nearly twice as many as those who donned uniforms, some 46,000, served the war effort by leaving their tribal homelands to work in war-related industry jobs, including 12,000 Indian women who took off-reservation jobs. For many of them, it was the first time they had seen a city or experienced life off-reservation as a member of a minority group.

As with the Indian school programs, an unanticipated consequence of the World War II experience was the development of Pan-Indianism. In 1944, the National Congress of American Indians was founded in Denver, Colorado. It began lobbying in

Washington, DC, adopting tactics similar to those of the NAACP. It was instrumental in the enactment of the Indian Claims Commission law and in convincing the Bureau of Indian Affairs to abandon the practice of treating Native Americans as wards of the state.

In 1946, Congress created the Indian Claims Commission to settle grievances, including treaty disputes, conflicts over Indian trust funds, and unresolved land claims, some dating back to colonial times. Originally the three-member commission was to work for five years, but so many claims were filed that Congress expanded it to a five-member commission, and it operated until 1978, with hundreds of complex cases still unresolved.

In 1952, the Bureau of Indian Affairs (BIA) began programs designed to assist Native Americans in relocating off-reservation. The 1962 Employment Assistance Program, for example, set up job assistance centers in a dozen major metropolitan areas, and by 1968, over 100,000 Native Americans had participated; over 200,000 had moved to urban areas, although about one-fourth of those returned to their reservations. One effect was to create a "brain drain" problem for reservations.

Box 5.4 offers a biography of Ada Deer, a Menominee Indian woman who successfully led the battle against the termination policy.

Also in the 1950s, the Eisenhower administration adopted the policy of *termination*. This policy remained in effect until it was halted by the Indian Self-Determination and Education Assistance Act of 1975, but by then 109 tribes were dissolved.

The increased urbanization of the Native-American population contributed to the Pan-Indian movement with such developments as the National Indian Youth Council (NIYC), the American Indian Movement (AIM), and the Council of Energy Resource Tribes (CERT).

The 1970s witnessed a spate of national legislative victories won by Native Americans. During the Nixon administration, two major laws were enacted: the Indian Education Act of 1972 and the Indian Financing Act of 1974. The Indian Self-Determination and Educational Assistance Act of 1975 was passed during the Carter administration. In 1978, Congress enacted the American Indian Religious Freedom Act, the Tribally Controlled Community College Assistance Act, and the Indian Child Welfare Act. In 1979, it passed the Indian Archaeological Resources Protection Act. In 1988, Congress passed the Indian Gaming Regulatory Act, resulting in 97 tribes in 22 states operating more than 200 casinos.

Nearly 60 percent of the native population now lives off-reservation, with their political activism and success in courts and statutes increasing considerably. More will be said of those developments in Chapter 8. Urbanization also contributed to higher rates of segmented assimilation, exemplified by the fact that by 1995 more than half of all Indians, both on- and off-reservation, were marrying non-Indians.

Today, the states with the highest Native-American populations are California, Oklahoma, Arizona, New Mexico, Alaska, and Washington, each with 100,000. The metropolitan areas with the largest populations are, in rank order, Los Angeles–Anaheim–Riverside, Tulsa, New York, Oklahoma City, San Francisco, Phoenix, Seattle–Tacoma, Minneapolis–St. Paul, Tucson, and San Diego. Despite the large migration to urban areas, reservations are unlikely to disappear. In fact, some 100 tribal groups are seeking official recognition, so the number of reservations is likely to increase.

Box 5.4   *Bio-Sketch: Ada Deer (1935–)*

Ada Deer was born on the Menominee Indian Reservation in northeastern Wisconsin in August 1935. Her mother, Constance Stockton (Wood) Deer, is an Anglo-American from Philadelphia and a former BIA nurse. Her father, Joseph Deer, who died at age 85 in 1994, was a nearly full-blooded Menominee Indian and an employee of the Menominee Indian Mills. Until Ada graduated from high school, she and her family lived in a log cabin near the Wolf River with no running water or electricity. She graduated from the Shawano and Milwaukee public schools in the top ten of her class and went on to the University of Wisconsin–Madison on a tribal scholarship. She was one of two Native Americans out of 19,000 students, and was the first Menominee to graduate from the university, receiving her B.A. in social work in 1957. In 1961, she became the first Native American to earn a M.S.W. from Columbia University.

After graduating, she was a social worker in New York City and in the Minneapolis Public Schools. She later worked with the Peace Corps in Puerto Rico. Between 1964 and 1967, Deer worked with the BIA in Minnesota as a community service coordinator. She then served as coordinator of Indian Affairs in the University of Minnesota's Training Center for Community Programs, and also served on a Joint Commission on the Mental Health of Children, Inc. In 1969 she became a member of the national board of Girl Scouts of the U.S.A., serving until 1975. She left to study at the American Indian Law program at the University of New Mexico, and briefly attended the University of Wisconsin–Madison law school, but left after one semester to take on an urgent tribal matter that became her major focus for several years.

As part of a national termination policy, in 1954 the U.S. Congress passed the Menominee Termination Act, imposing state jurisdiction and taxes that forced the tribe to sell off ancestral lands, and taking federal recognition away from the tribe, along with a host of benefits. The Menominee went from being prosperous to being Wisconsin's smallest and poorest county. Deer left law school to lead a campaign to regain tribal control and reverse termination. In 1970, she helped form the Determination of Rights and Unity for Menominee Shareholders (DRUMS) and organized a 220-mile march from Menominee county to the capital in Madison. From 1972 to 1973, Deer was the vice president and DC lobbyist for the National Committee to Save the Menominee People and Forest, Inc. From 1974 to 1976, she was the first woman to chair the Menominee Tribe. Tribal rights were restored in 1977. She then became a Senior Lecturer in the School of Social Work and the American Indian Studies Program at the University of Wisconsin–Madison, where she taught until 1993. She also served as legislative liaison to the Native American Rights Fund, was a candidate for Wisconsin secretary of state, a delegate-at-large at the Democratic National Convention, and vice-chair of the National Mondale-Ferraro Presidential Campaign. In 1992 she ran for Congress, narrowly losing in the Second Congressional District of Wisconsin.

In May 1993 she became the first woman to head the BIA. As head of the BIA she had to deal with many issues: budget reductions; conflicts with tribes and localities over land management, water resources, and mineral rights; tribal recognition; education; and religious freedom.

Her many awards include the following: Outstanding Young Woman of America (1966); White Buffalo Council Achievement Award and honorary doctorates from the University of Wisconsin–Madison and Northland College (1974); Woman of the Year for Girl Scouts of America and Wonder Woman Award (1982); Indian Council Fire Achievement Award (1984); National Distinguished Achievement Award from the American Indian Resources Institute (1991).

After leaving the BIA, she became the director of the American Indian Studies Program at the University of Wisconsin–Madison in January 1999. She also lectures in the School of Social Work there.

Sources: Bio-sketch by author, based on information from http://www.africanpubs.com/nativepubs/Apps/bios/0033DeerAda.asp; http://www.news.wisc.edu/view.html?get=2518; http://www.cic.uiuc.edu/programs/AmericanIndianStudiesConsortium/archive/ ConferencePresentation/AisSymposium; Carole Marsh, *Ada Deer: Notable Native American* (Gallopade, Int., 1998).

THE AMISH AND MENNONITES

Two ethno-religious subcultures that provide good examples of a minority following the strategy of physical separatism are the Amish and Mennonites. They reject the values of the majority culture, live in as rural and isolated a setting as they can find, reduce their contact with the majority culture to a minimum, and have struggled for over 400 years to maintain their separate cultures. As a scholar of the Mennonites says: "There is almost unanimous agreement within the sect that the regulation of their total physical and spiritual lives is necessary for the unity and continuity of their spiritual culture (Boyton 1986, vii). Likewise, scholars of the Amish characterize them as "a people of separation. Indeed, their entire history can be called a struggle to be separate. They are one of several Anabaptist groups that trace their origins to the Radical Reformation of sixteenth century Europe" (Kraybill and Olshan 1994, 1). By mainline church standards, the Amish and Mennonites are very small denominations organized in very small congregations. For example, the U.S. Census Bureau, in its *Statistical Abstract of the United States, 2000,* reports 81,000 Old Order Amish members in 898 congregations, and 92,000 Mennonites in 926 congregations. The National Congregations Study, 1999, had only 0.4 percent of its respondents listed as affiliates of two Mennonite denominations. By contrast, in the 1990 census data, all Christian Church adherents made up 56.6 percent of the total population.

The **Anabaptists**, or "rebaptizers," began as a reformation movement in 1525 in Zurich, Switzerland, preaching adult baptism as a public sign of Christian faith and stressing a double separation: church and state, and the separation of the church from the evils of the larger culture. The movement soon encountered severe persecution, as it seemed to threaten the very fabric of sixteenth-century society. Thousands were killed as both civil and religious authorities sought to repress the movement.

The Anabaptist sect known as Mennonites was named after Menno Simons, one of their prominent leaders and a bishop who united with a Dutch group of Anabaptists in 1536. After Zurich, the Netherlands became a second cradle of the movement. Today, Mennonites, Hutterites, and the Amish trace their religious heritage to the Anabaptist movement.

The Amish split off as a separate sect in 1693, in what is today the Alsace region of France. The Anabaptist leader, Jacob Ammann, began a new practice of community life that included social avoidance—shunning—of persons who had been excommunicated from the church, as well as advocating other practices that enforced even greater separation between the church and the majority society.

Both the Amish and the Mennonites migrated to the United States and Canada in the eighteenth century, frequently settling in the same geographic areas. Old Order Mennonites emerged as a conservative subgroup in the late nineteenth century when growing modernization led to schism in the church. Old Order Mennonite and Old Order Amish share similarities, including horse-and-buggy travel, plain dress, a conservative lifestyle, and the use of one-room parochial schools.

Amish society is organized on three levels: settlement, district, and affiliation. A settlement encompasses the general geographic area where Amish families live in proximity, varying considerably in size. Some twenty-five to thirty-five families compose a church district, the basic social unit of a settlement. Families within a district worship together in each other's homes. When the number of families grows too large to hold services in the home, it branches into two smaller districts. Thus, the church district becomes the primary social/religious unit—sort of parish, precinct, tribe, and club all wrapped up into a single social package. Church districts that are in fellowship with one another make up an affiliation, sharing similar church practices and exchanging ministers in their worship services. Congregational autonomy and loosely coupled affiliation engender considerable diversity in practice among the Amish churches. But they all share some common aspects of Amish identity:

> These common badges of Amish identity include the Pennsylvania German dialect, the use of horse-drawn transportation, the rejection of electricity from public utility lines, the use of homes for worship, plain dress, beards for men, a prayer cap for women, an eighth-grade education, and the use of horses for field work. There are of course many other distinctive markers of Amish lifestyles but these public symbols of identity are shared by most Amish groups across North America. What is remarkable, yes astonishing, is that the Amish have been able to preserve these common badges of separation without a centralized national structure to link the more than 900 congregations across more than 230 different geographic settlements in North America. (Kraybill and Olshan 1994, 4)

The Holdeman Mennonites and the Old Order Mennonites are more conservative than other Mennonite groups, having retained more of the original beliefs and behaviors of their sixteenth-century ancestors. The Holdeman Mennonites are named after John Holdeman who, with his followers, left the Old Mennonite church in 1859 to restore "the true church." It now has more than 10,000 persons in 100 congregations in the United States and Canada. Their beliefs and social practices serve as cultural markers: "Cultural boundary markers are merely restrictive behaviors which function symbolically to unify a subculture and separate it from the dominant society" (Boyton 1986, 11).

The first Amish settlement in the United States, the Northkill Settlement, a group of about 500, was in Berks County, Pennsylvania. At about the same time another settlement began in Lancaster County, which soon developed into a major area of settlement for Amish and Mennonite groups. These two settlements became the **mother colonies** of the Amish in America. Other settlements came about as both Amish and Mennonite groups expanded west and east, and a few to the south (Virginia and North Carolina). The Mennonites, who arrived first in 1710, tended to purchase unimproved property. The Amish more often bought land cleared by non-Amish. While there was some advantage to acquiring the somewhat improved farmland, the Mennonite communities tended to be on land of richer soil, and by the late 1700s were generally wealthier than the Amish (Nolt 1992).

Table 5.3 **Growth of Amish Population in North America, 1900–1992**

Year	*Estimated Population*	*Number of Church Districts*
1900	4,800	32
1910	8,550	57
1920	12,450	83
1930	16,500	110
1941	23,100	154
1951	30,300	202
1961	40,350	269
1971	55,050	367
1981	83,350	569
1991	134,700	898
1992	139,500	930

Source: Table by author; adapted from data in Donald Kraybill and Marc Olshan, eds., *The Amish Struggle with Modernity* (Hanover, NH: University Press of New England, 1994) 9.

A combination of high birth rates and low dropout rates resulted in vigorous growth, as illustrated by Table 5.3, which shows the growth in the Amish population throughout North America from 1900 to 1992.

Amish immigration from Europe came in four distinguishable periods: 1736–1770, when they settled mostly in Pennsylvania; 1804–1810, settling mostly in the Midwest and moving to areas also settled by groups expanding out from the Pennsylvania area; 1817–1860, when about 3,000 migrated directly to Ohio, Illinois, Indiana, Iowa, and New York; and 1860–1900, when some 50 families came and settled among established Amish communities.

The Mennonites of Indiana are descendants of Mennonite families who went there about 1840, except for three congregations who were composed wholly of people who came directly from Europe in 1838 (Wenger 1961).

The Amish and Old Order Mennonites remain separate through a well-defined moral order and lifestyle. The Amish use the **Ordnung**, the "understandings," to prescribe expectations of Amish life—the "do's" and "don'ts" of Amish practices. They form a major part of a comprehensive program of social control. Generally unwritten and passed on by oral tradition, the Ordnung comprises a body of communal understandings that cultivates group identity, cohesion, and order. They articulate the community's moral order and define the very essence of Amish identity. Table 5.4 lists a few examples of the practices either prescribed by the Ordnung (the do's), or practices prohibited by it (the don'ts).

These techniques of social control keep individuals in line with group goals and serve as cultural markers—barricades against the encroachment by the larger society's culture. Separatist groups, such as the Amish and Mennonites, employ at least five defensive tactics: symbolization of core values; centralized leadership; social sanctions; comprehensive socialization; and controlled interaction with outsiders (Kraybill 1989).

Table 5.4   Examples of Ordnung Practices

Prescribed Practices	*Prohibited Practices*
Color and style of clothing	Use of tractors for fieldwork
Men's hat styles	Ownership/use of automobiles
Color/style of buggies	Use of electricity from public power lines
Use of horses for field work	Filing a lawsuit
Steel wheels on machinery	Entering military service
Use of Pennsylvania German dialect	Ownership of computers, tvs, radios
Worship in homes	Central heating in homes
Order of worship service	Wall to wall carpeting
Unison singing, without instruments	Pipeline milking equipment
Menu of congregational meal	High school education
Marriage within the church	Air transportation
	Wearing/ownership of jewelry, even wedding rings and wrist watches
	Divorce

Source: Table by author; adapted from data in Kraybill and Nolt, 1995, p. 12.

The Amish and Mennonites not only resisted modernization, they also negotiated with it, adopting a process of cultural or structural bargaining wherein they sometimes compromised and at other times refused to concede.

The strains of coping with these strategies led to three internal divisions among the Old Order Amish in 1877, 1910, and 1966. In 1877, following some Amish divisions in the Midwest, two factions formed independent congregations using a meeting house for their worship services. The traditional Amish then became known as the Old Order Amish, or House Amish, because they continued to worship in their homes. About one-third of the original Amish continue in the "house-church" tradition; the rest developed into the "Church Amish," which finally merged with the "Old" Mennonites in the 1920s and are no longer identifiable today. The splinter groups, called Amish-Mennonite, or "Meeting House Amish," held their services in a church building, eventually becoming full-fledged Mennonites. A second division occurred in 1910 over the use of cars, telephones, and electricity. A liberal faction became known as the Beachy Church, affiliated today with the Beachy Amish Church. The Beachy Amish, which started as a liberalizing movement focused on softening the ban of the excommunicated, later adopted Sunday schools as well. The Beachy conference has become a more creative and growing movement, welcoming a number of Old Order Amish congregations desiring a more liberal church life and process. Often the Beachy Amish are merging with the Old Mennonite Church. The continuing loss of membership of the Old Order Amish to the more liberal groups has strained relationships among them. The third division came in 1966, when a group of so-called New Order Amish split over differences in the use of modern farm technology. The largest Mennonite group or conference in North America is the "Old" Mennonite Church (MC), or simply, "the Mennonite Church."

Coordination among Amish groups, often involving matters dealing with law or policy viewed as detrimental to all, led to the creation of six organizations with loosely coordinated activities that go beyond the scope of local districts. These organizations are unlike the formal bureaucratic structures of majority society. They are informal, flat, decentralized, small, and traditional.

Another example of the Amish coping with the broader culture is the dramatic change in their work patterns, especially since 1960. The pressures of suburbanization, declining farmland, rising land prices, and a burgeoning Amish population have made it increasingly difficult for young Amish couples to enter farming. The stereotypical image of the Amish is the farmer. Until 1970, nearly all of the Amish in Lancaster County were engaged in farming or in small crafts and enterprises linked to farming. Since 1970, the Amish have been creating small businesses and cottage industries that have flourished and provide much needed employment in the Amish communities. Now, less than half the Amish are in farming. Amish and Mennonites in Indiana have left their farms for factory work in the recreational vehicle and mobile home industries (Kraybill and Olshan 1994, 165–181). This non-farm occupational trend is more pronounced among Mennonites and is exemplified in Table 5.5, which lists the types of businesses found in a Mennonite settlement area in Mountain Lake, Minnesota, 1875–1985.

This transformation of Amish employment from farms to business will have a profound impact on Amish life, as well as on their relationship with the outside world.

> No longer barefoot farmers, whose peculiar ways can be attributed to rural naiveté, Amish entrepreneurs will be subject to the same legal and regulatory restrictions as their non-Amish competitors without the public indulgence they have sometimes enjoyed in the past. The power brokers of modern life and all their functionaries will no doubt insist that the Amish play on a level playing field despite the implications of their religious convictions. Many of the legal and political concessions that have been forged over the years have been based on the assumption that they were innocent farmers seeking to preserve a sharp separation from the world. That assumption will surely erode as they enter the fray of business. What, for example, might have been the outcome of the Supreme Court's 1972 decision in *Wisconsin v. Yoder* if less than half of the Amish had been farming at the time? (Kraybill and Nolt, in Kraybill and Olshan 1994, 162–163)

Conflict between the majority culture and the Amish and Mennonites centered on aspects of their beliefs that clash with the broader culture in ways the majority deems dangerous. Their pacifism caused them no end of problems during the time of the Civil War, when they refused to fight. The pressure was even greater during World War I, when the draft was employed. A few who were drafted served in noncombatant roles. Most, however, refused to participate at all.

> Despite the threats and pressure, young Amish draftees remained unwilling to fight, wear military uniforms or perform certain jobs which they felt were aiding the army's war-making ability. . . . Amish conscientious objectors received verbal abuse, beatings and wire-brush treatments. In addition, soldiers sometimes forcibly shaved the beards of the Amish. Many COs were made to stand for long periods of time in the sun, without refreshment. Those who refused to wear military uniforms were at times left in cold, damp cells with no clothing at all. Officers occasionally "baptized" Amish COs in camp latrines

Table 5.5   Mennonite and Non-Mennonite Entrepreneurs in Mountain Lake, Minnesota, 1875–1985

Business	Mennonite	Non-Mennonite	% Mennonite
Auto sales	7	2	70
Bakery	2	5	28
Bank	5	0	100
Barber shop	2	0	100
Blacksmith	5	2	71
Construction	11	4	66
Creamery/hatchery	4	3	57
Delivery/livery	6	3	66
Elevator	3	2	60
Garage	2	0	100
Hotel	2	0	100
Industry	7	2	70
Lumber	3	0	100
Machinery sales	8	2	80
Mills/feed	1	1	50
Newspaper	4	2	66
Photography	6	2	75
Repair Service	10	1	90
Restaurant	5	5	50
Stores, General	14	6	70
Department	5	1	83
Drug	2	4	33
Hardware	7	3	70
Furniture	3	1	75
Services, Ins., Real estate	4	3	57
Telephone	6	1	85
Undertaker	3	2	60
All Businesses	137	57	71

Source: Table by author; adapted from Table 12.4 in Redekop, 1989, p. 205.

in mockery of their Anabaptist beliefs. COs were stuck in abusive camp situations from the time of their induction until well after the war was over and demobilization began. For the Amish men who endured World War I camp experiences, the memories were powerful and unforgettable. (Nolt 1992, 226; see also Wenger 1961, 38–39)

Figure 5.1 provides a map of Mennonite settlements in the United States.

During World War I, they were suspected of being pro-German because they used German in their services and community life. They were hounded, two Mennonite

Figure 5.1   Mennonites in the United States

Source: Figure by author, data from Mennonite Weekly Review, June 20, 2005.

meeting houses were torched, and others were vandalized or posted with American flags.

Another conflict arose in 1955 when Congress extended the Social Security program to include self-employed farmers. The Amish had never taken part in the Social Security program, but suddenly participation became mandatory. When the Amish refused to pay to the fund, the IRS collected funds through their bank accounts. Some Amish closed their accounts. The government then foreclosed and sold several Amish farms to recover lost Social Security funds. The IRS forcibly collected from 130 Amish households. In 1965, Congress finally addressed the problem by including a provision of the Medicare Act that exempted self-employed Amish from both the Medicare and the Social Security systems.

The issue that aroused the most conflict was compulsory education. Old Order Amish and Old Order Mennonite parents refused to send their children to large, consolidated elementary schools or to high school. During the 1950s and 1960s, they had repeated run-ins with the law and were forced to pay fines and serve jail terms. Nearly every state that had Amish or Mennonite settlements experienced such clashes.

The Amish increasingly began to operate their own private schools. Such programs expanded rapidly. Sometimes compromises were negotiated with school officials. In Pennsylvania, the Amish were allowed, after completing eighth grade, to work at home and report to a special "vocational school" one morning per week until age fifteen. Several other states copied this method. The conflict was finally resolved by the U.S. Supreme Court. In 1967, a Lutheran pastor in Iowa, the Reverend William Lindholm, founded an interest group (the National Committee for Amish Religious Freedom) to work for Amish rights. They backed a case out of Wisconsin. Although they lost before the county court and the Wisconsin Supreme Court, they appealed to the U.S. Supreme Court and won their case in *Wisconsin v. Yoder* (1972). Since then, all states must allow the Old Order Amish the right to establish their own schools or to withdraw from compulsory public schools after the eighth grade.

BLACK NATIONALISM: MARCUS GARVEY AND "BACK TO AFRICA"

A portion of black Americans advocated a strategy of physical separatism. This chapter will focus on the most important such instance, the movement headed by Marcus Garvey, active in the United States during the 1920s.[5]

While Garveyism is a prototype example of **Black Nationalism**, Garvey certainly was not the first to argue the case for physical separatism, nor for a back to Africa tactic. An earlier if lesser known instance involved a free black Quaker from Philadelphia who was captain of a trade ship, the *Traveller*. Captain Paul Cuffe visited Sierre Leone in Africa in April 1811 to establish trade between the United States and Africa that did not involve the slave trade.

After that first trip, Captain Cuffe met with President James Madison, in May 1812, to discuss his plans to begin trade with the ultimate goal of enabling free blacks to return to Africa. President Madison, as did Thomas Jefferson, preferred a plan to remove blacks to Africa as a means of ending slavery in America. Cuffe declared that blacks "might rise to be a people in Africa, something they could not do in America" (Lamont 1986, 108). He helped found the African Institution of Philadelphia to promote such a plan, working mostly with the Quakers. He promoted Pan-Africanism. In 1816, the American Colonization Society began using him to promote racial separation in America, however, and he ceased promoting the plan. The black Quaker captain has been characterized as an early "voice from within the Veil," which was W. E. B. Du Bois's expression for oppressive white society.

A century later, Marcus Garvey's movement, the Universal Negro Improvement Association (UNIA), became the first mass movement among blacks in the United States, one that indeed had worldwide scope. As one of his biographers said: "Garvey's UNIA had collected more money and claimed a larger membership than any other Negro group either before or since" (Cronon 1969, 3).

Garvey was born in St. Ann's Bay, Jamaica, on August 17, 1887, the youngest of eleven children and descended from Maroons, African slaves who had successfully defied the Jamaican slave regime and set up virtually independent communities in the island's mountain regions from 1664 to 1765. In his teens he moved to Kingston and began work in a print shop where, at age twenty, he became the youngest foreman printer at a time when British and Canadian immigrants usually held such jobs. He was elected union leader during a strike that failed, and he was then fired and blacklisted. This experience made him skeptical of the labor movement and of socialism. He then

Marcus Garvey, founder and president of the UNIA (*Courtesy of the Library of Congress*)

began to work for a government printing office. It was during this period that he became increasingly aware of the injustices to blacks and began his opposition to British colonial rule.

In 1910, at age twenty-three, he began publishing his first newspaper, *Garvey's Watchman,* a small weekly. Thus began a career in journalism that continued for most of his life. He went on to Costa Rica, where he started a second paper, *La Nacion,* and also worked for *The Bluefield Messenger.* After a brief stint he moved to Panama, where he began publishing *La Prensa.* He traveled throughout South America, observing the poor treatment of blacks everywhere.

Garvey migrated to Europe and settled for a brief time in London, where he met an Egyptian nationalist, Duse Mohammad Ali, who expanded his knowledge of black subjugation throughout the world and who introduced him to the work of Booker T. Washington and his autobiography, *Up from Slavery.* It had a profound impact upon Garvey, and he determined to become a race leader. In 1914, he returned to Jamaica where, on August 1, he formed an international black organization designed to establish an independent black state—the Universal Negro Improvement and Conservation Association and African Communities League (known simply as the UNIA). Its motto was: "One God! One Aim! One Destiny!" As one of his biographers noted:

> The specifically racial character of Garveyite nationalism was a reaction to centuries of slavery, colonialism, and capitalist exploitation. This process involved the brutal enslavement of African people, their loss of territory, their arbitrary dispersal throughout the new world, the suppression of language, culture and kinship patterns and their victimization under the inhuman conditions of plantation slavery and the pernicious stigma of racial inferiority. (Lewis 1988, 125)

In 1916, at age twenty-eight, Garvey visited the United States, a move that was to be the decisive factor in his political career. He visited Tuskegee to pay his respects to his by then dead hero, Booker T. Washington. He toured thirty-eight states before settling in New York City, where he remained and worked, in Harlem, until 1927.

Initially, Garvey intended to raise funds in the United States and return to Jamaica and set up a school similar to Tuskegee. His oratorical skills attracted followers and attention. He faced immediate opposition from Harlem's black leadership, and he decided to remain in Harlem to build the UNIA chapter there. Within three weeks he claimed to have recruited 2,000 members, and by 1921 he estimated the worldwide membership of the UNIA at 6 million, though his figures have been much disputed and undoubtedly were inflated. In 1923, W. E. B. Du Bois stated that the UNIA had fewer than 20,000 members. Yet, by 1923, Garvey could reasonably claim to have many more members in the UNIA than all other Negro organizations combined (Brooks 1996, 132–142).

In 1919, he began his weekly paper, *The Negro World,* the official organ of the UNIA. With a weekly circulation estimated as high as 200,000, it was his greatest propaganda device and by far his most successful publishing venture. It appeared in English, French, and Spanish editions and lasted until 1933. It led to a new militancy in the Negro press during the 1920s.

In July 1919 Garvey bought a large auditorium in Harlem that he called Liberty Hall. It became the headquarters of the UNIA, and soon other branches opened their own Liberty Halls. These halls served multiple functions; Sunday morning worship, afternoon Sunday schools, public meetings at night, and concerts and dances were held there. Notice boards were put up where one could look for a room, a job, or a lost article. In localities where there were many people out of work during the winter, Black Cross nurses would organize soup kitchens. On freezing winter days stoves were kept going to accommodate the cold and homeless until they "got on their feet again." From 1919 to 1920, Garvey's UNIA and related ventures experienced a period of remarkable growth. The peak of his influence was a 1920 UNIA worldwide convention held at Liberty Hall in Harlem.

Garvey began a number of ventures. The Negro Factories Corporation was established to build and operate factories in major urban areas in the United States, South and Central America, the West Indies, and Africa. It developed a chain of grocery stores, a restaurant, a tailor shop, a hotel, a printing press, a doll factory, and a steam laundry in Harlem that employed 300 people. The UNIA established a motor corp, an African Legion, and the Black Cross nurses. A long-term goal of these ventures, and especially of the Black Star Shipping Line and the Liberia scheme, was to advance the organization of the UNIA and to aid ultimately in the "repossession of Africa by Africans."

His most notable undertakings were the basis for what became known as the Back to Africa movement: the Black Star Steamship Line and the Liberia scheme. Garvey's plan was to build an all-black steamship company that could link all the colored peoples of the world in commercial and industrial exchange. Begun in 1919, it was capitalized at one-half million dollars, with 100,000 shares selling for $5 each. The venture reflected Booker T. Washington's philosophy of blacks becoming independent of white capital. Its stock circulars appealed to racial pride.

Although connected to his Liberia scheme, the Black Star Line (BSL) was not for the purpose of mass transportation of blacks back to Africa but was a commercial venture to enhance justifiable racial pride and demonstrate black entrepreneurial and nautical skills. In promoting the BSL and the Negro Factories Corporation, Garvey made a clear statement on the "back-to-Africa" interpretation of his movement that his enemies on the right and left used to characterize the UNIA:

It is a mistake to suppose that I want to take the Negroes to Africa. I believe that the American Negroes have helped to establish the North American civilization and, therefore, have a perfect right to live in the United States and to aspire to equality of opportunities and treatment. Each Negro can be a citizen of the nation in which he was born or that he has chosen. But I foresee the building of a great state in Africa which, featuring in the concert of the great nations, will make the Negro race as respectable as the others. . . . Cuban Negroes will be favored by the building of this African state because when this state exists they will be considered and respected as descendants of this powerful country which has enough strength to protect them. (cited in Lewis 1988, 109; see also Cronon 1969)

His wife described the intention of the BSL enterprise:

The main purpose of the formation and promotion of the Black Star Line was to acquire ships to trade between the units of the Race—in Africa, the United States, the West Indies, and Central America, thereby building up an independent economy of business, industry, and commerce, and to transport our people on business and pleasure, without being given inferior accommodation or refusal of any sort of accommodation. (cited in White 1991, 86)

The 1920 UNIA convention provided fodder for his critics to label his movement the "back to Africa movement" by electing Garvey the "provisional president of the African Republic."

It was in connection with the Liberia scheme that his movement came to be known in the international press as the Back to Africa movement. In 1920, 1923, and 1924 the UNIA sent delegations to conduct negotiations with the Liberian government, first to establish trade and commerce ventures, but ultimately to create a black nation in Africa that could become the base of a worldwide black nationalism. The UNIA convention created a nobility, the "Knights of the Nile," with honors such as the "Distinguished Service Order of Ethiopia," and they issued a "Declaration of the Rights of the Negro Peoples of the World," which demanded that "Negro" be spelled with a capital N and which condemned European imperialism in Africa and lynchings in America.

Garvey himself traveled extensively to promote the BSL and the UNIA, including visits to Cuba, Jamaica, Costa Rica, Panama, and British Honduras. In 1922, he went to Georgia to meet with Edward Young Clarke, the Imperial Kleagle of the revived Ku Klux Klan, in an attempt to elicit Klan support for the UNIA's African program. Despite their opposing perspectives, they shared a common belief in racial purity and racial separation. Garvey stated: "Whilst the Ku Klux Klan desires to make America absolutely a white man's country, the UNIA wants to make Africa absolutely a black man's country" (cited in White 1991, 88).

In the mid-1920s, the UNIA grew extensively. Returning veterans from World War I (in which some 400,000 blacks served in the U.S. armed forces), proved to be fertile grounds for his appeal to Black Nationalism and black pride.

His Liberia scheme and his support for white segregationists such as the Ku Klux Klan and Mississippi Senator Theodore Bilbo, who actively opposed racial intermixing and also espoused the repatriation of black Americans to West Africa, demonstrated that in his zeal for black separatism, Marcus Garvey badly disregarded the sensibilities of the majority of American blacks. That misjudgment, and the repeated financial and legal difficulties of the BSL, which was economically unsound, led to his decline. The BSL's first ship, the *S.S. Yarmouth,* which became the *S.S. Frederick Douglass,* was never seaworthy and was in constant financial trouble. Purchased at an inflated price of $165,000, it was in constant need of repairs. Two other ships purchased by the line never realized a fraction of their purchase prices. The aptly named *Shadyside,* with less than five months of active service, cost the BSL $11,000 in operating losses. Likewise, the *Kanawha,* a steam yacht, was overpriced and operated briefly at a huge loss.

It was his promotion of the stock when the BSL's financial status was so clearly unable to match his promises that led to Garvey and three associates being arrested and charged with using the mails to defraud. His trial began in mid-May 1923, and he acted as his own lawyer, despite no law degree or legal training. His conceit and inexperience cost him dearly. Although the presiding judge gave him wide latitude and assistance in the conduct of the trial, he was found guilty and sentenced to five years in prison and a fine of $1,000.

Released on bond pending appeal, he continued his work with the UNIA, founded the Black Cross Navigation and Trading Company, and attempted to obtain permission from the Liberian government to establish a UNIA base there. The Firestone Rubber Company, which did extensive business in Liberia, put economic and political pressure on the Liberian government. The Liberian government changed its attitude toward Garvey and opposed his African colonization plan. In 1924, the federal government indicted him on perjury and income tax evasion charges as well. His 1925 appeal on the mail fraud conviction was rejected by the U.S. Circuit Court of Appeals, and he was sent to the federal penitentiary in Atlanta, where he remained from 1925 to 1927. His imprisonment earned him a martyr's image, but upon his release (with a presidential commutation of his sentence to time served), he was deported.

From 1927 to 1940 he tried to rebuild the UNIA, including developing new branches in Paris and London, where he set up an office in West Kensington. He held the 1929 UNIA convention in Kingston, Jamaica, but disputed with the American delegation when he refused to accept its demand to keep the headquarters in Harlem. His influence in the United States rapidly declined after that convention.

Marcus Garvey died on June 10, 1940, in West Kensington, England, at the age of 52, impoverished and without ever having set foot in Africa. Largely forgotten through the 1940s and 1950s, he was rediscovered in the 1960s, when a renewal of Black Nationalism inspired a reassessment. "Garvey's reputation as the outstanding father of Negro nationalism has grown in the years since his death" (Cronon 1969, 212).

Garvey promoted a zionist vision of Black Nationalism, an attempt to unite Negroes throughout the world. He, more than the black power theorists of the 1960s, deserves credit for the slogan "Black Is Beautiful." His significance was in demonstrating that a mass-membership organization of blacks was possible. He articulated the grievances of those blacks for whom the civil rights goals of desegregation and political rights were largely meaningless. The nationwide interest in the UNIA and its charismatic leader both aroused and reflected the disillusionment of blacks for whom "the promised land of the American city had turned into the squalid ghetto" (White

1991, 102). On a visit to Jamaica in 1965, Martin Luther King Jr. perhaps best summed up the leadership role of Marcus Garvey when he stated:

> Marcus Garvey was the first man of color in the history of the United States to lead and develop a mass movement. He was the first man on a mass scale and level to give millions of Negroes a sense of dignity and destiny, and make the Negro feel he is somebody. You gave Marcus Garvey to the United States of America, and gave to millions of Negroes . . . a sense of personhood, a sense of manhood, a sense of somebodiness. (cited in White 1991, 104; see also Sewell 1990)

Summary

This chapter discussed the strategy of physical separatism employed by racial/ethnic minorities who reject the norms, values, and customs of the majority society and desire to be physically isolated. Such groups seek frontier or rural areas with low enough density of population that they can fill in the area as a substantial numerical group of settlers. Often it is the very rejection by the majority society that determines their adoption of the separatist strategy. The actions of the majority certainly reinforce their isolation. Sometimes the majority forces them, as in the case of Native Americans, into isolation. Physical separatism is a tactic and strategy followed by groups who are small in size, making isolation viable. They are often an ethnoreligious group.

This chapter reviewed the experiences of the Mormons, Amish and Mennonites, Native Americans, and that faction among African Americans who followed Marcus Garvey during the 1920s.

Key Terms

anabaptists "Rebaptizers," a Protestant Reformation sect that developed in Switzerland in the sixteenth century.

Black Nationalism A separatist ideology that projects a collectivist economy and the cultural and political independence of a black nation-state, similar to Jewish Zionism.

celestial marriage The practice of marriages performed in the temples for time and eternity, a tenet of the Mormon church.

code talkers Native Americans who served in the U.S. armed forces during World War II and were communication specialists.

forced assimilation The use of law and formal government policy to deliberately suppress the culture of a minority group in order to force it to acculturate to the dominant society.

mother colonies The source colonies of the Amish and the Mennonites in America in Northkill and Lancaster, Pennsylvania.

Ordnung The "understandings" that prescribe the do's and don'ts of Amish life; part of their method of social control.

Pan-Indianism A sense of shared identity among Native Americans that transcends tribal boundaries; the movement to unify all "Indians" for common political action in dealing with the majority culture.

trust lands Term referring to American Indian reservations.

Review Questions

1. Discuss why the Mormon church/movement has so often splintered into subgroups.

2. To what extent do Mormons exemplify a "millennial" movement? Would you characterize the mainline Mormon Church (based in Salt Lake City, Utah) as a millennial movement today?

3. Compare the schism tendencies among the Mormons with those of the Amish and Mennonite churches. How do societal pressures to accommodate relate to schisms?

4. Discuss the periods of Amish immigration from Europe to the United States. How did their reasons for coming influence their separatist strategy?

5. What distinguishes the Old Order Amish from the New Order Amish?

6. What is the significance of *Wisconsin v. Yoder* (1972)?

7. When, where, and why was the first Indian reservation established?

8. What was the General Allotment Act? Why did it lead to the loss of so much Indian land?

9. Describe Pan-Indian organizations. Compare and contrast their various styles of coping with majority society.

10. What was the UNIA, and when, where, and by whom was it founded?

Notes

1. For more on the massacre and its aftermath, see Furniss (1960), Hirshon (1969), and Nelson (1963).

2. Lyman (1996, 19–21, 371).

3. For more on modern-day schisms, see Baer (1988).

4. See *Readers Digest*, "Through Indian Eyes," 1995, for an in-depth discussion of reservations and reservations policy.

5. On Garvey and black nationalism, see Cronon (1969), Lewis (1988), Sewell (1990), White (1991).

Additional Readings

Abanes, Richard. *One Nation under Gods: A History of the Mormon Church.* New York: Four Walls Eight Windows, 2002.

Boyton, Linda L. *The Plain People: An Ethnography of the Holdeman Mennonites.* Salem, WI: Sheffield, 1986.

Brooks, Roy L. *Integration or Separation? A Strategy for Racial Equality.* Cambridge, MA: Harvard University Press, 1996.

The Church of Jesus Christ of Latter-Day Saints. *Church History in the Fullness of Times.* Salt Lake City: The Church of Jesus Christ of Latter-Day Saints, 1989.

Davies, Douglas J. *The Mormon Culture of Salvation.* New York: Ashgate Publishing, 2000.

Deloria, Vine, Jr., and Daniel R. Wildcat. *Power and Place.* Golden, CO: American Indian Graduate Center and Fulcrum Resources, 2001.

Driedger, Leo, and Donald B. Kraybill. *Mennonite Peacemaking.* Scottsdale, PA: Herald Press, 1994.

Kohut, Andrew, John C. Green, Scott Keeter, and Robert C. Toth. *The Diminishing Divide: Religion's Changing Role in American Politics.* Washington, DC: Brookings Institution, 2000.

Kraybill, Donald B., and Marc O. Olshan, eds. *The Amish Struggle with Modernity.* Hanover, NH: University Press of New England, 1994.

Kraybill, Donald B., and Steven M. Nolt. *Amish Enterprises: From Plows to Profits.* Baltimore, MD: The Johns Hopkins University Press, 1995.

Launius, Roger D., and Linda Thatcher, eds. *Differing Visions: Dissenters in Mormon History.* Urbana, IL: University of Illinois Press, 1994.

Lewis, Rupert. *Marcus Garvey: Anti-Colonial Champion.* Trenton, NJ: Africa World Press, 1988.

Mauss, Armand. *The Angel and the Beehive: The Mormon Struggle with Assimilation.* Urbana, IL: University of Illinois Press, 1994.

Peters, Shawn Francis. *The Yoder Case: Religious Freedom, Education, and Parental Rights.* Lawrence: University Press of Kansas, 2003.

Sewell, Tony. *Garvey's Children: The Legacy of Marcus Garvey.* Trenton, NJ: Africa World Press, Inc., 1990.

Wiggins, Rosalind Cobb, ed. *Captain Paul Cuffe's Logs and Letters, 1807–1817.* Washington, DC: Howard University Press, 1996.

Wilkins, David E. *American Indian Politics and the American Political System.* Lanham, MD: Rowman and Littlefield, 2002.

Young, Ann Eliza. *Wife No. 19.* Republished, New York: Arno Press, 1972.

• *Reading 5.1*

Will Tribal Gaming Lead to Economic and Political Sovereignty?

The success and nearly nation-wide expansion of Indian gaming has revived concerns about and interest in the concept of Native-American tribal sovereignty. This aspect of American politics, unique to the American Indian experience, is related to prior forced geographical separation to "reservation" or "trust" lands. Ironically, it may emerge as the single most important development for their ultimate economic and political incorporation.

Sovereignty is a complex concept. In its simplest meaning, sovereignty may be defined as the accepted or legitimate right to rule. Sovereign power involves numerous dimensions: constitutional/legal, political, economic, moral, social, cultural, military, territorial, and environmental.

As a legal and diplomatic concept, sovereignty is most often associated with the nation-state, particularly with the system of nation-states that emerged in Europe as exemplified by the Peace of Westphalia, which established for Europeans "an international system based on a plurality of independent states, recognizing no superior authority over them" (Malanczuk, 1997, 11).

At first, these emerging nation-states recognized only other European states, organized as executive and legislative-based entities with powers concentrated in their sovereigns, then often kings. The system also led to their acceptance of a principle of international law—*terrae nulluis,* or the right to seize "territory allegedly belonging to nobody." (Malanczuk 1997, 19). It was used to justify the colonization of "discovered" territories by European imperial powers. When they began colonization of the Americas, they initially did not recognize the indigenous peoples of the Americas as having any state system when, in fact, there were such systems. The indigenous systems, however, were different from those of Europe. Where the European systems were executive and legislative-based, Native-American governments were based on judicial foundations. Native-American societies relied on principles of balance and tradition combined with kinship groups, personal autonomy, and a spiritual connection to politics and place (Wilkins 2002, 126; Deloria and Wildcat 2001, 2–3).

Perhaps the classic example of such a fully functional indigenous government—preexisting colonial America by several hundreds of years—was the Iroquois Confederacy (Wilkins 2002, 123–124), from which several ideas incorporated into the United States Constitution were drawn. Individual tribes occupying a vast and sparsely settled continent never presumed to unite into one general body controlling all indigenous people. Their *value system*, unlike that of the Western European states, neither wanted nor had a cultural imperative (such as "Manifest Destiny") to adopt a Westphalia-style system of European-like government structures. Euro-Americans, understanding "different" to be "inferior," eventually sought to destroy the indigenous systems of government, including legislation mandating changes in native tribal governments under the plenary power of Congress.

Native-American tribes are indigenous peoples, the original inhabitants of North America, and are nations; that is, separate peoples inhabiting specific territories over which they wielded some governmental control or jurisdiction. In other words, the sovereignty of tribes was not delegated to them by either the federal or state governments. It is original and inherent power. Tribal sovereignty has to do with a tribe's right to retain a measure of independence from outside entities. It involves the power to regulate one's internal affairs, including such authority as the ability to make and execute laws, to impose and collect taxes, and to make alliances with other governments (Wilkins 2002, 47–48).

As the national government of the United States increasingly interacted and dealt with existing tribal nations, it underwent a historical development of federal-tribal relationships that waxed and waned in the degree to which it recognized tribal sovereignty (Wilkins 2002, Table 4.1, 105). Over a period of many decades it negotiated a series of treaties, in excess of 300, with numerous native nations (see AIM; Berholz, Lyons).

These various hundreds of treaties, which are officially and legally binding, confirmed and recognized the nation-to-nation relationship between tribes and non-tribal parties to the treaty (the U.S. government, and later through agreements, with state governments, local governments, corporations, and so on). In the case of Indian tribes, the United States agreed to recognize Indian tribes' political, cultural, and land rights. By acknowledging such rights in its various treaties (and later, compacts or agreements), the United States voluntarily limited its own sovereignty. In short, tribal nations have an *extraconstitutional* relationship to the United States, one possessed by no other racial or ethnic minority group:

> "The United States has a unique relationship with Indian tribal governments as set forth in the Constitution of the United States, treaties, statutes, executive orders and court decisions. Since the formation of the Union, the United States has recognized Indian tribes as *domestic dependent nations* under its protection." (President William Jefferson Clinton, quoted in Wilkins 2002, 44).

When the federal government extends recognition by the United States to a tribal nation, it constitutes the *formal, diplomatic* acknowledgment by the federal government of that tribe's legal status as a sovereign. All such federally recognized tribes are thereby exempt from most state tax laws, enjoy sovereign immunity, and are not subject to the same constitutional constraints as are the federal and state governments. As of 2001, the Department of the Interior officially recognizes 561 indigenous entities among which are 332 Indian nations, tribes, bands, organized communities, and Pueblos in the lower 48 American states, and 229 Alaskan native villages or corporations. These 561 entities, then, comprise the indigenous peoples who are thereby eligible for the special programs and services provided by the United States to indigenous communities due to their status as Indians or Alaskan natives (Wilkins 2002, 14).

Tribal sovereignty, however, is more complex than just a legal doctrine or principle. It is a right that must be exercised to be sustained. Its power must be asserted from time to time in order to be recognized as legitimate by others. It is also an intangible and dynamic cultural force inherent in each indigenous community. But sovereignty does not "rest." It must be exercised to be sustained, and to enhance the political, economic, and cultural integrity of a given indigenous community. Tribal sovereignty is the basis upon which tribal governments relate to others: to their own citizens, to non-Indian residents of Indian trust lands, to adjacent local governments, to the various state governments within which are located the reservation territories or trust lands, to the federal government, to the corporate world with which they negotiate partnerships and business enterprises, and, indeed, even to the global community (Wilkins 2002, 48).

Tribal governments are nations inhabiting specific territories, variously referred to as reservations, trust lands, pueblos, or dependent communities. Within these native lands the constitution is for the most part inapplicable. This is because the political status of tribes pre-exists the constitution. Tribes have and sustain preexisting sovereignty and treaty-making powers. This means that the legally binding agreements of treaties results in the tribes having a political status that has been held by the courts to be higher than that of the states. American Indians have treble citizenship status since the 1920s: They are citizens of the United States, of the states in which they reside, and of their tribal nations. State and U.S. citizenship has been acknowledged by the U.S. Supreme Court as not incompatible with tribal existence (in *United States v. Nice,* (1916); see Wilkins 2002, 58).

Numerous tribal nations, as well as their individual members, however, have often suffered grievously, as has been illustrated, as a result of conflicting federal policies that have vacillated between respecting the internal sovereignty of tribes and seeking to destroy tribal sovereignty in order to forcibly assimilate individual Indians into the American body politic.

Key documents that form the legal basis for acknowledging tribal sovereignty are the Declaration of Independence of July 4, 1776; the Treaty with the Delaware Tribe, signed September 17, 1778 (7 Stat 13), which became the first Indian treaty written in formal diplomatic and legal language and as such was the model for literally over three hundred subsequent treaties negotiated with various tribes; the Northwest Ordinance of July 13, 1787; the U.S. Constitution of 1789, article 1, sections 2 and 8; the Treaty and Intercourse Act of July 22, 1790 (1 Stat 137); and two critically important U.S. Supreme Court decisions, *Cherokee Nation v. Georgia,* 1831 (30 U.S. [5 Pet] 1); and *Worcester v. Georgia,* 1832 (31 U.S. [6 Pet] 515).

Legislative, judicial, and executive orders have also been used to take away or severely limit sovereignty rights of Native Americans. Such major actions are exemplified by laws and public policy effects such as the Indian Removal Act of 1830; the suspension, in 1871, of all treaty making; the Major Crimes Act of 1885; the Allotment Act of 1887 (aka the Dawes Act); and the Termination Acts, Resolution 108, and Public Law 280, of 1953 (see Wilkins 2002, Table 4.1, 105).

These limiting policies have resulted in the current status of tribes as *domestic dependent nations,* wherein tribes are limited to exercising a reduced degree of internal sovereignty subject to federal dominance. While tribal sovereignty is an inherent and reserved power, individual tribal nations can only exercise those governmental powers that have been explicitly delegated to them by express Congressional action and consent. By contrast, state governments also have limited sovereignty, but they base that on the reserved and delegated powers specified in the Constitution.

In 1987, the Supreme Court opened increased opportunity to native sovereignty by its decision of *California v. Cabazon Band of Mission Indians*. Congress responded by enacting the Indian Gaming Regulation Act (IGRA), in 1988. This act regulated gaming and required tribes to negotiate compacts or agreements with state governments. The law, and Indian gaming enterprise, allowed tribes nonetheless to become heavily involved in state politics, in education decision making, and in attempts to influence the politics of the majority society. Gaming incomes provided tribes with the economic power to wield political influence in state and in local elections. It has also entailed conflicting tasks. Gaming tribes have to balance providing social services with running profitable businesses and competitive enterprises. Gaming operations often result in intratribal, intertribal, intergovernmental, and tribal-corporate conflicts when tribal government is also the chief employer. The considerable potential for wealth they entail, however, make them desirable enterprises upon which to base cultural and political power.

Some tribes have specifically rejected using gaming on their land—for cultural and moral reasons. Other tribes are essentially limited from using gaming enterprises due to financial constraints. Their reservation lands are not located near enough to major cities or major highway transportation routes to make them viable sites for gaming operations to be profitable.

Still other tribes have essentially "contracted out" the management of the gaming operations to majority society casino firms who enter into legal arrangements with the tribes, manage the casinos located on tribal land, and share a portion of the profits with the tribal governing body that in turn distributes the proceeds among tribal members. Such contracted-out casino operations often serve as a significant source of employment on tribal lands, both at the casinos and ancillary retail commercial enterprises, and at tribal government services made possible by gaming operation profits.

Sources: By author, with information from American Indian Movement (AIM), "The Trail of Broken Treaties" (October 31, 1972), available on-line at http://www.aimovement.org/archives/index.html; Charles D. Berholz, "American Indian Treaties and the Presidents," *Social Studies* 93, 5 (September/October, 2002): 218–227; President William Jefferson Clinton, Executive Order #13084, *Weekly Compilation of Presidential Documents* 34, no. 20 (May 18, 1988), 869; Vine Deloria and Daniel Wildcat, *Power and Place* (Golden, CO: Fulcrum Resources, 2001); Oren R. Lyons, et al., *Exiled in the Land of the Free* (Sante Fe, NM: Clear Light Publishers, 1992); Peter Malanczuk, *Akehurst's Modern Introduction to International Law,* 7th rev. ed. (New York: Routledge, 1997); David E. Wilkins, *American Indian Politics and the American Political System* (Lanham, MD: Rowman and Littlefield, 2002).

CHAPTER 6

•●•

THE STRATEGY OF SEPARATISM

Psychological Separatism

Closely related to the racial and ethnic groups discussed in Chapter 5 are groups espousing separatism but adopting a tactical approach of psychological means rather than physical isolation. Psychological separatism is often used by **millennial movements**, whose strong religious ideology provides the means by which the individual can develop a sort of psychological shell to isolate himself or herself from the influence of the majority society, even while living in its midst. Millennial movements are described in the end-of-chapter reading.

This chapter focuses on three prime examples of psychological separatism: the Nation of Islam, or Black Muslims, the Hasidic Jews, and the Jehovah's Witnesses. Brief references are made to other religious separatist movements, but these cases exemplify well the tactic and the difficulty of employing this tactic to retain separatism amidst the constant pressure from the majority culture to conform to its value system. It seems that over decades of time the psychological edge blurs and the sharpness of separatism dulls even for militant separatist minorities.

THE BLACK MUSLIMS

The Black Muslims exhibit distinct organizational and cultural norms that are specifically designed to compensate for the effects of discrimination. For a half-century, they withdrew from the ongoing polity. As a characteristic millennial movement, Black Muslim members are given a myth that accounts for their past in a manner that overcomes the psychological damage of racial discrimination while providing detailed lifestyle of guidelines for the present, and a glorious image of the future. One scholar describes the Nation of Islam (NOI) as follows:

> The rehabilitative effects of the movement on many members of the sect have been remarkable. From the nation's prisons and slums, the [Black] Muslims have recruited

drug addicts and pushers, prostitutes and pimps, alcoholics, criminals and the despairing ghetto residents alienated from society. These men and women have been transformed by the Muslims into employees of value in honest jobs, who conscientiously marry and raise a family. They obey the laws, save money, and tithe to their faith. They no longer drink, use drugs or tobacco, gamble, engage in sexual promiscuity, dance, take long vacations, steal, lie, nor exhibit idleness or laziness. Their women are models of domesticity: thrifty, keeping fastidiously clean homes, devoted to their mates and children. Instead of buying expensive clothes or cars, they pool their resources to help each other. Muslim families, even in the midst of the nation's worst slums, exhibit a healthy living standard. The movement has, in its own strange way, repaired some "irreparable" damages and saved some of the damned. (Litt 1970, 78–79)

The **Black Muslims** began in the 1930s. During the depression, various mystic, black nationalist, sectarian cults arose in the nation's urban ghettos. One of the precursors to the Black Muslims was the Moorish-American Science Temple movement, founded by Timothy Drew of North Carolina (1886–1929), who proclaimed himself Prophet Noble Drew Ali in Newark, New Jersey, in 1913 and opened the first branch of his movement in New York. Drew taught that Black Americans were really "Moorish Americans" or "Moors" and that he had been commissioned to preach Islam to Black Americans (Lincoln 1944, 52). Drew's movement soon had temples in Chicago, Detroit, and Pittsburgh, and gained from an influx of Garveyites in the late 1920s. Another was the Peace Mission movement of Father Divine, established on Long Island in 1919. He also instituted a collectivist economy that attracted many former Garvey followers to his blend of social and religious Black Nationalism. Father Divine's movement peaked between 1931 and 1936 with an estimated following of 1 million. The Ethiopian Pacific movement, founded in Chicago in 1932, attracted some 300 ex-Garveyites with a program of emigration and repatriation to Africa. All these movements echoed the Negro Convention movement of 1830 to 1860, which met annually and advocated repatriation or the possible creation of a black nation-state in Haiti. That movement ended with the Civil War.

The Black Muslims, first known as the Lost-Found Nation of Islam, and then simply the Nation of Islam (NOI), were first introduced to black Americans in 1930 with the arrival in Detroit's black ghetto of Wali D. Fard, also called Mr. W. Fard Muhammad or simply, Wallace. Under the leadership of Elijah Muhammad (nee Elijah Poole, 1897–1975), Fard's most trusted follower and his successor when Fard disappeared mysteriously in June 1934, the Nation of Islam developed into a well-known if controversial organization. At their height, Black Muslims were America's foremost Black Nationalist movement, with 69 temples in 27 states, and claiming a membership in excess of one million, roughly one-third of all American Muslims at the time (Brooks 1996, 143–155).

Fard was a disciple of Noble Drew Ali's Moorish-American Science Temple. His identity remains something of a mystery. He is thought to have been an Arab, claiming to have come from Mecca, but his true racial and even national origin is still not documented. Claiming to be Allah Incarnate, Fard assumed the leadership of the Noble Drew Ali's movement when the latter died in 1929. Fard went to Detroit in 1930, and between 1930 and 1933 he attracted a following of about 8,000 persons before he disappeared. In August of 1959, the FBI, in a failed attempt to discredit the Nation of

Islam, circulated a story alleging that Wallace D. Fard, founder of NOI, was Wallace Dodd Ford, a Caucasian.

With his disappearance, leadership of the movement passed to Elijah Poole, who changed his name to Elijah Muhammad, declaring he was "Allah's Prophet," the "Messenger of Allah" called to awaken the sleeping black nation and rid it of the whites' age-old domination. An early faction of Fard's movement followed Abdul Muhammad, another of his disciples, but that faction did not prosper (Lincoln, 1994 72–78). The Nation of Islam grew slowly but steadily during the 1930s and 1940s, appealing mostly to the black lower class. Temples were established in Chicago, Milwaukee, and Washington, DC. The black underclass provided fertile ground for the movement's growth. The nation's black ghettos with its large underclass provided great numbers of potential adherents in need of "being saved."

> Behind the ghetto's crumbling walls lives a large group of people who are more intractable, more socially alien and . . . hostile than almost anyone imagined. They are the unreachables: the American underclass . . . [whose] bleak environment nurtures values that are often at odds with those of the majority—even the majority of the poor . . . [It] produces a highly disproportionate number of the nation's juvenile delinquents, school dropouts, drug addicts and welfare mothers, and much adult crime, family disruption, urban decay, and demand for social expenditures.[1]

Black Muslims preached that whites were devils created by a black scientist named Yakub. Whites were considered to be mentally, physically, and morally inferior to blacks. Blacks were the "original man," the first people to inhabit the earth. Yakub's work was met with anger by Allah, who, in punishment, ordained that the white man would rule for 6,000 years over blacks. In this process blacks would suffer but thereby gain a greater appreciation of their spiritual worth by comparing themselves to whites. Blacks were members of the tribe of Shabazz. Black Muslims desired to free blacks from white influence and secure land for themselves within the continental United States. Preaching an assertive, militant separatism, they advocated a very Garvey-like form of group economy and black pride.[2]

Black Muslims advocated racial separatism and self-determination in a brand of black economic nationalism. They rejected the use of the term "Negro," favoring the use of "Afro American." They discarded black surnames as slave-names. They substituted the suffix X or a Muslim name, for example, Muhammad. Elijah Muhammad preached a mixture of unorthodox Islam with virulent black separatism. Their Black Nationalism blended the economic nationalism of Booker T. Washington and the cultural nationalism of W. E. B. Du Bois' "Negro Americanism."

> The so-called American Negro group . . . while it is in no sense absolutely set off physically from its fellow Americans, has nevertheless a strong, hereditary cultural unity born of slavery, of common suffering, prolonged proscription, and curtailment of political and civil rights. . . . Prolonged policies of segregation and discrimination have involuntarily welded the mass almost into a nation within a nation. (Du Bois, cited in Lincoln 1994, 43)

Black Muslims rejected both white society and the Judeo-Christian heritage underpinning the dominant culture and its value system. In their early years they used the

Elijah Muhammad is applauded by his followers during the annual convention in the Coliseum. (*UPI/Corbis/Bettmann*)

common terms for African Americans at the time, the Negro and Nigger. One of their proponents states the case for black nationalism and a new black religion as follows:

> As long as the Negro is in America there is no hope for him. The white man takes one Negro and kills the aspirations of a million others. The white man has successfully made the Negro into an individual for himself, and denied a nation of his own to the Negro. The Negro's worst enemy is his religion. The acceptance of Christianity killed his nationalism. Christianity is his worst poisonous enemy. There are over 700 denominations among Negroes and yet the Negroes have not founded a single denomination of their own. They get together to serve white gods. The Negro will never unite until the religious struggle is won. Ask a Negro what his problem is, he says, unity. He agrees with you but that is all. His case in America is hopeless. The NAACP is the Big Niggers' organization. It was founded by whites, the bosses are whites and Jews—the biggest thief there ever was. The Big Niggers, the NAACP, don't want Langer's Bill passed. The Jews don't want it passed. The Big Niggers want to get jobs here. They are not nationalists. They have no national program. They are not interested in the plight of the masses. The Big Niggers as a class don't think. Of course they get their diplomas and stand around like any other Negro for a job from the white man. Once a Negro reaches college level he is no good for anybody. They were brought here slaves, have remained slaves, and will remain slaves. (cited in Essien-Udom 1962, 55)

Temple 2, established in Chicago in 1934, functioned as the headquarters of the Nation of Islam, the "Mecca" of the movement. Chicago was a hotbed of Black Nationalism in the 1930s. It was home to the Abyssinian movement. This offshoot of Garvey's movement, the Peace Movement of Ethiopia, and the Moorish-American Temple movement were taken over by the Black Muslim movement. The Chicago temple experienced remarkable growth between 1946 and 1960. By 1960, it was a nationwide movement, growing from about 10,000 members to over 250,000 members.

The Black Muslim movement demands total commitment.[3] Black Muslims are not just a "Sunday religion"; they require a whole lifestyle change. For Black Muslims, their "Zion" is wherever whites are absent. In the words of Malcolm X, America's blacks are the "Lost Nation of Islam in North America." For them *black* is the ideal, the ultimate value. The black man is the primogenitor of *all* civilization, the "Chosen of Allah," and the rightful rulers of the planet earth.

In return for a total commitment to Islam, the movement provides its converts with an elaborate organization capable of maintaining a variety of institutional supports that radically change the member's lifestyle. Members are immersed in the new Muslim culture. The movement provides the temple, schools for children and adults, a well-disciplined security force known as the Fruit of Islam, and numerous daily or weekly publications filled with inspirational messages and Black Muslim ideology. The Nation of Islam publishes or published *Dispatch, Islamic News, Salaam,* and *Muhammad Speaks,* the latter of which once claimed a circulation of 600,000.

Women's auxiliaries teach homemaking skills, child care, and women's "proper role." Muslim children attend grade school and summer camps. Teenagers are provided with Muslim community centers. The movement offers employment training and runs a variety of retail and service businesses. Black Muslims have created their own "University of Islam" (actually no more than a high school). They strengthen the sense of collective identity by symbols that furnish deified objects for mass loyalty and expressions of aspirations. All nationalistic movements have flags or gods around which the faithful rally. The nationalist symbols for the Black Muslims are Allah, the star and crescent, their version of the Koran, and the Islamic tongue.

These cultural symbols, and the norms and values they embody and reinforce, help establish their **ethnic boundaries**. Such boundaries define the group. The ethnic boundary "canalizes social life—it entails a frequently quite complex organization of behavior and social relations" (Barth 1969, 15). The ethnic boundary both enables some relationships to exist and constrains or limits others. It is the device to distinguish the respective character of both intra- and intergroup relationships. Its list of prescribed and prohibited behavior and practices is similar to the Ordnung of the Old Order Amish discussed in Chapter 5.

These boundary markers are important to the movement's success in creating that psychological shell about each of its members. Black Muslim men adopt the Muslim name, are clean-shaven, and dress in dark, conservative suits, white shirts and ties, and with a small star and crescent button on their lapels. Black Muslim women wear a nunlike garb with full headdress and habit covering their arms and legs.

Changes in clothing style serve several identification functions. They reject the stereotypical flamboyant appearance of lower-class blacks. The sober neatness expresses strength and a new sense of dignity. The nunlike garb of the women again rejects the flashy and wild colors of the stereotypical black female. Their new dress stresses the protected, sequestered, and obedient role that women play in the Muslim life and family. The uniformity of both men and women heightens a sense of group cohesion and affords a readily detectable commonality that sets them apart from non-Muslims. Brothers and sisters are differentiated from all others, both other blacks and, of course, from the white majority society and culture.

Racial pride is stressed. Black features are upheld as the highest human representation of Allah. "Black Is Beautiful" is the prevailing aesthetic. Self-composure and control are maintained at all times. Young men conduct themselves with military-like bearing. Loud and boisterous behavior is forbidden, and displays of emotion are discouraged. A Black Muslim is told to listen to music quietly, without swaying or crooning. All these norms of behavior reject stereotypical images.

Black Muslims have numerous prescribed foods. A Muslim is forbidden to eat pork, seafood, or scavenger creatures. All "soul food" is held to be reminiscent of the slave past, so cornbread, black-eyed peas, collard greens, and opossum are prohibited. These dietary norms bolster members' new identity and help to eradicate the old. The result is a new sense of black self-worth. Black Muslims are taught that feeling inferior results in acting inferior, in accepting the white man's view of the black. Rejecting the stereotypes is their way of liberating the individual from the "slave mentality." As Elijah Muhammad stated it: "Love yourself and you will not need the white man's love."[4]

The Black Muslim movement distinguished itself from the civil rights groups by its emphasis on the individual rather than changes in the majority society's laws, policies, or customs. It stressed that responsibility for the betterment of the individual rests with the black man, not with white society. Black Muslims demand absolute separation of the black and white races. They are psychologically indrawn. They feel responsible only to each other and derive their satisfaction from their own mutual self-approval.

Black Muslim membership remains predominantly male and young. About 80 percent of its members are between eighteen and thirty-five years of age. Older persons who joined the movement tended to be ex-Garveyites or ex-Moorish Science Muslims. Table 6.1 provides a profile of Muslims in America today. The table includes members who are followers of Islam in Sunni and Shi'ite bodies, and in the Nation of Islam.

Converts to the Black Muslims, besides following a strict code of personal conduct, were forbidden to be involved in any political activity of the white dominant society, including service in the armed forces. Until they achieve their separate state, Black Muslims were to avoid any social or religious or political contact with whites. Even during the Great Depression, they refused to accept relief checks, Social Security numbers, or any form of federally sponsored employment (White 1991).

These tenets led to the first clash between the Black Muslims and the legal system of white society. In May 1942, Elijah Muhammad was arrested, charged with sedition for inciting his followers to resist the draft, and for tax evasion. He and 62 followers were convicted and sentenced to five years in the Federal Corrections Institute in Michigan. Eventually 100 of his followers were incarcerated for draft resistance. This incident resulted in the Black Muslim's outreach to recruit new members among criminals, delinquents, drug addicts and pushers, prostitutes and pimps (often while incarcerated), and the black underclass. They recruited recent immigrants to the northern cities from the segregated former confederate states of the South, most of whom were illiterate. As the movement developed temples in some dozen cities, it began to appeal to a broader spectrum of blacks, and its members took on increasingly "middle-class" lifestyles and norms of behavior.

Table 6.1   Profile of Muslims Compared to National Average

	Muslims	*National Average*
Group as a percentage of the nation as a whole	0.3%	—
Female	33%	52%
Black	64	10
Resident		
Northeast	41	21
Midwest	5	25
South	43	34
West	11	21
No High School Diploma	23	17
High School Diploma	25	35
Some College	31	26
College Graduate	21	21
Republican	19	29
Lean Republican	12	15
Independent	8	9
Lean Democrat	23	14
Democrat	38	32
Resident of a Large City	50	20
Suburban	20	22
Small City/Town	27	36
Rural	3	21
Family Income		
<$20,000	37	25
$20,000–$30,000	28	19
$30,000–$50,000	20	27
>$50,000	11	21
Age		
18–29	51	22
30–44	36	33
45–64	9	27
65 and older	5	17

Source: Table by author; based on data and table in Kohut, Green, Keeter, and Toth, *The Diminishing Divide*, 2000. Table A-13, data on pp. 154–155.

Among the young black male prisoners the Black Muslims recruited was its most successful proselytizer and effective preacher, Malcolm Little. He became Malcolm X. He was born in Omaha, Nebraska, in 1925, the son of a West Indian mother and a black American Baptist preacher, both ardent Garveyites. When Malcolm was very young, the family moved to Michigan, and he often went with his father to Universal Negro Improvement

Malcolm X, noted black Muslim leader (*Courtesy of the Library of Congress*)

Association (UNIA) missions. His father died when Malcolm was six. In his autobiography Malcolm claimed that his father was beaten and thrown to his death under a tram car by members of a local white supremacist group called The Black Legion. Allegedly, they had earlier burned the Little's house. Subsequent biographers have disputed that story.

Malcolm's budding oratorical skills were quickly noted and developed. He became the minister of the Philadelphia temple and then went on to Harlem, New York. In June 1954, he assumed command of the New York City temple. At Harlem's Temple 7, Malcolm X preached orthodox Black Muslim doctrine. He attracted followers by his militant condemnation of the civil rights movement's push for integration through nonviolent protest. He likened himself and Black Muslim leadership to slavery's "field Negro," and the civil rights leadership to the "house Negro." He called them "Uncle Toms" to his "new Negro." By 1964, Malcolm was the second most requested speaker on college campuses across the nation. He frequently wrote and was quoted in the Nation of Islam's national newspaper, *Muhammad Speaks*. Its circulation rose to about 900,000.

In the early 1960s, a strain developed between Malcolm X and the Nation of Islam, reflecting a growing envy by Elijah Muhammad of Malcolm X for his increasing popularity, and the increasing ideological differences between Malcolm X and the NOI. Elijah Muhammad's innermost circle of leadership at the Chicago headquarters was distrustful of Malcolm X, seeing him as a rival for leadership to Elijah's chosen heir-apparent, his seventh son, Wallace Deen Muhammad.

Malcolm X's thoughts and perspectives went through three periods. From 1952 to 1962, he espoused the orthodox theology of Black Nationalism. From 1962 to 1964,

"Pray keep moving, brother." (From *Herblock: A Cartoonist's Life* [Times Books, 1998]. Reprinted by permission of the Herb Block Foundation.)

he went through a period of transition, increasingly to one of secular Black Nationalism. From 1964 to his assassination, he advocated **pan-African internationalism**. By the early 1960s, Malcolm X questioned the theology of Elijah Muhammad, the Nation of Islam's programs, its refusal to become politically active, and its patriarchal attitude toward women. The Black Muslim program was politically and economically conservative, much like that of Booker T. Washington. Malcolm X advocated a more militant and politically activist stance. He was attracted to African socialism, and his view of whites shifted from that of "devils" to simply "hypocrites."

His open split with the NOI began in 1963, when he spoke out after the assassination of President John Kennedy, about which he had been ordered to refrain from public comment. He described the assassination as reaping what Kennedy had sown— in reference to the administration's involvement in the attempted assassination of Castro in Cuba and the assassinations of Patrice Lumumba in Africa and Ngo Dinh Diem in South Vietnam. In March 1964, Malcolm X announced his separation from the Nation of Islam. He set up his own movement, Muslim Mosque, Inc., to promote a more activist, direct-action approach to the racial problem. Disavowing nonviolence, he stated that if provoked by violence from whites, there would be retaliation. Elijah Muhammad called Malcolm X a "Judas," "Traitor," "Apostate," "Brutus," and "Benedict Arnold." The open split dismayed many Black Muslims (Kivisto 1995, 319).

Malcolm toured the Middle East and Africa (Ghana and Nigeria) and made a pilgrimage to Mecca, where he discovered "True Islam," and returned to the United States as a Sunni Muslim, adopting the name El Hajj-Malik El Shabazz. He openly changed his earlier positions and moved toward dealings with whites and with the mainstream civil rights movement. On his return he stated:

> Every time you see another nation on the African continent become independent, you know that Marcus Garvey is alive. All the freedom movement that is taking place right here in America today was initiated by the philosophy and teachings of Garvey. The entire Black Nationalist philosophy here in America rested upon the seeds that were planted by Marcus Garvey. (cited in White 1991, 156)

Malcolm's break with the Nation of Islam won him many admirers but few followers. In June 1964, he formed the **Organization of Afro-American Unity (OAAU).** It reflected Marcus Garvey's pan-Africanism. Malcolm took a second trip to Africa in 1964, attending a conference of the Organization of African Unity in Cairo. He flirted with socialism as an economic approach and articulated a strong anti-imperialism message.

The OAAU attracted a small following of about 900 persons, including some old-line Latino Garveyites, mostly Cubans and Panamanians. It published a newsletter, mostly a four-page mimeographed sheet with a circulation of only 200 to 300 copies, a far cry from the days when Malcolm's messages in *Muhammad Speaks* reached hundreds of thousands.

Malcolm articulated his pan-African internationalism in words that directly reflected the influence of Marcus Garvey:

> I believe that a psychological, cultural, and philosophical migration back to Africa will solve our problems. Not a physical migration, but a cultural, psychological and philosophical migration back to Africa—which means restoring our common bond— will give us the spiritual strength and the incentive to strengthen our political and social position here in America . . . and at the same time this will give incentive to many of our people to also visit and even migrate physically back to Africa, and those who stay here can help those who go back, and those who go back can help those who stay here, in the same way as the Jews who go to Israel. (cited in White 1991, 164)

After his split with the Nation of Islam, Malcolm was less prominent, certainly less so than his rival for leadership of the black civil rights movement, Dr. Martin Luther King Jr. After Dr. King was awarded the Nobel Peace Prize, Malcolm X said: "He got the Peace Prize; we got the problem. I don't want the white man giving me medals." He also recognized the varying roles that the black leadership played. In his final period he moved closer to the position of the civil rights movement. He realized that the more radical rhetoric of the Black Nationalists helped the King movement by contrast. "On another occasion, he looked a perceptive reporter in the eye and told him that the white power structure would turn a deaf ear to the demands of black moderates unless black extremists continued to threaten from the wings" (cited in Perry 1992, 349).

Like King, Malcolm X feared and anticipated his own assassination. The growing tension with his split from the Nation of Islam led to ever increasingly strong denunciations of Malcolm X by the NOI. His home was firebombed on February 14, 1965. Malcolm suspected, but the police could not prove, it was by the Nation of Islam's followers. Malcolm X was assassinated on February 21, 1965, by three NOI followers at a rally in New York City, held in a ballroom in Harlem.

The call for a separate black state, both by Malcolm X's OAAU and by the NOI, like Marcus Garvey's advocacy of such a state either in Africa or in some fenced-off portion of the United States, was unfathomable to most whites. To Garvey's followers and disciples, it remains a reasonable goal. In 1968, Malcolm's followers called for the creation of the Republic of New Africa.

> In the Black Belt, running through the five states that the Republic claims as the national territory of the Black Nation (Louisiana, Mississippi, Alabama, Georgia, and South Carolina), we have met all the criteria for land possession required of us by international practice, international law. We have incidentally met these tests too in many cities of the North . . . we give up these claims to these cities as *national* territory . . . in exchange for the five states of the deep South. (cited in Sales 1994, 176–177)

Malcolm X and his teachings were "rediscovered" in the 1990s. Today black youth searching for a "politics of liberation" have set Malcolm X as an icon equal to Dr. King in the pantheon of black heroes. Malcolm's evolution from Black Nationalism to pan-African internationalism, reflected in the OAAU, addressed the dilemma of the civil rights movement during the crucial period from 1963 to 1965. A more complete discussion of that period follows in Chapter 8.

After Malcolm's assassination, the Nation of Islam continued to be plagued by factionalism. In 1970, another prominent Black Muslim leader and rival to Elijah's son, Hamass Abdul Khaalis, was expelled from the group. He, too, set up a rival sect. He was denounced as a false prophet. The "Messenger's" triggermen shot his wife and daughter and drowned three of his children.

The Nation of Islam evolved in the 1970s. The Elijah Muhammad branch called itself the African Muslim Mission. After the death of Elijah Muhammad in 1975 and his son's selection as his successor, membership declined from over 250,000 to around 100,000. Wallace Deen Muhammad rejected much of his father's teachings. He nonviolently returned the Black Muslims to conventional Sunni Islam and opened the faith to people of all races, but it remained an African-American organization. In 1985, he formally dissolved the sect, leaving 200 mosques and worship centers to operate locally. Its members became integrated with mainstream Islam, referred to by its members as "the change," or "the second experience." He led upwards of 250,000 followers, and he preaches on Muslim life with a weekly television program. He is often considered the most prominent and respected indigenous Western Muslim leader. In 1992 he became the first Imam to give the invocation before the U.S. Senate (http:www.myss.com/worldreligions/Islam). At age sixty-nine, Imam W. Deen Muhammad retired as the spiritual head of the American Society of Muslims at their annual convention in Chicago, Illinois, on August 31, 2003 (*L.A. Times,* Monday, September 1, 2003, A-14).

The image of the Black Muslims changed as well. As the NOI de-emphasized, separatism elements within white majority society changed their view of the Black Muslims. A growing respect for the Nation of Islam's impressive use of capitalism to the organization's advantage, and for the strict moral code that its members follow, is evident in the mass media's coverage of the organization. Some of that more favorable image declined, however, in the post 9/11 era with a growing concern within majority society over international terrorism being linked to domestic cells of radical Sunni or Shi'ite followers. Box 6.1 presents a bio-sketch of Wallace Deen Muhammad, now known as Warith Deen Muhammad.

| **BOX 6.1** | ***BIO-SKETCH OF WARITH DEEN MUHAMMAD*** |

The Imam Warith Deen Muhammad was born Wallace Deen Muhammad in October, 1933, the son of Elijah Muhammad and his wife Clara. Elijah led the Nation of Islam from 1934 to his death in February, 1975. Wallace assumed leadership of the Nation of Islam upon his father's death. He soon rejected the literal meaning of his father's theology and the Black-separatist views, such as Elijah's teaching that Blacks were God's original people. Warith studied the Qu'ran and the life of the Prophet Mohammad, eventually accepting that whites were fellow worshippers and that Christians and Jews were people of the book. He forged closer ties with mainstream Muslim communities, of which there are an estimated 2 million in the United States.

Departing from his father's preaching and practice, in 1981 Wallace Muhammad declared that those who desire plural marriages are "cursed by God," and in 1983, claimed that Christians need not follow Islam. In 1984 he called for establishing his own school of thought, and by 1986 openly declared that the Muslim community had an obligation to serve the best interest of other communities— even Christian, Jewish, and the Socialist community. By 1991 he stated that Muslims should not proselytize non-Muslims to Islam. He endorsed Minister Farrakhan in 1992. He declared that though he loved their distinction as a people, he wanted racial dignity and racial and cultural distinction, but that Muslims also owed an allegiance to the Christian people and had to understand that Islam did not come to establish itself over everybody else.

Imam Muhammad gave the first-ever invocation in the United States Senate by a Muslim cleric, and in 1993 he gave an Islamic prayer during the first Inaugural Interfaith Prayer Service of President Clinton. While commemorating the seventieth anniversary of the Nation of Islam in America, in 2000, he publicly embraced and reconciled with Minister Louis Farrakhan at the annual Saviour Day convention in 1999. In 2000, he was selected to lead Washington area Muslims for Eid Al-Fitr Prayer at the DC armory. He currently emphasizes positive interfaith dialogue through nation-wide lecturing and involvement in the Focolare Movement. His message is no longer exclusively focused on the African American community and his movement in now inclusive of every race, although overwhelmingly Black. His teaching and lectures focus on both Muslim and non-Muslim audiences. He stresses the establishment of Muslim-owned business, schools, and communities in America.

Source: Bio-sketch by author, from information from the website: *www.allahuak.bar.net/wallace_deen_mohammad.htm*, accessed 3/19/2007; and en.wikipedia.org/wiki/Warith_Deen_Muhammad, accessed on 3/19/2007.

Much of that change and the new image of the Black Muslims can be attributed to the rise of Minister Louis Farrakhan, born Louis Eugene Walcott. In 1978 he formed a new Nation of Islam. His faction is now the most visible among the various Muslim groups within the black community. Minister Farrakhan, who as Louis X played a role at a Boston mosque much as Malcolm X had played in Harlem, opposed and eventually replaced Malcolm X at the Harlem mosque. Minister Farrakhan broke with Wallace Deen Muhammad in 1977. He named his faction the Nation of Islam, adopting the name and the orthodox ideals of Elijah Muhammad. He stresses black moral superiority. He continues the strong tradition of Garveyism by stressing black economic self-reliance; nontolerance for oppression and self-hatred; the belief that you cannot love your neighbor as yourself without first liking yourself and knowing who you are; and a belief that the sin of the Negro was that he failed to know himself. Neither he nor

Minister Louis Farrakhan speaks at a news conference in 1994. (*AP/Wide World Photos*)

his splinter group, however, has been recognized by orthodox Muslims in the Middle East or among orthodox Muslims in the United States. He has been widely criticized by non-Muslims for promoting separatism and anti-Semitism. His followers are estimated at about 20,000 members today.

Like Malcolm X, Minister Louis Farrakhan modified the Nation of Islam's isolation from politics. His endorsement of the Reverend Jesse Jackson in Jackson's bid for the Democratic Party's presidential nomination in both 1984 and 1988 dramatically exemplifies the change. It thrust Minister Farrakhan into the national limelight—and his anti-Semitic taint and rhetoric kept him there. His strong stands against drugs, abortion, and homosexuality emphasize anew the social conservatism of the Black Muslim tradition, as does his stress on self-help and bootstrap capitalism. In 1995, he called for, and led, the "Million Man March," which actively encouraged blacks to vote and to work for positive change. His career is highlighted in Box 6.2.

Black Muslims showed a typical softening of their separatism over time, as they changed from a revolutionary to an institutional force. They followed a path typical of millennial movements that are too weak to achieve their dreams of paradise and a black-nationalist state within the country, yet too strong and structured simply to wither away. By attaining structural stability and longevity, the movement began a process of transformation from separatism to accommodation. The very success of the movement in turning its members into "haves" rather than "have-nots," and the organizational structures that over time undercut the charismatic leadership of the movement, work to take the edge off the movement's separatist fervor. Instead of becoming a more radical sect, it is becoming more a "conservative, black self-improvement" group, more interested in material advances than in sacrificing the life of the movement for the sake of a black supremacist doctrine. As it increasingly developed its organizational structures—temples, schools, farms, stores, newspapers, and clothing businesses—the needs of those organizational structures modified the charismatic and separatist aspects of the sect toward a more accommodationist approach.

Eric Hoffer, the street corner philosopher, observed: "We are less willing to die for what we have or are than for what we wish to have and to be. It is a perplexing and unpleasant truth that when men already have something worth fighting for they do not feel like fighting" (Hoffer 1963, 134).

BOX 6.2   *BIO-SKETCH OF MINISTER LOUIS FARRAKHAN*

●

Louis Farrakhan was born Louis Eugene Walcott, in May, 1933 in the Bronx, New York. He was raised in the West Indian community in Roxbury, Massachusetts. His mother was an immigrant from Saint Kitts and his father was a Jamaican cab-driver from New York. As a young child of six he began playing the violin. By age 13 he played with the Boston College Orchestra and the Boston Civic Symphony, and by 14 had won national competitions and appeared on the Ted Mack Original Amateur Hour. He studied at the prestigious Boston Latin School and English High School and attended two years at Winston-Salem State University's teachers college. He became a professional musician, dancer, and calypso singer, recording several albums under the professional name, "The Charmer."

While performing in Chicago, and inspired by Malcolm X, Louis attended a Nation of Islam event—the annual Saviour's Day address by Elijah Muhammad. Walcott joined the NOI in July, 1955, taking the Muslim name of Louis X. Soon after, Elijah Muhammad declared all musicians had to give up the music world or leave the movement. Farrakhan gave up his music career and quickly moved up into leadership positions in the Nation of Islam. He became a Minister of the Boston Mosque, and in 1965 was appointed Minister of the influential Harlem Mosque, in which capacity he served until 1975.

When Elijah Muhammad died in 1975, Farrakhan underwent a crisis of faith. In 1977, after struggling with the changes being instituted in the NOI by Wallace Deen Muhammad, Farrakhan walked away from the movement, but in 1978 he and a small band of supporters decided to rebuild the original Nation of Islam under the foundations and teachings of Wallace Fard Muhammad and Elijah Muhammad. Farrakhan established a NOI newspaper entitled *The Final Call*.

He and his followers held the first annual Nation of Islam Saviours Day convention since 1975 in Chicago and at that event declared the restoration of the NOI under Elijah Muhammad's teachings. In 1991 Farrakhan reintroduced the Economic Program first established by Elijah Muhammad, and in 1993 he wrote the *Torchlight for America*, a compilation of the guiding principals of the NOI for the problems of America. In 1993 he led two groups visiting Gabon and the Second African-American Summit. In 1994 he led 2000 blacks to Accra, Ghana for the first ever NOI's International Saviour's Day, a five-day convention.

In 1995, he publicly reconciled with Malcolm X's family. This event marked the public repproachement between Farrakhan, the NOI, and the Shabazz family. The revived NOI established mosques and study groups in over 120 cities in America, Europe, the Caribbean, and missions in West Africa and South Africa.

In 1995, he also organized a broad coalition of some half-million black men to hold what was considered the largest march in American history, the so-called Million Man March. The movement's diminished separatism was evident in 1996, when he re-registered to vote, publicly endorsed the Jesse Jackson presidential campaign, and led a registration drive that resulted in an estimated 1.7 million black men voting in the 1996 presidential elections. In 1997, the NOI and the World Islamic People's Leadership, hosted an International Islamic Conference in Chicago, with Muslim scholars attending from Europe, Asia, Africa, and the Middle East, and attended by representatives who were Christian and Native American spiritual leaders.

In 2005, the tenth anniversary of the march was invoked with a second march, led by Farrakhan and the New Black Panther Party leader, Malik Zulu Shabazz, Al Sharpton, Senator Barack Obama (D-IL.) and other prominent black Americans, to commemorate the tenth anniversary of the first march.

Box 6.2, CONTINUED

Farrakhan was noted for his anti-white and anti-Semitic rhetoric, even being referred to as a "Black Hitler" by a Jewish journalist in *The Village Voice*. He reportedly declared Hitler a great man who "rose up the German nation from nothing," and that he was similar to Hitler in that he was rising up his people from nothing. In 2000, he stated that "White people are potential humans—they haven't evolved yet, alluding to the figure "Yakub" with reference to whites. In a *Meet the Press* interview in 1997, he defended the position that black people are the original people of the earth, but added that superiority and inferiority were determined by a people's righteousness, not by their color. He also stated, "any human being who gives himself over to the doing of evil could be considered a devil."

Source: bio-sketch by author; information from; *www.noi.org/mlfbio.htm;* accessed 3/19/2007; and en.wikipedia.org/wiki/Louis_Farrakhan, accessed 3/19/2007.

Black Muslims have shown increasing signs of accommodation since the mid-1970s. Instead of viciously attacking other civil rights groups that advocate an integrationist approach, as it had done in the early years of the movement to the mid-1960s, the Muslim press now gives such groups fair coverage. It decreased its emphasis on separatism in its publications. Accounts of integrationist battles now are often treated sympathetically and positively. The movement aligned itself with avowedly integrationist groups advocating a full-scale attempt to elect black officials, backing black candidates from mayors to Jesse Jackson's campaign for the presidency. The movement modified its stance regarding the "white devil." Increasingly, its press stresses "black pride" rather than "white hatred."

Another splinter group that has attracted a modest following is led by Jamil Abdullah Al-Amin, who in the 1960s was known as H. Rap Brown, a militant civil rights leader and Black Panther member. Most of the more than a dozen significant subgroups of Black American Muslims attend mainstream Islam temples. Some more theologically radical splinter groups survive, including the Moorish Science Temple of Noble Drew Ali (nee Timothy Drew, 1886–1929), founded in Newark, New Jersey, in 1913; and more recently, a new offshoot of the NOI called the Five Percenters, begun in Harlem in the 1960s. They combine extremist political ideology with esoteric Eastern theology. (http://www.myss.com/worldreligions/Islam. See also the Five Percenter's website http://www.allahsnation.net!)

The more mainline Muslims in America (Sunni and Shi'ia) are somewhat torn between remaining more detached if not separatist, or trying to pursue pluralism in their relations with the majority culture. Since the attacks of 9/11 and a subsequent increase in discrimination against them, some have turned to activism and lobbying, while others towards greater separatism. The next section briefly discusses American Muslims today.

American Muslims Today

Islam is the fastest growing major religion in the United States, with an estimated 6 to 6 and a half million adherents. Swelled by Muslim immigrants from across the globe and by high conversion rates, Islam has surpassed Judaism to become the largest religious minority in the United States. Their relative power, however, is low despite these numbers because they are substantially less well organized than other minority religious groups. The many and varied aspects of Islam, the different ethnic groups, the presence of so many apolitical members, and the more recent political mobilization of certain organizations have kept Muslims from unifying into a coherent community with a focused coping strategy. Different Muslim groups have pursued accommodation, separatism, and radicalism. The continuing immigration of Muslims and the competing leaderships among Muslim groups requires a common denominator of Islam to serve the broader Muslim community as a basis for unity.

At nearly 1.2 billion adherents, Islam is one of the largest religions in the world. They are found on all five continents, and some fifty countries of the world have a predominantly Muslim population, stretching from the West Coast of Africa to the islands in the Pacific Ocean. Islam is the second largest religion in Europe and Russia. These simple facts dispel a common American misperception that all Arabs are Muslims and that all Muslims are Arabs. In fact, only eighteen percent of all Muslims come from the Middle East. The majority live in South and Southeast Asia, in countries like Pakistan, India, and Indonesia.

Muslims believe in certain basic tenets that set them apart from other religions. First is their belief in monotheism and of Muhammad as the last Prophet in a line of Holy Messengers (including, for example, Adam, Noah, Abraham, Ishmael, Isaac, Jacob, Joseph, Moses, David, Solomon, Zacharia, John the Baptist, Jesus, and Muhammad). Muslims believe in the Qu'ran as the word of Allah, as expressed to Muhammad through the Archangel Gabriel starting in Christian Calendar Year 610 C.E. (Muslims, Jews, and Hindus all have different calendars based on their own beliefs). Other basic tenets include the belief in angels, a state of heavenly bliss, the existence of hell, and the Day of Judgment. They believe in five Pillars of Faith: 1) the Shahadah, or declaration of faith/belief; 2) the use of daily prayer or Salah, said five times a day at certain times; 3) Zakat, or the obligatory giving of charity which entails the expectation, if they can afford to do so, of contributing 2.5 percent of their income to the needy, and the idea that good deeds are an expression of charity; 4) the act of fasting from sunrise to sunset each day during the holy month of Ramadan; and 5) the Hajj, or Holy Pilgrimage to Mecca at least once in one's lifetime (although the sick, the elderly and the poor are excused if they cannot go).

Islam is one of three Abrahamic faiths, the other two being Judaism and Christianity. Muslims consider themselves as the natural progression of monotheistic religion. Jews and Christians are called by them "People of the Book." Muslims regard Jesus as the awaited Messiah, a Messenger and Prophet, born of a virgin mother, but not as the Son of God. Sermons and religious literature are presented in the language of those present, but ritual prayer and Qur'an recitation are in Arabic. The use of Arabic, and the Qur'an as a code for social conduct, establishes a special bond between all 1.2 billion Muslims worldwide.

Muslims are composed of different branches, schools of thought, languages, ethnicities, and historical, geographic, and cultural influences. The two major branches in Islam are the Shi'ia and Sunni communities. The main contention between the two branches rests with succession of the Prophet Muhammad. About ninety percent of all Muslims are Sunni. The other ten percent are Shi'ia, found mostly in Iraq, Iran, Lebanon, Yemen, and Bahrain (Hourani 1991, 59–62).

The dynamics among Muslims worldwide have been carried through immigration to the United States. The media tends to highlight any conflict that occurs between these two groups, but their differences are non-doctrinal in nature (Said 1997, 73–74). Sunni and Shi'ia Muslim communities in the United States commonly share the same mosques, especially in smaller communities. Shi'i majority mosques are growing in number in the larger Muslim-American populations as more immigrants settle. Many specific associations, schools of thought and strains of Islam, likewise, have developed specific mosques to serve their respective communities across the United States. They are most concentrated in twelve states, shown in Figure 6.1, which depicts the geographical distribution of American Muslim voters in those states, the highest reporting in a survey conducted by the Council on American-Islamic Relations (CAIR).

Another interaction that has carried over is the establishment of Sufi Orders in the United States. Sufism is a mystical variant of Islam centered on meditation and self-expression. Its growth has paralleled the New Age Movement in the United States, although it has been in existence in the United States since 1910 when a famous Sufi teacher from India, Hazrat Inayat Khan, taught his message for nearly twenty-five years. His group still exists in small numbers today (Beverly 2003, 26).

In addition to the traditional Muslim groupings, homegrown variants are notable as well. African American Islamic movements generally grew out of political frustration in the segregation era when their quest for an identity separate from white America led them to Islam. Rejecting Christian churches they found apologetic, the new associations, as we have seen above, based their religion on a combination of black nationalism, black empowerment, and certain tenets of Islam. Interpretations of Islam within the various Black Muslim groups varied widely and mainstream Sunni Muslims have shunned a few of them for their unorthodoxy.

Muslims came to the United States during the Great Migration in the late 1800s and early 1900s, and the majority arrived from Greater Syria and spoke Arabic. Identifiable Muslim communities developed slowly within Arab-American communities. Even though African American Muslims started erecting mosques before the 1920s, the first permanent mosque in the United States was built in 1923 in Cedar Rapids, Iowa. Still in existence, it is often referred to as the "Mother Mosque of America." The quota provisions of the Johnson-Reed Act of 1924 severely restricted immigration from what were then considered to be non-desirable places, including Southern and Eastern Europe, Asia, and the Middle-East. As a result, Muslim immigration to the United States slowed to a trickle. Without a continued flow, many Muslim communities stagnated. Muslim names were quickly Americanized and intermarriage between Muslims and non-Muslims increased (i.e. segmented assimilation). When their immigration increased markedly after the 1965 immigration act was passed, Islam in America began to grow again.

The new post-1965 immigrants differed from their predecessors. Most of the new Arab immigrants were Palestinian and Lebanese. Many Muslims in the new flow,

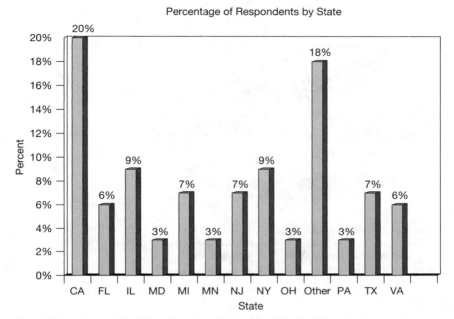

Figure 6.1   Geographical Distribution of American Muslim Voters Percentage of Respondents by State

Source: Figure by author, adapted from report of the Council on American-Islamic Relations, data from 2004 Election.*http://www.cair-net.org/* accessed April 27, 2007.

however, came from other parts of the Arabic speaking world. Slightly different from Greater Syrian Arabs in terms of idiom and food, these groups established separate identities and associations based on their specific ethnicity or nationality first, and only secondly through religion. Over time, these Arabic-speaking groups in the new wave slowly incorporated into the larger, established Arabic-Muslim community. Figure 6.2 presents a pie chart of world religions, showing the status of Islam as the second largest religious denomination in the world today.

Among those in the post-1965 wave, more varied groups of Muslims came looking for a better life. Some were refugees escaping violence in their homelands. Others came seeking better economic opportunities. Refugee groups included: Lebanese from the 1975–1990 Civil War; Palestinians from the West Bank and Gaza Strip; displaced Kurds and Shi'ia from Iraq; war-weary Afghanis; survivors from the 1992–1995 war in Bosnia; and other smaller influxes. Among those pursuing economic opportunities were large numbers of professionals from Pakistan and India who entered under the third preference category. Highly educated but with little chance of advancement at home, they immigrated to the United States under favorable conditions and have become highly successful. Since the terrorist attacks of September 11, 2001, however, immigration from "high risk" countries (defined by the DHS as Muslim majority countries) has slowed significantly. The new Department of Homeland Security designated

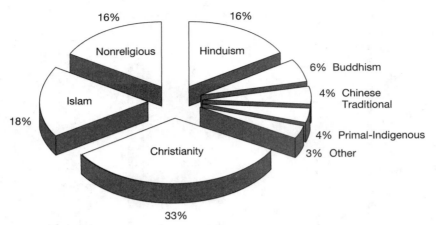

Figure 6.2   World Religions Today
Christianity includes: Catholic, Protestant, Eastern Orthodox, Pentecostal, AIC's,
Latter-Day Saints, Jehovah's Witnesses, nominal, etc.
Nonreligious includes: "none," agnostics, secular humanists, atheists, etc.

Source: Figure by author, adapted from report by the Council on Arab-Islamic Relations. Data from
2000 Election Survey, *http://www.cair-net.org/* accessed May 24, 2007.

two groups for special registration. Those who chose not to register were immediately
deported upon apprehension. The unfavorable social climate and the threat of deportation keep the American Muslim community in a state of flux.

American Muslims have begun to mobilize politically, channeling their resources
to fight negative stereotypes of Islam and to lobby immigration policy and U.S. foreign policy vis-à-vis the Middle East. A study by the Council on American-Islamic
Relations (CAIR) notes that only seven percent of mosques list only one ethnic group
as their congregation. Close to ninety percent of the 1,200 American mosques have a
mix of South Asian, African Americans, and Arabs. The study also found conversion
rates are at the highest levels yet recorded. Although the majority of new converts are
African American, a sizable number of Anglos and Hispanics convert to Islam. The
number of Latino Muslims is estimated between 25,000 and 60,000 (Bagby, Perl, and
Froehle 2001, 3). Muslim organizations are also gaining members and political strength,
such as CAIR, the Muslim Pacific Affairs Committee, the Institute of Islamic Information and Education, and the Islamic Society of North America.

Hasidic Jews

Another example of separatism in a religious sect whose members, like the Black Muslims, are immersed in the heart of urban America is the Hasidic Jews of Brooklyn, New
York. Like the Black Muslims, they exemplify a psychological approach to separatism
and have successfully maintained, for over a century, a religious/ethnic subculture all
the while living amidst the majority culture.

Geography professor Joshua Comenetz estimates today's Hasidic (also spelled Chasidic, from the Hebrew word meaning pious) population at about 180,000, or three percent of the approximately 6 million Jews in the United States (*http://www .news.ufl.edu/2006/11/27/hasidic-jews/*, accessed 3/19/2007). Professor Comenetz estimates there are also about 180,000 ultra-Orthodox Jews who are not Hasidic. Like all ultra-Orthodox Jews, they do not seek converts so the growth of their population is almost entirely due to births. They are a rapidly growing population, doubling every twenty years because they tend to have many children (families average 4–6 children), while non-Orthodox Jewish groups have flat or falling rates. Their growth rate is leading many Hasidic Jews to leave their traditional neighborhoods in Brooklyn to set up communities in the rural suburbs. Hasidic Jews believe in living close together, within walking distance of their synagogue, so even the rural settlements of Hasidic villages tend to consist of closely spaced apartment or row-houses, rather than the big houses with big yards typical of the American suburban archetype. This rural shift represents something of the opposite of "suburban sprawl."

An outsider visiting their Brooklyn neighborhood would be immediately struck by its Hasidic look—an island of traditional Jewishness amid the larger, racially diverse, working and middle-class neighborhoods. Signs on stores in the neighborhood are all in Yiddish and Hebrew; the men wear long beards and black garb, while the women were scarves or wigs and dress in modest clothing. Even the fast-food restaurants serve kosher food. School buses ramble by filled with noisy children, and other special buses carry Hasidic men into Manhattan to work. Their distinctiveness from the majority American culture is palpable—from their apparent community tightness, to the ever-present consciousness of the group. Men and women obviously live in different spheres, and by custom and religious law follow very different roles. The high degree of ritual and religious observance permeates every corner. Hasidic Jews follow all the 613 commandments found in the Torah, some positive and some negative, and include everything from giving to charity, to not mixing wool and linen; from strictly practicing kosher dietary laws, to refraining from any work on the Sabbath, to following the laws regulating sexual behavior, to studying the Torah and loving and fearing God. Hasidic Jews live in a traditional, patriarchal system.

They differ from Orthodox Jews in several ways. At its core, Hasidism is mystical and enthusiastic, radiating an interest in the inner transformative experience, a personal connection to God and to others in their community. It emphasizes the importance of inner intent when carrying out ritual obligations—attempting to invest even neutral activity with pious intention. Another primary distinction of Hasidism from other Jewish traditions and culture is the social and spiritual role of the rebbe. The rebbe is both a community leader and a holy man, a mystic and teacher who bridges man and God and serves as the center of the Hasidic community. Their rebbes are expected to provide a wide range of services to their community: blessing proposed marriages, choosing an occupation, providing spiritual inspiration and moral guidance for every aspect of everyday life. The word "rebbe" means "rabbi" in Yiddish and is distinctively Hasidic. Its meaning of teacher among the Hasidic Jews implies a man trained as a teacher. Historically, each rebbe came to be known by the town in which their court was located in Eastern Europe: the Lubavitch from Lubavitch in Russia; the Satmar from Satu Mare in Hungary; the Bobover from the Polish town of Bobova, and so on. The different courts developed some ideological distinctiveness and even some rivalry, but never so seriously as to challenge a shared Hasidic identity.

Hasidism developed a long and rich tradition of using dance, song, and storytelling arts cultivated as aids in the service of God. They believe wholeheartedly in personal participation in worship that uplifts the Hasid toward the divinity; toward achieving a state of adhering, cleaving, or becoming one with God. Hasidic Jews believe that each individual has a responsibility to seek out the "divine sparks" hidden within all creation (*www.pbs.org/alifeapart/intro_2.html*, accessed 3/19/2007).

This growth in ultra-orthodox Jews trend portends significant changes. In fifty years ultra-Orthodox Jewish groups will constitute a majority of U.S. Jews, marking a profound cultural and political change. Ultra-Orthodox Jews tend to be politically conservative, and send their children to religious schools, making them more sympathetic to faith-based initiatives identified with the Republican Party. They believe in a strict interpretation of the laws and ethics of the Torah, the first five books of the Bible. Hasidic Jews oppose contraception, abortion, and divorce, although they do not absolutely ban them. Hasidic Jews have large, traditional, patriarchal families with most Hasidic women working in the home, although they are not forbidden from entering the workplace. Although they live apart culturally, they are politically active in voting in majority society elections. Hasidism is aimed not at dogmatic or ritual reform, but at a deeper psychological one. It aims not to change the belief, but the believer. It seeks psychologically to create a new type of religious man: one who places emotion above reason and rites, and religious exaltation above knowledge.

It should not be surprising to most readers that Jews would be classified as an ethnic minority group. This recognizes that, nationally, Jews are a small percentage of the total population—about 3 percent. Jewish immigration prior to 1880 was small. Most Jews came from Germany, among them prominent "forty-eighters." The first big wave of Jewish immigration came between 1880 and 1920, mostly from Eastern Europe.

Jews can be divided by religious affiliation into three subgroups: Orthodox, Reformed, and Conservative. Orthodox Jews sometimes contain distinct "sects," such as the Hasidim, who are highly visible because of their distinctive dress, hairstyle, the character of their worship, a strong sense of "peoplehood," and a dogma that operates as a self-segregating force and a divisive factor between gentile and Jew. Their sense of peoplehood figures both in the discrimination they have experienced and in their manner of coping with it.

Their "in-group" sense is reflected in strongly cohesive family units, a cultural opposition to marriage to gentiles, a high proportion of self-employment and avoidance of economic contact with the gentile society, and their being stereotyped by majority society as "excessively clannish" (Marden and Meyer 1968).

Today there are 3,727 synagogues in the United States. Among them, total Orthodox synagogues number 1,501, or just over 40 percent of all U.S. synagogues. Total Reform synagogues number 976, or just over 26 percent, and total Conservative number 865, or just over 23 percent. The rest are more splinter synagogues, like the Agudath Israel, the Reconstructionist, the Sephardi, the Traditional, the Humanistic, the Gay/Lesbian, and the Jewish Renewal. Among the Orthodox are the Hasidic synagogues, the Lubavitch/Chabad (at 346), or some mixed synagogues, the Orthodox Union and Lubavitch (4), and the Young Israel and Lubavitch (2) (Singer and Grossman 2002, 128–129).

Hasidism is distinctive from other Jewish traditions based on beliefs and philosophy:

1. Their belief in miracle workers.
2. Their distinctive way of dress that outwardly signifies their piety.
3. Their core philosophy that God permeates all physical objects in nature, including all living things: that "God is all and all is God," in the words of Baal Shem Tov.
4. Their teaching that there are sparks of goodness in all things, which can be redeemed to perfect the world.
5. Revival—Hasidism came to revive the Jews physically and spiritually.
6. Piety beyond the letter of the law—Hasidism demands and aims at cultivating this extra degree of piety.
7. Refinement—teaching that one should strive to improve one's character by learning new habits and manners designed to change a person completely in the quality, depth, and maturity of one's nature by internalizing and integrating the perspective of Hasidic philosophy.
8. Demystification—believing that the esoteric teachings of Kabbalah can be made understandable to everyone, adding depth and vigor to one's ritual observance. http://en.wikipedia.org/wiki/Hasidic_Judaism. Accessed 3/19/2007).

Negative stereotyping is among the more pronounced forms of anti-Semitism in the United States. Gordon Allport (1958), in his classic *The Nature of Prejudice,* lists the most common stereotypical images ascribed to Jews in the United States: shrewd, mercenary, industrious, grasping, intelligent, ambitious, sly, loyal to family ties, persistent, talkative, aggressive, and very religious. Jews are often viewed as clannish, in control of everything, underhanded in business, overbearing, dirty, sloppy or filthy, energetic and smart, and loud and noisy.

In the United States, anti-Semitism ebbs and flows with social conditions that increase or decrease levels of fear among non-Jews. Chronic fear raises anxiety. Anxiety causes prejudice to rise, manifested in increased discrimination against Jews. Any strong emotions can trigger anti-Semitism. Greed leads to desiring what belongs to others. If a group's self-esteem falls, they can raise it by thinking they are better than Jews. Anti-Semitism can be traced to the post–Civil War period of economic displacement. The 1870s were an economically troubled decade in which many of the old upper-class families were being replaced by the new industrial elite. By the 1880s, when such displacement was considerable, the waves of East European Jews provided a convenient scapegoat for a society undergoing the pangs of industrialization.

The Bolshevik revolution and the rise of Communism led to the disintegration of the Hasidic centers in the Ukraine, such as Chabad, Breslov, Chernobyl, and Ruzhin. The Holocaust brought the final destruction to all Hasidic centers in Eastern Europe, and the survivors moved to Israel and to the United States and established new centers of Hasidism modeled on their originals.

After World War I, a strong and open anti-Semitism appeared. Such feelings were at their height in the 1920s and 1930s, when World War I and then the Great Depression upset so many socioeconomic positions. Much of the agitation for passage of the Immigration Act of 1921 and the Johnson-Reed Act of 1924 (the Quota Acts) was clearly anti-Semitic in nature. The only lynching of an American Jew—Leo Frank, a manager of an Atlanta pencil factory—took place in 1915. Although the lynching was attributed to Tom Watson, a Georgia Populist, the more intense anti-Semitism of the 1920s was a product of the revived Ku Klux Klan. Klan publications *Searchlight* and *Fiery Cross* linked communism to Jewishness. This same era linked anti-Semitism with anti-Bolshevik and anti-German attitudes of the World War I era. The infamous *Protocols of the Elders of Zion,* a fabrication of czarist Russia, was widely distributed by the Fellowship Forum. Henry Ford contributed to this anti-Semitic campaign through publication of the *Dearborn Independent,* described as "the most consistent and widespread anti-Semitic agitation that America has yet known. It touched off other movements and gave aid and comfort to lesser demagogues" (Janowsky 1964, 190).

In 1877, the prominent New York banker and President Grant's nominee for secretary of the treasury, Joseph Seligman, was refused accommodations at the Grand Hilton Hotel in Saratoga Springs. By the 1920s, discrimination in social clubs, hotels, and resorts was commonplace. A popular ditty sung by members of college fraternities around the turn of the century reflects this type of social anti-Semitism: "Oh, Harvard's run by millionaires, And Yale is run by booze, Cornell is run by farmer's sons, Columbia's run by Jews. So give a cheer for Baxter Street, Another one for Pell, And when the little sheenies die, Their souls will go to hell."

Discrimination against Jews in the United States has been pervasive and persistent. While undoubtedly more moderate than in Europe, American anti-Semitism has sometimes been more intense if less violent than against other religious minorities. No violent mob actions of burning down synagogues, attacking rabbis, or lynching Jews have occurred in the United States, even during times of intense anti-Semitism marked by desecration of Jewish cemeteries and synagogues. In the United States, anti-Semitism has been more subtle, if nonetheless pervasive. It was into that background of more general anti-Semitism that Hasidic Jews migrated when they came to the United States during World War II.

Hasidic Jews in the United States are most notably settled in Brooklyn, New York. They are viewed as being ultra-orthodox Jews from Eastern Europe who continue to use their Old World garb and customs. Survivors of the Holocaust, they are seen largely as a "sect" by the broader American culture and even by many Reform Jews.

The Hasidic movement began in the mid-eighteenth century in what is today Poland, Belorussia, and Ukraine. At the time these areas had the largest concentrations of Jews anywhere in the world. Living in Jewish **shtetls** (villages), they were generally very poor and forbidden by law to own land. Hasidism began with a small group of rabbis searching for a way to renew the fervor of the Jewish people, among them was Israel ben Eliezer, who came to be known as Baal Shem Tov (meaning Master of the Good Name) and is considered the founder of Hasidism. He first rose to prominence as a healer and miracle worker. He was thirty-six years old in 1734, when he began traveling from village to village as his fame for mysticism and miracles spread. Using parables and talmudic folktales, he brought the classical Jewish mystical themes in stories that even uneducated people could understand. Shortly before his death, in 1760, he selected certain disciples to succeed him in spreading Hasidism, generating a group of remarkable leaders who became known as **rebbes**. They attracted many followers to Hasidism, and eventually a majority of Jews in Ukraine, Galicia, Belarus, and central Poland were Hasidic. The movement also had sizable groups of followers in Hungary, and began spreading to Western Europe and to the United States during the large waves of Jewish emigration in the 1880s.

The institution of the rebbe was central to the expansion of the Hasidic movement. Each rebbe was close to Baal Shem Tov and highly influenced by his daily routines and devotion. They provided Hasidic guidance in every sphere of daily life. Viewed as intercessors in the heavenly courts and as teachers of mysteries through study and meditation, they became figures of wisdom in each community they founded. Each Hasidic group evolved into a dynastic court composed of the rebbe and his followers.

Eventually, nearly half of East European Jewry became allied with the movement (Mintz 1968). Among the leading rebbes emerged Rabbi Schneur Zalman of Liady, who became the founder of the Lubavitch Hasidim—today the largest group of Hasidic Jews. Despite a period of sustained persecution that saw him twice imprisoned by the czar's government, Rabbi Zalman refused to leave Russia. When some 300 Hasidim fled to the Holy Land in 1777, Rabbi Zalman remained. He used his organizational skills to establish a pattern of leadership that became the model for successive generations of Lubavitcher rebbes and, indeed, the Hasidic movement more generally. Leadership was transmitted through lineage. Rebbes were the sons or sons-in-law of their predecessors. The new generation of Hasidic rebbes provided mystical-oriented writings and tales.

In the early 1800s, when all of Europe was undergoing massive change, the Hasidic Jews remained unswerving in their allegiance to traditional Judaism and its laws. Even after World War I and the Communist revolution in Russia, which shattered the Hasidic way of life, Rabbi Yosef Schneersohn, the sixth Lubavitcher rebbe, refused to leave. During the period of severe Communist government repression, he became the unofficial head of all Russian Jewry. In 1927 he was arrested as a "counterrevolutionary" and imprisoned. International protest succeeded in winning his release and permission to leave Russia. He moved first to Latvia and then to Poland. Seeing no hope for Judaism to flourish in Russia, he encouraged all Hasidim to emigrate if possible. With the Nazi invasion of Poland in 1939, Rabbi Schneersohn fled to New York in 1940.

He established what became the world headquarters of the Lubavitch Hasidic group in Crown Heights, Brooklyn. He appointed his son-in-law, Rabbi Manachem Schneersohn, to organize three Chabad (Hasidic movement) divisions: publishing, educational outreach missions, and social services. A small nucleus of young Chabad-trained rabbis founded yeshivas in a dozen cities across the country, circulating Hasidic texts, prayer books, and periodicals. After the death of Rabbi Yosef Schneersohn in 1950, Rabbi Manachem Schneersohn, at the age of forty-six, reluctantly accepted the position of the seventh Lubavitcher rebbe. For the next forty years he led the Hasidic group through a period of rapid growth.

Other Hasidic courts were established as rebbes fled the Holocaust in Eastern Europe. Groups of Hasidic Jews settled in London, Montreal, Jerusalem, and Benei Brak in Israel. But for most, Brooklyn, New York, became the end of their exodus from war-torn Europe. Several surviving rebbes became the heart of new settlements in the United States: the Satmar and Klausenberger rebbes in Williamsburg; the Lubavitcher and Bobover rebbes in Crown Heights, and the Stoliner rebbe in Boro Park. In all, some forty courts began to function. To keep their beliefs intact, they were aware that they had to resist the acculturating pressures that had reshaped the lives of earlier Jewish

Rabbi Yosef Schneersohn (1880–1950), Rebbe of the Lubavitch Dynasty of Hasidic Jews in Brooklyn, New York (drawing by *Michael C. LeMay*)

immigrants who were becoming increasingly secularized. The courts continued to grow. By 1970, an estimated 50,000 Hasidic Jews resided in New York, with courts ranging from the Satmar with over 1,300 families to several courts of between 100 and 500 families. In 1967, the Lubavitcher rebbe, Manachem Schneersohn, was the leader of an estimated 250,000 people, the world's largest Hasidic group. Worldwide, there are courts in Israel, Canada, England, South America, and Russia.

The first attempt to found a Hasidic village in the United States was at New Square, in the Rockland County township of Ramapo, New York, just over an hour's drive from New York City. Started in 1956, it is a suburban village of about 130 families and a population of under 1,000, accepting the leadership of Rebbe Squarer. It was officially incorporated as a village in 1961. Although none of the villagers were followers of Rebbe Squarer in Europe, they joined the new Squarer court after becoming attracted to the rebbe or to the idea of living in a completely Hasidic village. Rebbe Squarer died in March 1968, and his son was proclaimed his successor at the funeral.

Whether in the midst of Brooklyn, New York, or in a small village of 1,000, the Hasidic Jews live in a world apart. They establish strong communities of believers who interact mostly within the community, are generally self-employed in various trades, and live and marry within the Hasidic culture. They maintain their cultural identity by living apart from the broader culture, even if living within its midst.

Orthodox Jewish children attend special schools to meet minimal educational requirements. Their strong devotion to religious study is reflected in the following comment of a Hasidic Jew: "Look at Freud, Marx, Einstein—all Jews who made their mark on the non-Jewish world. To me, however, they would have been much better off studying in a **yeshiva** [a Jewish religious school]. What a waste of three fine Talmudic minds" (cited in Schaefer 1998, 414).

Although they maintain strict cultural separatism, Hasidic Jews participate in local elections and some are employed at jobs outside their ethnic enclave. All such activities are shaped by their self-reliance and orthodoxy. Like the Amish and Mennonites, they maintain a high degree of cultural identity despite living within the heart of the majority culture.

The relationship between Jews and black Americans was severely strained by events that highlighted alleged black anti-Semitism, as well as anti-black feelings among Jewish Americans. The strain developed when the Black Muslim and Black Panther movements supported Arabs in the Middle East, to the point of calling for Israel to surrender. The relationship was strained further during Jesse Jackson's presidential campaign when his off-the-record reference to Jews as "hymies" and the openly anti-Semitic remarks by the Nation of Islam Minister Louis Farrakhan were reported in the media. In his 1988 campaign, Jesse Jackson purposely distanced himself from Minister Farrakhan and the Nation of Islam rhetoric by avowing that the "sons and daughters of the Holocaust and the sons and daughters of slavery must find common ground again." In 1991, an incident in New York City added fuel to the fires of tension between blacks and Jews when a Hasidic Jew ran a red light, killing a black child, and the ambulance that normally served the Hasidic community failed to pick up the child. Tempers in the black neighborhood rose to a fever pitch, and an Australian Jew was stabbed to death. That was followed by several days of rioting in the Brooklyn neighborhood of Crown Heights with much destruction of Hasidic Jewish property, some vandalism of Jewish cemeteries, and incidents of black-on-Jew violence.

Hasidic Jews have been remarkably successful in their use of psychological separatism by maintaining a degree of involvement in the majority society while retaining their distinctive subculture to an amazing degree.

JEHOVAH'S WITNESSES

Another example of a millennial religious group that exemplifies considerable use of psychological separatism is the Jehovah's Witnesses. They grew out of the nineteenth century Millerite and Bible Student millennial movements. They are perhaps most known for their door-to-door preaching, their objection to blood transfusions, their not celebrating birthdays or national holidays, and their proselytizing through their religious magazines, *The Watchtower* and *Awake!*

They adopted their present name in 1931, under their then president Joseph Franklin Rutherford. They proport themselves to be the restoration of true, first-century Christianity. According to their website, as of 2006, there were 6.7 million members worldwide as "active members," that is, those who have reported preaching activity in approximately 91,000 congregations in 235 countries speaking 340 languages. In the United States, as of 2000, they estimate one million members. Only the United States, Brazil, and Mexico claim active Witness numbers in excess of half a million. Jehovah's Witnesses are aggressive proselytizers, adding about 300,000 new members annually. After growth rates that peaked at 9 percent per year in the 1970s, their growth has averaged about 2 percent per annum since 1999. They claim 16.6 million attended the Witnesses' annual Memorial in 2006, which would involve inactive members not involved in preaching nor submitting reports. They hold training five times a week at their "Kingdom Halls," and claim to average about 45 new congregations a year being formed. In 2000, in the United States alone, a reported 988,000 Witnesses spent an estimated 181 million hours in field service (door-to-door witnessing and "bible studies"). They assert themselves to be the sole Christian religion and authority as well as God's mouthpiece or prophet.

They originated with the religious movement known as Bible Students, founded in the late 1870s by Charles Taze Russell. Russell organized a Bible study group of Second Adventists, which arose after the Millerite Great Disappointment, in Pittsburgh, Pennsylvania. The 1870s were a decade in which bible studies and an interest in biblical prophecy were widespread in the United States. In 1876 Russell and Nelson Barbour predicted the visible return of Christ in 1873. When that failed to occur, Russell revised the prediction to 1874. After Barbour's second disappointment, the group decided Christ had returned *invisibly* to Earth in 1874. They differed with Second Adventists in teaching that all humankind descended from Adam would be given a second opportunity to live in paradise on earth. A gathering of the saints up into heaven was predicted for 1878, then again for 1914 when the final end of the rule of human governments would begin, marking a forty-year period from 1874.

In 1879, Russell split with Barbour and began publishing his own magazine, *Zion's Watch Tower and Herald of Christ's Presence*, now known simply as *The Watchtower*. Russell held with the Adventists a rejection of the traditional view of Hell, and by 1882 rejected the doctrine of the Trinity. Calling himself "Pastor Russell," he formed the legal entity and tax exempt non-profit organization, in 1881, The Watch Tower Bible and Track Society of Pennsylvania (now headquartered in New York City). In 1914, Russell founded the International Bible Students Association in the United Kingdom. Indeed, in the past, Jehovah's Witnesses have gone by several names: Millennial Dawn, People's Pulpit Association, The Brooklyn Tabernacle, as well as the International Bible Students Association. He authored a six-volume series called *Studies in Scriptures*. Russell died in October, 1916, and the presidency passed to Joseph Franklin Rutherford.

A schism erupted in the movement when Rutherford succeeded Russell as president. In 1931, those who supported Rutherford took the name *Jehovah's Witnesses* and those who did not support him formed the Pastoral Bible Institute which published its own religious journal, and schisms ensued in congregations worldwide as a result. Rutherford removed four of the seven members of the Board of Directors and the schism came to a head with Rutherford's release of his book *The Finished Mystery* in July, 1917. Pacifist teachings in his book led to Rutherford and the new Board of Directors being indicted for violation of the Espionage Act in May, 1918. They were found guilty and sentenced to twenty years in prison, but in March, 1919, the judgment was reversed and they were released from prison and the charges dropped.

The movement's emphasis on house-to-house preaching began in 1922 and between 1925 and 1933, significant changes in doctrine were promulgated. Failed predictions and evolving doctrinal changes continued to splinter the church. By 1933, Jehovah's Witnesses were teaching that 1914 was the beginning of Christ's invisible presence on earth and his enthronement as King and the start of the "final days" instead of the terminal date in their chronology. Under Rutherford's leadership, the group grew from about 21,000 in 1917 to 115,000 when he died in 1942. Rutherford was succeeded in the presidency by Nathan Homer Knorr, who founded the Watchtower Bible School of Gilead to train missionaries, and a Theocratic Ministry School to train congregational preaching and teaching. They struggled with the majority society over free speech and religion doctrines such as pacifism, refusal to salute the flag, and opposition to blood transfusions. In 1943 they won a Supreme Court decision in *West Virginia State Board of Education vs. Barnette*, which ruled school children of Jehovah's Witnesses could not be compelled to salute the flag. During Knorr's presidency, church membership grew to over 2 million. Another failed prediction for 1975 led to a drop off in membership.

In 1976, the leadership of the church was reorganized and the power of the presidency passed on to the Governing Body of Jehovah's Witnesses and doctrinal and organizational decisions since have been made by the governing body who also supervise the writing of the *Watchtower* publications. They no longer teach that the generation of people living in 1914 will survive until Armageddon but continue to preach "the nearness of Jehovah's day of judgment." In 2000, three new non-profit corporations were organized to represent the denomination in legal matters: Christian Congregation of Jehovah's Witnesses, which coordinates all services, preaching activity, door-to-door preaching, circuit and district conventions and so on; the Religious Order of Jehovah's Witnesses, which coordinates the activities of those involved in full-time service, including pioneers, missionaries, and circuit and district overseers; and Kingdom Support Services, Inc., which controls the construction of new Kingdom Halls and other facilities and holds the titles to Society-owned vehicles. Their three major publications are *The Watchtower*, a magazine published since 1879 as their main journal and which is considered authoritative; *Awake!*, a general interest magazine with a wider scope than *The Watchtower* that has articles on nature, and geography with a religious slant and is published monthly in 81 languages; and the *New World Translation of the Holy Scriptures*, their translation of the bible, last revised in English in 1984.

Table 6.2 lists a brief summarization of Jehovah's Witnesses teachings, many of which are controversial and have led to their conflicts with majority society. In that regard, of particular note is their objection to blood transfusions for religious reasons. They interpret the Bible literally and accept the entire Bible canon, although they acknowledge that biblical writers used symbolism, parable, figures of speech, and poetry. They maintain the bible alone should be used for determining issues of doctrine, but that the interpretation of scripture and the codification of doctrines is the responsibility of the Governing Body of Jehovah's Witnesses.

Witnesses are politically neutral, believing their allegiance belongs to God's Kingdom which they view as an actual government. Thus they refrain from saluting the flag or singing nationalistic songs which they hold tantamount to idol worship. They obey all laws and pay taxes as long as these do not violate what they view as God's law. They refuse to participate in military service, even if such is compulsory in nature, and until 1996 also refused alternatives to such service. They are detached from secular politics, and are discouraged from voting although not strictly prohibited from doing so, and do not object to voting on non-political issues. They do not stand for any political office. Jehovah's Witnesses have variously predicted the end of times (the world) for 1914, 1918, 1925, 1975, and 1989.

They maintain congregational discipline through formal controls administered by leaders of the congregation that range from restriction of duties to excommunication,

Table 6.2   What Jehovah's Witnesses Teach

1. There is one God in one person; there is no Trinity.
2. The Holy Spirit is God's impersonal active force, not alive.
3. Jehovah's first creation was "his only begotten son" the Archangel Michael who was used in creating all other things, and who became Jesus at his incarnation. Jesus was only a perfect man, not God in the flesh. He is the only means to approach God in prayer and is the means of salvation for all worthy mankind and is the mediator of the new covenant which limits those going to heaven, whose number is 144,000.
4. Jesus did not rise from the dead in his physical body but was born again and raised "not a human creature, but a spirit."
5. Jesus did not die on the cross, but on a stake.
6. Jesus began his invisible rule on earth in 1914. The last days began in 1914 and Armageddon is imminent. All other religions are false and will come under attack by governments worldwide. After all false religion is destroyed, governments will also face destruction and all those not deemed faithful by God will be destroyed with no hope of resurrection.
7. Jesus' ransoming sacrifice did not include Adam.
8. Jehovah's Witnesses are the self-proclaimed prophets of God and the only true church and the only channel of God's truth, and only church members will be saved.
9. Good works are necessary for salvation. Salvation is by faith and by what you do. It is possible to lose your salvation.
10. The soul ceases to exist after death. Hades or Sheol is the designated common grave of all mankind.
11. There is no hell where the wicked are punished.
12. Only 144,000 Jehovah's Witnesses will go to heaven and be born again; and only 144,000 may take communion. The vast majority of Jehovah's Witnesses expect to live on a renewed paradise on earth.
13. Blood transfusions are a sin.
14. The cross is a pagan symbol and should not be used.
15. The universe is billions of years old; each of the 6 days of creation was 7000 years long and therefore man was created toward the end of the 42,000 years of earth's preparation.
16. Jehovah's Witnesses refuse to vote, salute the flag, sing the national anthem, celebrate Christmas or birthdays, or serve in the armed forces.
17. Man was entrusted with the obligation and charged with the duty of overseeing the creation of the earth.
18. Homosexuality and premarital sex are considered sins and abortion is considered murder.
19. Modesty in dress and grooming is stressed and gambling is strictly forbidden.
20. Weddings, anniversaries, and funerals are observed, but birthdays, Thanksgiving, and Christmas are regarded as unchristian and not celebrated.
21. Marriages are monogamous and the family structure is patriarchal with the husband the final authority on family decisions.

Summary by author, from: http://www.carm.org/jw/doctrines.htm.

known as disfellowship, and shunning by the congregation. Marking is used for a clear violation of scriptural principles short of seriousness warranting disfellowship. Reproof involves sins more serious than ones for which one might be marked and are administered as a last resort before disfellowship and shunning.

Summary

This chapter examined the use of psychological separatism as a tactic of religious/ethnic subcultures to cope with their minority status. It examined the cases of Black Muslims, contrasted with mainstream Muslims today, with Hasidic Jews, and with Jehovah's Witnesses. It stressed their use of ethnic boundary markers to create a psychological shell around individual members, both to set themselves apart from the majority culture whose values they reject and to protect themselves from the psychological harm that can be caused by the prejudice and discrimination they endure. Black Muslims, Hasidic Jews, and Jehovah's Witnesses show remarkable persistence in maintaining their distinctive identity despite the acculturation pressures of the majority society. They illustrate the difficulty of this tactical approach to separatism, and exhibit signs of increased accommodation among their members. All have experienced schisms and factionalism. None has escaped some degree of segmented acculturation among its members. The religious nature of sects like the Black Muslims, Hasidic Jews, and Jehovah's Witnesses, much like the Amish and Mennonites, is an essential element in their ability to maintain a subculture over a long time, as well as a source of their rejection of the value system of the majority society.

Key Terms

Black Muslims   Also known as the Nation of Islam; a religious Islamic sect advocating Black Nationalism, founded in Detroit in 1930.

ethnic boundaries   The aspect of an ethnic group subculture that defines it and sets it apart from all other cultures; a complex organization of behaviors and social relationships that control intra- and interethnic social relations.

millennial movement   A religious movement with a myth of the past and glorious vision of the future with a prescribed plan for the present designed to bring the future vision to fruition.

Organization of Afro-American Unity (OAAU)   A group founded by Malcolm X in 1964 just before his assassination.

Pan-African internationalism   The ideology to which Malcolm X evolved in his political thinking at the time of his assassination.

rebbes   The leadership group of the Hasidic Jewish sect; a leading rabbi around whom a "court" is formed in a Hasidic community.

shtetls   Jewish villages or ghettos of Eastern Europe, mostly in Russia and Poland.

yeshiva   A Jewish religious school of Orthodox Jewry formed to study the Talmud.

Review Questions

1. When and where did the Black Muslim movement begin? How is it related to Garveyism?
2. What ethnic boundary markers distinguish Black Muslims? Which ones characterize the Hasidic Jews?
3. What is the OAAU? How is it philosophically similar to or different from the NOI?
4. When and where did the Hasidic movement begin? How does it maintain its identity in the highly secular world of New York City?

5. Which group, the Black Muslims, the Hasidic Jews, or the Jehovah's Witnesses would you argue has more successfully employed psychological separatism?

6. Discuss the boundary markers used by Jehovah's Witnesses to set themselves apart.

7. Compare and contrast religious groups using physical separatism with those using the psychological tactic or approach.

8. The problem of schism or factionalization appears more obvious among Black Muslims than among Hasidic Jews? Why so?

9. Hasidic Jews have economically incorporated but not civically so. How have they maintained their separatism in the political arena even while economically incorporating to a far greater degree?

10. As more Black Muslims embrace orthodox Islam, is their ability to maintain psychological separatism inevitably lost or at least greatly hampered? How and why so?

Notes

1. "The American Underclass." *Time,* August 19, 1977, 140.

2. For accounts of the Black Muslim movement, see Essien-Udom (1962), Lincoln (1994), Perry (1996), and White (1991).

3. See Litt (1970); see also LeMay (1985) and Lincoln (1994).

4. See Bill Turque, "Playing a Different Tune." *Newsweek,* June 28, 1993, 30–31; and Don Terry. "Minister Farrakhan: Conservative Militant." *New York Times,* March 3, 1994, A-1, A-10.

Additional Readings

Bagby, Ihsan, Paul M. Perl, and Bryan T. Froehle. *The Mosque in America: A National Portrait.* Washington, DC: Council of American-Islamic Relations, 2001.

Beverly, James A. *Islamic Faith in America.* New York: Facts on File, 2003.

Bowman, Robert M., Jr. *Understanding Jehovah's Witnesses.* Grand Rapids, MI.: Baker Book House, 1992.

Brooks, Roy L. *Integration or Separation? A Strategy for Racial Equality.* Cambridge, MA: Harvard University Press, 1996.

Curtis, Edward E., IV. *Islam in Black America.* Albany: State of New York University Press, 2002.

DeCarlo, Louis A., Jr. *Malcolm and the Cross.* New York: New York University Press, 1998.

Hoffman, Edward. *Despite All Odds: The Story of Lubavitch.* New York: Simon & Schuster, 1991.

Hourani, Albert. *A History of the Arab Peoples.* New York: Warner Books, 1991.

Jacobson, Simon. *Towards a Meaningful Life: The Wisdom of the Rebbe.* New York: William Morrow, 1995.

Landes, Richard, ed. *Encyclopedia of Millennialism and Millennial Movements.* New York: Routledge, 2000.

Marsh, Clifton E. *The Lost-Found Nation of Islam in America.* Lanham, MD: Scarecrow Press, 2000.

Myers, Walter Dean. *Malcolm X: A Fire Burning Brightly.* New York: Harper Collins, 2000.

Penton, M. James, *Apocalypse Delayed: The Story of Jehovah's Witnesses.* Toronto: Toronto University Press, 1997.

Rashad, Adib. *The History of Islam and Black Nationalism in America.* Beltsville, MD: Writers, Inc., 1991.

Said, Edward. *Covering Islam: How the Media and the Experts Determine How We See the World.* New York: Vintage Books, 1997.

Shabazz, Ilyasah. *Growing Up X.* New York: One World, Ballantine Publishing Group, 2002.

Singh, Robert. *The Farrakhan Phenomenon.* Washington, DC: Georgetown University Press, 1997.

Smith, Jane I. *Islam in America.* New York: Columbia University Press, 1999.

Sniderman, Paul M., and Thomas Piazza. *Black Pride and Black Prejudice.* Princeton, NJ: Princeton University Press, 2002.

• *Reading 6.1*

The Basics of Millennial Movements

Millennial movements may be nationalistic (political), religious, or social in nature and all take on some blending of all three elements. They emphasize an apocalyptic vision of the end of times or of the eventual triumph of the movement in some glorious future, often expressed in long term views—in thousands of years. Be it a Hitler establishing a Third Reich that was to reign for a thousand years, or a Moses leading his people across the desert to the promised land where the chosen people were to establish their kingdom, or a Charles Russell preaching the second coming of Christ in 1914 to establish God's Kingdom on earth to thereafter last for eternity, millennial movements are characterized by a leader, a prophet, who projects a glorious future for the select of those chosen members of the movement. As Litt (1970) notes:

> "Whether the prophet is Treitschke, Dostoevsky, Hitler, Moses, Mazzini, Mussolini or Elijah Muhammad, the myth of the past and the illusion of the future remain a remarkably consistent, nationalistic, mass movement formula. To convince an alienated people of their worth and unity, one must remind them of their sacred origin. To explain the disheartening realities of their present plight, one must convince them of their natural superiority and ferret out corrupters and devils. To gird them for the trials ahead, one must reveal a glorious destiny ordained from the beginnings of time. Past, present, and future must intermingle in one expression of Divine intent."

They are movements comprised of persons who feel under attack by a "they" group of powerful forces bent on destroying their way of life or removing them from their land. They are a people who long to return to some sort of idealized past golden age. Those in a Christian tradition typically identify themselves with the oppressions and deliverance of the Israelites of the Old Testament. Given their vision of the future, they are also referred to as revitalization movements.

Many such movements are "catastrophic" millennial movements in that they await some sort of divine intervention to remove their oppressors and establish the millennial kingdom, or they are revolutionaries who fight to eliminate their oppressors. Examples of **nativist** millennial movements include the Xhosa Cattle-Killing movement of South Africa, the Israelites massacred by police at Bulhock, South Africa, the Native American Ghost Dance movement related to the massacre of the Lakota Sioux at Wounded Knee, the Taiping revolutionaries in China, the German Nazis and the American Neo-Nazis. The Freeman, involved in a standoff with FBI agents in Montana in 1996 are part of a diffuse Euro-American nativist millennial movement that includes not only the Neo-Nazis, but also Identity Christians, Odinists, and other racist and anti-Semitic white Americans who feel oppressed by the bureaucracies of the federal government and regard themselves as the natives of this land, expressed in the conviction that whites are the true Israelites given the promised land of America by Yahweh.

Black nationalist millennial movements include the Moorish-American Science Temple movement, Father Divine's Peace Mission Movement, the Ethiopian Pacific Movement, the Abyssinian Movement, the Peace Movement of Ethiopia, Black Nationalism, and a spin-off of the Nation of Islam, the Five Percenters. The Five Percenters, for example, believe that all blacks are themselves Gods and black women are Earths. They take the name Five Percenters from the belief that eighty-five percent of the world is unaware of God and therefore incapable of salvation; that ten percent of the world's people are aware of God, yet teach that He cannot be physically seen; and that they, the remaining five percent, must become the righteous teachers for the rest. All these black nationalist movements blend a nationalism identity with a religious expression, a means of personal salvation, and of establishing a glorious paradise on earth for their followers.

As social and sometimes ethno-religious movements, millennial movements can give rise to cults and sects. **Cults** are typically small groups of people who hold a system of religious worship or ritual, often living in a colony with a charismatic leader who indoctrinates the members with unorthodox or extremist views, practices, or beliefs. They commonly have secret practices and rites known only to the initiated. **Sects** are typically religious bodies that form in small to medium sized groups that break away from an established orthodoxy or church. Sects are characterized by having a common leadership, a strong set of opinions, philosophical doctrines, religious principles and practices, and often associated political principles. A member of a sect, or sectarian, is a person who is blindly and narrow-mindedly devoted to a sect. Cults can grow into sects in size. Sects that survive their leader and grow in size can come to be viewed as denominations, for example, as did the Mormons.

Some sects call themselves Christian and use the Bible as sacred scripture and may have the name of Christ in their title but are not considered Christian by the more orthodox or mainline denominations because they believe Jesus Christ was not God, or that he is God as much as anyone is God. Examples of such sects of Christianity are the Mormons, Jehovah's Witnesses, the Unification Church (more commonly known as Moonies after their founder, Sun Myung Moon), New Age, Christian Science Church, Church of Scientology, Worldwide Church of God, Unitarian Church, Universalism, Unity School of Christianity, and Socinianism. Other Christian cults, historically, are Gnosticism, Neo-Gnostics, and Agnosticism.

Sometimes the cults, emerging out of millennial movements, take on a dark side when their leader leads them to mass suicide in the name of their faith. A classic example of such destructive cults is the People's Temple Christian Church, led by Jim Jones, who preached an eclectic mix of Pentecostalism, imminent second coming of Christ, Christian social gospel, socialism, communism, and utopianism. He gradually taught what he called "the Translation" in which the group, dying together in mass suicide, would move to another planet in mass bliss. In 1978, this resulted in the mass suicide/homicide of 914 followers at their commune in Guyana. Other suicidal cults with millennial movement aspects are: the Branch Davidians led by David Koresh with 82 deaths; the Family, led by Charles Manson that led to 8 deaths; Jeffrey Lundgren's Mormon splinter group that resulted in 5 deaths; the Order of the Solar Temple, with 53 deaths between 1994 and 1997, whose suicide members believed they were moving on to Sirius; Heaven's Gate, which in 1997 led to 39 suicide deaths of cult followers who believed they were exiting their human vehicles so that their souls could go on a journey aboard a spaceship they believed to be following the comet Hale-Bopp; the Aum Shinrikyo cult in Japan that perpetrated the Tokyo subway gas attack in 1995; Snake Handlers; the Movement of Restoration of the Ten Commandments, that resulted in 924 deaths in Uganda in March, 2000; the Family International, also called the Children of God, which emphasizes the imminent Second Coming and in 2005 encouraged suicide; and the Falun Gong, which in 2001 led to the self-immolation in Tiananmen Square in Beijing, China, involving six Falun Gong followers.

Source: Essay by author LeMay. Examples drawn from: *http://www.religion-cults.com/; http://en.wikipedia.org/wiki/Cult_suicide;* and from Catherine Wessinger, *How the Millennium Comes Violently: From Jonestown to Heaven's Gate.* New York: Seven Bridges Press, 2000; and Catherine Wessinger, ed., *Millennialism, Persecution, and Violence: Historical Cases.* Syracues: Syracuse University Press, 2000.

●

CHAPTER 7

● ● ●

OLD-STYLE RADICALISM

Some racial and ethnic minorities neither accept the values of the dominant culture and try to assimilate into it, nor reject the value system and attempt to isolate themselves from it by physical or psychological means. Some groups reject the value system of the majority society and seek to radically alter it. They strive to replace some part of the dominant culture's values with their own. This chapter explores three radical ideologies as prominent examples of groups attempting to recruit converts from among the nation's minorities: Socialism, Communism, and Fascism/Nazism. Each saw minorities as sources of adherents upon which to build their movements to where they could seize power and impose their values. None succeeded, but they made an effort and had an indirect impact on the dominant culture.

Chapters 5 and 6 discussed separatism noting that most groups opting for this strategy were religious sects. Religion provided a sufficiently powerful motivation for members of these groups to pursue and sustain, often for decades or even hundreds of years, a separatist ideology in the face of societal pressures to conform to the dominant society's norms and values. Groups pursuing the strategy of radicalism rely on *political ideology*, held with near-religious fervor, to provide their members with the motivation and means to follow this tactical response.

Radical political parties in American politics are just one type of "third" or "minor" political party. These third or minor parties failed to thrive and become majority parties because they never attracted enough followers to the polls to dominate, or even to secure a foothold in some region long and strong enough to build to a major political party movement. Several of the third parties died off precisely because their narrow base of appeal rejected immigrants and minority groups as unworthy of incorporation into the body politic. Prominent among such anti-immigrant or anti-minority parties were the Whig Party in the 1840s, the Know Nothing Party in the 1850s, the Prohibition Party of the 1880s, the People's Populist Party of the 1890s, and to some degree, the Progressive Party of the 1920s and 1930s.

Another set of third or minor parties are those who advocated a radical political ideology but who sought to woo racial and ethnic minorities, hoping to base a winning coalition upon the foundations they felt could be provided by these ethnic groups. Because they never succeeded in attracting the potentially large following among the racial or minority groups to whom they appealed, they disappeared from the political scene or remained a consistently minor party.

This chapter explores these cases, starting with socialism, then communism, and closing with an examination of fascism, in both the Italian and German variations. What is particularly interesting is that while they proposed what was, for their time, a radical ideology that, if accepted, would have drastically altered American culture and society, they pursued that goal using standard political behavior and methods. These "isms" sought mass followings by using standard political behavior targeted at the nation's racial and ethnic minorities. Political ideologies of the extreme left exhibited some commonalities. They favored destruction of the existing system and replacement of it with a variation of Marxism. They were generally nonreligious but claimed to love humanity and to be working for the betterment of human kind; and they were generally internationalist in outlook, with the central bodies or factions within them aligned with one or more foreign powers. Exemplary organizations would include the Communist Party USA, the Young Communist League, the Spartacist League, the Workers League, the Communist Workers Party, the Marxist-Leninist Party USA, the Revolutionary Communist Party, the All African People's Revolutionary Party, the Progressive Labor Party, the Socialist Workers Party, the Workers World Party, and so on (George and Wilcox 1992, 454–455).

SOCIALISM

The earliest *ism* to develop in America was socialism.[1] It sought converts especially among immigrant groups, notably Germans, Russians, Scandinavians, Slavs, and East European Jews. While socialism appealed in areas where radical agrarianism was strong, its weakness was in being perceived as a foreign-born political ideology. Equally important to its ultimate failure was the factional strife that split and weakened the socialist movement throughout its history. The earliest stages of the movement in the United States were characterized by a struggle between Marxist Socialists and Lassalleans. The Lassalleans were Socialist followers of the German Socialist Ferdinand Lassalle. They advocated reform rather than revolution.

Among the 1848 immigrant wave were German immigrants who espoused Marxism. They were the force in developing Marxist thought in America in the nineteenth century. Forerunners of both the Socialists and Communists in the United States, they settled in large numbers in a half-dozen large cities in which Socialism arose: New York, Philadelphia, St. Louis, Milwaukee, Cincinnati, and Chicago (see, for example, Judd 1989). They were a prominent faction of the national labor organization movement, strong in certain trade associations and unions.

The first distinctly Marxist-Socialist organization was the Proletarian League, founded in New York City in June 1852 by two German immigrants, Joseph Weydemeyer and F. A. Sorge. After 1857, other Marxist-Socialist organizations arose, calling themselves Communist clubs, in New York City, Chicago, Milwaukee, and Cincinnati, where there were large German immigrant settlements.

The Panic of 1873 was followed by large-scale and at times violent labor unrest. In the Pennsylvania mines a radical Irish immigrant group, the Molly Maguires, arose, soon after the Know Nothing movement evaporated. They remained a secret organization responsible for many murders, maimings, bombings, and arsons. Today they would be referred to as a terrorist organization. In 1874 the Pinkerton agency infiltrated their operations. They disbanded in 1877 after a number of their leading members were arrested, jailed, and a few even executed (George and Wilcox 1992, 20).

Extensive labor strife, including nation-wide railroad strikes in 1877, led to the founding and growth of the Socialist Labor Party (1876 to 1890). The Socialist Labor Party was handicapped in achieving broad social appeal by the very basis of its organizational strength—its highly German immigrant composition. Its peak membership was about 3,000. The party quickly split into factions when those advocating anarchosyndicalism established the Revolutionary Socialist Labor Party.

The labor movement was struggling to become national. In 1869, the Knights of Labor was formed. It peaked at about 700,000 members in 1886. On May 4, 1886, the Haymarket Square bombing killed seven policemen and injured sixty people. An immediate reaction resulted in the Knights of Labor losing over 178,000 members. Although not justified in reality, the majority society press generally linked, in the minds of many, anarchism, socialism, and trade unionism.

In 1881, the American Federation of Labor (AFL) was formed in Pittsburgh, and the Knights of Labor gradually died out as the AFL grew to nearly 600,000 members by 1900. The Workingman's Party of the United States began in 1876, and the Social Labor Party of North America in 1877. In the 1890s, the Western Federation of Miners became one of the strongest and most radical of American unions. As America industrialized, social upheaval, labor strife, and the struggle to adjust to millions of immigrants fed the Socialist movement: "American socialism flourished in a few decades after the time of the robber barons, the brutalities of Social Darwinism, rapid industrialization, shameless strikebreaking, labor spying. Coarsely primitive in its accumulations, early industrial capitalism could easily be taken as the enemy by everyone within, and a good many without, the Party" (Howe 1985, 16).

German workers in Milwaukee, Chicago, Detroit, and Cincinnati, and Jewish workers in New York provided the shock troops of the Socialist Party. They remained the most loyal, supplied the party with most of its money and manpower, showed the fewest number of defections, and provided most of its leadership. Finns, Russians, and Slavs supplied important contingents to the party. The Socialist Labor Party included Jews, Germans, Poles, Czechs, Slavs, Hungarians, South Slavs, and Russians. German and Jewish immigrants were the most important in overall numbers and in leadership positions in the party. These groups formed a solid base upon which industrial trade unions and Socialist parties developed. Given historical backgrounds of persecution in their homelands, they were accustomed to organizing. By World War I, Jewish needleworkers were solidly organized into the International Ladies' Garment Workers Union; the furriers and the hatters unions were notably Socialist. Union members read Socialist newspapers. German workers dominated several trade unions, for example, printers, bakers, and brewers. They forged an iron-clad combination of organization and ideology, no easy task (Draper 1957, 31–32).

In 1890, Daniel DeLeon joined the Socialist Labor Party, serving as editor of its paper, *Weekly People*. A dominant force in the party, he oversaw its decline from 1890 to 1900. DeLeon organized the Socialist Trades and Labor Alliance, whose membership was heavily foreign-born (German, Jewish, Scandinavian, and Polish). He criticized the American Federation of Labor (AFL) organization as "labor lieutenants of capital" and the "aristocracy of labor" (Draper 1957, 29). By 1900, his Socialist Labor Party declined to less than 6,000 members in twenty-six states and mustered less than 80,000 votes in the 1900 national election. He exemplified the use and the limitations of the old-style radicalism approach, and its appeal to the German and Jewish immigrant minority groups.

The Socialist Labor Party was weakened by its position on the **"Negro question."** Both its leaders and its rank-and-file members simply believed Negroes were inferior to whites. They did not attempt to recruit black members (Record 1951). DeLeon developed the tactic of "boring from within." Socialist members joined trade unions to take them over. When that failed, they attempted to form a rival to the AFL, the Socialist Trades and Labor Alliance. The party remained an ideological-based labor union and political movement typical of small third parties.

In 1900, the Socialist Labor Party split. One faction continued to follow DeLeon; the other led to the creation of the Socialist Party, formally established in St. Louis in 1901, with Leon Greenbaum as its national secretary and Eugene Debs as its outstanding mass personality and perennial presidential candidate.[2] The Socialist Democratic Party, as it was called in 1900, picked Debs to run for president, with Job Harriman for vice-president. Other leaders of the new party were Morris Hillquit, a Russian-born attorney and ardent Socialist in New York, and Victor Berger, a German Socialist active in Milwaukee (Draper 1957, 27–28).

Eugene Debs was born in Terre Haute, Indiana, on November 5, 1855.[3] His parents were immigrants from Alsace (in present-day France) who came to the United States in 1849. Debs was fluent in French and German, as well as his native English. Debs lost his railroad fireman job during the depression that followed the Panic of 1873. In 1875, he became a labor organizer of the Brotherhood of Locomotive Firemen (BLF). By 1879, he was active in Democratic politics and was elected to the Indiana state legislature in 1883. In 1880, he became editor of the union magazine and national secretary/treasurer. In 1893, Debs organized the American Railway Union (ARU), pushing the concept of forming an industry-wide union for all railroad workers.

The unsuccessful Pullman strike in 1894 was a disaster that essentially ended the union. Debs was jailed for six months for violating an injunction. In 1897, Debs became a Socialist, beginning a 30-year career of carrying the dual message of industrial unionism and socialism to Americans. He constantly stressed that the movement had to be both economic and political in character. In his words: "I am a proletarian revolutionist . . . opposed to every war but one; I am for that war with heart and soul, and that is the world wide war of the social revolution" (cited in George and Wilcox 1992, 25)

A spellbinding speaker, a follower described him: "I was a young man at the time and had heard a good many speakers before," he avowed, "but Debs was something out of the ordinary. He held the audience in a trance with his tall figure and long arms waving" (cited in Brommel 1978, 63). Debs pushed various Progressive Era reform measures.

His ideas, considered so radical in his day, eventually became standard American political values: the abolition of child labor; the right of women to vote; the graduated income tax; the direct election of U.S. senators; unemployment insurance; employer liability laws; establishment of national departments of education and of health; attacks on Jim Crowism; support of equal rights for blacks; and prison reform.

The American Socialist Party depended heavily on and sought immigrants as converts to its cause. These immigrant groups formed associations linked to the Socialist parties of their respective native countries. Federations of the foreign-language workers played a special role in American socialism. Pathbreakers in linking language federations and the American Socialist Party were the Finnish Socialists. Socialism was part of their immigrant baggage, involving a radical break with old traditions: Finnish Socialists preached atheism and science as well as socialism. Their membership strength grew from anticlericalism as much as from specific labor grievances.

Debs sought to recruit blacks, but both he and the party considered the "Negro problem" one of class, not race, a view dictating a strategy of working-class organizations. As Debs said: "The Socialist Party is the party of workers regardless of race, color, and creed. In mill and mine, shop and farm, office and school, the workers can assert their united power, and through the Socialist Party establish a cooperative commonwealth forever free from human exploitation and class rule" (cited in Record 1951, 101).

Debs failed to gain widespread support within the party for recruiting blacks and was unsuccessful in efforts to attract a large number of blacks to the cause: "Negroes were too preoccupied with staying alive and praising God (in that order) to give time to the building of a new society. Coupled with this was their reluctance to invite the stigma of radicalism when the stigma of race was already overwhelming. The fact that it (the Socialist Party) gave deference to southern mores by organizing separate locals below the Mason-Dixon line did not enhance its appeal to Negroes" (Record 1951, 11).

Despite Debs's untiring efforts, the American Socialist Party was never able to gain mass appeal. In its presidential bids the party never got more than 6 percent of the vote, that in its high-tide year of 1912. In 1912, Debs received his largest electoral support, over 80,000 votes for president, representing one-tenth of his total national vote, from Oklahoma, Texas, Arkansas, and Louisiana. Oklahoma had the strongest state party organization in the Socialist Party, with over 961 locals and 12,000 dues-paying members. In 1914, they had over 100 people elected to local office and even six to the state legislature.

The Socialist Party's inner diversity developed schismatic factionalism that led to catastrophe after 1912. The party split began at the 1912 convention when the left wing, enraged over the question of the party's position on the United States entering World War I in 1917, left the party. It split further when the Communist Party was established in 1919–1920.

The party's decline was also influenced by Debs's evangelism. His very fervor allowed him to see only two choices: capitalism, which he characterized as the devil's spawn, and socialism, his angelic promise. He could never breach the gap between factions of the party advocating violent activism (the syndicalists/anarchists) and those advocating political reform and close cooperation with the trade/skilled craft unionism movement. The 1912 split was partly over relations with the AFL and the labor union movement generally. In 1912, the AFL had fewer than 1 million members and confined

Shown here is a 1904 Socialist Party campaign poster. (*Eugene V. Debs Foundation*)

itself to skilled craftsmen. The Socialists called Samuel Gompers a "reactionary." Both Debs and Victor Berger attacked him for his "class collaboration." This threatened a labor movement that included anti-Socialist elements, especially large numbers of Catholics (Lipset and Marks, 2000).

By 1912, factions within the Socialist Party were increasingly unwilling or unable to work together. One faction, the so-called **Sewer Socialists**, were largely German Americans in Milwaukee. Their leftist critics sneeringly called them by that title. They had little of the millennial zeal that marked the Debsian cadres in the West and Southwest. They lived in close and effective harmony with their local trade unions. Ironically, these often "foreign-born" (German) immigrants showed a keener appreciation of changes in American society than such completely indigenous radicals as the "Texas Reds," the "Oklahoma Rebels," and the "Colorado syndicalists." Sewer Socialists proved they knew how to win elections (George and Wilcox 1992, 24–25; Draper, 1957, 27–28). Box 7.1 presents a bio-sketch of their leader, Victor Berger, who held the highest elected office achieved by any socialist—United States Representative from Milwaukee. His career illustrates their electoral success but also the problems radicals such as the socialists faced not only in attracting votes and minority group support, but from overt discrimination that spilled over into the political arena.

Another faction involved Jewish immigrant socialists in New York, Yiddish-speaking and distinctively Jewish in the flavor of their organization. They were militant garment workers. Their leader, Morris Hillquit, tried to steer the movement between the extremes of antipolitical syndicalism and incoherent reform. A third faction were Christian Socialists of Populist agrarianism.

A fundamentalist and radical faction was the Western syndicalists, a good example of a millennialist movement. In 1905, they formed the Industrial Workers of the

Box 7.1   *Bio-Sketch of Victor L. Berger*

Victor Louis (Luitpold) Berger was born in 1860 in Austria-Hungary. He attended the universities at Budapest and Vienna, and he and his parents immigrated to the United States in 1878, first settling in Bridgeport, Connecticut. He moved to Milwaukee, Wisconsin in 1881 to work as a school teacher and a newspaper editor, publishing several papers in both English (the *Social-Democrat* Harold, 1901–1913; and the *Milwaukee Leader,* 1911–1929), and the German-language *Wisconsin Vorwaerts,* meaning Forward, 1892–1911). He was a labor-leader with the Milwaukee Federated Trades council and through them tied to the socialist movement.

Victor Berger was a delegate to the People's Party Convention held in St. Louis in 1896, and from that helped organize (with Eugene Debs, Morris Hillquit, and others) the Social Democratic Party in 1897, which later was known simply as the Socialist Party.

The Milwaukee Socialists became known as the "sewer socialists" with their back-to-basic reform strategy and legacy that sought to reform the more dire conditions resulting from the industrial revolution, and for pushing local reforms such as cleaning up neighborhoods and factories with a new sanitation system, community parks, and an improved public education system (he and other German immigrants, for example, first started the "kindergarten" system). In economic policy, they proposed, as did socialists generally, replacing the capitalist system with a planned economy of state-owned industries that would protect workers from an increasingly oppressive business class. They did not advocate violent change, however, instead supporting the achievement of their goals through public opinion education and via the ballot box, and more efficient administration of government, especially at the local level. Victor Berger became the symbol of the Milwaukee Socialism movement. He ran for Congress in 1904, but lost that election. In 1910, however, he was elected to represent Wisconsin's fifth Congressional district and was the first socialist to serve in the U.S. Congress. He pushed for voting rights for the District of Columbia, and what for his time were radical proposals such as eliminating the presidential veto, and the social takeover of major industries. He gained national attention pushing for an old-age pension (what eventually became the Social Security program), the first of its kind introduced into Congress. He lost his re-election bids in 1912, 1914, and 1916, but remained active in Wisconsin and in national Socialist Party politics. When World War I broke out, his German heritage and socialist views of the war led him to oppose the war, and when the United States entered that conflict and Congress passed the Espionage Act of 1917, Berger and many other Socialists were indicted under the act in 1918. He was convicted and sentenced to 20 years in prison in 1919, but the conviction was appealed and overturned in 1921. Despite his being indicted at the time, the people of Milwaukee elected him to the House of Representatives in 1918, but when he arrived in the capital to claim his seat, Congress formed a special committee to determine whether a convicted felon and war opponent should be seated. In 1919, Congress ruled he could not, and declared the seat vacant. A special election was held to fill the seat, and the voters elected Berger again. The House again refused to seat him and the seat remained vacant until 1921, when a Republican, William Stafford, was elected to the seat.

Berger defeated Stafford in 1922, and was reelected in 1924 and 1926 and after the war-time hysteria had passed, he was seated and served his terms. He again proposed an old-age pension, and what was then considered radical proposals such as unemployment insurance and public housing, recognition of the Soviet Union, and revision of the Versailles Treaty. He was defeated in his re-election bid in 1928 by Republican Stafford, and returned to Milwaukee to continue his career as a newspaper editor until his death in a streetcar accident in 1928.

Source: Bio-sketch by author, with information from: http://www.wisconsinhistory.org/turningpoints/tp-043/?acton-more_essay, accessed 3/22/2007; and http://en.wikipedia.org/wiki/Victor_Berger. Accessed 3/22/2007.

World (IWW), known as the **Wobblies**. This group used verbal violence and advocated "direct action"—the use of violence and force to further the revolution (George and Wilcox 1992, 26–27; Draper 1957, 135–136). Its leaders were William Haywood, Charles Ruthenberg, and William Foster, all of whom later became Communists.

The IWW led a textile strike in 1912. Its radicalism prevented its establishment as a lasting union. In 1912, its membership exceeded 14,000; a year later it had declined to 700. It reached out to blacks, attempting to organize both unskilled and semiskilled workers with no racial lines. Very critical of the AFL for its racial policies, the Wobblies trained and used Negro organizers, such as Ben Fletcher, who recruited both blacks and whites. He led the IWW to control of the Philadelphia docks and won an increase in wages from .25 an hour to .65 cents an hour in 1916. He symbolized the IWW's efforts to improve race relations and to end disunity among workers by creating working-class solidarity. The IWW sponsored anti-racist forums to educate the rank-and-file membership. The high point of working-class solidarity remained on the Philadelphia docks. A more national approach failed due to xenophobic reaction to World War I, economic scapegoating, and the repeal of civil rights, tying socialism to unionism and their "siding with the Axis nations and plotting to render America weaker." In the 1919 hysteria, Fletcher and many Wobblies were arrested and sent to prison for treason. Fletcher landed in Leavenworth prison with hundreds of other Wobblies, charged with speaking out against the war, dodging the draft, refusing to sign no-strike contracts, and engaging in "criminal syndicalism." Several states passed laws to outlaw the IWW (http://www.iww.org/culture/biography/BenFletcher1.shtml. Accessed 3/22/2007). Despite its efforts to do so, however, it never achieved a large black membership. Blacks were never more than 5 to 10 percent of its membership.

After the split in 1912, the Socialist Party made a concerted effort to win over blacks. It played a central role in the formation of the NAACP, began to organize black dockworkers in New Orleans, and recruited blacks into the United Mine Workers. In 1915, it helped organize the International Trade Union Educational League to organize Negro workers. In 1917, it made its most serious effort when A. Philip Randolph and Chandler Owen established *The Messenger* and served as its editors. These outreach efforts failed to attract enough new members to make up for those lost because of Debs's anti-war position, which damaged the party's electoral support, led to the imprisonment of many of its leaders, and led to the eventual decline of the party.

Although the socialist movement failed to attract large numbers of African Americans to the cause, they did recruit some who became prominent leaders in the movement. Box 7.2 presents a Bio-Sketch of perhaps the most famous and effective black socialist leader—A. Philip Randolph. His story personifies their attempt, and the religious-like fervor with which movement members embraced the socialist ideology as well as the difficulty the movement experienced in winning large numbers to the cause.

Box 7.2   *BIO-SKETCH OF A. PHILIP RANDOLPH*

•

Asa Philip Randolph was born in April 1889 in Crescent City, Florida, the son of an A.M.E. minister. He moved to New York City's Harlem in 1911, intent on becoming an actor. While at City College of New York, he switched to political science and economics. While studying at City College, he met Chandler Owen, a sociology and political science student at Columbia University. Together they began, in 1917, to publish *The Messenger*, a radical magazine out of Harlem that espoused their socialist views. In 1918, he and Chandler Owen were charged with breaking the law under the Espionage Act, although they were not convicted. In *The Messenger*, in 1919, Randolph stated that the IWW was the only major labor organization in the United States that drew no race or color lines. He ran several times for elective office on the socialist ticket, but never succeeded in being elected. Randolph helped organize blacks working in the laundry, clothes, and cinema industries.

Randolph became a very effective union organizer, founding the Brotherhood of Sleeping Car Porters in 1929, the first serious effort to organize employees of the Pullman Company, which employed a large number of African Americans. The organization effort took years and was a bitter struggle, but the union finally won bargaining rights in 1935 and achieved their first contract in 1937. Randolph arranged for the Brotherhood to associate with the American Federation of Labor, but later moved the union to the Congress of Industrial Organizations when the AFL failed to fight discrimination in its own ranks.

Randolph emerged as one of the most effective and visible spokespersons for African American civil rights and, when the United States entered World War I, Randolph proposed a "March on Washington" to protest racial discrimination in the armed forces. He cancelled the march when President Franklin Roosevelt issued the Fair Employment Act in June, 1941. In 1947, he formed the Committee Against Jim Crow in the Military Service, later called the League for Non-Violent Civil Disobedience. President Harry Truman reacted positively to the campaign and abolished racial segregation in the armed forces by executive order in 1948. In 1950, Randolph, Roy Wilkins of the NAACP, and Arnold Aronson of the National Jewish Community Relations Council formed the Leadership Conference on Civil Rights which soon became the premier civil rights coalition, and was involved in coordination of virtually every civil rights law since 1957.

In 1963, Randolph, King, and others organized the March on Washington for Jobs and Freedom, drawing an estimated 400,000 people, both blacks and whites, at which Dr. King delivered his famous, "I Have a Dream Speech." Randolph came to the forefront of national attention as the civil rights movement gained momentum in the early 1960s when he often addressed the nation on behalf of African Americans engaged in the struggle for voting rights and an end to segregation and discrimination in public accommodations, working closely with Bayard Rustin and the AFL-CIO. Philip Randolph died in New York on May 16, 1979.

Source: Bio-sketch by author, information from: http://en.wikipedia.org/wiki/A_Philip_Randolph, accessed 3/22/2007; and in http://www.spartacus.schoolnet.co.uk/USArandolph.htm, accessed 3/22/2007.

Just as the industrial labor union movement divided into two major factions, the American Federation of Labor and the Congress of Industrial Organizations, so the Socialist Party split in two in 1912. Haywood and Foster left the party in 1912, forming the Syndicalist League of North America in Chicago. After a brief attempt to keep them in the party, Debs shifted his support to mend differences with Hillquit and

Berger in 1913. During 1912–1915, as World War I raged in Europe, Debs became a militant pacifist and led the Socialist Party to become an anti-war movement.

When the United States entered World War I, on April 6, 1917, the Socialist Party held its convention in St. Louis and opposed the war in a statement known as the "Majority Report" and by a national referendum of its members who voted for the anti-war resolution by a vote of 11,041 to 782. The party had been slowly recovering from the 1912 split. Its membership rose from just over 79,000 in 1915, to over 80,000 in 1917, and to just short of 105,000 in 1919. By war's end almost every Socialist leader was prosecuted under the Espionage Act: Victor Berger, Kate Richards O'Hare, Adolph Geuner, Charles Ruthenberg, and Eugene Debs. Only Hillquit, stricken with tuberculosis, was spared.

The Socialist Party was attacked as being pro-German. Debs was arrested following an anti-war speech he gave in 1918, and sentenced, under the Espionage Act, to ten years in prison. In March 1919 his conviction was upheld by the U.S. Supreme Court. The party was further split when its left wing walked out, held its own convention, and voted to affiliate with the Communist Internationale, forming the Communist Party.

In 1920, the Socialist Party again nominated Debs for president. Although he was serving his term in a federal prison, he was allowed to issue a once-per-week statement for the campaign. He won nearly 1 million votes. The party launched a campaign to have him pardoned. President Harding ordered Debs released (a commutation, not a pardon) at Christmastime in 1921. In 1922, Debs tried to revive the Socialist Party of America, then down to a mere 7,793 members, almost half of whom were foreign-language affiliates. He specifically rejected joining the Communist Party. In 1924, Debs supported Robert La Follette and the new Progressive Party.

In 1926, he wrote a pamphlet appealing to American labor in defense of Sacco and Vanzetti. Eugene Debs died on October 20, 1926. The Socialist Party continued its factional strife. In 1934, Upton Sinclair, the novelist who had run for office as a Socialist, entered and won the California Democratic primary for governor. Norman Thomas followed Debs as the party's leader, as the leading American socialist, pacifist, and a six-times candidate for president on the Socialist Party of America ticket (from 1928 to 1948), but Thomas never received the votes of Debs' high point. Thomas, too, was unable to heal the factional strife. The son of a Presbyterian minister, he received his degree from Princeton University in 1905, and was ordained a Presbyterian minister himself in 1911, from the Union Theological Seminary. He was instrumental in the Social Gospel movement and liberal politics, blending religious fervor with his socialist political ideology. He also ran, unsuccessfully, for Governor of New York in 1924, and for Mayor of New York City in 1925 and 1929.

Figure 7.1 presents the Socialist Party's presidential vote cast for selected years, 1896–1936, with the percent of the popular vote those total votes cast represented.

The party was torn between whether to support President Roosevelt and the New Deal evolutionary programs in support of labor, or whether, along with the Popular Front period of communism, to ally itself with local union groups, the American Labor Party, the Farmer-Labor Party, and the like. In these allied groups, the party was never a dominant force, although it played a significant role in some coalitions.

Table 7.1 summarizes the party's tickets from 1900 to 1956, listing the party's candidates for President and Vice-President over those years.

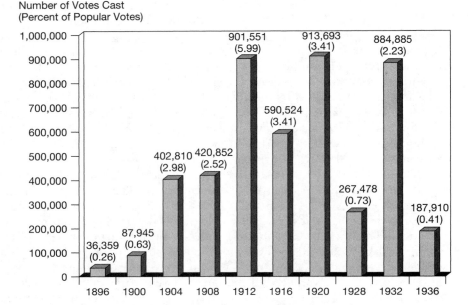

Figure 7.1   The Socialist Party Presidential Vote, Selected Years 1896–1936

Source: Figure by author. Data on number/percent of votes cast from: http:www.uselectionsatlas.org/
Results/accessed 5/17/2007.

Communism

The Communist Party in America grew out of the Socialist Party movement, with members drawn from the mostly foreign-language affiliations of the Socialist Labor Party.[4] Nathan Glazer describes its birth:

> The most important step to a proper understanding of the question "who" became Communists and "why" is to realize that for certain social groups, for certain milieux, it was neither eccentric nor exceptional to become a communist. The great majority of these members came from the Socialist Party. In January 1919, this party had almost 110,000 members. In May and June of that year, great blocs of the membership were expelled or suspended for allegiance to the Left Wing that was forming in response to the Bolshevik revolution. By July 1919, the membership was down to 40,000. . . . As the entire [Communist] party emerged from the underground, it had about 12,000 members. At this time, in 1922, the Socialist Party had about the same number of members. (1961, 39)

The Communist Party in America was always small. At its peak it had fewer than 100,000 members, and its card-carrying membership was never more than 40,000. Numbers and votes were not the critical aspects of the movement. It targeted for recruitment the most exploited and oppressed because they were considered potentially the best, most loyal, and most dependable workers: white Euro-ethnic immigrants and the American Negro (Buhle, 1987).

Table 7.1 Socialist Party Presidential Tickets, 1900–1956

Presidential Election Year	Nominees for President, Vice-President
1900	Eugene Debs and Job Harriman
1904	Eugene Debs and Ben Hanford
1908	Eugene Debs and Ben Hanford
1912	Eugene Debs and Emil Seidel
1916	Allan Benson and George Kirkpatrick
1920	Euguene Debs and Seymour Stedman
1924	Robert LaFollete Sr. and Burton K. Wheeler (Progressive)
1928	Norman Thomas and James H. Mauer
1932	Norman Thomas and James H. Mauer
1936	Norman Thomas and George Nelson
1940	Norman Thomas and Maynard Krueger
1944	Norman Thomas and Darlington Hoopes
1948	Norman Thomas and Tucker Smith
1952	Darlington Hoopes and Samuel Friedman
1956	Darlington Hoopes and Samuel Friedman

Source: Table by author, information from http://en.wikipedia.org/wiki/Socialist_Party_America.

Two American Communist parties were formed in 1919. One emerged from the left wing of the Socialist Party (the IWW) and the Socialist Labor Party. The other arose in the Workers International Industrial Union and responded to the appeal of the Communist Internationale. The Communist Labor Party was the foreign-language-federation-dominated faction from the Socialist Labor Party. It met in Chicago and claimed about 10,000 members. The Communist Party of America was the Michigan federationist group, claiming about 58,000 members. A partial merger between the groups was effected when the United (or Centrist) Communist Party was set up in July 1920 in New York City (Draper 1957, 164–175).

All the factions were driven underground when Attorney General A. Mitchell Palmer led hundreds of raids during the "Red Scare" summer of 1919. These raids resulted in over 10,000 persons being arrested in 70 cities. Over 500 aliens were deported, 249 alone aboard the "Soviet Ark" ship, the *Buford*. In the hysteria of 1919, the Socialist congressman from Milwaukee, Victor Berger, was refused his elected seat in the House of Representatives. Five Socialist assemblymen were denied their seats in the New York state legislature. In the delirium of anti-communism, Palmer even claimed that the Communist Party had 1 million members. The various surviving Communist Party factions met in New York City in 1922 and formed the Worker's Party of America. It claimed a membership of 25,000 by 1923.

The most striking characteristic of the Communist Party in the 1920s was its overwhelmingly new-immigrant membership. The Communist Party worked with the foreign-language groups active in the Socialist movement and in the industrial union movement because they provided the party with three key elements: money, access to the industrial worker class, and the movements' cadres of rank-and-file members.

While the white ethnic predominance of party membership caused white-black membership strains, it reflected the predominance of such white ethnics in the primary target group of the party, the "American industrial proletariat." As a report of the Sixth Convention noted: "We face the fact that the working class of this country, in its national composition, consists of a majority of foreign born. For example, we find that 67 percent of the oil workers are foreign born, 62 percent of the packing house workers, 61 percent of the miners. We find textile workers over 60 percent, steel workers over 60 percent. . . . The party was a working class party because the greater part of its membership came from certain immigrant communities" (cited in Glazer 1961, 76).

After World War I, the Third Internationale of the Communist Party believed, as did the party in the United States, that world revolution was at hand, European nations were collapsing, and the United States was on the eve of a social revolution.

The left wing of the Socialists, in June 1920, organized the Proletarian Party of America, but the new party was expelled from the Communist Party. The two factions of the party failed to effectively unite, and by 1921 the movement experienced a multiplication of Communist sects and organizations: the Industrial Communist Party, the Rummager League, the Worker's Council, the American Labor Alliance, the United Communist Party, and the African Black Brotherhood (which did not survive the year, as only a few Communists were initially attempting to carry on agitation among the nation's Negro workers). Of the twelve Communist organizations that began in 1921, eight of which were political, seven failed or merged, so that at the end of 1921 only six remained: the Communist Party, the United Communist Party, the Proletarian Party, the American Labor Alliance, the Worker's Council, and the Arbeiter Bildungs Vereine (former German Socialists).

American Communists of all types were profoundly affected by the barren results. American labor simply was not responding to their propaganda and policies. After World War I, all labor organizations declined: The IWW declined rapidly from its peak of about 60,000; the AFL had 4 million members in 1920 but was down to 2.9 million by 1923; the Socialist Labor Party, which only had 11,000 members in 1912, was down to 2,000 by 1920; and the Socialist Party, likewise, fell from over 80,000 before World War I to just over 26,000 by 1920.

The American Communist Party, which the Worker's Party began to call itself by 1923, had a decidedly middle-class membership, which differentiated it from almost every other Communist Party in the Western world. This reflected the middle-class status of its Jewish members, which by 1925 were second only to the Finnish members. Although Communist Party members were but a miniscule percentage of American Jews, those Jews who were Communist were a significant (about 9) percentage of the party.

By the early 1920s, the party was making a concerted effort to attract African Americans. The founders of the American Communist Party were radicals of European origin, and their initial expectation had been that they would first revolutionize white workers and then go on to bring the gospel of Marx and Lenin to people of color. They considered the Negro an organizing asset and were anxious to enlist the support of the African-American organizers in the IWW. Taking their lead from Lenin's analysis of imperialism and the national and colonial question, they proposed to direct much of their energy toward developing the oppressed Negroes into a revolutionary force. Since blacks were clearly the most oppressed group in the United States, the party thought them to be one of the greatest potential resources for its program, and it actively tried to recruit black leadership, consistently made the "Negro question" a major issue in its program, and issued a stream of special books and pamphlets on the subject.

At the Fourth Congress of the Comintern, in 1922, American Communists John Reed and Claude McKay contributed resolutions on Garveyism, recognizing the legitimacy of the black anti-colonial and anti-imperialist struggle. The congress put a high priority on recruitment of African Americans to the party (Draper 1960, 300–314).

In their efforts during the 1920s and 1930s to appeal to blacks and to progressive whites troubled by the flagrant racial injustices of American and South African society, Communists enjoyed a special advantage. No one else in those decades was fighting so intently and assertively for the abolition of segregation and the complete equality of the races. (Frederickson 1995, 180)

Despite the party's overtures and attempts to infiltrate the UNIA, Marcus Garvey, by 1925 and while in prison, explicitly rejected working with them:

> Communism among Negroes in 1920–1921 was represented in New York by such Negroes as Cyril Briggs, and W. A. Domingo, and my contact and experience of them and their methods are enough to keep me shy of that kind of communism for the balance of my natural life. . . . The American Negro is warned to keep away from communism, as it is taught in this country. (cited in Lewis 1988, 134)

While the Communist Party had an advantage in its uncompromising position of antiracism, its major liability was the approach it used. The party shifted directions in its appeal to the black struggle in response to changes in the party line coming from Moscow. In two decades, from the late 1920s to 1950s, it adopted five major strategy shifts, giving the American party the image of being mere agents of Moscow, tools of the Soviet Union. Rupert Lewis (1988) argues that the conflict between the rank-and-file white and black members of the party and the party's stumbling over how to deal with the Garvey movement were significant reasons for the party's failure to win over a large black following.

Its main source of African-American members was the **African Blood Brotherhood (ABB)**, created in 1919 after the Socialist Party split. Most of the Brotherhood leaders were Socialists drawn to the promise of the Bolshevik revolution (Draper 1957, 387). The Brotherhood specifically rejected Garvey's program. Instead, it favored organizing a militant program to win black freedom in the United States. Although the Brotherhood supplied relatively few party members, it was among the first to join the party and made up the core of the black Communist leadership for many years.

The Worker's Party members were unofficially involved in the Federated Farmer–Labor Party founded July 3, 1923, in Chicago. It had an estimated 600,000 members—miners, machinists, needleworkers, carpenters, metalworkers, the 87,000-strong West Virginia Federation of Labor, and the 210,000-strong AFL-affiliated unions. The Federated Farmer–Labor Party endorsed Senator Robert LaFollette, who made one of the strongest third-party efforts of the twentieth century, polling 4,826,382 votes, or 16.5 percent of the total cast. The Worker's Party refused to endorse him and instead ran its own candidate, William Foster, who received a mere 33,316 votes in the 13 states where the party was on the ballot. Like some other third-party movements, it was more committed to ideological purity than to winning elections.

Among the earliest of the members who rose to become prominent within the Worker's Party was Cyril Briggs, who founded the African Blood Brotherhood, edited *The Crusader,* a monthly magazine of the left, and was a regular contributor to *The Messenger,* the Socialist magazine edited by Chandler Owen and A. Philip Randolph. Another was poet Claude McKay, the most notable black intellectual associated with the party in the early 1920s and who was associate editor of *The Liberator.* Another ABB member who became an early Communist leader was Harry Haywood, of the IWW. Edward Doty commanded the Chicago post and organized independent unions in Chicago. Other members included Richard Moore, Otto Huiswood, Grace Campbell, Otto Hall, and S. V. Phillips. The ABB never had more than 2,000 members, about 150 to 200 of whom joined the party.

In 1924, an All-Race Assembly, also known as the **Sanhedrin**, met in Chicago. It had 250 delegates from 20 states representing 61 national black organizations. It was the first united front of blacks in which the Communist Party participated officially. The Worker's Party sent Lovett Fort-Whiteman, Gordon Owens, and S. V. Phillips; the African Blood Brotherhood was represented by Otto Huiswood.

The party was instrumental in establishing the American Negro Labor Congress in 1925, the first significant effort by the party to organize the black masses. Convened in October, also in Chicago, six of the seventeen signers were Communist Party members. The strategy of using the Sanhedrin and the American Negro Labor Congress exemplified the "bore from within" tactic of the party. Organized labor and the Communist Party essentially used one another in this strategy.

In 1928, the Communist Party launched its "Negro self-determination" phase, a shift that certainly surprised most black Communists in the United States. This effort was led by Cyril Briggs. In *The Crusader,* Briggs called for self-determination for blacks in an independent society in the nation, while continuing to advocate cooperation with radical whites to overthrow capitalism. The other leading advocate of self-determination was Harry Haywood, another leading force in the ABB, who joined the Young Communist League in 1923 and the Communist Party in 1925. He was sent to Moscow in 1926 for training. He characterized African Americans as members of an "oppressed nation," and argued for "self-determination for the black belt." The Sixth Congress of the International voted that Negro self-determination must be a party goal in the United States and South Africa. It ruled out working with the NAACP, UNIA, or the ANLC (American Negro Labor Congress). Communists were to denounce such movements and to discredit them in any way they could.

This new strategy was a response to the failure to recruit a significant black following in the 1920–1928 period. Their lack of success in attracting black unionists differed little from that of their fellow white members. In 1925, they set up the International Labor Defense (ILD) and selected a black lawyer, William L. Patterson, as its executive secretary. The American Negro Labor Congress was mostly a paper organization of sweeping promises but little performance. By 1928, it claimed a membership of 14,000, but its total black membership was between 150 and 200, largely from the black belt of the deep South (Foner and Allen 1987, 63).

The self-determination phase was the party's attempt to attract a mass following among America's black population. It had noted the success of Marcus Garvey's movement in attracting a mass following among lower- and lower-middle-class blacks, the very classes it was targeting, who had found in Garvey's promises of a new land an escape from the harsh realities of segregation. After his imprisonment, Garvey's organization began to deteriorate, and the Communists shifted from their original position of not opposing him and his movement to one of being increasingly critical of him and of "Negro Zionism."

When the Sixth World Congress laid down its program of self-determination, the CPA responded with its black belt program, defining the basis for a separate Negro nation: "In the economic and social conditions and class relations of the Negro people there are increasing forces that serve as a basis for the development of a Negro nation (a compact mass of farmers on a contiguous territory, semi-feudal conditions, complete segregation, common traditions of slavery, the development of distinct class and economic ties, etc." (Record 1951, 59).

Despite its criticism of the Garvey movement as "Negro Zionism," the party's self-determination and black republican program had a distinctly Garvey look. Both the new Communist view and the UNIA stressed the distinct culture of the Negro; both held that common racial features were a basis for a nation-state, and both noted that the Negro had a "natural area" for the location of a state—in Africa according to Garvey and in the black belt of the United States for the Communists. Neither program could overcome the basic African-American attitude that:

> It is conceivable that conditions might become so intolerable for Negroes in the United States that the black man would seek refuge on other shores. It is extremely doubtful that any significant support for a colonization or repatriation movement could be developed among Negroes under present conditions. However, the glamour of a black state, either here as a 49th state or in Africa, as an independent nation, has not caught the imagination of the Negro—either of the Negro intellectual or the Negro in the mass. The Negro in his customs, in his thinking, and in his aspirations is an American, and he regards America as his home. He lacks even those religious ties that would attract the Jewish refugee to Palestine. If the Negro is to be gotten out of America he will have to be driven out. Only when racial persecution becomes so efficiently brutal, so thoroughly institutionalized that life for the Negro will become impossible here, will there be any likelihood that the black American will seek refuge elsewhere. (Ralph Bunch, cited in Record 1951, 42)

During the 1928–1935 phase, Communists, with a revolutionary self-determination program, stood in opposition to practically all the Negro betterment, interracial, and nationalist organizations. The party failed to see merit in any of their programs. It lumped them together as conscious conspiracies to defeat the potentially radical Negro masses. In its view, only the party was right, only it had the correct theory, and only the party alone had the correct program of action. Communists blessed only those extensions of themselves: the League for the Struggle of Negro Rights, the International Labor Defense, and the Trade Union Unity League.

The 1930s witnessed the biggest success the Communist Party experienced in winning credibility among black Americans. It set up the League for the Struggle of Negro Rights in 1930. Although its obvious character as a front organization of the party prevented it from developing true mass support, the depression released radical impulses that had been held in check during the prosperity and conservative probusiness climate that prevailed during the 1920s. The Communist-led **Sharecropper's Union of Alabama** had no chance of reaching the bulk of the black farmers in the state, but it persisted in some counties for several years despite horrendous violence and intimidation against it. At its peak, in 1935, it may have had as many as 8,000–10,000 members (Draper 1960, 354). Its leader, Hosea Hudson, was one of a few black Alabamians able to substitute Marx and Lenin for Christ or the dictatorship of the proletariat for the millennium. Unquestionably, the party's greatest gains were made in the large urban industrial centers where relief programs were more acute and where the large concentrations of the unemployed provided a solid base for the party's organizational efforts.

The party recruited and developed some key black leaders. Negro journalists, intellectuals, and trade unionists went to Moscow for training. Among them were James W. Ford, the party's vice-presidential candidate in 1932; Eugene Gordon, a journalist; and William L. Patterson, who became the secretary of the International Labor Defense. Young Negro trade unionists were targeted by the Trade Union Educational League. The American Negro Labor Congress selected and trained radical Negro unionists. James Ford entered the party in 1926 and was a delegate to the Fourth World Congress of the Red International Labor Unions. In 1928, he was a delegate to the Sixth World Congress of the Communist Internationale. Shortly afterward he assumed the post of Negro Organizer for the Trade Union Unity League. In 1932, the Foster/Ford ticket received 102,991 votes.

The most successful effort by the party in increasing its visibility and its credibility among blacks was its role in the defense of the Scottsboro Boys, led by the International Labor Defense (ILD).[5] Its involvement helped develop a conviction among blacks by the mid-1930s that the Communists were the boldest and most effective advocates of equal citizenship for African Americans. Although the case won it no judicial victory or mass membership, it enabled the Communist Party to develop a much more favorable image. As Nathan Glazer points out, by "capturing" the Scottsboro case, the party could, for the first time, enter Negro churches and other organizations to raise money for the defense. The sums raised were considerable, and most of it could go to support a staff of Communist organizers and fundraisers. The ILD was on the constant lookout for victims of injustice who might allow them to take over their defense.

The Scottsboro case significantly aided black recruitment. A big recruiting drive in 1930 brought in 6,197 new members, including the first big wave of Negro members, at 1,300. But turnover of Negro members was particularly high, and it took a few years before Negro membership rose above 1,000. Chicago was particularly effective in recruiting Negro members; New York lagged. In May 1935, the party reported 2,227 Negro members, 8 percent of the party membership at the time. Among recruits, 15 percent were blacks. This was the pattern of Negro recruitment into the party for many years. The party steadily recruited about twice as many Negro members as the rolls showed at any time. In a big recruiting drive in 1938, it was announced that 2,890 (17 percent of all new recruits) were Negro and that the Negro membership of the party was 5,000. Yet, in 1942, the party still had only 3,200 Negro members, about 7 percent of total membership. It is doubtful that the Negro membership ever rose much above this percentage. The party made continuous efforts to recruit and retain blacks. It aimed at a high percentage of blacks at its conventions as delegates, committee chairs,

James Ford, Communist Party vice-presidential nominee, 1936 (*California State University–San Bernardino*)

and national standing committee members. Nonetheless, it failed to achieve a high percentage of black members at any time.

A 1953 study by the FBI determined that of the 5,395 "leading members of the Communist Party," 411 were black, about 8 percent of the leadership. While a sizable proportion (about their proportion of the total population), it was not "high." Still, no other predominantly white party or, indeed, any social movement in the United States, had that percentage of blacks among its leadership. The party faced a difficulty in reaching out to blacks, cited by analysts of the party and recognized in its official organs as well—the attitudes of many of its members. This problem was called the "sin" of **white chauvinism**.

Throughout the 1920s, the party struggled with the white chauvinism issue. There was feuding in its day-to-day operations at the local branch level to carry over a biracial pattern. In the mid-1920s the party tried, for a time, to organize separate black and white unions, such as the American Negro Labor Congress. In 1925 it approved a program that went beyond the labor question to cover the broad field of black rights in all aspects.

The Congress failed to attract a mass following among blacks. A major lesson to be learned from both the Sanhedrin and the congress was that the Negro question could not be relegated to a separate compartment, even if placed in the hands of black Communists.

In the mid-1930s, the party launched a new strategy and effort—the United Front phase. The American Communist Party decided it could work with middle-class black reform groups. It sought to work with unions and organizations like the NAACP and the National Negro Congress. During this phase it made a significant contribution to the cause of African-American liberation through its success in helping to influence organized labor to open its ranks to blacks. The party transformed the Trade Union Educational League into the Trade Union Unity League (TUUL). Its task was to create a trade union center that could unite all revolutionary unions, minority groups, and individual militants, and to infiltrate the "reformist" unions against the AFL bureaucracy.

The Popular Front period of communism (1936–1938) saw the party infiltrate the institutions and organizations of the New Deal, and it allied itself with local political groups, with the Socialist Party, the American Labor Party, the Farmer–Labor Party, and the like. While in none of these efforts was it dominant, it did become a significant force. Its greatest success during the period of the Popular Front was in the newly formed CIO unions, which at one time had 60 Communists among 200 full-time organizers. This phase not only represented a shift in strategy, it was a period when the party itself changed in its composition. As Nathan Glazer noted: "During the thirties, the party was transformed from a largely working-class organization to one that was one-half middle-class. . . . In 1938, the breakdown of the occupations of a large group of new recruits (17,000) showed 22 percent in middle-class categories. In 1941, no less than 44 percent of the party was reported as professional and white collar" (p. 114).

What success the Popular Front policy had can be attributed to its leader, Earl Browder. In the election of 1940, the Communist Party ticket of Earl Browder for president and James Ford for vice-president garnered only 46,251 votes, but he was an effective proponent of the Popular Front line. In the Popular Front era, while working cooperatively with other groups, especially the union movement and particularly the CIO, the party enjoyed some success and access that until then had eluded all its efforts. Glazer describes some very human aspects of that development:

> Let us not forget a simple fact that some historians of American communism do tend to forget; communists, even communist leaders, remain human beings—often enough fanatical, often enough with moral sensibilities coarsened, but, still, human beings susceptible to the desires and needs that most of us experience. A second-level party leader who had been section organizer, say, in Cleveland during the early thirties and had led demonstrations that brought him stitches in his head and months in jail, might now find it exceedingly pleasant to be leading a party that had opened an attractive headquarters, enjoyed good relations with local politicians and trade-union leaders, and could attract seven or eight thousand people to a rally when Earl Browder came to Cleveland. A section organizer in Harlem, where the Party had counted a mere straggle of comrades during the early thirties, might now find it decidedly pleasant to be able to reach Adam Clayton Powell on the phone whenever he chose, to enroll hundreds of new black members, and to lure a brilliant array of Harlem talent when the party ran a big social event. An old, battered activist could now feel a sense of growing authority in heading, say, a large Massachusetts local of the electrical workers' union, or a local of the California maritime workers' union, sheltered within the CIO and favored, more or less, by John L. Lewis. As for the top union leaders who belonged or were close to the Communist Party, men like Julius Emspak, Joseph Curran, Harry Bridges, and Mike Quill—they were starting to enjoy the taste of real power. They were negotiating contracts that covered thousands of members; were disposing of significant sums of money (some of it drained off to the party and its front groups); were dealing and wheeling with other union leaders and political figures who wanted their support. Respectability, comfort, secretaries, good salaries, docile staffs, admiring followers—all came together to soften and allure. (pp. 100–101)

The radical change in membership in the party from old-line, working-class radicals to middle-class and lower professional workers contributed to a new phase that appealed to blacks by purging its members of the "sin" of white chauvinism, and by selecting a black, James Ford, as its vice-presidential nominee.

Earl Browder led the party into the early 1940s in a revisionist phase he called "organized capitalism," and by 1944 the party reached its peak in official membership. In the 1944 convention, Foster claimed 80,000 members, about 14 percent of whom were blacks. He claimed they became about 33 percent of the party by 1945 (Glazer 1961, 146–47).

In 1940, A. Philip Randolph, then the Democratic Socialist president of the National Negro Congress, resigned over the peace resolution passed that year. His resignation was a turning point in the development of the black protest movement since it turned one of the most effective and charismatic protest leaders into an uncompromising anti-Communist. His call for a March on Washington, even though cancelled, was important in that it foreshadowed the growth of the more militant, nonviolent civil rights movement of the post World War II era from which the Communists were excluded. When the Communist Party savaged Randolph, its image among African Americans suffered greatly.

The party line, and its appeal, held only while the United States and the Soviet Union were allies against Nazism during World War II. After the war, the rise of the Iron Curtain, and the Cold War, the Communist Party in the United States shifted its line yet again. William Foster opposed Browder, and the party expelled Browder in 1946, adopting a stronger leftist line and developing new leadership. The party underwent critical self-evaluation, again focused to a great degree on the Negro question. Harry Haywood published his book, *Negro Liberation,* and the party went through another phase of rooting out white chauvinism.

In 1948, the Communist Party backed the Progressive Party and its nomination of Henry Wallace for president (against Harry Truman). Wallace's campaign was supposedly controlled by the Communist Party, which is a major reason why the NAACP would not be associated with it, and why black "revolutionary antagonists" like W. E. B. Du Bois and Paul Robeson were attracted to it (Wynn, 1955). The Progressive Party aggressively sought, yet failed to achieve, a significant black vote, winning less than 14 percent of the votes in Harlem.

Paul Robeson was the expatriate black artist and avowed Communist who had returned from France to the United States in 1939 to fight fascism. He created the Council on African Affairs. It was labeled as a subversive organization and placed on the U.S. attorney general's list of such organizations after the war. W. E. B. Du Bois was a former NAACP leader who increasingly moved to the left in the 1940s. In 1950 he was indicted for "failure to register as an agent of a foreign principal" (i.e., Moscow) for his work with another Communist front group, the Peace Information Center. He was tried on those charges in November 1951 but was acquitted.

In July 1948, twelve members of the Communist Party, including William Foster and Eugene Dennis, were indicted for violation of the Alien Registration Law of 1940, better known as the Smith Act. They were convicted and sentenced to five years in prison and fined $10,000 each. The Federal Court of Appeals affirmed those convictions in 1951, and the U.S. Supreme Court upheld them in October 1951. After the Supreme Court decision, the FBI arrested many other Communists, announcing that it had "43,000 communists under surveillance." It used the McCarren Walter Act of 1952 to deport foreign-born Communists.

In terms of its appeal to blacks, the American Communist Party staggered into the postwar era with a number of handicaps. Due to its party line shifts and its attacks

"It's OK—we're hunting Communists." (From *Herblock Special Report* [W.W. Norton, 1974]. Reprinted by permission of the Herb Block Foundation.)

on the NAACP and Randolph's March on Washington, it was seen as less militant than those organizations. Its position on "self-determination for the black belt," restored to party prominence by Harry Haywood, was rejected by an increasingly urbanized black population that during the war had moved to the urban industrial North in a mass migration that then made the black belt strategy seem unreal. The failure of all but a tiny minority of blacks to vote for the Progressive Party in 1948 showed clearly that the party carried little weight in the black community.

The foreign-language members of the party shared in its general postwar decline, although at a slower pace. Being more isolated, socially, linguistically, and by age, from the mainstream of American public opinion, their rate of defection from the party was slower. Some clung to the party in fear, since many had belonged to the International Workers Order and other such organizations judged to be subversive in the 1950s. Others had never become citizens and were being deported or feared deportation and separation from their families. The party characterized itself as the defender of the rights of the foreign-born. By the 1950s, the foreign-language groups had little to offer the party. They were aged and no longer dominated the work force, having declined in size and proportion to those working in heavy industry. Their sole virtue for the party was that they were faithful, but that faithfulness was greatly taxed by developments in the mid-1950s.

The Communist Party made a strong appeal to white ethnics, especially from South, Central, and East European countries, and it had a small degree of success in attracting membership from those groups. These were the members who dominated the party and its cadres throughout its history in America. Party membership, nonetheless, was never more than a tiny percentage of those foreign-born, at its height never more

Box 7.3   *BIO-SKETCH OF ANGELA DAVIS (1944–)*

●

Angela Davis was born in January, 1944, in Birmingham, Alabama, the youngest child of Frank and Sallye Davis. Her father owned a gas station and her mother was a school teacher, so the family was comfortable financially, living in a middle-class area of Birmingham. Her mother taught her reading, writing, and arithmetic before she entered school.

While in elementary school, she joined her mother in civil rights demonstrations. In high school she became an organizer. At age fifteen, on an American Friends Service Scholarship, Davis moved to New York to attend a progressive private school, the Elizabeth Irwin High School. A proverbial "hotbed of radicals," the school's faculty were persons often blacklisted from other public schools for their leftist political beliefs. Davis was ready to be a radical herself and she joined Advance, a Marxist-Leninist group. She entered Brandeis University where she excelled academically and spent her junior year at the Sorbonne in Paris. There her political activity increased to an intense level.

In 1963, four girls whom Davis had known were killed in a Birmingham church bombing attributed to the Klan, and Davis's radicalism became personal. In her senior year she studied under philosopher Herbert Marcuse. His belief in the responsibility of the individual to rebel against injustice profoundly affected Davis. She graduated from Brandeis in 1965 with a degree in French and left the United States to study philosophy in Europe. At Goethe University in Frankfurt she joined a socialist student group to protest the Vietnam War. Davis returned to the states in 1967, to study further under Marcuse, who was then at the University of California at San Diego. She immediately became active in the civil rights movement there. She attended a workshop sponsored by the Student Nonviolent Coordinating Committee (SNCC) in Los Angeles where she met Kendra and Franklin Alexander, Black Panther members also active in SNCC and in the Communist Party. She joined the Party and in 1969 traveled to Cuba.

In 1969, with a Master's degree and courses toward a Ph.D. completed, Davis was hired to teach philosophy at UCLA. She was a popular teacher but her Communist Party membership was revealed and the UCLA board of regents and then-governor Ronald Reagan fired her. She challenged the dismissal in court and won. After she was reinstated, her classes were monitored as the board of regents sought a way to fire her. She became more involved with the Black Panthers, especially with prison inmates, whom she viewed as prisoners of class war. She joined the cause of the "Soledad Brothers." Speeches she gave in their defense, along with her lack of a doctorate, led the board of regents to deny her a new contract.

In 1970, when a gun registered to her was used by her friend Jonathan Jackson in a Marin County Courthouse shootout that resulted in the death of two prisoners, a judge, and Jackson himself, Davis went underground. The professor of philosophy whose crime consisted of owning a gun used in a crime was placed on the FBI's ten-most-wanted list. Charged by California with kidnapping, conspiracy, and murder, she was captured in New York after two months underground and put in jail without bail. A "Free Angela" movement erupted, the slogan appearing on urban walls, bumper stickers, and in newspapers. Her face appeared on posters and T-shirts. In February of 1972 she was released on $102,000 bail. At her subsequent trial she was acquitted of all charges. Governor Reagan and the board of regents voted that she would never be employed to teach at a university supported by the state of California.

Davis went on writing and lecturing extensively, remaining politically active. She ran for vice president of the United States in 1980 and again in 1984 on the Communist Party ticket. Her books

Box 7.3, CONTINUED

·

include *If They Came in the Morning* (1971), *Women, Race, and Class* (1983), *Women, Culture, and Politics* (1989), and her best-selling autobiography *Angela Davis: An Autobiography* (1988).

Sources: Bio-sketch by author, information from Jack Salzman, ed., *African American History* (New York: Simon & Schuster, 1996), 233–234; http://www.speakersandartists.org/People/AngelaDavis.html; http://search.eb.com/blackhistory/micro/161/4.html.

than tens of thousands among tens of millions. Likewise was the case of its appeal to black Americans. In the late 1960s and early 1970s, the Marxist-Leninist perspective would again inform the thinking of a few black radicals, as we shall see more fully in Chapter 8. It was a major element in the ideology of the Black Panther Party, for instance; but with the conspicuous exception of Angela Davis, no prominent black activist or black intellectual formally affiliated with the remnant of the diehard loyalists that were the American Communist Party after 1960. (See Box 7.3.)

FASCISM

Our last example of old-style radicalism appealing to ethnic minorities in the United States is fascism, whose appeal was limited to three white ethnic target groups: Italians, Germans, and white Russians. This section briefly examines Italian fascism and German Nazism.

The Italian Fascist movement was launched in Italy in 1919 (Magil and Stevens, 1938; Salvemini, 1977). It had the support of industrialists and stressed government policy that favored big business. It endorsed and relied on a totalitarian method of ruling society. As in Nazi Germany, Italian Fascists glorified war and adopted an expansionist foreign policy.

In America, fascism arose after World War I, responding to the economic dislocations of the postwar economy, particularly the Great Depression. In October 1922, after Mussolini came to power in Italy, his government established a Secretariat General of the Fasci Abroad to use consuls of the foreign office to spread fascism abroad. It targeted particularly the huge Italian population in the United States (some 5 million immigrants by then). In 1923, it entrusted the fascio of New York with acting as the central fascio of the Italian **fasci** (fascist organization) in North America.

The director of the Bureau of Italians Abroad, who later served as a consul of the Italian government to the United States, described its tactics:

> The Bureau of Italians Abroad, faithful to the directions by which the Duce wanted to reattach the Italian Communities abroad to the life of our nation, has devised new instruments and sharpened and perfected those already on hand. Each Fascio abroad . . . is a center of the faith that has . . . put Italy back on the map among the peoples of the world. The Fascist Regime has increased the number and scope of the Italian schools abroad. . . . Lectures in the Italian language in foreign universities and regular courses in Italian language for foreigners not only help to spread our language and culture, but fan the spark of Fascist thought in the modern world. (Salvemini 1977, 190)

The bureau worked with the Dante Alighieri Society to coordinate action. It used a foreign section of the National Union of Discharged Officers to create and maintain a bond of national and military solidarity among the ex-officers to be intimately united to the Fascist fatherland. Through its propaganda, the Bureau for Italians Abroad coordinated the tools to keep alive in the communities of emigrants love for the fatherland and faith in the Fascist regime, and to stress the achievements of Fascist Italy. The bureau maintained strict watch over the Italian newspapers. Orators were sent from Rome to inspire fellow Italians, bring them support, and maintain ties to Italy. The Bureau of the Consuls organized annual celebrations like the birthday of fascism, the March on Rome, and Victory Day in Italian communities abroad, with orators selected by and sent from Rome. It organized group excursions of Italian émigrés to Italy, published school textbooks, purposely edited, illustrated, and printed for Italian schools abroad.

The Bureau of the Consuls immediately began to infiltrate the many Italian-American organizations in the United States. The **Order of the Sons of Italy** was first established in New York in 1914, with 316 lodges. By 1918, it had grown to 590 lodges and a membership of 125,000. By 1924, in New York alone, it had 1,110 lodges with 160,000 members and claimed a nationwide membership of 300,000. After Mussolini came to power, his government financially backed its growth (Salvemini 1977). Giovanni Di Silvestro, a "Venerable" of the Sons of Italy, declared in 1922 that the "Order of the Sons of Italy is today a Fascio for the safety of Italy and America." He remained a pillar of fascism in the United States until 1935, when he suddenly left the Order under suspicion of having embezzled funds.

From 1922 to 1923, the Italian fascio of New York directed all of the Fascist movements in the United States. By 1923, however, it became clear that the directors in New York were incapable of coping with the multiplying local fasci. The national directorate of the Fascist Party in Italy dissolved the Fascio of New York and reorganized it. It delegated control of the Fascist organizations all over North America to the eleven-member Fascist Central Council (Salvemini 1977, 52).

In July, 1925 the Fascist League of North America set up subordinate organizations like the Court of Discipline, a Central Committee for Press and Propaganda, and a Nationalist Fascist Party in the United States. It began publishing *Il Carrocio*. The directorate of the League was appointed from Rome and it clearly acted as an agent of the Fascist government. It soon was publishing several daily newspapers, such as *Progresso Italo-Americano, Il Bulletino della Sera,* and *Il Corriere d'America.* It published two weekly newspapers, *Nuova Italia,* and the *Bulletin of the Fascist League of America,* and several monthly magazines: *Il Grido, Grido della Stripe, Giovinessa, Il Vittoriale, Italia Madre, L'Italia Nostra,* and *Noi.*

The Fascist League and its successor, the Lictor Federation, created organizations or infiltrated established organizations to promote the Fascist movement, such as the Fascist Italian Union, the Italian War Veterans Federation, the Italian Chamber of Commerce, the Italian Historical Society of Rhode Island, the New York Fascio Benito Mussolini, the Fascist Association of Italian Journalists, the Yearbook of Italian Press, the Order of the Sons of Italy, the Dante Alighieri Society, the Victor Emmanuel III Foundation, the Fascist Longshoremen Federation of North America, the Italian Medical Association, the Italy-America Society, and the Black Shirts. All became sources of Fascist propoganda in America.

The triumphal year for fascism in America was 1929, when the movement had grown beyond the capabilities of the Fascist League of North America to direct it, and it was disbanded and replaced by the Lictor Federation. The league claimed 12,000 members in 1929, although that claim was probably exaggerated. The Sons of Italy claimed 300,000 at the time, when their actual number was closer to 150,000.

The Black Shirts youth organization first appeared in New York City in July 1923. By 1927, at their Brooklyn meeting, they were 2,000 strong. By the late 1930s, anti-Fascists Salvemini and Girolamo Valenti reported to the U.S. Congress, in a hearing before the Un-American Activities Committee, on a decade-long study of Fascist activities abroad. Valenti produced a briefcase of documents and affidavits proving that Italian consular officials were intimidating Italian Americans reluctant to go along with the Fascist party line. Valenti told the committee:

> Italian-American Black Shirt legions, 10,000 strong, are marching in America with the same resounding tread as those of the goose-stepping detachments of German-American Bund storm troopers. Behind this Black Shirt parade are more than 100,000 Americans of Italian descent who are willing to be seen at the public manifestations of some 200 Fascist organizations throughout the United States. . . . Another 100,000 fall within the influence of the powerful organs of propaganda emanating from well-knit and centralized fascistic forces that are mind-conditioning American citizens and swerving their allegiance to Italian dictatorship under the thumping fist of Mussolini. (Salvemini 1977, xxxiii; see also MacDonnell 1995, 75–76, "The Italian Fifth Column")

The appeal of fascism, particularly after the post–World War I economic dislocations and the Great Depression, went beyond Italian Americans. By the 1930s, a number of "American" organizations developed or took on increasingly fascist tones. In 1932, an openly Fascist magazine, *The American Guard*, was launched by the Swastika Press. Terrorist organizations like the Black Legion, the White Legion, the White Crusaders, and the Knights of the White Camelia joined the revived Ku Klux Klan as reactionary groups composed mostly of native-born whites. These groups claimed membership in the thousands, even to 10,000 members (MacDonnell 1995, 45–46). Other American groups supporting the Fascist line were the Liberty League, the Friends of New Germany (FONG), the Silver Shirts, the Sentinels of the Republic, and the Southern Committee to Uphold the Constitution. American-born Lawrence Dennis became the theoretician of American fascism, and Father Charles Coughlin, characterized as an American version of Paul Goebbels, Hitler's propagandist, established the National Union for Social Justice, openly preaching a Fascist message (MacDonnell 1995, 34–38; 45–46). Nor was Father Coughlin the only such Christian demagogue to espouse fascism. In 1939 a small ultra-reactionary group splintered off from the Christian Front and formed the Christian Mobilizers, an extreme anti-Semite group led by Joseph McWilliams, whom radio commentator Walter Winchell colorfully labeled, "Joe McNazi." Similarly, the Reverend Gerald Winrod led the Defenders of Christian Faith, who in 1932 organized a paramilitary organization, the Khaki Shirts (MacDonnell 1995, 38–39).

In 1934, the Liberty League was founded, backed by the DuPonts, Lloyds, Mellons, and other wealthy businessmen. The Sentinels of the Republic, founded in 1922, was an anti-Semitic organization revived in the 1930s with the financial backing of the Liberty League. The Crusaders, founded in 1929, were organized along pseudo-military lines, with a "national commander," "battalions," and "battalion commanders."

In 1935, the Farmer's Independence Council, an extreme right group appealing to farmers, was formed.

The Ku Klux Klan, revived in 1915, grew from a few thousand to several million members nationwide by 1932. The Black Legion used terrorism and had an estimated 40,000 members in Michigan in 1931. The Silver Shirts, begun in Asheville, North Carolina, by William Dudley Pelley, blended anti-Semitism and anti-black sentiment into a Nazi-inspired terrorist group (MacDonnell 1995, 45–46). He became a leading fascist pamphleteer. Pelley embodied the blending of race appeal and political ideology with religious fervor. Box 7.4 presents his bio-sketch.

The Reverends Coughlin and Gerald Smith used demagoguery during the 1936 election campaign. As described by A. B. Magil and Henry Stevens:

> The anti-New Deal diatribes of the Hearst press were mild in comparison [to] two men of God, Father Coughlin and Reverend Gerald Smith. Smith is a truly remarkable rabble-rouser, and during the campaign he ripened his fascism by adding those ingredients that Huey Long had lacked: extreme national chauvinism, anti-Semitism and, above all, Red-baiting. His and Coughlin's speeches had a bloodthirstiness reminiscent of the days when Hitler was promising that the heads of the Weimer Republic "Marxists" would roll in the sand. . . . A United Press dispatch of September 25, 1936 quoted [Coughlin] as saying: "When any upstart dictator in the United States succeeds in making this a one-party form of government, when the ballot is useless, I shall have the courage to stand up and advocate the use of bullets." Since Coughlin and his Liberty League allies had already discovered the "dictator" occupying the White House, his meaning was clear. The statement shocked the country and was undoubtedly instrumental in losing many votes for Lemke (p. 190). Father Coughlin had secretly backed the formation of a third party movement, the Union Party, which ran the populist congressman, and former Republican, from North Dakota, William Lemke. (MacDonnell 1995, 36–37)

By 1930, German and Italian Fascist movements linked several organizations designed to promote fascism, notably the American National Socialist Leagues, the Friends of New Germany, and the U.S. Fascists. Russian "White Guard" fascism was the target of the National Revolutionary Fascist Party, begun by a naturalized American citizen, Anatase Vonsiatsky. Avowedly Fascist organizations worked through English-speaking front organizations serving as "transmission belts" to the broader American culture and society. Prominent among those from the Italian Fascist movement were the Italy-America Society, the Institute of Italian Culture, and the Italian Historical Society.

During the Great Depression, influential American politicians adopted a demagogic approach, promoting an extreme right wing ideology as the way to solve the ills of American society. Most notable were Huey Long, former governor and then U.S. Senator from Louisiana; Francis Townsend, whose "economic reform" movement claimed 3 and one-half million followers; and Theodore Bilbo. Indeed, Senator David Reed (R–PA), known as the "Mellon Man," an acknowledged spokesman for big business, announced on the floor of the Senate that "if this country ever needed a Mussolini, it needs one now." Demarest Lloyd, a wealthy businessman and financial supporter of the Liberty League, published in his magazine, *Affairs,* a call for Congress to abdicate to a small group of "patriotic men" (i.e., the American Fascist Party) (Magil and Stevens 1938, 79).

The early 1930s witnessed an assault on civil liberties and democratic rights. Growing numbers of workers and farmers were driven to loudly demand relief, and government

Box 7.4   *BIO-SKETCH OF WILLIAM DUDLEY PELLEY*

Born in March of 1890 in Massachusetts, William Dudley Pelley was raised as a son of a Southern Methodist minister who went on to become a leading American Fascist and founder of the Silver Legion.

Pelley grew up in poverty and was largely self-educated. He soon honed his writing skills, however, and by World War I had traveled extensively and published articles in national publications, serving as a foreign correspondent in Europe and Asia, and especially in Russia where he developed a deep hatred for communism and Jews.

Pelley returned to the states in 1920 and began writing for the film industry, producing numerous screen plays. He also became a popular novelist. He nearly died in 1928 and had an "out-of-body" experience and began writing metaphysical pamphlets.

When the Great Depression began in 1929, Pelley turned to politics and moved to Asheville, North Carolina where he founded Galahad College in 1932, which specialized in correspondence, "Social Metaphysics," and "Christian economics." He founded Galahad Press which published political and metaphysical texts and magazines, newspapers, and books. In 1933, when Hitler seized power in Germany, Pelley formed a political movement and began the Silver Legion (also known as the Silver Shirts and "Christian Patriots"), named for their Nazi-like silver uniforms. The Legion had a scarlet L emblazoned on its flags and uniforms and Pelley founded chapters in virtually every state.

He traveled extensively about the country in the 1930s, orchestrating mass rallies, lectures, and public speeches attempting to attract followers to his organization and converts to his political ideology of anti-Communism, anti-Semitism, extreme patriotism, and isolationism in foreign policy. Pelley viciously opposed Franklin Roosevelt and the New Deal and in 1936 he founded the Christian Party and ran for president. In 1940 his Asheville headquarters was raided by federal marshals and some of his followers were arrested and his property seized. He was called to testify before the House Un-American Activities Committee and charged with tax evasion. Despite these setbacks, Pelley continued to oppose the Roosevelt Administration and its strained foreign policy relations with Germany and Japan.

The 1941 attack on Pearl Harbor led to the immediate collapse of the Silver Legion. Pelley continued to attack Roosevelt in a new magazine, *Roll Call*. Pelley was arrested, charged with treason and sedition in April, 1942, and after a bitter public trial, sentenced to 15 years in prison. He remained in prison until 1950, when his family and friends raised enough money to mount an appeal. He was paroled in 1951 on condition that he never engage in political activity. He returned to Noblesville where he founded Soulcraft Press and began publishing metaphysical and political magazines and books, served as something of a cult leader, supposedly channeling spiritual revelations from "higher intelligences." He continued writing against Roosevelt and his legacy and espoused virulent anti-UN, pro-segregation, and anti-Semitic political publications. Security fraud charges were brought against him while he lived in Asheville, but before any trial he died, in Noblesville, on July 1, 1965 at age 75.

Source: bio-sketch by author from information in http://en.wikipedia.org/wiki/William_Dudley_Pelley, accessed 3/22/2007.

authorities increasingly resorted to force in dealing with such demonstrations. In scores of cities, unemployment demonstrations were broken up with police bullets and tear gas. Armed troops were sent out against strikers. Negro sharecroppers attempting to organize unions were hunted down, and hundreds were lynched. Waves of aliens were deported. State governments revived old criminal syndicalism and sedition statutes, and professional patriots clamored for new repressive laws.

Italian-American fascism reached its peak of activity during 1933–1934, when Mussolini appointed Antonio Grossardi the Italian consul general. Under his auspices, Fascist celebrations and demonstrations increased rapidly in number, size, and significance. The movement was especially active in trying to influence U.S. foreign policy vis-à-vis Italy. As did the party in Italy, the Fascist Party in the United States created a dual hierarchy of party and government officials and leaders to direct efforts to influence U.S. policy and politics.

Ambassadors, consuls, and consular agents, as official representatives of the Italian government, were bound by rules of diplomatic behavior. The secretaries of the fasci, although also representatives of the Fascist regime, had no diplomatic character, and were free to carry on activities forbidden to the former. The abnormal situation of the fasci in America and in all foreign countries, consisted precisely in the fact that, according to the law of the countries where the fasci were established, they were only private associations, whereas according to the Italian law they were organs of the Fascist regime . . . their constitutions were dictated by the head of the Italian government, and they had as their basic duty, "obedience to the Duce and to Fascist law." (Salvemini 1977, 61)

There was an anti-Fascist movement in the Italian-American community, most notably the Mazzini Society, created by Gaetano Salvemini; serious opposition to fascism also formed within the labor union movement. But this was by no means a cohesive and unified resistance. As early as 1923, various radicals of Communist, Socialist, syndicalist, and anarchist persuasion formed the Anti-Fascist Alliance of North America (AFANA). It was supported by the New York Federation of Labor, Amalgamated Clothing Workers of America (ACWA), and the International Ladies' Garment Workers Union.

In 1925, Frank Ballanco of the ACWA and Girolamo Valenti launched *Il Nuovo Mondo,* a daily newspaper aimed at reconciling the divisive factions with the anti-Fascist left. Efforts to create a unified front proved unsuccessful, and by 1926, the Socialist-liberal elements split from AFANA and created the Anti-Fascist Federation for the Freedom of Italy.

The turning point for the Fascist movement in the United States came with the Italio-Ethiopian war. Until late 1935 and early 1936, the Fascists controlled a majority of Italian-American organizations, as discussed earlier. With Italy's invasion of Ethiopia, however, Mussolini lost America in a few weeks, and all the prestige he had managed to build up over the many years of Fascist propaganda was dissipated. The movement managed to hold a few huge demonstrations in early 1936, and the Fascists claimed allegiance of 250,000 members in all of their various organizations in 1936, but by the fall of that year the movement was clearly dying.

The American people did not take the road of Father Coughlin in the 1936 elections. Nor did they take the road of communism since this was not an issue in the balloting, despite the strenuous efforts of Coughlin, Hearst, and the Liberty Leaguers to identify Roosevelt and every progressive idea with communism. The American people indicated unmistakably their rejection of all that the Coughlin-Hearst-Liberty League crowd represented and their desire to retire Father Coughlin permanently from political life. In place of the 9,000,000 votes that the radio priest had, in the height of self-intoxication, promised personally to deliver for Lemke, the latter received a total of only 891,858 and did not carry a single state. Four days after the election, Coughlin, in a nationwide broadcast, announced his retirement acknowledging that more than 90 percent of his own followers had deserted him on election day (Magil and Stevens 1938, 191).

The 1936 election showed dramatically the decline of fascism's appeal in the United States. After World War II it was ended completely.

As long as Mussolini remained nonbelligerent and no clash with the policies of the United States seemed possible, the Fascist-pacifist attitude could be maintained without undue difficulty. The end of Mussolini's non-belligerency, the harsh condemnation uttered by President Roosevelt against him, and the consent given by the overwhelming majority in this country to the president's judgment, brought about a serious dislocation in Fascist activities (Salvemini 1977, 245).

After Pearl Harbor, when the United States entered the war against the Axis Powers, Italian-American fascism was finished as a viable political ideology that could appeal to Americans of Italian descent. By early in the war, military necessity forced the Germans into Italy and Mussolini was seen as a mere flunky of Hitler. Italy became, in fact, occupied German territory.

Nazism

As Italian fascism sought to develop a mass movement among Italian immigrants, the Nazi movement appealed to German immigrants, white Russian immigrants, and their American-born children. Since there were more immigrants to the United States from Germany than from any other single nation (in 1910 an estimated 10 million, of whom about 2.5 million were foreign-born), its potential was enormous (MacDonnell 1995, 21). As with fascism, however, Nazism's appeal was short-lived and never very successful. It was quickly seen as a mere tool of a foreign power (Higham 1985).

The potential for political power by appealing to rather substantial ethnic groups lay not only on its size, but also on its existing ethnic-based organizational array. German Americans were joiners: "German Americans formed themselves into a wide-range of social, charitable, and civic organizations. In 1914, the German American Central Alliance was the largest of these organizations in the country" (MacDonnell 1995, 22).

The largest and most influential Nazi organization in the United States was the German-American Bund. It began in July 1933 as the Association of the Friends of New Germany. Working with the United German Societies of Chicago and of New York, it was re-formed as the German-American Bund in 1936, under Fritz Kuhn, a naturalized citizen born in Munich in 1896. He was soon replaced by Gerhardt Kunze, a Nazi spy. White Russians formed a significant part of the Bund in a section headed by James Wheeler-Hill, who, despite his decidedly non-Slavic name, was a white Russian. In 1936, the FBI reported the membership of the Bund at 8,000 (MacDonnell: 42–45). Through the Bund, parties were held on German steamships while they were in U.S. ports, where German Americans were wined and dined and addressed by representatives of various Nazi organizations. Hitler followed Mussolini's example by creating a Foreign Division of the National Socialist Party (Gau Ausland) under its director, Ernst Wilhelm Rohle. Its official purpose was to bring all those of German citizenship living outside Germany into the ranks of the National Socialist Party. The Nazi government took over the League of German Societies Abroad, established in 1892, to promote cultural relations between Germany and other countries, and fashioned it into an agency of propaganda. This organization, and a number of others, were coordinated into the League for Germans Abroad, which sought allegiance among all so-called "Volksgenossen," or racial comrades. Stuttgart was officially designated as the city of foreign Germans. Annual conventions held there attracted 70,000 or more persons from all over Europe and America.

Various other agencies of the German government, the Student Exchange Service, the Academic Exchange Service, and lecture bureaus and travel organizations established German racial groups devoted to the interests of the German Reich. German newspapers in the United States were supplied with free news services, German schools with free educational materials, and German radio listeners with special short-wave broadcasts. This propaganda was directed toward one goal: to instill in the American citizen of German descent a consciousness of the German "race" and a feeling of allegiance toward the German Reich.

The Bund faced a problem in appealing to German Americans or even to their parents who were German immigrants, however, in that so many had come to America to escape the very totalitarianism that the Bund was peddling. The Nazi movement quickly established organizations to appeal to German-American youth. The Brown Shirts began a summer camp for youth, Camp Hindenberg, in Grafton, Wisconsin. Others were set up outside Philadelphia, in Detroit, and on Long Island. Children attending the camps were taught to regard Hitler as their leader and to believe that the principles of government espoused by him were superior to those of the democratic American government.

The Nazis worked with and financially supported America First, a propaganda campaign to keep the United States out of the war in Europe. The FBI, however, immediately infiltrated the Nazi movement and began tracking it. Frederich Aughagen, a Nazi agent who was arrested in September 1941, testified that America First was an agency of the German government. FBI Director J. Edgar Hoover agreed. The Detroit headquarters of Henry Ford and Father Coughlin were the center of the activities of the America First campaign, which by 1941 had a membership list of 25,000 names. Henry Ford and James D. Mooney, then chairman of General Motors, were so valued for their work with America First that they were awarded the Order of Merit of the Golden Eagle by Adolf Hitler himself.

German propagandists in America sought to soothe public opinion and encourage isolationism. They established the German Library of Information as a front to promote an isolationist line. More significantly, they used a German agent, George Sylvester Viereck, who was a press officer with the German embassy, to secretly manage the pro-Nazi and anti-British U.S. senator from Minnesota, Ernest Lundeen. He was under the direct pay of the Nazis who used his free mailing privileges as a member of Congress to distribute isolationist propaganda financed directly by the German embassy. Lundeen served as chair of the Make Europe Pay Its War Debts Committee, which insisted that Great Britain and France pay their World War I debt to the United States. His ideas and articles were published by a German propaganda publisher, Flanders Hill, as part of a Nazi conspiracy to infiltrate and influence Capitol Hill.

The most strongly Fascist intellectual in the pro-Nazi American movement was Lawrence Dennis, a U.S. Department of State employee and close friend of Senator Burton K. Wheeler, U.S. senator from Montana. Dennis wrote the book *The Coming American Fascism*. The American Nazi movement promoted the cause of Major General George Van Horn Moseley for president as the "solution to America's problems," and briefly attempted to launch him as a candidate to oppose Roosevelt. For his role in the "Capitol Hill conspiracy," Dennis and twenty-seven others working for the government were indicted, in July 1942, on sedition charges.

Using front organizations, Nazi propaganda was published through various outlets. Through the German-American Alliance of Chicago, the party put out a Nazi paper, *Free American*. It also regularly fed information to the flagrantly Nazi magazine *Social Justice*, published by Father Charles Coughlin. In it, Father Coughlin recommended that the United States become a "fascist corporate state" in which democracy would be perfected. A regular contributor was "Leon Hamilton," whose real name was Father Jean Baptiste Duffee. Duffee was the contact between Father Coughlin and Boris Brasal, the white Russian forger who was the true author of the "Protocols of the Learned Elders of Zion." This famed anti-Semitic forgery was reprinted in *Social Justice* and was widely circulated through the publishing house of William Dudley Pelley, the leader of the Gestapo-like Silver Shirts.

Another Nazi front organization, the American Fellowship Forum, established the magazine *Today's Challenge*. It regularly published the writings of Charles Lindbergh and members of America First. These propaganda efforts were directed by several Nazi agents: George Sylvester Viereck, Manfred Zapp, Hans Thomsen, and Friedrich Aughagen.

The Bund was badly damaged by events in Europe. Krystallnacht, the "Night of the Broken Glass," when Nazis looted and destroyed Jewish temples, proved a disaster for Fritz Kuhn, the Bund's head. He continued to organize public displays, even after the German government had ordered him to downplay such activity. On February 22, 1939, George Washington's birthday, he organized the "single most striking display of Nazism in the history of the United States": a huge rally at Madison Square Garden in New York City, which 22,000 people attended. Kuhn's self-indulgence led the Nazi government to have him replaced. They exposed him for misappropriation of Bund funds, and in December 1939 he was sent to Sing Sing prison for two and a half years for embezzlement.

In 1938 the Federal Bureau of Investigation uncovered a substantial Nazi spy ring in a celebrated case known as the Rumrich Spy Case (MacDonnell 1995, 49–61). It exposed Nazi foreign intelligence operatives serving as spies, and many of their American allies, a number of whom were connected to the German-American Bund.

In 1939, after the German invasion of Poland, the Nazi occupation force found files in the Warsaw office of the Polish Foreign Ministry clearly indicating that President Roosevelt intended to push the United States into World War II against the Axis and on the side of the Allies. The German government published the documents in a "White Book" designed to undercut President Roosevelt's re-election in 1940. The report of the German Foreign Office was published throughout the world and caused an immediate sensation. The White Book showed conclusively that the American president planned to bring the country into the war at a time when the majority of the population, and of the Congress, supported peace and neutrality. Roosevelt denounced the documents as forgeries, as did Secretary of State Cordell Hull. The Nazis also leaked embarrassing documents and statements by Joseph Kennedy, then ambassador to the Court of St. James. In early 1940, the German charge d'affairs, Hans Thomsen, leaked the documents to the press through pro-Nazi publishers like Ralph Strassburger, owner of the *Norristown Times Herald*. The leaks, however, failed to impede Roosevelt's re-election.

The German-American Bund formally dissolved itself on December 8, 1941, the day after the Pearl Harbor attack (MacDonnell 1995, 45). When the United States declared war against Japan and Germany, the FBI swept up and arrested many German spies. It uncovered plots to kill President Roosevelt and the king and queen of England. The bureau linked John Koos, a Ukrainian white Russian who worked for Henry Ford, to a Ukrainian terrorist group in Detroit, connecting them to Father Coughlin and Marion Stevens Vonsiatsky, wife of a white Russian count who was a financial supporter of America First. It arrested Lucy Boehmler, an American woman who was a Nazi spy and had smuggled, through the Nazis to Japan, the secret U.S. defense plans and installations for Pearl Harbor.

World War II completely ended Nazi influence in the United States as a political movement to appeal to German Americans. By 1943, America First was discredited and could do little more than express its annoyance with the war.

In the 1960s, a brief neo-Nazi political movement, led by the "sixties Führer," George Lincoln Rockwell, surfaced in reaction to the civil rights movement. Today, neo-Nazi skinheads carry on the tradition, but the movement is small and largely an expression of anti-black racism rather than a fully Fascist political ideology. Officially known as the National Socialist Movement, it is the largest Nazi Party in the U.S. today, led by Commander Jeff Schoep.

SUMMARY

This chapter examined the approach of old-style radicalism. Sometimes racial and ethnic groups reject the value system of the dominant society and seek to replace its values with their own. The chapter focused on three such cases, the radical ideological "isms": socialism, communism, and fascism in both the Italian and German inspired movements. The cases showed the limited appeal of these radical political ideologies among the racial and ethnic minority groups they targeted.

Socialism attempted to win over a mass following primarily among ethnic groups comprising white Euro-Americans, particularly those immigrants who came from Scandinavia and from South, Central, and Eastern Europe. Developing in the late 1800s, the Socialist movement in America peaked in the American Socialist Party during the 1912 election, when Eugene Debs attracted 6 percent of the total vote cast in the presidential election, when the party elected over 1,000 local officials, and when the party's official membership exceeded 100,000.

Socialism failed to attract a true mass following in part because of the basic conservatism of the very immigrants it was trying to organize and because of its own internal factionalism and tendency to schism. By the end of the 1920s, socialism ceased to be a significant political movement. Although it lost its electoral battles, in a sense it won its war in that, subsequently, Progressive and liberal Democratic Party reforms enacted most of its proposals for reform. Many of its values have become part of the American political mainstream.

Communism arose in the 1920s. Like the Socialist movement from which it emerged, it targeted immigrants from South, Central, and Eastern Europe and native-born Americans who were involved in the radical industrial union movement. It aggressively sought to win a mass following among black Americans. As with socialism, communism failed to win over any significant following among its targeted groups due to their basic cultural, economic, and religious conservatism. It failed to develop a good organizational base from which to work with blacks. Its reliance on ethnic foreign-language associations to reach white Euro Americans foundered on factionalism, schism, and bewildering shifts in tactical approaches following the changing party line of the Communist Internationale. The Communist Party never achieved even half the size of the Socialist Party. It was suppressed and simply withered away by the 1950s.

Fascism was a movement of even shorter duration, existing in America only during the inter-war years (1920–1945). Italian fascism appealed to Italian immigrants and Italian Americans. Nazism worked with white Russians and Germans. Fascism never overcame its image of being the mere tool of a foreign power and never attracted more than 1 to 5 percent of its targeted groups. Fascism and Nazism died out with the entrance of the United States into World War II.

KEY TERMS

African Blood Brotherhood (ABB)   A radical black organization that had strong Communist Party ties in the 1920s.

fasci   Plural for Fascist; persons who adhered to the Fascist ideology.

"Negro question"   Term used by the Communist Party as to how best to appeal to American Negroes and what the appropriate role of blacks was in the United States.

Order of the Sons of Italy   The largest Italian-American ethnic organization, strongly infiltrated by the Fascists during the 1920s and 1930s.

Sanhedrin   The All-Race Assembly, a conference held in Chicago in 1924.

Sewer Socialists   The German Socialists of Milwaukee who won local office by stressing practical political reforms and services.

Sharecropper's Union of Alabama   A failed attempt by the Communist Party to win support of rural blacks in the South during the 1930s.

white chauvinism   A "sin" within the Communist Party during the late 1930s and 1940s in which white ethnic Communist members were opposed to working closely and equally with black Communist members.

Wobblies   Members of the radical industrial union, the International Workers of the World (IWW).

REVIEW QUESTIONS

1. Describe the struggles among competing factions that characterized the earliest stages of socialism in the United States.
2. Discuss the reforms advocated by the Socialist Eugene Debs that eventually became accepted as mainstream American policy. Why did they fail to win widespread support in the 1920s?
3. Describe the factors over which the Socialist Party split.

4. What white Euro-American ethnic groups were the strongest foreign-language components of the Socialist and the Communist parties of America?

5. Discuss three major reasons why the Communist Party, despite vigorous efforts, failed to win significant support among black Americans.

6. What was the peak or triumphal year for fascism in America? Why did it have appeal at that time?

7. Name three prominent American national elected officials who became associated with the American Fascist movement.

8. What event proved to be the turning point leading to the decline of the American Fascist movement?

9. Discuss the American industrialists prominently allied with the American Nazi movement. What organizations and media outlets did they found or use to spread Nazi propaganda?

10. Among the three major "isms" discussed in this chapter, socialist groups have achieved a greater degree of civic incorporation. What evidence from the chapter can you cite to substantiate that assessment?

NOTES

1. For in-depth discussions of socialism and other radical movements in the United States, see Aveling and Moore (1969), Foster (1952), and O'Neal and Warner (1947).

2. Eugene Debs was the Socialist Party's presidential candidate in 1900, 1904, 1908, 1912, and 1920. He declined to run in 1916, instead making a failed attempt to be elected to Congress.

3. See Brommel (1978), Constantine (1995), and Tussey (1970) on Debs.

4. See Ford (1938), Foster (1952), Frederickson (1955, 201); Glazer (1961, 173–74); and Record (1951).

5. For this assessment, see also Aveling and Moore (1969), Buhle (1987), Foster (1952), and O'Neal and Warner (1947).

ADDITIONAL READINGS

Cannistraro, Philip, and Gerald Meyer, eds. *The Lost World of Italian American Radicalism.* Westport, CT: Praeger Press, 2003.

Constantine, J. Robert, ed. *Gentle Rebel: Letters of Eugene V. Debs.* Urbana and Chicago: University of Illinois Press, 1995.

Foner, Philip S., and Herbert Shapiro, eds. *American Communism and Black Americans: A Documentary History, 1930–1934.* Philadelphia, PA: Temple University Press, 1991.

George, John, and Laird Wilcox. *Nazis, Communists, Klansmen and Others on the Fringe: Political Extremism in America.* New York: Prometheus Books, 1992.

Judd, Richard W. *Socialist Cities: Municipal Politics and the Grass Roots of American Socialism.* New York: State University of New York Press, 1989.

Lipset, Seymour Martin and Gary Marks. *It Didn't Happen Here: Why Socialism Failed in the United States.* New York: W.W. Norton, 2000.

Record, Wilson. *The Negro and the Communist Party.* Chapel Hill: University of North Carolina Press, 1951.

Salvemini, Gaetano. *Italian Fascist Activities in the United States.* New York: Center for Migration Studies, 1977.

Schonback, Morris. *Native American Fascism During the 1930s and 1940s: A Study of Its Roots, Its Growth and Its Decline.* New York: Garland Press, 1985.

Solomon, Mark. *The Cry Was Unity: Communism and African Americans, 1917–1936.* Jackson: University Press of Mississippi, 1998.

• *Reading 7.1*

The Communist Party
and the Scottsboro Defense

Perhaps the most effective instrument employed by the Communist Party in its Negro program during the 1928–1934 period was the International Labor Defense (ILD). This organization had not been widely known among Negroes or whites until its participation in the famed Scottsboro cases, beginning in 1931. The Scottsboro trials grew out of the indictment of nine Negro youths for the alleged rape of two white women (who were later shown to be of unsavory repute) on a freight train bound from Chattanooga to Huntsville, Alabama, in late March of 1931.

The chances for a fair trial, always slim for Negroes in Alabama, in this instance were practically nonexistent. The NAACP quickly intervened in the case, and its attorneys were assigned to handle the defense. During the first trial the Party and the ILD carried on an intensive propaganda campaign in which southern injustice and the ineptness of the NAACP defense were the principal themes. As the trial neared its close, the ILD in New York addressed a telegram to the presiding judge in which it advised him that he would be held "personally responsible unless the defendants were immediately released." The boys were summarily convicted, and eight were given the death sentence. Then began the first of a long series of appeals to the higher courts.

While the appeals were pending the ILD sent its representatives to the parents of the condemned boys and persuaded them that the ILD rather than the NAACP should thereafter handle the cases. This maneuver, perhaps more than any other act of the Communists, indicated the contempt in which they held the moderate organizations; it indicated also the extent to which the Party was willing to go in obtaining participation in trials of such obvious propagandistic value. "It was a sorry spectacle," said Henry Lee Moon—the scramble of the Communists to wrest the defense of the hapless boys from the control of the NAACP. To accomplish this end the whole propaganda machinery of the party was turned loose in a campaign to discredit the Association's leadership. Stunned by the violence of this attack, not only upon the principles and policies of their organization, but also upon their personal integrity, the leaders of the NAACP were bewildered and in the end relinquished the defense to the ILD. The Communists maintained that legal defense had to be supplemented by international propaganda. American consulates, legations, and embassies were picketed and stoned in many parts of the world. Mass meetings of protest were held in the capitals of Europe and Latin America at which resolutions demanding the freedom of the Scottsboro boys were passed. Letters, telegrams, and cablegrams poured in upon the president of the United States, the governor of Alabama, the presiding judge, and other state officials, demanding the immediate release of the boys. This propaganda was effective in exposing the hypocrisy of American justice, but it did not gain the freedom of the boys. Only after it had ceased was a compromise effected that resulted in the release of four of the accused.

Having withdrawn from the case, the NAACP had nothing further to do with the Scottsboro matter until 1935. At this time, with the ILD facing failure in its efforts to obtain the freedom of the defendants, and with the new line of cooperation having been laid down to the Party and the ILD by the Communist International, the Communists agreed to share the case with the NAACP and other organizations; out of this grew a new Scottsboro defense committee. Among the participating organizations were the American Civil Liberties Union, Methodist Federation for Social Service, League for Industrial Democracy, Church League for Industrial Democracy, and the National Urban League, the latter in an advisory capacity.

During some four years in which the ILD had almost exclusive control of the Scottsboro defense, it widely employed the technique of "mass pressure" described earlier. The general position of the Party among Negroes was undoubtedly strengthened as a result, although it is highly doubtful whether its efforts were of any direct benefit to the defendants in the case. Scottsboro was not only publicized by the Communists among Negroes in the United States but, because of the ILD's connections with Communist agencies throughout the world, it became a global *cause célèbre*. In the fundraising campaigns and at the protest rallies staged from San Francisco to New York, the ILD had an excellent opportunity to explain its larger program and the Communist cause to Negroes. "To the Communists," said Henry Lee Moon, "the whole campaign was much more than a defense of nine unfortunate lads. It was an attack upon the system that had exploited them, fostered the poverty and ignorance in which they were reared, and finally victimized them by legal proceedings that were a mockery of justice. It was a case made to order for the Communists and well worth the scramble they made for the privilege of representing the defendants. They made the most of it."

For the Communist Party no intrinsic issues of justice were involved. It viewed the Negroes as victims of a capitalist economic order and the courts as one of its institutional extensions. The Scottsboro victims could be liberated only by an effective challenge to the economic order outside the limits of the regular judicial process. It is significant, however, that the ILD retained exceptionally able lawyers to handle the actual court proceedings. But basically, the Communists regarded Scottsboro as only a steppingstone for organizing the unemployed, recruiting Negro workers and sharecroppers, and building a mass Communist organization among colored Americans.*

Scottsboro had values for the Party outside the propaganda field; one of these values could be expressed in cash. How many of the thousands of dollars raised by the ILD, the Communist Party, and other Communist organizations involved with the Scottsboro defendants actually went for defending them we have no way of knowing. The Party's ideological bookkeeping was frequently confused with the more regular forms of financial accounting. A thousand dollars raised for the Scottsboro boys' defense could be just as legitimately spent for pamphlets advocating self-determination for Negroes in the Black Belt as for the payment of lawyers' fees. And we have no way of estimating how much of these funds were used for activities having an even remoter connection with the Scottsboro case.

*Ford, for example, as late as 1935 declared: "Properly brought forward not by liberal humanitarian methods, but as a support to the struggles of the working class, the correctness of our fight for Scottsboro can be shown to even the most backward worker. Similarly, among liberal groups who still believe in democracy and civil rights, support will be gained when the fight for Scottsboro is presented as inseparably bound up with the rights of the Negro people and the maintenance of civil rights. Scottsboro is bound up with the national liberation of the Negro people and with the struggle of the entire American working class for the dictatorship of the proletariat—Soviet Power." (James W. Ford, "The United Front in the Field of Negro Work," *Communist* 14, no. 2, February 1935: 174)

Such statements as the above indicated also the confusion within Party ranks concerning the pursuit of revolutionary as opposed to united front objectives during the first phase of the 1934–1939 period.

The Party also reaped an organizational windfall from the case. It attempted to follow up protest and fundraising meetings with the building of local branches of the Communist Party and the Young Communist League. Party functionaries were instructed to employ the Scottsboro trials as a means for building Communist strength in the various communities. It was possible to get a hearing in the name of Scottsboro when a reference to self-determination would have been hooted down or tolerated in stony silence. The Party was aware of the organizational implications of the case, even if few other organizations were.

In trying to pass final judgment on the role of the Communists and the ILD in the Scottsboro case from the standpoint of their effectiveness in obtaining legal justice for the defendants, we are involved largely in speculation. It is not possible to predict what would have happened had the ILD not intervened, or, having intervened, if it had not attempted to employ the technique of mass pressure. The extremes of complete exoneration or the death penalty were possible; where the verdict would have come to rest between these two poles is a conjectural matter. How effective the propaganda campaign of the Party was in influencing the courts we have no way of knowing.

Source: C. Wilson Record, *The Negro and the Communist Party,* pp. 86–88. Copyright © 1951 by the University of North Carolina Press. Used by permission of the publisher.

CHAPTER 8

— • ● • —

NEW-STYLE RADICALISM

Some racial and ethnic minority groups reject the values and norms of the majority society and seek to change them by radically altering the majority's culture. Chapter 7 discussed groups with a radical ideology who sought to bring about change by the standard tactic of electoral politics. They pursued a tactic of "third party" movements. This chapter examines groups seeking to change majority society values through radical political behavior, which may range from nonviolent civil disobedience to the use of radical rhetoric and even to physical violence. This strategy is illustrated by discussing the black, brown, and red power movements of the late 1950s through the early 1970s, and by the newer protest groups of the 1980s and of today.

Proponents of radical politics used different tactics to reach their goal of resistance and protest aimed at drastically altering public policy. Among the earliest advocates of this strategy was W. E. B. Du Bois, a historian and sociologist at Atlanta University. In 1905, he and a small group of African-American intellectuals met in Niagara Falls, Canada. The Niagara movement rejected moderation and compromise. Instead, it called for radical change that would end African-American inferior status, loss of voting rights (disenfranchisement), Jim Crow laws, segregated schools, inhumane conditions in southern prisons, denial of equal job opportunities, and segregation of African Americans in the federal armed forces. Out of this meeting came the establishment, on February 12, 1909, the one-hundredth anniversary of Lincoln's birth, of the National Association for the Advancement of Colored People (NAACP). It has led various campaigns to establish African-American rights through legal action. In 1915, it achieved its first major victory in one of hundreds of cases pursued at all levels of government when the U.S. Supreme Court declared unconstitutional the grandfather clause of the Oklahoma state constitution.

THE MODERN BLACK CIVIL RIGHTS MOVEMENT

In many respects the modern black civil rights movement grew out of events precipitated by World War II.[1] Black soldiers served in the war, especially after President Harry Truman integrated the armed forces by Executive Order 9981 in 1948. When they came back from the war they were unwilling to accept the status of the pre-war years. During the war, large numbers of blacks moved north to work in industry and jobs opened up by the war effort. Blacks from the south experienced a lifestyle of far less severe racial discrimination and segregation. They would no longer meekly accept Jim Crowism.

By 1940, a host of black organizations united to demand full and equal service in the military, and to end discrimination in employment in the defense industries. A planned March on Washington signaled a change in black protest thought and strategy. In early 1941, A. Philip Randolph issued a call and began plans for 10,000 Negroes to march on the nation's capital to demand their rights. The march was conceived as an all-black action by and for the black masses. Reflecting the bottom-up approach, it anticipated the black protest actions of the 1950s and 1960s. The march was canceled when President Franklin Roosevelt established a federal Fair Employment Practices Commission in 1941. A. Philip Randolph accepted that compromise in achieving their goals. The ideals and idea of the march were neither lost nor forgotten, and it inspired the March on Washington held in 1963.

Bayard Rustin, a follower and confidant of Randolph, served in 1941, as the youth director for the march. He had been a communist youth organizer in New York in the late 1930s. Rustin broke with the communists after Pearl Harbor, in 1941, and became a stern critic of them the rest of his life, although his affiliation with them came back to haunt him and the civil rights movement in the early 1960s (Anderson, 1998, 263).

In 1943, Randolph began to plan a campaign of civil disobedience, following the Gandhi movement in India, to expressly attack segregation and discrimination in the northern states. The Congress of Racial Equality (CORE), founded in 1942–1943, grew out of a pacifist organization, the Fellowship of Reconciliation. Its founder was James Farmer, a black Louisianan. Combining the nonviolent, direct-action techniques of Gandhi with the sit-down strikes of the 1930s, it developed the "sit-in." CORE concentrated on attacking discrimination in places of public accommodation. It engaged in its first sit-ins in 1943, using the tactic against a segregated restaurant in Chicago. In 1947, it sponsored a "journey of reconciliation," a forerunner to the freedom rides of 1961. The integrated bus trip through the upper South tested compliance with a decision, *Morgan v. Virginia* (1946) that had banned segregation in interstate transportation. The sit-in tactics of the 1940s were used in the north and typically by the youth of the movement like Bayard Rustin and Ella Baker. In the 1960s, they would inspire the youth of the movement then to use this tactic in the segregated South to great effect despite deadly violence against them.

The black civil rights movement was propelled forward by the 1954 Supreme Court decision, *Brown v. Board of Education of Topeka, Kansas,* in which the NAACP won its greatest legal battle against de jure (by law) segregation when the Court finally overturned the separate-but-equal doctrine of *Plessy v. Ferguson* (1896). Where *Plessy* had established a constitutional principle that served to underpin Jim Crowism and the pervasive use of de jure segregation, *Brown* gave constitutional blessing to the effort and

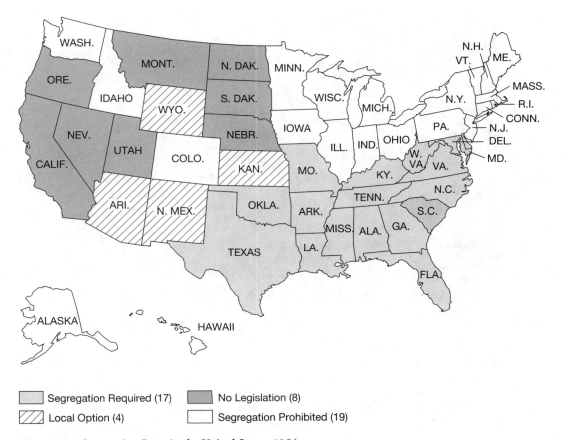

	Segregation Required (17)		No Legislation (8)
	Local Option (4)		Segregation Prohibited (19)

Figure 8.1   Segregation Laws in the United States, 1954
Source: Thomas R. Dye, *Understanding Public Policy,* 9th ed. © 1998 by Prentice-Hall, Inc. Reprinted by permission.

policy of racial desegregation. *Brown* failed to be immediately enforced, and little practical change resulted from it. It would take more than a decision by the nine justices of the Supreme Court to seriously alter the norms, values, and institutionalized racism of a nation. It would take a truly national mass movement (Schaefer 1998, 204). Figure 8.1 presents a map of the United States showing the segregated states, the local segregated states, and the non-segregated states as of 1954, which were overturned by the *Brown* decision.

The direct-action approach ignited a truly national mass movement with the 1955–1956 bus boycott in Montgomery, Alabama. The protest action was precipitated in early December 1955, when Mrs. Rosa Parks, a 43-year-old black seamstress, refused a bus driver's order to give up her seat to a white man. She had been ejected several times before for refusing to obey the Alabama segregation ordinance requiring that blacks give up their seats to whites when ordered to do so by a white bus driver. This ordinance enacted provisions of a 1945 Alabama state law requiring the Alabama Public Service Commission to enforce racially segregated seating on all bus companies

Rosa Parks (*Courtesy of the Library of Congress*)

under its jurisdiction. Mrs. Parks was arrested, charged with breaking the law, and fined $14. Box 8.1 presents her bio-sketch and her impact on the civil rights movement. The bus boycott ensued, and the Reverend Dr. Martin Luther King Jr. emerged as a national figure. His organization, the Southern Christian Leadership Conference (SCLC), which he began in 1957, moved to the forefront of the civil rights movement.

Nonviolent, direct-action protest became a popular tactic to fight segregation across the nation. Its most effective use was in the South against de jure segregation. The 1960s saw new groups and leaders emerge. In April 1960, the Student Nonviolent Coordinating Committee (SNCC) was organized in Raleigh, North Carolina. This group of militant college students was organized by Ella Baker, a tough-minded, hard-drinking NAACP activist with a leftist past. She was the inspiration, in 1960, for founding the SNCC at her alma mater, Shaw University, in Raleigh, North Carolina. SNCC led the first sit-ins in the South, in Greensboro, North Carolina, in 1960. The college youth of SNCC became known as the "shock troops" of the civil rights movement (Levine 2000, 84–85; 96, 123). A similarly militant group, the Congress of Racial Equality (CORE) began its freedom rides into Alabama and Mississippi in 1961.

The Montgomery bus boycott was launched when Mrs. Jo Ann Robinson, an English teacher at Alabama State College, an active member of the Dexter Avenue Baptist Church, and president of the Women's Political Council, a local black women's organization founded in 1946, and Edgar Nixon, president of the local chapter of the International Brotherhood of Sleeping Car Porters and a leading force in the Montgomery chapter of the NAACP, activated a group of black ministers to form the Montgomery Improvement Association (MIA) to direct and coordinate what became a 382-day boycott of the City Lines bus company. The city's black churches united behind the boycott,

BOX 8.1
BIO-SKETCH OF ROSA PARKS

Born Rosa Louise McCauley in February, 1913 in Tuskegee, Alabama, Rosa Parks came from a poor family and humble background, yet she went on to become an icon of the civil rights movement and the first woman ever to lie in state in the capitol rotunda, an honor normally used for Presidents of the United States. The United States Congress recognized her as the "Mother of the Modern-Day Civil Rights Movement." Her father was a carpenter and her mother a grade school teacher. When her parents separated, Rosa and her mother moved to the Montgomery area and she grew up on a farm with her maternal grandparents. She was a life-long member of the African Methodist Episcopal Church (AME.), was home-schooled by her mother, and, as a teenager, at the Industrial School for Girls in Montgomery (a facility burned twice by arsonists) although she had to drop out before graduating with a high school degree to care first for her grandmother, then for her ailing mother.

At the time, Jim Crow laws segregated all aspects of life for blacks, including public transportation. Indeed, as she was growing up in the highly segregated Montgomery area she experienced the Ku Klux Klan marches in front of her house, so the blatant racism was impossible to ignore. In 1932 she married Raymond Parks, a local barber and an active member of the National Association for the Advancement of Colored People (NAACP). Raymond had actively raised funds for the Scottsboro Boys, a group of black men falsely accused of raping two white women. Rosa worked several jobs, including domestic work and as a hospital aide. She finished her high school studies in 1933, when only about 7% of African Americans had a high school diploma. A feisty woman, despite Jim Crow laws making it so difficult to accomplish, Rosa Parks managed to register to vote on her third try.

Rosa joined the NAACP in 1943, and went on to serve as the Montgomery chapter's secretary. In 1944 she worked for a time at Maxwell Air Force Base where the trolley was integrated, an experience she noted as "opening her eyes up." A Montgomery municipal ordinance stipulated the first four rows of bus seats were reserved for whites, and buses had a "colored" section beginning from the back of the bus. These sections were not fixed, however, and the conductors could move the "colored section" sign depending on the number of riders. Generally, about 75 percent of the public bus riders were African American. The law prohibited black people from sitting across the aisle from white people. When the whites filled the first four rows, additional white passengers moved toward the middle section, and the bus driver or conductor ordered black passengers to move to the back or stand to vacate rows of seats for the whites.

On December 1, 1955, after a long day of work at the Montgomery Fair department store, Parks took a bus home and was sitting in the first row of seats designated for blacks. When the whites-only seats filled and two or three white men were standing, the conductor, James F. Blake, ordered four blacks to vacate their seats and stand in the back of the bus. Three black men complied, but Rosa Parks refused. Blake called a police officer who arrested Parks for violation of Chapter 6 of the segregation law of the Montgomery City code. She spent the night in jail before being bailed out by some NAACP staff, and was fined $10 plus $4 in court costs.

The NAACP announced a bus boycott at the Mt. Zion AME church, and a front-page story in *The Montgomery Advertiser* helped spread the word. A number of church leaders formed the Montgomery Improvement Association (MIA) which came to be led by Dr. Martin Luther King Jr. They distributed 35,000 leaflets promoting the boycott. Some 40,000 black commuters car-pooled or walked to work, some as far as 20 miles. The boycott lasted 382 days. Some segregationists responded with violence—bombing or burning black churches and the homes of Dr. King, Rev. Ralph Abernathy,

Box 8.1, CONTINUED

and E. D. Nixon. The boycott, however, led to Dr. King's founding the Southern Christian Leader-ship Conference and moving to the forefront of the Civil Rights Movement.

On November 13, 1956 the United States Supreme Court declared the bus segregation laws (Title 48, Code of Alabama, and sections 10 and 11 of Chapter 6 of the Code of the City of Montgomery) unconstitutional (applying the precedent of *Brown v. Board of Education*). The court order arrived in Montgomery on December 20, 1956, and the bus boycott ended the next day. The ruling was greeted with white snipers firing on buses, and into King's home, and several churches and the homes of black ministers were bombed, including those of Dr. King and Rev. Abernathy. Rosa lost her job with the department store, and her husband was forced to quit his job, and the Parks moved to Hampton, Virginia in 1957, and then moved on to Detroit.

Rosa worked as a seamstress until 1965 when she joined the staff, as a secretary/receptionist, of U.S. Representative John Conyers. She worked for Conyers until she retired in 1988. In 1992 she wrote *Rosa Parks: My Story*, an autobiography. In 1995 she published her memoirs, *Quiet Strength*, detail-ing the role her faith played in her life.

As an icon of the Civil Rights Movement, Rosa Parks received many honors late in her life. In 1979 the NAACP gave her its highest honor, the Spingarn Medal, and in 1980, the Martin Luther King Award. She was inducted into the Michigan Women's Hall of Fame in 1983. She received the Rosa Parks Peace Prize in Stockholm, in 1994. In 1996, President Clinton presented her the Presidential Medal of Freedom, the highest honor bestowed by the Executive Branch. In 1998 the National Under-ground Railroad Freedom Center named her as the first recipient of the International Freedom Con-ductor Award. In 1999 the United States Congress awarded her its highest honor, the Congressional Gold Medal. *Time* magazine hailed her as one of the 20 most influential and iconic figures of the twentieth century. In 2000, Alabama awarded her the Alabama Academy of Honor and the first Gov-ernor's Medal of Honor for Extraordinary Courage.

Rosa Parks died on October 24, 2005. The U.S. Congress allowed her body to lie in honor in the U.S. Capitol Rotunda, the first woman, and the first black who had not been a government official, to be so honored. On October 30, 2005 President Bush ordered all flags to be flown at half-mast in her honor and memory. The Metro Transit of King County (Montgomery's bus line) placed stickers on the first forward facing seat of all its buses in her memory, and on the fiftieth anniversary of her arrest, President Bush directed that a statue of Parks be placed in the United States Capitol's National Statuary Hall.

Source: Bio-sketch by author, based on information from: *http://en.wikipedia.org/wiki/RosaParks*; and *http://www.achievement .org/autodoc/page/par0bio-1*accessed 3/27/2007.

providing crucial meeting places and fundraising efforts for a city that did not have a black-owned radio station or newspaper. The vast majority of the city's bus passengers were blacks, and the bus line stood to lose $3,000 a day in revenues, and the city its part of $20,000 a year in taxes from the bus line. Downtown merchants could antici-pate in excess of $1 million in lost sales if the boycott proved effective.

The MIA's demands were a modest modification of the city's bus segregation prac-tices. It asked only for concessions granted by other southern cities, notably by Baton

Rouge, Louisiana, two years earlier. It simply demanded seating on a first-come, first-served basis within segregated seating areas, greater courtesy from bus drivers, the hiring of black bus drivers for predominantly black routes, the seating of blacks from the back of the bus forward, and the seating of whites from the front of the bus backward, without a designated section always to be kept clear for each race. Dr. Martin Luther King Jr., then a 26-year-old minister who had arrived in Montgomery only a year before, was unanimously elected president of the MIA.

Montgomery's black churches became the organizational base for an elaborate carpool system for blacks who refused to use the bus line. King was arrested for an alleged speeding offense, and in January 1956 his home was bombed. A grand jury indicted 115 blacks for breaking a 1921 antilabor law by supporting the bus boycott. King continued to preach nonviolent civil disobedience and began to work closely with Dr. Ralph Abernathy, pastor of the First Baptist Church. According to King's own account, he was first alerted to the parallels between their bus boycott and Gandhi's strategy in India by a white woman, Miss Juliette Morgan. In a letter to the editor of the *Montgomery Advertizer*, she wrote:

> The Negroes of Montgomery seem to have taken a lesson from Gandhi—and our own Thoreau, who influenced Gandhi. Their task is greater than Gandhi's, however, for they have greater prejudice to overcome. One feels that history is being made in Montgomery these days. It is hard to imagine a soul so dead, a heart so hard, a vision so blinded and provincial as to not be moved with admiration at the quiet dignity, discipline and dedication with which the Negroes have conducted this boycott. (cited in White 1991, 121)

In 1956 a federal district court ruled that the city ordinance violated the U.S. Constitution. The boycott continued while the city appealed. The U.S. Supreme Court, in *Gales v. Browder*, declared Alabama's state and local laws upholding segregation on buses to be unconstitutional. The MIA prepared the black community for desegregation, urging them to behave courteously and to pray for guidance to commit to complete non-violence (White 1991, 121).

The desegregation order for Montgomery's buses led to retaliatory violence against blacks, including fire-bombing of Negro churches. Blacks did not respond to violence with violence. They accepted the MIA's approach of relying upon the power of moral suasion (Cross 1984, 47).

In 1957, King, Abernathy, and other black clergymen, with advice from Bayard Rustin and Stanley Levison, began the Southern Christian Leadership Conference (SCLC) (Levine 2000, 91–115). Its strategy was to use nonviolent protest throughout the South to oppose racial segregation in all its forms. Stanley Levison, an early adviser to Martin Luther King Jr., was a white, Jewish lawyer and an alleged Communist. He was the target of J. Edgar Hoover and the FBI's campaign to discredit King. Bayard Rustin was a black intellectual and man of letters, publisher of the Socialist magazine *Liberation*. An early and key adviser to Martin Luther King Jr., he was openly gay, and this caused much criticism for King's tolerance of homosexuals. The FBI also dredged up his earlier affiliation with the Communist Party, in an attempt to discredit King and the SCLC. Rustin's brief dalliance with the party in the late 1930s was like that of many young idealists of the time, and clearly inspired by their prominent role in the

Martin Luther King Jr. (*Courtesy of the Library of Congress*)

Scottsboro Case (Anderson 1998, 46). He was a member and organizer of the Young Communist League at City College in New York from 1938 to 1941, but he broke with the party in 1941, after the attack on Pearl Harbor and when the party leadership pressured him to cease his efforts to have the U.S. military desegregated. Rustin served time briefly in a federal prison, from March, 1944 to July, 1945, as a conscientious objector. His firmly held moral principles led him to refuse to cooperate with the draft (Levine 2000, 1).

Dr. King's nonviolent philosophy rested on six key principles: active resistance to evil, attempts to win over one's adversaries through understanding, attacking forces of evil rather than people, willingness to accept suffering without retaliation, refusing to hate one's opponent, and the conviction that the universe is on the side of justice.

King spoke in Washington, DC, in May 1957, joining other more prominent black leaders in a "Prayer Pilgrimage." He authored a book, *Stride Toward Freedom*, describing the Montgomery boycott and articulating his nonviolent civil disobedience philosophy. He was stabbed in 1959 by a deranged black woman, while signing copies of his book in a New York City bookstore. He travelled to India, visiting Gandhi's shrine. In November 1959 he resigned as pastor of the Dexter Avenue Church and moved to Atlanta to concentrate entirely on the SCLC movement.

In 1960 the sit-in tactic was pioneered at Greensboro, North Carolina, when a group of students from the Agricultural and Technical College sat in at a Woolworth's segregated lunch counter and demanded service. These sit-in demonstrations were soon followed by "wade-ins" at city swimming pools and segregated beaches, by "stand-ins" at segregated churches, and by the famous freedom rides on interstate buses. Students at Raleigh, North Carolina, led by Ella Baker, met in April 1960 and formed the Student Nonviolent Coordinating Committee (SNCC), an organization that King tried to shape in the image of the SCLC. The students accepted and used his nonviolent philosophy but, at Ella Baker's urging, they maintained a separate identity. They soon moved beyond King's cautious approach, which they considered too conciliatory and unrealistic.

SNCC sought to create a rationale for activism by adopting ideas from the Gandhian independence movement, from American traditions of pacifism, and from Christian idealism as formulated by the Congress of Racial Equality (CORE), Fellowship of Reconciliation (FOR), and Southern Christian Leadership Conference (SCLC). SNCC was less willing than other civil rights groups to impose its ideas on local black leaders or to restrain southern black militancy. As the shock troops of the civil rights movement, SNCC activists worked in areas, such as rural Mississippi, considered too dangerous by other organizations. SNCC developed a new phase when its members resolved their differences by addressing the need for black power and black consciousness, by separating themselves from white people, and by building black-controlled institutions. After his election as chairman of SNCC in May 1966, Stokely Carmichael popularized the organization's new separatist orientation. He and other workers, however, were less able to formulate a set of ideas that could unify blacks.

During the 1960 presidential campaign, when King was given a four-month prison sentence for an alleged driving offense in Georgia, Democratic candidate Senator John F. Kennedy intervened and won his early release. In gratitude, Martin Luther King, Sr. quietly backed the senator and urged blacks to support him. Kennedy narrowly won; his 68 percent of the black vote provided a crucial margin in that victory. President Kennedy, however, was slow to push civil rights. In 1961, CORE sponsored a series of freedom rides into the South to test compliance with the Supreme Court's decision on desegregating interstate travel. They were met with violence in Alabama and Mississippi. CORE's and SNCC's more militant tactics drew King into the fray as he attempted to regain leadership of the civil rights coalition.

From winter 1961 to summer 1962, King led a mass direct-action campaign in Albany, Georgia, to integrate its public facilities and its police department. The campaign stalled, in part due to the rivalry among SNCC, SCLC, and local black leadership. James Foreman, of SNCC, did not want King in Albany, believing it should be a grass-roots-led campaign. King was arrested and jailed, but later released. The local police chief wisely did not use violence against protesters, avoiding media exposure and possible federal intervention. Attorneys for the city secured a federal court injunction halting the demonstration for ten days, draining momentum from the demonstrations. The city closed its parks rather than integrate them. When the library was integrated, the city simply removed all its chairs. The Albany campaign failed, although King and SCLC learned valuable lessons from it.

King's next campaign, in Birmingham, Alabama, in 1962–1963, was better organized and conducted. New staff members were brought in who had practical experience in voter registration drives and freedom rides. They made the organization more effective and efficient. They and King realized that protest was an effective tactic only if it elicited brutality and oppression from the white power structure, creating what King called "creative tension." Attacks by whites on peaceful, nonviolent protesters attracted media coverage, resulting in national outrage and federal intervention.

The South's major industrial city, Birmingham, was a fortress of racial segregation pledged to resist change. Eugene "Bull" Connor exercised total power and had earlier closed city parks rather than integrate them. Seventeen black churches and homes of civil rights leaders had been bombed and no arrests made. Local college students began a boycott of Birmingham stores and staged sit-ins at segregated restaurants. King and SCLC were invited to direct the campaign. They issued three demands: integration of lunch counters, fitting rooms, rest rooms, and drinking fountains in department stores; increased hiring of blacks in the local labor market; and the creation of a biracial committee to work out a timetable to desegregate other areas of the city.

Boycotts, sit-ins, and street demonstrations were used in Birmingham. King was arrested and jailed and not allowed to contact a SCLC lawyer. President Kennedy intervened again. King's activities were harshly criticized by a group of eight local white clergymen, describing him as an outsider and extremist. King's response was to write what became the classic statement and an eloquent justification of civil disobedience and use of nonviolent protest. (See a summary of his famous "Letter from a Birmingham Jail" in the reading at the end of Chapter 8.) His "Letter" is both an emotional and a philosophical explanation for the strategy of new-style radicalism. Summarizing why racial and ethnic groups might be compelled to use civil disobedience, it moves the reader to see how such attempts to awaken the conscience of a nation can be a powerful means of effective protest politics. It evokes themes King used in his famous "I Have a Dream" speech in 1963.

Released, King left Birmingham while the protest continued. Hundreds of black schoolchildren were used in direct confrontation with white authorities. Bull Connor met them with fire hoses, police dogs, clubs, and electric cattle prods. Over 20,000 persons participated in Birmingham's demonstrations. Many were arrested and jailed. Ten lost their lives. Thirty-five homes and churches were bombed. Reports by the national press and television shocked the nation. Bull Connor was viewed as a bigot, and the federal government sent in Burke Marshall, head of the Civil Rights Division of the Justice Department, to negotiate a settlement with the city. Only some SCLC goals were met, and King was criticized for accepting the compromises. The Birmingham case illustrates well the difficulty of sustaining a nonviolent protest effort.

Before his assassination, President Kennedy, prodded by the Birmingham demonstrations, introduced sweeping civil rights legislation to the Congress. The Birmingham campaign put King back into the leadership of the civil rights coalition. In August 1963, the various national civil rights groups organized a March on Washington. An estimated quarter-million people, some 20 percent of whom were white, converged on the nation's capital to demand passage of the civil rights bill. During the march King delivered, from the steps of the Lincoln Memorial, his "I Have a Dream" speech, now widely considered one of the greatest speeches of the twentieth century.

Bayard Rustin was an important leader in organizing the August 28, 1963, March on Washington. He took A. Philip Randolph's dream of 1941 and helped bring it to successful fruition in 1963. Another leader and follower of Dr. Martin Luther King Jr., Andrew Young described the importance of the March on Washington as follows: "The March transformed what had been a Southern movement into a national movement that helped to achieve the Civil Rights Act of 1964 and the Voting Rights Act of 1965" (in Anderson 1998, 263).

The FBI undertook a campaign of spying, wiretapping, and disinformation designed to discredit King, but it failed to dissuade or discredit him. In 1964, King made the cover of *Time* magazine when he was awarded the Nobel Peace Prize.

SCLC launched a protest campaign in St. Augustine, Florida. The local campaign ended in stalemate, but the SCLC leadership believed it pushed President Lyndon Johnson to secure enactment of the 1964 Civil Rights Act, the most sweeping civil rights law ever passed by the Congress. The "Freedom Project," a voter registration drive in Mississippi, was directed by a coalition of SNCC, CORE, NAACP, and SCLC. It challenged the all-white Mississippi delegation to the Democratic National Convention. President Johnson refused to allow the "Freedom Democrats" voting rights at the convention, but negotiated a compromise covering future conventions and allowing two Freedom Democrats to sit in the convention as delegates-at-large with full voting rights. King and SCLC, Roy Wilkins and NAACP, James Farmer and CORE, and Bayard Rustin all favored accepting the compromise. SNCC, angered by the treatment of the Mississippi Freedom Democratic Party (MFDP), increasingly drew away from King and SCLC, viewing them as too conservative. In 1965, however, SCLC joined CORE and SNCC in a voter registration drive in Selma, Alabama.

King led a march from Selma to Montgomery, drawing national media attention. SNCC leadership was upset with King's refusal to break through a police barricade. His presence dramatized an already violent confrontation. Sheriff James Clark was provoked into violence against the demonstrators on "Bloody Sunday," at the Edmund Pettis Bridge, where demonstrators were tear-gassed and beaten by mounted police. C. T. Vivian of SCLC had been publicly assaulted by Clark, and the murder of a white Unitarian minister, James Reeb, by Selma whites moved President Johnson to call Congress into special session to enact a new voting rights bill.

A federal court approved the Selma-to-Montgomery march, and President Johnson activated the Alabama state militia to protect the procession. On March 25, 1965, Dr. King spoke to a crowd of 25,000 from the capital steps in Montgomery, bringing the civil rights movement back to the scene of the bus boycott a decade earlier. The Selma march culminated the civil rights movement in the South and was King's finest hour. President Johnson signed the Voting Rights Act into law on August 6—a direct result of the Selma campaign.

The 1964 and 1965 laws resulted in a dramatic closing of the gap between black and white voter turnout. The Civil Rights Acts of 1964 and 1965 solidified black voting support for Democrats. Their support for Democratic presidential candidates remained in the 82 percent to 94 percent range from the 1960s into the new century, even as that party's white coalition weakened and fell.

Passage of the 1964 and 1965 acts meant only the end of de jure (by law) segregation, not of de facto (by custom) segregation. Racial separation and inequality continued. Black leaders, aware of the discrepancy between what had been accomplished regarding legal discrimination and the lack of improvement in the day-to-day lives of blacks, increasingly shifted their focus to the Northeast and Midwest. In 1966, King led SCLC demonstrations in Chicago, attempting to end its status as the "most segregated city in America." The Reverend Jesse Jackson launched "Operation Breadbasket," using consumer boycotts against white employers who practiced hiring discrimination. SCLC soon discovered its tactics did not transfer easily from the rural South to the urban North. Black ministers lacked the prestige they enjoyed in the South, and black churches were less efficient at organizing protests. Ill-prepared and inadequately briefed, SCLC workers were not even dressed for Chicago's harsh winters. Black street gangs rejected King's philosophy of nonviolent protest. The SCLC campaign achieved little and called King's philosophy, strategies, and leadership into question.

The growing split between SNCC and the SCLC deepened in 1966. James Meredith began his one-man "March Against Fear." When Meredith was shot, Martin Luther King of SCLC, Stokely Carmichael of SNCC, and Floyd McKissick of CORE finished his march. Carmichael's use of the slogan "black power" became a source of tension with King. He opposed use of the slogan because of its connotations of racial separatism and apparent acceptance of violence. In 1967, King began speaking out against the war in Vietnam, arousing hostile press commentary. The FBI intensified its surveillance of SCLC and of King.

In February 1968, black sanitation workers in Memphis, Tennessee, went on strike to win union recognition and improve working conditions. King viewed the strike as the beginning of a SCLC project, the "Poor People's Campaign." He went to Memphis in support of the strikers. On April 3, he delivered a speech to a small but enthusiastic audience, referring to the increasing number of threats made on his life. His speech became known as the "I've Been to the Mountaintop" address. On April 4, he was shot and killed by a white sniper on the balcony of his motel. His martyrdom touched off a wave of violence across the nation in which 20 people died. Following King's death, 300 black and white ministers marched on city hall in Memphis demanding recognition of the union. Local businessmen urged a settlement. The passage of the 1968 Civil Rights Act, incorporating a fair housing proposal, was eased through Congress in the period of sympathy King's assassination provoked. Eighteen years later, Dr. King was recognized as the only non-president and only the second citizen (George Washington was the first) to be celebrated with a personal national holiday. After King's assassination, the leadership of SCLC shifted to Dr. Ralph Abernathy. Its overall influence and visibility quickly declined as rival leaders, organizations, and approaches advanced to the forefront of the civil rights movement.

Social and economic gains did not keep pace with political change. De facto segregation in schools, ongoing occupational discrimination, and much slower change in the social norms gave rise to frustration and to increasingly radical tactics.

As black protest groups proliferated and more varied tactics were used, the advances made by blacks fell short of expectations. Frustrations grew. The ideology and rhetoric of the movement became angrier. Radical protest leaders like H. Rap Brown decried nonviolence, chanting "Burn, baby, burn" during urban riots. Malcolm X of the Black Muslims exemplified the belief that racism was so deeply ingrained in white America that appeals to conscience would fail to bring fundamental change. From this mood the rhetoric of black power emerged in the summer of 1966. It expressed disillusionment and alienation from white America and pride in black independence and self-respect. Phrases like "black power," "black is beautiful," and "black consciousness" were soon expressed by the full range of black organizations. Black Power became associated with fringe groups emerging from CORE and SNCC. The Black Panthers illustrate this trend.

The late 1960s witnessed an increase in violent behavior as well as rhetoric. From 1963 through 1968, hundreds of riots rocked the cities of America, in sharp contrast to the previous fifty-year period when there were only seventy-six major racial disturbances. Moreover, the very nature of the urban violence—in its scope, intensity, and targets—was far different from the earlier riots of this century, 1900–1940. One study for 1967 alone identified 257 "disorders" in 173 cities that resulted in 87 deaths, injury to over 2,500, and 29,200 arrests. After King's assassination, more cities (369) erupted in riots than in all of 1967. They reached small as well as large cities; one-fourth of the riots took place in cities under 25,000 in population.

The riots were more intense and destructive. The Watts riot of 1965 lasted five days, destroyed $40 million in property, left a burned area in excess of 45 square miles with 34 dead, of whom 31 were black. Over 1,100 were injured and 1,600 arrested. The national guard used 3,000 troops, with local police providing 1,400 officers and the state sending 500 state troopers. More than 10,000 demonstrators confronted over 15,500 police and national guard troops. The Newark riot of 1967 required 4,000 officers to quell it. Twenty-six persons, of whom 21 were black, perished in that riot. Detroit erupted in 1967. Its five-day riot was the worst of all. Of the 43 dead, 39 were black. Fifteen thousand police officers were used to restore order. Some 1,300 buildings were destroyed and 2,700 businesses looted; property damage exceeded $500 million. The army and the national guard were called into fifteen cities. The property damage alone in eight riots that year amounted to in excess of $250 million. In July 1967, President Johnson created a National Advisory Commission on Civil Disorders to study the riots, determine what happened, why, and what could be done to prevent them.

Within the majority society a popular explanation for the outbreak of the riots was called the "riffraff," or "rotten apples" theory. This view saw riot participants as unemployed youth with criminal records who vastly outnumbered the African Americans who repudiated the looting and the arson. This theory left white society untouched. The black community viewed the riots and rioters with more sympathetic understanding. Rioters were not merely the poor and uneducated, but also working-class, middle-class, educated residents of the black ghetto areas.

Another explanation for the riots involves a theory of **rising expectations** coupled with **relative deprivation**. This view sees riots as emerging from frustrations that resulted as the standards of blacks improved after World War II and as the civil rights movement promised increased change. Black expectations for progress rose exponentially. Black incomes rose, but so did white incomes. The gap between black and white income did not close causing an increased sense of relative deprivation—the conscious feeling of negative discrepancy between legitimate expectations and present actualities. Not only were black lives relatively unchanged, the existing social structure seemed to hold no prospect for improvement. When their frustration levels reached a flash point, incidents such as the assassination of Dr. King set off the riots.

Another explanation has been termed a developing national consciousness. Media coverage of the civil rights movement, especially on national television, created a national interest and racial identity that transcended community boundaries. Blacks had become acutely aware not of deprivation unique to their own neighborhood but of the deprivation characteristic of all urban ghettos. Nearly every black community became a powder keg ready to explode.

In the late 1960s, a more militant phase of the black civil rights movement emerged, one advocating, if not using, violent behavior to bring about a radical change in majority society. Its adherents espoused and used the term **black power**, which came to symbolize this end of the spectrum of new-style radicalism. The term itself was not new. It can be traced back to the early 1900s, for example, in Garvey's movement. Its renewed usage, however, was popularized during the SNCC-CORE-SCLC campaign in Mississippi in 1966. It is generally attributed to Stokely Carmichael, who became its chief advocate. He defined it as "the ability of black people to politically get together and organize themselves so that they can speak from a position of strength rather than a position of weakness" (cited in Kitano 1997, 131). Within the black community, the black power ideology came to mean a sense of black control over the community and an effort to instill self-pride. The term gained wide acceptance among blacks, although whites tended to view it and its usage as a form of **reverse discrimination** or reverse racism.

The black power term and ideology was explained and developed in a book by that title written by Stokely Carmichael and Charles V. Hamilton (1967). It was more popularly associated with two divergent groups: the Nation of Islam and the Black Panther Party. The Black Muslims used the term in an avowedly separatist movement. They used it to justify their goals of political and economic separatism. Black power was a "dramatically defiant" term that came to symbolize the more militant phase of the civil rights movement. It increasingly represented a rejection of integrationist objectives.

The Black Panther Party popularized the term as but one aspect of its symbolic radicalism and militancy. In 1966, the party arose in Oakland, California, founded by Huey Newton and Bobby Seale. In their radical rhetoric, the Black Panthers condemned capitalism, defied white racist society, and promised to respond to violence with violence. Wearing black leather jackets and berets, adopting paramilitary titles (minister of defense), and sporting rifles over their shoulders, they were seen as the leading black nationalist group in the country. In their programs, however, they were clearly reformist rather than revolutionary. They developed many community service programs, such as breakfast programs for schoolchildren. Their service to the black community inspired emulation by the Chinese Americans, Chicanos, and Puerto Ricans.

The Black Panthers were willing to work within the political system. Co-founder Bobby Seale ran for mayor of Oakland (unsuccessfully), and Eldridge Cleaver, their minister of information (propaganda), ran for U.S. president. Their former defense minister, Bobby Rush, eventually became the deputy chairman of the Illinois State Democratic Party. In 1992, he was elected to the U.S. Congress. The Black Panthers were willing to form alliances with other groups, including political reform and integration groups, as well as with more radical organizations: Students for a Democratic Society, the Peace and Freedom Party, the Communist Party of the United States, the Young Lords, and the Young Patriots.

The Black Panthers exemplify the fate that often awaits a racial or ethnic minority group that is "defiantly militant" and uses the radical rhetoric of violence. The majority culture responds with repression rather than reform. Their militancy meant the Black Panthers became the target of both local and federal police agencies. The FBI conducted an extensive campaign of surveillance against them, and secretly plotted and executed a campaign of disinformation to discredit them publicly. Local police departments simply suppressed them. Between 1968 and 1970, dozens of Black Panthers were killed and thousands of others arrested. "One notorious case was the 1969 killing of Mark Clark and Fred Hampton by the Chicago police, who fired between 800 and 1,000 rounds of ammunition into the victims' apartment" (Kivisto 1995, 320). By 1971 the party split. Eldridge Cleaver went into exile in Algiers. Another faction concentrated on less radical rhetoric, pushing black pride and service to the black community instead.

It is arguable that this more militant phase of the black civil rights movement, despite its brief period, generated some results. Just as the ending of de jure segregation in the form of Jim Crowism can be attributed to the nonviolent civil disobedience phase, certain economic gains can be attributed to the more violent phase of the urban riots and the radical rhetoric used by groups such as the Black Panthers and the Symbionese Liberation Army (SLA). Frances Fox-Piven and Richard Cloward, in their book *Regulating the Poor* (1971), argue that the expansion of the welfare rolls and the social service programs of the Johnson administration's War on Poverty was a political response to political disorder.

The gains and changes made as a result of the protest politics of the 1960s and into the early 1970s enabled the change in strategy and tactics that developed from the mid-1970s and since. Economic, political, and social incorporation was notable. For example, economic progress was significant: From 1965 to 1970, black incomes gained 13 percent on whites'. Political electoral success followed as well. Black elected officials in the South increased ninefold in ten years, although black gains, power, and influence slid backward during the 1980s and the Reagan and Bush administrations.

African-American voting behavior began to close the gap with that of white voters throughout the 1980s and into the new century. By the 2000 presidential election African-American voting turnout was 54 percent, compared to 56 percent among white voters. They also increasingly became associated with Democratic Party voting. Whereas the African-American vote split 71 percent to John Kennedy versus 29 percent for Richard Nixon in 1960, by the 2000 election it rose to 89 percent for Gore to a mere 8 percent for Bush and 2 percent for Ralph Nader (1960 and 2000 National Election Surveys). Their participation in government also rose dramatically. The percentage of African Americans in the federal bureaucracy rose from essentially zero in 1900, to about 12 percent in 1960, to over 17 percent by 1990 (Hayes 1941, 1; King 1995, 221–237; Walton and Smith 2000, 250). Table 8.1 shows their considerable gain in Congressional representation. It presents the African-American members of the 110th Congress as members of the Congressional Black Caucus. The Caucus began in 1969. Its founding members were: Shirley Chisholm, William Clay, Sr., George Collins, John Conyers, Ronald Dellums, Charles Diggs, Augustus Hawkins, Ralph Metcalfe, Parren Mitchell, Robert Nix, Charles Rangel, Louis Stokes, and Washington, DC delegate, Walter Fauntroy. Although officially non-partisan, there have only been three Republicans elected to Congress since the caucus was formed: Senator Edward Brooke of

Table 8.1   Members of the Black Congressional Caucus, 110th Congress

Name	State	Party	Congressional District
Senate			
Barack Obama	Illinois	Democrat	
House of Representatives			
Sanford Bishop	Georgia	Democrat	Second
Corrine Brown	Florida	Democrat	Third
G. K. Butterfield	N. Carolina	Democrat	Second
Julia Carson	Indiana	Democrat	Seventh
Donna Christian-Christensen, Delegate	U.S. Virgin Islands	Democrat	At-large
Yvette Clark	New York	Democrat	Eleventh
William Lacy Clay Jr.	Missouri	Democrat	First
Emanuel Cleaver II V.C.	Missouri	Democrat	Fifth
James E. Clyburn	S. Carolina	Democrat	Sixth
John Conyers, Dean	Michigan	Democrat	Fourteenth
Elijah Cummings	Maryland	Democrat	Seventh
Artur Davis, Secretary	Alabama	Democrat	Seventh
Danny Davis, Secretary	Illinois	Democrat	Seventh
Keith Ellison	Minnesota	Democrat	Fifth
Chaka Fattah	Pennsylvania	Democrat	Second
Al Green	Texas	Democrat	Ninth
Alcee Hastings	Florida	Democrat	Twenty-third
Jesse L. Jackson Jr.	Illinois	Democrat	Second
William J. Jefferson	Louisiana	Democrat	Second
Eddie Bernice Johnson	Texas	Democrat	Thirtieth
Hank Johnson	Georgia	Democrat	Fourth
Stephanie Tubbs Jones	Ohio	Democrat	Eleventh
Carolyn Cheeks Kilpatrich, Chairwoman	Michigan	Democrat	Thirteenth
Barbara Lee, First Vice-Chair	California	Democrat	Ninth
Sheila Jackson Lee, Whip	Texas	Democrat	Eighteenth
John Lewis	Georgia	Democrat	Fifth
Kendrick Meeks, Foundation Chairman	Florida	Democrat	Seventeenth
Gregory Meeks	New York	Democrat	Sixth
Juanita Millender-McDonald	California	Democrat	Thirty-seventh
Gwen Moore	Wisconsin	Democrat	Fourth
Eleanore Holmes-Norton, Delegate	District of Columbia	Democrat	At-large
Donald M. Payne	New Jersey	Democrat	Tenth
Charles Rangel	New York	Democrat	Fifteenth
Bobby Rush	Illinois	Democrat	First
Bobby Scott	Virginia	Democrat	Third
David Scott	Georgia	Democrat	Thirteenth

Table 8.1 Members of the Black Congressional Caucus, 110th Congress

Name	State	Party	
Bennie Thompson	Mississippi	Democrat	Second
Edolphus Towns	New York	Democrat	Tenth
Maxine Walters	California	Democrat	Thirty-fifth
Diane Watson	California	Democrat	Thirty-third
Mel Watt	N. Carolina	Democrat	Twelfth
Albert Wynn	Maryland	Democrat	Fourth

Source: Table by author, from http://www.answers.com/topic/congressional-black-caucus, accessed 3/28/2007.

Massachusetts, Rep. Gary Franks of Connecticut, and Rep. J. C. Watts Jr. of Oklahoma, who did not join the caucus because of its Democratic affiliation and goals. It has grown in size and clout from 13 members to its present 43 members.

BROWN POWER: THE HISPANIC PROTEST MOVEMENT

Although some are reluctant to admit it, the brown power movement resulted from Hispanics' adoption of the black civil rights movement's strategy and tactics.[2] Brown power advocates learned from the experience of black militants. The success of the black civil rights movement unquestionably inspired the Chicano adoption of brown power and protest politics, including boycotts, marches, church-based organization of protest activities, and the taking over of buildings in protest of discrimination.

In the early 1960s, Mexican Americans were even lower than black Americans in terms of income, housing, and formal educational status. The brown power and Chicano movement erupted across the nation, manifested in farm workers' strikes in California, in the land grant struggle in New Mexico, in the revolt of the young Chicano electorate in Crystal City, Texas, and in school walkouts in Denver and Los Angeles. As the black civil rights movement gave rise to newly-formed civil rights organizations and new leaders, so the Hispanic movement was led by new leaders and groups.

Early on the black power movement was led by groups tactically conservative and accommodationist (NAACP, Urban League, etc.). So too was the Hispanic movement. Among the earliest such organizations were the League of United Latin American Citizens (LULAC), the G.I. Forum, the Order of the Sons of America (La Orden de los Hijos de America), and the Community Service Organization (CSO).

Hispanic protest events followed a curve similar to that exhibited by the earlier black civil rights movement. There were zero Hispanic protests in 1960. That number rose to 35 in 1965, more than doubled again to 90 in 1970, peaked at 110 in 1973, then began to ease off, falling to 90 in 1975, 52 in 1978, and to 15 in 1980 (Nagel 1996; Wilkins 2002, 219).

The Order of the Sons of America (OSA) was organized in San Antonio, Texas, in 1918 and was open only to U.S. citizens. LULAC began in 1928–1929 in Corpus

Christi, Texas, and was strongly assimilationist. It began in the wake of a racial attack by the Ku Klux Klan that spread across Texas just after World War I. LULAC began as a self-proclaimed defensive and patriotic organization. The Klan held sway over much of East Texas, and the previously staunchly Democratic state had voted for Herbert Hoover in the presidential election of 1920 because of the Klan's hatred of the Catholic "papist" nominee on the Democratic ticket, Al Smith. LULAC used the name "Latin-American citizens" in order to avoid using "Mexican American," then decidedly not in vogue. LULAC soothed jittery anti-Mexican sentiment then evident in much of Texas by a pledge of loyalty. Reflecting the "Four Freedoms" of World War II, LULAC set goals of reverence for their racial heritage; equal protection under the law; eradication of discrimination, and political unification by participating in all local, state, and national elections.

After World War I several Hispanic or Latino organizations developed, most notably the Community Service Organization (CSO), from which arose Congressman Eduardo Roybal and Cesar Chavez, the G.I. Forum, the Council of Mexican-American Affairs, and the Mexican American Political Association (MAPA). The Community Service Organization can be traced to the pioneer of nonviolent confrontation politics, Saul Alinsky. His Chicago-based Industrial Areas Foundation had a West Coast organizer, Fred Ross, who served as a guiding spirit to the budding CSO. Congressman Roybal described its founding when, in 1947, he first ran for the Los Angeles City Council. Although he lost that race, he and his campaign forces decided they needed a community group, which became the CSO. In his words, "We thought of it and we organized it. Of course, others helped. But we did it" (Steiner 1969, 180).

In the postwar era, returning veterans organized to elect Chicanos. Middle-class Chicanos used CSO as a political lever to help elect Roybal. It became innovative yet cautious, tempering its boldness with politeness. The barrio youth looked upon the CSO as too middle class and mainline. Its membership dropped off markedly during the 1960s—by 75 percent, from 12,000 to 4,000. Its membership was elderly. Young Chicanos were joining more militant groups.

The Chicano movement began using the term *Chicano* as a matter of self-pride, much as blacks began referring to themselves as blacks or African Americans instead of Negroes. Like the black civil rights movement, it was a national, mass membership movement evident in both rural areas and urban barrios.

Another use of the bottoms-up approach was the rural movement that began with a union-led campaign to organize migrant workers. Its leader, Cesar Chavez, went on to become the best known Chicano leader. Like Dr. Martin Luther King Jr., he was an authentic "man of the people" in the traditional sense of those words—a charismatic leader who came from a rural, migrant, working-class background and who understood and commanded the loyalty of those he led. The co-founder, with Cesar Chavez, of the United Farm Workers was Dolores Huerta. She is featured in Box 8.2.

Chavez's movement, often referred to as "La Causa," began in September 1965. In Delano, California, a strike by Filipino workers harvesting grapes, who belonged to the Agricultural Workers Organizing Committee (AWOC), expanded to include Mexican migrant workers. The migrant workers earned an annual average income of $1,378.

BOX 8.2   *BIO-SKETCH OF DOLORES FERNANDEZ HUERTA (1930–)*

Born in April, 1930, in Dawson, New Mexico, where her family roots go back to the seventeenth century, Dolores Huerta was the daughter of a miner and migrant agricultural worker. She is the mother of 11 children, with 14 grandchildren, and 4 great-grandchildren. Her family moved to Stockton, California, where she grew up. In the 1950s, while helping to organize the Community Service Organization (CSO), she met Cesar Chavez. When he left the CSO in 1962 to organize farm workers, she left with him and has since dedicated herself to serving agricultural workers through the United Farm Workers (UFW). At various times organizer, lobbyist, and picket captain, Dolores spent most of the 1960s organizing migrant workers in Stockton and Modesto. She went to the UFW's central headquarters at Delano, California, and became Cesar Chavez's most trusted and valuable associate. In 1963, she was instrumental in securing AFDC benefits for farm workers in California. She played an important role in the negotiation of contracts that brought an end to the five-year-long Delano Grape Strike in 1970 and in the ensuing off-and-on again lettuce strike in the Salinas valley. Experienced in all aspects of union organizing, Dolores Huerta served as vice-president of the UFW (1970–1973) and is the First Vice President Emeritus of the UFW, AFL-CIO. She served as a spokesperson for the union, developer of labor contracts, chief negotiator, boycott strategist, and lobbyist. She is credited with contributing importantly to the UFW policy of nonviolence. As an advocate for farm worker rights, she has been arrested twenty-two times for nonviolent peaceful union activities.

In 1984 the California Senate bestowed on her the Outstanding Labor Leader Award. In 1993, Dolores was inducted into the National Women's Hall of Fame, and that same year received the American Civil Liberties Union Roger Baldwin Medal of Liberty Award. She also received the Eugene V. Debs Foundation Outstanding American Award, and the Ellis Island Medal of Freedom Award. She is the recipient of the Consumer's Union Trumpeter's Award. In 1998 she was one of three *Ms. Magazine*'s "Women of the Year" and of the *Ladies Home Journal*'s "100 Most Important Women of the 20th Century." She has been awarded three honorary doctorate degrees.

She currently serves as secretary-treasurer of the United Farm Workers, vice-president for the Coalition for Labor Union Women, vice-president of the California AFL-CIO, and is a board member for the Fund for the Feminist Majority, which advocates for the political and equal rights for women. She serves on such other boards as: Democratic Socialists of America, Latinas for Choice, FAIR (Fairness in Media Reporting), and Center for Voting and Democracy. In the past she has served on such federal commissions as Minority Apprentice Programs, 1965; Advisory Committee on Immigration, 1980; and Commission of Agricultural Workers, 1988 to 1993. She was a member of two California state commissions: Industrial Welfare Commission, 1960, and Board of Directors of the California State Library Service, 1980–1982. In 2003 California Governor Gray Davis appointed her to the University of California Board of Trustees.

Sources: Bio-sketch by author with information from http://www.ufw.org/dh.htm; Matt S. Meier, *Mexican American Biographies* (Westport, CT: Greenwood Press, 1988), 106–107.

La Huelga, the strike, soon developed into La Causa, a social movement that used strikes and boycotts against lettuce and grape growers. A coalition of organized labor, liberal clergy, radicals, and student groups began when Cesar Chavez formed the National Farm Workers Association (NFWA). Even the city of Boston experienced a symbolic demonstration, a "Boston Grape Party" that evoked the revolutionary spirit of the Boston Tea Party.

Striking grape pickers took on powerful economic forces with but $85 in their treasury, arrayed against the multi-billion-dollar giants of California's agribusiness. The union grew dramatically. By fall, 2,000 workers in the Delano area alone had joined the NFWA, and 5,000 workers signed to have NFWA or AWOC represent them. By winter, the strike became a national boycott. The AFL-CIO gave $5,000 a month so the strikers could receive $5 per week strike pay. In March 1966, they organized a three-hundred-mile march, the Pilgrimage to Sacramento. The strike evolved into a movement as university students and barrio youth joined the workers. La Huelga became a crusade that literally changed lives.

Like the black civil rights campaigners, striking migrant workers faced violence. One striking worker suffered broken legs when he was run over with a truck driven by a strike-breaker. Three strikers riding in a car were run off the road. Picketers were beaten, and they had guns discharged over their heads. Forty-four strikers were arrested for refusing to remain silent on the picket line. The sheriff's officer from Kern County came to the picket lines and said they could not use the word *huelga*. The strikers refused to give up using the word so the forty-four were jailed.

Like King and SCLC, Chavez and UFW were committed to nonviolence. He testified regarding the violence used against them before a special subcommittee of labor that investigated the strike (Steiner 1969, 370). When the Chicano youth began using the term **La Raza**, which though translated as "the race" was used by them in the sense of "our people," Cesar Chavez was quick to distinguish its meaning as other than a racist term. "When *La Raza* means or implies racism, we don't support it. But if it means our struggle, our dignity, or our cultural roots, then we're for it" (Chavez 1984, 137).

During the five-year strike against the growers, the "association" evolved into a union, then a social protest movement, a mass protest civil rights group (by 1967, it had 17,000 members in California alone), and then into a community organizing force. The strike went from the grape to the lettuce fields, and the Delano plan spread from California to the Southwest to the nation.

Just as SCLC inspired the development of SNCC and the increased militancy of CORE and the Black Panthers, so did La Causa. The strike got everyone excited. University students organized. Chicano leaders in the cities and universities struck out in new directions. Out of the upheavals came dozens of new barrio and university clubs. The Brown Berets was an organization of young Chicanos from the barrios of Los Angeles. Styled after the Black Panthers, they were a militant Chicano group. University students were especially outspoken and active. The United Mexican American Students (UMAS) in California and the National Organization of Mexican American Students (NOMAS, literally, "no more") in Texas were but two of more than thirty groups organized on campuses. University and barrio youth talked and marched together. David Sanchez, prime minister of the Brown Berets, talked to students at

"And remember, nothing can be accomplished by taking to the streets." (From *Straight Herblock* [Simon & Schuster, 1964]. Reprinted by permission of the Herb Block Foundation.)

UCLA, while the members of UMAS walked the picket lines of the campesinos of Delano and beside the Brown Berets protesting school conditions in East Los Angeles.

A similar sense of inspiring militancy arose from the New Mexico land grant movement and its colorful leader, Reies Lopez Tijerina, known as "El Tigre" (the Tiger). A native Texan, he began the militant Alianza Federal de Mercedes on February 2, 1962. He first tried to work through the courts, asserting claims to land taken illegally from Mexicans living in Texas and New Mexico after the Treaty of Guadalupe Hidalgo. His movement was inspired by the black civil rights movement. "We are expecting this great change. The Negroes are expecting this great change, they feel it. That's why they are jumping, breaking the barriers, and yelling, and respecting *nothing* that gets in their way. Because the Negroes can *feel* the future. And so can we, the New Breed" (cited in Steiner 1969, 88). Black power became the model used to promote a new sense of Brown Power.

The Treaty of Guadalupe Hidalgo guaranteed the land rights to Mexicans living in what became California and New Mexico. Tijerina argued that those treaty rights, "consecrated by the law of nations," were stolen in land grabs after the Mexican-American War. Those lands ranged across Texas, New Mexico, Arizona, California, Nevada, Utah, Colorado, and north into Wyoming. They made up an area larger than any of the nations of Europe except Russia, and larger than most other nations of the world. Property rights guaranteed by the treaty if held to be legally valid were no small real estate matter.

Records of the land grants were destroyed, but they were known to number over 1,700. Profits from Anglos' seizing land grant property were enormous, as the grants covered an estimated 20 million acres in Texas and New Mexico and 10 million acres in California. Tijerina argued the lands were stolen by Anglos, such as Thomas Catron, the "king of the Santa Fe ring." By filing a "patenting" and paying some well-placed bribes, he acquired some 593,000 acres with a single piece of paper. Some 34,653,340 acres of land grants land were brought to the Court of Private Land Claims. It validated only 1,934,986 acres, about 6 percent.

In launching his land grant movement Tijerina argued that Chicanos had to demand their rights, to fight for them, to be willing if need be to die for them. "Look at the black man. He has become free, free in spirit. He has lost his fear of the 'white power.' He is clean of fear and terror. And when you are free of these things you become filled with anger. You strike out for freedom. Anger is a manifestation that you know you are right and you wish to tear down the system that enslaved you" (Steiner 1969, 64).

The barrios' newspaper in Los Angeles, *La Raza,* voiced a growing sentiment for Tijerina and Corky Gonzales: "'We've been waiting since 1846 for real men.'; The barrio newspaper hails 'El Tigre' and 'Corky,' Reies Tijerina and Rodolfo Gonzales, as a 'new and militant type of leadership' that youth 'admire and respect.' . . . These men have said and done things Chicanos have only mumbled and have said under their breath, but didn't have the 'Guts' or the 'Machismo' to say out loud. These men are real men: They are both *machos.*" (Steiner 1969, 195).

The newspaper *El Grito de Norte* described the farmers of Tierra Amarilla (a small town in New Mexico) setting up a farmer's co-op that had near its door the defiant slogan "Che is alive and farming in Tierra Amarillo." In the nearby city of Santa Rosa, a Chicano student helped rural villagers construct a stone schoolhouse. He described his work as follows: "School? It is not just a school. It is one battle in our fight for self-determination. 'La Raza Arriba!' the student says. 'Our people arise'" (Steiner 1969, 41).

El Tigre was an evangelical minister and spoke with the fiery intensity of a preacher using the podium as his pulpit. When court action failed to restore lands, he adopted the tactics of civil disobedience. In October 1966, he led a group that occupied the Echo Amphitheater at Kit Carson National Forest. In protest, they burned down a guard post, and Tijerina was arrested for vandalism. In November 1967, he and four members of Alianza were convicted on one or more counts for the Echo Amphitheater takeover. Tijerina was convicted of assaulting two forest rangers and burning two national forest signposts (in retaliation for Anglos burning down the barns of two co-op farmers). On June 5, 1967, while out on bail awaiting appeal, he led an attack on the courthouse of the county seat at Tierra Amarilla, New Mexico. The state government sent 400 national guardsmen, 200 state troopers, 2 tanks, and several helicopters. He was arrested and charged with wounding two officers, and kidnaping for taking two hostages. The kidnaping charge was reduced to false imprisonment. Though released on bail, none of his fiery oratory was quenched. Tensions were high during his trial for the Tierra Amarilla takeover. On the wall of an abandoned gas station near the court someone had written, "If Tijerina goes to jail—WAR!" After a brief deliberation the jury found him not guilty. Released, he participated in the Poor People's March on Washington in 1968.

In 1969, Tijerina was sent to federal prison for two years for the Kit Carson National Forest incident. His health declined. He was released early after promising not to hold any office with the Alianza movement. While Tijerina was in jail, Alianza suffered attacks. In April 1968, a former sheriff's deputy bombed the Alianza headquarters, but bungled the job and blew off his right hand. The police, following a trail of blood, arrested him in his blood-spattered car, finding yet another stick of dynamite in a lunch box in the car. Charges of using a "deadly weapon" were dismissed, and a grand jury cleared him of a "dangerous use of explosives charge." He was sentenced to a mere sixteen hours of community service at the county medical center.

In the winter of 1968, rifle shots from a speeding car shattered the headquarters' office windows. There were no arrests. In June 1969, terrorists shot up a crowded hall during an Alianza meeting. Again, no arrests were made. Repeated bombings, rock throwing, and shooting amounted to a campaign of terror against Alianza. Cars were burned. Arsonists set fire to the villagers' health clinic. Tijerina's children were threatened with kidnaping and murder. An Alianza car was tear-gassed with members in it—but again, no arrests were made.

The Minutemen are a paramilitary, white extremist group who are racist and advocate the violent overthrow of the U.S. government. During the campaign of terror, an extremist Minutemen leader, Robert DePugh, and his chief assistant, Walter Peyson, were caught by the FBI in a small New Mexico town near Albuquerque. Their cache of arms and bombs was so large its description filled twenty-four typed pages in the police report. Maps of the land grant villages were found, as well as thousands of rounds of ammunition. A list of Minutemen membership found there suddenly vanished amid rumors that local law enforcement officers were in on it. A security chief of Alianza was warned that opponents of Tijerina were going to assassinate him. After their arrest, the Minutemen leaders were taken out of state. Tijerina's office was bombed three times, once while his wife and children were present, although no one was injured. Like Martin Luther King Jr., Tijerina was accused of being a Communist. District Attorney Alfonso Sanchez, with whom Tijerina fought in the Tierra Amarilla incident, implied that Alianza villagers were training for a revolution. Tijerina scoffed at such charges: "I don't know much about communism or Marxism. Communism is just another European political system to me, just as corrupt as any other political system. We don't need it. . . . The old powers are dying . . . we are being born. The Communists are no threat to the rich, the oppressors, in New Mexico. We are a threat to them" (Steiner 1969, 89).

The Alianza movement crumbled without Tijerina's active leadership. In 1979, the courts did consider the land grant issue, but no victories were won. Tijerina now lives a lonely and isolated life in a small New Mexico town. Nonetheless, he activated ethnic pride and inspired new leadership.

Another Chicano leader was Rodolfo "Corky" Gonzales, founder of the Crusade for Justice, a Chicano youth group centered in Denver, Colorado. In the 1960 presidential election, Gonzales had been a district captain of the Denver Democratic Party, as its Viva Kennedy coordinator. He worked for the War on Poverty Program in Denver from 1961 through 1965, when he resigned to begin the Crusade for Justice. He helped organize the Poor People's March on Washington, DC, and he and Reies Tijerina led the delegation of Chicanos from the Southwest. The Crusade started as a civil rights group but quickly developed into a wide-ranging barrio group stressing self-defense. It had its own security force whose aim was not only to protect the barrio but to safeguard its activists. It was praised by the Washington, DC, police force for its work in maintaining good order during the Poor People's March. By 1967, the Crusade claimed a membership of 1,800.

Corky Gonzales adopted the term **Aztlan** at the first national Chicano conference, held in Denver in 1969. He used the term and popularized it. Many scholars believe the Aztlan of the Aztecs was actually within present-day Mexico. Nonetheless, the term came to be used to refer to the "lost lands" of northern Mexico that are now the southwestern United States. Aztlan became a kind of Utopia or Eden. The Chicano activists converted that ancient idealized landscape into an ideal of a modern homeland where they hoped to fulfill their people's (La Raza's) political, economic, and cultural destiny.

Gonzales inspired the Crusade for Justice with the fervor of nationalism. On Palm Sunday, 1969, he convened a national gathering of barrio youth at the Chicano Youth Federation Conference to the cries of "*Raza! Raza! Raza!*" From the conference various campus groups merged into the more militant Estudiantil Chicano de Aztlan (MECHA), the Chicano Student Movement of Aztlan. Corky Gonzales and the conference inspired groups such as UMAS, MAYO, and the Brown Berets. (McClain and Steward 1995, 50–51; 203–205). Corky Gonzales rejected integration as fruitless. He characterized it as the "small end of a funnel" wherein a few Chicanos may make it, but the rest of the people would stay behind at the bottom. He praised the youth for demanding a revolutionary change, not merely putting water on a fire. He challenged them to teach their people, rather than trying to educate a racist majority; to be proud of their values and their culture. Perhaps his most lasting contribution was helping to organize La Raza Unida. At the Denver, Colorado, conference he issued a ringing declaration of independence for Mexican Americans: "We have to start judging our lives with new values. . . . The Anglos consider us conquered citizens, but we are not second class citizens. We must declare that our rights under the Treaty of Guadalupe Hidalgo be recognized, that the educational system be changed and include bilingual teaching and the history of the Mexican American. Que viva la raza y la revolucian!" (Steiner 1969, 324).

The La Raza Unida Conference in 1967 in El Paso, Texas, inspired numerous new leaders and groups. Jose Angel Gutierrez, who helped organize La Raza Unida, led a Chicano voter revolt in 1970 in Crystal City, Texas. Although the small city had a population that was 80 percent Mexican American, it had a 100 percent Anglo government. Organizing La Raza Unida as a third party, Gutierrez and La Raza ran candidates for local office, organized community co-ops, supported Chicano business, and led boycotts against hostile merchants. The **La Raza Unida Partido** (the People's Party or LRU) won numerous city offices, essentially capturing the government of Crystal City.

Like black youth in SNCC and CORE, militant Chicano youth challenged their leaders and showed little patience with the efforts of the veteran Chicano leaders. Jose Angel Gutierrez of San Antonio, president of the Mexican American Youth Organization (MAYO), challenged the crowds in the barrio gym: "We are going to march and you can join us. But if you don't, you will be left behind." Another young leader, Phil Castruita of the United Mexican American Students (UMAS), a California State University group, remarked matter-of-factly, "The young Chicanos see this conference [the hearings and La Raza Unida] as the last chance you older Chicanos have to come through. If nothing happens from this you'll have to step aside or we'll walk over you" (Steiner 1969, 238–239).

The **barrio** of Los Angeles is the third largest city of Mexican residents in the world, exceeded only by Guadalajara and Mexico City. Over 1 million Mexicans live in Los Angeles. By themselves they would constitute one of the ten largest cities in the United States. Los Angeles is the capital of La Raza. It is to the Chicano what Boston is to the Irish American and New York City is to the American Jew (Steiner 1969).

In March 1968 the barrio of Los Angeles experienced student protest when some 15,000 Chicano students walked out of five Los Angeles high schools and staged what they called a "blowout." Their "strike" had closed classes throughout the barrio. Police and sheriff's deputies blockaded the neighborhood, arresting both students and some teachers. The teenagers held up hastily drawn posters voicing their frustrations: "Education not contempt," "Education not eradication," "Teachers si, bigots no!" "Que paso? Free speech!" "We are not 'Dirty Mexicans,'" "Our kids don't have blue eyes, but they do go overseas," "School, not prison," and "Is this a holiday?"

Student leaders issued a list of demands for textbook and curriculum revisions to show Mexican contributions to America, the transfer of teachers who evidence prejudice, the building of swimming pools in all East Los Angeles schools, unlocked rest rooms, and all campuses being open and fences removed. The L. A. Teachers Association and Local 1021 of the American Federation of Teachers supported demands for more bilingual and bicultural training of school personnel, more Spanish-language library and textbook matter, and better food in the cafeterias.

The city responded by arresting thirteen student leaders of the blowout and their teacher, Sal Castro. Charged with conspiracy to disturb the educational process, they were jailed. The barrio newspaper, *La Raza,* chortled that there were "thirteen Aztec gods," that those arrested were a select and prophetic number, and their arrest showed the ignorance of the Board of Education of the Chicano heritage. The paper called the students the "cream of their crop" who were "pushed out" of their schools. Numerous groups came to the defense of those arrested: the Congress of Mexican American Unity, UMAS, Cesar Chavez's United Farm Workers, the Council of Churches of Southern California, the Pacific Southwest Council of the Union of American Hebrew Congregations, the local American Federation of Teachers, the NAACP, and the Black Congress. After a year's delay, protests by thousands of barrio residents, and dozens of subsequent arrests, the "thirteen" were brought to trial, convicted, fined, and placed on three-years probation forbidding them to enter any barrio school unless on official business. When the Board of Education voted to suspend the teacher, students and parents staged a week-long sit-in at the board offices. Upon their return, the bemused members of the board voted to reinstate the teacher. Students were appeased but still angry, promising more blowouts if the board did not act on their demands.

In the fall of 1969, Chicano students across the country declared a national walkout in celebration of Mexican Independence Day on September 17. In Denver, Colorado, school officials agreed to the students' demand by holding a special assembly in a high school that had been the site of a riot the previous spring, allowing the blowout student leaders to address the student body, an unprecedented action by the school board in recognition of the Chicano students' views. There were numerous walkouts, blowouts, and student marches from Texas to California. Student activists demanded community control of barrio schools and new curricular changes to recognize the teaching, language, and cultural heritage of Mexican Americans. The barrio classroom became an arena of the movement's struggles. In the streets, Chicano youth organized the Brown Berets. Wearing berets and gun belts and slinging rifles on their shoulders, barrio militants embraced the style and tactics of the Black Panthers. Just as the Black Panthers popularized the term "black power," the Brown Berets used their version, "brown power."

While Reies Tijerina was free on bond, he visited Los Angeles and spoke at a MAPA meeting. He appeared several times in the area, flanked by Brown Beret bodyguards. He embraced and praised Black Nationalist leaders and stirred young militants with hints of violence and calls for valor, for a willingness to die, if need be, for La Causa. Louis Valdez, then a young Chicano leader of MAPA and a disciple of Cesar Chavez, spoke to the same rally. Wearing a Che Guevara outfit, he attacked the "*bagachos*" (a Chicano term for Anglos), showing a militancy more typical of the fiery Tijerina and the Brown Berets than of Cesar Chavez.

The Brown Berets supported high school student blowout demonstrations, economic boycotts, political drives, and street demonstrations. Their motto was "To Serve, Observe, Protect." They monitored especially the Los Angeles police department, which they accused of harassment and having an agenda to destroy their group. Like the Black Panthers, they adopted paramilitary titles. "Field Marshall" Jose is quoted on the misperception of La Raza as a racist expression: "You are using the white people's words. English, you see . . . English is a racist language. That is why they sound the same, brown power, black power. In Spanish we don't say a color. We say the power of the people—La Raza" (Steiner 1969, 116–117).

The chairman of the Mayor's Youth Advisory Council became the "prime minister" of the Brown Berets. When asked, "Who organized them?" he replied, "The police organized them." The Brown Berets saw their struggle with the police as "fighting like the Indian fought—for motherland." The Los Angeles police arrested sixty-five members of the Brown Berets. White police were characterized as bigots with guns who saw Chicanos as brown faces, not human beings. Chicanos perceived the police as having the attitude that they could treat Chicanos any way they wanted and get away with anything; as creating violence not preventing it; and as building community animosity rather than community relations. "More Chicanos are killed by cops on the streets in the Southwest than any other minority group in the population," wrote a young man in the barrio newspaper. He called it "Chicano birth control."

In the 1970s, paralleling the development of the Black Panthers, the Brown Berets evolved into a community service movement. Many of its members hung up their berets and guns and became part of La Junta, setting up community programs, stressing pride in their heritage and history, and working towards goals by conducting themselves in a free and democratic manner in keeping with the great traditions of the Americas (Steiner 1969, 111–12).

In New York City and Chicago, the Puerto Rican community formed its version of the Black Panthers and the Brown Berets: the Young Lords. In the Puerto Rican area of Manhattan known as "El Barrio," or Spanish Harlem, Puerto Rican power arose among students in 1968–1969. They were concerned with many of the same issues that agitated New York's Black Harlem: poor schools, bad housing, and widespread poverty. The Puerto Rican Young Lords of New York and of Chicago adopted a radically militant paramilitary style. In 1968, they occupied a church in Harlem and staged militant actions around two city hospitals. In the spring of 1969, they demonstrated at Queens College and City College, supporting militant Puerto Rican college students in their demonstrations in association with black youth demonstrations. In April 1969, they took over the Second City-Wide Puerto Rican Conference of New York. In June 1969, they marched in the streets.[3]

Despite its militancy and celebration of brown power, the reality of Hispanic power is more potential than actual. Since 1980, the more radical groups have given way to Hispanic organizations following a more political accommodationist route: PASSO, MAPA, MASA, MAYO, and UMAS all used standard electoral politics. MECHA continues its more militant voice, but it too organizes campus and community groups and stresses Chicano pride more than violent or radical reform. The Mexican-American Legal Defense and Education Fund (MALDEF), founded in 1967, developed a strategy based on court cases and voter drives, developing into an Hispanic version of the NAACP. Likewise, the American Coordinating Council on Political Education (ACCPE) launched a nationwide Hispanic voter registration drive (McClain and Steward 1995, 204–205).

Political organization and action brought measurable results. From 1970 to 1988, Hispanic elected officials increased from less than 800 to over 3,400. Hispanic elected officials served prominently in the Clinton administration, for example Henry Cisneros, secretary of housing; Frederico Peña, White House chief of staff; and Antonia Novella, surgeon general. Hispanic members in the House of Representatives established the Hispanic Caucus. It grew from a mere handful in the 1970s to the current 19 in 2002. Table 8.2 lists the Hispanic members of the 110th Congress. Box 8.3 presents the bio-sketch of Rep. Lucille Roybal-Allard of the 34th District of California. Her career illustrates the pay-off in electoral success of the Hispanic power movement as she is the first Mexican-American woman elected to Congress and the first woman to serve as chairperson of the Hispanic Congressional Caucus.

RED POWER: THE NATIVE-AMERICAN PROTEST MOVEMENT

Like Hispanics, the Native-American movement turned to a more radical and militant strategy by using a variation of the tactics developed by the black civil rights movement. Like Hispanics, the Native-American civil rights movement began in the early 1960s.

The "red power" theme did not develop until the pan-Indian movement arrived (creating organizations that crossed or spanned tribal or "national" boundaries). Again,

Table 8.2   Hispanic Caucus Members, 110th Congress

Name	Ethnic Origin	State	Party	
Senate				
Bob Menendez	Cuban	New Jersey	Democrat	
John Salazar	Mexican	Colorado	Democrat	
House of Representatives Officers				**District**
Joe Baca, Chair	Mexican	California	Democrat	Forty-third
Raul Grijalva, Vice-Chair	Mexican	Arizona	Democrat	Seventh
Lucille Roybal-Allard, Whip	Mexican	California	Democrat	Thirty-fourth
Members				
Xavier Beccerra	Mexican	California	Democrat	Thirty-first
Dennis Cardoza	Mexican	California	Democrat	Eighteenth
Jim Costa	Mexican	California	Democrat	Twentieth
Henry Cuellar	Mexican	Texas	Democrat	Twenty-eighth
Charles Gonzales	Mexican	Texas	Republican	Twentieth
Gene Green	Mexican	Texas	Democrat	Twenty-ninth
Luis V. Gutierrez	Puerto Rican	Illinois	Democrat	Fourth
Ruben Hinojosa	Mexican	Texas	Democrat	Fifth
Grace Napolitano	Mexican	California	Democrat	Thirty-eighth
Solomon Ortiz	Mexican	Texas	Democrat	Twenty-seventh
Ed Pastor	Mexican	Arizona	Democrat	Fourth
Silvestre Reyes	Mexican	Texas	Democrat	Sixteenth
Robert Salazar	Mexican	Colorado	Democrat	Fifth
Linda T. Sanches	Mexican	California	Democrat	Thirty-ninth
Loretta Sanchez, resigned January 31, 2007	Mexican	California	Democrat	Forty-seventh
Jose Serrano	Puerto Rican	New York	Democrat	Sixteenth
Hilda Solis	Mexican	California	Democrat	Thirty-second
Nydia Velazquez	Puerto Rican	New York	Democrat	Twelfth
Nonvoting Delegate in the House				
Carlos Romero-Barcelo	Puerto Rican	Puerto Rico	DNP/Dem.	At-large

Source: Table by author, data from http:en.wikipedia.org/wiki/Congressional_Hispanic_Caucus. Accessed 3/28/2007.

World War II played a key role in the organizational development of the pan-Indian movement. In 1944, the National Congress of American Indians was organized in Denver, Colorado, the first truly viable national pan-Indian organization. This organization was integrationist rather than radical. Like the NAACP, it used the courts and lobbied for legislation. At a June 1961 national conference held in Chicago, 500 delegates from 90 communities attended. Four young militants addressed the conference, calling the leadership "Uncle Tomahawks."

Ten young leaders split off and met in Gallup, New Mexico, to form the National Indian Youth Council, led by Mel Thom, a Pauite graduate student. While stressing the

Box 8.3

BIO-SKETCH OF LUCILLE ROYBAL-ALLARD

Lucille Roybal-Allard was born in June, 1941 in Boyle Heights, California, the daughter of Representative Edward Roybal. Educated at the Ramona Convent Secondary School, she then graduated from California State University, Los Angeles. She worked as an Assistant Director for the Alcoholism Council of East Los Angeles United Way, where she focused on fund raising and public relations. She is married to Edward Allard.

She began a career in politics as a member of the California State Assembly from 1986 to 1992. In 1992 she became the first Mexican-American woman elected to Congress, and the second Latina (after Ileana Ros-Lehtinen), and served with Nydia Valasquez of New York City. Her district is over 77 percent Hispanic, the highest of any district in California. She ran for the House from the 34th Congressional District after her father retired from an adjacent district. She has compiled a solid liberal voting record and has worked on immigration issues. She served a term as chairwoman of the Hispanic Caucus, and as chairperson of the California Congressional Delegation (1998–1999). She is active on the Congressional Children's Working Group, the Democratic Homeland Security Task Force, and the Livable Communities Task Force, and sits on the House Appropriations Committee and its subcommittees on Homeland Security, on Labor, Health and Human Services, and on Transportation, Treasury, Housing and Urban Development; and on the Standards of Official Conduct committee. She represents well the transition of Hispanics from protest politics to standard electoral politics and is one of the highest-level serving Latinas in American politics.

Source: Bio-sketch by author, based on data from the 2006 Almanac of American Politics: 252–254; from *http:// www.sourcewatch.org/index.php?title=Lucille_Roybal-Allard*; and from *http://en.wikipedia.org/wiki/Lucille_Roybal-Allard*, accessed 3/28/2007.

spirit of red power, tactically they first pointed to the 370 existing treaties and simply advocated that the government enforce laws already on the books. They began using more active protest actions. From 1961 through 1970, various groups staged 194 instances of Native-American protest. The term "Red Power" is generally attributed to Vine Deloria Jr., a member of the Standing Rock Sioux and then executive director of the National Council of American Indians, who used it in a 1966 speech (Wilkins 2002, 218).

Like SNCC and the black power movement, the young and more militant Indian leaders began their first use of direct-action protest, in this case by organizing "fish-ins" in 1964 in the Seattle, Washington, area. In 1968, the U.S. Supreme Court upheld their treaty rights to fish. They led a similar fish-in campaign in Wisconsin from 1968 through 1991 to gain traditional (and treaty-protected) rights through a combination of demonstrations (spear fishing) and court actions. In Wisconsin, the Chippewas started the dispute by asserting their spear-fishing rights. A number of Wisconsin "anti-native" groups developed: the Wisconsin Alliance for Rights and Resources and Protect

American Rights and Resources. Soon whites were sporting racist signs that proclaimed "Save a Walleye, Spear an Indian," and "Spear a Pregnant Squaw, Save a Walleye," and bumper stickers that read "Indian Niggers" and "Red Niggers." The Chippewas waged a nine-year legal battle to ensure their treaty rights to fish and hunt.

What became the best known of the radical protest pan-Indian groups, the American Indian Movement (AIM), began in the summer of 1968 in Minneapolis, Minnesota. Its founders were Clyde Bellecourt, a Chippewa; Dennis Banks, an Anishinabe Ojibwa; and Russell Means, an Oglala Lakota Sioux. They were born on reservations but lived in urban areas. They began by stressing community service programs: monitoring police violence against Indians, alcohol rehabilitation programs, and school reform.

Their militant protests began when they linked up with a group calling itself the Indians of All Tribes, which staged a 19-month (November 1969 through May 1971) takeover of Alcatraz Island in San Francisco Bay. Red Power was truly born with this action. The radical youth castigated all Indians who sympathized with the Bureau of Indian Affairs as "Uncle Tomahawks," and "apples" (red on the outside but white on the inside). They laid claim to the island with the takeover, asserting rights under an 1868 treaty that promised to return unused federal property to Indian control. This protest action drew worldwide attention to their cause.

AIM had a knack for selecting an appropriate symbolic gesture that would maximize the power of publicity. On Thanksgiving Day 1970, they seized the *Mayflower* replica and painted Plymouth Rock red. On the Fourth of July they organized a "counter-celebration" at Mount Rushmore in the sacred Black Hills of South Dakota. In 1972, AIM and eight other Native-American organizations began the extensive protest they called the "Trail of Broken Treaties." It started on the West Coast and picked up Native Americans at various reservation stops along the way. On November 1, 1972, it ended at Washington, DC, where 500 demonstrators seized the Bureau of Indian Affairs headquarters, occupied its offices for six days, and rummaged through and released embarrassing files.

By far their most militant protest action occurred in 1973 when they staged a "takeover" of Wounded Knee, South Dakota. The ten-week siege began when Dennis Banks and Russell Means organized demonstrations at the Pine Ridge and Rosebud reservations to protest the failure of authorities to arrest the suspected murderers of Raymond Yellow Thunder. He was a 51-year-old Sioux who had been stripped of his pants and assaulted by a group of drunken whites at the local American Legion Hall. His frozen body was later found in the back of a pickup truck. They chose Pine Ridge for the symbolic value of the site. Wounded Knee, on the Pine Ridge Reservation, was the site of the 1890 massacre of 250 Sioux old men, women, and children at what white soldiers had termed the last "battle" of the Plains Indians Wars (Brown 1971).

The dispute leading to the siege began when Richard Wilson and the tribal elders banned AIM activities at the Pine Ridge Reservation. In February 1973, Banks and Means led a group of 300 AIM members who took over the tiny hamlet, which they occupied for 70 days, during which time two of their members were killed. The FBI arrested the demonstrators, and although AIM's goals were not met, the incident did focus national attention on conditions of reservation life.

AIM's radicalism spurred Indian pride. Even assimilated Indians began to return to their native culture: "I watched what they were doing, and I could see the pride in

Chief Big Foot was one of the 250 Native Americans (all elderly men, women, and children) killed in the 1890 massacre at Wounded Knee. (*Smithsonian Institution, National Anthropological Archives, Bureau of American Ethnology Collection*)

these young men and women. . . . Then I looked at myself. I was making money and living in white suburbia. . . . I started letting my hair grow long, and I stopped wearing a tie and started to sort of de-program myself" (*Reader's Digest* 1995, 366).

Although arrested and charged for the Wounded Knee siege, Means and Banks were cleared of any crimes for it. They were later imprisoned for other crimes and AIM's protest actions quieted down in the mid-1970s. AIM spent much time and effort during the period 1976–1994 to win the release of one of their leaders, Leonard Peltier, who was sentenced to two consecutive life terms for the murder of two FBI agents on the Pine Ridge Reservation. In 1994, these efforts culminated in the "Walk for Justice."

Like the black and Hispanic civil rights movements, the Native-American movement shifted its focus and tactics during the late 1970s and throughout the 1980s to the court and legislative arenas (Cornell 1988). It scored some significant victories in both areas. Native Americans fought legal battles over lands they claimed were taken in direct violation of treaty agreements. Over the course of two decades various Indian tribes sued a number of states over land, often settling the disputes when the courts awarded them millions of dollars in compensation for the lost land. They used court action in Maine, Massachusetts, Rhode Island, New York, South Carolina, Washington, South Dakota, Alaska, and even against the South Pacific Transportation Company, which settled with the Walker River Paiutes for $1.2 million over a land dispute.

The Alaska dispute exemplifies many of these long, drawn-out court battles over land. In 1970, the Alaskan Federation of Natives (AFN) took court action to stop what they termed the biggest land-grab in the history of the United States. They were disputing state seizure of 53,000 million acres of land. The 1971 Alaskan Claims Settlement Act awarded 44 million acres to the Inuits, Aleuts, and Eskimos and a cash settlement of nearly $1 billion. Further reforms in 1988 helped safeguard the original act, but as a major trade-off, the Alaskan Native Americans surrendered future claims to all aboriginal lands.

David Wilkins usefully distinguishes four major types of Indian political mobilization. He describes *intratribal groups,* wherein segments of tribes, frustrated by the direction of their tribal leaders, organize to confront the existing tribal power structure. He exemplifies this type by the Navajo Native American Church, the Diné Coalition and Diné C.A.R.E. (also two Navajo groups, the first organized against coal gasification programs, the latter as Citizens Against Ruining the Environment) (Wilkins 2002, 203).

Wilkins's second type are *tribal groups*—those 561 and counting recognized by the U.S. government (Wilkins 2002, 34).

His third type he calls *intertribal coalitions and alliances.* These are exemplified by such organizations as the Great Lakes Intertribal Council, the Alaska Native Brotherhood and Sisterhood, the Northwest Indian Fisheries Commission, the Council of Energy Resource Tribes, and the National Council of American Indians, which is the oldest, largest, and most representative intertribal interest group and was founded in 1944 (Wilkins 2002, 205–206). Box 8.4 presents an argument by controversial Professor Ward Churchill that emphasizes the offensive and racist nature of such majority society cultural practices.

The final type categorized by Wilkins is *Pan-Indian or Supratribal Organizations.* These organizations are made up of individual Indian members, often urban Indians, who join the organizations to promote goals they see as important to all Indian tribes, but are not organized nor pursued on a tribal representative basis. Examples of Pan-Indian groups are: the National Indian Youth Council (NIYC, 1961), the Alaska Federation of Natives (1966), the American Indian Movement (1968), the Indians of All Tribes (1969), the Native American Rights Fund (1970), the United Native Americans and the Institute for the Development of Indian Law (both 1971), the International Indian Treaty Council (1974), the Women of All Red Nations (1975), and the Indian Law Resource Center (1977) (Wilkins 2002, 208–213). The Council of Energy Resource Tribes (CERT) typifies these Pan-Indian groups in its approach and tactics.

In 1974, the pan-Indian organization, CERT, formed to press legal claims and to protect Indian lands from exploitation. It fought to ensure a fair return to tribes when natural resources were developed. It began with the twenty-five largest tribes; by 1990, over forty-five tribes had joined. In 1991, funds awarded to the Sioux tribes over a Black Hills land suit amounted to $330 million. As of 1995 the Sioux had refused to accept payment, insisting on control of the land rather than a cash settlement.

This period also saw Native Americans securing a number of legislative victories:

1. Indian Civil Rights Act of 1968, which reversed the termination policies of the 1950s and increased the number of Native Americans serving in the Bureau of Indian Affairs and other related federal agencies
2. Indian Education Act of 1972
3. Indian Self-Determination and Education Assistance Act of 1975
4. Indian Child Welfare Act of 1978, which halted the long-standing practice of forcing assimilation of Native Americans by mandatory attendance at boarding schools
5. Indian Religious Freedom Act of 1978, designed to protect sacred sites and allow certain religious practices (use of eagle feathers, the use of peyote), but rendered nearly ineffective by subsequent (1990s) court rulings

---

BOX 8.4   STICKS AND STONES . . . AND THE HURT OF NAME-CALLING

•

In recent years Native Americans have protested the use of Indian names and mascots by various sports teams—names such as the Atlanta "Braves," the Washington "Redskins," the Kansas City "Chiefs," the Florida State "Seminoles," and the Lamar Colorado High School "Savages," and mascots with head dress and beads, spears, and "warpainted" faces using gestures like the "tomahawk chop." Team owners and players, university officials, and many fans disagree with the position taken by Russell Means of the American Indian Movement and by the related American Indian Anti-Defamation Council. They insist that the use of these names and mascots is just "good, clean fun," and not intended to be offensive.

But such behavior *is* offensive. Imagine the uproar if we used comparable names and symbols for other racial and ethnic groups. As Indian author Ward Churchill put it, would society tolerate a football team called the "Niggers," with a half-time show featuring a simulated stewing of the opposing team's coach in a pot of boiling water while players danced around it garbed in leopard skins and wearing bones in their noses? What would be the reaction to such names as the San Diego "Spics" or the Wisconsin "Wetbacks"? How about a basketball team called the Gonzaga "Gooks"? Would Jews accept the name Kansas City "Kikes"? How would Italian Americans react to the Daytona "Dagos," or Polish Americans to the Pittsburgh "Polacks"? What about rechristening the Fighting Irish of Notre Dame the "Drunken Irish," or the "Papist Pigs"? Would society think it was just "good, clean fun" to call a women's basketball team the Detroit "Dykes"? These offensive examples illustrate why Native Americans are concerned. What is unacceptable for other racial and ethnic minorities ought to be equally unacceptable in their case.

In 1946 the Nuremberg Trials convicted and hanged a Nazi, Julius Streicker, for "crimes against humanity." Streicker published a tabloid titled *Der Sturmer*, in which he penned a series of anti-Semitic editorials, "news" stories, and cartoons depicting Jews in a derogatory fashion. He was prosecuted for propaganda that "dehumanized" Jews in the German public's mind, thereby creating the atmosphere that contributed to the holocaust, wherein some six million Jews and several million Gypsies, Poles, Slavs, homosexuals, and other "untermenschen" (subhumans) were exterminated. Russell Means and Ward Churchill have shown the parallels to the U.S. policy to "exterminate red savages." They note that from the year 1500, when Europeans arrived, the indigenous American Indian population was reduced from about 12.5 million to 250,000 at the beginning of the twentieth century. The majority society accepted the opinion that "the only good Indian was a dead Indian." The U.S. Army perpetrated numerous massacres of Indians— at Horsehoe Bend, Bear River, Sand Creek, Washita River, Marias River, Camp Robinson, and Wounded Knee. Native Americans were forcibly removed from the east and force-marched two thousand miles to the west in what today we would justifiably refer to as "ethnic cleansing." Native Americans were forcibly "assimilated." Their native culture was suppressed in reservation schools, where children were forced to adopt the Anglo culture. Indeed, for over a century the U.S. government implemented a national policy that today would fit actions specifically prohibited by Article II of the UN Genocide Convention.

Data published by the U.S. government show that Native Americans have the lowest annual and lifetime per capita incomes of any group. They suffer the highest rates of infant mortality and death by exposure, malnutrition, and diseases related to alcoholism and substance abuse. Native American men living on reservations have a life expectancy of forty-five years, and women of forty-eight years.

Thus, Native Americans are right to want the U.S. public to consider the implications of the use of derogatory names and images. We need to think about the real situation of American Indians and understand that the treatment of them in U.S. culture is not "good, clean fun." Such practices cause pain and suffering and are as much a crime against humanity as was the treatment of the Jews in Nazi Germany. Native Americans have every right to call a halt to such practices.

Source: Box by author, adaptation of the ideas of Ward Churchill in "Crimes against Humanity," *Z Magazine* (March 1993): 43–47.

6. 1988 Indian Gaming Regulation Act, which resulted, by 1994, in 23 states having Native-American–operated gaming on their reservations netting some $600 million for the 200 tribes involved. (Wilkins 2002, xxv).

Table 8.3 lists the names and tribal affiliations of Native Americans elected to various state legislature.

The Clinton administration appointed Ada Deer, a Menominee Indian leader who had led the fight against the Termination Act, director of the Bureau of Indian Affairs. In 1994, in a symbolic show of support for Native Americans, President Clinton hosted a conference of 547 leaders of the federally recognized tribes. It was the largest Native-American meeting with a U.S. president.

The 1980s saw Native-American organizations, both intertribal and Pan-Indian groups, split in their goals. Some were largely "reformative" in their goals. They were accommodationist and sought to "improve" the conditions of life for Native Americans through reforms won by legislation or court action. This approach is exemplified by former Senator Ben Nighthorse Campbell (R–Co), who in 1992 became the first Native American elected to the U.S. Senate. In contrast were the **transformative goals** of anti-assimilationist and anti-acculturationist groups (such as AIM), who sought a fundamental restructuring of Native-American–white relations. In the 1990s, AIM again attracted national media attention with a series of protests against the various national sports franchises (baseball, basketball, football) that use Native-American logos and mascots in racially offensive ways. They objected to the use of the tomahawk chop and degrading caricatures that embody mocking stereotypes. Although spokespersons for the teams responded that such usage was not racist or intentionally offensive, AIM leaders such as Russell Means argued they clearly were racist. Table 8.4 presents Native Americans who have served or are serving in the U.S. Congress.

As with the Black and the Brown Power movements, the more radical politics of the Red Power movement waned after 1980. The court and legislative victories of the movement modified the status and enabled a greater degree of economic and political incorporation. The tribes with gaming operations acquired considerable economic resources and success. They applied their new-found economic clout to wielding electoral power.

SUMMARY

Not all minority groups choose assimilation or the accommodationist approach. This chapter reviewed three groups that pursued new-style radicalism: blacks, Hispanics, and Native Americans. The black civil rights movement arose during the late 1950s and 1960s. It developed new tactics and organizations to pursue nonviolent protest politics. The chapter explored such groups as SCLC, SNCC, CORE and their use of sit-ins, freedom rides, and protest marches that peacefully confronted de jure segregation and Jim Crowism. It focused on the groups and leaders who developed and articulated the strategy of new-style radicalism, setting the model with black power that inspired subsequent movements. It discussed the use of more radical protest politics, focusing on the Black Panthers and on urban riots of the late 1960s as political protests.

Table 8.3 Native-American State Legislators, 1999–2001

State	Body	Name	Tribe	Party	First Elected
Arizona	House	Sylvia Laughter	Navajo	Democrat	1999
		Deborah Norris	Tohono O'Odham	Democrat	1997
		Sally Gonzalez	Pascua Yaqui	Democrat	1997
	Senate	Jack Jackson	Navajo	Democrat	1999
Alaska	House	Irene Nicholai	Athabascan	Democrat	1992
		Bill Williams	Tlingit	Democrat	1980
		Albert Kookesh	Tlingit	Democrat	1996
		Beverly Masek	Athabascan	Republican	1994
		Reggie Joule	Inupiat Eskimo	Democrat	1996
		Mary Sattler	Yup'ik Eskimo	Democrat	1999
	Senate	Lyman Hoffman	Yup'ik Eskimo	Democrat	1994
		Al Adams	Inupaic	Democrat	1980
		Georgiana Lincoln	Athabascan	Democrat	1992
Montana	House	Jay Stovall	Crow	Republican	1993
		Bill Eggars	Crow	Democrat	1999
		Carol Juneau	Mandan Hidatsa	Democrat	1999
		Frank Smith	Assiniboine	Democrat	1999
New Mexico	House	Leo Watchman	Navajo	Democrat	1993
		James Madelena	Jemez Pueblo	Democrat	1985
		Ray Begay	Navajo	Democrat	1999
		Lynda Lovejoy	Navajo	Democrat	1989
	Senate	John Pinto	Navajo	Democrat	1977
		Leo Tsosie	Navajo	Democrat	1993
North Carolina	House	Ronnie Sutton	Lumbee	Democrat	1991
North Dakota	House	Les LaFountain	Chippewa	Democrat	1995
Oklahoma	House	Kelley Haney	Seminole Creek	Democrat	1987
South Dakota	House	Ron Volesky	Standing Rock Sioux	Democrat	1980
		Richard Hagen	Oglala Sioux	Democrat	1982
	Senate	Paul Valandra	Rosebud Sioux	Democrat	1990

Source: Table by author from data in Paula D. McClain, *Can We All Get Along?* Second Edition. 1995. Reprinted by permission of Westview Press, a member of Perseus Books, L.L.C.

The chapter then went on to the development of brown power, emphasizing the Chicano protest movement. It discussed both rural and urban variations, drawing close parallels between the Hispanic movement and the black civil rights movement. It described various groups and leaders who promoted strikes, boycotts, land grant protests, and the young urban Chicano groups that sprang up in the nation's barrios.

Finally, it described the red power protest movement of Native Americans. Describing the various protest organizations of the pan-Indian movement, it showed how they

Table 8.4   Native Americans Who Have Served in the U.S. Congress

Name	Tribe	State	Years Served
Senate			
Matthew Stanley Quay	Abenaki/Delaware	Pennsylvania	1887–1899; 1901–1904
Charles Curtis	Kaw-Osage	Kansas	1907–1913; 1915–1929
Robert Owen	Cherokee	Oklahoma	1907–1925
Ben Nighthorse Campbell	N. Cheyenne	Colorado	1992–1998; 1998–2004
House of Representatives			
Charles Curtis	Kaw-Osage	Kansas	1893–1907
Charles D. Carter	Choctaw	Oklahoma	1907–1927
W. W. Hastings	Cherokee	Oklahoma	1915–1921; 1923–1935
William G. Stigler	Choctaw	Oklahoma	1944–1952
Benjamin Reifel	Rosebud Sioux	S. Dakota	1961–1971
Ben Nighthorse Campbell	N. Cheyenne	Colorado	1987–1992

Source: Table by author, from data in Paula D. McClain, *Can We All Get Along?* Second Edition. 1995 Reprinted by permission of Westview Press, a member of Perseus Books, L.L.C.

modified and adapted protest politics to suit their needs and aspirations. It assessed the failures and accomplishments of the red power movement.

KEY TERMS

Aztlan   The "lost land" of Mexico, the present-day Southwest of the United States.

barrio   The neighborhood or urban village; the Hispanic section of a major urban area in the United States.

black power   Ability of black people to get together politically and organize to speak from a position of strength rather than weakness.

La Huelga   "The strike."

La Raza   "The race" or "the people," the Chicano term for Mexicans, Mexican Americans.

La Raza Unida (Partido)   "The united race" or "united people." It also refers to the political party formed by Chicanos, mostly in Texas.

relative deprivation   Sociological theory; mostly refers to black income relative to white income.

reverse discrimination   Programs of preference toward minorities, held to constitute discriminatory treatment of the white majority.

rising expectations   The conscious feeling of negative discrepancy between legitimate expectations and present actualities.

transformative goals   Goals seeking a fundamental restructuring of Native-American–white relations.

REVIEW QUESTIONS

1. Discuss two pre–World War II black civil rights organizations that were accommodationists. Compare them to two more militant organizations formed in the 1960s.

2. Which U.S. Supreme Court decision established the separate-but-equal doctrine? Discuss its role in inspiring the new black civil rights movement.

3. What was the most sweeping civil rights law ever enacted by the U.S. Congress? What protest actions were critically instrumental in its enactment?

4. Describe the assimilationist Hispanic groups of the pre-1960s era.

5. Which Chicano leader became the best known, often characterized as the Martin Luther King Jr. of the Chicano movement? What organization did he lead? What tactics did he use?

6. What takeover protest brought the New Mexico land grant protest to national attention? When and why did it die off?

7. In the Chicano movement, to what does Aztlan refer? What militant Chicano youth organization did this concept inspire? What tactics do they use?

8. Specify any two pan-Indian organizations. Compare and contrast them in style and tactics with black or Chicano groups.

9. What is the most notably militant pan-Indian organization? Discuss its style and tactics. What black and Chicano groups does it resemble?

10. Compare the "black power," "brown power," and "red power" movements. Which of the three resulted in the greater degree of civic incorporation? What evidence from this chapter can you cite to exemplify why you so rate each movement?

NOTES

1. The volumes on the civil rights movement and its personalities are too numerous to cite here, but see, in particular, Branch (1988), Cross (1984), and White (1991). See also Carson (1981), Gonzales (1996), Kitano (1997), Kivisto (1995), LeMay (1985), Marger (2003), and Schaefer (1998).

2. See note 1. See also, for in-depth treatments of the struggle, Burma (1970), Chavez (1984), and Steiner (1969).

3. See Howard (1983) and Fitzpatrick (1968) for accounts of the activities of Puerto Ricans in New York City.

ADDITIONAL READINGS

Anderson, Carol. *Eyes Off the Prize: The United Nations and the African American Struggle for Human Rights, 1944–1955.* New York: Cambridge University Press, 2003.

Anderson, Karen. *Changing Woman: A History of Racial Ethnic Women in Modern America.* New York: Oxford University Press, 1997.

Andreas, Peter, and Thomas J. Biersteker, eds. *The Rebordering of North America: Integration and Exclusion in a New Security Context.* New York: Routledge, 2003.

Chalmers, David. *Backfire: How the Ku Klux Klan Helped the Civil Rights Movement.* Lanham, MD: Rowman and Littlefield, 2003.

Cornell, Stephen. *The Return of the Native: American Indian Political Resurgence.* New York: Oxford University Press, 1988.

Crawford, Vicki, Jacqueline Anne Rouse, and Barbara Woods, eds. *Women in the Civil Rights Movement: Trailblazers and Torchbearers, 1941–1965.* Berkeley: University of California Press, 1998.

Fixico, Donald. *The American Indian Mind in a Linear World.* New York: Routledge, 2003.

Glusker, Ann. *Fertility Patterns of Native and Foreign-Born Women: Assimilating to Diversity.* New York: LFB Publishing, 2003.

Henton, Tim B., Bruce A. Chadwick, and Cardell K. Jackson. *Statistical Handbook on Racial Groups in the United States.* Phoenix, AZ: The Oryx Press, 2000.

Meier, Matt S., and Margo Gutierrez, *Encyclopedia of Mexican-American Civil Rights Movement.* Westport, CT: Greenwood Press, 2000.

Morehouse, Maggi M. *Fighting in the Jim Crow Army: Black Men and Women Remember World War II.* Lanham, MD: Rowman and Littlefield, 2000.

Nagel, Joane. *American Indian Ethnic Renewal: Red Power and the Resurgence of Identity and Culture.* New York: Oxford University Press, 1996.

Rasmussen, R. Kent. *Farewell to Jim Crow: The Rise and Fall of Segregation in America.* New York: Facts on File, 1997.

Robnett, Belinda. *How Long? How Long? African-American Women in the Struggle for Civil Rights.* New York: Oxford University Press, 2000.

Swain, Carol M. *The New White Nationalism in America: Its Challenge to Integration.* New York: Cambridge University Press, 2002.

Wilkins, David E. *American Indian Politics and the American Political System.* New York: Rowman and Littlefield, 2002.

• *Reading 8.1*

Martin Luther King, Jr.: "Letter from a Birmingham Jail"

My dear fellow clergymen:
While confined here in the Birmingham city jail, I came across your recent statement calling my present activities "unwise and untimely." Seldom do I pause to answer criticism of my work and ideas. . . . But since I feel that you are men of genuine good will and that your criticisms are sincerely set forth, I want to try to answer your statement in what I hope will be patient and reasonable terms. . . .

I think I should indicate why I am here in Birmingham, since you have been influenced by the view which argues against "outsiders coming in." . . . I am here because I have organizational ties here. . . . But more basically, I am in Birmingham because injustice is here . . .

Moreover, I am cognizant of the interrelatedness of all communities and states. I cannot sit idly by in Atlanta and not be concerned about what happens in Birmingham. Injustice anywhere is a threat to justice everywhere. We are caught in an inescapable network of mutuality, tied in a single garment of destiny.

Whatever affects one directly, affects all indirectly. Never again can we afford to live with the narrow, provincial "outside agitator" idea. Anyone who lives inside the United States can never be considered an outsider anywhere within its bounds.

You deplore the demonstrations taking place in Birmingham. But your statement, I am sorry to say, fails to express a similar concern for the conditions that brought about the demonstrations.

I am sure that none of you would want to rest content with the superficial kind of social analysis that deals merely with effects and does not grapple with underlying causes. It is unfortunate that demonstrations are taking place in Birmingham, but it is even more unfortunate that the city's white power structure left the Negro community with no alternative.

In any nonviolent campaign there are four basic steps: collection of the facts to determine whether injustices exist; negotiation; self-purification; and direct action. We have gone through all these steps in Birmingham.

There can be no gainsaying the fact that racial injustice engulfs this community. Birmingham is probably the most thoroughly segregated city in the United States. Its ugly record of brutality is widely known. Negroes have experienced grossly unjust treatment in the courts. There have been more unsolved bombings of Negro homes and churches in Birmingham than in any other city in the nation. These are the hard, brutal facts of the case . . .

On the basis of these conditions, Negro leaders sought to negotiate with city fathers. But the latter consistently refused to engage in good-faith negotiation. Then, last September, came the opportunity to talk with leaders of Birmingham's economic community.

In the course of the negotiations, certain promises were made by the merchants—for example, to remove the stores' humiliating racial signs.

On the basis of these promises, the Reverend Fred Shuttlesworth and the leaders of the Alabama Christian Movement for Human Rights agreed to a moratorium on all demonstrations. As the weeks and months went by, we realized that we were the victims of a broken promise. A few signs, briefly removed, returned; the others remained.

As in so many past experiences, our hopes had been blasted, and the shadow of deep disappointment settled upon us. We had no alternative except to prepare for direct action, whereby we would present our very bodies as a means of laying our case before the conscience of the local and the national community.

Mindful of the difficulties involved, we decided to undertake the process of self-purification. We began a series of workshops on nonviolence, and we repeatedly asked ourselves: "Are you able to accept blows without retaliation?" "Are you able to endure the ordeal of jail?". . .

You may well ask, "Why direct action? Why sit-ins, marches, and so forth? Isn't negotiation a better path?" You are quite right in calling for negotiation. Indeed, this is the very purpose of direct action. Nonviolent direct action seeks to create such a crisis and foster such a tension that a community which has constantly refused to negotiate is forced to confront the issue. It seeks so to dramatize the issue that it can no longer be ignored.

My citing the creation of tension as part of the work of the nonviolent resister may sound rather shocking. But I must confess that I am not afraid of the word "tension." I have earnestly opposed violent tension, but there is a type of constructive, nonviolent tension which is necessary for growth.

Just as Socrates felt that it was necessary to create a tension in the mind so that individuals could rise from the bondage of myths and half-truths to the unfettered realm of creative analysis and objective appraisal, so must we see the need for nonviolent gadflies to create the kind of tension in society that will help men rise from the dark depths of prejudice and racism to the majestic heights of understanding and brotherhood.

The purpose of our direct-action program is to create a situation so crisis-packed that it will inevitably open the door to negotiation. I therefore concur with you in your call for negotiation. Too long has our beloved Southland been bogged down in a tragic effort to live in monologue rather than dialogue.

One of the basic points in your statement is that the action that I and my associates have taken in Birmingham is untimely. Some have asked: "Why didn't you give the new city administration time to act?" The only answer that I can give to this query is that the new Birmingham administration must be prodded about as much as the outgoing one, before it will act. . . .

We have not made a single gain in civil rights without determined legal and non-violent pressure. . . . Lamentably, it is an historical fact that privileged groups seldom give up their privileges voluntarily. Individuals may see the moral light and voluntarily give up their unjust posture; but, as Reinhold Niebuhr has reminded us, groups tend to be more immoral than individuals.

We know through painful experience that freedom is never voluntarily given by the oppressor. It must be demanded by the oppressed. Frankly, I have yet to engage in a direct-action campaign that was "well timed" in view of those who have not suffered unduly from the disease of segregation.

For years now I have heard the word "Wait!" It rings in the ear of every Negro with piercing familiarity. This "Wait!" has almost always meant "Never." We must come to see, with one of our distinguished jurists, that "justice too long delayed is justice denied."

We have waited for more than 340 years for our constitutional and God-given rights. The nations of Asia and Africa are moving with jetlike speed toward gaining political independence, but we still creep at horse-and-buggy pace toward gaining a cup of coffee at a lunch counter. Perhaps it is easy for those who have never felt the stinging darts of segregation to say, "Wait."

But when you have seen vicious mobs lynch your mothers and fathers at will and drown your sisters and brothers at whim;

when you have seen hate-filled policemen curse, kick and even kill your black brothers and sisters;

when you see the vast majority of your twenty million Negro brothers smothering in an airtight cage of poverty in the midst of an affluent society;

when you suddenly find your tongue twisted and your speech stammering as you seek to explain to your six-year-old daughter why she can't go to the public amusement park that has just been advertised on television, and see tears welling up in her eyes when she is told that Funtown is closed to colored children, and see ominous clouds of inferiority beginning to form in her little mental sky, and see her beginning to distort her personality by developing an unconscious bitterness toward white people;

when you have to concoct an answer for a five-year-old son who is asking, "Daddy, why do white people treat colored people so mean?";

when you take a cross-country drive and find it necessary to sleep night after night in the uncomfortable corners of your automobile because no motel will accept you;

when you are humiliated day in and day out by nagging signs reading "white" and "colored";

when your first name becomes "nigger," your middle name becomes "boy" (however old you are) and your last name becomes "John," and your wife and mother are never given the respected title "Mrs.";

when you are harried by day and haunted by night by the fact that you are a Negro, living constantly at tiptoe stance, never quite knowing what to expect next, and are plagued with inner fears and outer resentments;

when you are forever fighting a degenerating sense of "nobodiness"—then you will understand why we find it difficult to wait.

There comes a time when the cup of endurance runs over, and men are no longer willing to be plunged into the abyss of despair. I hope, sirs, you can understand our legitimate and unavoidable impatience.

You express a great deal of anxiety over our willingness to break laws. This is certainly a legitimate concern. Since we so diligently urge people to obey the Supreme Court's decision of 1954 outlawing segregation in the public schools, at first glance it may seem rather paradoxical for us consciously to break laws.

One may well ask: "How can you advocate breaking some laws and obeying others?" The answer lies in the fact that there are two types of laws: just and unjust. I would be the first to advocate obeying just laws. One has not only a legal but a moral responsibility to obey just laws. Conversely, one has a moral responsibility to disobey unjust laws. I would agree with St. Augustine that "an unjust law is no law at all."

Now, what is the difference between the two? How does one determine whether a law is just or unjust? A just law is a man-made code that squares with the moral law or the law of God. An unjust law is a code that is out of harmony with the moral law.

To put it in the terms of St. Thomas Aquinas: An unjust law is a human law that is not rooted in eternal law and natural law. Any law that uplifts human personality is just. Any law that degrades human personality is unjust.

All segregation statutes are unjust because segregation distorts the soul and damages the personality. It gives the segregator a false sense of superiority and the segregated a false sense of inferiority. . . .

Let us consider a more concrete example of just and unjust laws. An unjust law is a code that a numerical or power majority group compels a minority group to obey but does not make binding on itself. This is *difference* made legal. By the same token, a just law is a code that a majority compels a minority to follow and that it is willing to follow itself. This is *sameness* made legal.

Let me give another explanation. A law is unjust if it is inflicted on a minority that, as a result of being denied the right to vote, had no part in enacting or devising the law. Who can say that the legislature of Alabama which set up that state's segregation laws was democratically elected?

Throughout Alabama all sorts of devious methods are used to prevent Negroes from becoming registered voters, and there are some counties in which, even though Negroes constitute a majority of the population, not a single Negro is registered. Can any law enacted under such circumstances be considered democratically structured?

Sometimes a law is just on its face and unjust in its application. For instance, I have been arrested on a charge of parading without a permit. Now, there is nothing wrong in having an ordinance which requires a permit for a parade. But such an ordinance becomes unjust when it is used to maintain segregation and to deny citizens the First-Amendment privilege of peaceful assembly and protest.

I hope you are able to see the distinction I am trying to point out. In no sense do I advocate evading or defying the law, as would the rabid segregationist. That would lead to anarchy.

One who breaks an unjust law must do so openly, lovingly and with a willingness to accept the penalty. I submit that an individual who breaks a law that conscience tells him is unjust, and who willingly accepts the penalty of imprisonment in order to arouse the conscience of the community over its injustice, is in reality expressing the highest respect for law.

Of course, there is nothing new about this kind of civil disobedience. It was evidenced sublimely in the refusal of Shadrach, Meshach, and Abednego to obey the laws of Nebuchadnezzar, on the ground that a higher moral law was at stake. It was practiced superbly by the early Christians, who were willing to face hungry lions and the excruciating pain of chopping blocks rather than submit to certain unjust laws of the Roman Empire.

To a degree, academic freedom is a reality today because Socrates practiced civil disobedience. In our own nation, the Boston Tea Party represented a massive act of civil disobedience.

We should never forget that everything Adolf Hitler did in Germany was "legal" and everything the Hungarian freedom fighters did in Hungary was "illegal." It was "illegal" to aid and comfort a Jew in Hitler's Germany. Even so, I am sure that, had I lived in Germany at the time, I would have aided and comforted my Jewish brothers. If today I lived in a Communist country where certain principles dear to the Christian faith are suppressed, I would openly advocate disobeying that country's anti-religious laws.

I must make two honest confessions to you, my Christian and Jewish brothers. First, I must confess that over the past few years I have been gravely disappointed with the white moderate. I have almost reached the regrettable conclusion that the Negro's great stumbling block in his stride toward freedom is not the White Citizen's Councilor or the Ku Klux Klanner, but the white moderate, who is more devoted to "order" than to justice; who prefers a negative peace which is the absence of tension to a positive peace which is the presence of justice; who constantly says, "I agree with you in the goal you seek, but I cannot agree with your methods of direct action"; who paternalistically believes he can set the timetable for another man's freedom; who lives by a mythical concept of time and who constantly advises the Negro to wait for a "more convenient season."

Shallow understanding from people of good will is more frustrating than absolute misunderstanding from people of ill will. Lukewarm acceptance is much more bewildering than outright rejection.

I had hoped that the white moderate would understand that law and order exist for the purpose of establishing justice and that when they fail in this purpose they become the dangerously structured dams that block the flow of social progress.

I had hoped that the white moderate would understand that the present tension in the South is a necessary phase of the transition from an obnoxious negative peace, in which the Negro passively accepted his unjust plight, to a substantive and positive peace, in which all men will respect the dignity and worth of human personality.

Actually, we who engage in nonviolent direct action are not the creators of tension. We merely bring to the surface the hidden tension that is already alive. We bring it out in the open, where it can be seen and dealt with. Like a boil that can never be cured so long as it is covered up but must be opened with all its ugliness to the natural medicines of air and light, injustice must be exposed, with all the tension its exposure creates, to the light of human conscience and the air of national opinion, before it can be cured.

In your statement you assert that our actions, even though peaceful, must be condemned because they precipitate violence. But is this a logical assertion? Isn't this like condemning a robbed man because his possession of money precipitated the evil act of robbery? . . .

We must come to see that, as the federal courts have consistently affirmed, it is wrong to urge an individual to cease his efforts to gain his basic constitutional rights because the quest may precipitate violence. Society must protect the robbed and punish the robber.

I had also hoped that the white moderate would reject the myth concerning time in relation to the struggle for freedom. . . . Actually, time itself is neutral; it can be used either destructively or constructively. More and more I feel that the people of ill will have used time much more effectively than have the people of good will. We will have to repent in this generation not merely for the hateful words and actions of the bad people, but for the appalling silence of the good people.

Human progress never rolls in on wheels of inevitability; it comes through the tireless efforts of men willing to be co-workers with God, and without this hard work, time itself becomes an ally of the forces of stagnation. We must use time creatively, in the knowledge that the time is always ripe to do right.

Now is the time to make real the promise of democracy and transform our pending national elegy into a creative psalm of brotherhood. Now is the time to lift our national policy from the quicksand of racial injustice to the solid rock of human dignity.

You speak of our activity in Birmingham as extreme. At first I was rather disappointed that fellow clergymen would see my nonviolent efforts as those of an extremist. I began thinking about the fact that I stand in the middle of two opposing forces in the Negro community.

One is a force of complacency, made up in part of Negroes who, as a result of long years of oppression, are so drained of self-respect and a sense of "somebodiness" that they have adjusted to segregation; and in part of a few middle-class Negroes who, because of a degree of academic and economic security and because in some ways they profit by segregation, have become insensitive to the problems of the masses.

The other force is one of bitterness and hatred, and it comes perilously close to advocating violence. It is expressed in the various black nationalist groups that are springing up across the nation, the largest and best-known being Elijah Muhammad's Muslim movement. Nourished by the Negro's frustration over the continued existence of racial discrimination, this movement is made up of people who have lost faith in America, who have absolutely repudiated Christianity, and who have concluded that the white man is an incorrigible "devil."

I have tried to stand between these two forces, saying that we need emulate neither the "do-nothingism" of the complacent nor the hatred and despair of the black nationalist. For there is the more excellent way of love and nonviolent protest. I am grateful to God that, through the influence of the Negro church, the way of nonviolence became an integral part of our struggle.

If this philosophy had not emerged, by now many streets of the South would, I am convinced, be flowing with blood. And I am further convinced that if our white brothers dismiss as "rabble-rousers" and "outside agitators" those of us who employ nonviolent direct action, and if they refuse to support our nonviolent efforts, millions of Negroes will, out of frustration and despair, seek solace and security in black-nationalist ideologies—a development that would inevitably lead to a frightening racial nightmare.

Oppressed people cannot remain oppressed forever. The yearning for freedom eventually manifests itself, and that is what has happened to the American Negro. Something within has reminded him of his birthright of freedom, and something without has reminded him that it can be gained. Consciously or unconsciously, he has been caught up by the Zeitgeist, and with his black brothers of Africa and his brown and yellow brothers of Asia, South America and the Caribbean, the U.S. Negro is moving with a sense of great urgency toward the promised land of racial justice.

If one recognizes this vital urge that has engulfed the Negro community, one should readily understand why public demonstrations are taking place. The Negro has many pent-up resentments and latent frustrations, and he must release them. So let him march; let him make prayer pilgrimages to the city hall; let him go on freedom rides—and try to understand why he must do so.

If his repressed emotions are not released in nonviolent ways, they will seek expression through violence; this is not a threat but a fact of history. So I have not said to my people, "Get rid of your discontent." Rather, I have tried to say that this normal and healthy discontent can be channeled into the creative outlet of nonviolent direct action. And now this approach is being termed extremist.

But though I was initially disappointed at being categorized as an extremist, as I continued to think about the matter I gradually gained a measure of satisfaction from the label.

Was not Jesus an extremist for love: "Love your enemies, bless them that curse you, do good to them that hate you, and pray for them which despitefully use you, and persecute you."

Was not Amos an extremist for justice: "Let justice roll down like waters and righteousness like an ever-flowing stream.". . .

And John Bunyan: "I will stay in jail to the end of my days before I make a butchery of my conscience."

And Abraham Lincoln: "This nation cannot survive half slave and half free." And Thomas Jefferson: "We hold these truths to be self-evident, that all men are created equal. . . ."

So the question is not whether we will be extremists, but what kind of extremists we will be. Will we be extremists for hate or for love? Will we be extremists for the preservation of injustice or for the extension of justice?. . . Perhaps the South, the nation, and the world are in dire need of creative extremists.

I had hoped that the white moderate would see this need. Perhaps I was too optimistic; perhaps I expected too much. I suppose I should have realized that few members of the oppressor race can understand the deep groans and passionate yearnings of the oppressed race, and still fewer have the vision to see that injustice must be rooted out by strong, persistent, and determined action.

I am thankful, however, that some of our white brothers in the South have grasped the meaning of this social revolution and committed themselves to it. They are still all too few in quantity, but they are big in quality. Some—such as Ralph McGill, Lillian Smith, Harry Golden, James McBride Dabbs, Ann Braden, and Sarah Patton Boyle—have written about our struggle in eloquent and prophetic terms.

Others have marched with us down nameless streets of the South. They have languished in filthy, roach-infested jails, suffering the abuse and brutality of policemen who view them as "dirty nigger-lovers." Unlike so many of their moderate brothers and sisters, they have recognized the urgency of the moment and sensed the need for powerful "action" antidotes to combat the disease of segregation.

Let me take note of my other major disappointment. I have been so greatly disappointed with the white church and its leadership.

Of course, there are some notable exceptions. I am not unmindful of the fact that each of you has taken some significant stands on this issue. I commend you, Reverend Stallings, for your Christian stand on this past Sunday, in welcoming Negroes to your worship service on a nonsegregated basis. I commend the Catholic leaders of this state for integrating Spring Hill College several years ago.

But despite these notable exceptions, I must honestly reiterate that I have been disappointed with the church. I do not say this as one of those negative critics who can always find something wrong with the church. I say this as a minister of the gospel, who loves the church; who was nurtured in its bosom; who has been sustained by its spiritual blessings and who will remain true to it as long as the cord of life shall lengthen.

When I was suddenly catapulted into the leadership of the bus protest in Montgomery, Alabama, a few years ago, I felt we would be supported by the white church. I felt that the white ministers, priests and rabbis of the South would be among our strongest allies. Instead, some have been outright opponents, refusing to understand the freedom movement and misrepresenting its leaders; all too many others have been more cautious than courageous and have remained silent behind the anesthetizing security of stained-glass windows.

In spite of my shattered dreams, I came to Birmingham with the hope that the white religious leadership of this community would see the justice of our cause and, with deep moral concern, would serve as the channel through which our just grievances could reach the power structure. I had hoped that each of you would understand. But again I have been disappointed.

I have heard numerous southern religious leaders admonish their worshipers to comply with a desegregation decision because it is the law, but I have longed to hear white ministers declare: "Follow this decree because integration is morally right and because the Negro is your brother."

In the midst of blatant injustices inflicted upon the Negro, I have watched white churchmen stand on the sideline and mouth pious irrelevancies and sanctimonious trivialities. In the midst of a mighty struggle to rid our nation of racial and economic injustice, I have heard many ministers say: "Those are social issues, with which the gospel has no real concern." And I have watched many churches commit themselves to a completely otherworldly religion which makes a strange, un-Biblical distinction between body and soul; between the sacred and the secular. . . .

I hope the church as a whole will meet the challenge of this decisive hour. But even if the church does not come to the aid of justice, I have no despair about the future. I have no fear about the outcome of our struggle in Birmingham, even if our motives are at present misunderstood. We will reach the goal of freedom in Birmingham and all over the nation, because the goal of America is freedom.

Abused and scorned though we may be, our destiny is tied up with America's destiny. Before the pilgrims landed at Plymouth, we were here. For more than two centuries our forebears labored in this country, without wages; they made cotton king; they built the homes of their masters while suffering gross injustice and shameful humiliation—and yet out of a bottomless vitality they continued to thrive and develop.

If the inexpressible cruelties of slavery could not stop us, the opposition we now face will surely fail. We will win our freedom because the sacred heritage of our nation and the eternal will of God are embodied in our echoing demands.

Before closing I feel impelled to mention one other point in your statement that has troubled me profoundly. You warmly commended the Birmingham police force for keeping "order" and "preventing violence."

I doubt that you would have so warmly commended the police force if you had seen its dogs sinking their teeth into unarmed, nonviolent Negroes. I doubt that you would so quickly commend the policemen if you were to observe their ugly and inhumane treatment of Negroes here in the city jail; if you were to watch them push and curse old Negro women and young Negro girls; if you were to see them slap and kick old Negro men and young boys; if you were to observe them, as they did on two occasions, refuse to give us food because we wanted to sing our grace together. I cannot join you in your praise of the Birmingham police department.

It is true that the police have exercised a degree of discipline in handling the demonstrators. In this sense they have conducted themselves rather "nonviolently" in public. But for what purpose? To preserve the evil system of segregation.

Over the past few years I have consistently preached that nonviolence demands that the means we use must be as pure as the ends we seek. I have tried to make clear that it is wrong to use immoral means to attain moral ends. But now I must affirm that it is just as wrong, or perhaps even more so, to use moral means to preserve immoral ends. . . . As T. S. Eliot has said, "The last temptation is the greatest treason: to do the right deed for the wrong reason."

I wish you had commended the Negro sit-inners and demonstrators of Birmingham for their sublime courage, their willingness to suffer, and their amazing discipline in the midst of great provocation. One day the South will recognize its real heroes. They will be the James Merediths, with the noble sense of purpose that enables them to face jeering and hostile mobs, and with the agonizing loneliness that characterizes the life of the pioneer. They will be old, oppressed, battered Negro women, symbolized in a seventy-two-year-old woman in Montgomery, Alabama, who rose up with a sense of dignity and with her people decided not to ride segregated buses, and who responded with ungrammatical profundity to one who inquired about her weariness: "My feets is tired, but my soul is at rest."

They will be the young high school and college students, the young ministers of the gospel and a host of their elders, courageously and nonviolently sitting in at lunch counters and willingly going to jail for conscience' sake. One day the South will know that when these disinherited children of God sat down at lunch counters, they were in reality standing up for what is best in the American dream and for the most sacred values in our Judaeo-Christian heritage, thereby bringing our nation back to those great wells of democracy which were dug deep by the founding fathers in their formulation of the Constitution and the Declaration of Independence.

Never before have I written so long a letter. I'm afraid it is much too long to take your precious time. I can assure you that it would have been much shorter if I had been writing from a comfortable desk, but what else can one do when he is alone in a narrow jail cell, other than write long letters, think long thoughts and pray long prayers? . . .

Yours for the cause of peace and brotherhood,
Martin Luther King, Jr.

CHAPTER 9

ARENAS OF THE STRUGGLE

Previous chapters focused on the nature of racial and ethnic relations in America and on the strategies and tactics adopted by various minority groups to cope with the effects of their status. Certain public policy areas move to the forefront of relations between the two cultures. A minority group is categorized as such precisely because it lacks sufficient political power to influence certain policy areas to its benefit or because it is unable to restrain the majority culture from using public policy to its detriment. Majority society employs public policy to treat members of the minority in a negatively differential manner. The majority develops a degree of structural or institutionalized discrimination against the minority. Certain public policy areas become arenas of the struggle over power relations between the majority and minority groups.

When a minority group strives to change its minority power status, whether through accommodation, separatism, or radicalism, it does so by using those strategies to influence public policy. Several policy areas can be viewed as more important arenas of conflict in minority/majority relations. While virtually any policy area can be used by the majority society to "keep a minority in its place," and while a minority may seek to influence any number of policy areas more likely to respond to its particular needs, capabilities, or resources, this chapter focuses on six policy areas especially important to their struggle: education, employment, housing, immigration, law enforcement, and political participation.

The chapter highlights aspects of each policy arena used to discriminate against minority groups in American society. It shows that some minority groups have sought to influence those policy areas to redress their minority status and mitigate related problems. When some in majority society are convinced a "problem" exists and change is needed, they advocate or support proposals for change in one or more of these six policy areas.

EDUCATION

Of these six areas critically important to majority/minority relations, none is more basic or significant in its impact than that of education. Discrimination in educational opportunity is the primary method to enforce minority status. Poor educational background influences occupational and income opportunities, related housing options, and the social status of the individual.

Segregation in schools has been the most pronounced and longstanding form of institutionalized discrimination. The segregation of Native Americans within special reservation schools and the segregation of Chinese and Japanese students from the 1880s to 1920s in California, exemplify de jure segregation; that is, formal segregation based on law. The most significant use of de jure segregation, both in terms of numbers and of impact, was directed against black Americans.

Despite the Fourteenth Amendment, reconstruction had clearly failed by 1877. Southern states increasingly enacted what came to be known as Jim Crow laws which segregated all aspects of life, including education. Jim Crow laws effectively kept blacks in second-class citizenship status. Although the Fourteenth Amendment states: "No State shall make or enforce any law which shall abridge the privileges or immunities of citizens of the United States; nor shall any State deprive any person of life, liberty or property, without due process of law; nor any person within its jurisdiction the equal protection of the law, . . ." the Supreme Court ruled state laws segregating the races were constitutional as long as persons in each of the segregated races were protected equally. This "separate but equal" legal doctrine became the Court's interpretation of the Fourteenth Amendment in *Plessy v. Ferguson* (163 U.S. 537, 1896). This doctrine gave a constitutional blessing to de jure segregation—to all Jim Crow laws. It led to extensive segregation of all public facilities, especially schools. Segregated facilities are seldom, if ever, equal in reality. Black schools, as were Indian and Asian schools in the West, were poorer in physical aspects. They had dilapidated and overcrowded buildings, smaller libraries and gyms, and fewer supplies. Their teachers were paid lower salaries, were often less qualified, and taught restricted curriculum.

The status of de jure segregation as of 1954, when *Brown vs. Board of Education* was decided was that then seventeen states *required* segregation by law, and Congress required segregation of public schools in the District of Columbia; four states had enabling laws allowing local school districts to impose segregation; sixteen states *prohibited* segregation; and the remaining eleven states were simply silent on the matter (in 1954 there were only 48 states. Alaska and Hawaii, were added in 1960).

The NAACP fought to overturn *Plessy* and end de jure segregation by using federal power via the courts to overrule the states. Before 1950 the NAACP achieved very limited success. Two cases had ruled that blacks must be admitted to white law schools because comparable black law school facilities were not available (*Missouri ex rel. Gaines v. Canada* [1938], and *Sepuel v. University of Oklahoma* [1948]). Their impact was minimal as they set a very limited precedent based, as it was, on the absence of a black facility.

The first real dent in the wall of separation erected by the legal doctrine of "separate-but-equal" was delivered in the *Sweatt v. Painter* (1950) ruling. Although the Court refused to overturn *Plessy* directly, it ordered the admission of black students to the University of Texas law school on the grounds that segregated *professional* schools were *necessarily unequal*. The Court's test of "true equality" included such factors as the school's reputation, the experience of the faculty, and the school's traditions, prestige, and standing in the community. The Court stopped short of a full reversal of *Plessy.* A question remained as to whether such tests—virtually impossible to meet— would apply also to primary and secondary schools. *Sweatt* led to immediate and significant improvements in black schools in the South, as southern states scrambled to upgrade their black schools to come closer to apparent equality in conditions and facilities.

The NAACP pressed its frontal attack on *Plessy* by support of litigation in five border area school districts where conditions were more nearly equal (Delaware, District of Columbia, Kansas, South Carolina, and Virginia). They sought a ruling upholding their contention that *segregation per se* was unconstitutional. On May 17, 1954, the Court so ruled in its famous *Brown v. Board of Education of Topeka, Kansas* decision. The *Brown* case was historic. Not only was *Plessy* overturned, but in arriving at its decision, the Court deliberately underplayed the importance of legal precedent, using instead social and psychological evidence to determine the detrimental effects of segregation on black children. It stated that in public education the doctrine of separate but equal had no place. Segregated facilities were *inherently unequal.* The Court held de jure segregation deprived those segregated the equal protection of the law guaranteed by the Fourteenth Amendment.

The ruling became a watershed case. Just as *Plessy* established a constitutional underpinning to segregation based on the separate but equal doctrine, the *Brown* ruling that segregation was inherently unequal gave the constitutional basis for overturning all Jim Crow laws. The Court moved thereafter to end legal segregation in transportation, public parks, playgrounds, golf courses, and bathing beaches. *Brown* did not immediately end segregation in schools, but it struck the death knell for de jure segregation. The victory precipitated the black civil rights movement. It legitimated their concerns and protests over second-class citizenship implicit in a segregated society and sparked the use of mass political protest actions to seek equality in public and private life. While the significance of the historic decision was tremendous—in a single blow it struck down the laws of twenty-one states and the District of Columbia—its effects were less immediate. In allowing for its implementation to proceed "with all deliberate speed," the Court opened the door to the use of litigation, obstruction, and delays by those states resisting desegregation.

Nine "border-area" states (Arizona, Delaware, Kansas, Kentucky, Maryland, Missouri, New Mexico, Oklahoma, and West Virginia) and the District of Columbia decided not to resist desegregation, and progress proceeded fairly well in those places. The eleven states of the South, the old Confederacy, resisted desegregation. These states employed a number of delaying tactics. Only 2 percent of their black students were attending integrated schools by 1964.

Some states passed new laws creating an endless series of litigation. Other states established "private" schools in which the state paid the tuition of white students attending such schools. Still others revised their compulsory attendance laws so that no child was

Thurgood Marshall, U.S. Supreme Court Justice
(*Courtesy of the Library of Congress*)

compelled to attend integrated schools. Some resisted on the grounds of protecting public safety by interposing the state between the schools and federal authority. Most successful of all was the tactic of revising "pupil placement law." Each child was guaranteed freedom of choice in selecting his or her school. Most students chose to attend the school they had previously attended. This ploy maintained segregation by de facto rather than de jure methods. Resistance also took the form of violence. Prominent examples of violent resistance to court-ordered desegregation occurred in Clinton, Tennessee, in 1956; in Little Rock, Arkansas, in 1957; in New Orleans in 1960; and at the University of Mississippi at Oxford in 1962. Both Presidents Eisenhower and Kennedy countered violence with the use of federal troops to ensure compliance with the Supreme Court's ruling.

Real change began only after passage of the 1964 Civil Rights Act and the 1965 Elementary and Secondary Education Act (ESEA). Title VI of the Civil Rights Act specified the termination of federal aid to states and communities that resisted compliance with court-ordered desegregation. ESEA provided sufficient public school funding to make the threat compelling. The monetary threat moved desegregation plans along more than all prior federal court actions. The U.S. Office of Education (then within the Department of Health, Education, and Welfare) required desegregation plans from seventeen states that had previously used de jure segregation. In three years, desegregation of schools in those states increased eightfold. By 1970, the South had more black students attending integrated schools than did the states of the North. This situation demonstrated that the real equality issue was de facto segregation, which was far more difficult to overcome.

The Commission on Civil Rights reported in 1967 that 75 percent of black elementary school children in seventy-five large cities attended schools whose student body was 90 percent or more black. Reducing such segregation would be no easy task.

President Lyndon B. Johnson signed the Civil Rights Act of 1968. (*Courtesy of the Library of Congress*)

Attempts to deal with de facto segregation required that school officials classify their students on the basis of race and use race as a category in school placement. Effective reduction of de facto racial segregation seemed to need busing. Opposition to busing was widespread and often violent. Boston was the site of long and violent confrontations over busing. Black parents often opposed busing as much as did white parents. The nation witnessed the revival of the Ku Klux Klan and its spread north as cities across the country grappled with busing plans to desegregate schools of central city and suburb.

In *Swann v. Charlotte-Mecklenberg Board of Education* (402 U.S. 1, 1971), the Court ruled that where no present or past actions of state and local governments were used to create racial imbalance, there was no affirmative duty to correct racial imbalance. Where such imbalance resulted from discriminatory laws by states or local school districts, then school officials had a duty to eliminate vestiges of segregation which could entail busing and deliberate racial balancing to achieve integration. The *Swann* decision affected southern schools. In the North, where no history of de jure segregation was evident, the Court ruled 5–4 (in *Milliken v. Bradley* [418 U.S. 717, 1974]) that the Fourteenth Amendment does not require busing across city/suburban school district lines to achieve integration. *Milliken* meant that the nation's mostly black central cities surrounded by white suburbs would remain segregated de facto because there simply were not enough white students living in the central city boundaries to achieve anything near a balanced integration. The Supreme Court ruled that since "state sanctioned discrimination" (de jure) has been removed "as far as practicable," lower federal courts could dissolve racial balancing plans even though some imbalances caused by

Table 9.1   Educational Attainment of Persons 25 Years or Older by Race, 1960–2004

Year	Total	White	Black
Completed 4 Years of High School or More			
1960	41.1	43.2	20.1
1965	49.0	51.3	27.2
1970	52.3	54.5	31.4
1975	62.5	64.5	42.5
1980	66.5	68.8	51.2
1985	73.9	75.5	59.8
1990	77.6	79.1	66.2
1995	80.9	82.0	73.8
1996	81.7	82.8	74.3
1997	82.1	83.0	74.9
1998	82.8	83.7	76.0
1999	83.4	84.3	77.0
2000	84.1	84.9	78.5
2004	85.2	86.8	80.6
Completed 4 Years of College or More			
1960	7.7	8.1	3.1
1965	9.4	9.9	4.7
1970	10.7	11.3	4.4
1975	13.9	14.5	6.4
1980	16.2	17.1	8.4
1985	19.4	20.0	11.1
1990	21.3	22.0	11.3
1994	22.2	22.9	12.9
1995	23.0	24.0	13.2
1996	23.6	24.3	13.6
1997	23.9	24.6	13.3
1998	24.4	25.0	14.7
1999	25.2	25.9	15.4
2000	25.6	26.1	16.5
2004	24.2	18.4	12.3

Source: U.S. Bureau of the Census, *Statistical Abstract of the United States, 2006,* Table 214, p. 148 (http://www.census.gov/).

racially separate housing patterns continued to exist (in *Board of Education v. Dowell* [U.S. 1991 111 S.Ct. 630]; see also *Missouri v. Jenkins* [1995]). Table 9.1 presents the educational attainment levels of white versus black students from 1960 to 2004. Although the gap between the two narrows over the decades, a persistent gap of 5 to 6 percent continues to exist.

Many educators attribute the rise in achievement levels among blacks, while similar levels for whites have run slightly higher or held steady, to integration. Progress has been dramatic where past segregation had been deeply rooted. In many communities opposition was intense. When Boston began busing about half of Boston's 94,000 students in 1974, whites stoned school vehicles, and several empty ones were overturned and set afire. Many whites simply left the public school system. White enrollment dropped from 70 percent in 1974 to 27 percent by 1985 (Dye 1998). Proponents of mandatory busing argue that it is the only efficient way to achieve integration, since most residential areas remain very segregated. Opponents charge that forced busing is divisive, costly, and counterproductive, since it prompts white flight from the public school system, leaving those schools even more segregated.

The Reagan administration promoted voluntary plans like those used in Buffalo and Milwaukee. Its Justice Department led the anti-busing drive. The administration favored voluntary programs like the so-called *magnet schools*. These provide intensive instruction in subjects like the fine arts. The administration viewed them as being ultimately more effective. Such programs are costly and federal desegregation support has been cut drastically. Voluntary plans have not worked in many large cities and some courts have dismissed them as ineffective. White resistance to school integration has been declining steadily, if slowly, since the *Brown* decision. The continued presence of the gap in formal education is significant given the pronounced trend in American society toward more formal education.

Table 9.2 presents summary data on the enrollment status by race, Hispanic origin, and sex, 1975 and 2004, again illustrating the gap between white and minority enrollments across sex, race, and ethnic lines.

EMPLOYMENT

From the days of slave labor through the era of "No Irish Need Apply" to the present, discrimination in employment opportunity has been a recurrent aspect of majority/minority relations. Job discrimination has been institutionalized, sometimes manifested in formal policy, such as specific laws. Usually it is enforced through labor union training practices (apprenticeships), educational entrance barriers, and informal hiring practices of majority member employers. The "last hired, first fired" norm has been and continues to be a problem for the nation's minorities.

The Irish were initially limited to periodic work, low pay, and constant job threat explicitly implemented by the common use of the "No Irish Need Apply" signs, as were Jews, who experienced both the signs and job advertisements that read "Christians Only" or "Gentiles Only." The use of the padrone constituted a formalized system of occupational discrimination for Greeks and Italians. Even the Foran Act of 1885, which forbade contract labor and was aimed at the padrone system, constituted a formalized pattern of discrimination.

Institutionalized racism was based on formal acts of job discrimination. Blacks were legally enslaved for a time. Even after slavery was abolished, blacks were kept out of many jobs by Jim Crow legislation that reinforced informal norms. In California, racism led to the Foreign Miners Tax of 1885, which, coupled with violence, kept the

Table 9.2   Enrollment Status by Race, Hispanic Origin, and Sex, 1975, 2004

Characteristic	Percent HS Graduates		Percent College Graduates	
	1975	2004	1975	2004
Total	78.0	85.2	33.5	27.7
White	80.6	85.8	34.6	24.2
Hispanic	57.2	58.4	24.4	12.1
Male	76.6	74.4	35.4	41.7
White	79.7	75.3	36.9	41.8
Black	55.0	67.3	23.9	36.9
Hispanic	54.6	51.9	25.2	20.1
Female	79.2	79.5	31.8	45.8
White	81.4	80.4	32.4	47.0
Black	65.0	73.0	25.8	35.0
Hispanic	59.3	59.4	23.6	24.8

Source: U.S. Census Bureau, *Statistical Abstract of the United States: 2001.* Adapted by author from Table 259, p. 163. [Update to 2004 data from 2006 Abstract.]

Chinese out of the mine fields. The Chinese and Japanese were restricted from certain occupational endeavors by the California Alien Land Act of 1913. That law was upheld as constitutional in *Ozawa v. United States* (1921). In 1923, California strengthened such legal restrictions by plugging several loopholes in the 1913 act. Similar laws were enacted in Arizona, Idaho, Louisiana, Montana, New Mexico, and Oregon. The reservation policy of the 1870s legally forced occupational restrictions on Native Americans. As with race, formal or legal barriers in the job market have been used for gender, age, and sexual preference. Women and persons over 65 years of age face legal barriers in occupational opportunity in the Social Security laws. The firings of gays from certain jobs has been legally upheld, even when the dismissal was based solely on the person's sexual preference.

Most job discrimination is informal. Informal mechanisms include (1) restrictions in job training conducted by labor unions; (2) educational barriers that denied certain minorities the educational backgrounds required for many jobs; and (3) informal hiring practices of majority employers. Informal mechanisms enforced society's norms by denying equal opportunity in employment. Because these norms are informally enforced, they cannot be directly measured. That they have and continue to operate, however, cannot be denied.

Indirect evidence of informal discrimination is pervasive and persuasive. Patterns of minority employment demonstrate discrimination unmistakably. Exceptionally large percentages of minority group members in specific and limited occupations indicate **occupational niches** typical of minority groups. Employment discrimination is channeling large numbers of such persons into those jobs. While minority members voluntarily enter such occupations, they are jobs that are attractive because a pattern of

Box 9.1 *Employment Discrimination: Special Occupational Niches*

National Origin Groups

Greeks	Restaurants, confectionaries, candy stores, construction
Hispanics	Migrant farm work, low-skilled blue-collar urban jobs
Hungarians	Unskilled labor in heavy industry—steel, rubber, mines
Irish	Unskilled—mines, railroads, police, fire, stevedores, domestic service
Italians	Truck farming, restaurants, wine, barbers
Poles	Truck gardening, domestics, unskilled labor in mines, steel
Russians	Unskilled labor—mines, construction, tailors, furriers

Religious Groups

Amish and Mormons	Agriculture
Jews	Garment and cigar industries, retail sales, theater, music

Racial Groups

Blacks	Blue-collar unskilled jobs to low-skilled menial jobs, migrant farm work, tenant farming, domestic service
Chinese	Restaurants, laundries, domestic service, import/export gift shops
Japanese	Gardening, truck farming, fishing

Other Groups

Gender—Women: Nursing, elementary school teachers, typists, data entry, secretaries, hairdressers, waitresses, telephone operators

Sexual Preference: Bookkeeping, dress design, window display, hairdressers, interior decorating, art, theater, music

discrimination closed off access to alternative occupations of equal or better opportunity. Box 9.1 shows the types of niches common to various minorities. It is but one indirect measure of pervasive job discrimination. Subsequent data show additional evidence.

Another indicator of occupational discrimination is the status of several racial and ethnic minorities compared to the total population. Racial and ethnic minorities are clearly underemployed as managers, professionals, and executives, and disproportionately employed in low-paying service occupations. Likewise, unemployment rates for blacks continue to be higher than for whites, consistently being about twice the rate of whites. In 2004, black unemployment rates were 8.1 percent, compared to only 3.9 percent for whites (*Statistical Abstract of the U.S.*, 2006). Black unemployment in relation to white unemployment has remained remarkably consistent over the past forty years. Government programs to mitigate discrimination against minorities apparently have done little. During recessions, minorities carry the brunt of the unemployment burden.

Steps to reverse the effects of occupational discrimination include a series of congressional actions and Supreme Court decisions addressing the problems of informal but structured job discrimination. Congress took action with various "War on Poverty" programs in the 1960s, designed to provide training to aid the underemployed and the unemployed to develop needed job skills; for example, the Job Corps and the Neighborhood Youth Corps projects conducted by the Office of Economic Opportunity, the Comprehensive Employment Training Act (CETA), and Public Service Employment (PSE).

The most significant action against employment discrimination was the Civil Rights Act of 1964, which created the Equal Employment Opportunity Commission (EEOC), charged with implementing policy to end discrimination by any employer or labor union with twenty-five or more persons. While the EEOC could not require specific quotas or even preferential treatment from the mere fact of racial imbalance, the commission used imbalance as evidence of discrimination. Title VII of the 1964 Civil Rights Act is the major anti-discrimination law in the employment sector. Its implementation has led to some improvement. In overall rates of participation in the labor force, for example, African-American rates are equal to those of whites: as of 2004, 66.8 percent for whites compared to 67 for blacks (*Statistical Abstract of the U.S.*, 2006, table 580: 389).

The law assumes that if discrimination were not at work, members of the targeted groups (e.g., blacks, Hispanics, women) would be present in various sectors of society in rough proportion to their numbers in society at large. This **proportionality criterion** served as the basis for the EEOC treatment plans and represented a shift in the conceptualization of what constitutes "equality," from equality under the law to equality of opportunity to equality of well-being.

Policies to attain this goal of equality of material well-being came to be collectively known as **affirmative action**, a search for compensatory justice for the persisting effects of past institutionalized discrimination. Affirmative action includes any program designed to get minority persons past institutionalized barriers that previously would have stopped them. These programs are concentrated in educational and employment structures where such barriers existed. The *logic* of affirmative action is that a cycle of discrimination affects minority persons, and that cycle must be broken. If poor education leads to poor jobs, to low income and poor housing, which leads back to poor education, then one might improve the whole chain by breaking one link. A better job leads to better housing, a more middle-class lifestyle, and better schools, which all lead to better education and a new generation that would no longer need affirmative action. The cycle has been broken. Affirmative action is, in short, an attempt to force structural (in this case, economic) incorporation.

Attempts to achieve better racial and gender balance in employment and in education led to various preference plans. These were challenged in a number of cases:

Bakke (1978), *Weber* (1979), *Stotts* (1984), and *Crosen* (1989). The Office of Federal Contract Compliance and the EEOC began a process of court battles by setting guidelines that held that any test for employment, promotion, or membership in a union that disproportionately failed members of designated groups constituted evidence of illegal discrimination unless the job relevance of the test could be shown. The employer has the burden of proof to show that those who scored higher on the test or selection criteria actually performed better in the role for which they were selected.

In *Griggs v. Duke Power* (401 U.S. 424, 1971), the Court upheld those guidelines and threatened the legality of virtually every performance criteria. Three "suspect" categories were identified by the Court: race, gender, and alienage. In *Craig v. Boren* (429 U.S. 190, 1976), the Court set standards for when gender may be used to classify people. The government has to convince the Court that its purpose is an important one and that gender classification is "substantially related" to achieving that purpose. In *Washington v. Davis* (44 LW 4789, 1976), the Court further muddied the waters in a case concerning a Washington DC police officer test. Although four times as many blacks as whites failed to pass the written test, the Court nonetheless decided that this failure rate was not in and of itself evidence to invalidate the test. Unlike the *Griggs* decision, this one relied on the due process clause, not Title VII, which did not apply to governmental units. The Court ruled that under due process a test used for employment purposes is presumed valid unless the *intent to discriminate* is shown. It is exceedingly difficult to prove intent to discriminate and that criterion shifts the burden of proof from the employer to the applicant.

The situation was further complicated by several challenges to various racial preference plans. In *DeFunis v. Odegaard* (416 U.S. 312, 1974), the Court essentially dodged the question by ruling that the DeFunis challenge of the University of Washington's Law School preferential admissions program was a moot question, since, by the time the case had reached the Court, DeFunis, who had been ordered admitted by the state trial court, was ready to graduate. In the case of *Bakke v. Regents of the University of California, Davis* (438 U.S. 265, 1978), the Court decided on the admission criterion and procedures of the medical school at Davis. Alan Bakke had been denied admission although he clearly had higher scores on his GPA and Medical College Aptitude test than did a number of minority applicants who were admitted under the school's set-aside quota system of 16 placements out of 100 to be used for nonwhites. The *Bakke* decision, in a 5–4 split found the school's program invalid on equal protection grounds. It objected to the *fixed-quota* system. In *Firefighters Local Union v. Stotts* (1984), the Supreme Court decided that a city could not lay off white firefighters with greater seniority in order to retain black firefighters with less seniority. In *Richmond v. Crosen* (1989), it ruled that Richmond, Virginia's set-aside program mandating 30 percent of all city construction contracts must go to specified racial minorities violated the equal protection clause. In *Wards Cove v. Antonio* (1989), the Court reiterated its *Bakke* position that any rigid numerical quota was suspect of reverse discrimination. It held that the burden of proof of unlawful discrimination should be shifted from the defendant (the employer) to the plaintiff (the person claiming to have suffered discrimination).

During the Reagan and Bush administrations the executive branch also shifted on affirmative action. Under President Reagan, the budgets and staffs of key civil rights agencies were cut dramatically, busing was opposed, and the EEOC filed 50 percent fewer discrimination suits against employers. Government cases against school desegregation and housing discrimination dropped to a fraction of previous administrations. Under Reagan, the Justice Department terminated suits based on statistical evidence of discrimination and focused only on individual cases where intent to discriminate could be proven. President George H. Bush (Bush I) vetoed the Civil Rights Act of 1990 as a "quota bill" (although he signed essentially the same bill in 1991). He appointed conservative judges to the federal bench, including Justice Clarence Thomas, an adamant opponent of affirmative action, as his sole appointment to the Supreme Court.

In 1991, Congress passed the Civil Rights Act. It shifted the burden of proof back to employers, but the Supreme Court, in *Adarand Constructors v. Pena* (1995), weakened affirmative action by ruling that race-based policies, such as preferences for minority contractors, must survive strict scrutiny. The government had to show that affirmative action programs serve a compelling government interest and are narrowly tailored to identifiable past discrimination.

The cumulative effect of these cases was to maintain a highly modified affirmative action structure. While strict quotas in preference plans may violate either the Civil Rights Act or the Constitution, other uses of race or gender for "benign" purposes of racial or gender balance seem acceptable. Critics of affirmative action continue to press opposition. They hold such plans to be a denial of meritocracy, inconsistent with equality under the law, and penalizing competitive success by its performance standards. In 2003, the U.S. Supreme Court struck down some aspects of the University of Michigan Law School's affirmative action program while acknowledging it could still consider race as one criteria among several in determining acceptance of applicants (*Grutter v. Bollinger* [2003]).

All affirmative action programs raise an issue that they inherently involve conflicting rights and the difficulty of pursuing group goals at the expense of the individual. When society seeks a goal of social policy involving the redistribution of material well-being, it involves a **zero-sum situation** wherein whatever new benefits are accorded to some must be taken away from others. What one group gains another must lose. Although the history of discrimination against groups clearly establishes an argument for some sort of compensatory justice, the confusion between bigotry and discrimination of groups and of individuals within groups muddies the concept of justice. The white race in the aggregate may be guilty of discrimination, but individuals—Alan Bakke, Brian Weber, or Marco DeFunis—pay the debt, even though they did not personally discriminate. Nor do benefits of affirmative action necessarily flow to the most disadvantaged individuals in society. The hard-core unemployed seldom get to professional schools under such programs. Such programs tend to benefit middle-class members of the designated groups. To change the rules of the game and deny benefits to the Bakkes of society, ones to which they were entitled under the old rules, is seen by many as the denial of their rights, that is, reverse discrimination.

Racial preferences were further muddied when Angel Luevano challenged, under Title VII of the Civil Rights Act, the use of the Professional and Administrative Career Examination (PACE) by the Office of Personnel Management on the grounds that a disproportionate number of blacks and Hispanics failed the test. The failure rate for all applicants on PACE was about 60 percent, while the failure rate for blacks was around 95 percent. Recall that *Griggs* held that the employer must show the job relevance for any hiring criteria that disproportionately failed targeted groups, while the *Davis* precedent held that when the due process clause of the Constitution is used, no such requirement exists. The plaintiffs in *Luevano v. Campbell* (1981) relied on Title VII even though the employer in this case was the federal government. The case was settled out of court by the Reagan administration with an agreement to phase out the PACE test and replace it with "alternative examining procedures" that have no "adverse impact" on blacks and Hispanics. In the agreement, *adverse impact* was defined to mean a failure to be hired at the same rate as whites. The government agreed to hire certain categories of individuals without reference to test scores (for example, Spanish-speaking people when knowledge of Spanish is an asset), and to strive to have blacks and Hispanics make up at least 20 plus percent of the work force at the GS-5 level and higher. This amounts to a quota that *Bakke* seemed to forbid and that has been alleged to constitute reverse discrimination against whites explicitly banned by Title VII.

Box 9.2 shows that a wide gap on race and gender remains in the U.S. work force. Using 1995 annual salary data from the U.S. Census Bureau, the National Committee on Pay Equity shows the continued impact of race and gender discrimination in employment. Table 9.3 presents the unemployment rates by race and sex, 1980–2004, indicating minorities continue to be the last hired and the first fired.

Table 9.4 presents poverty rates, by race and Hispanic origin. One way minority groups can cope with private sector job discrimination is by entrepreneurship. Table 9.5 shows the number of U.S. firms by race, Hispanic origin, sex, and various minority-owned firms as of 1997.

Minority groups often cope with the negative income effects of employment discrimination by increasing family income by having more members of a family, sometimes even an extended family, working and pooling their resources. Table 9.6 shows the median income of households by race and Hispanic origin in constant (2000) dollars from 1980 to 2000.

Nor has the wage gap disappeared over the past decades. Women's earnings as a percentage of men's earnings, for example, was 63.9 percent in 1955, 60.8 percent in 1960, 60.0 percent in 1965, 59.4 percent in 1970, 58.8 percent in 1975, 60.2 percent in 1980, 64.5 percent in 1985, 71.6 percent in 1990, and 71.4 percent in 1995 (Ibid).

HOUSING

Housing is another area of extensive discrimination. This pattern is particularly evident regarding racial minorities. Housing remains highly segregated despite federal action by the courts and Congress designed to end de jure segregation in housing. This section reviews how segregation became the established pattern, and efforts passed to mitigate it.

Spatial isolation (segregation) is a powerful indicator of a group's general position in society. It influences a variety of social phenomena: intermarriage, linguistic assimilation, and even the maintenance of a group's distinctive occupational composition. Most minorities in the United States experienced housing segregation, some largely through self-segregation for security, and others through de jure segregation, such as Native Americans on reservations. Be it the "Little Italy" of East Coast cities, the Chinatowns of Los Angeles and San Francisco, or the black ghettos of the nation's major

Box 9.2

Report Of The National Committee On Pay Equity Data, 1996

1. *The U.S. labor force is occupationally segregated by race and sex*

- In 1995, women constituted 46.0 percent of all workers in the civilian labor force (over 57 million women).[1]
- People of color constituted 14.7 percent of all workers (over 18 million workers).[2]
- Labor force participation is almost equal among white women, black women, and women of Hispanic origin. In 1995, 59.5 percent of black women (7.6 million), 52.6 percent of Hispanic women (4.8 million), and 59.0 percent of white women (50 million) were in the paid labor force.[3]
- In 1995, women were

  98.5 percent of all secretaries

  93.1 percent of all registered nurses

  96.8 percent of all child care workers

  88.4 percent of all telephone operators

  74.7 percent of all teachers (excluding colleges and universities)

  82.9 percent of all data entry keyers
- Women were only

  13.4 percent of all dentists

  8.4 percent of all engineers

  26.2 percent of all lawyers and judges

  12.9 percent of all police and detectives

  8.9 percent of all precision, production, craft, and repair workers

  24.4 percent of all physicians[4]

2. *Economic status*

- Over 12 million women work full-time in jobs that pay wages below the poverty line (in 1995 for a family of three the poverty line was $12,158 per year). They work in jobs such as day care, food counter, and many service jobs. Many more women than men are part of the working poor (125 percent of the poverty level) and work in jobs such as clerical, blue collar, and sales positions.[5]
- In 1995, married couple families had a median income of $47,062 while female-headed families had a median income of only $19,691.[6]

3. *The wage gap is one of the major causes of economic inequality in the United States today*

- In 1995, all men working year-round full-time were paid a median salary of $31,496 per year.
- All women, working year-round full-time, were paid a median salary of $22,497 per year.
- On average, women earned only 71.4 cents for each dollar that a man earned.

(continued)

Box 9.2, CONTINUED

                                              ●

[1]U.S. Department of Labor, Bureau of Labor Statistics, 1995 Annual Average Tables, from the January 1996 issue of *Employment and Earnings,* Table 2.

[2]Ibid., Table 3.

[3]Ibid., Tables 3 and 4.

[4]Ibid., Table 11.

[5]*Poverty in the United States,* U.S. Department of Commerce, Bureau of the Census, Current Population Reports, Consumer Income, Series P-60-194, Table 1; and *Money Income in the United States: 1995,* Current Population Reports, Consumer Income, Series P-60-193, Table 10.

[6]*Money Income in the United States: 1995,* U.S. Department of Commerce, Bureau of the Census, Current Population Reports, Consumer Income, Series P-60-193, Table 5.

Table 9.3   Unemployment Rates, Persons 16 or Older, by Race and Sex, 1980–2004

Year	Blacks	Whites	Hispanic	Male	Female
1980	14.3%	6.3%	10.1%	6.9%	7.4%
1985	15.1	6.2	10.5	7.0	7.4
1990	11.4	4.8	8.2	5.7	5.6
1995	10.4	4.9	9.3	5.6	5.6
1997	10.0	4.2	7.7	4.9	5.0
1998	8.9	3.9	7.2	4.4	4.6
1999	8.0	3.7	6.4	4.1	4.3
2000	7.6	3.5	5.7	3.9	4.1
2004	10.4	4.8	7.0	5.6	5.4

Source: U.S. Bureau of the Census, *Statistical Abstract of the United States, 2006.* Adapted by author, from Table 610, p. 409.

Table 9.4   Number of Poor and Poverty Rate by Race and Hispanic Origin, 2003

Number	2003 Average (in thousands)	Value (percent)
All Races	35,864	12.7
White	21,652	10.1
Non-Hispanic White	16,436	8.6
Black	8,441	24.7
American Indian/Alaska Native	530	24.5
Asian/Pacific Islander	1,348	11.5
Hispanic	8.544	21.9

Source: Table by author, with data from *Statistical Abstract of the U.S.*, 2006, Table 37, pp. 40–41.

Table 9.5   U.S. Firms by Race, Hispanic Origin, and Sex—Minority Owned, 1997

	Number of Firms (1,000)
White/Non-Hispanic	17,317
Hispanics	1,200
Black	823
American Indian	197
Asian/Pacific Islanders: Total	913
Asian Indian	167
Chinese	253
Filipino	85
Japanese	86
Korean	136
Vietnamese	98
Other Asian	71
	Number of Firms
Women-Owned, All Industries	5,417,034
Hispanic-Owned Firms	1,199,896
Black-Owned Firms	823,499
Asian/Pacific-Owned Firms	912,960
American Indian/Alaska-Owned Firms	197,300

Source: Table by author, data from *Statistical Abstract of the United States, 2006.*
Tables 748, p. 518.

Table 9.6   Money Income of Families—Median Income by Race and Hispanic Origin in Constant U.S. (2000) Dollars, 1980–2003

Median Family Income in 12 Months, U.S. Dollars

Year	All Families	White	Black	Asian Pacific Islanders	Hispanic
1980	$41,830	$43,583	$25,218	NA	$29,281
1985	42,564	44,739	25,761	NA	29,200
1990	45,392	47,398	27,506	$54,243	30,085
1991	44,514	46,798	26,689	50,750	29,596
1992	44,129	46,659	25,463	50,985	28,421
1993	43,472	46,226	25,338	52,290	27,822
1994	44,638	47,058	28,427	53,087	27,990
1995	45,599	47,884	29,160	52,050	27,588
1996	46,240	48,925	28,993	53,679	28,618
1997	47,687	50,026	30,603	55,478	30,111

(continued)

Table 9.6   Money Income of Families—Median Income by Race and Hispanic Origin in Constant U.S. (2000) Dollars, 1980–2003   (*continued*)

Median Family Income in 12 Months, U.S. Dollars

Year	All Families	White	Black	Asian Pacific Islanders	Hispanic
1998	49,317	51,729	31,027	55,742	31,243
1999	50,594	52,945	32,846	58,208	32,727
2000	50,890	53,256	34,192	61,511	35,054
2003	52,273	55,938	34,608	63,883	35,600

Source: U.S. Bureau of the Census, *Statistical Abstract of the United States, 2006,* Table 37, p. 41.

cities, most minorities have experienced some combination of voluntary and induced housing segregation.

The concentration of minorities in central cities is a product of the availability of low-priced rental units in older, run-down sections of the central city; the heavy outflow of the middle-class white population to the surrounding suburbs, and the policies of public and private real estate owners and developers.

Black isolation was not always so intense. At the turn of the century, Stanley Lieberson's study (1980) shows that in the North, there were higher levels of segregation among the South, Central, and East European groups than among blacks. Italians and Russians were more isolated than blacks. Lieberson found black isolation to be rather slight in 1890 among the seventeen leading cities of the North and West. The average black, working as a domestic servant and living in the white home, lived in a ward where over 90 percent of the population was not black. Although black isolation increased in the next decade, in five or six cities there were actual declines in the degree of black isolation. From 1910 to 1930, however, extensive increases in black isolation occurred. A massive migration of blacks from the rural South to the urban North led to sharp increases in anti-black sentiment and attempts by whites to maintain the degree of isolation existing before that migration began (Brooks 1996, 47). The isolation of new immigrant groups declined as second and third generations were able to move out of ethnic enclaves. Those enclaves developed into black ghettos.

The sharp increase in black isolation affected jobs and education and indicates that the social position of blacks in the North deteriorated drastically at the turn of the century. Historian Allan Spear (1967), in his study of the growth of Chicago's black ghetto, distinguishes it from ethnic enclaves:

> The Chicago experience, therefore, tends to refute any attempt to compare Northern Negroes with European immigrants. Unlike the Irish, Poles, Jews, or Italians, Negroes banded together not to enjoy a common linguistic, cultural, and religious tradition, but because a systematic pattern of discrimination left them no alternative. . . . The persistence of the Chicago Negro ghetto, then, has not been merely the product of a special historical experience. From its inception, the Negro ghetto was unique among the city's ethnic enclaves. It grew in response to an implacable white hostility that has

not basically changed. In this sense it has been Chicago's only true ghetto, less the product of voluntary development within than external pressure from without. (pp. 228–229)

Several policy devices ensured black isolation. The restrictive covenant used by real estate agencies and enforced by the courts typically read as follows: "No part of the land hereby conveyed shall ever be used or occupied by or sold, demised, transferred, conveyed unto, or in trust for, leased or rented or given to Negroes, or to any person or persons of Negro blood or extraction, or to any person of the Semitic race, blood, or origin which racial description shall be deemed to include Armenians, Jews, Hebrews, Persians, and Syrians" (cited in Dye 1971).

The National Association of Real Estate Boards (NAREB) in its Code of Ethics explicitly required "a realtor should never be instrumental in introducing into a neighborhood . . . members of any race or nationality, or any individuals whose presence will clearly be detrimental to property values in the neighborhood" (cited in Brooks 1996, 50). The NAREB's racist policy reinforced housing segregation long after 1950.

Other practices of ghettoization included large lot zoning, which keeps lower income (i.e., nonwhite) families out of suburbs; illegal collusion among real estate agents, who refuse to sell to blacks; and the lack of enforcement of housing codes, which virtually encourages slum development. Municipal property tax policy penalizes improvements and rewards slum landlords who poorly maintain their properties. The use of "earnings power" as a measure of determining the value of a property in condemnation proceedings favors those who overcrowd their buildings. Capital gains taxes and depreciation policies favor slum owners. The location of public housing projects concentrated in central city neighborhoods helps maintain the ghetto pattern.

From late 1930 to mid-1960, the federal government encouraged the ghetto by requiring "homogeneous neighborhoods" in its mortgage policies within Federal Housing Administration, Federal National Mortgage Association, and G.I. bill programs. These programs helped finance white flight to the suburbs. Although the making of a ghetto was not an *intended* impact, it was the *direct consequence* of programs subsidizing white flight to the suburbs. In 1962 alone, "the federal government spent $820 million to subsidize housing for the poor (this includes public housing, public assistance, and tax deductions). That same year at least an estimated $2.9 billion was spent to subsidize housing for the middle and upper income families" (Schon 1969, 208; Brooks 1996, 50–58).

Once developed, the economics of the ghetto encouraged their continuation. Segregation was the single most important factor making slums profitable. Slum profits depend on collusion between city agencies and slum landlords. In return for nonenforcement of codes, slum lords take the blame for the slums and enable the city to evade the political ire of ghetto residents (Tabb 1970; Gordon 1977).

Black ghettos reflect the shift from the rural South to the urban North, where discrimination practices forced them into the central city locations. From 1950 to 1970, black population grew by 25.4 percent, compared to a white growth rate of 17.6 percent. Where 87 percent of the nation's blacks lived in the South in 1900, less than half live there today. Blacks make up just over 12 percent of the population. They make up a much larger share of the nation's large cities. Numerous studies indicate the larger the city, and the larger the percentage of a single minority group in that city, the greater the segregation. This is particularly the case when the minority is racially-defined.

High residential segregation has consequences for a wide variety of related events: school isolation; restrictions of opportunities because of minimal contacts with whites, marking the racial population as distinct and different; and restricted opportunities to live near all sorts of employment found at great distance from the black ghettos. Racial residential isolation reinforces differences between whites and racial minorities and intensifies ethnic bonds.

Despite several decades of policy attempts to redress segregation, change has taken place slowly. The 1948 Supreme Court decision *Shelly v. Kramer* overturned the use of restrictive covenants as unconstitutional. Southern community attempts to legalize zoning for the purpose of residential segregation were ended by subsequent court action. But while Jim Crow de jure segregation in housing may have ended, blacks and whites are still largely segregated de facto.

Black attempts to integrate previously all-white areas adjacent to predominantly black areas elicit white flight. Generalizing this reaction, known as the **tipping mechanism**, led to uncovering the principal dimensions of such expected behavior. Attempts to alter the way in which the housing market currently operates to enforce the concentration of blacks into inner city enclaves remains politically explosive.

In 1966, President Johnson first requested open housing legislation. His bills died in the House in 1966 and 1967, in part because of entrenched opposition from the real estate industry that lobbied against enactment of any fair housing law. The National Association of Real Estate Boards published a "Property Owners Bill of Rights" opposing those bills. The Civil Rights Act of 1968 finally established a fair housing law. Coming after the assassination of Dr. Martin Luther King, Jr., the measure was passed in part as a memorial to him. It prohibited the following forms of discrimination: (1) the refusal to sell or rent a dwelling to any person because of race, color, religion, or national origin; (2) discrimination against a person in terms, conditions, or privileges of the sale or rental of a dwelling; (3) indicating a preference or discrimination on the basis of color, race, creed, or national origin in advertising the sale or rental of a dwelling; and (4) inducing **block-busting** techniques of real estate selling. The law covered all apartments and houses rented or sold by real estate developers or agents. It exempted private homes sold without real estate agents and apartments with less than five rental units where the landlord maintained his or her own residence in the building.

The federal government worked at cross-purposes to this law by concentrating public housing projects in central city locations. Only one of the nation's twenty-four largest cities—Cincinnati—built public housing units outside the central city. The Department of Transportation spends billions of dollars constructing metropolitan expressways that encourage urban sprawl and promote white flight to the suburbs, in addition to promoting the outflow of commercial interests that follow the white middle-class exodus. This leads to further racial segregation and reduces the number of jobs available to minorities trapped in central cities. FHA mortgage programs encouraged white flight to the suburbs. HUD, by tearing down slum housing and replacing it with civic centers and upper-middle-class developments, displaced the poor.

After the 1968 Civil Rights Act, also known as the Fair Housing Act, the most notable federal attempts at anti-discrimination laws were the Equal Credit Opportunity Act, 1975; the Home Mortgage Disclosure Act, 1976; and the Community Reinvestment Act, 1977. These laws had mixed results. A 1992 study in Boston found Black or Hispanic applicants 60 percent more likely to be denied a mortgage loan than a similarly situated white applicant. For example, 17 percent of black/Hispanic applicants, compared to 11 percent of white applicants, were denied loans even having the same obligations ratios, credit history, loan to value of house, and property characteristics as white applicants (Brooks 1996, 66).

Despite decades of efforts to end segregation and promote fair housing, contradictory policy action and inaction resulted in many ghetto areas remaining virtually untouched. Some progress has been evident, especially since 1980. For the 1980 census, four racial groups were identified for study: white, Negro or black, American Indian or Alaska Native, and Asian or Pacific Islander. In addition, one ethnic group, Spanish or Hispanic origin, was designated. The census bureau has been studying trends in residential segregation since then. This section closes with a brief summation of the results. The census bureau uses five indexes to measure segregation: a dissimilarity index (measuring an evenness dimension, an isolation index (exposure dimension), a delta index (examining the concentration dimension), the absolute centralization index (measuring the centralization dimension), and a spatial proximity index (studying the clustering dimension).

In the most recent census bureau study, the trend for African Americans was clearest of all—declines in segregation were evident over the 1980 to 2000 period across all dimensions. Despite the declines, however, residential segregation was still higher for African Americans than for other groups across all measures. Hispanics were the next most highly segregated, followed by Asians/Pacific Islanders, and then American Indian and Alaska Natives. Asian and Pacific Islanders and Hispanics experienced increases in segregation across some of the dimensions. Increases were generally larger for Asians than for Hispanics. In terms of trends across the five dimensions, declines in segregation were most evident in centralization, where all groups experienced declines over the 1980 to 2000 period. Three of the four groups experienced declines in concentration. Trends for the evenness and clustering dimensions were split. Exposure (the isolation dimension) was the one dimension where increasing segregation was the norm during the period, with only African Americans experiencing a slight decline in it (http://www.census.gov/hhes/www/housing/resseg/chl.html).

Blacks are the most residentially segregated group. They had the highest mean index scores for all metropolitan areas for all five indexes and for all three censuses (1980, 1990, 2000). Hispanics were the second most segregated group, with the second highest mean index scores for all five indexes and for all three censuses. Asians and Pacific Islanders were more residentially segregated than American Indians and Alaska Natives, as measured by four of the five indexes for all years, both for all metropolitan and for selected metropolitan areas. The one exception was spatial proximity. Trends for each of the groups are summarized in the text that follows.

Blacks grew in number over the period from 26.5 million in 1980 to 30.0 million in 1990, and to 36.4 million in 2000. They comprised 11.7 percent of the U.S. population in 1980, 12.1 percent in 1990, and 12.9 percent in 2000. About 86.5 percent of blacks lived in metropolitan areas in 2000. The largest metropolitan areas (those with 1 million or more in population) had higher segregation than middle-sized ones (500,000 to 999,999), which, in turn, had higher segregation than the smallest metropolitan areas. The pattern held for all indexes and for all three years. In 2000, the West region had the lowest level of residential segregation for three of the five indexes, and the South was lowest for the remaining two. The Midwest had the highest level of residential segregation for four of the five indexes, and the Northeast had the highest level for the remaining one. Generally speaking, as the percentage of the population that is black increased, blacks were less likely to be evenly spread (dissimilarity), less likely to share common neighborhoods (isolation), less concentrated in dense areas (delta), less likely to be centralized (absolute centralization index), and more likely to live near other blacks (spatial proximity index).

Across the five indexes, the top ten most segregated metropolitan areas for blacks in 2000 were, in order, (1) Milwaukee-Waukesha, (2) Detroit, (3) Cleveland-Lorain-Elyria, (4) St. Louis, (5) Newark, (6) Cincinnati, (7) Buffalo-Niagara Falls, (8) New York, (9) Chicago, and (10) Philadelphia. The latter two are roughly tied with Kansas City, New Orleans, and Indianapolis. The top ten most segregated metropolitan areas for blacks, then, were in the older Northeast to Midwest "rust-belt" region that has lost population in recent decades.

When using all five indexes, the five least segregated metropolitan areas for blacks were, in order, Orange County, San Jose, Norfolk-Virginia Beach-Newport News, Tampa-St. Petersburg-Clearwater, and San Diego (the latter two being roughly tied with Providence-Fall River-Warwick). All but one of the least segregated metropolitan areas for blacks were in the West and South, where metropolitan areas have tended to gain population. Residential segregation for blacks decreased in the 1980–1990 period and continued apace during the 1990–2000 period, with most strides being made in the West and South, particularly in California, Florida, and Texas. The reduction of African-American residential segregation can best be characterized as remaining slow but steady.

American Indians/Alaska Natives numbered 4.1 million in the 2000 census, of which 34 percent lived outside metropolitan areas. Ten metropolitan areas had at least 3 percent or more American Indians/Alaska Natives in the 1980 census. In decreasing order, and using 2000 census percentages, these were Tulsa, OK (10.7 percent); Anchorage, AK (10.4 percent); Rapid City, SD (9.9 percent); Fort Smith, AR-OK (8.0 percent); Lawton, OK (7.0 percent); Albuquerque, NM (6.6 percent); Great Falls, MT (5.7 percent), Yakima, WA (5.6 percent); Bellingham, WA (3.8 percent); and Yuma, AZ (2.2 percent in 2000, but 3.6 percent in 1980). Using the dissimilarity index (the most widely used), American Indian and Alaska Natives declined in segregation in 1980, 1990, and 2000 in all metropolitan areas. However, these metropolitan areas accounted for only 12.7 percent of their population, and only 19.4 percent of metropolitan-residing American Indian and Alaska Natives. Middle-sized metropolitan areas had lower residential segregation than did larger or smaller ones across all five indexes. In all three census years, the four metropolitan areas in Oklahoma (in the South region) had substantially lower levels of residential segregation for all five indexes than the eight in the West. Using the dissimilarity index, Yakima was the most segregated metropolitan area for them in 2000, followed by Fort Smith and Phoenix-Mesa. The least segregated in 2000 was Oklahoma City, followed by Tulsa and Lawton. Residential segregation trends for them over the 1980–2000 period shows a mixed pattern. On the dissimilarity index, they register a moderate reduction of 6 to 11 percent from 1980 to 1990, and from 4–10 percent from 1990 to 2000. Other residential segregation indexes, however, show different patterns, with some showing an increase over the period. Overall, metropolitan areas in Oklahoma seem the least segregated for them.

Asian American/Pacific Islanders grew from 3.5 million (1.5 percent of the U.S. population) in 1980 to 7.3 million (2.9 percent) in 1990, to just under 13 million (4.5 percent) in 2000. Metropolitan areas with the greatest growth between 1980 and 2000 experienced the largest increase in isolation, and some increases in dissimilarity and spatial proximity. Those with the lowest rate of growth experienced more modest changes in segregation over the two decades. In all, twenty metropolitan areas have at least 3 percent or more Asians and Pacific Islanders. The five most segregated areas (using dissimilarity) were, in order, New York, San Francisco and Houston (tied), Los Angeles-Long Beach, and San Diego. Using all five indexes, the most segregated include four of the five, with San Francisco at number one and San Jose moving into the top five, and Houston, at number six, essentially tied with San Jose and Los Angeles. The least segregated areas were (dissimilarity index) Portland-Vancouver, Seattle-Bellevue-Everett, Nassau-Suffolk, Newark, Bergen-Passaic, and Detroit. In sum, over the two decades, they experienced increased segregation on three of the five indexes, no change in a fourth index, and a slight decline in the fifth. The more Asian and Pacific Islanders in an area as a percentage of the population, the more they are isolated and the more they tend to live with one another. Asians as a group were more segregated in 2000 than were Pacific Islanders.

Census 2000 showed that Hispanics already are the largest minority in the United States. About 14.5 million persons identified themselves as Hispanic in 1980 (then 6.4 percent of the population). This number grew to 22.4 million in 1990 (over a 50 percent increase, and to 9.0 percent of the total population). In 2000 they were at 35.3 million (or 12.5 percent of the total population). As with Asians, the highest level of residential segregation among Hispanics was in areas with the highest percentage Hispanics. In 2000, the dissimilarity index was 10 percent higher in areas where the population was 17.5 percent or more (the highest quartile) than in areas that were under 3.9 percent Hispanic (the lowest quartile). Medium-sized areas tended to have lower levels of segregation than did areas of larger or smaller size.

The five most segregated metropolitan areas, using the dissimilarity index, were, in order, Providence-Fall River-Warwick, New York, Newark, Hartford, and Los Angeles-Long Beach. Using all five indexes, the five most segregated areas for Hispanics in 2000 were, in order, New York, Providence, Phoenix, Los Angeles, Chicago and Newark (tied). The top ten were rounded out by Denver, Riverside-San Bernardino, and Houston, and five others roughly tied for tenth. The five least segregated metropolitan areas for Hispanics in 2000 were, in order, St. Louis, Seattle-Bellevue-Everett, Fort Lauderdale, Portland-Vancouver, and Baltimore.

Overall, trends for the 1980 to 2000 period are a bit mixed. Increases slightly outnumber declines when all measures are considered, with evidence of a slight decline in the South, increases for medium-sized metropolitan areas, and increases in metropolitan areas with large percentages of Hispanics. While New York continues to be the most segregated large metropolitan area for Hispanics (Puerto Ricans), as it has been for two decades, several others showed some significant changes. The Providence area, for example, became more segregated and Miami much less so (http://www.census.gov/hhes/ and http://www/housing/resseg/ch6.html).

IMMIGRATION

Immigration policy is important in race relations because it is *intermestic*, that is, it blends both international and domestic policy concerns. Immigration to the United States is a primary source of minority groups. Immigration policy plays a **gatekeeping** role significantly determining the composition of the flow (LeMay 2006). It has long been an area of intense struggle. From 1820, when the nation first began keeping count of immigration, to 2004, over 72 million persons have immigrated here. In terms of sheer numbers, the United States is by far the largest immigrant-receiving nation in the world.

This section discusses phases in immigration policy and the link between policy and the resulting composition of the flow. Immigration policy reflects the perceived needs of the nation as those needs shift over time in response to changing economic and social conditions. It reflects reactions to the changing nature and composition of immigrant waves. Various cultural, economic, ethnic, and foreign policy issues played key roles in the debates over immigration policy. Immigration policy trends seem to be cyclical.

Shifts in policy reflect conflicting value perspectives that tug and pull at one another. On the one hand, immigrants are valued as a source of industry and renewed vitality, a desirable infusion of new blood into the American stock, enriching the heritage and spurring new economic growth. This perspective forms the traditional base for a more open immigration policy. Presidents from George Washington to George W. Bush have affirmed we are a nation of immigrants, one of asylum for which immigration expresses and confirms the American spirit of liberty for all. The other perspective calls for varying degrees of restrictions. Its proponents fear strangers who cannot, or in their view should not, be incorporated. They fear the dilution of American culture; that so vast an influx will destroy the economy or severely depress wages and working conditions. They advocate restrictive immigration policy to avoid such dire effects (see, for instance, Huntington 2004).

Changes in immigration policy can result in dramatic shifts in the size and composition of the flow. The gatekeeping function suggests the use of "door" imagery to characterize U.S. immigration policy.

We distinguish five phases in immigration policy. Phase 1, from 1820 to 1880, we term the **open-door era**. During this era, policy had few restrictions; almost all who sought entrance were allowed in. Some state governments sent agents to Europe to recruit immigrants. Phase 2, the **door-ajar era**, lasted from 1880 to 1920. It saw the beginnings of effective restrictions, although the door was open to most. Phase 3, the **pet-door era**, lasted from 1920 to 1950, when the national origins quota system formed U.S. immigration policy. A highly restrictive approach to immigration, it allowed in only a favored few. Phase 4, the **dutch-door era**, lasted from 1950 to 2000, establishing more open policy than during the quota years, allowing for an increase in total immigration, but favoring those who entered "at the top" by allowing large refugee flows under special provisions. Phase 5, the **storm-door era**, characterizes the policy since 2000. It responds to and allows an increased number, many of whom come and go in large numbers often annually, and many illegally.

The "asylum" view determined policy in the open-door era. Little opposition to this policy was even voiced at first. In 1790, when the nation took its first census, it recorded a population of 3,227,000, mostly the descendants of seventeenth- and eighteenth-century arrivals or recent immigrants themselves. More than 75 percent were of British origin; about 8 percent were of German origin; the rest were Dutch, French, or Spanish in origin, or black slaves and Native Americans. This population occupied a vast, sparsely settled land rich in soil and natural resources. The population density in 1790 was only 4.5 persons per square mile. There was an obvious need for labor to build cities, clear farms, and defend against Indians and European colonial powers.

Congress passed laws regulating naturalization. The first act (1 Stat. 104, 1790) was very liberal, requiring only a two-year residency and the renunciation of former allegiances. In 1795, turmoil in Europe raised fears and Congress passed a more stringent act requiring five years' residency and a renunciation of foreign titles as well as allegiances. In 1798, Congress, then under the control of the Federalists, raised the residency to fourteen years (1 Stat. 566). It passed the Alien Acts, allowing the president to deport any alien considered to be a threat to the nation. These acts were permitted to expire when the Jeffersonian Democratic Republicans replaced the Federalists in power. In 1802, an act reinstated the five-year provisions of the 1795 law. In 1819, Congress passed a law requiring the listing of all entering ship passengers, which indicated their sex, occupation, age, and country to which they belonged (3 Stat. 489).

During the 1830s and 1840s, a wave of largely Catholic immigrants set off a dramatic xenophobic reaction. They were easy scapegoats to blame for problems of a rapidly urbanizing and industrializing country. They were alleged to be importing crime and drunkenness. Social reformers desiring to preserve the nation's institutions and Protestant evangelicals seeking to save the nation's "purity" joined forces to form anti-immigration associations like the Secret Order of the Star Spangled Banner, which became the Know Nothing political party. These groups advocated restrictive immigration policy and more stringent naturalization laws. Xenophobia led to violent attacks on churches and convents and inflammatory anti-Catholic literature. Such nativist sentiment did not prevail over public policy, however, as the more politically and economically powerful of the native stock continued supporting more open immigration to supply cheap labor for the explosively expanding cities and factories. Economic needs, coupled with the philosophic idealism regarding America as the land of opportunity and freedom, prevailed over the narrow views of the anti-Catholic movement.

The discovery of gold in California in 1848 drew a vast population west. The post–Civil War period created an insatiable need for immigrants. The transcontinental railroad building boom opened up vast lands to settlement. Massive numbers of unskilled laborers were needed to mine the coal and ore, work the mills, and staff the factories of Civil War–generated production. These forces drew Chinese immigrants to the West Coast. The composition of European immigrants also began to change, with those from South, Central, and Eastern Europe outnumbering those from Western Europe.

The changing flow of immigration, coupled with economic recessions and a depression during the 1870s, renewed political pressures for restrictions. A law banning the immigration of convicts and prostitutes was passed in 1875, and the 1880s ushered in a new phase in immigration policy, the "door-ajar era." Ironically, at the very time the Statue of Liberty was erected symbolizing the nation being open to the "poor and the oppressed" of the world, the "new" immigrants were raising fear and dislike among many in the native stock. The more "alien" characteristics of the newcomers—strange coloring, physiques, customs, and languages—renewed fears that such strangers were unable to assimilate. A spate of pseudo-scientific studies by historians, sociologists, and biologists attacked the new immigrants as biologically and racially inferior. Racist fervor led to the first blatantly restrictionist immigration law, the Chinese Exclusion Act of 1882 (22 Stat. 58; 8 U.S.C.).

Passage of the 1882 immigration acts did not satisfy the restrictionists. The continued large flow of immigrants from 1880 to 1890 resulted in further efforts to change immigration policy, focusing on a new device—literacy. The first literacy bill was introduced in Congress in 1895, where it quickly passed both houses but was vetoed by President Cleveland. In 1906, another comprehensive immigration act was proposed that included both a literacy test for admission and an English-language test for naturalization. Nativist forces were joined by labor unions in advocating this policy. The budding unionization movement feared the economic threat to wage scales and working conditions implicit in unrestricted immigration. Business leaders opposed the new law, wanting to avoid any limitation of new, cheap, and pliable labor.

Restrictionists succeeded in passing the literacy requirements for entrance and the language requirement for naturalization, but again the law was vetoed. In 1907, Congress established the Dillingham Commission to study the impact of immigration. The Dillingham Commission adopted pseudo-scientific, racist theories prevalent at the time. Its recommendations, published in 1911, called for a literacy test and other highly restrictive legislation. The war in Europe, however, generated economic growth and labor demands, both of which ran counter to restrictive policy. The growing political power of the new immigrant groups, coupled with business demand for new labor, preserved a more free-entry policy. In 1912, Congress again passed a literacy bill, and President Taft successfully vetoed it. In 1915, another bill passed, this time being vetoed by President Wilson. After the United States entered World War I, Congress passed and successfully overrode yet another veto. The 1917 law finally made literacy an entrance requirement (39 Stat. 874; 8 U.S.C.). It codified a list of aliens to be excluded, virtually banned all immigration from Asia, and culminated in restrictive policy being accepted broadly throughout society.

A frenzy of anti-German activity resulted in an "Americanization" movement to educate the foreign-born in American language and customs. Between 1919 and 1921, twenty states passed laws creating Americanization programs. Even industry, for the first time, took a more restrictionist view, resulting in a new phase of immigration policy, the national origins quota system.

Two restrictionist groups—organized labor and the nativist "100 Percenters"—called for the suspension of all immigration. Labor feared the job competition of immigrants who enhanced the realignments occurring in the postwar economy. The 100 Percenters simply feared the European ideas, most notably the "red-menace of Bolshevism," that would contaminate society's institutions and customs. The Senate led the way, designing a bill to reduce total immigration and to change the composition of those who were allowed to enter. The Quota Act of 1921 (42 Stat. 5; 8 U.S.C. 229) contained many of the ideas proposed by the Dillingham Commission. It was designed to ensure access for immigrants from North-Western Europe while restricting those from South, Central, and Eastern Europe and continuing the total ban on Asian immigration. In 1921, Congress passed and President Harding signed into law a measure introducing the national origins quota device. In 1924, this concept was expanded by enactment of the Johnson-Reed Act, known as the National Origins Quota Act (43 Stat. 153; 8 U.S.C. 201). It established an annual immigration limit of 150,000 Europeans, a total ban on Japanese, the issuance of visas against set quotas rather than upon arrival, and quotas based on the number of each nationality in the overall population, providing for the admission of immigrants until 1927 by annual quotas of 2 percent of the proportion of the U.S. population based on the 1890 census. It was amended in 1929 when the quotas were permanently set. This remained in effect until 1952. Emigration from Europe declined during the Great Depression of the 1930s, reducing overall immigration for three decades.

The first pressures to revise the quota system began during the 1940s in reaction to World War II. The need for alien labor resulted in enactment of the "bracero" program, a temporary workers program that imported labor mostly from Mexico to fill wartime needs. Congress responded to our wartime alliance with China to repeal the 60-year ban of Chinese immigration. News of the Holocaust at the end of the war helped induce President Truman to issue a directive admitting 40,000 war refugees. Congress reacted to the problems of soldiers who had married overseas by passing the War Brides Act in 1945 (59 Stat. 659; 8 U.S.C. 232) allowing 120,000 alien wives, husbands, and children of members of the Armed Forces to immigrate to the United States separate from the quota system. Truman initiated a refugee law, the Displaced Persons Act (62 Stat. 1009). Passed by Congress in 1948, it allowed the admission of over 400,000 displaced persons through the end of 1951 by "mortgaging" their entry against future quotas foreshadowing the "dutch-door era," when special provisions enabled easy entry of various favored groups.

In 1952, Congress passed the Immigration and Nationality Act, also known as the McCarran-Walter Act (66 Stat. 163). It consolidated previous immigration laws into a single statute, retained aspects of the national origins quota system, but also set up a system of preferences for certain skilled labor and for the relatives of U.S. citizens and permanent resident aliens. It set a limit of 150,000 on immigration from the Eastern Hemisphere and retained the unlimited number for the Western Hemisphere. It set a small quota for Asian immigration, a "Pacific Triangle" provision. In 1953 President Truman appointed a commission to study immigration and naturalization policy that recommended a more liberalized approach.

During the Cold War, Congress enacted measures in response to foreign policy issues. In 1956 and 1957, it passed laws allowing Hungarian "refugee-escapees" displaced by their failed revolution to enter and established a category for refugees fleeing Communist-dominated countries or countries in the Middle East (72 Stat. 419). In 1960, Congress passed the Refugee Fair Share Act, providing a temporary program for World War II refugees and displaced persons still in United Nations refugee camps (74 Stat. 504). In 1962, Congress enacted the Migration and Refugee Assistance Act, responding to refugees fleeing Communist Cuba.

Congress comprehensively revised immigration policy with the Immigration and Nationality Act of 1965 (79 Stat. 911). This new law reflected the civil rights era in much the same way as the McCarran-Walter Act reflected the Cold War period. A healthy and expanding economy eased fears of job competition among organized labor forces. The new law abolished the national origins quota system, replacing it with an overall limit of 160,000 to be distributed on the basis of a limit of 20,000 persons per country for all nations outside the Western Hemisphere and an overall limit of 120,000 on Western Hemisphere nations without individual national limits. It established a seven-category system of preferences for the Eastern Hemisphere, giving first preference to reuniting families and a high preference for certain desired occupational skill categories. The ending of the open-door policy for Western Hemisphere nations was a compromise to get the bill passed. The bracero program was ended in 1964. That and the closing of the open door to Western Hemisphere countries, led to a backlog of applicants from Latin America and renewed problems of undocumented (illegal) aliens from those countries. In 1976, Congress reacted to such pressures by amending the 1965 law. It set immigration limits for both hemispheres to 20,000 per country, on a first-come, first-served basis. It set a worldwide limit of 290,000 and retained the seven-category preference system of the 1965 act.

Special "parole" programs to handle massive waves of refugees from Cuba, Vietnam, and the Soviet Union were enacted instead of any blanket revisions in overall legal immigration policy. This approach became increasingly inadequate to handle what was becoming a recurring "special" situation, and Congress passed the Refugee Act of 1980 (94 Stat. 102), providing an ongoing mechanism for the admission of and aid to refugees, removal of previous geographic and ideological restrictions, and the setting of a total allocation for such refugee admissions at 50,000 annually through 1982. It set up a system for reimbursement to states and voluntary associations for financial and medical assistance they provided to refugees, and signaled a renewed concern for reexamining immigration policy.

Beginning in 1973, a decade of "stagflation," characterized by high inflation and high unemployment, coupled with continued massive illegal immigration, led to calls for a major revision in immigration policy. In 1984 alone, the Immigration and Naturalization Service apprehended over 1.2 million undocumented aliens, an astonishing 34 percent increase over two years. Broad support and bipartisan efforts for immigration reform developed in response. It became increasingly clear that the United States could not adequately patrol its more than 5,000 miles of border. The combined illegal and legal immigration rate exceeded the peak years of the early 1900s, representing an estimated 40 to 50 percent of the U.S. annual population increase.

Another commission was established to study the problem—the Select Commission on Immigration and Refugee Policy (SCIRP). Its recommendations ushered in a new direction in policy exemplified by the Immigration Reform and Control Act (IRCA) of 1986 (100 Stat. 3360). It enacted a new balance in the opposing values pursued over the years. On the one hand, it attempted to control illegal immigration by strengthening the border patrol and cutting down on incentives for new entrants by placing stiff penalties on potential employers—fines and even prison terms for employers who knowingly hire or recruit undocumented aliens for employment. The stiffer and restrictionist-oriented employer sanctions provision was balanced by an amnesty provision. Over 3 million previously illegal aliens were granted amnesty and allowed legal status as resident aliens. This approach of attempting to decrease immigration by decreasing the economic incentives for immigration was a new direction in immigration policy.

Legal immigration was further amended by the Immigration Act of 1990 (104 Stat. 4981), which among other provisions established a sort of lottery for immigrants and set up a new category for persons willing to invest millions into the economy and create new jobs. In 1994, California entered the picture with its attempt to restrict immigration to that state. Using the initiative process, in November, 1994, California voters passed a measure, officially entitled the "Save Our State Initiative," but more commonly known as Proposition 187, by nearly 60 percent. The measure required state and local agencies to report to the INS any persons "suspected of being illegal," to prevent illegal aliens from receiving benefits or public services in the State of California. Among its many provisions, it restricted children of aliens from schools, increased punishments for the manufacture, sale, or distribution of false citizenship or resident alien documents, increased criminal penalties for alien smuggling, made it a crime to use false documents, established verification requirements for state and local officials, excluded illegal aliens from most public social services, including health services except in cases of emergency or communicable diseases, and excluded illegal aliens from postsecondary education. Immediately challenged by the League of United Latin American Citizens (LULAC), much of the new law was overturned in federal district court as unconstitutional infringement of congressional power (*LULAC et al. v. Wilson et al.* 908 F. Supp. 755 C.D.Cal. 1995: 787–791). Figure 9.1 depicts *legal* immigration flows to the United States, from 1901 to 2004.

The successful use of Proposition 187 by California Governor Pete Wilson to ride the issue back into the governorship sent a loud and clear message to Congress to do something about illegal immigration. In 1996, Congress enacted the Personal Responsibility and Work Opportunity Act, a welfare reform act that contained provisions aimed at both legal and illegal immigrants (110 Stat. 2105). Later in 1996, Congress passed a more restrictive legal immigration law, the Illegal Immigration Reform and Immigrant Responsibility Act (110 Stat. 3009). These laws had a temporary impact on the numbers of illegal and legal immigrants and they enacted most of the restrictive measures of Proposition 187. The new laws strained families in the United States split in their status (with one or more members being here legally, but others illegally). As economic conditions improved by 2000, Congress eased up a bit by passing, on December 21, 2000, the Legal Immigration and Family Equity Act (LIFE). This act impacted about 640,000 undocumented aliens, allowing them to apply for visas without first leaving the United States.

The combination of increased restrictions and denial of benefits to illegals and even to some legal resident aliens entailed in Proposition 187 and in the two 1996 Congressional acts, plus the over three million persons who had earlier been given amnesty by IRCA in 1986 and were by 1997 qualified to seek naturalization, combined to dramatically increase the number of persons naturalized during the final years of the twentieth century. An upsurge in naturalizations spiked to nearly 1.2 million in 1999, and over 1 million in 2001. Those being naturalized shifted in the region of birth to those from Mexico, Asia, and South America, with a dramatic decline in those from Europe. In 1990 Mexico was the top sending country with 22 percent of the total foreign-born. By 2000, Mexican immigrants accounted for 30 percent of the total, and Mexico alone accounted for 43 percent of the growth in the immigration population between 1990 and 2000. Several states in which Mexican immigrant influx is especially pronounced registered significant increases. In Arizona, for example, immigrants from Mexico grew from 5 percent to 67 percent of the foreign born, and in Texas they went from 59 percent to 65 percent of the total.

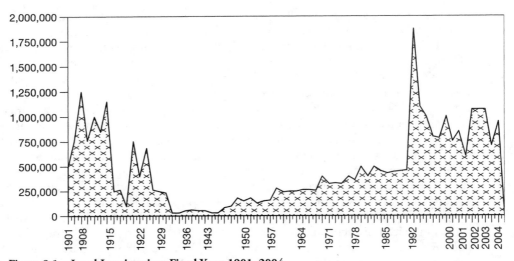

Figure 9.1   Legal Immigration: Fiscal Years 1901–2004

Source: Figure by author. Adapted from U.S. Department of Justice, "Legal Immigration, Fiscal year 2001," Annual report (August 2002), updated to 2004 by Annual Report data.

Figure 9.2 shows dramatically the rapid growth of Mexicans in the United States, showing the Mexican-born population in the nation and graphing their percent of the foreign-born population from 1850 projected to 2010. Total *legal* immigration to the United States increased from 2000 to 2004, the last year for which we have firm data, as follows: 2000, 850,000; 2001, 1,064,000; 2002, 1,064,000; 2003, 706,000; and 2004, 946,000 (from the *Statistical Abstract of the United States, 2006*, data taken from Table 5, p. 9.)

Table 9.7 shows the breakdown of the officially estimated 7 million unauthorized immigrants to the United States in 2000 by selected countries of origin and by state in which they resided in 2000.

After the attacks of 9/11 on the New York City World Trade Center Twin Towers and on the Pentagon in Washington, DC, Congress quickly and overwhelmingly passed two laws with considerable implications for future immigration, and particularly for illegal aliens and for legal immigrants from the Middle East. The first was the USA Patriots Act of 2001 (HR 3162). It is a lengthy 288 pages. Its key immigration-related provisions broaden the definition of terrorism, expand grounds for inadmissibility to include aliens suspected of being involved in terrorist activity or who publicly endorsed such, and required the attorney general to detain aliens he certified as threats to national security. About a year later Congress passed the second law, the Homeland Security Act of 2002 (HR 5005). It establishes the new Department of Homeland Security. It is a massive law, over 400 printed pages long, and it merges twenty-two federal agencies and results in the most extensive reorganization of the federal bureaucracy since the creation of the Department of Defense after World War II. It creates within the new department two bureaus, each headed by an Undersecretary: the Directorate of Border and Transportation Security, and a Bureau of Citizenship and Immigration services. Relevant here is their likely impact on immigration. The USA Patriots Act gives the attorney general

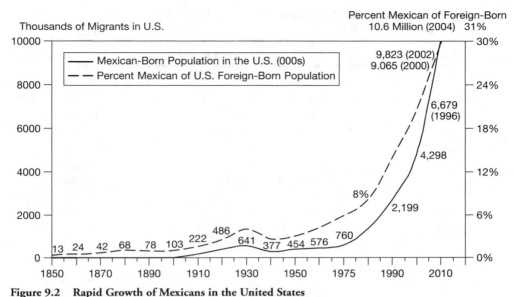

Figure 9.2   Rapid Growth of Mexicans in the United States

Source: Figure by author. Adapted from figure presented by Robert Suro, Pew Hispanic Center, at The Regional Conference on Illegal Immigration (NCLS, Denver, CO: December 12, 2005).

and the Justice Department rather sweeping new powers to arrest anyone suspected of terrorism. It also enhances the Department of Justice's expedited removal powers. The new Department of Homeland Security includes an enhanced Border Patrol operation. These two laws ushered in a new era of immigration policy, the "storm-door" era.

Changing regulations making it easier for the INS to remove aliens, and conditions inducing more voluntary departures, contributed to dramatic increases in aliens expelled or who voluntarily departed. For example, from 1981 to 1990, there were 232 formal removals and 9,961,912 voluntary departures. Those numbers really sky-rocketed during the most recent decade of 1991 to 2000, when there were 939,749 formal removals and 13,587,684 voluntary departures (Annual Report, BCIS, accessed on-line at http://www.immigration.gov/graphics/, p. 17).

Illegal immigration, complex refugee issues, and the continued pressure for high levels of legal immigration to the United States made immigration policy more complex and less predictable. Immigration policy swings between intense moral links to the American creed and an ongoing struggle over who and how many the economy could afford and society could effectively absorb. Immigration policy is an area in the struggle between the nation's racial and ethnic minorities and the majority because it so clearly affects the very nature of the nation of people the United States will be in the future. Ultimately, the key to understanding immigration policy is the disparities in power among the competing groups who seek to influence that balance. The interplay among such groups determines how wide open or closed will be the doors to the nation at any given period of time. Figure 9.3 depicts the unauthorized alien residents, their arrivals and more recent redistribution across many more states, 1980 to 2004.

Table 9.7 **Estimated Unauthorized Immigrants by Selected States and Country of Origin, 2000**

State		*Country of Origin*	
California	2,209,000	Mexico	4,808,000
Texas	1,041,000	El Salvador	189,000
New York	489,000	Guatemala	144,000
Illinois	422,000	Columbia	141,000
Florida	337,000	Honduras	138,000
Georgia	263,000	China	115,000
New Jersey	226,000	Ecuador	108,000
N. Carolina	206,000	Dom. Rep.	91,000
Colorado	144,000	Philippines	85,000
Washington	136,000	Brazil	77,000
Virginia	103,000	Haiti	76,000
Nevada	101,000	India	70,000
Oregon	90,000	Peru	61,000
Massachusetts	87,000	Korea	55,000

Source: Table by author, data from *Statistical Abstract of the United States, 2006,* Table 5, p. 9.

LAW ENFORCEMENT

The relationship between the police and the minority population is often characterized by a hostility and distrust on both sides. While a majority of black and white citizens have a positive attitude toward the police, the most anti-police groups are young adult males, especially young black males.

In 2002, Human Rights Watch reported that "out of a total population of 1,976,019 incarcerated in the United States in adult facilities, 1,239,946 (63 percent) are blacks or Latinos, though these groups constitute only 25 percent of the national population" (Brewster and Stowers 2004, 200). Their 2002 report highlights the racial and ethnic divide in the law enforcement arena. For example, in 12 of the American states, black men are incarcerated at rates between 12 and 16 times greater than those of white men. In 15 states, black women are incarcerated at rates between 10 and 35 times greater than those of white women. In 6 states, black youth under 18 are incarcerated in adult facilities at 12 to 25 times greater than those of white youth. In 10 states, Latino men are 5 to 9 times more likely than white men to be incarcerated, and in 8 states, Latina women are incarcerated 4 to 7 times more often than white women (Brewster and Stowers 2004, 201–202). This pattern, moreover, has grown steadily since 1990. The links between race or ethnicity and crime vary and the reasons are many, including racism, family patterns, levels of poverty, increased numbers of broken homes, the effects of central-city decaying schools, and so on. The social sciences have long noted a strong association between crime rates and socio-economic status, although there is no clear-cut consensus as to the "causes" of crime.

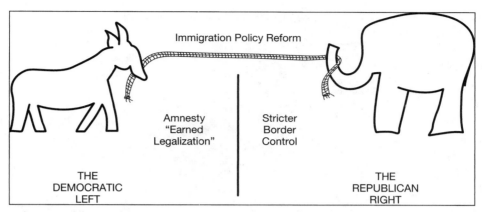

Immigration Policy Reform

Amnesty
"Earned
Legalization"

Stricter
Border
Control

THE
DEMOCRATIC
LEFT

THE
REPUBLICAN
RIGHT

Is there no middle ground?
Source: By author.

In large measure the animosity between the law enforcement and racial and ethnic minorities reflects two-sided prejudice. Racism runs deep in American society and can be explosive. When racial prejudice becomes uncontrolled, as during a race riot, racial violence runs loose in the streets. It unleashes a degree of fear and hatred that can turn even warm human beings, black as well as white, into cold perpetrators of violence. Tragically, it is often the innocent who are victims during violent outbreaks. Riots exacerbate the antipathy between police and minorities and have often begun with an encounter between police and ghetto residents. The police served as the "flash point" for minority anger, the formation of mobs, and the resulting disorder.

Minority hostility toward police reflects a long history of discrimination. Blacks remember the mistreatment of their southern past where de jure segregation was often brutally enforced by the police. The lynching of minority persons accused of crime was the worst of such behavior made possible only because law enforcement agencies stood aside and let the mobs work their will. "From 1882 to 1959, 2,595 Negroes were lynched in nine Southern states. No white person was ever punished for these offenses" (Edwards 1982, 25).

Pervasive racial conflict reflects the often common anti-minority attitudes among police personnel. When the civil rights movement first arose, the attitude of the police was apparent. It engendered a reciprocal feeling among blacks both North and South. "Every time illegal violence is employed against civil rights demonstrations anywhere, it increases animosity against police everywhere. The dogs that Police Chief T. Eugene "Bull" Connor set on young Negroes in Birmingham, Alabama, in 1963, probably caused more physical injury to police officers in other cities in the long run than to the demonstrators they were pictured as attacking" (Edwards 1982, 17).

Numerous studies indicate a widespread prejudice among police against minorities, particularly blacks.[1] A President's Crime Commission Task Force found that 72 percent of the police officers it interviewed in three major cities exhibited prejudice against blacks in their responses to task force observers. Blacks and whites manifest sharply different positions in their attitudes and experience with police. Studies indicate a widespread problem of police abuse and excessive use of force. Reports on police

Most Unauthorized Arrived Since 1990

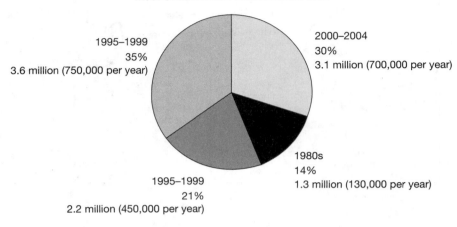

1995–1999
35%
3.6 million (750,000 per year)

2000–2004
30%
3.1 million (700,000 per year)

1980s
14%
1.3 million (130,000 per year)

1995–1999
21%
2.2 million (450,000 per year)

10.3 Million Unauthorized in March 2004

(Demographic estimates based on March 2004 CPS with allowance for omissions.)
Pew Hispanic Center

**Major Redistribution Away from
Big Six Settlement States**

Percent of Total Unauthorized Migrant Population

☐ 1990
▮ 2002–2004

	CA	NY	TX	FL	IL	NJ	All Other
1990	45%	15%	11%	9%	4%	4%	12% / 400,000
2002–2004	24%	7%	14%	9%	4%	4%	39% / 3.0 Million

Figure 9.3   Unauthorized Alien Residents, Arrivals and Redistribution

Source: Figure by author. Adapted from figures presented by Roberto Suro, Pew Hispanic Center, Presentation at the Regional Conference on Illegal Immigration, NCLS, Denver, Colorads,: December 12, 2005.

brutality show that it is common and that the lower class bears the brunt of victimization. Officers tend to mistreat citizens of the same race: 67 percent of citizens victimized by white police officers were white, 71 percent of citizens victimized by black officers were black (Lipsky 1970, 74). A similar gap between white and Hispanic populations in regard to attitudes toward the police is evident. For example, in a 1999 report, when asked if the person thought the police in their community might stop and arrest the person when that person is completely innocent, 22 percent of Hispanic respondents reported being so afraid, compared to 14 percent of white respondents (*Hispanic Americans: A Statistical Sourcebook,* 187).

The commission's most troubling finding was that in a third of the cases where excessive use of force was evident, it took place in the police station after the arrest, when the police officer should have been in control. Highly publicized incidents, like the beatings of blacks in major cities like Los Angeles, New York, Chicago and so on confirm the worst fears among the nation's minorities.

The ghetto setting ensures conflict in that residential segregation and density problems mean blacks are more likely than whites to come into adversarial contact with the police. A study of 600 police officers in three major cities with large black populations found that three-fourths of white officers working in predominantly black areas expressed prejudiced views of blacks. Twenty-eight percent of black officers in the study did so as well. Mark Levy concludes that the problem is not one of a few bad eggs but rather of a police system that is racist in its recruitment, training, socialization, and assignment patterns (Ruchelman 1973, 80). The very existence of the ghetto as the center of intense crime aggravates the systematic nature of police/minority conflict. Metropolitan areas have a violent crime rate five times higher and a property crime rate twice as high as those of the smaller city or rural area.

The adversarial relationship is compounded by the role police play in the ghetto. The police serve as buffers. Their job is to minimize crime where possible and to contain it where it is less likely to be a threat to the person or property of the majority members of society. This means the police officer comes quite literally to personify "the law." The officer becomes the symbol of authority, empowered to use his gun when necessary. He becomes the symbol and agent of the sovereign right of the state to take lives if need be. Ghetto residents react to that role. Their frustrations and anger are directed toward the police like lightning to the rod. The pervasive animosity in the ghetto is transferred to the police. Enmity provides ghetto residents a release from pent-up frustrations that seethe and boil over into race riots.

The structure of the judicial system exacerbates the problem. Policy concerning so-called victimless crime enhances the likelihood of police/minority conflict by concentrating many of the resources of the entire judicial system, most especially law enforcement, on the control of crimes of prostitution, public intoxication, and sexual perversions. The war on drug abuse consumes the vast proportion of court time in any large city, time that might otherwise be devoted to more swiftly prosecuting perpetrators of crimes against person or property. Add to the court time the use of the resources of the prosecutor's office, court-appointed defense attorneys, and police time spent on victimless crime, and the total mounts dramatically. These laws demean law enforcement officers who consort with prostitutes, gamblers, and drug pushers in order to catch them. This reinforces their attitudes against "social undesirables." Police arrest streetwalkers but rarely expensive call girls; blacks, Hispanics, and lower-class whites for public intoxication but seldom middle-class whites unless when driving. Victimless crime encourages organized crime. Organized crime "syndicates" provide "victimless" crime activities as a "service."

These laws fail to prevent the conduct they proscribe. It is arguable whether they even reduce significantly such behavior. The need to enforce such laws puts the police into sustained conflict with minorities. For the police, who often witness the ghetto resident in the context of breaking the law, anti-minority attitudes are confirmed and reinforced. To the ghetto resident, the police are viewed as "The Man," whose only contact is when they bust somebody for something often culturally viewed as "no real crime." Minority persons are far more likely to be arrested, prosecuted, and convicted than are members of the white majority. The nation's prison population is vastly disproportionately Black and Hispanic. For minorities, that fact confirms racial/ethnic bias. For the white majority, it confirms the view that minorities cause the crime epidemic.

Violent crime is often regionally located, in the large metropolitan areas where the racial/ethnic concentrations are found. Higher violent crime rates are found in the South, in the East Coast's larger metropolitan area states, and in the Midwest states of Michigan (Detroit) and Illinois (Chicago).

There is a strong association between increases in immigration and minority group conflict with law enforcement. The number of noncitizens (legal and illegal aliens) who have been processed in the federal criminal justice system has increased on average 10 percent annually since the 1980s. Non-citizens comprise, on average, 15 percent of the federal prison population. As of June, 2001, the number of noncitizens incarcerated in federal prisons had increased a whopping 53 percent since 1994 (growing from 18,929 in 1984 to 35,629 in 2001). Whereas immigrants comprise only 9.3 percent of the total U.S. population, they make up 29 percent of federal inmates (Brewster and Stowers 2004, 204).

Immigrants who are racial or ethnic minorities link directly to another growing aspect of minority group/law enforcement relations—that of racial profiling. *Racial profiling* has been defined by New York City Police Commissioner Raymond Kelly, in March 2002, as "the use of race, color, ethnicity, or national origin as the determinative factor for initiating police action" (cited in Levine 2004, 65). Several studies have focused on the issue, about which there is considerable debate as to its extent and validity. A New Jersey study found that eight of ten stops and searches of automobiles by state troopers on the New Jersey turnpike were of African-American and Hispanic drivers and a Maryland state study on Interstate 95 found that although 17 percent of drivers were black, 75 percent of those stopped and searched were black (Sugrue, 2004: 66 and 71 respectively). Other states' findings of similar results include Ohio, Texas, and North Carolina. Allegations about the extensive use of racial profiling have risen, especially since 9/11, as have subsequent allegations of racial profiling being used against Arab Americans, and persons appearing to be of Middle Eastern heritage (Levine 2004, 66).

David Harris contends that there are five good reasons for police not to use racial profiling: (1) It is, simply put, poor policing policy; (2) it causes deep cynicism among blacks about the fairness and legitimacy of law enforcement and courts; (3) police can reduce crime rates without use of racial profiling; (4) community policing is a better approach; and (5) not using it "keeps the feds out" (Levine 2004,: 70–81).

An issue similar to that of racial profiling that goes directly to the majority society and law enforcement relations with racial and ethnic minorities is that of the growing incidence of *hate crimes*. In 2000, the FBI collected statistics on hate crimes from nearly 12,000 law enforcement agencies serving over 238 million inhabitants. Table 9.8 reports on the number of incidents, offenses, victims, and known offenders by bias motivation (hate crimes) in 2003.

Minorities are not only more likely to be victims of hate crimes, they are more likely to be victims of crime in general, and of violent crime in particular. Table 9.9 briefly lists the victimization rates of all crime and of violent crime, by characteristics of the victim as of 2003.

Persons incarcerated in federal and state prisons have been growing at steadily increasing rates since 1980. Table 9.10 reports the number of federal and state prisoners from 1980 to 2003 and their rate per 100,000 estimated U.S. population. Both the number and the rate have increased dramatically over the two decades reported in Table 9.10.

Finally, racial and ethnic minority persons, when compared to their percent of the population, are more likely than are whites to be sentenced to death and to be actually executed. Table 9.11 details those facts by reporting on prisoners sentenced to death by characteristics of the prisoner, 1980 to 2003, and prisoners actually executed under civil authority, 1985 to 2004.

What, if anything, can be done to reduce this seemingly inherent conflictual relationship? Three major reforms have been suggested to improve police/minority relations:

1. Hiring more minority officers: a city's police force should mirror the racial diversity of its citizenry.
2. More sensitivity and stress training of police officers and judicial system staff.
3. The use of the "neighborhood police" assignment pattern especially in large cities. Use more patrolmen who walk the neighborhood beat and know the people they serve, and vice versa.

Attempts to implement such reforms have resulted in the dramatic increase in minority police officers in the nation's major cities and the sharp decrease in fatal police shootings. But some scholars of police/community relations are less optimistic about how much improvement such "reforms" bring. They argue that the conflict will continue as long as the police must be the buffers, the social brokers and urban colonial guards of society. Police departments, moreover, attract **stratiphiles**, individuals who are extraordinarily disposed to the forces and commitments that flow from social stratification. They are also marginal men. In the ghetto, police are often viewed as pariahs, judas-goats, and sacrificial lambs. This is doubly so for the black officer, who often feels a double marginality, rejected by both blacks and many white officers, sometimes viewed as traitors to their race. Officers who regularly work the ghetto, be they black or white, can become ghettoized: coming to feel rejected, abused, exploited, alienated, and even powerless. Even black officers sometimes become abusive toward ghetto residents.

Another common proposal for reform is the civilian review board. Such boards have not been very successful, and few metropolitan areas have established them. Clearly they are not panaceas. Where established—in Philadelphia and Rochester, for example—they

Table 9.8   Hate Crimes: Numbers Reported, Offenses, Victims, and Known Offenders by Bias Motivation, 2003

Total Bias Motivation	Incidents	Offenses	Victims	Known Offenders
Race Total	7,531	8,775	9,166	6,978
Ethnic/National Origin	1,033	1,245	1,335	1,128
Religion	1,343	1,428	1,492	573
Sexual Orientation	1,246	1,439	1,488	1,318
Disability	46	53	56	44

Source: U.S. Census Bureau, *Statistical Abstract of the United States, 2006.* Adapted by author from Table 305, p. 200.

Table 9.9   Victimization Rates of All Crime and Violent Crime by Type of Victim, 2003

Characteristic of Victims	All Crime	All Crimes of Violence
Male	23.3	22.6
Female	20.2	19.0
White	22.1	21.5
Black	30.7	29.1
Other	16.9	16.0
Hispanic	25.3	24.2
Non-Hispanic	23.0	22.3

Source: U.S. Census Bureau, *Statistical Abstract of the United States, 2006.* Adapted by author from Table 308, p. 201.

are faulted for being inadequately staffed, relying on the police for the investigation of the police. They have not prevented riots in those cities. They often lack remedial powers, only being able to investigate and advise (Edwards 1982).

Police are rarely convicted and punished on the basis of citizen complaints, by internal affairs division investigation, or by outside police civilian review boards. The police reform movement has generally persuaded state, local, and even federal authorities that they should handle complaints against the police. Out of a deep concern for the reputation of the department, internal affairs units and special squads have on occasion used reprehensible tactics to discourage citizens from filing complaints against officers. Critics list many devices used: threatening citizens with criminal libel; forcing them to take lie detector tests; employing disorderly conduct charges and resisting arrest charges against them, or threatening to do so; intimidating them or their witness if they do file charges; refusing access to counsel or to files; and developing expensive, complicated, and protracted procedures.

The police reform movement has called for greater police "professionalism." This approach is very expensive. In New York City, in one decade, the police force increased by 18 percent and its costs rose by 96 percent. Various police scholars and critics are

Table 9.10   Federal and State Prisoners, Number and Rate, 1980–2003

Year	Total Number	Rate
1980	315,974	139
1981	353,673	154
1982	395,516	171
1983	419,346	179
1984	443,398	188
1985	480,568	202
1986	522,084	217
1987	560,812	231
1988	603,732	247
1989	680,907	276
1990	739,980	297
1991	789,610	313
1992	846,277	332
1993	932,074	359
1994	1,016,691	389
1995	1,137,722	411
1996	1,195,498	427
1997	1,245,402	461
1998	1,304,074	477
1999	1,321,137	478
2000	1,331,278	470
2001	1,345,217	470
2002	1,380,516	476
2003	1,409,280	482

Source: U.S. Census Bureau, *Statistical Abstract of the United States, 2006.* Adapted by author from Table 339, p. 215.

pessimistic about the value of "professionalism" reforms. They have not prevented riots, reduced significantly the allegations of police abuse, or improved ghetto residents' attitudes toward the police. A major federal policy response to the urban riots was the Crime Control and Safe Streets Act of 1968, which created the Law Enforcement Assistance Administration (LEAA). This law poured millions of federal dollars into local police departments with an approach that critics allege is inefficient. Most of the money spent, at least early on, was on expensive "hardware" and on a repressive response to police minority relations.[1] So long as crime and disorder are disproportionately to be found among young lower-class males, and so long as Blacks and Hispanics remain over-represented in young gangs, the police are going to be adversaries.

While law enforcement, like housing, is a policy arena that shows precious little improvement in minority/majority relations, political participation is one showing the most positive change.

Table 9.11   Prisoners on Death Row, 1980–2003, and Prisoners Executed, by Sex and Race, 1985–2004

							Prisoners on Death Row							
Prisoners	1980	1990	1991	1992	1993	1994	1995	1996	1997	1998	1999	2000	2001	2002	2003
Total	688	2,346	2,466	2,575	2,727	2,905	3,064	3,242	3,328	3,465	3,527	3,593	3,577	3,562	3,374
White	418	1,368	1,450	1,508	1,575	1,653	1,732	1,833	1,864	1,917	1,948	1,990	1,968	1,939	1,878
Black/ Other	270	978	1,016	1,067	1,152	1,252	1,332	1,409	1,409	1,548	1,579	1,603	1,608	1,623	1,496

Source: Statistical Abstract of the U.S., 2006, Table 340, p. 215.

Prisoners Executed, 1985–2004

Year	Total	Male	Female	White	Black
1985	18	18	—	11	7
1986	18	18	—	11	7
1987	25	25	—	13	12
1988	11	11	—	6	5
1989	16	16	—	8	8
1990	23	23	—	16	7
1991	14	14	—	7	7
1992	31	31	—	20	11
1993	38	38	—	23	14
1994	31	31	—	20	11
1995	56	56	—	33	22
1996	45	45	—	31	14
1997	74	74	—	45	27
1998	68	66	2	48	18
1999	98	98	—	61	33
2000	85	83	2	48	36
2001	66	63	3	48	17
2002	71	69	2	53	18
2003	65	65	—	44	20
2004	59	59	—	39	19
Total	4,803	4,761	42	2,358	2,338

Source: U.S. Census Bureau, *Statistical Abstract of the United States, 2006.* Adapted by author from Table 342 p. 216.

POLITICAL PARTICIPATION

This section traces changes in American public policy regarding political participation. It shows how the United States changed from a society that systematically disenfranchised its minority population to one that now guarantees basic civil rights of participation. Dramatic improvements have been made in the actual participation by minorities—increases in their voting registration and turnout rates and in the success of electing, from among their own, officials to public office.

Many minority groups exhibit considerable political incorporation. For some ethnic minorities, such progress was critical to their segmented assimilation, or even full assimilation.

Earlier chapters described varying but consistently low levels of political participation by minority groups in the United States. Much of that low level of participation is undoubtedly related to low socioeconomic status. Social science scholars studying political participation view *socioeconomic status (SES)* as the most important determinant of political participation. The consensus among scholars about its importance is referred to as the *standard SES model.* Simply put, the higher one's SES, the more likely one is to vote, and vice versa.

Ethnicity has been shown to have an independent impact on political participation. Policy has been used by majority society to disenfranchise ethnic minorities. Ethnicity and race have been instrumental in developing an association between low SES and low levels of participation. The right to vote is a primal act of democratic citizens. The loss of suffrage endangers all other rights. It is central to a group's ability to protect itself against biased public policy (Sigler 1975, 113).

Majority society uses laws, public policy, and informal measures such as violence and intimidation, to deny participation to minority groups. Such devices and practices as the poll tax, literacy tests, white primary, racial gerrymandering, and registration laws have all been used to disenfranchise minorities. Threats of being fired from one's job and the sheer use of terror by nighttime visits from robed Ku Klux Klan members have denied the vote to many.

Women were denied the right to vote until the Nineteenth Amendment passed in 1920. Asian immigrants, denied citizenship by law, were thereby denied the vote. Native Americans could not vote, except for their tribal leadership, until Congress finally passed the Indian Citizen Act in 1924. Even then, some states limited them from participation in state and local elections until the 1940s. The most extensive use of public policy to disenfranchise minorities involved the various Jim Crow laws aimed at blacks. So intense was racial (and sex) discrimination that, at one time, seventeen states permitted male aliens to vote but denied American women and black citizens the right to do so.

Immediately after the Civil War, three constitutional amendments passed that abolished slavery and guaranteed citizenship to all persons born or naturalized in the United States, and specifically prohibited the denial of the right to vote to any citizen on the basis of race. Enjoyment of this basic right by blacks was short-lived. When federal troops left the South in the late 1870s, southern whites re-established political control over the black population in the South, effectively denying them the vote until the mid-1960s. Although southern blacks continued to vote, sometimes in fairly sizable numbers, until well into the 1880s and 1890s, by the 1890s most of the former

Confederate states passed laws segregating public facilities and eroding their participation. The first objective of the white supremacy movement was to disenfranchise blacks.

At first, Congress attempted to deal with the South's efforts to curtail black voting rights. Congress passed the Enforcement Act of 1870 to give clear "teeth" to the Fifteenth Amendment. A hostile Supreme Court effectively scuttled the law in 1876 (in *United States v. Reese*, 92 U.S. 214). The Court argued that the right to vote was not conferred to anyone by the Fifteenth Amendment since the right to vote was not derived from the states. In 1894, Congress repealed the Enforcement Act, thereby leaving black voting rights to the mercies of the Court. Despite the clear intent of the Fifteenth Amendment, most of the nation's blacks living in the South were denied the right to vote prior to the mid-twentieth century. Several Supreme Court decisions led to that development. In 1883, the civil rights cases decided that the Constitution gave Congress no expressed or implied powers to pass laws prohibiting discrimination practiced by private individuals. In *Hurtado v. California* (1894), the Court ruled that the Fourteenth Amendment's due process clause did not make the Bill of Rights binding on state governments. It took forty years for the Court to reverse itself.

A common device used in the South to strip blacks of the vote was the **literacy test**. These tests originated in the North—in Connecticut and Massachusetts—and only later came to the South. They were first developed to screen out the new immigrants and deny them the vote. Southern states soon seized on them as effective devices against their black populations. The tests were upheld by the Supreme Court in 1898 (*Williams v. Mississippi*, 170 U.S. 218), but they were "fraud, and nothing more" (Key 1949, 576).

Another effective device was the **poll tax**, used by eleven southern states. In several cases the tax was made retroactive—that is, the citizen desiring to vote not only had to pay the poll tax for that year but for past years for which he or she had been eligible to vote. The poll tax prevented large numbers of poor whites as well as blacks from voting in the South. It was upheld by the Supreme Court in 1937 (in *Breedlove v. Suttles*, 302 U.S. 277). Only in 1966 did the Court finally reverse itself and declare the poll tax invalid (in *Harper v. Virginia Board of Elections*, 383 U.S. 663).

A blatant form of legal disenfranchisement of the black was the **grandfather clause**, used in seven southern states. It allowed a registrant to vote without barriers if one's grandfather could do so. Since the grandfathers of blacks had been slaves legally barred from voting, this device blatantly denied blacks that right. In 1915, the Supreme Court finally struck down such laws, based on an Oklahoma case that exempted whites from a literacy test on the basis of a grandfather clause (in *Guinn v. United States*, 238 U.S. 347). Oklahoma quickly passed a new registration law that continued to deny blacks the vote until it, too, was finally overturned in 1939 (in *Lane v. Wilson*, 307 U.S. 268, 275).

The **white primary** was a popular disenfranchisement device in many southern states, because Democratic Party turnout was so solid that an aspiring politician effectively had to win the Democratic Party nomination to win office. The primary election became the real election. The general election merely rubber-stamped the selection made in the primary. By legally banning blacks from the primary, southern states denied blacks an effective vote in the general election. The Supreme Court first ruled that there was no national authority to regulate primary elections (*Newberry v. United States,* 256 U.S. 232, 1921). In 1927, that ruling was modified by *Nixon v. Herndon,* which invalidated a Texas law that flatly prohibited blacks from voting in the state's Democratic primary. Texas responded by authorizing the executive committees of the state's parties to prescribe voting qualifications in primary elections. In 1932, that law was struck down in *Nixon v. Condon* (286 U.S. 73). Texas then set up the Democratic Party as a "private club," whose members could be limited to whites only. At first, the Court upheld the law, deciding such action was discrimination by a private organization rather than by a state (see *Grovey v. Townsend,* 295 U.S. 45, 1935; and *Breedlove v. Suttles,* 302 U.S. 277, 280, 1937). The white primary was finally ruled unconstitutional in any form when the Supreme Court reversed itself in the 1944 case of *Smith v. Allwright* (285 U.S. 355).

Racial gerrymandering was ruled unconstitutional by the Court in *Gomillion v. Lightfoot* (364 U.S. 339, 1960). This decision overturned an Alabama legislative redistricting plan that designed voter districts in a manner the Court ruled was clearly intended to diffuse black votes. With virtually every Jim Crow law being overturned, the white majority turned increasingly to more indirect methods. Registration laws still remain a hurdle to the poor, and intimidation still is used to suppress black registration, and as recently as the 2000 presidential elections and particularly in Florida, many blacks complained of hostile and uncooperative attitudes at polling sites (Brooks 1996, 87–88).

Intimidation worked because of the South's history of violence against blacks who dared to participate. From the 1880s through the 1920s, the Ku Klux Klan used a systematic campaign of violence against blacks to "keep them in their place." From 1889 to 1918, a total of 3,224 blacks were lynched. In the late 1940s, Congress became involved in the process. President Truman supported bills in 1948 that ensured fair employment and fair elections, outlawed the poll tax, cracked down on violence and lynchings, eliminated segregation in interstate commerce and advocated creation of a permanent Civil Rights Commission. The South's power in the Senate blocked passage of his proposals, but clearly the pressure was on Congress to act.

In 1962, Congress passed the Twenty-fourth Amendment outlawing the poll tax in national elections. It was ratified by the states in 1964. In 1966, the Supreme Court, in *Harper v. Virginia Board of Elections,* applied it to state and local elections as well. That decision effectively brought an end to all poll taxes in the United States.

The civil rights movement, through direct-action tactics, pressured Congress to enact legislation ending de jure segregation. In 1963, the Birmingham demonstrations ignited protests across the nation, culminating in the March on Washington in August of that year. More than 200,000 blacks and whites participated. Dr. Martin Luther King Jr. delivered his famous "I Have a Dream" address. In response to the march, President Kennedy sent a strong civil rights bill to Congress, which passed after his assassination as the Civil Rights Act of 1964. The act was hailed as the most sweeping civil rights law enacted in American history. Its various titles and provisions did much to end all Jim Crow practices in the South. The act contained several provisions touching directly on participation. Title I concerned literacy tests, making it unlawful, when determining whether an individual was qualified by state law to vote in any federal election, to apply any standard, practice, or procedure different from those applied to other individuals within the same county. It required written literacy tests and exempted any individual who had completed sixth grade in any English-speaking school as being presumed literate.

Title V of the act empowers the U.S. Commission on Civil Rights, first established by the Civil Rights Act of 1957, to investigate deprivations of the right to vote. The law was immediately challenged, but the entire act was upheld as constitutional in *Heart of Atlanta Motel v. United States* (379 U.S. 241); and in *Katzenbach v. McClung* (379 U.S. 241)—both decided in 1964.

Local registrars in the South still barred blacks by an endless variety of registration barriers. Congress reacted by passing the Voting Rights Act of 1965. This law was the first truly effective tool for protecting the voting rights of minority citizens. Congress extended the act in 1970, 1975, and 1982. It has both permanent and temporary provisions.[2] The permanent or general provisions of the act (1) ensure that length-of-residency requirements will not prevent any citizen from voting in presidential elections; (2) prohibit anyone from denying an eligible citizen the right to vote or from interfering with or intimidating anyone from seeking to register or to vote; and (3) forbade the use of literacy tests or other devices as qualifications for voting in any federal, state, local, general, or primary election. The temporary or special "triggering" provisions applied to those states or counties where (1) literacy tests or similar devices were enforced as of November 1, 1964, and (2) where fewer than 50 percent of the voting-age residents were registered or had cast ballots in the 1964 presidential election. In such jurisdictions, the attorney general of the United States, upon evidence of voter discrimination determined by him, was empowered to replace local registrars with federal examiners who were authorized to abolish literacy tests, waive poll taxes, and register voters under simpler federal procedures. Although quickly challenged, the law was upheld in *South Carolina v. Katzenbach* (383 U.S. 301).

A third triggering device was added in 1975 concerning minority languages. It was added to ensure that citizens are not deprived of the vote because they cannot speak, read, or write English. A jurisdiction is covered by the language provision if (1) in November 1972, more than 5 percent of the voting-age population in that jurisdiction were members of a single-language minority (specified as American Indian, Asian Americans—Chinese, Japanese, Filipino, Koreans—Alaskan Natives, or persons of Spanish heritage), and the jurisdiction provided English-only election material and less than 50 percent of the voting-age population registered or voted in the 1972 presidential election; or (2) more than 5 percent of the voting-age population in a jurisdiction are members of a single-language minority and the illiteracy rate for that minority population is higher than the national illiteracy rate, such rate being defined as failure to complete the fifth grade.

The two trigger provisions brought under their special coverage the entire states of Alabama, Georgia, Louisiana, Mississippi, South Carolina, and Virginia, about forty counties in North Carolina, and a scattering of counties in Arizona, Hawaii, and Idaho. Hundreds of observers and federal examiners were sent to those jurisdictions. Special language provisions affected more jurisdictions including local governments in California, Massachusetts, and Kansas.

Section V of the act requires all jurisdictions covered under its first and second trigger provisions to submit in advance any proposed changes in their election laws or procedures to the federal government for approval. The intent of this provision is to prevent new discrimination practices from replacing old ones—a common cycle prior to the 1965 act. Section V further places the burden of proof on covered jurisdictions that neither the purpose nor effect of proposed changes in their election system is discriminatory.

The impact of the 1964 and 1965 laws has been dramatic. Whereas only 5 percent of voting-age blacks were registered to vote in the eleven southern states in 1940, black registration rose to 45 percent in 1964 and to 57 percent in 1968. In Mississippi, before the 1965 act, only 6.7 percent of the voting age blacks were registered. By 1972, that number had jumped to 60 percent. Georgia's rate rose from 27 percent in 1965 to nearly 68 percent in 1972. Overall, black registration rates in the South have approached the level of white rates for the first time since Reconstruction. In the Southwest, after the 1975 language provision was added, Hispanic registration rose from 44 percent in 1976 to 59 percent in 1980. The closing of the gap between white and minority (black and Hispanic) registration and voter turnout from 1972 to 2004 is shown in Table 9.12.

Registration and voting increases showed up in similarly dramatic strides in the number of successfully elected black officials. In 1962, there were only 72 black elected officials in the South. A decade later there were over 2,500; by 2000 over 9,000. These data are detailed in Table 9.13. As of 2001, the top five states as ranked by the number of black elected officials are as follows: (1) Missouri, 897; (2) Alabama, 731; (3) Louisiana, 701; (4) Illinois, 621; and (5) Georgia, 582 (U.S. Census Bureau, *Statistical Abstract of the United States*, 2002, Table 391, p. 252).

Currently, African Americans face two major problems in the political arena: discrimination associated with casting the ballot (a "right to vote" problem), and the ability to muster enough political clout to protect or promote their interests (a "voting power," or "dilution" problem) (Brooks 1996, 276). The dilution problem manifests itself in various devices to weaken African-American voting power: the use of at-large electoral districts, single-shot voting, decreasing the size of the governing body, using exclusive "slating" groups, and gerrymandering (Brooks 1996, 91–94). The use of "at-large" districts to dilute African-American voting power was evident for many years. In 1986 the U.S. Supreme Court established the standard for determining whether or not vote dilution claims based on the use of at-large or multimember districts violated the Voting Rights Act in *Thornburg v. Gingles,* 478 U.S. 30 (1986). And for many years blacks lost political clout by facing racially gerrymandered districts designed to make sure they did not elect black candidates. In recent years, racial gerrymandering has been used to try to assure them of a safe district. Racial redistricting to create "safe" minority districts, however, has been constrained by the U.S. Supreme Court decision *Miller v. Johnson* 115 S. Ct. 2475 (1995), which applied a strict scrutiny test to racial gerrymandering. In *Shaw v. Reno* 113 S. Ct. 2816 (1993) the Supreme Court ruled that white voters could challenge bizarrely shaped voting districts that had large black majorities, as in the North Carolina plan at issue there.

Hispanic voters in the Southwest still face gerrymandering barriers. *Citizen participation,* a journal on voting behavior, found sixty-six counties in Texas and California that were racially gerrymandered against Mexican Americans. Increased voter registration drives and voter turnout are less effective when the vote is diluted by

Table 9.12   Voter Participation by Group, 1972–2004

	1972		1992		1996		2000		2002		2004	
	Registered	Voted	Registered	Voted	Registered	Voted	Registered	Voted	Registered	Voted	Registered	Voted
Whites	73.4%	64.5%	70.1%	63.3%	67.7%	56.0%	65.6%	56.4%	63.1%	44.1%	67.9%	60.3%
Hispanics	44.4	37.5	35.0	28.9	35.7	26.7	34.9	27.5	32.6	18.9	34.3	28.0
Blacks	65.5	63.0	68.2	61.3	65.9	50.6	63.9	59.7	58.8	39.7	64.4	56.3

Source: U.S. Bureau of the Census, *Statistical Abstract of the United States, 2006,* Table 405, p.263.

Table 9.13   Black Elected Officials, 1970–2001

Year	Total	Congress/State Legs.	City and County	Law Enforcement	Education
1970	1,469	179	715	213	362
1980	4,890	326	2,832	526	1,206
1990	7,335	436	4,485	769	1,645
1995	8,385	604	4,954	987	1,840
1997	8,617	613	5,056	996	1,952
1998	8,830	614	5,210	998	2,008
1999	8,896	618	5,354	997	1,927
2000	9,001	621	5,420	1,037	1,923
2001	9,061	633	5,456	1,044	1,928

Source: U.S. Census Bureau, *Statistical Abstract of the United States, 2006,* Table 403, p. 262.

gerrymandering. Discriminatory redistricting schemes have plagued Hispanic political advancement for some time, especially in Texas. The Southwest Voter Registration Education Project (SVREP) has been involved in thirty-six lawsuits alleging gerrymandering in Colorado, New Mexico, and Texas. Most were settled out of court.

Both blacks and Hispanics launched drives to overcome such obstacles. The Voter Education Project (VEP), begun in 1962, was rejuvenated in the 1980s. Jesse Jackson's two presidential campaigns scored impressive gains in new black registrations, with estimates of over 2 million new voters turning out during the primary elections in which he ran.

The potential of such programs is considerable. Hispanics can provide the swing vote in states like Texas and California, which alone account for nearly one-third of the votes needed to be elected president. The SVREP campaign scored considerable success, and the results of its litigation efforts are impressive. In Texas, for example, Medina County had not reapportioned since the turn of the century. When SVREP sued and the district was redrawn, three Mexican Americans were elected to office,

Table 9.14   Hispanic Public Elected Officials by Office, 1985–2004

Year	Total	Legislative and State Executive	City/County	Judicial/Law Enforcement	Education and School Boards
1985	3,147	129	1,316	517	1,185
1988	3,360	135	1,425	574	1,228
1989	3,783	143	1,724	575	1,341
1990	4,004	144	1,819	583	1,458
1991	4,202	151	1,867	596	1,588
1992	4,994	150	1,908	628	2,308
1993	5,170	182	2,023	633	2,332
1994	5,549	199	2,197	651	2,412
2000	5,205	223	1,846	454	2,682
2004	4,651	231	2,059	638	1,723

Source: U.S. Census Bureau, *Statistical Abstract of the United States, 2006.* Adapted by author from Table 403, p. 262.

Table 9.15   Voting and Percent Registered Voters, by Sex, Race and Hispanic Origin, 2004

Characteristic	Number Voting	Percent Registered to Vote
Male	103,800,000	64.0
Female	111,900,000	67.6
White	176,600,000	67.9
Black	24,900,000	64.4
Hispanic	27,100,000	34.3

Source: Table by author, from data in *Statistical Abstract of the United States,* 2006, Table 405, p.263.

the first in the county's history. In Victoria County, where minorities are 30 percent of the population, a Chicano county commissioner was elected and the city council forced to go from an at-large to a single-member district structure. Victories such as these set off a chain reaction: When Mexican Americans have a better chance of winning elections, they register and turn out to vote in even greater numbers. The Mexican American Legal Defense Education Fund and the Texas Rural Legal Aid have used suits to challenge at-large election structures and racial gerrymandering in Texas.

Hispanic voters have been making great strides in recent years. Table 9.14 lists the number of Hispanic public elected officials, by office, 1985 to 2004. As of 2004, the top five states in rank order of number of Hispanic elected officials are (1) Texas, 1,828; (2) Illinois, 1,190; (3) California, 767; (4) New Mexico, 618; and (5) Colorado, 151 (U.S. Census Bureau, *Statistical Abstract of the United States, 2006,* Table 403, p. 262).

Table 9.15 shows the numbers voting and the percent of registered voters by sex, race, and Hispanic origin as of 2004, the most recent year for which such data is available.

Table 9.16   Members of Congress—Selected Characteristics, 1983–2003

Member of Congress	Male	Female	Black	API	Hispanic
Representatives					
98th Cong. 1983	413	21	21	3	8
99th Cong. 1985	412	22	21	5	10
100th Cong. 1987	412	23	23	6	11
101st Cong. 1989	408	25	24	6	10
102nd Cong. 1991	407	28	26	5	11
103rd Cong. 1993	388	47	38	7	17
104th Cong. 1995	388	47	40	7	17
106th Cong. 1999	379	56	39	6	19
107th Cong. 2001	381	82	39	7	19
108th Cong. 2003	376	59	39	5	22
Senators					
98th Cong. 1983	98	2	—	2	—
99th Cong. 1985	98	2	—	2	—
100th Cong. 1987	98	2	—	2	—
101st Cong. 1989	98	2	—	2	—
102nd Cong. 1991	98	2	—	2	—
103rd Cong. 1993	93	7	1	2	—
104th Cong. 1995	92	8	1	2	—
106th Cong. 1999	91	9	—	NA	—
107th Cong. 2001	87	13	—	NA	—
108th Cong. 2003	86	14	—	2	—

Source: U.S. Census Bureau, *Statistical Abstract of the United States, 2006.* Adapted by author from Table 395, p. 257.

Finally, Table 9.16 illustrates the electoral gains made by several minority groups in terms of election of members to the Congress from 1983 to 2003. It serves as an indicator of the degree of political incorporation of those groups.

SUMMARY

This chapter examined public policy in six arenas in which the struggle between majority and minority society takes place: education, employment, housing, immigration, law enforcement, and political participation. In each, laws and policy were used by the majority to relegate certain racial and ethnic groups to second-class status. Minority groups struggled in each policy area to bring about changes to end or reduce de jure or institutionalized discrimination against them.

The chapter documented gains made by minorities in education and employment. The chapter also illustrated that comparatively little progress has been made in coping with ethnic and racial housing segregation, an arena largely impacted by de facto discrimination through norms and customs rather than de jure segregation. It discussed five phases of U.S. immigration policy, linking each to the flows of immigration and how changes in those policy phases influenced the composition of subsequent immigration flows. It discussed the arena of law enforcement and the nearly warlike relationship that has developed between the police and racial minorities. Finally, the chapter reviewed how Jim Crow laws were used to disenfranchise blacks and other ethnic minorities, and how changes in civil rights laws enacted since the 1960s have resulted in rather dramatic increases in their political participation and electoral success—demonstrating how various minority groups have achieved political incorporation.

KEY TERMS

affirmative action   Government programs designed to get minority persons past prior institutionalized barriers in education and employment in an attempt to force structural assimilation.

block busting   A device by which real estate agencies encourage minority members to purchase homes in a previously all-white neighborhood in order to reach the tipping point and set off white flight, thus generating large-scale sales of real estate in an area.

door-ajar era   The second phase of immigration policy, from 1880 to 1920, during which the beginnings of restrictive immigration policies were enacted.

dutch-door era   The fourth phase of immigration policy, from 1950 to 1985, in which the quota system was replaced by the "preference system" and special refugee/asylum laws.

gatekeeping   The function of immigration policy to determine who is or is not allowed to enter the United States as a permanent immigrant.

grandfather clause   A device used to disenfranchise blacks in the South; only persons whose grandfathers voted could vote, thus blacks whose grandfathers were slaves and could not vote were denied registration.

literacy tests   A "test" one had to pass to prove literacy in order to vote; used against blacks in the South.

occupational niche   Jobs in which members of particular racial or ethnic minorities work in highly disproportionate numbers. They serve as indirect evidence of pervasive employment discrimination.

open-door era   The first phase of U.S. immigration policy, from 1820 to 1880, in which immigration policy was virtually unrestricted.

pet-door era   The third phase of immigration policy, from 1920 to 1950, during which severe restriction was imposed via the national origins quota system.

poll tax   A tax one had to pay in order to vote; used mostly in the South to disenfranchise blacks.

proportionality criterion   A measure of inequality used to establish occupation discrimination; it would look critically at employers or job classifications in which minority members fall far below their proportion of the appropriate labor market.

racial gerrymandering   Drawing electoral district lines in such a way as to diffuse or dilute a certain racial or ethnic group's vote.

storm-door era   Beginning with the USA Patriots Act and the Homeland Defense Act in 2001, a new era of immigration policy with heightened restriction and easier repatriation.

stratiphiles   Individuals who are extraordinarily disposed to the forces of social stratification, such as many police officers.

tipping mechanism   A factor in racial segregation; the point at which an influx of blacks or another ethnic minority will trigger widespread white flight out of a neighborhood.

white primary   Primary elections in the one-party South open to voting by whites only; another device used to disenfranchise blacks during the Jim Crow era.

zero-sum situations   Whenever the benefits accorded to some must be taken away from others; one person's or group's gain is another person's or group's loss.

REVIEW QUESTIONS

1. Discrimination in which policy area is the primary method by which minority status is enforced?

2. Compare/contrast the *Plessy v. Ferguson* with the *Brown v. Board of Education* cases. How and why did the Supreme Court rule in each case? What were the consequences of these two watershed Supreme Court decisions?

3. Describe the proportionality criterion and how it affects affirmative action programs.

4. Discuss three Supreme Court decisions that concerned reverse discrimination. How has the concept of affirmative action evolved over time?

5. Which public policy area remains today as the most racially segregated area in U.S. society?

6. Describe the five eras of U.S. immigration policy. How did each era affect the flow of immigration to the United States?

7. Name four anti-immigrant nativist groups. How did they inject concepts of race into U.S. immigration policy?

8. Specify two groups that entered the United States in large numbers under special "parole" status. How has that special status affected their ability to assimilate into U.S. society?

9. Discuss the devices used to "demagnetize" the pull of the U.S. economy in immigration laws enacted during the 1980s and 1990s. Why do they not seem to be working?

10. Rank-order the six "arenas" discussed in this chapter in terms of their degrees of incorporation having been achieved. What statistical evidence used in the chapter would you cite to justify your rankings?

NOTES

1. See the reservations of Gordon Misner and Jerry Wilson in "Reform at a Standstill," in Fogelson (1977); and the criticisms of Burton Levy, Arthur Niederhoffer, and Jerome Skolnick, in Levy (1968). See also Dye (1998), and Sindler (1977).

2. See "Open Door Policy for Voting Rights." *National Voter* (Spring 1981): 1–2; and Dye (1971). See also U.S. Commission on Civil Rights, *Report of the Commission, 1975* (Washington, DC: U.S. Government Printing Office, 1975).

Additional Readings

Brewster, Lawrence and Genie N. L. Stowers. *The Public Agenda: Issues in American Politics,* 5th ed. New York: St. Martin's Press, 2004.

Cohen, Joshua, Jefferson Decker, and Joel Rogers, eds. *A Way Out: America's Ghettos and the Legacy of Racism.* Princeton, NJ: Princeton University Press, 2003.

Cottrol, Robert J., Raymond T. Diamond, and Leland B. Ware. *Brown v. Board of Education: Caste, Culture, and the Constitution.* Lawrence: University Press of Kansas, 2003.

Cussak, Lance, and Milton Heumann. *Good Cop, Bad Cop: Racial Profiling and Competing Views of Justice in America.* New York: P. Lang, 2003.

Frazier, John, Florence Margai, and Eugene Tettrey-Fio. *Race and Place: Equity Issues in Urban America.* Boulder, CO: Westview Press, 2003.

Free, Marvin D. Jr. *Racial Issues in Criminal Justice: The Case of African Americans.* Westport, CT: Praeger Press, 2003.

Gertenfeld, Phyllis B. *Hate Crimes: Causes, Controls, and Consequences.* Thousand Oaks, CA: Pine Forge Press, Sage Publications, 2003.

Herivel, Tara and, Paul Wright, eds. *Prison Nation: The Warehousing of America's Poor.* New York: Routledge, 2003.

LeMay, Michael. *U.S. Immigration: A Reference Handbook.* Santa Barbara, CA: ABC-CLIO, 2004.

LeMay, Michael. *Guarding the Gates: Immigration and National Security.* Westport, CT.: Praeger Security International, 2006.

LeMay, Michael. *Illegal Immigration: A Reference Handbook.* Santa Barbara, CA: ABC-CLIO, 2007.

Menfield, Charles E. *Representation of Minority Groups in the U.S.: Implications for the Twenty-First Century.* Lanham, MD: University Press of America, 2001.

Neubeck, Kenneth J. *Welfare Racism: Playing the Race Card against America's Poor.* New York: Routledge, 2003.

Pei-Te, Lien. *The Making of Asian America Through Political Participation.* Philadelphia, PA: Temple University Press, 2002.

Pincus, Fred L. *Reverse Discrimination: Dismantling the Myth.* Boulder, CO: Lynne Rienner, 2003.

Pitts, Winfred E. *A Victory of Sorts: Desegregation in a Southern Community.* Lanham, MD: University Press of America, 2003.

Sidney, Mara S. *Unfair Housing: How National Policy Shapes Community Action.* Lawrence, KS: University Press of Kansas, 2003.

Tomasson, Richard F., Faye J. Crosby, and Sharon D. Herzberger. *Affirmative Action: The Pros and Cons of Policy Practice,* rev. ed. Lanham, MD: Rowman and Littlefield, 2001.

• *Reading 9.1*

American Diversity into the Twenty-First Century

The United States enters the twenty-first century with a population in excess of 280 million, of which over 80 million are considered members of a minority group. The number of legal immigrants to the United States, including those coming as refugees and those seeking asylum, has been about 800,000 to over 1 million annually for the decade of the 1990s. In addition, an estimated 4 million to 5 million undocumented aliens continue to live and work in the United States. These demographic trends pose a number of challenges to American society and raise a number of public policy questions.

American society has made a number of substantial gains and changes in its minority/majority relationships. As America began the decade of the 1960s, Jim Crowism was alive and well, with numerous legal and other barriers to African-American political participation. Today no legal barriers remain to their participation, and their actual involvement has essentially closed the gap with that of white political participation. The 1960s witnessed a society with few significant protections for minority groups. Today there are many significant protections. The 1960s began with virtually no equal employment opportunity for blacks and other minorities. Today, equal opportunity is the law, and affirmative action programs are in place if under increasing attack. In the 1960s there were no bilingual education programs required and they were seldom available. Today bilingual education is required in many school districts and by a number of states. The 1960s began with rampant discrimination in housing. Today, such discrimination is illegal if still all too common. In 1960, as this chapter showed, there were few African Americans and other minorities in public office. Today, black, Hispanic, and Asian elected officials number in the many thousands, having been elected to political office at all levels of government. In 1960, minorities were registered at less than half that of whites, and voted at a rate of 20 to 30 percent less than that of whites. Today the voter turnout among many minorities is very close to that of whites. In 1960, women had little or no legislative protection against employment discrimination. Today, women are protected against discrimination in employment by both federal and state laws. Despite these gains, however, as this entire book has shown, racism in America is persistent.

In the nearly 400 years since the first slaves were brought to America, and almost 50 years since Rosa Parks touched off the Montgomery bus boycott, American society remains racially divided. Paradoxically, race both defines and in some ways unites society because racism still matters to so many. Race-based thinking permeates our laws and public policy. Racial grievance impacts our politics in diverse ways. African Americans demonstrate against their role as one of this nation's historical victims even while whites complain and vote to end affirmative action programs they hold constitute reverse discrimination.

A 1997 Gallup poll demonstrated the gap in black and white attitudes. Where less than half of blacks felt that they were treated the same as whites, over 75 percent of whites believed they now were so treated. Whereas only 45 percent of blacks agreed they were treated fairly on the job, over 74 percent of whites agreed. Whereas over 60 percent of blacks agreed that they were treated less fairly by police, only 30 percent of whites so believed. Where 63 percent of blacks agreed that they had as good a chance as whites to get quality education, nearly 80 percent of whites believed they did. Where 58 percent of blacks agreed they had an equal chance with whites to get quality housing, over 86 percent of whites thought they did. Whereas only 33 percent of blacks agreed that the quality of life for blacks had improved over the past ten years, nearly 60 percent of whites felt that it had done so. Where 60 percent of blacks felt government should make every effort to improve conditions for blacks, only 43 percent of whites agreed. When asked, should the government not make any special efforts to aid blacks, that they should help themselves, 30 percent of blacks agreed, while nearly 60 percent of whites agreed (Gallup Poll Social Audit on Black/White Relations in the United States, June 1997). Similarly, a 1995 *Newsweek* poll found that 86 percent of blacks rated race relations in the United States as "only fair" or as "poor."

Yet opinion polls show acceptance of interracial marriage and the willingness to reside in mixed-race neighborhoods has never been higher. America is beginning to change its two-way definition of race. Racial identity is being blurred. The sense that race is physical, fixed, immutable, and primarily a matter of skin color is being replaced with a sense that race is as much a matter of ideology and identity as skin pigmentation, that race is a social construct—a mixture of prejudice, superstition, and myth. And now, some thirty years after the last state anti-miscegenation law was struck down, an increasingly interracial generation is demanding its place in American society.

Racial thinking, as this book has shown, has been modified by the changing nature of the racial composition in American society, reflecting the past three decades of immigration from Africa, Asia, and Latin America. The additional 18 million people who came since 1965 have been largely "people of color." Blacks are nearly 13 percent of the total population. Hispanics, at over 25 million, are nearly 10 percent, and are projected to be the nation's largest minority by 2010. Hispanics, however, are themselves a disparate collection of nationalities reflecting various descendants of Europeans, African slaves, and Native Americans. The new (post-1965) immigrants number nearly 4 million from Asia.

All of this means an era of increasing multiethnic and multiracial diversity. It raises questions as to whether American society can absorb the increasingly diverse demographic changes. The arrival of these tens of millions of new immigrants from racially mixed sources undermines the de facto consensus as to what "race" means in American society. Demand for more flexible definitions of race are prevalent. The Association of Multi-Ethnic Americans successfully lobbied to add a multiracial category to the year 2000 census. Changing the census form helps acknowledge the nation's increasing diversity. In the 1990 census, Americans wrote in the blank on the form to identify "other" with nearly 300 "races," some 600 Indian tribes, over 70 Latin groups, and some 75 combinations of multiracial ancestry.

There will be political consequences to the significant number of Americans who checked the multiracial block, as census-based formulas are used to distribute federal aid in varied ways and programs. Some African Americans fear that the biracial category may erode black solidarity and voting clout due to "defections" to the multiethnic status.

This chapter has amply presented evidence of African-American political gains since 1965. The mere handful of black elected officials then have been succeeded by over 9,000 today. Hispanic officeholders grew from just over 3,000 in 1985 to nearly 5,000 today. Progress in such electoral strength demonstrates that as America enters the twenty-first century, minority group politics will remain persistent and increasingly potent. Clearly, the perennial struggle described throughout this volume will continue vibrantly active into the first decades of the next century. These trends beg the question of whether a black person can be elected president, or whether the American presidency will continue to be held only by white, non-Jewish, and non-Hispanic males. The Gallup polling organization asked, between 1937 and 1987 (since which time it no longer asks the question), the following question: "If your party nominated a generally well-qualified man for president who happened to be black [Jew], would you vote for him?" Or, "If your party nominated a woman for president, would you vote for her if she were qualified for the job?" Whereas nearly 70 percent opposed voting for a black for president in 1937, less than 15 percent admitted to opposing doing so in 1987. Where just less than 50 percent opposed voting for a Jew in 1937, less than 10 percent were opposed to doing so in 1987. Where nearly 55 percent of Americans opposed voting for a woman for president in 1958, less than 15 percent were so opposed in 1987. Perhaps the first decade of the new century will witness the election of the first minority person as president of the United States. Recent public opinion polls suggest more Americans are willing to vote for a black (Senator Barack Obama) than ever before, and more willing to do so than to vote for a person espousing the Mormon faith.

Bibliography

Abanes, Richard. *One Nation under Gods: A History of the Mormon Church.* New York: Four Walls Eight Windows, 2002.

Allport, Gordon. *The Nature of Prejudice.* New York: Doubleday, 1958.

Anderson, Charles. *The Political Economy of Social Classes.* Englewood Cliffs, NJ: Prentice Hall, 1974.

Anderson, Carol. *Eyes Off the Prize: The United Nations and the African American Struggle for Human Rights, 1944–1955.* New York: Cambridge University Press, 2003.

Anderson, Jervis. *Bayard Rustin: Troubles I've Seen.* Berkeley, CA: University of California Press, 1998.

Anderson, Karen. *Changing Woman: A History of Racial Ethnic Women in Modern America.* New York: Oxford University Press, 1997.

Andreas, Peter, and Thomas J. Biersteker, eds. *The Rebordering of North America: Integration and Exclusion in a New Security Context.* New York: Routledge, 2003.

Armor, John, and Peter Wright. *Manzanar.* New York: Times Books, 1988.

Arrington, Leonard, and Davis Bitton. *The Mormon Experience,* 2nd ed. Chicago, IL: University of Illinois Press, 1992.

Aveling, Edward and Samuel Moore. *Dialectical Marxism.* New York: Basic Books, 1969.

Baer, Hans. *Recreating Utopia in the Desert: A Sectarian Challenge to Modern Mormonism.* Albany, NY: State University of New York Press, 1988.

Bagby, Ihsan, Paul M. Perl, and Bryan T. Froehle. *The Mosque in America: A National Portrait.* Washington, DC: Council of American-Islamic Relations, 2001.

Banton, Michael. *Race Relations.* London: Tavistock, 1967.

Banton, Michael. *Racial Theories.* New York: Cambridge University Press, 1987.

Barth, Ernest, and Donald Noel. "Conceptual Frameworks for the Analysis of Race Relations: An Evaluation." *Social Forces* 50 (1972): 333–347.

Barth, Fredrik. *Ethnic Groups and Boundaries.* Boston, MA: Little, Brown, 1969.

Berholz, Charles D., "American Indian Treaties and the Presidents." *Social Studies* 93, 5 (September/October, 2002): 218–227.

Berle, Adolph. *Power without Property.* New York: Harcourt, Brace & World, 1959.

Berry, Brewton. *Race and Ethnic Relations.* Cambridge, MA: Addison-Wesley, 1958.

Bernstein, Mary. "Celebration and Suppression: The Strategic Use of Identity by the Lesbian and Gay Movement." *The American Journal of Sociology,* 103 (3, November, 1997): 531–65.

Beverly, James A. *Islamic Faith in America.* New York: Facts on File, 2003.

Blalock, Hubert M. *Toward a Theory of Minority Group Relations.* New York: Wiley, 1967.

Blalock, Hubert M. *Race and Ethnic Relations.* Englewood Cliffs, NJ: Prentice-Hall, 1982.

Blasius, Mark. "An Ethos of Lesbian and Gay Existence." *Political Theory,* 20 (4, November, 1992): 642–71.

Bogardus, E. S. "Stereotypes vs. Sociotypes." *Sociology and Social Research* 34 (March 1950): 286–291.

Bonacich, Edna. "A Theory of Middleman Minorities." *American Sociological Review* 38 (1973): 583–594.

Bonacich, Edna. "Advanced Capitalism and Black/White Race Relations in the U.S.: A Split Labor Market Interpretation." *American Sociological Review* 41 (February 1976): 34–51.

Bonacich, Edna, and John Modell. *The Economic Basis of Ethnic Solidarity: Small Business in the Japanese-American Community.* Berkeley, CA: University of California Press, 1980.

Boyton, Linda. *The Plain People: An Ethnography of the Holdeman Mennonites.* Salem, WI: Sheffield, 1986.

Bowman, Robert M. Jr. *Understanding Jehovah's Witnesses.* Grand Rapids, MI: Baker Book House, 1992.

Branch, Taylor. *Parting the Waters: America in the King Years, 1954–1963.* New York: Simon & Schuster, 1988.

Brewster, Lawrence, and Genie N. L. Stowers. *The Public Agenda: Issues in American Politics,* 5th ed. New York: St. Martin's Press, 2004.

Brommel, Bernard. *Eugene V. Debs: Spokesman for Labor and Socialism.* Chicago, IL: Charles H. Kerr, 1978.

Brooks, Roy L. *Integration or Separation? A Strategy for Racial Equality.* Cambridge, MA: Harvard University Press, 1996.

Browder, Earl. *The People's Front.* New York: International Publishers, 1938.

Brown, Dee. *Bury My Heart at Wounded Knee.* New York: Holt, Rinehart & Winston, 1971.

Browning, Rufus, Dale Rogers Marshall, and David Tabb (eds). *Racial Politics in American Cities.* New York: Longman, 1997.

Buhle, Paul. *Marxism in the United States.* London: Verso, 1987.

Burma, John H., ed. *Mexican-Americans in the United States.* New York: Harper & Row, 1970.

Calavita, Kitty. *Inside the State: The Bracero Program, Immigration and the INS.* New York: Routledge, 1992.

Carmichael, Stokely, and Charles V. Hamilton. *Black Power: The Politics of Liberation in America.* New York: Vintage, 1967.

Cannistraro, Philip, and Gerald Meyer, eds. *The Lost World of Italian American Radicalism.* Westport, CT: Praeger Press, 2003.

Carson, Clayborne. *In Struggle: SNCC and the Black Awakening of the 1960s.* Cambridge, MA: Harvard University Press, 1981.

Chalmers, David. *Backfire: How the Ku Klux Klan Helped the Civil Rights Movement.* Lanham, MD: Rowman and Littlefield, 2003.

Chavez, John R. *The Lost Land: The Chicano Image of the Southwest.* Albuquerque, NM: University of New Mexico Press, 1984.

Citrin, Jack, Amy Lehrman, Michael Murakami, and Kathryn Pearson. "Testing Huntington: Is Hispanic Immigration a Threat to American Identity?" *Perspectives on Politics.* 5 (1), March, 2007: 31–48.

The Church of Jesus Christ of Latter-Day Saints. *Church History in the Fullness of Times.* Salt Lake City, Utah: The Church of Jesus Christ of Latter-Day Saints, 1989.

Church, Ward. "Crimes against Humanity." *Z Magazine,* March 1993, 43–47.

Cohen, Joshua, Jefferson Decker, and Joel Rogers, eds. *A Way Out: America's Ghettos and the Legacy of Racism.* Princeton, NJ: Princeton University Press, 2003.

Collins, Barry. *Social Psychology.* Reading, MA: Addison-Wesley, 1970.

Conover, Ted. *Coyotes: A Journey Through the Secret World of America's Illegal Aliens.* New York: Vintage Books, 1987.

Constantine, J. Robert, ed. *Gentle Rebel: Letters of Eugene V. Debs.* Urbana, IL: University of Illinois Press, 1995.

Cornell, Stephen. *The Return of the Native: American Indian Political Resurgence.* New York: Oxford University Press, 1988.

Cottrol, Robert J., Raymond T. Diamond, and Leland B. Ware. *Brown v. Board of Education: Caste, Culture, and the Constitution.* Lawrence, KS: University Press of Kansas, 2003.

Cox, Oliver C. *Caste, Class and Race: A Study in Social Dynamics.* New York: Doubleday, 1948.

Crawford, Vicki, Jacqueline Anne Rouse, and Barbara Woods, eds. *Women in the Civil Rights Movement: Trailblazers and Torchbearers, 1941–1965.* Berkeley, CA: University of California Press, 1998.

Cronon, E. David. *Black Moses: The Story of Marcus Garvey and the Universal Negro Improvement Association.* Madison, WI: University of Wisconsin Press, 1969.

Cross, Theodore. *The Black Power Imperative.* New York: Faulkner, 1984.

Curtis, Edward E. IV. *Islam in Black America.* Albany, NY: State of New York University Press, 2002.

Cussak, Lance, and Milton Heumann. *Good Cop, Bad Cop: Racial Profiling and Competing Views of Justice in America.* New York: P. Lang, 2003.

Dahrendorf, Ralf. *Class Conflict in Industrial Society.* Stanford, CA: Stanford University Press, 1939.

David Reimers. *Natives and Strangers,* 2nd ed. New York: Oxford University Press, 1990.

Davies, Douglas J. *The Mormon Culture of Salvation.* New York: Ashgate Publishing, 2000.

Davis, Kingsley, and Wilbert E. Moore. "Some Principles of Stratification." *American Sociological Review* 10 (1945): 242–249.

DeCarlo, Louis A. Jr. *Malcolm and the Cross.* New York: New York University Press, 1998.

Deloria, Vine Jr., and Daniel R. Wildcat. *Power and Place.* Golden, CO: American Indian Graduate Center and Fulcrum Resources, 2001.

DeSipio, Louis. *Counting on the Latino Vote: Latinos as a New Electorate.* Charlottesville, VA: University of Virginia Press, 1996.

DeSipio, Louis. "Immigrant Organizing, Civic Outcomes: Civic Engagement, Political Activity, National Attachments, and Identity in Latino Immigrant Communities." Center for the Study of Democracy, University of California Irvine, 2002.

Dinnerstein, Leonard, and Frederick C. Jaher. *Uncertain Americans.* New York: Oxford University Press, 1977.

Dinnerstein, Leonard, and David M. Reimers. *Ethnic Americans,* 3rd ed. New York: Harper & Row, 1988.

Dollard, John, et al. *Frustration and Aggression.* New Haven, CT: Yale University Press, 1939.

Draper, Theodore. *The Roots of American Communism.* New York: Viking Press, 1957.

Draper, Theodore. *American Communism and Soviet Russia.* New York: Viking Press, 1960.

Driedger, Leo, and Donald B. Kraybill. *Mennonite Peacemaking.* Scottsdale, PA: Herald Press, 1994.

Durkheim, Emile. *The Study of Sociology.* New York: Free Press, 1964.

Dye, Thomas. *The Politics of Equality.* Indianapolis, IN: Bobbs-Merrill, 1971.

Dye, Thomas, *Understanding Public Policy,* 9th ed. Upper Saddle River, NJ: Prentice Hall, 1998.

Easton, David. *A Framework for Political Analysis.* Englewood Cliffs, NJ: Prentice Hall, 1965.

Edwards, George. *The Politics of the Urban Frontier.* New York: Institute of Human Relations Press, 1982.

Essien-Udom, E. U. *Black Nationalism: A Search for an Identity in America.* Chicago, IL: University of Chicago Press, 1962.

Fairchild, Henry. *Greek Immigration.* New Haven, CT: Yale University Press, 1911.

Feagin, Joe R., and Clairice Feagin. *Racial and Ethnic Relations,* 5th ed. Englewood Cliffs, NJ: Prentice Hall, 1996.

Federal Writer's Project. *The Italians of New York.* New York: Arno Press, 1969.

Fichter, Joseph. *Social Relations in an Urban Parish.* Urbana, IL: University of Illinois Press, 1954.

Fisher, Peter. *The Gay Mystique.* New York: Stein and Day, 1975.

Fitzpatrick, Joseph P. "Intermarriage of Puerto Ricans in New York City." *American Journal of Sociology* 71 (1968): 395–406.

Fixico, Donald. *The American Indian Mind in a Linear World.* New York: Routledge, 2003.

Fogelson, Robert M. *Big City Police.* Cambridge, MA: Harvard University Press, 1977.

Foner, Philip S., and James Allen, eds. *American Communism: A Documentary History, 1919–1929.* Philadelphia, PA: Temple University Press, 1987.

Foner, Philip S., and Herbert Shapiro, eds. *American Communism and Black Americans: A Documentary History: 1930–1934.* Philadelphia, PA: Temple University Press, 1991.

Ford, James. *The Negro and the Democratic Front.* New York: International Publishers, 1938.

Foster, William Z. *History of the Communist Party in the United States.* New York: International Publishers, 1952.

Fox-Piven, Frances, and Richard A. Cloward. *Regulating the Poor.* New York: Random House, 1971.

Fox-Piven, Frances, and Richard A. Cloward. *The Politics of Turmoil.* New York: Vintage, 1975.

Frazier, John, Florence Margal, and Eugene Tettrey-Fio. *Race and Place: Equity Issues in Urban America.* Boulder, CO: Westview Press, 2003.

Frederickson, George M. *Black Liberation.* New York: Oxford University Press, 1995.

Free, Marvin D. Jr. *Racial Issues in Criminal Justice: The Case of African Americans.* Westport, CT: Praeger Press, 2003.

"Fresh Faces for an Old Struggle." *Time,* August 22, 1983, 32–33.

Fuchs, Lawrence. *The American Kaleidoscope: Race, Ethnicity, and Civil Culture.* Hanover, NH: University Press of New England, 1990.

Furniss, N. F. *The Mormon Conflict: 1850–1859.* New Haven, CT: Yale University Press, 1960.

Fushfield, Daniel R. *The Basic Economics of the Urban Racial Crisis.* New York: Holt, Rinehart & Winston, 1973.

George, John, and Laird Wilcox. *Nazis, Communists, Klansmen and Others on the Fringes: Political Extremism in America.* New York: Prometheus Books, 1992.

Geron, Kim. *Latino Political Power.* Boulder, CO. Lynne Rienner Publishers, 2005.

Gerstle, Gary, and John Mollenkopf, eds. *E Pluribus Unum? Contemporary and Historical Perspectives on Immigrant Political Incorporation.* New York: Russell Sage Foundation, 2001.

Gertenfeld, Phyllis B. *Hate Crimes: Causes, Controls, and Consequences.* Thousand Oaks, CA: Pine Forge Press, Sage Publications, 2003.

Glazer, Nathan. *The Social Basis of American Communism.* New York: Harcourt, Brace & World, 1961.

Glazer, Nathan, and Daniel Moynihan. *Ethnicity: Theory and Experience.* Cambridge, MA: Harvard University Press, 1975.

Glusker, Ann. *Fertility Patterns of Native and Foreign-Born Women: Assimilating to Diversity.* New York: LFB Publishing, 2003.

Gonzales, Juan. *Racial and Ethnic Groups in America,* 3rd ed. Dubuque, IA: Kendall/Hunt, 1996.

Gordon, David. *Problems in Political Economy and Urban Perspectives.* Lexington, MA: D. C. Heath, 1977.

Gordon, Milton. *Assimilation in American Life.* New York: Oxford University Press, 1964.

Greenstein, Frederick. *The American Party System and the American People.* Englewood Cliffs, NJ: Prentice Hall, 1970.

Haider-Markel, Donald P., and Kenneth J. Meier, "The Politics of Gay and Lesbian Rights: Expanding the Scope of the Conflict." *The Journal of Politics,* 58 (2, May, 1996): 332–49.

Hamamoto, Darrell. "Black-Korean Conflict in Los Angeles." *Z Magazine,* July 1, 1992, 61–62.

Handlin, Oscar. *The Uprooted.* Boston, MA: Little, Brown, 1951.

Hardy, B. Carmon. *Solemn Covenant: The Mormon Polygamous Passage.* Chicago, IL: University of Illinois Press, 1992.

Hayes, L. J. *The Negro Federal Government Worker.* Washington, DC: Howard University Press, 1941.

Henton, Tim B., Bruce A. Chadwick, and Cardnell K. Jackson. *Statistical Handbook on Racial Groups in the United States.* Phoenix, AZ: The Oryx Press, 2000.

Herivel, Tara, and Paul Wright, eds. *Prison Nation: The Warehousing of America's Poor.* New York: Routledge, 2003.

Hernstein, Richard. "I.Q." *Atlantic Monthly,* September 1971, 43–64.

Higham, Charles. *American Swastika.* New York: Doubleday, 1985.

Hirshon, Stanley. *The Lion and the Lord.* New York: Knopf, 1969.

Hoffer, Eric. *True Believer.* New York: Harper & Row, 1963.

Hoffman, Edward. *Despite All Odds: The Story of Lubavitch.* New York: Simon & Schuster, 1991.

Hollifield, James. "Migrants to Citizens: The Politics of Immigration in France and the United States." Paper delivered at the Annual Meeting of the American Political Science Association, Atlanta, August 31–September 3, 1989.

Horne, Gerald, and Mary Young, eds. *W. E. B. Dubois: An Encyclopedia.* Westport, CT: Greenwood Press, 2001.

Hornor, Louise L., ed. *Hispanic Americans: A Statistical Sourcebook.* Palo Alto, CA: Information Publications, 2002.

Hosokawa, William. *Nisei: The Quiet Americans.* New York: William Morrow, 1969.

Hourani, Albert. *A History of the Arab Peoples.* New York: Warner Books, 1991.

Howard, John R., ed. *Awakening Minorities.* New Brunswick, NJ: Transaction Books, 1983.

Howe, Irving. *Socialism in America.* New York: Harcourt Brace Jovanovich, 1985.

Huntington, Samuel. *Who Are We? The Challenge to American National Identity.* New York: Simon & Schuster, 2004.

Immigration Plus. *Immigration and Illegal Aliens: Burden or Blessing?* Farmington Hills, MI: Thomson/Gale, 2006.

"Intermarried with Children." *Time Special Issue* 142 (November 1993): 64.

Iorrizzo, Luciano, and Salvatore Mondello. *The Italian Americans.* New York: Twayne, 1971.

Jacobson, Simon. *Toward a Meaningful Life: The Wisdom of the Rebbe.* New York: William Morrow, 1995.

Janowsky, Oscar. *The American Jews: A Reappraisal.* Philadelphia, PA: Jewish Publication Society of America, 1964.

Jensen, Arthur. "How Much Can We Boost IQ and Scholastic Achievement?" *Harvard Educational Review* 39 (Winter 1969): 1–13.

Jim-Kyung Yoo. *Korean Immigrant Entrepreneurs: Networks and Ethnic Resources.* Ames, IA: Blackwell Publishing, Garland Studies in Entrepreneurship, 1998.

Judd, Richard W. *Socialist Cities: Municipal Politics and the Grass Roots of American Socialism.* New York: State University of New York Press, 1989.

Katz, Daniel, and Kenneth Braley. "Verbal Stereotypes and Racial Prejudice." In Eleanor Mausby, Theodore Newcomb, and Eugene Hartley, eds., *Readings in Social Psychology,* pp. 40–46. New York: Holt, Rinehart & Winston, 1958.

Key Jr., Validimer Orlando. *Southern Politics in the State and Nation,* New York: Knopf, 1949.

Kim, Hyung-Chan, ed. *The Korean Diaspora.* Santa Barbara, CA: ABC-CLIO, 1977.

King, Desmond. *Separate and Unequal: Black Americans and the U.S. Federal Government.* London: Oxford University Press, 1995.

King, Martin Luther Jr. "Letter from a Birmingham Jail." *American Visions* (January/February 1986): 52–59.

Kinloch, Graham. *The Dynamics of Race Relations: A Sociological Analysis.* New York: McGraw-Hill, 1974.

Kitano, Harry. *Japanese-Americans: The Evolution of a Subculture.* Englewood Cliffs, NJ: Prentice Hall, 1976.

Kitano, Harry. *Race Relations,* 5th ed. Upper Saddle River, NJ: Prentice Hall, 1997.

Kivisto, Peter. *Americans All.* Belmont, CA: Wadsworth, 1995.

Kohut, Andrew, John C. Green, Scott Keeter, and Robert C. Toth. *The Diminishing Divide: Religion's Changing Role in American Politics.* Washington, DC: Brookings Institution, 2000.

Kottak, Conrad Phillip, and Kathryn A. Kozaitis. *On Being Different.* Boston, MA: McGraw-Hill, 1999.

Kraybill, Donald. *The Riddle of the Amish Culture.* Baltimore, MD: Johns Hopkins University Press, 1989.

Kraybill, Donald, and Marc Olshan, eds. *The Amish Struggle with Modernity.* Hanover, NH: University Press of New England, 1994.

Kraybill, Donald B., and Steven M. Nolt. *Amish Enterprises: From Plows to Profits.* Baltimore, MD: The Johns Hopkins University Press, 1995.

Kung, Shien Woo. *Chinese in American Life.* Seattle, WA: University of Washington Press, 1962.

Kurokawa, Minako, ed. *Minority Responses.* New York: Random House, 1970.

Lamont, Thomas. *Rise to Be A People.* Urbana, IL: University of Illinois Press, 1986.

Landes, Richard, ed. *Encyclopedia of Millennialism and Millennial Movements.* New York: Routledge, 2000.

Latham, Earl. *The Group Basis of Politics.* Amherst, NY: Cornell University Press, 1965.

Launius, Roger. *Joseph Smith III: Pragmatic Prophet.* Urbana, IL: University of Illinois Press, 1988.

Launius, Roger, and Linda Thatcher, eds. *Differing Visions: Dissenters in Mormon History.* Urbana, IL: University of Illinois Press, 1994.

LeMay, Michael. *The Struggle for Influence.* Lanham, MD: University Press of America, 1985.

LeMay, Michael. *From Open Door to Dutch Door.* New York: Praeger, 1987.

LeMay, Michael. *U.S. Immigration: A Reference Handbook.* Santa Barbara, CA: ABC-CLIO, 2004.

LeMay, Michael. *Guarding the Gates: Immigration and National Security.* Westport, CT.: Praeger Security International, 2006.

LeMay, Michael. *Illegal Immigration:* A Reference Handbook. Santa Barbara, CA.: ABC-CLIO, 2007.

Levine, Daniel. *Bayard Rustin and the Civil Rights Movement.* New Brunswick, NJ: Rutgers University Press, 2000.

Levine, Edward M. *The Irish and the Irish Politicians.* Notre Dame, IN: University of Notre Dame Press, 1966.

Levine, Herbert M., ed. *Point-Counterpoint,* 7th ed. Belmont, CA: Wadsworth/Thomson Learning, 2004.

Levine, Robert A., and Donald Campbell. *Ethnocentrism.* New York: Wiley, 1972.

Levy, Burton, ed. *Riots and Rebellion: Civil Violence in the Urban Community.* Beverly Hills, CA: Sage Publications, 1968.

Levy, Mark, and Michael Kramer. *The Ethnic Factor: How American Minorities Decide Elections.* New York: Simon & Schuster, 1973.

Lewis, Rupert. *Marcus Garvey: Anti-Colonial Champion.* Trenton, NJ: Africa World Press, 1988.

Lieberman, Robert C. *Shifting the Color Line.* Cambridge, MA: Harvard University Press, 1998.

Lieberson, Stanley. *A Piece of the Pie.* Berkeley, CA: University of California Press, 1980.

Light, Ivan, and Edna Bonacich. *Immigrant Entrepreneurs: Koreans in Los Angeles, 1965–1982.* Berkeley, CA: University of California Press, 1988.

Lincoln, C. Eric. *The Black Muslims in America,* 3rd ed. Trenton, NJ: Africa World Press, 1994.

Lipset, Seymour M. and Gary Marks. *It Didn't Happen Here: Why Socialism Failed in the United States.* New York: W.W. Norton, 2000.

Lipsky, Michael. *Law and Order Police Encounters.* Chicago, IL: Aldine, 1970.

Litt, Edgar. *Ethnic Politics in America.* Glenview, IL: Scott Foresman, 1970.

Lopata, Helen Z. *Polish-Americans.* Englewood Cliffs, NJ: Prentice Hall, 1976.

Lyman, Edward L. *San Bernardino: The Rise and Fall of a California Community.* Salt Lake City, UT: Signature Books, 1996.

MacDonnell, Francis. *Insidious Foes.* New York: Oxford University Press, 1995.

Magil, A. B., and Henry Stevens. *The Perils of Fascism.* New York: International Publishers, 1938.

Malanczuk, Peter. *Akehurst's Modern Introduction to International Law, 7ᵗʰ rev. ed.* New York: Routledge, 1997.

Marden, Charles, and Gladys Meyer. *Minorities in American Society.* New York: Van Nostrand, 1968.

Marger, Martin N. *Race and Ethnic Relations,* 64th ed. Belmont, CA: Wadsworth, 2003.

Marsh, Carole. *Ada Deer: Notable Native American.* Gallopade, Int., 1998.

Marsh, Clifton E. *The Lost-Found Nation of Islam in America.* Lanham, MD: Scarecrow Press, 2000.

Matras, Judah. *Social Inequality, Stratification, and Mobility.* Englewood Cliffs, NJ: Prentice Hall, 1975.

Mauss, Armand. *The Angel and the Beehive: The Mormon Struggle with Assimilation.* Urbana, IL: University of Illinois Press, 1994.

McClain, Paula D. and Steward, J. *Can We All Get Along? Racial and Ethnic Minorities in American Politics.* Boulder, CO: Westview Press, 1995.

McConkie, Bruce R. *Mormon Doctrine.* Salt Lake City, UT: Bookcraft, 1966.

McElroy, John H. *Divided We Stand.* Lanham, MD.: Rowman and Littlefield, 2006.

McIntosh, Peggy. *White Privilege: Unpacking the Invisible Knapsack, Independent School,* Winter, 1990.

McLemore, Dale S. *Racial and Ethnic Relations in America,* 2nd ed. Boston, MA: Allyn & Bacon, 1983.

Meier, Matt S., and Margo Gutierrez. *Encyclopedia of Mexican-American Civil Rights Movement.* Westport, CT: Greenwood Press, 2000.

Mena, Jesus. "Activists Discuss Latino Political Power." http://www.ksg.harvard.edu/news/2003/latino_forum_0410403.htm.

Menfield, Charles E. *Representation of Minority Groups in the U.S.: Implications for the Twenty-First Century.* Lanham, MD: University Press of America, 2001.

Merton, Robert. "Discrimination and the American Creed." In R. M. MacIver, ed., *Discrimination and National Welfare,* pp. 99–126. New York: Harper & Row, 1949.

Min, Pyong Gap, ed. *Asian Americans.* Newbury Park, CA: Sage, 1995.

Mintz, Jerome R. *The Legends of Hasidim.* Chicago, IL: University of Chicago Press, 1968.

Morehouse, Maggi M. *Fighting in the Jim Crow Army: Black Men and Women Remember World War II.* Lanham, MD: Rowman and Littlefield, 2000.

Morrison, Toni. "On the Back of Blacks." *Time Special Issue* 142 (November 1993): 57.

Moskos, Charles C. *Greek Americans.* Englewood Cliffs, NJ: Prentice Hall, 1980.

Myers, Walter Dean. *Malcolm X: A Fire Burning Brightly.* New York: HarperCollins, 2000.

Nagel, Joanne. *American Indian Ethnic Renewal: Red Power and the Resurgence of Identity and Culture.* New York: Oxford University Press, 1996.

Nelli, Humbert S. *Italians in Chicago, 1830–1930.* New York: Oxford University Press, 1970.

Nelson, John. *Fifty Years on the Trail.* Norman, OK: University of Oklahoma Press, 1963.

Neubeck, Kenneth J. *Welfare Racism: Playing the Race Card against America's Poor.* New York: Routledge, 2003.

Nevins, Joseph. *Operation Gatekeeper: The Rise of the Illegal Aliens and the Making of the U.S.-Mexico Boundary.* New York: Routledge, 2002.

Noel, Donald. "A Theory of the Origin of Ethnic Stratification." *Social Problems* (Fall 1968): 157–172.

Nolt, Steven M. *A History of the Amish.* Intercourse, PA: Good Books, 1992.

O'Dea, Thomas F. *The Mormons.* Chicago, IL: University of Chicago Press, 1957.

O'Grady, Joseph D. *How the Irish Became Americans.* New York: Twayne, 1973.

Omi, Michael, and Howard Winant. *Racial Formation in the United States,* 2nd ed. New York: Routledge, 1994.

O'Neal, James, and G. A. Warner. *American Communism.* Westport, CT: Greenwood Press, 1947.

Palmore, Erdman B. "Ethnophaulism and Ethnocentrism." *American Journal of Sociology* 67 (January 1962): 442–445.

Park, Robert E. "The Nature of Race Relations." In Edgard T. Thompson, ed., *Race Relations and Race Problems,* pp. 3–45. Durham, NC: Duke University Press, 1939.

Park, Robert E. *Race and Culture.* New York: Free Press, 1950.

Parrillo, Vincent. *Strangers to These Shores.* New York: Wiley, 1985.

Parrillo, Vincent. *Diversity in America.* Thousand Oaks, CA: Pine Forge Press, 1996.

Parsons, Talcott. "A Revised Analytical Approach to the Theory of Social Stratification." In Reinhard Bendix and Seymour Lipset, eds., *Class Status and Power: A Reader in Social Stratification.* New York: Free Press, 1953.

Peach, C. "Which Triple Melting Pot? A Re-Examination of Ethnic Intermarriage in New Haven, 1900–1950." *Ethnic and Racial Studies* 3 (1980): 1–16.

Pei-Te, Lien. *The Making of Asian America through Political Participation.* Philadelphia, PA: Temple University Press, 2003.

Penton, M. James. *Apocalypse Delayed: The Story of Jehovah's Witnesses.* Toronto, ON: Toronto University Press, 1997.

Perry, Bruce. *Malcolm: The Life of a Man Who Changed Black America.* Barrytown, NY: Station Hill Press, 1992.

Perry, Theresa. *Teaching Malcolm X.* New York: Routledge, 1996.

Peters, Shawn Francis. *The Yoder Case: Religious Freedom, Education, and Parental Rights.* Lawrence, KS: University Press of Kansas, 2003.

Pincus, Fred L. *Reverse Discrimination: Dismantling the Myth.* Boulder, CO: Lynne Rienner, 2003.

Pitts, Winfred E. *A Victory of Sorts: Desegregation in a Southern Community.* Lanham, MD: University Press of America, 2003.

Rashad, Adib. *The History of Islam and Black Nationalism in America.* Beltsville, MD: Writers Inc., 1991.

Rassmussen, R. Kent. *Farewell to Jim Crow: The Rise and Fall of Segregation in America.* New York: Facts on File 1997.

Reader's Digest. *Through Indian Eyes.* Pleasantsville, NY: Reader's Digest, 1995.

Record, Wilson. *The Negro and the Communist Party.* Chapel Hill, NC: University of North Carolina Press, 1951.

Redekop, Calvin Wall. *Mennonite Society.* Baltimore, MD: The Johns Hopkins University Press, 1989.

Reeves, Keith. *Voting Hopes or Fears? White Voters, Black Candidates, and Racial Politics in America.* New York: Oxford University Press, 1997.

Reuter, E. B. *Race and Cultural Contacts.* New York: McGraw-Hill, 1934.

Riis, Jacob. *How the Other Half Lives.* New York: Dover, 1971.

Robnett, Belinda. *How Long? How Long? African-American Women in the Struggle for Civil Rights.* New York: Oxford University Press, 2000.

Rose, Peter. *They and We.* New York: McGraw-Hill, 1990.

Rosen, Bernard, and H. J. Crockett Jr. *Achievement in American Society.* Cambridge, MA: Schenman, 1969.

Rostow, Eugene. "Our Worst Wartime Mistake." *Harper's Magazine,* September 1945, 193–201.

Ruchelman, Leonard. *Who Rules the Police?* New York: New York University Press, 1973.

Said, Edward. *Covering Islam: How the Media and the Experts Determine How We See the World.* New York: Vintage Books, 1997.

Sales, William H. Jr. *From Civil Rights to Black Liberation: Malcolm X and the Organization of Afro-American Unity.* Boston, MA: South End Press, 1994.

Salvemini, Gaetano. *Italian Fascist Activities in the United States.* New York: Center for Migration Studies, 1977.

Salzman, Jack, ed. *African American History.* New York: Simon & Schuster, 1996.

Schaefer, Richard. *Racial and Ethnic Groups,* 7th ed. New York: HarperCollins, 1998.

Schermerhorn, Richard A. *Comparative Ethnic Relations.* New York: Random House, 1970.

Schmidt, Ronald. "The Political Incorporation of Recent Immigrants: A Framework for Research and Analysis." Paper presented at the Annual Meeting of the American Political Science Association, Atlanta, August 31–September 3, 1989.

Schonback, Morris. *Native American Fascism During the 1930s and 1940s: A Study of Its Roots, Its Growth, and Its Decline.* New York: Garland Press, 1985.

Segura, Gary M., and Shaun Bowler, eds. *Diversity in Democracy: Minority Representation in the United States.* Charlottesville, VA: University of Virginia Press, 2005.

Sewell, Tony. *Garvey's Children: The Legacy of Marcus Garvey.* Trenton, NJ: Africa World Press, 1990.

Shabazz, Ilysah. *Growing Up X.* New York: One World, Ballantine Books, 2002.

Shaheen, Jack. *The T.V. Arab.* Bowling Green, OH: Bowling Green University Press, 1984.

Sidney, Mara S. *Unfair Housing: How National Policy Shapes Community Action.* Lawrence: University Press of Kansas, 2003.

Sigler, Jay A. *American Rights Policy.* Homewood, IL: Dorsey Press, 1975.

Sindler, Allan, ed. *America in the Seventies: Problems, Policies and Politics.* Boston, MA: Little, Brown, 1977.

Singh, Robert. *The Farrakhan Phenomenon.* Washington, DC: Georgetown University Press. 1997.

Singer, David and Lawrence Grossman (eds.). *American Jewish Yearbook, 2002.* New York: American Jewish Committee, 2003.

Smith, Jane I. *Islam in America.* New York: Columbia University Press, 1999.

Sniderman, Paul M., and Thomas Piazza. *Black Pride and Black Prejudice.* Princeton, NJ: Princeton University Press, 2002.

Solomon, Mark. *The Cry War Unity: Communism and African Americans, 1917–1936.* Jackson, MS: University Press of Mississippi, 1998.

Soloutos, Theodore. *The Greeks in the United States.* Cambridge, MA: Harvard University Press, 1964.

Spear, Allan H. *Black Chicago: The Making of a Negro Ghetto.* Chicago, IL: University of Chicago Press, 1967.

Steiner, Stan. *La Raza*. New York: Harper & Row, 1969.

Stokes, Atiya Kai, "Latino Group Consciousness and Political Participation." *American Politics Research*, 2003, 31 (4): 361–378.

Stowers, Genie. "Cuban Political Incorporation into Miami Politics: A Model for the 'New Immigrants.'" Paper presented at the Annual Meeting of the American Political Science Association, Atlanta, August 31–September 3, 1989.

Sugrue, Thomas J., "Driving While Black: The Car and Race Relations in Modern America." *Automobile in American Life and Society,* 2004 at: http://www.autolife.umd.umich.edu/.

Suro, Roberto. "Latino Power?" *The Washington Post.* Sunday, June 26, 2005: B1.

Swain, Carol M. *The New White Nationalism in America: Its Challenge to Integration.* New York: Cambridge University Press, 2002.

Tabb, William. *The Political Economy of the Black Ghetto.* New York: W.W. Norton, 1970.

Tanner, Annie Clark. *A Mormon Mother: An Autobiography.* Salt Lake City, UT: Tanner Trust Fund, University of Utah Library, 1976.

Tarrow, Sidney. *Power in Movement: Social Movements, Collective Action, and Politics.* New York: Stein and Day, 1994.

Terry, Don. "Minister Farrakhan: Conservative Militant." *New York Times,* March 3, 1994, A1, A10.

"The American Underclass." *Time,* August 19, 1977, 14–27.

Thernstrom, Stephen. *The Harvard Encyclopedia of American Ethnic Groups.* Cambridge, MA: Harvard University Press, 1980.

Thompson, William. *Native-American Issues.* Santa Barbara, CA: ABC-CLIO, 1996.

Tomasson, Richard F., Faye J. Crosby, and Sharon D. Herzberger. *Affirmative Action: The Pros and Cons of Policy Practice,* rev. ed. Lanham, MD: Rowman and Littlefield, 2001.

Torrow, Sidney. *Power in Movement: Social Movements, Collective Action, and Politics.* New York: Cambridge University Press, 1994.

Turque, Bill. "Playing a Different Tune." *Newsweek,* June 28, 1993, 30–31.

U.S. Department of Commerce. Bureau of the Census. American Community Survey (ACS). http://www.censess.gov/acs/www/

U.S. Department of Commerce. Bureau of the Census. *1990 Census of Population: Social and Economic Characteristics.* Washington, DC: U.S. Government Printing Office, 1990.

U.S. Department of Commerce. Bureau of the Census. *Statistical Abstract of the United States, 1993.* Washington, DC: U.S. Government Printing Office, 1993.

U.S. Department of Commerce. Bureau of the Census. *Statistical Abstract of the United States, 2001.* Washington, DC: U.S. Government Printing Office, 2001.

U.S. Department of Commerce. Bureau of the Census. *Statistical Abstract of the United States, 2002.* Washington, DC: U.S. Government Printing Office, 2002.

U.S. Department of Commerce. Bureau of the Census. *Statistical Abstract of the United States, 2006.* Washington, DC: U.S. Government Printing Office, 2006.

U.S. Department of Commerce. Bureau of the Census. *Current Population Reports. P-25.* Washington, DC: U.S. Government Printing Office, 1995.

Van den Berghe, Pierre. *Race and Racism.* New York: Wiley, 1971.

Vecoli, Rudolph, and Joy K. Lintelman. *A Century of American Immigration, 1884–1984.* Minneapolis, MN: University of Minnesota Continuing Education and Extension, 1984.

Wagner, Brian. "Immigration Reform Debate Prompts Political Action by Latinos," August 4, 2006. http://www.voanews.com, accessed 5/9/2007.

Wallace, Irving. *The Twenty-Seventh Wife*. New York: Simon & Schuster, 1961.

Walton, Hanes Jr., and Robert C. Smith. *American Politics and the African American Quest for Universal Freedom*. New York: Longman, 2000.

Warner, Lloyd, and Leo Srole. *The Social System of American Ethnic Groups*. New Haven, CT: Yale University Press, 1945.

Welch, Susan, et al. *American Government*, 6th ed. Belmont, CA: Wadsworth, 1998.

Wenger, John. *The Mennonites in Indiana and Michigan*. Scottsdale, PA: Herald Press, 1961.

Wessel, B. B. *An Ethnic Survey of Woonsocket, Rhode Island*. Chicago, IL: University of Chicago Press, 1931.

Wessinger, Catherine. *How the Millennium Comes Violently: From Jonestown to Heaven's Gate*. New York: Seven Bridges Press, 2000.

Wessinger, Catherine, ed. *Millennialism, Persecution, and Violence: Historical Cases*. Syracuse, NY: Syracuse University Press, 2000.

White, John. *Black Leadership in America*, 2nd ed. New York: Longman, 1991.

Wiggins, Rosalind Cobb, ed. *Captain Paul Cuffe's Logs and Letters, 1808–1817*. Washington, DC: Howard University Press, 1996.

Wilkins, David E. *American Indian Politics and the American Political System*. Lanham, MD: Rowman and Littlefield, 2002.

Williams, Robin Jr. *The Reduction of Intergroup Tension*. New York: Social Science Research Council, 1947.

Wilson, William J. *The Truly Disadvantaged*. Chicago, IL: University of Chicago Press, 1987.

Woodward, C. Vann. *The Strange Career of Jim Crow*, commemorative ed. New York: Oxford University Press, 2001.

Wright, Peter, and John Armor. *Manzanar*. New York: Random House, 1989.

Wynn, Daniel Webster. *The NAACP versus Negro Revolutionary Protest*. New York: Exposition Press, 1955.

Young, Ann Eliza. *Wife No. 19*. Hartford, CT: Dustin, Gilmann and Company, 1878; Republished, New York: Arno Press, 1972.

Young, Kimball. *Isn't One Wife Enough?* New York: Henry Holt and Company, 1954.

Zenner, Walter. *Minorities in the Middle: A Cross-Cultural Analysis*. Albany, NY: State University of New York Press, 1991.

Author Index

A

Abenes, Richard, 176, 177, 181
Allport, Gordon, 13, 66, 233
American Community Survey, 72, 79
American Indian Movement, 211
American Legal Defense and Education Fund, 121
Amor, John, 83
Anderson, Carol, 218
Anderson, Jervis, 5, 284, 290, 292

B

Bagby, Ihsan, 230
Banton, Michael, 36, 38–39
Barkan, Elliott, 74
Barth, Ernest, 44
Berholz, Charles, 205, 211
Bernstein, Mary, 160, 162
Beverly, James, 228
Blalock, Hubert, 44, 91
Blasius, Mark, 160–161
Bonacich, Edna, 45, 91, 121
Boyton, Linda, 194
Braley, Kenneth, 51
Brewster, Lawrence, 360, 364
Brommel, Bernard, 249
Brooks, Roy, 347–49, 371
Buhle, Paul, 256

C

Calavita, Kitty, 109
Chavez, John, 302

Church of Jesus Christ of the Latter Day Saints, History, 175
Churchil, Ward, 315
Citrin, Jack, 35
Cloward, Richard, 297
Conover, Ted, 109
Cornell, Stephen, 313
Crockett, H.J., 41–42
Cronon, E. David, 200, 203, 204
Cross, Theodore, 289

D

Dahrendorf, Ralf, 44
Davies, Douglas, 171
Deloria, Vine, Jr., 208, 211
Department of Homeland Security Yearbook, 2004, 111
DeSipio, Louis, 147, 166–68
Dinnerstein, Leonard, 99, 103, 130, 184
Dollard, John, 42
Draper, Theodore, 248, 251, 253, 257, 259
Dye, Thomas, 153, 336, 347

E

Easton, David, 45
Edwards, George, 361, 366
Essein-Udom, E. U., 215

F

Fairchild, Henry Pratt, 98, 102
Feagin, Joe, and Clarice, 23, 40, 41

Fichter, Joseph, 10, 41
Fisher, Peter, 159, 160, 161
Foner, Philip S., 260
Ford, James W., 282
Fox-Piven, Francis, 297
Frederickson, George, 259
Froehles, Bryan, 230
Fuchs, Lawrence, 126

G

Gallagher, Charles, 44
George, John, 247–48, 249, 251, 253
Geron, Kim, 165–168
Glazer, Nathan, 43, 256, 258, 264–65
Gordon, David, 347
Gordon, Milton, 7, 35–38, 40, 41, 42–43, 123
Green, John C., 218
Greenstein, Fred, 57, 59

H

Haider-Markel, Donald, 161
Hammomoto, Darrell, 121
Hardy, B. Carmon, 174, 177
Hayes, L. J., 297
Higham, Charles, 274
Hirshon, Stanley, 193
Hispanic Americans: A Statistical Yearbook, 364
Hoffer, Eric, 224
Hollifield, James, 40
Hornor, Louise, 150

Subject Index